Table of Contents

1. Foundations of Interpersonal Communication
Joseph A. Devito

1

2. Culture and Interpersonal Communication
Joseph A. Devito

29

3. Perception of the Self and Others in Interpersonal Communication
Joseph A. Devito

57

4. Listening in Interpersonal Communication
Joseph A. Devito

87

5. Verbal Messages
Joseph A. Devito

113

6. Nonverbal Messages
Joseph A. Devito

147

7. Emotional Messages
Joseph A. Devito

183

8. Conversational Messages
Joseph A. Devito

209

9. Interpersonal Relationship Stages, Theories, and Communication
Joseph A. Devito

243

10. Interpersonal Conflict and Conflict Management
Joseph A. Devito

273

Glossary of Interpersonal Communication Concepts and Skills
Joseph A. Devito

297

References
Joseph A. Devito

315

Index

343

II

Pearson New International Edition

The Interpersonal Communication Book
Joseph A. DeVito
Thirteenth Edition

Pearson Education Limited
Edinburgh Gate
Harlow
Essex CM20 2JE
England and Associated Companies throughout the world

Visit us on the World Wide Web at: www.pearsoned.co.uk

 ISBN 10: 1-292-02516-6
ISBN 13: 978-1-292-02516-2

British Library Cataloguing-in-Publication Data
A catalogue record for this book is available from the British Library

Printed in the United States of America

Foundations of Interpersonal Communication

From Chapter 1 of *The Interpersonal Communication Book*, Thirteenth Edition. Joseph A. DeVito. Copyright © 2013 by Pearson Education, Inc. All rights reserved.

Foundations of Interpersonal Communication

Why Study Interpersonal Communication

The Nature of Interpersonal Communication

Elements of Interpersonal Communication

Principles of Interpersonal Communication

Pearson Education

2:13 / 5:00

Ryan wants to ask Professor Starck for a recommendation for a summer internship, but isn't sure how to approach him. He considers the effect of the various elements of communication on the outcome as he contemplates his communication choices. See how his choices play out in the video, "Ryan Asks for a Recommendation" (www.mycommunicationlab.com).

Why read this chapter?

Because you'll learn about:

- the benefits you'll derive from studying interpersonal communication.
- what interpersonal communication is and how it works.

Because you'll learn to:

- communicate with a clear understanding of the elements of interpersonal communication.
- communicate with an understanding of the principles of interpersonal communication.

This chapter introduces the study of interpersonal communication and explains why interpersonal communication is so important. The chapter examines the nature of this unique form of communication, its elements, and its principles.

Why Study Interpersonal Communication

Fair questions to ask at the beginning of this text and this course are "What will I get out of this?" and "Why should I study interpersonal communication?" One very clear answer is given by the importance of interpersonal communication: it's a major part of human existence that every educated person needs to understand. Much as you need to understand history, science, geography, and mathematics, for example, you need to understand how people interact (how people communicate interpersonally)—whether face-to-face or online.

You'll find answers to these questions throughout this text; you'll recognize the situations discussed and the skills suggested as crucial to your personal and social as well as professional success.

Personal and Social Success

Your personal success and happiness depend largely on your effectiveness as an interpersonal communicator. Close friendships and romantic relationships are made, maintained, and sometimes destroyed largely through your interpersonal interactions. Likewise, the success of your family relationships depends heavily on the interpersonal communication among members. For example, in a survey of 1,001 people over 18 years of age, 53 percent felt that a lack of effective communication was the major cause of marriage failure—significantly greater than money (38 percent) and in-law interference (14 percent) (How Americans Communicate, 1999).

Likewise, your social success in interacting with neighbors, acquaintances, and people you meet every day depend on your ability to engage in satisfying conversation—conversation that's comfortable and enjoyable.

Alexander Walter/Taxi/Getty Images

VIEWPOINTS One study found that 80 percent of young adult women consider a spouse who can communicate his feelings more desirable than a man who earns a good living (www.gallup.com). How important, compared to all the other factors you might take into consideration in choosing a partner, is the ability to communicate? What specific communication skills would you consider "extremely important" in a life partner?

Professional Success

The ability to communicate interpersonally is widely recognized as crucial to professional success (Morreale & Pearson, 2008). From the initial interview at a college job fair to interning to participating and then leading meetings, your skills at interpersonal communication will largely determine your success.

One study, for example, found that among the 23 attributes ranked as "very important" in hiring decisions, "communication and interpersonal skills" was at the top of the list, noted by 89 percent of the recruiters. This was a far higher percentage of recruiters than noted "content of the core curriculum" (34 percent), or "overall value for the money invested in the recruiting effort" (33 percent) (Alsop, 2004). Interpersonal skills offer a "key career advantage for finance professionals in the next century" (Messmer, 1999), play an important role in preventing workplace violence (Parker, 2004), reduce medical mishaps, and improve doctor–patient communication (Smith, 2004; Sutcliffe, Lewton, & Rosenthal, 2004), and are one of six areas that define the professional competence of physicians and trainees (Epstein & Hundert, 2002). In a survey of employers who were asked what colleges should place more emphasis on, 89 percent identified "the ability to effectively communicate orally and in writing" the highest of any skills listed (Hart, 2010). And, in that same survey, the largest number of employers (84 percent), when asked what would prepare college students for success, identified "communication skills." The importance of interpersonal communication skills extends over the entire spectrum of professions.

Clearly, interpersonal skills are vital to success. Understanding the theory and research in interpersonal communication and mastering its skills go hand in hand (Greene & Burleson, 2003). The more you know about interpersonal communication, the more insight and knowledge you'll gain about what works and what doesn't work. The more skills you have within your arsenal of communication strategies, the greater your choices for communicating in any situation. In a nutshell, the greater your knowledge and the greater the number of communication choices at your disposal, the greater the likelihood that you'll be successful in achieving your interpersonal goals. This concept of choice figures into many of the principles and skills discussed throughout this text. You might even look at this text and your course as enlarging your interpersonal communication choices, giving you a greater number of options than you had before your formal exposure to the study of interpersonal communication.

As a preface to an area of study that will be enlightening, exciting, and extremely practical, examine your assumptions about interpersonal communication by taking the accompanying self-test.

INTERPERSONAL CHOICE POINTS

Throughout this text you'll find marginal items labeled Interpersonal Choice Points. *These items are designed to encourage you to apply the material discussed in the text to specific interpersonal situations by first analyzing your available choices and then making a communication decision.*

INTERPERSONAL CHOICE POINTS

Communicating an Image

A new position is opening at work, and you want it. Your immediate supervisor will likely be the one to make the final decision. What are some of the things you can do to help secure this new position?

Test Yourself   What Do You Believe about Interpersonal Communication?

Respond to each of the following statements with T if you believe the statement is usually true or F if you believe the statement is usually false.

_____ 1. Good communicators are born, not made.

_____ 2. The more you communicate, the better at it you will be.

_____ 3. In your interpersonal communications, a good guide to follow is to be as open, empathic, and supportive as you can be.

_____ 4. The best guide to follow when communicating with people from other cultures is to ignore the differences and treat the other person just as you'd treat members of your own culture.

_____ 5. Fear of meeting new people is detrimental and must be eliminated.

_____ 6. When there is conflict, your relationship is in trouble.

How Did You Do? As you probably figured out, all six statements are generally false. As you read this text, you'll discover not only why these beliefs are false but also the trouble you can get into when you assume they're true. For now, and in brief, here are some of the reasons each of the statements is generally false:

(1) Effective communication is a learned skill; although some people are born brighter or more extroverted, all can improve their abilities and become more effective communicators.

(2) It's not the amount of communication people engage in but the quality that matters; if you practice bad habits, you're more likely to grow less effective than more effective, so it's important to learn and follow the principles of effectiveness (J. O. Greene, 2003; Greene & Burleson, 2003).

(3) Each interpersonal situation is unique, and therefore the type of communication appropriate in one situation may not be appropriate in another.

(4) This assumption will probably get you into considerable trouble, because people from different cultures will often attribute different meanings to a message; members of different cultures also follow different rules for what is and is not appropriate in interpersonal communication.

(5) Many people are nervous meeting new people, especially if these are people in authority; managing, not eliminating, the fear will enable you to become effective regardless of your current level of fear.

(6) All meaningful relationships experience conflict; relationships are not in trouble when there is conflict, though dealing with conflict ineffectively can often damage the relationship.

What Will You Do? This is perhaps, then, a good place to start practicing the critical thinking skill of questioning commonly held assumptions about interpersonal communication and about yourself as an interpersonal communicator. Consider, for example, what other beliefs you have about communication and about yourself as a communicator. How do these beliefs influence your communication?

The Nature of Interpersonal Communication

Although this entire text is in a sense a definition of interpersonal communication, a working definition is useful at the start. **Interpersonal communication** is *the verbal and nonverbal interaction between two (or sometimes more than two) interdependent people.* This relatively simple definition implies a variety of characteristics to which we now turn.

Interpersonal Communication Involves Interdependent Individuals

Interpersonal communication is the communication that takes place between people who are in some way "connected." Interpersonal communication would thus include what takes place between a son and his father, an employer and an employee, two sisters, a teacher and a student, two lovers, two friends, and so on. Although largely dyadic (two-person) in nature, interpersonal communication is often extended to include small intimate groups such as the family. Even within a family, however, the communication that takes place is often dyadic— mother to child, father to mother, daughter to son, and so on.

In much the same way that Facebook may have changed the definition of friendship, it may also have changed the definition of interpersonal communication. Sending a message to your closest 15 friends who then respond to you and the others would be considered interpersonal communication by some theorists and not by others. Collective chats, on the other hand, would also be considered interpersonal communication.

Not only are the individuals simply "connected"—they are also interdependent: What one person does has an impact on the other person. The actions of one person have consequences for the other person. In a family, for example, a child's trouble with the police will affect the parents, other siblings, extended family members, and perhaps friends and neighbors.

Interpersonal Communication Is Inherently Relational

Because of this interdependency, interpersonal communication is inevitably and essentially relational in nature; interpersonal communication takes place within a relationship—it impacts the relationship, it defines the relationship.

The communication that takes place in a relationship is in part a function of that relationship. That is, the way you communicate is determined in great part by the kind of relationship that exists between you and the other person. You interact differently with your interpersonal communication instructor and your best friend; you interact with a sibling in ways very different from the ways in which you interact with a neighbor, a work colleague, or a casual acquaintance. You interact on Facebook and Twitter in ways very different from the way you interact in a face-to-face situation.

But also notice that the way you communicate, the way you interact, will influence the kind of relationship you develop. If you interact with a person in friendly ways, you're likely to develop a friendship. If you regularly exchange hateful and hurtful messages, you're likely to develop an antagonistic relationship. If you regularly express respect and support for each other, a respectful and supportive relationship is likely to develop. This is surely one of the most obvious observations you can make about interpersonal communication. And yet, many people seem not to appreciate this very clear relationship between what they say and the relationships that develop (or deteriorate).

Interpersonal Communication Exists on a Continuum

Interpersonal communication exists along a continuum (see Figure 1) that ranges from relatively impersonal to highly personal (Miller, 1978, 1990). At the impersonal end of the spectrum, you have simple conversation between people who really don't know each other—the server and the customer, for example. At the highly personal end is the communication that takes place between people who are intimately interconnected—a father and son, two long-time lovers, or best friends, for example. A few characteristics distinguish the impersonal from the personal forms of communication.

- **Role versus personal information.** Notice that in the impersonal example, the individuals are likely to respond to each other according to the *roles* they are currently playing; the server treats the customer not as a unique individual but as one of many customers. And the customer, in turn, acts towards the server not as a unique individual but as he or she would act with any server. The father and the son, however, react to each other as unique individuals. They act on the basis of *personal information*.
- **Societal versus personal rules.** Notice too that the server and the customer interact according to the *rules of society* governing the server–customer interaction. The father and the son, on the other hand, interact on the basis of *personally established rules*. The way they address each other, their touching behavior, and their degree of physical closeness, for example, are unique to them and are established by them rather than by society.
- **Social versus personal messages.** Still another difference is found in the messages exchanged. The messages that the server and customer exchange, for example, are themselves

FIGURE 1
An Interpersonal Continuum

Here is one possible interpersonal continuum. Other people would position the relationships differently. You may want to try constructing an interpersonal continuum of your own relationships.

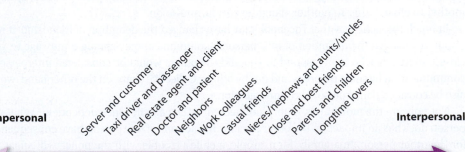

Impersonal

Server and customer
Taxi driver and passenger
Real estate agent and client
Doctor and patient
Neighbors
Work colleagues
Casual friends
Nieces/nephews and aunts/uncles
Close and best friends
Parents and children
Longtime lovers

Interpersonal

TABLE 1	Impersonal and Interpersonal Communication	

Impersonal Communication	Interpersonal Communication
Social role information: you interact largely on the basis of the social roles you occupy—for example, server and customer, cab driver and passenger.	**Personal information:** you interact largely on the basis of personal roles—for example, friends, lovers, parents and children, cousins.
Social rules: you interact according to the social rules defining your interaction; for example, as a server, you would greet the customers, hand them menus, and ask if there was anything else you could do.	**Personal rules:** you interact according to the personal rules you both have established rather than to any written rules set down by society; for example, the mother and daughter follow the rules they themselves have established over the years.
Social messages: you exchange messages in a narrow range of topics—you talk to the server about food and service, not about your parents' divorce—with little emotion and little self-disclosure.	**Personal messages:** you exchange messages in a broad range of topics—you talk about food and also about your parents' divorce—with much emotion and self-disclosure.

impersonal; there is little personal information exchanged and there is little emotional content in the messages they exchange. In the father–son example, however, the messages may run the entire range and may at times be *highly personal* with lots of personal information and lots of emotion.

Table 1 offers a brief comparison and summary of impersonal and interpersonal communication.

Interpersonal Communication Involves Verbal and Nonverbal Messages

Interpersonal interaction involves the exchange of both verbal and nonverbal messages. The words you use as well as your facial expressions, your eye contact, and your body posture—in face-to-face interaction—and your online text, photos, and videos send interpersonal messages. Likewise, you receive interpersonal messages through all your senses—hearing, vision, smell, and touch. Even silence sends interpersonal messages. These messages, as you'll see throughout this course, will vary greatly depending on the other factors involved in the interaction. You don't talk to a best friend in the same way you talk to your college professor or your parents.

One of the great myths in communication is that nonverbal communication accounts for more than 90 percent of the meaning of any message. Actually, it depends. In some situations the nonverbal signals will indeed carry more of your meaning than the words you use, perhaps in expressing strong emotions. In other situations, however, the verbal signals will communicate more information, as when, for example, you talk about accounting or science. Most often, of course, they work together.

Interpersonal Communication Takes Place in Varied Forms

Interpersonal communication often takes place face-to-face, as when we talk with other students before class, interact with family or friends

Joseph A. DeVito

over dinner, or trade secrets with intimates. And, interpersonal communication often takes place over some kind of computer network, through texting, e-mailing, posting to Facebook, phoning, and tweeting. Some of these forms are **synchronous**; they allow you to communicate in real time; the messages are sent and received at the same time as in face-to-face and phone messages. Other forms are largely **asynchronous**; they do not take place in real time. For example, you might poke someone on Facebook today who may not see it until tomorrow and may not poke you back until the next day. Similarly, you might find a tweet or a blog post today that was actually written weeks or even years ago. Table 2 identifies some of the major similarities and differences between face-to-face and online communication.

Interpersonal Communication Involves Choices

The interpersonal messages that you communicate are the result of choices you make. Many times we don't think of what we say or don't say as involving a choice—it seems so automatic that we don't think of it as under our conscious control. At other times, the notion of choice is paramount in our minds—do you admit your love openly and if so where and when do you do it? What do you say when you face the job interviewer? Part of the purpose of this text is to present you with a wide variety of interpersonal communication choices and the reasons why, in some situations, some choices work better than others.

Look at it this way: Throughout your interpersonal life and in each interpersonal interaction, you're presented with **choice points**—moments when you have to make a choice as to who you communicate with, what you say, what you don't say, how you phrase what you want to say, and so on. This course and this text aim to give you reasons (grounded in communication theory and research discussed throughout the text and highlighted in the Understanding Interpersonal Theory & Research boxes) for the varied choices you'll be called upon to make in your interpersonal interactions. The course and text also aim to give you the skills you'll need to execute these well-reasoned choices (many of which are written into the text and some of which are highlighted in the Understanding Interpersonal Skills boxes).

Plampy/Shutterstock

When you have to make a choice and don't make it, that in itself is a choice.
—*William James*

Elements of Interpersonal Communication

The model presented in Figure 2 is designed to reflect the circular nature of interpersonal communication; both persons send messages simultaneously rather than in a linear sequence where communication goes from person 1 to person 2 to person 1 to person 2 and on and on. Each of the concepts identified in the model and discussed here may be thought of as a universal of interpersonal communication, in that it is present in all interpersonal interactions: (1) source–receiver, (2) encoding–decoding, (3) messages (and the metamessages of feedback and feedforward), (4) channels, (5) noise, (6) contexts, and—though not indicated in the diagram but an overriding consideration in all interpersonal communication, (7) ethics.

Source–Receiver

Interpersonal communication involves at least two people. Each individual performs source functions (formulates and sends messages) and also performs receiver functions (perceives and comprehends messages). The term **source–receiver** emphasizes that both functions are performed by each individual in interpersonal communication.

Who you are, what you know, what you believe, what you value, what you want, what you have been told, and what your attitudes are all influence what you say, how you say it, what

| TABLE 2 | Face-to-Face and Computer-Mediated Communication | |

Throughout this text, face-to-face and computer-mediated communication are discussed, compared, and contrasted. Here is a brief summary of just some communication concepts and some of the ways in which these two forms of communication are similar and different.

Human Communication Element	Face-to-Face Communication	Computer-Mediated Communication
Sender • Presentation of self and impression management • Speaking turn	• Personal characteristics (sex, approximate age, race, etc.) are open to visual inspection; receiver controls the order of what is attended to; disguise is difficult. • You compete for the speaker's turn and time with the other person(s); you can be interrupted.	• Personal characteristics are hidden and are revealed when you want to reveal them; anonymity is easy. • It's always your turn; speaker time is unlimited; you can't be interrupted.
Receiver • Number • Opportunity for interaction • Third parties • Impression formation	• One or a few who are in your visual field. • Limited to those who have the opportunity to meet; often difficult to find people who share your interests. • Messages can be overheard by or repeated to third parties but not with complete accuracy. • Impressions are based on the verbal and nonverbal cues the receiver perceives.	• Virtually unlimited. • Unlimited. • Messages can be retrieved by others or forwarded verbatim to a third party or to thousands. • Impressions are based on text messages and posted photos and videos.
Context • Physical • Temporal	• Essentially the same physical space. • Communication is synchronous; messages are exchanged at the same (real) time.	• Can be in the next cubicle or separated by miles. • Communication may be synchronous (as in chat rooms) or asynchronous (where messages are exchanged at different times, as in e-mail).
Channel	• All senses participate in sending and receiving messages.	• Visual (for text, photos, and videos) and auditory.
Message • Verbal and nonverbal • Permanence	• Words, gestures, eye contact, accent, vocal cues, spatial relationships, touching, clothing, hair, etc. • Temporary unless recorded; speech signals fade rapidly.	• Words, photos, videos, and audio messages. • Messages are relatively permanent.

messages you receive, and how you receive them. Likewise, the person you're speaking to and the knowledge that you think that person has will greatly influence your interpersonal messages (Lau, Chiu, & Hong, 2001). Each person is unique; each person's communications are unique.

FIGURE 2
A Model of Interpersonal Communication

After you read the section on the elements of interpersonal communication, you may wish to construct your own model of the process. In constructing this model, be careful that you don't fall into the trap of visualizing interpersonal communication as a linear or simple left-to-right, static process. Remember that all elements are interrelated and inter-dependent. After completing your model, consider, for example: (1) Could your model also serve as a model of intrapersonal communication? A model of small group, public, or mass communication? (2) What elements or concepts other than those noted here might be added to the model?

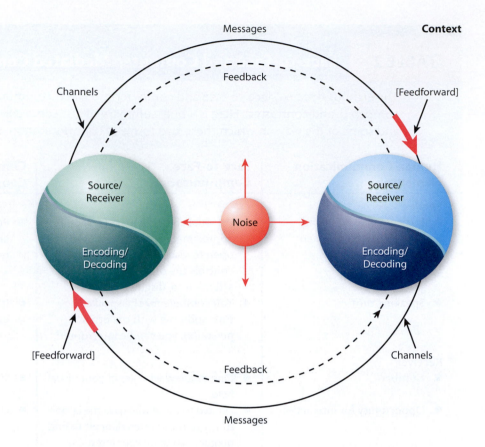

Danny Feld/ABC/Newscom

VIEWPOINTS What characters in television sitcoms or dramas do you think demonstrate superior interpersonal competence? What characters demonstrate obvious interpersonal incompetence?

Your ability to communicate effectively (as source and receiver) is your interpersonal **competence** (Spitzberg & Cupach, 1989; Wilson & Sabee, 2003). Your competence includes, for example, the knowledge that in certain contexts and with certain listeners one topic is appropriate and another isn't. Your knowledge about the rules of nonverbal behavior—for example, the appropriateness of touching, vocal volume, and physical closeness—is also part of your competence. In short, interpersonal competence includes knowing how to adjust your communication according to the context of the interaction, the person with whom you're interacting, and a host of other factors discussed throughout this text.

You learn communication competence much as you learn to eat with a knife and fork—by observing others, by explicit instruction, and by trial and error. Some individuals learn better than others, though, and these are generally the people with whom you find it interesting and comfortable to talk. They seem to know what to say and how and when to say it.

Not surprisingly, there's a positive relationship between interpersonal competence on the one hand and success in college and job satisfaction on the other (Rubin & Graham, 1988; Wertz, Sorenson, & Heeren, 1988). So much of college and professional life depends on interpersonal competence—meeting and interacting with other students, teachers, or colleagues; asking and answering questions; presenting

Understanding Interpersonal Skills

MINDFULNESS

Mindfulness is a state of mental awareness; in a mindful state you're conscious of your reasons for thinking or communicating in a particular way. And, especially important in interpersonal communication, you become aware of your choices. You act with an awareness of your available choices. Its opposite, **mindlessness**, is a lack of conscious awareness of your thinking or communicating (Langer, 1989). To apply interpersonal skills appropriately and effectively, you need to be mindful of the unique communication situation you're in, of your available communication options or choices, and of the reasons why one option is likely to prove better than the others (Burgoon, Berger, & Waldron, 2000; Elmes & Gemmill, 1990; Langer, 1989). You can look at this textbook and this course in interpersonal communication as means of awakening your mindfulness about the way you engage in interpersonal communication. After you complete this course and this text, you should be much more mindful about all your interpersonal interactions, which will prove beneficial in all your interpersonal interactions (Carson, Carson, Gil, & Baucom, 2004; Sagula & Rice, 2004).

Increasing Mindfulness. To increase mindfulness in general, try the following suggestions (Langer, 1989).

- **Create and recreate categories**. Learn to see objects, events, and people as belonging to a wide variety of categories. Try to see, for example, your prospective romantic partner in a variety of roles—child, parent, employee, neighbor, friend, financial contributor, and so on. Avoid storing in memory an image of a person with only one specific label; if you do, you'll find it difficult to recategorize the person later.
- **Be open to new information and points of view**, even when these contradict your most firmly held stereotypes. New information forces you to reconsider what might be outmoded ways of thinking. New information can help you challenge long-held but now inappropriate beliefs and attitudes. Be willing to see your own and others' behaviors from a variety of viewpoints—especially from the perspective of people very different from yourself.
- **Beware of relying too heavily on first impressions** (Chanowitz & Langer, 1981; Langer, 1989). Treat your first impressions as tentative—as hypotheses that need further investigation. Be prepared to revise, reject, or accept these initial impressions.

In addition, consider a few suggestions specific to communication. Ask yourself these questions (Burgoon, Berger, & Waldron, 2000).

- Can the message be misinterpreted? What can you do to make sure it's interpreted correctly? For example, you can paraphrase or restate the message in different ways or you can ask the person to paraphrase.
- When there's a continuous communication pattern—as there is in an escalating conflict in which each person brings up past relationship injustices—ask yourself if this pattern is productive and, if not, what you can do to change it. For example, you can refuse to respond in kind and thereby break the cycle.
- Remind yourself of what you already know about a situation, recall that all communication situations are different, and ask yourself how you can best adapt your messages to this unique situation. For example, you may want to be especially positive to a friend who is depressed but not so positive to someone who betrayed a confidence.
- Think before you act. Especially in delicate situations (for example, when expressing anger or when conveying commitment messages), it's wise to pause and think over the situation mindfully (DeVito, 2003b). In this way you'll stand a better chance of acting and reacting appropriately.

Working with Interpersonal Skills

Reflect on your own tendencies to communicate mindlessly and mindfully. Do you regularly examine your choices, before you send your message? In which situations are you more apt to communicate mindlessly? For example, when compared to face-to-face communication, are you more or less mindful when communicating on Facebook, Twitter, or other social networking sites? If there is a difference, why do you suppose it exists? Do you communicate mindfully with certain people and mindlessly with others?

information or argument—that you should not find this connection surprising. Interpersonal competence also enables you to develop and maintain meaningful relationships in friendship, love, family, and work. Such relationships, in turn, contribute to the lower levels of anxiety, depression, and loneliness observed in interpersonally competent people (Spitzberg & Cupach, 1989).

Encoding–Decoding

Encoding refers to the act of producing messages—for example, speaking or writing. **Decoding** is the reverse and refers to the act of understanding messages—for example, listening or reading. By sending your ideas via sound waves (in the case of speech) or light waves (in the case of writing), you're putting these ideas into a code, hence *en*coding. By translating sound or light waves into ideas, you're taking them out of a code, hence *de*coding. Thus, speakers and writers are called encoders, and listeners and readers are called decoders. The term encoding–decoding is used to emphasize that the two activities are performed in combination by each participant. For interpersonal communication to occur, messages must be encoded and decoded. For example, when a parent talks to a child whose eyes are closed and whose ears are covered by stereo headphones, interpersonal communication does not occur because the messages sent are not being received.

Messages

Messages are signals that serve as stimuli for a receiver and are received by one of our senses—auditory (hearing), visual (seeing), tactile (touching), olfactory (smelling), gustatory (tasting), or any combination of these senses. You communicate interpersonally by gesture and touch as well as by words and sentences. The clothes you wear communicate to others and, in fact, to yourself as well. The way you walk communicates, as does the way you shake hands, tilt your head, comb your hair, sit, smile, or frown. Similarly, the colors and types of cell phones, the wallpaper and screen savers on your computer, and even the type and power of your computer communicate messages about you. The photo and background theme you choose for your Twitter page reveals something about yourself beyond what your actual tweets reveal. Tweeters with the generic white bird photo and standard background communicate something quite different from the Tweeters who customize their pages with clever photos, original backgrounds, and sidebars. The same is true of Facebook pages. All of these signals are your interpersonal communication messages.

Interpersonal communication can take place by phone, through prison cell walls, through webcams, or face-to-face. Increasingly, it's taking place through computers, through Facebook and Twitter.

Messages may be intentional or unintentional. They may result from the most carefully planned strategy as well as from the unintentional slip of the tongue, lingering body odor, or nervous twitch.

Messages may refer to the world, people, and events as well as to other messages (DeVito, 2003a). Messages that are about other messages are called **metamessages** and represent many of your everyday communications; they include, for example, "Do you understand?" "Did I say that right?" "What did you say?" "Is it fair to say that . . .?" "I want to be honest," "That's not logical." Two particularly important types of metamessages are feedback and feedforward.

Feedback Messages Throughout the interpersonal communication process, you exchange feedback—messages sent back to the speaker concerning reactions to what is said (Clement & Frandsen, 1976). **Feedback** tells the speaker what effect she or he is having on listeners. On the basis of this feedback, the speaker may adjust, modify, strengthen, deemphasize, or change the content or form of the messages.

Feedback may come from yourself or from others. When you send a message—say, in speaking to another person—you also hear yourself. That is, you get feedback from your own messages: You hear what you say, you feel the way you move, you see what you write. In addition to this self-feedback, you get feedback from others. This feedback can take many forms. A frown or a smile, a yea or a nay, a pat on the back or a punch in the mouth are all types of feedback. Sometimes feedback is easy to identify, but sometimes it isn't (Skinner, 2002). Part of the art of effective communication is to discern feedback and adjust your messages on the basis of that feedback.

Feedforward Messages **Feedforward** is information you provide before sending your primary message (Richards, 1951). Feedforward reveals something about the message to come. Examples of feedforward include the preface or table of contents of a book, the opening paragraph of a chapter or post, movie previews, magazine covers, e-mail subject headings, and introductions in public speeches. Feedforward may serve a variety of functions. For example, you might use feedforward to express your wish to chat a bit, saying something like "Hey, I haven't seen you the entire week; what's been going on?" Or you might give a brief preview of your main message by saying something like "You'd better sit down for this; you're going to be shocked." Or you might ask others to hear you out before they judge you.

VIEWPOINTS The "feedback theory of relationships" holds that satisfying friendships, romantic relationships, or workplace relationships may be characterized by feedback that is positive, person-focused, immediate, low in monitoring, and supportive—and that unsatisfying relationships are characterized by feedback that is negative, self-focused, non-immediate, high in monitoring, and critical. How effective is this theory in explaining relationships with which you're familiar?

Wrangler/Shutterstock

Channel

The communication **channel** is the medium through which messages pass. It's a kind of bridge connecting source and receiver. Communication rarely takes place over only one channel; two, three, or four channels are often used simultaneously. For example, in face-to-face interaction, you speak and listen (vocal–auditory channel), but you also gesture and receive signals visually (gestural–visual channel), and you emit odors and smell those of others (chemical–olfactory channel). Often you communicate through touch (cutaneous–tactile channel). When you communicate online, you often send photo, audio, or video files in the same message or, in the case of Twitter, links to these additional files. In most situations, a variety of channels are involved.

Another way to think about channels is to consider them as the means of communication: for example, face-to-face contact, telephone, e-mail and snail mail, Twitter, instant messaging, news postings, Facebook, film, television, radio, smoke signals, or fax—to name only some.

Note that the channel imposes different restrictions on your message construction. For example, in e-mail you can pause to think of the right word or phrase, you can go on for as short or as long a time as you want without any threat of interruption or contradiction, and you can edit your message with ease. In face-to-face communication your pauses need to be relatively short. You don't have the time to select just the right word or to edit, though we do edit a bit when we review what we said and put it in different words.

At times, the channel is physiologically damaged. For example, for individuals with visual difficulties, the visual channel is impaired, so adjustments

INTERPERSONAL CHOICE POINT
Channels
You want to ask someone for a date and are considering how you might go about this. What are your choices among channels? Which channel would be the most effective? Which channel would provoke the least anxiety?

13

have to be made. Table 3 gives you an idea of how such adjustments can make interpersonal communication between persons with and without visual impairment more effective.

Noise

Technically, **noise** is anything that distorts a message—anything that prevents the receiver from receiving the message. At one extreme, noise may prevent a message from getting from source to receiver. A roaring noise or line static can easily prevent entire messages from getting through to your telephone receiver. At the other extreme, with virtually no noise interference, the message of the source and the message received are almost identical. Most often, however, noise distorts some portion of the message a source sends as it travels to a receiver.

Four types of noise are especially relevant. It's important to identify these types of noise and, when possible, to reduce their effects.

- **Physical noise** is interference that is external to both speaker and listener; it impedes the physical transmission of the signal or message. Examples include the screeching of passing cars, the hum of a computer, sunglasses, extraneous messages, illegible handwriting, blurred type or fonts that are too small or difficult to read, misspellings and poor grammar, and pop-up ads. Still another type of physical noise is extraneous information that makes what you want to find more difficult, for example, spam or too many photos on Facebook.
- **Physiological noise** is created by barriers within the sender or receiver, such as visual impairments, hearing loss, articulation problems, and memory loss.
- **Psychological noise** is mental interference in speaker or listener and includes preconceived ideas, wandering thoughts, biases and prejudices, closed-mindedness, and extreme emotionalism. You're likely to run into psychological noise when you talk with someone who is closed-minded or who refuses to listen to anything he or she doesn't already believe.
- **Semantic noise** is interference that occurs when the speaker and listener have different meaning systems; examples include language or dialectical differences, the use of jargon or overly complex terms, and ambiguous or overly abstract terms whose meanings can be easily misinterpreted. You see this type of noise regularly in the medical doctor who uses "medicalese" without explanation or in the insurance salesperson who speaks in the jargon of the insurance industry.

As you can see from these examples, noise is anything that hinders your receiving the messages of others or their receiving your messages.

A useful concept in understanding noise and its importance in communication is *signal-to-noise ratio*. In this term the word *signal* refers to information that you'd find useful, and *noise* refers to information that is useless (to you). So, for example, a blog post that contains lots of useful information would be high on signal and low on noise; messages that contain lots of useless information (spam is probably the best example) would be high on noise and low on signal.

All communications contain noise. Noise cannot be totally eliminated, but its effects can be reduced. Making your language more precise, sharpening your skills for sending and receiving nonverbal messages, and improving your listening and feedback skills are some ways to combat the influence of noise.

Context

Communication always takes place in a **context**, or environment, that influences the form and content of your messages. At times this context isn't obvious or intrusive; it seems so natural that it's ignored—like background music. At other times the context dominates, and the ways in which it restricts or stimulates your messages are obvious. Compare, for example, the differences among communicating in a funeral home, football stadium, formal restaurant, and a rock concert. The context of communication has at least four dimensions, all of which interact with and influence each other.

Throughout the text you'll find invitations to visit The Communication Blog (tcbdevito.blogspot.com) for additional coverage of a topic and relevant websites. Comment as you wish and read the comments of others.

Noise of a somewhat different type is discussed in "The Chain Letter as Dysfunctional Communication" at tcbdevito.blogspot.com. What's your opinion of the chain letter? Are there some chain letters that you view more positively than others?

INTERPERSONAL CHOICE POINT

Noise Reduction

Looking around your classroom (or your room, if you're taking the course online), what are some of the things you can do to reduce physical noise?

TABLE 3

INTERPERSONAL COMMUNICATION TIPS
Between People with and People without Visual Impairments

Louis Braille
EMG Education Management Group

Helen Keller as a young child portrayed in the film, *The Miracle Worker*
The Everett Collection

Ray Charles
AFP/Getty Images

David Paterson, former governor of New York
Getty Images

People vary greatly in their visual abilities: some are totally blind, some are partially sighted, and some have unimpaired vision. Ninety percent of people who are "legally blind" have some vision. All people, however, have the same need for communication and information. Here are some tips for making communication better between those who have visual impairments and those without such difficulties.

If you're the person without visual impairment and are talking with a visually impaired person:

Generally	Specifically
Identify yourself.	Don't assume the visually impaired person will recognize your voice.
Face your listener; you'll be easier to hear.	Don't shout. Most people who are visually impaired are not hearing impaired. Speak at your normal volume.
Encode into speech all the meanings you wish to communicate.	Remember that your gestures, eye movements, and facial expressions cannot be seen by the visually impaired.
Use audible turn-taking cues.	When you pass the role of speaker to a person who is visually impaired, don't rely on nonverbal cues; instead, say something like "Do you agree with that, Joe?"
Use normal vocabulary and discuss topics that you would discuss with sighted people.	Don't avoid terms like "see" or "look" or even "blind." Don't avoid discussing a television show or the way your new car looks; these are normal topics for all people.

If you are a person with visual impairment and are talking with a person without visual impairment:

Help the sighted person meet your special communication needs.	If you want your surroundings described, ask. If you want the person to read the road signs, ask.
Be patient with the sighted person.	Many people are nervous talking with people who are visually impaired for fear of offending. Put them at ease in a way that also makes you more comfortable.
Demonstrate your comfort.	When appropriate, let the other person know that you're comfortable with the interaction, verbally or nonverbally.

Sources: These suggestions were drawn from a variety of sources: www.cincyblind.org, www.abwa.asn.au/, www.mass.gov, www.ndmig.com, and www.batchelor. edu.au/disability/communication.

Physical Dimension

The *physical dimension* is the tangible or concrete environment in which communication takes place—the room, hallway, or park; the boardroom or the family dinner table. The size of the space, its temperature, and the number of people present in the physical space would also be part of the physical dimension. In print media such as magazines or newspapers, context includes the positioning of stories and news articles; an article on page 37 is identified as less important than an article on page 1 or 2. Twitter's restriction of messages to 140 characters or fewer is an especially good example of the physical dimension influencing the message; Twitter requires you to abbreviate your message, while having coffee at Starbucks seems to encourage the opposite.

Temporal Dimension

The *temporal dimension* has to do not only with the time of day and moment in history but also with where a particular message fits into the sequence of communication events. For example, a joke about illness told immediately after the disclosure of a friend's sickness will be received differently than the same joke told in response to a series of similar jokes. Also, some channels (for example, face-to-face, chat rooms, and instant messaging) allow for synchronous communication in which messages are sent and received simultaneously. Other channels (for example, letter writing, e-mail, and social networking postings) are asynchronous; messages are sent and received at different times.

Comstock/Thinkstock

VIEWPOINTS In a class discussion of ethics, your instructor presents the following possible ethical guidelines: (1) Behavior is ethical when you feel in your heart that you're doing the right thing, (2) Behavior is ethical when it is consistent with your religious beliefs, (3) Behavior is ethical when it's legal within society, (4) Behavior is ethical when the majority of people would consider it ethical, and (5) Behavior is ethical when the end result is in the interest of the majority. How would you respond to these guidelines? Would you accept any as an accurate statement of what constitutes ethical behavior? Would you reject any? Why?

Social–Psychological Dimension

The *social–psychological dimension* includes, for example, status relationships among the participants, roles and games that people play, norms of the society or group, and the friendliness, formality, or gravity of the situation. Social networks such as Facebook and Myspace are informal and largely-for-fun communication; LinkedIn and Plaxo, on the other hand, are primarily for serious business-oriented communication.

Cultural Dimension

The *cultural context* includes the cultural beliefs and customs of the people communicating. When you interact with people from different cultures, you may each follow different rules of communication. This can result in confusion, unintentional insult, inaccurate judgments, and a host of other miscommunications. Similarly, communication strategies or techniques that prove satisfying to members of one culture may prove disturbing or offensive to members of another. In fact, research shows that you lose more information in an intercultural situation (approximately 50 percent) than in an intracultural situation (approximately 25 percent) (Li, 1999).

For a self-test on what is and what is not ethical, see "ABCD: Ethics" at tcbdevito.blogspot.com. Add your own comments.

Ethics

Because communication has consequences, interpersonal communication also involves **ethics**; each communication act has a moral dimension, a rightness or wrongness (Tompkins, 2011; Neher & Sandin, 2007). Communication choices need to be guided by ethical considerations as well as by concerns with effectiveness and satisfaction. Some research finds important cross-cultural similarities in this regard; for example, it's been proposed that there are certain universal ethical principles that are held by all cultures, such as that you should tell the truth, have respect for another's dignity, and not harm the innocent (Christians & Traber, 1997). Ethics is therefore included as a foundation concept of interpersonal communication.

Ethics in Interpersonal Communication

ETHICAL QUESTIONS

- What obligations do you have to keep a secret? Can you identify situations in which it would be unethical not to reveal information you promised to keep secret?
- What are your ethical obligations as a listener?
- Are ethical principles objective or subjective? For example, if lying is unethical, is it unethical in all situations? Or would your answer depend on the circumstances?
- What are your ethical obligations to reveal personal information to a relationship partner?
- Are there ethical and unethical ways to engage in conflict and conflict resolution?

As you read these questions, think about your own ethical beliefs and how these beliefs influence the way you'd answer the questions.

ETHICAL CHOICE POINT

You're ready to enter into a permanent romantic relationship and are being pressured to talk about yourself. What can you do ethically to avoid revealing personal information that you just aren't ready to talk about? What can you ethically keep hidden? What types of information are you ethically obligated to reveal?

In thinking about these ethical issues, we may take an objective or a subjective view of ethics. An objective view argues that morality is absolute and exists apart from the values or beliefs of any individual or culture: The same standards apply to all people in all situations at all times. In this view, if lying, false advertising, using illegally obtained evidence, or revealing secrets is unethical, then any such behavior is unethical regardless of the circumstances surrounding it or the context in which it occurs. In a strict objective view, the end doesn't justify the means; you cannot justify an unethical act regardless of how good or beneficial its results (or ends) might be.

A subjective view argues that what is or is not ethical depends on the culture's values and beliefs as well as the particular circumstances. Thus, a subjective position would claim that lying may be wrong to win votes or sell cigarettes, but that white lies may be quite ethical if their purpose is to make someone feel better and if the deceptions do no harm.

Principles of Interpersonal Communication

Now that the nature of interpersonal communication and its elements are clear, we can explore some of the more specific axioms or principles that are common to all or most interpersonal encounters. These axioms are largely the work of the transactional researchers Paul Watzlawick, Janet Helmick Beavin, and Don D. Jackson, presented in their landmark *Pragmatics of Human Communication* (1967; Watzlawick 1977, 1978).

Interpersonal Communication Is a Transactional Process

A **transactional perspective** views interpersonal communication as (1) a process with (2) elements that are *inter*dependent. Figure 3 visually explains this transactional view and distinguishes it from two earlier views of how interpersonal communication works.

Interpersonal Communication Is a Process   Interpersonal communication is best viewed as an ever-changing, circular process. Everything involved in interpersonal communication is in a state of flux: You're changing, the people you communicate with are changing, and your environment is changing. Sometimes these changes go unnoticed and sometimes they intrude in obvious ways, but they're always occurring.

Understanding *Interpersonal Theory & Research*

COMMUNICATION THEORIES AND RESEARCH

A **theory** is a generalization that explains how something works—for example, gravity, blood clotting, interpersonal attraction, or communication. Academic writers usually reserve the term *theory* to refer to a well-established system of knowledge about how things work or how things are related that is supported by research findings. **Research** is a systematic process of discovering an answer (or answers) to a question (in scientific terms, an hypothesis). Through research, theories are developed, refined, and, in some cases, discarded.

The theories and research you'll encounter in this text explain how communication works—for example, how you accommodate your speaking style to your listeners, how communication works when relationships deteriorate, or how and why people disclose their normally hidden selves.

Despite their many values, however, theories don't reveal truth in any absolute sense. Rather, theories reveal some degree of accuracy, some degree of truth. In the natural sciences (such as physics and chemistry), theories are extremely high in accuracy. In the social and behavioral sciences (such as communication, sociology, and psychology), the theories are far less accurate in describing or in predicting how things work. Nevertheless, theories provide enormous insights into the world of interpersonal communication and interpersonal relationships.

Not surprisingly, interpersonal communication theories often have practical implications for developing your own skills. For example, theories of interpersonal attraction offer practical insight into how to make yourself more attractive to others; theories of nonverbal communication will help you use and decipher nonverbal behaviors more accurately. The more you know about the theories and research explaining how communication works, the more likely you'll be able to use them to build your own interpersonal communication skills.

Working with Theories and Research

Try working with theories in these three steps: (1) Select a theory that you have about some aspect of social networking communication (Women have more friends on Facebook than men; or The more time spent on computer-mediated communication, the less time spent on face-to-face communication; or any belief you have about social networking); (2) examine the various data bases for research on your question; (3) draw a conclusion, an answer to your research question. This would be the general plan for researching what is already known.

If you discovered that there is no research that will answer your question, then your third step would be to develop a research plan for testing your theory (for example, you might examine the Facebook pages of men and women for the number of friends listed or you might develop a questionnaire that asks about time spent on various communication activities). In Step 4 you would execute the plan. And, in Step 5 you would draw your conclusions or answer your research question.

FIGURE 3

The Linear and Transactional Views of Interpersonal Communication

The top figure represents a linear view of communication in which the speaker speaks and the listener listens. The bottom figure represents a transactional view, the view favored by most communication theorists, in which each person serves simultaneously as speaker and listener; at the same time that you send messages, you also receive messages from your own communications as well as from the reactions of the other person(s).

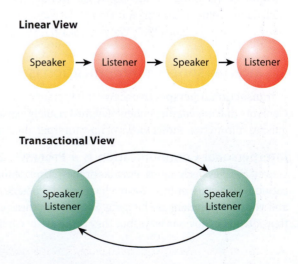

Linear View

Speaker → Listener → Speaker → Listener

Transactional View

Speaker/Listener   Speaker/Listener

One person's message serves as the stimulus for another's message, which serves as a stimulus for the first person's message, and so on. Throughout this circular process, each person serves simultaneously as a speaker *and* a listener, an actor *and* a reactor. Interpersonal communication is a mutually interactive process.

Elements Are Interdependent   In interpersonal communication, not only are the individuals interdependent, as noted earlier, but the varied elements of communication also are interdependent. Each element—each part—of interpersonal communication is intimately connected to the other parts and to the whole. For example, there can be no source without a receiver; there can be no message without a source; there can be no feedback without a receiver. Because of interdependency, a change in any one element causes changes in the others. For example, you're talking with a group of fellow students about a recent examination, and your teacher joins the group. This change in participants will lead to other changes—perhaps in the content of what you say, perhaps in the manner in which you express it. But regardless of what change is introduced, other changes result.

Interpersonal Communication Is Purposeful

The interpersonal communication act is purposeful; each interpersonal interaction has a purpose or, more often, a combination of purposes. Five such purposes can be identified: to learn, to relate, to influence, to play, and to help.

To Learn   Interpersonal communication enables you to learn, to better understand the external world—the world of objects, events, and other people. When you read the tweets from your followers, you're learning about them but also about the world they live in—whether it's down the road or across an ocean. Although a great deal of information comes from the media, you probably discuss and ultimately learn or internalize information through interpersonal interactions. In fact, your beliefs, attitudes, and values are probably influenced more by interpersonal encounters than by the media or even by formal education.

Most important, however, interpersonal communication helps you learn about yourself. By talking about yourself with others, you gain valuable feedback on your feelings, thoughts, and behaviors. Through these communications, you also learn how you appear to others—who likes you, who dislikes you, and why. This function, you'll note, is written into the very fabric of Facebook, Twitter, and blogs, where commenting, recommending, and liking for a post can be indicated so easily.

To Relate   Interpersonal communication helps you relate. You communicate your friendship or love through your interpersonal communication; at the same time, you react and respond to the friendship and love messages of others. When you poke someone on Facebook, you're indicating your desire to relate to that person, to communicate with him or her. Such communication is at the heart of one of the greatest needs people have: to establish and maintain close relationships. You want to feel loved and liked, and in turn you want to love and like others. Such relationships help to alleviate loneliness and depression, enable you to share and heighten your pleasures, and generally make you feel more positive about yourself.

To Influence   Very likely, you influence the attitudes and behaviors of others in your interpersonal encounters. You may

Maslov Dmitry/Shutterstock

VIEWPOINTS   How would you explain interpersonal communication or interpersonal relationships in terms of metaphors, such as a seesaw, a ball game, a flower, ice skates, a microscope, a television sitcom, a work of art, a book, a rubber band, or a software program?

wish others to vote a particular way, try a new diet, buy a new book, listen to a record, see a movie, take a specific course, think in a particular way, believe that something is true or false, or value some idea—the list is endless. A good deal of your time is probably spent in interpersonal persuasion. Some researchers, in fact, would argue that all communication is persuasive and that all our communications seek some persuasive goal.

This influencing function is seen on social media sites in at least two different ways: (1) direct influence attempts (advertisements or friends urging you to sign up for a cause or to join a group) and (2) indirect influence attempts (reading that your friends have seen a particular movie and enjoyed it, or a news feed announcing that one of your friends has joined a cause or bought a ticket to a play or concert, or is signing up for a particular group or cause).

To Play   Talking with friends about your weekend activities, discussing sports or dates, telling stories and jokes, tweeting, and posting a clever joke or photo on some social media site, and in general just passing the time are play functions. Far from frivolous, this extremely important purpose gives your activities a necessary balance and your mind a needed break from all the seriousness around you. In online communication, perhaps the most obvious forms of play are the interactive games in a real or virtual reality environment. In the process, interestingly enough, players develop useful skills such as the ability to take the perspective of another person (Tynes, 2007). And even certain forms of cyberflirting may be viewed as play (Whitty, 2003b).

To Help   Therapists of various kinds serve a helping function professionally by offering guidance through interpersonal interaction. But everyone interacts to help in everyday encounters: You console a friend who has broken off a love affair, counsel another student about courses to take, or offer advice to a colleague about work. Social media websites such as LinkedIn and Plaxo and even Facebook and Twitter are used extensively for securing the help of others and giving help to others. Success in accomplishing this helping function, professionally or otherwise, depends on your knowledge and skill in interpersonal communication.

DPiX Center/Shutterstock

Interpersonal Communication Is Ambiguous

An ambiguous message is a message that can be interpreted as having more than one meaning. Sometimes **ambiguity** occurs because people use words that can be interpreted differently. Informal time language offers good examples; for example, *soon, right away, in a minute, early, late,* can easily be interpreted very differently by different people. The terms are ambiguous. A more interesting type of ambiguity is grammatical ambiguity. You can get a feel for this type of ambiguity by trying to paraphrase—rephrase in your own words—the following sentences:

- What has the cat in its paws?
- Visiting neighbors can be boring.
- They are frying chickens.

Each of these ambiguous sentences can be interpreted and paraphrased in at least two different ways:

- What monster has the cat in its paws? What is the cat holding in its paws?
- To visit neighbors is boring. Neighbors who visit are boring.
- Those people are frying chickens. Those chickens are for frying.

Although these examples are particularly striking—and are the work of linguists who analyze language—some degree of ambiguity exists in all interpersonal communication: All messages are ambiguous to some degree. When you express an idea you never communicate your meaning exactly and totally;

VIEWPOINTS How would you describe the optimum level of relationship ambiguity? For example, would you want to be certain about everything? Be kept in the dark about certain things?

rather, you communicate your meaning with some reasonable accuracy—enough to give the other person a reasonably clear idea of what you mean. Sometimes, of course, you're less accurate than you anticipated. Perhaps your listener "gets the wrong idea" or "gets offended" when you only meant to be humorous, or the listener "misunderstands your emotional meaning." Because of this inevitable uncertainty, you may qualify what you're saying, give an example, or ask, "Do you know what I mean?" These additional explanations help the other person understand your meaning and reduce uncertainty (to some degree).

This quality of ambiguity makes it extremely important to resist jumping to conclusions about the motives of a speaker. For example, if someone doesn't poke you back, it may mean that the person is not interested in communicating with you, or it may be a function of information overload or a lack of knowledge in how to poke back or being away from the computer. Similarly, if someone unfollows you on Twitter or defriends you on Facebook, it may simply be a mistake. Meaning is in the person, not in the words or in the photos posted.

Similarly, all relationships contain uncertainty. Consider one of your own close interpersonal relationships and answer the following questions, using a six-point scale with "1" meaning that you are completely or almost completely uncertain about the answer and "6" meaning that you are completely or almost completely certain of the answer.

- What can or can't you say to each other in this relationship?
- Do you and this person feel the same way about each other?
- How would you and this person describe this relationship?
- What is the future of the relationship?

It's very likely that you were not able to respond with 6s for all four questions, and equally likely that the same would be true for your relationship partner. Your responses to these questions—adapted from a relationship uncertainty scale (Knoblock & Solomon, 1999)—and similar other questions illustrate that you probably experience some degree of uncertainty about (1) the norms that govern your relationship communication (question 1), (2) the degree to which you and your partner see the relationship in similar ways (question 2), (3) the definition of the relationship (question 3), and (4) the relationship's future (question 4).

The skills of interpersonal communication presented throughout this text may be looked at as means for appropriately reducing ambiguity and making your meaning as unambiguous as possible (when you want it to be unambiguous).

Interpersonal Relationships May Be Symmetrical or Complementary

Interpersonal relationships can be described as either symmetrical or complementary (Bateson, 1972; Watzlawick, Beavin, & Jackson, 1967). In a **symmetrical relationship**, the two individuals mirror each other's behavior (Bateson, 1972). If one member nags, the other member responds in kind. If one member is passionate, the other member is passionate. If one member expresses jealousy, the other member also expresses jealousy. If one member is passive, so is the other. The relationship is one of equality, with the emphasis on minimizing the differences between the two individuals.

Note, however, the problems that can arise in this type of relationship. Consider the situation of a couple in which both members are very aggressive. The aggressiveness of one person fosters aggressiveness in

INTERPERSONAL CHOICE POINT
Reducing Relationship Ambiguity
You've gone out with someone for several months and want to reduce ambiguity about the future of the relationship and discover your partner's level of commitment. But you don't want to scare your partner. What are some things you can say or do to find answers to your very legitimate questions?

INTERPERSONAL CHOICE POINT
Reducing Negative Symmetry
You're dating a person you really like and find yourself in a symmetrical relationship, especially when it comes to things like aggressiveness and jealousy; it sometimes spirals out of control. What are some of the things you might do to lessen these unpleasant spirals?

the other, which fosters increased aggressiveness in the first individual. As this cycle escalates, the aggressiveness can no longer be contained and the relationship is consumed by the aggression.

In a **complementary relationship**, the two individuals engage in different behaviors. The behavior of one serves as the stimulus for the other's complementary behavior. In complementary relationships, the differences between the parties are maximized. The people occupy different positions, one superior and the other inferior, one passive and the other active, one strong and the other weak. At times, cultures establish such relationships—for example, the complementary relationship between teacher and student or between employer and employee.

Interpersonal Communication Refers to Content and Relationship

Messages may refer to the real world (content messages); for example, to the events and objects you see before you. At the same time, however, they also may refer to the relationship between the people communicating (relationship messages). For example, a judge may say to a lawyer, "See me in my chambers immediately." This simple message has both a content aspect, which refers to the response expected (namely, that the lawyer will see the judge immediately), and a relationship aspect, which says something about the relationship between the judge and the lawyer and, as a result of this relationship, about how the communication is to be dealt with. Even the use of the simple command shows that there is a status difference between the two parties. This difference can perhaps be seen most clearly if you imagine the command being made by the lawyer to the judge. Such a communication appears awkward and out of place because it violates the normal relationship between judge and lawyer.

In any two communications, the **content dimension** may be the same, but the relationship aspect may be different, or the relationship aspect may be the same and the content dimension different. For example, the judge could say to the lawyer, "You had better see me immediately" or "May I please see you as soon as possible?" In both cases, the content is essentially the same; that is, the message about the expected response is the same. But the **relationship dimension** is quite different. The first message signifies a definite superior–inferior relationship; the second signals a more equal relationship, one that shows respect for the lawyer.

Similarly, at times the content is different but the relationship is essentially the same. For example, a daughter might say to her parents, "May I go away this weekend?" or "May I use the car tonight?" The content of the two questions is clearly very different. The relationship dimension, however, is the same. Both questions clearly reflect a superior–inferior relationship in which permission to do certain things must be secured.

Many problems between people result from failure to recognize the distinction between the content and relationship dimensions of communication. Consider the following interchange:

Dialogue	*Comments*
He: I'm going bowling tomorrow. The guys at the plant are starting a team.	He focuses on the content and ignores any relationship implications of the message.

She: Why can't we ever do anything together?

She responds primarily on a relationship level, ignores the content implications of the message, and expresses her displeasure at being ignored in his decision.

He: We can do something together anytime; tomorrow's the day they're organizing the team.

Again, he focuses almost exclusively on the content.

This example reflects research findings that men generally focus more on the content while women focus more on the relationship dimensions of communication (Ivy & Backlund, 2000; Pearson, West, & Turner, 1995; Wood, 1994). Once you recognize this difference, you may be better able to remove a potential barrier to communication between the sexes by being sensitive to the orientation of the opposite sex. Here is essentially the same situation but with added sensitivity:

Dialogue

Comments

He: The guys at the plant are organizing a bowling team. I'd sure like to be on the team. Would it be a problem if I went to the organizational meeting tomorrow?

Although focused on content, he is aware of the relationship dimensions of his message and includes both in his comments—by acknowledging their partnership, asking if there would be a problem, and expressing his desire rather than his decision.

She: That sounds great, but I was hoping we could do something together.

She focuses on the relationship dimension but also acknowledges his content orientation. Note, too, that she does not respond as though she has to defend her emphasis on relationship aspects.

He: How about you meet me at Joe's Pizza, and we can have dinner after the organizational meeting?

He responds to the relationship aspect—without abandoning his desire to join the bowling team—and incorporates it.

She: That sounds great. I'm dying for pizza.

She responds to both messages, approving of his joining the team and their dinner date.

Arguments over the content dimension are relatively easy to resolve. Generally, you can look up something in a book or ask someone what actually took place. It is relatively easy to verify disputed facts. Arguments on the relationship level, however, are much more difficult to resolve, in part because you may not recognize that the argument is in fact a relational one. Once you realize that, you can approach the dispute appropriately and deal with it directly.

Interpersonal Communication Is a Series of Punctuated Events

Communication events are continuous transactions. There is no clear-cut beginning and no clear-cut end. As participants in or observers of the communication act, you segment this continuous stream of communication into smaller pieces. You label some of these pieces causes or stimuli and others effects or responses.

Consider an example. A married couple is in a restaurant. The husband is flirting with another woman, and the wife is talking to her sister on her cell phone. Both are scowling at each other and are obviously in a deep nonverbal argument. Recalling the situation later, the husband might observe that the wife talked on the phone, so he innocently flirted with the other woman. The only reason for his behavior (he says) was his anger over her talking on the phone when they were supposed to be having dinner together. Notice that he sees his behavior as a response to her behavior. In recalling the same incident, the wife might say that she phoned her sister when he started flirting. The more he flirted, the longer she talked. She had no intention of calling anyone until he started flirting. To her, his behavior was the stimulus and hers was the response; he caused her behavior. Thus, the husband sees the sequence as going from phoning to flirting, and the wife sees it as going from flirting to phoning. This example is depicted

For an application of some of these principles to a letter to Dear Abby, see "It's about communication, Abby" at tcbdevito.blogspot.com. How would you have answered this writer's letter?

FIGURE 4
Punctuation and the Sequence of Events

(A) Shows the actual sequence of events as a continuous series of actions with no specific beginning or end. Each action (phoning and flirting) stimulates another action, but no initial cause is identified.

(B) Shows the same sequence of events as seen by the wife. She sees the sequence as beginning with the husband's flirting and her phoning behavior as a response to that stimulus.

(C) Shows the same sequence of events from the husband's point of view. He sees the sequence as beginning with the wife's phoning and his flirting as a response to that stimulus.

Try using this three-part figure, discussed in the text, to explain what might go on when a supervisor complains that workers are poorly trained for their jobs and when the workers complain that the supervisor doesn't know how to supervise.

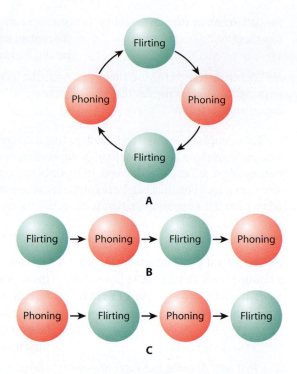

visually in Figure 4 and is supported by research showing that, among married couples at least, the individuals regularly see their partner's behavior as the cause of conflict (Schutz, 1999).

This tendency to divide communication transactions into sequences of stimuli and responses is referred to as **punctuation** (Watzlawick, Beavin, & Jackson, 1967). Everyone punctuates the continuous sequences of events into stimuli and responses for convenience. Moreover, as the example of the husband and wife illustrates, punctuation usually is done in ways that benefit the self and are consistent with a person's self-image.

Understanding how another person interprets a situation, how he or she punctuates, is a crucial step in interpersonal understanding. It is also essential in achieving empathy (feeling what the other person is feeling). In all communication encounters, but especially in conflicts, try to see how others punctuate the situation.

Interpersonal Communication Is Inevitable, Irreversible, and Unrepeatable

Interpersonal communication cannot be prevented (is inevitable), cannot be reversed (is irreversible), and cannot be repeated (is unrepeatable). Let's look briefly at each of these qualities and their implications.

Inevitability   Often communication is thought of as intentional, purposeful, and consciously motivated. In many instances it is. But the **inevitability** principle means that in many instances you're communicating even though you might not think you are or might not even want to be. Consider, for example, the new editorial assistant sitting at the desk with an "expressionless" face, perhaps staring out the window. Although this assistant might say that she or he is not communicating with the manager, the manager may derive any of a variety of messages from this behavior—for example, that the assistant lacks interest, is bored, or is worried about something. In any event, the manager is receiving messages even though the assistant might not intend to communicate. In an interactional situation, all behavior is potentially communication. Any aspect of your behavior may communicate if the other person gives it message value. On the other hand, if the behavior (for example, the assistant's looking out the window) goes unnoticed, then no communication will have taken place.

Further, when you are in an interactional situation, your responses all have potential message value. For example, if you notice someone winking at you, you must respond in some way. Even if you don't respond openly, that lack of response is itself a response and it communicates (assuming it is perceived by the other person).

Irreversibility   The processes of some systems can be reversed. For example, you can turn water into ice and then reverse the process by melting the ice. Moreover, you can repeat this reversal of ice and water as many times as you wish. Similarly, you can authorize and then deauthorize an app on Facebook as many times as you wish. Other systems, however, are irreversible. In these systems, the process can move in only one direction; it cannot go back again. For example, you can turn grapes into wine, but you cannot reverse the process and turn the wine back into grapes. It's similar to naming or selecting a category for your Facebook page; once you publish it, you cannot unpublish either, short of deleting the entire page and starting over. Similarly, you can post a message on Facebook and then delete the message but you cannot delete the memory of those who already read the message.

Interpersonal communication is irreversible. This quality of **irreversibility** means that what you have communicated remains communicated; you cannot *un*communicate. Although you may try to qualify, negate, or somehow reduce the effects of your message, once it has been sent and received, the message itself cannot be reversed. In interpersonal interactions (especially in conflict), you need to be especially careful that you don't say things you may wish to withdraw later. Similarly, commitment messages, such as "I love you," must be monitored lest you commit yourself to a position you may be uncomfortable with later.

Face-to-face communication is evanescent; it fades after you have spoken. There is no trace of your communications outside of the memories of the parties involved or of those who overheard your conversation. In computer-mediated communication, however, the messages are written and may be saved, stored, and printed. Both face-to-face and computer-mediated messages may be kept confidential or revealed publicly. But computer messages may be made public more easily and spread more quickly than face-to-face messages. Also, in communicating on Facebook, for example, it's relatively easy to intend to send a message to one person but actually send it to an entire group. Written messages provide clear evidence of what you have said and when you said it.

Because electronic communication often is permanent, you may wish to be cautious when you're e-mailing, posting your profile, or posting a message. Consider the following:

- Electronic messages are virtually impossible to destroy. Often e-mails that you think you deleted or a post you wrote in anger will remain on servers and workstations and may be retrieved by a clever hacker or may simply be copied and distributed to people you'd rather not have see what you wrote.
- Electronic messages can easily be made public. Your post on your blog or on a social networking site can be sent to anyone. Your rant about a former employer may reach a prospective employer, who may see you as a complainer and reject your job application. In fact, employers regularly search such sites for information about job candidates.
- Electronic messages are not privileged communication; they can easily be accessed by others and be used against you. And you'll not be able to deny saying something; it will be there in black and white.

Unrepeatability   In addition to being inevitable and irreversible, interpersonal communication is unrepeatable. The reason for this quality of **unrepeatability** is simple: Everyone and everything is constantly changing. As a result, you can never recapture the exact same situation, frame of mind, or relationship dynamics that defined a previous interpersonal act. For example, you can never repeat the experience of meeting a particular person for the first time, comforting a grieving friend, or resolving a specific conflict. And, as you surely know, you never get a second chance to make a first impression.

See "social media warnings" at tcbdevito.blogspot.com for some added insights into the dangers of posting inappropriate photos and messages on your social media site. Do you think this concern is warranted? Overblown?

You can, of course, try again, as when you say, "I'm sorry I came off so forward; can we try again?" But notice that even when you say this, you don't erase the initial impression. Instead, you try to counteract the initial (and perhaps negative) impression by going through the motions once more. In doing so, you try to create a more positive impression, which you hope will lessen the original negative effect—and which often does.

Summary

 Use your smartphone or tablet device (or log on to mycommunicationlab.com) to hear an audio summary of this chapter.

These chapter summaries are designed to refresh your memory of the topics covered in the chapter. Note that the major heads of the chapter are repeated here to better connect them and the summary propositions.

This chapter introduced the importance of interpersonal communication, its essential nature, its elements, and some of its major principles.

Why Study Interpersonal Communication

1. Intellectual benefits include a deeper understanding of yourself and others and of relationships.
2. Practical benefits include personal, social or relationship, and professional benefits.

The Nature of Interpersonal Communication

3. Interpersonal communication is communication between two or more interdependent individuals.
4. Interpersonal communication is inherently relational.
5. Interpersonal communication exists on a continuum from relatively impersonal to intimate.
6. Interpersonal communication involves both verbal and nonverbal messages.
7. Interpersonal communication can take place, and interpersonal relationships can develop, through face-to-face interactions as well as those you have on the Internet.
8. Interpersonal communication can range from extremely ineffective to extremely effective.

Elements of Interpersonal Communication

9. The source–receiver concept emphasizes that you send and receive interpersonal messages simultaneously.
10. Encoding–decoding involves putting meaning into verbal and nonverbal messages and deriving meaning from the messages you receive from others.
11. Messages are the signals that serve as stimuli for a receiver; metamessages are messages about other messages. Feedback messages are messages that are sent back by the receiver to the source in response to the source's messages. Feedforward messages are messages that preface other messages and ask that the listener approach future messages in a certain way.
12. Channels are the media through which messages pass and which act as a bridge between source and receiver; for example, the vocal–auditory channel used in speaking or the cutaneous–tactile channel used in touch.
13. Noise is the inevitable physical, physiological, psychological, and semantic interference that distorts messages.
14. Context is the physical, social–psychological, temporal, and cultural environment in which communication takes place.
15. Ethics is the moral dimension of communication, the study of what makes behavior moral or good as opposed to immoral and bad.

Principles of Interpersonal Communication

16. Interpersonal communication is a transactional process. Interpersonal communication is a process, an ongoing event, in which the elements are interdependent; communication is constantly occurring and changing. Don't expect clear-cut beginnings or endings or sameness from one time to another.
17. Interpersonal communication is purposeful. Five purposes may be identified: to learn, relate, influence, play, and help.
18. Interpersonal communication is ambiguous. All messages are potentially ambiguous; different people will derive different meanings from the "same" message. There is ambiguity in all relationships.
19. Interpersonal relationships may be symmetrical or complementary; interpersonal interactions may stimulate similar or different behavior patterns.
20. Interpersonal communication refers both to content and to the relationship between the participants.
21. Interpersonal communication is punctuated; that is, everyone separates communication sequences into stimuli and responses on the basis of his or her own perspective.
22. Interpersonal communication is inevitable, irreversible, and unrepeatable. When in an interactional situation, you cannot not communicate; you cannot uncommunicate; and you cannot repeat exactly a specific message.

Key Terms

These are the key terms discussed in this chapter.

ambiguity
asynchronous
  communication
channel
choice points
competence
complementary
  relationship
content dimension

context
decoding
encoding
ethics
feedback
feedforward
inevitability
interpersonal
    communication

irreversibility
messages
metamessages
mindfulness
mindlessness
noise
punctuation
relationship dimension
research

source–receiver
symmetrical relationship
synchronous
  communication
theory
transactional perspective
unrepeatability

MyCommunicationLab Explorations

MyCommunication**Lab**®

Communication Choice Points

Revisit the chapter-opening video, "Ryan Asks for a Recommendation." Recall from the video that Ryan, a communication major, needs a letter of recommendation for a summer internship. Ryan decides to ask Professor Starck, a popular instructor who he previously had in class. Ryan tries three different approaches to ask for a letter of recommendation, with varying degrees of success. "Ryan Asks for a Recommendation" looks at how the elements of communication play into an effective message, including context, feedback, feedforward, noise, and the communication channel. It also previews how expectations and politeness may affect the receiver and the message.

Log on to mycommunicationlab.com to view the video for this chapter, "Ryan Asks for a Recommendation," and then answer the related discussion questions.

Additional Resources

A variety of exercises, identified at the end of each chapter and available on the MyCommunicationLab website, will help you gain a deeper understanding of the concepts in this chapter and help you to apply this material to your own interpersonal interactions.

1 Models of Interpersonal Communication asks you to draw a model of interpersonal communication that will visualize and explain a specific interpersonal situation. **2** How Would You Give Feedback? and **3** How Would You Give Feedforward? provide practice in examining the types of feedback and feedforward you have available. **4** Ethics in Interpersonal Communication asks you to consider what you feel is an ethical response in a variety of interpersonal situations. **5** How Can You Respond to Contradictory Messages? looks at types of situations that may call for you to respond to contradictory meanings. **6** I'd Prefer to Be is an icebreaker that will help you get to know others in the class and at the same time explore factors that can influence your interpersonal communication. **7** Applying the Axioms and **8** Analyzing an Interaction provide opportunities to examine how the axioms may be applied to actual interpersonal situations.

Culture and Interpersonal Communication

From Chapter 2 of *The Interpersonal Communication Book*, Thirteenth Edition. Joseph A. DeVito. Copyright © 2013 by Pearson Education, Inc. All rights reserved.

Culture and Interpersonal Communication

Culture

Cultural Differences

Principles for Effective Intercultural Communication

Pearson Education

Charles will be meeting Mei Li's extended family for the first time, and both he and Mei Li are a bit nervous. They consider how the differences in their cultures may affect their relationship and their communication choices. Watch the video clips to see how Charles' and Mei Li's relationship is affected by their communication choices in the video, "Meet the Family" (www.mycommunicationlab.com).

Why read this chapter?

Because you'll learn about:

- the nature of culture.
- the ways in which cultures differ.
- the principles of intercultural communication.

Because you'll learn to:

- communicate with an appreciation of cultural influences and differences.
- communicate more effectively in intercultural communication situations.

This chapter discusses one of the foundation concepts of interpersonal communication, culture—an often misunderstood concept. More specifically, this chapter explains the nature of culture and its relationship to interpersonal communication, the major differences among cultures and how these differences affect interpersonal communication, and the ways you can improve your own intercultural communication.

Forestpath/Shutterstock

 Culture

Culture is defined as (1) the relatively specialized lifestyle of a group of people (2) that is passed on from one generation to the next through communication, not through genes.

(1) Included in a social group's "culture" is everything that members of that group have produced and developed—their values, beliefs, artifacts, and language; their ways of behaving; their art, laws, religion, and, of course, communication theories, styles, and attitudes.

(2) Culture is passed on from one generation to the next through communication, not through genes. Culture is not synonymous with race or nationality. The term *culture* does not refer to color of skin or shape of eyes, as these are passed on through genes, not communication. Of course, because members of a particular ethnic or national group are often taught similar beliefs, attitudes, and values, it's possible to speak of "Hispanic culture" or "African American culture." It's important to realize, however, that within any large group—especially a group based on race or nationality—there will be enormous differences. The Kansas farmer and the Wall Street executive may both be, say, German American, but may differ widely in their attitudes, beliefs, and lifestyles. In some ways the Kansas farmer may be closer in attitudes and values to a Chinese farmer than to the New York financier.

In ordinary conversation *sex* and *gender* are often used synonymously. In academic discussions of culture, however,

VIEWPOINTS ⬧ Consider two opposing views on culture: cultural evolution and cultural relativism. The *cultural evolution* approach (often called social Darwinism) holds that much as the human species evolved from earlier life forms to Homo sapiens, cultures also evolve. Under this view, some cultures may be considered advanced and others primitive. Most contemporary scholars reject this view, however, because the judgments that distinguish one culture from another have no basis in science and are instead based on individual values and preferences.

Cultural relativism theory, on the other hand, holds that all cultures are different but that no culture is either superior or inferior to any other (Berry, Poortinga, Segall, & Dasen, 1992; Mosteller, 2008). Before reading any further, how would you explain the nature of culture and how it developed and how it's passed on from one generation to another?

they're more often distinguished. *Sex* refers to the biological distinction between male and female; sex is determined by genes, by biology. *Gender*, on the other hand, refers to the "social construction of masculinity and femininity within a culture" (Stewart, Cooper, & Stewart, 2003). Gender (masculinity and femininity) is what boys and girls learn from their culture; it's the attitudes, beliefs, values, and ways of communicating and relating to one another that boys and girls learn as they grow up.

Because of this, although sex is transmitted genetically and not by communication, gender may be considered a cultural variable—largely because cultures teach boys and girls different attitudes, beliefs, values, and ways of communicating and relating to others. Thus, you act like a man or a woman in part because of what your culture has taught you about how men and women should act. This does not, of course, deny that biological differences also play a role in the differences between male and female behavior. In fact, research continues to uncover biological roots of male/female differences we once thought were entirely learned (McCroskey, 1998).

Enculturation, Ethnic Identity, and Acculturation

Culture is transmitted from one generation to another through **enculturation**, the process by which you learn the culture into which you're born (your native culture). Parents, peer groups, schools, religious institutions, government agencies, and the media are the main teachers of culture.

Through enculturation you develop an **ethnic identity**, a commitment to the beliefs and philosophy of your culture that, not surprisingly, can act as a protective shield against discrimination (Chung & Ting-Toomey, 1999; R.M. Lee, 2005). The degree to which you identify with your cultural group can be measured by your responses to questions such as the following (from Ting-Toomey, 1981). Using a five-point scale, with 1 meaning "strongly disagree" and 5 meaning "strongly agree," indicate how true of you these statements are:

_____ 1. I am increasing my involvement in activities with my ethnic group.
_____ 2. I involve myself in causes that will help members of my ethnic group.
_____ 3. It feels natural being part of my ethnic group.
_____ 4. I have spent time trying to find out more about my own ethnic group.
_____ 5. I am happy to be a member of my ethnic group.
_____ 6. I have a strong sense of belonging to my ethnic group.
_____ 7. I often talk to other members of my group to learn more about my ethnic culture.

High scores (say, 4s and 5s) indicate a strong commitment to your culture's values and beliefs; low numbers (1s and 2s) indicate a relatively weak commitment.

As you can imagine, you acquire your ethnic identity from family and friends who observe ethnic holidays, patronize ethnic parades, and eat ethnic foods; from your schooling where you learn about your own culture and ethnic background; and from your own media and Internet exposure. Ethnic identity can turn into ethnocentrism if you begin looking at your culture's practices as the only right ways to behave or seeing the practices of other cultures as inferior.

A different process of learning culture is **acculturation**, the process by which you learn the rules and norms of a culture different from your native culture. In acculturation your original or native culture is modified through direct contact with or exposure to a new and different culture. For example, when immigrants settle in the United States (the host culture), their own culture becomes influenced by the host culture. Gradually, the values, ways of behaving, and beliefs of the host culture become more and more a part of the immigrants' culture. At the same time, of course, the host culture also changes as it interacts with the immigrants' culture. Generally, however, the culture of the immigrant changes more.

INTERPERSONAL CHOICE POINT

Violating Cultural Norms or Expectations

You're invited to a holiday party by people you recently met at school. Having lots of money yourself and not knowing much about anyone else, you buy a really expensive present. As the gifts are being opened, you notice that everyone gave very inexpensive items—a photograph, a book, a scented candle. Your gift is next. What are some of the things you can do to lessen the effect of your choice, which is sure to seem very strange to everyone else?

The reasons for this are that the host country's members far outnumber the immigrant group and that the media are largely dominated by and reflect the values and customs of the host culture (Kim, 1988, 2001).

New citizens' acceptance of the new culture depends on many factors (Kim, 1988). Immigrants who come from cultures similar to the host culture will become acculturated more easily. Similarly, those who are younger and better educated become acculturated more quickly than do older and less well-educated people. Personality factors also play a part. Persons who are risk takers and open-minded, for example, have greater acculturation potential. Also, persons who are familiar with the host culture before immigration—through interpersonal contact or through media exposure—will be acculturated more readily.

The Relevance of Culture

Because of (1) demographic changes, (2) increased sensitivity to cultural differences, (3) economic interdependency, (4) advances in communication technology, and (5) the fact that communication competence is specific to a culture (what works in one culture will not necessarily work in another), it's impossible to communicate effectively without being aware of how culture influences human communication.

Demographic Changes Most obvious, perhaps, are the vast demographic changes taking place throughout the United States. Whereas at one time the United States was a country largely populated by Europeans, it's now a country greatly influenced by the enormous number of new citizens from Latin and South America, Africa, and Asia. The same demographic shift is noticeable on college campuses. These changes have brought different interpersonal customs and the need to understand and adapt to new ways of communicating.

VIEWPOINTS What's in a name? Some researchers prefer to use the term *subculture* to refer to smaller cultures within larger cultures; other researchers do not use the term, feeling that it implies that some cultures are less important than others. Some researchers prefer to use the term *co-culture* to refer to a variety of cultures coexisting side by side, whereas others think this term is imprecise because all cultures coexist (Lustig & Koester, 2010); these theorists prefer simply to refer to all cultures as cultures. How do you feel about the terms *subculture*, *co-culture*, and just plain *culture*?

Adisornfoto/Shutterstock

Sensitivity to Cultural Differences As a people we've become increasingly sensitive to cultural differences. American society has moved from an assimilationist attitude (people should leave their native culture behind and adapt to their new culture) to a perspective that values cultural diversity (people should retain their native cultural ways). We have moved from the metaphor of the melting pot, in which different cultures blended into one, to a metaphor of a spaghetti bowl or tossed salad, in which there is some blending but specific and different tastes and flavors still remain. In this diverse society, and with some notable exceptions—hate speech, racism, sexism, homophobia, and classism come quickly to mind—we are more concerned with saying the right thing and ultimately with developing a society where all cultures coexist and enrich one another. As a bonus, the ability to interact effectively with members of other cultures often translates into financial gain and increased employment opportunities and advancement prospects as well.

Economic and Political Interdependence Today, most countries are economically dependent on one another. Our economic lives depend on our ability to communicate effectively across different cultures. Similarly, our political well-being depends in great part on that of other cultures. Political unrest in any place in the world—South Africa, Eastern Europe, Asia, and the Middle East, to take a few examples—affects our own security. Intercultural communication and understanding seem more crucial now than ever.

VIEWPOINTS Assume you're a judge and the following case is presented to you (*Time*, December 2, 1993, p. 61): A Chinese immigrant killed his wife in New York because he suspected her of cheating. A "cultural defense" was offered, essentially claiming that infidelity so shames a man that he is uncontrollable in his anger. Would this cultural defense have influenced your judgment? In the actual case, influenced by an anthropologist's testimony that infidelity is so serious in Chinese culture that it pushed the defendant to commit the crime, the judge sentenced the defendant to five years' probation. How do you feel about "cultural defenses" in general? Are there some cultural defenses you'd accept and others you would not?

Spread of Technology The rapid spread of technology has made intercultural communication as easy as it is inevitable. News from foreign countries is commonplace. You see nightly—in vivid detail—what is going on in remote countries, just as you see what's happening in your own city and state. Of course, the Internet has made intercultural communication as easy as writing a note on your computer. You can now communicate just as easily by e-mail or any social network site with someone in Asia or Europe, for example, as you can with someone living a few blocks away or in the next dorm room.

Culture-Specific Nature of Interpersonal Communication Still another reason why culture is so important is that interpersonal competence is culture-specific; what proves effective in one culture may prove ineffective in another. Many Asians, for example, often find that the values they were taught—values that promote cooperation and face-saving but discourage competitiveness and assertiveness—work against them in cultures that value competition and outspokenness (Cho, 2000). The same would be true for executives from the United States working in Asia. An example of these differences can be seen in business meetings. In the United States corporate executives get down to business during the first several minutes of a meeting. In Japan business executives interact socially for an extended period and try to find out something about one another. Thus, the communication principle influenced by U.S. culture would advise participants to get down to the meeting's agenda during the first five minutes. The principle influenced by Japanese culture would advise participants to avoid dealing with business until everyone has socialized sufficiently and feels well enough acquainted to begin negotiations.

Another example: Giving a birthday gift to a close friend would be appreciated by many; but Jehovah's Witnesses would frown on this act because they don't celebrate birthdays (Dresser, 2005). Neither principle is right, neither is wrong. Each is effective within its own culture and ineffective outside its own culture.

The Aim of a Cultural Perspective

Because culture permeates all forms of communication, it's necessary to understand its influences if you're to understand how communication works and master its skills. As illustrated throughout this text, culture influences communications of all types (Jandt, 2007; Moon, 1996). It influences what you say to yourself and how you talk with friends, lovers, and family in everyday conversation (for example, Shibazaki & Brennan, 1998). It influences how you interact in groups and how much importance you place on the group versus the individual. It influences the topics you talk about and the strategies you use in communicating information or in persuading. It influences how you use the media and the credibility you attribute to them.

Consider attitudes toward age. If you were raised in the United States, you probably grew up with a youth bias (young is good, old is not so good)—an attitude the media reinforce daily—and might well assume that this preference for youth would be universal across all cultures. But it isn't; and if you assume it is, you may be in for intercultural difficulties. A good example is the case of the American journalist in China who remarked that the government official he was talking with was probably too young to remember a particular event—a comment that would be taken as a compliment by most youth-oriented Americans. But to the Chinese official the comment appeared to be an insult, a suggestion that the official was too young to deserve respect (Smith, 2002).

You need cultural understanding to communicate effectively in a wide variety of intercultural situations. Success in interpersonal communication—at your job and in your social and personal life—will depend in great part on your understanding of and your ability to communicate effectively with persons who are culturally different from yourself. Daily, the media bombard you with evidence of racial tensions, religious disagreements, sexual bias, and, in general, the problems caused when intercultural communication fails.

This emphasis on culture does not imply that you should accept all cultural practices or that all cultural practices will necessarily be equal in terms of your own values and beliefs (Hatfield & Rapson, 1996). Nor does it imply that you have to accept or follow all of the practices of your own culture. For example, even if the majority in your culture find cockfighting acceptable, you need not agree with or follow the practice. Nor need you consider this practice equal to a cultural practice in which animals are treated kindly. You can reject capitalism or communism or socialism regardless of the culture in which you were raised. Of course, going against your culture's traditions and values is often very difficult. But it's important to realize that culture influences, it does not determine, your values or behavior. Often personality factors (your degree of assertiveness, extroversion, or optimism, for example) will prove more influential than culture (Hatfield & Rapson, 1996).

As demonstrated throughout this text, cultural differences exist throughout the interpersonal communication spectrum—from the way you use eye contact to the way you develop or dissolve a relationship (Chang & Holt, 1996). Culture even influences your level of happiness, which in turn influences your attitudes and the positivity and negativity of your messages (Kirn, 2005). But these differences should not blind you to the great number of similarities existing among even the most widely separated cultures. When discussing differences, remember that these are usually matters of degree rather than all-or-none. For example, most cultures value honesty, but some cultures give it greater emphasis than others. In addition,

For a similar example of cultural differences see Intercultural Communication: Gaining Weight? at tcbdevito.blogspot.com. Have you ever witnessed or been a part of such cultural misunderstandings?

Ethics in Interpersonal Communication

CULTURE AND ETHICS

One of the most shocking revelations to come to world attention after the events of September 11, 2001, was the way in which women were treated under Taliban rule in Afghanistan: Females could not be educated or even go out in public without a male relative escort, and when in public had to wear garments that covered their entire body.

Throughout history there have been cultural practices that today would be judged unethical. Sacrificing virgins to the gods, burning people who held different religious beliefs, and sending children to fight religious wars are obvious examples. But even today there are practices woven deep into the fabric of different cultures that you might find unethical. A few examples:

- bronco riding and bullfighting, practices involving inflicting pain and even causing the death of horses and bulls
- "female circumcision," in which part or all of a young girl's genitals are surgically altered so that she can never experience sexual intercourse without extreme pain, a practice designed to keep her a virgin until marriage
- the belief and practice that a woman must be subservient to her husband's will
- the practice of wearing fur—which in some cases means killing wild animals and in others raising animals so they can be killed when their pelts are worth the most money

ETHICAL CHOICE POINT

You're talking with new work colleagues who are discussing one of these practices with great approval; your colleagues argue that each culture has a right to its own practices and beliefs. Given your own beliefs about these issues and about cultural diversity, what ethical obligations do you have to speak your mind without—you hope—jeopardizing your new position?

advances in media and technology and the widespread use of the Internet are influencing cultures and cultural change and are perhaps homogenizing different cultures to some extent, lessening differences and increasing similarities.

Cultural Differences

For effective interpersonal communication to take place in a global world, goodwill and good intentions are helpful—but they are not enough. If you're going to be effective, you need to know how cultures differ and how these differences influence communication. Research supports several major cultural distinctions that have an impact on communication: (1) individualist or collectivist orientation, (2) emphasis on context (whether high or low), (3) power structure, (4) masculinity–femininity, (5) tolerance for ambiguity, (6) long- and short-term orientation, and (7) indulgence and restraint. Each of these dimensions of difference has significant impact on all forms of communication (Gudykunst, 1994; Hall & Hall, 1987; Hofstede, Hofstede, & Minkov, 2010). Following the major researchers in this area, these differences are discussed in terms of countries, even though in many cases different nations have very similar cultures (and so we often speak of *Hispanic culture*, which would include a variety of countries). In other cases, the same country includes varied cultures (for example, Hong Kong, although a part of China, is considered separately because it has a somewhat different culture) (Hofstede, Hofstede, & Minkov, 2010).

Before reading about these dimensions, take the accompanying self-test. It will help you think about your own cultural orientations and will personalize the text discussion and make it more meaningful.

Test Yourself   What's Your Cultural Orientation?

For each of the items below, select either *a* or *b*. In some cases, you may feel that neither *a* nor *b* describes yourself accurately; in these cases simply select the one that is closer to your feeling. As you'll see when you read this next section, these are not *either/or* preferences, but *more-or-less* preferences.

1. Success, to my way of thinking, is better measured by
   a. the extent to which I surpass others.
   b. my contribution to the group effort.
2. My heroes are generally
   a. people who stand out from the crowd.
   b. team players.
3. If I were a manager, I would likely
   a. reprimand a worker in public if the occasion warranted.
   b. always reprimand in private regardless of the situation.
4. In communicating, it's generally more important to be
   a. polite rather than accurate or direct.
   b. accurate and direct rather than polite.
5. As a student (and if I feel well informed), I feel
   a. comfortable challenging a professor.
   b. uncomfortable challenging a professor.
6. In choosing a life partner or even close friends, I feel more comfortable
   a. with just about anyone, not necessarily one from my own culture and class.
   b. with those from my own culture and class.

7. In a conflict situation, I'd be more likely to
   a. confront conflicts directly and seek to win.
   b. confront conflicts with the aim of compromise.
8. If I were a manager of an organization, I would stress
   a. competition and aggressiveness.
   b. worker satisfaction.
9. As a student, I'm more comfortable with assignments in which
   a. there is freedom for interpretation.
   b. there are clearly defined instructions.
10. Generally, when approaching an undertaking with which I've had no experience, I feel
    a. comfortable.
    b. uncomfortable.
11. Generally,
    a. I save money for the future.
    b. I spend what I have.
12. My general belief about child rearing is that
    a. children should be cared for by their mothers.
    b. children can be cared for by others.
13. For the most part,
    a. I believe I'm in control of my own life.
    b. I believe my life is largely determined by forces out of my control.
14. In general,
    a. I have leisure time to do what I find fun.
    b. I have little leisure time.

How Did You Do?

- Items 1–2 refer to the **individualist–collectivist orientation**; *a* responses indicate an individualist orientation, and *b* responses indicate a collectivist orientation.
- Items 3–4 refer to the **high- and low-context** characteristics; *a* responses indicate a high-context focus, and *b* responses indicate a low-context focus.
- Items 5–6 refer to the **power distance** dimension; *a* responses indicate greater comfort with a low power distance, and *b* responses indicate comfort with a high power distance.
- Items 7–8 refer to the **masculine–feminine** dimension; *a* responses indicate a masculine orientation; *b* responses, a feminine orientation.
- Items 9–10 refer to the **tolerance for ambiguity** or uncertainty; *a* responses indicate high tolerance, and *b* responses indicate a low tolerance.
- Items 11–12 refer to the **long- or short-term orientation**; *a* responses indicate long-term orientation, and *b* responses indicate short-term orientation.
- Items 13–14 refer to **indulgent and restraint orientation**; *a* responses indicate indulgent, and *b* responses indicate restraint cultures.

What Will You Do? Understanding your preferences in a wide variety of situations as culturally influenced (at least in part) is a first step to controlling them and to changing them should you wish to do so. This understanding also helps you modify your behavior as appropriate for greater effectiveness in certain situations. The remaining discussion in this section further explains these orientations and their implications.

Individual and Collective Orientation

Cultures differ in the way in which they promote individualist and collectivist thinking and behaving (Hofstede, Hofstede, & Minkov, 2010; Singh & Pereira, 2005). An **individualist culture** teaches members the importance of individual values such as power, achievement, hedonism, and stimulation. Examples include the cultures of the United States, Australia, United Kingdom, Netherlands,

VIEWPOINTS ✛ It's been argued that in the United States women are more likely to view themselves as interdependents, having a more collectivist orientation, whereas men are more likely to view themselves as independents, having a more individualist orientation (Cross & Madson, 1997). Does your experience support this?

Canada, New Zealand, Italy, Belgium, Denmark, and Sweden. A **collectivist culture**, on the other hand, teaches members the importance of group values such as benevolence, tradition, and conformity. Examples of such cultures include Guatemala, Ecuador, Panama, Venezuela, Colombia, Indonesia, Pakistan, China, Costa Rica, and Peru.

One of the major differences between these two orientations is the extent to which an individual's goals or the group's goals are given greater importance. Of course, these goals are not mutually exclusive—you probably have both individualist and collectivist tendencies. For example, you may compete with other members of your basketball team for the most baskets or most valuable player award (and thus emphasize individual goals). At the same time, however, you will—in a game—act in a way that will benefit the entire team (and thus emphasize group goals). In actual practice, both individual and collective tendencies will help you and your team each achieve your goals. Yet most people and most cultures have a dominant orientation. In an individualist culture members are responsible for themselves and perhaps their immediate family. In a collectivist culture members are responsible for the entire group.

In some instances these tendencies may come into conflict. For example, do you shoot for the basket and try to raise your own individual score, or do you pass the ball to another player who is better positioned to score and thus benefit your team? You make this distinction in popular talk when you call someone a team player (collectivist orientation) or an individual player (individualist orientation).

Success in an individualist culture is measured by the extent to which you surpass other members of your group; you take pride in standing out from the crowd. And your heroes—in the media, for example—are likely to be those who are unique and who stand apart. In a collectivist culture success is measured by your contribution to the achievements of the group as a whole; you take pride in your similarity to other members of your group. Your heroes are more likely to be team players who don't stand out from the rest of the group's members.

Distinctions between in-group members and out-group members are extremely important in collectivist cultures. In individualistic cultures, which prize each person's individuality, the distinction is likely to be less important. In fact, closely related to individualism and collectivism is universalism and exclusionism (Hofstede, Hofstede, & Minkov, 2010). A universalist culture (highly correlated with individualism) is one in which people are treated as individuals, rather than in terms of the groups (racial, sexual, national, for example) to which they

The key to your universe is that you can choose.
—*Frederick Carl Frieseke*

belong. A universalist orientation teaches a respect for other cultures, other beliefs, and other ways of doing things. An exclusionist orientation (highly correlated with collectivism) fosters a strong in-group affiliation with much less respect for out-group members. Special privileges are reserved for in-group members while indifference, impoliteness, and, in some cases, even hostility are directed at members of other cultures.

Table 1 compares and summarizes the differences between individualist and collectivist cultures.

High- and Low-Context Cultures

Cultures also differ in the extent to which information is made explicit, on the one hand, or is assumed to be in the context or in the persons communicating, on the other. In a **high-context culture** much of the information in communication is in the context or in the person—for example, information that was shared through previous communications, through assumptions about each other, and through shared experiences. The information is thus known by all participants, but it is not explicitly stated in the verbal message. In a **low-context culture** most of the information is explicitly stated in the verbal message; in formal transactions it will be stated in written (or contract) form.

High-context cultures are also collectivist cultures (Gudykunst & Kim, 1992; Gudykunst, Ting-Toomey, & Chua, 1988). These cultures (Japanese, Arabic, Latin American, Thai, Korean, Apache, and Mexican are examples) place great emphasis on personal relationships and oral agreements (Victor, 1992). Low-context cultures are also individualist cultures. These cultures (German, Swedish, Norwegian, and American are examples) place less emphasis on personal relationships and more emphasis on verbalized, explicit explanation—for example, on written contracts in business transactions.

A frequent source of intercultural misunderstanding that can be traced to the distinction between high- and low-context cultures is seen in face-saving (Hall & Hall, 1987). People in high-context cultures place a great deal more emphasis on face-saving, on avoiding one's own or another's possible embarrassment. For example, they're more likely to avoid argument for fear of causing others to lose face, whereas people in low-context cultures (with their individualist orientation) will use argument to make a point. Similarly, in high-context cultures criticism should take place only in private. Low-context cultures may not make this public–private distinction. Low-context managers who criticize high-context workers in public will find that their criticism causes interpersonal problems—and does little to resolve the difficulty that led to the criticism in the first place (Victor, 1992).

Members of high-context cultures are reluctant to say no for fear of offending and causing the person to lose face. So, for example, it's necessary to understand when the Japanese

INTERPERSONAL CHOICE POINT

Giving Directions in High- and Low-Context Situations

To further appreciate the distinction between high and low context, consider giving directions to some specific place on campus (such as the cafeteria) to someone who knows the campus and who you can assume knows the local landmarks (which would resemble a high-context situation) and to a newcomer who you cannot assume is familiar with campus landmarks (which would resemble a low-context situation). What are some of the ways you could give directions to each of these individuals? What are the major ways in which they differ?

TABLE 1   Individualist and Collectivist Cultures

This table summarizes some of the major features of individualist and collectivist cultures. You may find it helpful to construct similar tables for the other cultural differences discussed in this chapter.

	Individualist Cultures	Collectivist Cultures
Cultural Trait	An **individualist culture** teaches members the importance of individual values such as power, achievement, hedonism, and stimulation.	A **collectivist culture** teaches members the importance of group values such as benevolence, tradition, and conformity.
Representative Cultures	United States, Australia, United Kingdom, Netherlands, Canada, New Zealand, Italy, Belgium, Denmark, and Sweden	Guatemala, Ecuador, Panama, Venezuela, Colombia, Indonesia, Pakistan, China, Costa Rica, and Peru
Interpersonal Implications	You: ■ measure success by the extent to which you surpass others. ■ take pride in standing out from the crowd. ■ have heroes who are unique and who stand apart. ■ place little importance on the distinction between in-group and out-group.	You: ■ measure success by the extent to which you contribute to the group's goals. ■ take pride in being a group member. ■ have heroes who are group oriented. ■ place great importance on the distinction between in-group and out-group.

executive's *yes* means *yes* and when it means *no*. The difference is not in the words used but in the way in which they're used. It's easy to see how the low-context individual may interpret this reluctance to be direct—to say *no* when you mean *no*—as a weakness or as an unwillingness to confront reality.

Power Distance

Power distance refers to how power is distributed in a society. In some cultures power is concentrated in the hands of a few, and there's a great difference between the power held by these people and the power of the ordinary citizen. These are called **high-power-distance cultures**. The ten countries with the highest power distance are Malaysia, Slovakia, Guatemala, Panama, the Philippines, Russia, Romania, Serbia, Suriname, and Mexico (Hofstede, Hofstede, & Minkov, 2010; Singh & Pereira, 2005). In **low-power-distance cultures,** power is more evenly distributed throughout the citizenry. The ten countries with the lowest power distance are Austria, Israel, Denmark, New Zealand, Switzerland, Ireland, Sweden, Norway, Finland, and Great Britain (Hofstede, Hofstede, & Minkov, 2010; Singh & Pereira, 2005). In a list of 76 countries, the United States ranks 59th (58 nations are higher in power distance). These differences affect communication in numerous ways. For example, in high-power-distance cultures there's a great power distance between students and teachers; students are expected to be modest, polite, and totally respectful. In low-power-distance cultures (and you can see this clearly in U.S. college classrooms), students are expected to demonstrate their knowledge and command of the subject matter, participate in discussions with the teacher, and even

Kathy Willens/AP Photos

challenge the teacher—something many high-power-distance culture members wouldn't even think of doing.

Friendship and dating relationships also will be influenced by the power distance between groups (Andersen, 1991). In India, for example, such relationships are expected to take place within your cultural class. In Sweden a person is expected to select friends and romantic partners not on the basis of class or culture but on the basis of such individual factors as personality, appearance, and the like.

Low-power-distance cultures expect you to confront a friend, partner, or supervisor assertively; in these cultures there is a general feeling of equality that is consistent with assertive behavior (Borden, 1991). High-power-distance cultures, on the other hand, view direct confrontation and assertiveness negatively, especially if directed at a superior.

Masculine and Feminine Cultures

Especially important for self-concept is the culture's attitude about gender roles; that is, about how a man or woman should act. In fact, a popular classification of cultures is in terms of their masculinity and femininity (Hofstede, Hofstede, & Minkov, 1998, 2010). When denoting cultural orientations, the terms *masculine* and *feminine* should not be interpreted as perpetuating stereotypes but as reflecting some of the commonly held assumptions of a sizable number of people throughout the world. Some intercultural theorists note that equivalent terms would be *achievement* and *nurturance*, but because research is conducted under the terms *masculine* and *feminine* and because these are

VIEWPOINTS In 1995 the Emma Lazarus poem inscribed on the Statue of Liberty was changed. The original last five lines of the poem, "The New Colossus," had been as follows, but in 1995 the words in brackets were deleted:
Give me your tired, your poor, Your huddled masses yearning to breathe free, [The wretched refuse of your teeming shore,] Send these, the homeless, tempest-tost, to me: I lift my lamp beside the golden door. The late Harvard zoologist Stephen Jay Gould, commenting on this change, noted that the poem no longer represented what Lazarus wrote. "The language police triumph and integrity bleeds," said Gould (1995). Yet it is true that calling immigrants "wretched refuse" is insulting; if Lazarus had been writing in 1995, she probably wouldn't have used that phrase. Would you have supported deleting the line?

the terms you'd use to search the electronic databases, we use these terms here (Lustig & Koester, 2010).

A highly **masculine culture** values aggressiveness, material success, and strength. A highly **feminine culture** values modesty, concern for relationships and the quality of life, and tenderness. The 10 countries with the highest masculinity score are (beginning with the highest) Japan, Austria, Venezuela, Italy, Switzerland, Mexico, Ireland, Jamaica, Great Britain, and Germany. The 10 countries with the highest femininity score are (beginning with the highest) Sweden, Norway, the Netherlands, Denmark, Costa Rica, Yugoslavia, Finland, Chile, Portugal, and Thailand. Of the 53 countries ranked, the United States ranks 15th most masculine (Hofstede, Hofstede, & Minkov, 2010).

Masculine cultures emphasize success and so socialize their members to be assertive, ambitious, and competitive. For example, members of masculine cultures are more likely to confront conflicts directly and to fight out any differences competitively; they're more likely to emphasize conflict strategies that enable them to win and ensure that the other side loses (win–lose strategies). Feminine cultures emphasize the quality of life and so socialize their members to be modest and to highlight close interpersonal relationships. Feminine cultures, for example, are more likely to utilize compromise and negotiation in resolving conflicts; they're more likely to seek solutions in which both sides win (win–win strategies).

VIEWPOINTS The theory of cultural imperialism argues that certain developed countries, such as those of North America and Western Europe, dominate the cultures of countries importing their products, especially their Internet and media. What do you think of the influence that media and the Internet are having on native cultures throughout the world? How do you evaluate this trend? Do you see advantages? How does this influence what you believe and feel about cultures other than your own?

Giulio Andreini/Marka/Alamy

Similarly, organizations can be viewed as masculine or feminine. Masculine organizations emphasize competitiveness and aggressiveness. They stress the bottom line and reward their workers on the basis of their contributions to the organization. Feminine organizations are less competitive and less aggressive. They emphasize worker satisfaction and reward their workers on the basis of the needs of workers.

High-Ambiguity-Tolerant and Low-Ambiguity-Tolerant Cultures

Levels of **ambiguity tolerance** vary widely among cultures. In some cultures people do little to avoid uncertainty, and they have little anxiety about not knowing what will happen next. In some other cultures, however, uncertainty is strongly avoided and there is much anxiety about uncertainty.

High-Ambiguity-Tolerant Cultures Members of high-ambiguity-tolerant cultures don't feel threatened by unknown situations: Uncertainty is a normal part of life, and people accept it as it comes. The 10 countries with highest tolerance for ambiguity are Singapore, Jamaica, Denmark, Sweden, Hong Kong, Ireland, Great Britain, Malaysia, India, and the Philippines; the United States ranks 11th.

Because high-ambiguity-tolerant culture members are comfortable with ambiguity and uncertainty, they minimize the importance of rules governing communication and relationships (Hofstede, Hofstede, & Minkov, 2010; Lustig & Koester, 2010). People in these cultures readily tolerate individuals who don't follow the same rules as the cultural majority, and may even encourage different approaches and perspectives.

Students from high-ambiguity-tolerant cultures appreciate freedom in education and prefer vague assignments without specific timetables. These students want to be rewarded for creativity and readily accept an instructor's lack of knowledge.

Photos 12/Alamy

Low-Ambiguity-Tolerant Cultures Members of low-ambiguity-tolerant cultures do much to avoid uncertainty and have a great deal of anxiety about not knowing what will happen next; they see uncertainty as threatening and as something that must be counteracted. The 10 countries with the lowest tolerance for ambiguity are Greece, Portugal, Guatemala, Uruguay, Belgium, Malta, Russia, El Salvador, Poland, and Japan (Hofstede, Hofstede, & Minkov, 2010).

Low-ambiguity-tolerant cultures create clear-cut rules for communication that must not be broken. For example, students from strong-uncertainty-avoidance cultures prefer highly structured experiences with little ambiguity; they prefer specific objectives, detailed instructions, and definite timetables. An assignment to write a term paper on "anything" would be cause for alarm; it would not be clear or specific enough. These students expect to be judged on the basis of the right answers and expect the instructor to have all the answers all the time (Hofstede, Hofstede, & Minkov, 2010).

Long- and Short-Term Orientation

Another interesting distinction is that between long- and short-term orientation. Some cultures teach a **long-term orientation**, an orientation that promotes the importance of future rewards and so, for example, members of these cultures are more apt to save for the future and to prepare for the future academically (Hofstede, Hofstede, & Minkov, 2010). The most long-term oriented countries are South Korea, Taiwan, Japan, China, Ukraine, Germany, Estonia, Belgium, Lithuania, and Russia. The United States ranks 69th out of 93 countries, making it less long-term than most countries. In these cultures, marriage is a practical arrangement rather than one based on sexual or emotional arousal, and living with extended family (for example, in-laws) is common and considered quite normal. These cultures believe that mothers should be at home with their children, that humility is a virtue for both men and women, and that old age should be a happy time of life.

Cultures fostering a **short-term orientation** (Puerto Rico, Ghana, Egypt, Trinidad, Nigeria, Dominican Republic, Colombia, Iran, Morocco, and Zimbabwe are the top ten) look more to the past and the present. Instead of saving for the future, members of this culture spend their resources for the present and, not surprisingly, want quick results from their efforts. These cultures believe and teach that marriage is a moral arrangement, living with in-laws causes problems, children do not have to be cared for by their mothers (others can do that), humility is a virtue only for women (not men), and old age is an unpleasant time of life.

These cultures also differ in their view of the workplace. Organizations in long-term-oriented cultures look to profits in the future. Managers or owners and workers in such cultures share the same values and work together to achieve a common good. Organizations in short-term-oriented cultures, on the other hand, look to more immediate rewards. Managers and workers are very different in their thinking and in their attitudes about work.

Even in educational outlook there are significant differences. Students in long-term cultures will attribute their success or failure in school to their own efforts, while students in short-term cultures will attribute their success or failure to luck or chance.

Another perspective on this difference is offered by a study that asked Asian (long-term cultures) and American (short-term culture) executives to rank order those values they

TABLE 2	Values of the Workplace
This table presents the six highest ranked values (beginning with the highest ranked value) by Asian and American executives (Hofstede, Hofstede, & Minkov, 2010). Notice that "hard work" makes both lists but in very different positions.	

Values Selected by Asian (Long-Term Orientation) Executives	Values Selected by American (Short-Term Orientation) Executives
Hard work	Freedom of expression
Respect for learning	Personal freedom
Honesty	Self-reliance
Openness to new ideas	Individual rights
Accountability	Hard work
Self-discipline	Personal achievement

considered most important in the workplace. The top six responses are presented in Table 2 and show a dramatic difference between the two cultural groups.

Indulgence and Restraint

Cultures also differ in their emphasis on indulgence or restraint (Hofstede, Hofstede, & Minkov, 2010). Cultures high in **indulgence** are those that emphasize the gratification of desires; they focus on having fun and enjoying life. Venezuela, Mexico, Puerto Rico, El Salvador, Nigeria, Colombia, Trinidad, Sweden, New Zealand, and Ghana are the top 10 in indulgence; the United States ranks 15th out of 93 countries, making it considerably more indulgent than most countries. These cultures have more people who are happy, which depends on two major factors:

- **Life control.** This is the feeling that you may do as you please (at least to a significant degree), that you have freedom of choice to do or not do what you want.
- **Leisure.** This is the feeling that you have leisure time to do what you find fun.

In addition, members of indulgent cultures have more positive attitudes, greater optimism, and are more likely to remember positive emotions. They also have a more satisfying family life and loose gender roles (for example, household tasks are shared by both partners).

Cultures high in **restraint** (Pakistan, Egypt, Latvia, Ukraine, Albania, Belarus, Lithuania, Bulgaria, Estonia, and Iraq are the top ten), on the other hand, are those that foster the curbing of such gratification and its regulation by social norms. Restraint cultures have more people who are unhappy: people who see themselves as lacking control of their own lives and with little or no leisure time to engage in fun activities. In contrast to indulgent cultures, members of cultures high in restraint are more cynical, pessimistic, and are less likely to remember positive emotions. They have less satisfying family lives, rigid gender roles, and an unequal distribution of household tasks.

As you might expect, indulgent cultures do not place great value on thrift; instead the value is on spending to gratify one's needs. Restrained cultures place a great value on thrift. Also predictable is the finding that indulgent cultures place great importance on friendship and having lots of friends whereas restrained cultures place less importance on friendships. Although there are no studies offering evidence, it's likely that the Facebook pages of indulgent culture members will have a lot more friends than will those of members of restrained cultures. And, not so predictably perhaps, is the finding that death rates from cardiovascular diseases are significantly higher in restrained than in indulgent cultures, and significantly more indulgent culture members describe their health as "very good" (Hofstede, Hofstede, & Minkov, 2010).

Principles for Effective Intercultural Communication

Intercultural communication refers to communication between persons who have different cultural beliefs, values, or ways of behaving. The model in Figure 1 illustrates this concept. The circles represent the cultures of the individual communicators. The inner circles identify the communicators (the sources/receivers). In this model each communicator is a member of a different culture. In some instances the cultural differences are relatively slight—say, between persons from Toronto and New York. In other instances the cultural differences are great—say, between persons from Borneo and Germany, or between persons from rural Nigeria and industrialized England.

Understanding *Interpersonal Skills*

CULTURAL SENSITIVITY

Cultural sensitivity is an attitude and way of behaving in which you're aware of and acknowledge cultural differences; it's crucial for such global goals as world peace and economic growth as well as for effective interpersonal communication (Franklin & Mizell, 1995). Without cultural sensitivity there can be no effective interpersonal communication between people who are different in gender or race or nationality or affectional orientation. So be mindful of the cultural differences between yourself and the other person. The techniques of interpersonal communication that work well with European Americans may not work well with Asian Americans; what proves effective in Japan might not in Mexico. The close physical distance that is normal in Arab cultures may seem too familiar or too intrusive in much of the United States and northern Europe. The empathy that most Americans welcome may be uncomfortable for most Koreans, Japanese, or Chinese.

Increasing Cultural Sensitivity. This chapter has identified many guidelines for more effective intercultural communication, and among them are recommendations that constitute the best advice for achieving cultural sensitivity:

- **Prepare yourself.** Read about and listen carefully for culturally influenced behaviors.
- **Recognize your fears.** Recognize and face your own fears of acting inappropriately toward members of different cultures.
- **Recognize differences.** Be mindful of the differences between yourself and those from other cultures.
- **Recognize differences within the group.** At the same time that you recognize differences between yourself and others, recognize that there are often enormous differences within any given cultural group.
- **Recognize differences in meaning.** Words don't always mean the same thing to members of different cultures.
- **Be rule conscious.** Become aware of and thinking mindfully about the cultural rules and customs of others.

Working with Interpersonal Skills

How would you rate your own cultural sensitivity? Try to recall situations in which you were and situations in which you weren't culturally sensitive. What happened in each? Can you identify one situation that could have been improved with the additional of cultural sensitivity?

FIGURE 1

A Model of Intercultural Communication

This model of intercultural communication illustrates that culture is a part of every communication act. More specifically, it illustrates that the messages you send and the messages you receive will be influenced by your cultural beliefs, values, and attitudes. Note also that the circles overlap to some degree, illustrating that no matter how different the cultures of the two individuals are, there will always be some commonalities, some similarities, along with differences.

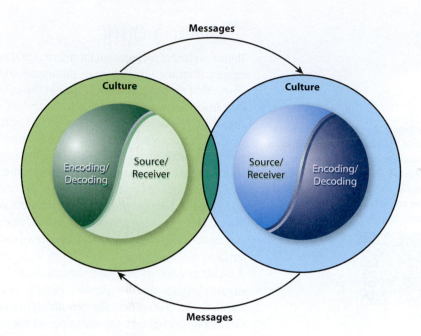

The following categories of communication all may be considered "intercultural" and can all be improved with the application of the general principles of intercultural communication discussed in this section:

- Communication between cultures—for example, between Chinese and Portuguese, or between French and Norwegian individuals or groups
- Communication between races (sometimes called *interracial communication*)—for example, between people of African American and Asian American heritages
- Communication between ethnic groups (sometimes called *interethnic communication*)—for example, between Vietnamese Americans and German Americans
- Communication between people of different religions—for example, between Roman Catholics and Episcopalians, or between Muslims and Jews
- Communication between nations (sometimes called *international communication*)—for example, between the United States and Argentina, or between Lybia and Italy
- Communication between smaller cultures existing within the larger culture—for example, between doctors and patients, or between research scientists and the general public
- Communication between a smaller culture and the dominant culture—for example, between homosexuals and heterosexuals, or between older people and the younger majority
- Communication between genders—between men and women

Regardless of your own cultural background, you will surely come into close contact with people from a variety of other cultures—people who speak different languages, eat different foods, practice different religions, and approach work and relationships in very different ways. It doesn't matter whether you're a longtime resident or a newly arrived immigrant: You are or soon will be living, going to school, working, and forming relationships with people who are from very different cultures. Your day-to-day interpersonal interactions are sure to become increasingly intercultural.

Drawing on the work of numerous intercultural researchers, let's consider several guidelines designed to increase the chances for effective intercultural communication (Barna, 1997; Lustig & Koester, 2010; Ruben, 1985; Spitzberg, 1991).

INTERPERSONAL CHOICE POINT

Putting Your Foot in Your Mouth

At work you tell an ageist joke, only to discover later that it has been resented and clearly violated the organizational norms for polite and unbiased talk. What are some of the things you might say to make this situation a little less awkward and less potentially damaging to your relationships with coworkers?

Educate Yourself

There's no better preparation for intercultural communication than learning about the other culture. Fortunately, there are numerous sources to draw on. View a documentary or movie that presents a realistic view of the culture. Read material about the culture by persons from that culture as well as by "outsiders" (e.g., Foster, 2004). Scan magazines and websites from the culture. Talk with members of the culture. Chat in international chat rooms. GeoSurf™ from your Facebook page or from your browser. Another fun way to educate yourself is with geotagging, which enables you to access tweets from the part of the world you're interested in to see what the people are doing and thinking about. Another way is to join a Facebook group focusing on the culture in which you're interested. Read materials addressed to people who need to communicate with those from other cultures. Books on the subject include: *Essential Do's and Taboos: The Complete Guide to International Business and Leisure Travel* (Axtell, 2007); *Managing Cultural Differences: Global Leadership Strategies for Cross-Cultural Business Success* (Moran, Harris, & Moran, 2010), *Global Business Etiquette: A Guide to International Communication and Customs* (Martin & Chaney, 2008); *Managing Across Cultures: the Seven Keys to Doing Business With a Global Mindset* (Solomon & Schell, 2009), *Global Negotiation: The New Rules* (Graham & Hernandez Requejo, 2008), and *Dubai & Co.: Global Strategies for Doing Business In The Gulf States* (Rehman, 2007). You can find a great many more such works at Amazon.com (www.amazon.com) or Barnes and Noble (www.bn.com), for example.

Another part of this preparation is to recognize and face your own fears, which can stand in the way of effective intercultural communication (Gudykunst, 1994; Shelton & Richeson, 2005; Stephan & Stephan, 1985). For example, you may fear for your self-esteem. You may become anxious about your ability to control the intercultural situation, or you may worry about your own level of discomfort. You may fear saying something that will be considered politically incorrect or culturally insensitive and thereby losing face.

You may fear that you'll be taken advantage of by a member of another culture. Depending on your own stereotypes, you may fear being lied to, financially duped, or made fun of. You may fear that members of this other group will react to you negatively. You may fear, for example, that they will not like you or may disapprove of your attitudes or beliefs or perhaps even reject you as a person. Conversely, you may fear negative reactions from members of your own group. They might, for example, disapprove of your socializing with the culturally different.

Some fears, of course, are reasonable. In many cases, however, such concerns are groundless. Either way, they need to be assessed logically and their consequences weighed carefully. Then you'll be able to make informed choices about your communications.

Still another way to educate yourself is to understand and anticipate culture shock, a topic considered in the accompanying Understanding Interpersonal Theory & Research box.

Recognize Differences

To communicate interculturally you need to recognize the differences between yourself and people from other cultures, the differences within the other cultural group, and the numerous differences in meaning.

Differences between Yourself and the Culturally Different
A common barrier to intercultural communication occurs when you assume that similarities exist and that differences do not. This is especially true of values, attitudes, and beliefs. You might easily accept different hairstyles, clothing, and foods. In basic values and beliefs, however, you may assume that deep down all people are really alike. They aren't. When you assume similarities and ignore differences, you'll fail to notice important distinctions and when communicating will convey to others that your ways are the right ways and that their ways are not important to you. Consider this example. An American invites a Filipino coworker to dinner. The Filipino

See "Intercultural Communication Taboos" at tcbdevito.blogspot.com for additional examples of the problems you can get into when cultural expectations are violated. Have you violated any cultural taboos lately?

Understanding Interpersonal Theory & Research

CULTURE SHOCK

Culture shock is the psychological reaction you experience when you're in a culture very different from your own (Ward, Bochner, & Furnham, 2001; Wan, 2004). Culture shock is normal; most people experience it when entering a new and different culture. Nevertheless, it can seem unpleasant and frustrating when you lack knowledge of the rules and customs of the new society. You may not know such basic things as how to ask someone for a favor or pay someone a compliment, how to extend or accept an invitation for dinner, or how early or how late to arrive for an appointment.

Culture shock occurs in four stages (Oberg, 1960). These stages are useful for examining many encounters with the new and the different. Going away to college, moving in with a romantic partner, or joining the military, for example, can also result in culture shock.

- **Stage One: The Honeymoon.** At first you experience fascination, even enchantment, with the new culture and its people.
- **Stage Two: The Crisis.** Here, the differences between your own culture and the new setting create problems. Feelings of frustration and inadequacy come to the fore. This is the stage at which you experience the actual shock of the new culture.
- **Stage Three: The Recovery.** During this period you gain the skills necessary to function effectively. You learn the language and ways of the new culture. Your feelings of inadequacy subside.
- **Stage Four: The Adjustment.** At this final stage, you adjust to and come to enjoy the new culture and the new experiences. You may still experience periodic difficulties and strains, but on the whole, the experience is pleasant.

People may also experience culture shock when they return to their original culture after living in a foreign culture, a kind of reverse culture shock (Jandt, 2004). Consider, for example, Peace Corps volunteers who work in rural and economically deprived areas. On returning to Las Vegas or Beverly Hills, they too may experience culture shock. A sailor who serves long periods aboard ship and then returns to an isolated farming community may experience culture shock. In these cases, however, the recovery period is shorter and the sense of inadequacy and frustration is less.

Working with Theories and Research

Among the ways recommended to manage the inevitable culture shock are: (1) Familiarize yourself with the host nation, (2) form friendship networks to assist you in adjusting, (3) interact with members of the culture and your hosts, and (4) be open to seeking professional help in adjusting to cultural problems (Constantine, Anderson, Berkel, Caldwell, & Utsey, 2005; Britnell, 2004; Chapdelaine & Alexitch, 2004). In what other ways might you effectively manage culture shock?

politely refuses. The American is hurt and feels that the Filipino does not want to be friendly. The Filipino is hurt and concludes that the invitation was not extended sincerely. Here, it seems, both the American and the Filipino assume that their customs for inviting people to dinner are the same when, in fact, they aren't. A Filipino expects to be invited several times before accepting a dinner invitation. When an invitation is given only once it's viewed as insincere.

Here's another example. An American college student hears the news that her favorite uncle has died. She bites her lip, pulls herself up, and politely excuses herself from the group of foreign students with whom she is having dinner. The Russian thinks: "How unfriendly." The Italian thinks: "How insincere." The Brazilian thinks: "How unconcerned." To many Americans, it's a sign of bravery to endure pain (physical or emotional) in silence and without any outward show of emotion. To members of other groups, such silence is often interpreted negatively to mean that the individual does not consider them friends who can share such sorrow. In many other cultures, people are expected to reveal to friends how they feel.

Differences within the Culturally Different Group

Within every cultural group there are vast and important differences. As all Americans are not alike, neither are all Indonesians, Greeks, Mexicans, and so on. When you ignore these differences—when you assume that all persons covered by the same label (in this case a national or racial label) are the same—you're guilty of stereotyping. A good example of this is seen in the use of the term "African American." The term stresses the unity of Africa and of those who are of African descent and is analogous to "Asian American" or "European American." At the same time, it ignores the great diversity within the African continent when, for example, it's used as analogous to "German American" or "Japanese American." More analogous terms would be "Nigerian American" or "Ethiopian American." Within each culture there are smaller cultures that differ greatly from each other and from the larger culture.

Differences in Meaning

Meaning exists not in words but in people. Consider, for example, the differences in meaning that exist for words such as *religion* to a born-again Christian and an atheist, and *lunch* to a Chinese rice farmer and a Madison Avenue advertising executive. Even though the same word is used, its meanings will vary greatly depending on the listeners' cultural definitions.

The same is true of nonverbal messages. For example, a child who avoids eye contact with an adult may be seen in one culture as deference (the child is showing respect for the older person) and in another as disrespect or even defiance (the child is indicating a lack of concern for what the older person is saying).

Confront Your Stereotypes

Stereotypes, especially when they operate below the level of conscious awareness, can create serious communication problems (Lyons & Kashima, 2003). Originally, the word *stereotype* was a printing term that referred to the plate that printed the same image over and over. A sociological or psychological **stereotype** is a fixed impression of a group of people. Everyone has attitudinal stereotypes—images of national groups, religious groups, or racial groups or perhaps of criminals, prostitutes, teachers, or plumbers. Consider, for example, if you have any stereotypes of, say, bodybuilders, the opposite sex, a racial group different from your own, members of a religion very different from your own, hard drug users, or college professors. It is very likely that you have stereotypes of several or perhaps even of all of these groups. Although we often think of stereotypes as negative ("They're lazy, dirty, and only interested in getting high"), stereotypes also may be positive ("They're smart, hardworking, and extremely loyal").

If you have these fixed impressions, you may, on meeting a member of a particular group, see that person primarily as a member of that group. Initially this may provide you with some helpful orientation. However, it creates problems when you apply to that person all the characteristics you assign to members of that group without examining the unique individual. If you meet a politician, for example, you may have a host of characteristics for politicians that you can readily apply to this person. To complicate matters further, you may see in the person's behavior the manifestation of various

For a brief rant on stereotyping of men, see "Stereotyping in Cartoons," etc., at tcbdevito .blogspot.com. Can you add any examples from your own experience where stereotyping was involved?

Photos 12/Alamy Clearviewstock/Shutterstock

VIEWPOINTS ⬥ The stereotype of the male generally defines him as logical, decisive, aggressive, insensitive, unemotional, non-nurturing, talented mechanically, and impatient. The stereotype of the female generally defines her as illogical, variable, nurturing, emotional, sensitive, untalented mechanically, and impatient (Cicarelli & White, 2012). Do your acquaintances maintain any of these stereotypes? What are some of the implications of thinking through these stereotypes?

characteristics that you would not see if you did not know that the person was a politician. In online communication, because there are few visual and auditory cues, it's not surprising to find that people form impressions of online communication partners with a heavy reliance on stereotypes (Jacobson, 1999).

Consider, however, another kind of stereotype: You're driving along a dark road and are stopped at a stop sign. A car pulls up beside you and three teenagers jump out and rap on your window. There may be a variety of possible explanations. Perhaps they need help or they want to ask directions. Or they may be about to engage in carjacking. Your self-protective stereotype may help you decide on "carjacking" and may lead you to pull away and into the safety of a busy service station. In doing that, of course, you may have escaped being carjacked—or you may have failed to help people who needed assistance.

Stereotyping can lead to two major barriers. The tendency to group a person into a class and to respond to that person primarily as a member of that class can lead you to perceive that a person possesses certain qualities (usually negative) that you believe characterize the group to which he or she belongs. Then you will fail to appreciate the multifaceted nature of all people and all groups. For example, consider your stereotype of someone who is deeply into computers. Very likely your image is quite different from the research findings on such individuals, which show that in fact they are as often female as male and are as sociable, popular, and self-assured as their peers who are not into heavy computer use (Schott & Selwyn, 2000).

Stereotyping also can lead you to ignore the unique characteristics of an individual; you therefore may fail to benefit from the special contributions each person can bring to an encounter.

Reduce Your Ethnocentrism

Ethnocentrism is the tendency to see others and their behaviors through your own cultural filters, often as distortions of your own behaviors. It's the tendency to evaluate the values, beliefs, and behaviors of your own culture as superior—as more positive, logical, and natural than those of other cultures. For example, highly ethnocentric individuals would think that other cultures should be more like theirs, that people from other cultures often don't know what's good for them, that the lifestyles of people in other countries are not as good as theirs, and that people from other cultures are not as smart or trustworthy as people from their own culture (Neuliep & McCroskey, 1997). To achieve effective interpersonal communication, you need to see yourself and others as different but as neither inferior nor superior. You need to become aware of the potential blinders that ethnocentrism might impose—admittedly, not a very easily accomplished task.

But ethnocentrism also can create considerable problems. Although the research is not conclusive, it appears that it may create obstacles to communication with those who are culturally different from you. It can also lead to hostility toward outside groups and may blind you to seeing other perspectives, other values, other ways of doing things (Neuliep & McCroskey, 1997; Cashdan, 2001; Jörn, 2004).

Ethnocentrism exists on a continuum (see Figure 2). People aren't either ethnocentric or not ethnocentric; rather, most are somewhere between

John Birdsall/The Image Works

VIEWPOINTS What other suggestions would you offer for decreasing ethnocentrism, increasing cultural awareness and sensitivity, and making intercultural communication more satisfying and more productive?

49

FIGURE 2
The Ethnocentric Continuum

This figure ethnocentrism? Middle? High? What accounts for these differences? This figure draws on the work of sev summarizes some of the interconnections between ethnocentrism and communication. In this figure, five areas along the ethnocentrism continuum are identified; in reality, there are as many degrees as there are people. The "Communication Distances" are general terms that highlight the attitude that dominates that level of ethnocentrism. Under "Communications" are some of the major ways people might interact given their particular degree of ethnocentrism. Can you identify your own degree of ethnocentrism on this continuum? For example, are there groups toward which you have low eral intercultural researchers (Lukens, 1978; Gudykunst & Kim, 1992; Gudykunst, 1991).

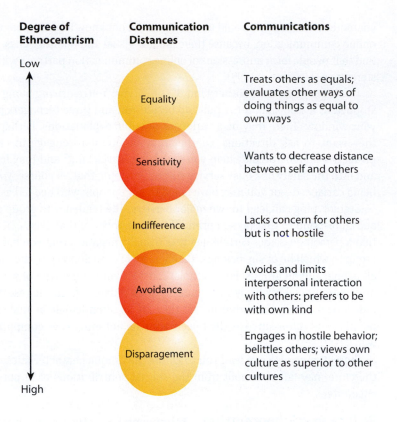

Degree of Ethnocentrism	Communication Distances	Communications
Low	Equality	Treats others as equals; evaluates other ways of doing things as equal to own ways
	Sensitivity	Wants to decrease distance between self and others
	Indifference	Lacks concern for others but is not hostile
	Avoidance	Avoids and limits interpersonal interaction with others: prefers to be with own kind
High	Disparagement	Engages in hostile behavior; belittles others; views own culture as superior to other cultures

these polar opposites. Of course, your degree of ethnocentrism varies, depending on the group on which you focus. For example, if you're Greek American, you may have a low degree of ethnocentrism when dealing with Italian Americans but a high degree when dealing with Turkish Americans or Japanese Americans. Most important for our purposes is that your degree of ethnocentrism (and we are all ethnocentric to at least some degree) will influence your interpersonal interactions.

There is nothing wrong with classifying. In fact, it's an extremely useful method of dealing with any complex matter; it puts order into thinking. The problem arises not from classification itself but from applying an evaluative label to a class and using that label as an "adequate" map for each and every individual in the group.

Adjust Your Communication Intercultural communication (in fact, all interpersonal communication) takes place only to the extent that one person can understand the meanings of the words and nonverbals cues of the other—that is, only to the extent that the two individuals share the same system of symbols. Because no two people share the identical meaning system for symbols, each person needs to adjust in all interpersonal interactions, but especially, perhaps, in intercultural interactions. Figure 3 illustrates the connection between degrees of cultural difference and the degree of adjustment that will be necessary for successful communication.

Parents and children, for example, not only have different vocabularies but also, even more importantly, have different meanings for some of the terms they have in common. People in close relationships—either as intimate friends or as romantic partners—realize that learning the other person's signals takes a long time and, often, great patience. If you want to understand what another person means—by smiling, by saying "I love you," by ar-

FIGURE 3
Cultural Differences and Interpersonal Adjustment

As you can see from this diagram, the greater the cultural differences, the greater the communication adjustment you'll need to make in order to accomplish your interpersonal goal. Try identifying a specific interpersonal encounter in which little adjustment would be necessary and another in which a great deal of adjustment would be necessary. In what ways are these situations different?

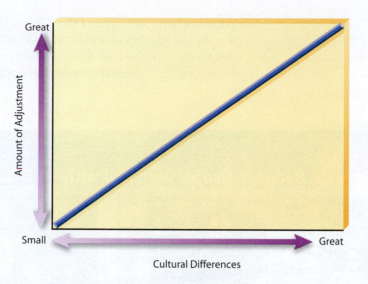

guing about trivial matters, by self-deprecating comments—you have to learn their system of signals.

This principle is especially important in intercultural communication—largely because people from different cultures use different signals and/or use the same signals to signify quite different things. As previously mentioned, focused eye contact means honesty and openness in much of the United States. But in Japan and in many Hispanic cultures that same behavior may signify arrogance or disrespect if it occurs between a youngster and someone significantly older.

Part of the art of intercultural communication is learning the other person's signals, how they're used, and what they mean. Furthermore, you have to share your own system of signals with others so that they can better understand you. Although some people may know what you mean by your silence or by your avoidance of eye contact, others may not. You cannot expect others to decode your behaviors accurately without help.

An interesting theory focusing on adjustment is *communication accommodation theory*. This theory holds that speakers will adjust to or accommodate the speaking style of their listeners to gain, for example, social approval and greater communication efficiency (Giles, 2008; Giles & Ogay, 2007). For example, research shows that when two people have a similar speech rate, they're attracted more to each other than to people with dissimilar rates (Buller, Le-Poire, Aune, & Eloy, 1992). Another study found that roommates who had similar communication competence and were both low in verbal aggressiveness were highest in roommate liking and satisfaction (Martin & Anderson, 1995). People even accommodate in their e-mail. For example, responses to messages that contained politeness cues were significantly more polite than responses to e-mails that did not contain such cues (Bunz & Campbell, 2004).

As you adjust your communications, recognize that each culture has its own rules and customs for communicating (Barna, 1997; Ruben, 1985; Spitzberg, 1991). These rules identify what is appropriate and what is inappropriate (Serewicz & Petronio, 2007). Thus, for example, in American culture you would call a person you wished to date three or four days in advance; in certain Asian cultures you might call the person's parents weeks or even months in advance. In American culture you say, as a general friendly gesture and not as a specific invita-

INTERPERSONAL CHOICE POINT
Misusing Linguistic Privilege
You enter a group of racially similar people who are using terms normally considered offensive to refer to themselves. Trying to be one of the group, you too use such terms—but are met with extremely negative nonverbal feedback. What are some things you might say to lessen this negative reaction and to let the group know that you don't normally use such racial terms?

tion, "Come over and pay us a visit." To members of other cultures, this comment is sufficient for the listeners to actually visit at their convenience. A good example of a series of rules for an extremely large and important culture appears in Table 3, "Interpersonal Communication Tips between People with and without Disabilities."

TABLE 3	INTERPERSONAL COMMUNICATION TIPS **Between People with and without Disabilities**

Christopher Reeve
Andy King/AP Photos

Franklin Delano Roosevelt
New York Daily News

Stephen Hawking
Andrew Parsons/PA Photos/Landov

Trevor Snowden
Andy King/AP Photos

Here we look at communication between those with general disabilities—for example, people who use wheelchairs or who have cerebral palsy—and those who have no such disability. The suggestions offered here are considered appropriate in the United States, although not necessarily in other cultures. For example, most people in the United States accept the phrase "person with mental retardation," but the term is considered offensive to many in the United Kingdom (Fernald, 1995).

If you're the person without a general disability:

Generally	Specifically
Use person-first language where the person, rather than the disability, is emphasized.	Avoid terms that define the person as disabled. Avoid such expressions as "the disabled man" or "the handicapped child." Instead, using "person-first" language, say "person with a disability."
Respect assistive devices, such as wheelchairs, canes, walkers, or crutches.	Don't move these out of your way; they're for the convenience of the person with the disability. Avoid leaning on a person's wheelchair; it's similar to leaning on a person.
Shake hands with the person with the disability if you shake hands with others in a group.	Don't avoid shaking hands because the individual's hand has lost some normal function, for example.
Avoid talking about the person with a disability in the third person.	For example, avoid saying, "Doesn't he get around beautifully with the new crutches." Direct your comments directly to the individual. Even if the person has an interpreter, direct your comments to the person with the disability, not the interpreter.

Don't assume that people who have a disability are intellectually impaired.	Slurred speech—such as may occur with people who have cerebral palsy or cleft palate—should not be taken as indicating a low-level intellect. Be careful not to talk down to such individuals as, research shows, many people do (Unger, 2001).
When you're not sure of how to act, ask.	For example, if you're not sure if you should offer walking assistance, say, "Would you like me to help you into the dining room?" And, more important, accept the person's response. If he or she says no, then that means no; don't insist.
Maintain similar eye level.	If the person is in a wheelchair, for example, it might be helpful for you to sit down or kneel down to get onto the same eye level.
If you're the person with a general disability:	
Communicate your feelings.	For example, if you want someone to speak in a louder voice, ask. If you want to relax and have someone push your wheelchair, say so.
Be patient and understanding.	Many people mean well but may simply not know how to act or what to say. Put them at ease as best you can.
Demonstrate your own comfort.	If you detect discomfort in the other person, you might talk a bit about your disability to show that you're not uncomfortable about it—and that you understand that others may not know how you feel. But you're under no obligation to educate the public, so don't feel this is something you should or have to do.

Sources: These suggestions are based on a wide variety of sources, including www.empowermentzone.com/etiquet.txt (the website for the National Center for Access Unlimited), www.disabilityinfo.gov, www.drc.uga.edu, www.ndmig.com, and www.ucpa.org/.

Summary

Use your smartphone or tablet device (or log on to mycommunicationlab.com) to hear an audio summary of this chapter.

This chapter explored the nature of culture and identified some key concepts and principles that explain the role of culture in interpersonal communication.

Culture

1. Culture is the relatively specialized lifestyle of a group of people (values, beliefs, artifacts, ways of behaving) that is passed from one generation to the next by means of communication, not through genes.
2. Enculturation is the process through which you learn the culture into which you're born; ethnic identity is a commitment to the ways and beliefs of your culture; and acculturation is the process by which you learn the rules and norms of a culture that is different from your native culture and that modifies your original or native culture.

3. An individual's cultural beliefs and values will influence all forms of interpersonal communication and therefore need to be considered in any full communication analysis.
4. Culture is especially relevant today because of the demographic changes, increased sensitivity to cultural variation, economic interdependency among nations, advances in communication technology which make intercultural communication easy and inexpensive, and the fact that communication effectiveness in one culture may not be effective in another.

Cultural Differences

5. In high-power-distance cultures, power is concentrated in the hands of a few and there is a great difference between those with and those without power. In low-power-distance cultures, the power is more equally shared throughout the citizenry.

6. Highly masculine cultures view men as strong, assertive, and focused on success and view women as modest, tender, and focused on the quality of life. Highly feminine cultures view men and women more similarly.
7. Cultures differ greatly in their level of tolerance for ambiguity.
8. A collectivist culture emphasizes the group and subordinates the individual's goals to those of the group. An individualist culture emphasizes the individual and subordinates the group's goals to the individual's.
9. In high-context cultures, much of the information is in the context; in low-context cultures, information is explicitly stated in the verbal message.

Principles for Effective Intercultural Communication

10. Intercultural communication is communication between people who have different cultures, beliefs, values, and ways of behaving.
11. Some intercultural communication guidelines include: Educate yourself; recognize differences (between yourself and others, within the culturally different group, and in meanings); confront your stereotypes; reduce your ethnocentrism; and adjust your communication.

Key Terms

acculturation
ambiguity tolerance
collectivist culture
culture
enculturation
ethnic identity
ethnocentrism
feminine culture

high-context culture
high-power-distance
 cultures
individualist culture
indulgence
intercultural
 communication
low-context culture

low-power-distance
 cultures
long-term orientation
masculine culture
power distance
restraint
short-term orientation
stereotype

MyCommunicationLab Explorations

MyCommunicationLab®

Communication Choice Points

Revisit the chapter-opening video, "Meet the Family." Recall from the video that Charles was meeting Mei Li's extended family for the first time, and both he and Mei Le were a bit nervous. "Meet the Family" explores the options you have for communicating in a cultural setting that is different from the one you grew up in. Illustrated here are choices that are both effective and ineffective communication among friends, romantic partners, and families.

Log on to mycommunicationlab.com to view the video for this chapter, "Meet the Family," and then answer the related discussion questions.

Additional Resources

These exercises enable you to explore a wide variety of cultural issues and their relationships to interpersonal communication.

1 Random Pairs sets up specific intercultural dyads and asks you to consider how these dyads might influence communication. **2** Cultural Beliefs asks you to examine some of your own cultural beliefs. **3** From Culture to Gender explores the relationship of culture to gender beliefs. **4** Cultural Identities lets you explore the strengths in the cultures represented by class members and others. **5** The Sources of Your Cultural Beliefs explores the origins of your own beliefs about a wide variety of issues. **6** Confronting Intercultural Obstacles presents situations that can cause intercultural conflict and asks you how you'd head off potential conflicts or resolve them.

Perception of the Self and Others in Interpersonal Communication

From Chapter 3 of *The Interpersonal Communication Book*, Thirteenth Edition. Joseph A. DeVito. Copyright © 2013 by Pearson Education, Inc.

Perception of the Self and Others in Interpersonal Communication

The Self in Interpersonal Communication

Perception in Interpersonal Communication

Impression Formation

Impression Management: Goals and Strategies

Pearson Education

Mike would like to ask Chloe, a classmate from his biology class, out on a date so that he can get to know her better. See how various strategies for how to approach her work out for him in the video, "Mike Tries to Get a Date" (www.mycommunicationlab.com).

Because you'll learn about:

- self-concept, self-awareness, and self-esteem.
- what is perception and how it operates.
- how we form impressions of people on the basis of their communications.

Because you'll learn to:

- increase your self-awareness and self-esteem.
- perceive people more accurately.
- communicate the impressions we want others to have of us.

This chapter discusses two interrelated topics—the self (including self-concept, self-awareness, and self-esteem) and the nature of perception. Then these concepts are applied by looking at the ways in which you form impressions of others and how you manage the impressions of self that you convey to others.

The Self in Interpersonal Communication

Let's begin this discussion by focusing on several fundamental aspects of the self: self-concept (the way you see yourself), self-awareness (your insight into and knowledge about yourself), and self-esteem (the value you place on yourself). In these discussions you'll see how these dimensions influence and are influenced by the way you communicate.

Self-Concept

You no doubt have an image of who you are; this is your **self-concept**. It consists of your feelings and thoughts about your strengths and weaknesses, your abilities and limitations, and your aspirations and worldview (Black, 1999). Your self-concept develops from at least four sources: (1) the image of you that others have and that they reveal to you, (2) the comparisons you make between yourself and others, (3) the teachings of your culture, and (4) the way you interpret and evaluate your own thoughts and behaviors (see Figure 1).

Others' Images According to Charles Horton Cooley's (1922) concept of the *looking-glass self*, when you want to discover, say, how friendly or how assertive you are, you look at the image of yourself that others reveal to you through the way they treat you and react to you (Hensley, 1996). You look especially to those who are most significant in your life. As a child, for example, you look to your parents and then to your teachers. As an adult, you may look to your friends, romantic partners, and colleagues at work. If these important others think highly of you, you'll see this positive image of yourself reflected in their behaviors; if they think little of you, you'll see a more negative image.

Social Comparisons Another way you develop your self-concept is by comparing yourself with others. When you want to gain insight into who you are and how effective or competent you are, you probably look to your peers. For example, after an examination you probably want to know how you performed relative to the other students in your class. If you play on a baseball team, it's important to compare your batting average with those of others on the team. You gain an additional perspective when you see your score in comparison with the scores of your peers.

FIGURE 1
The Sources of Self-Concept

This diagram depicts the four sources of self-concept, the four contributors to how you see yourself: (1) others' images of you; (2) social comparisons; (3) cultural teachings; and (4) your own observations, interpretations, and evaluations. As you read about self-concept, consider the influence of each factor throughout your life. Are the influences of each factor likely to change with age? For example, do the same factors influence you in the same way they did when you were a preteen? Which will likely influence you the most 25 or 30 years from now?

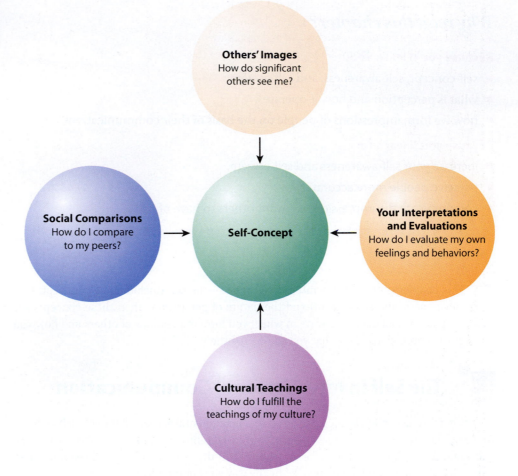

On social media sites social comparisons are easy; you can compare the number of friends you and others have on Facebook or the number of followers you have on Twitter. Some websites provide social comparisons and indicate your rank in terms of influence in the Twitter-verse based on such factors as the number of times that others talk about you, a measure that is often very different from the number of followers. For example, as of March 2011, Lady Gaga and Justin Bieber were the two most followed persons on Twitter but neither made the top ten list in influence. Rafinha Bastos and Chad Ochochinco (two Brazilian celebrities) were the most influential—more people tweeted about them than about any others (Leonhardt, 2011).

If you want to feel good about yourself, you may compare yourself to those you know are less effective than you. If you want a more accurate and objective assessment, you'd compare yourself with your peers, with others who are similar to you.

Cultural Teachings Through your parents, teachers, and the media, your culture instills in you a variety of beliefs, values, and attitudes—about success (how you define it and how you should achieve it); about your religion, race, or nationality; about the ethical principles you should follow in business and in your personal life. These teachings provide benchmarks against which you can measure yourself. For example, achieving what your culture defines as success will contribute to a positive self-concept. A perceived failure to achieve what your culture promotes (for example, not being in a permanent relationship by the time you're 30) may contribute to a negative self-concept.

Self-Evaluations Much in the way others form images of you based on what you do, you also react to your own behavior; you interpret and evaluate it. These interpretations and evaluations help to form your self-concept. For example, let us say you believe that lying is wrong. If you lie, you will evaluate this behavior in terms of your internalized beliefs about lying. You'll thus react negatively to your own behavior. You may, for example, experience guilt if your behavior contradicts your beliefs. In contrast, let's say you tutor another student and help him or her pass a course. You will probably evaluate this behavior positively; you will feel good about this behavior and, as a result, about yourself.

Self-Awareness

Your **self-awareness** represents the extent to which you know yourself. Understanding how your self-concept develops is one way to increase your self-awareness: The more you understand about why you view yourself as you do, the more you will understand who you are. Additional insight is gained by looking at self-awareness through the Johari model of the self, or your four selves (Luft, 1984).

Your Four Selves Self-awareness is neatly explained by the model of the four selves—the Johari window. This model, presented in Figure 2, has four basic areas, or quadrants, each of which represents a somewhat different self. The Johari model emphasizes that the several aspects of the self are not separate pieces but are interactive parts of a whole. Each part is dependent on each other part. Like that of interpersonal communication, this model of the self is transactional.

Each person's Johari window will be different, and each individual's window will vary from one time to another and

VIEWPOINTS Do you engage in downward social comparison (comparing yourself to those you know are inferior to you in some way) or in upward social comparison (comparing yourself to those who you think are better than you) (Aspinwall & Taylor, 1993)? What are the purposes of these comparisons?

WilleeCole/Shutterstock

FIGURE 2
The Johari Window

Visualize this model as representative of yourself. The entire model is of constant size, but each section can vary from very small to very large. As one section becomes smaller, one or more of the others grows larger. Similarly, as one section grows, one or more of the others must get smaller. For example, if you reveal a secret and thereby enlarge your open self, this shrinks your hidden self. Further, this disclosure may in turn lead to a decrease in the size of your blind self (if your disclosure influences other people to reveal what they know about you but that you have not known). How would you draw your Johari window to show yourself when interacting with your parents? With your friends on Facebook or other social media site? With your college instructors? The name *Johari*, by the way, comes from the first names of the two people who developed the model, Joseph Luft and Harry Ingham.

Source: Group Processes: An Introduction to Group Dynamics, 3d ed. by Joseph Luft, 1984, p. 60. Reprinted by permission of Mayfield Publishing Company, Mountain View, CA.

From Luft, Joseph, Group Processes, 3/e, p. 60. Copyright © 1984. Reprinted with permission from The McGraw-Hill Companies

	Known to Self	Not Known to Self
Known to Others	**Open Self** Information about yourself that you and others know	**Blind Self** Information about yourself that you don't know but that others do know
Not Known to Others	**Hidden Self** Information about yourself that you know but others don't know	**Unknown Self** Information about yourself that neither you nor others know

FIGURE 3

Johari Windows of Different Structures

Notice that as one self grows, one or more of the other selves shrink. Assume that these models depict the self-awareness and self-disclosure of two different people. How would you describe the type of communication (especially self-disclosure) that might characterize each of these two people?

From Luft, Joseph, Group Processes, 3/e, p. 60. Copyright © 1984. Reprinted with permission from The McGraw-Hill Companies

Open self Information about yourself that you and others know

Blind self Information about yourself that you don't know but that others do know

Hidden self Information about yourself that you know but others don't know

Unknown self Information about yourself that neither you nor others know

Open self Information about yourself that you and others know

Blind self Information about yourself that you don't know but that others do know

Hidden self Information about yourself that you know but others don't know

Unknown self Information about yourself that neither you nor others know

from one interpersonal situation to another. Figure 3, for example, illustrates two possible configurations.

- **The open self** represents all the information about you—behaviors, attitudes, feelings, desires, motivations, and ideas—that you and others know. The type of information included here might range from your name, skin color, and sex to your age, political and religious affiliations, and financial situation. Your open self will vary in size depending on the situation you're in and the person with whom you're interacting. Some people, for example, make you feel comfortable and supported; to them, you open yourself wide, but to others you may prefer to leave most of yourself closed.

- **The blind self** represents all the things about you that others know but of which you're ignorant. These may include relatively insignificant habits like saying "You know," gestures like rubbing your nose when you get angry, or traits such as a distinct body odor; they also may include things as significant as defense mechanisms, fight strategies, or repressed experiences.

- **The hidden self** contains all that you know of yourself and of others that you keep secret. In any interaction, this area includes everything you don't want to reveal, whether it's relevant or irrelevant to the conversation. At the extremes of the hidden-self spectrum, we have the overdisclosers and the underdisclosers. The overdisclosers tell all. They tell you their marital difficulties, their children's problems, their financial status, and just about everything else. The underdisclosers tell nothing. They talk about you but not about themselves.

- **The unknown self** represents truths about yourself that neither you nor others know. Sometimes this unknown self is revealed through temporary changes brought about by special experimental conditions such as hypnosis or sensory deprivation. Sometimes this area is revealed by certain projective tests or dreams. Mostly, however, it's revealed by the fact that you're constantly learning things about yourself that you didn't know before (things that were previously in the unknown self)—for example, that you become defensive when someone asks you a question or voices disagreement, or that you compliment others in the hope of being complimented back.

Growing in Self-Awareness   Here are five ways you can increase your self-awareness:

- **Ask yourself about yourself**. One way to ask yourself about yourself is to take an informal "Who Am I?" test (Bugental & Zelen, 1950; Grace & Cramer, 2003). Title a piece of paper "Who Am I?" and write 10, 15, or 20 times "I am . . ." Then complete each of the sentences. Try not to give only positive or socially acceptable responses; just respond with what comes to mind first. Take another piece of paper and divide it into two columns; label one column "Strengths" and the other column "Weaknesses." Fill in each column as quickly as possible. Using these first two tests as a base, take a third piece of paper, title it "Self-Improvement Goals," and complete the statement "I want to improve my . . ." as many times as you can in five minutes. Because you're constantly changing, these self-perceptions and goals also change, so update them frequently. Also, see the photo caption on the following page.

■ **Listen to others.** You can learn a lot about yourself by seeing yourself as others do. In most interpersonal interactions, people comment on you in some way—on what you do, what you say, how you look. Sometimes these comments are explicit; most often they're found in the way others look at you, in what they talk about, in their interest in what you say. Pay close attention to this verbal and nonverbal information.

■ **Actively seek information about yourself.** Actively seek out information to reduce your blind self. You need not be so obvious as to say, "Tell me about myself" or "What do you think of me?" But you can use everyday situations to gain self-information: "Do you think I was assertive enough when asking for the raise?" Or "Would I be thought too forward if I invited myself for dinner?" Do not, of course, seek this information constantly; your friends would quickly find others with whom to interact.

■ **See your different selves.** Each person with whom you have an interpersonal relationship views you differently; to each you're a somewhat different person. Yet you are really all of these selves, and your self-concept will be influenced by each of these views as they are reflected back to you in everyday interpersonal interactions. For starters, visualize how you're seen by your mother, your father, your teachers, your best friend, the stranger you sat next to on the bus, your employer, your neighbor's child. The experience will give you new and valuable perspectives on yourself.

■ **Increase your open self.** When you reveal yourself to others and increase your open self, you also reveal yourself to yourself. At the very least, you bring into clearer focus what you may have buried within. As you discuss yourself, you may see connections that you had previously missed, and with the aid of feedback from others you may gain still more insight. Also, by increasing the open self you increase the likelihood that a meaningful and intimate dialogue will develop, which will enable you to get to know yourself better. This important process is called self-disclosure.

VIEWPOINTS Your cultural background will significantly influence your responses to this simple "Who Am I?" test. In one study, for example, participants from Malaysia (a collectivist culture) and from Australia and Great Britain (individualist cultures) completed this test. Malaysians produced significantly more group self-descriptions and fewer idiocentric self-descriptions than did the Australian or British respondents (Bochner, 1994; also see Radford, Mann, Ohta, & Nakane, 1993). If you completed the "Who Am I?" test, can you identify responses that were influenced by your cultural orientation, particularly your collectivist-individualist orientation? Did other cultural factors influence your statements?

Nigel Hicks/Dorling Kindersley

Self-Esteem

Self-esteem is a measure of how valuable you think you are. If you have high self-esteem, you think highly of yourself; if you have low self-esteem, you tend to view yourself negatively. Before reading further about this topic, consider your own self-esteem by taking the accompanying self-test, "How's Your Self-Esteem?"

Test Yourself   How's Your Self-Esteem?

Respond to each of the following statements with T for true if the statement describes you at least some significant part of the time, or with F for false if the statement describes you rarely or never.

_____ 1. Generally, I feel I have to be successful in all things.

_____ 2. Several of my acquaintances are often critical or negative of what I do and how I think.

_____ 3. I often tackle projects that I know are impossible to complete to my satisfaction.

_____ 4. When I focus on the past, I focus more often on my failures than on my successes and on my negative rather than my positive qualities.

_____ 5. I make little effort to improve my personal and social skills.

How Did You Do? "True" responses to the questions would generally suggest ways of thinking that can get in the way of building positive self-esteem. "False" responses would indicate that you are thinking much like a self-esteem coach would want you to think.

What Will You Do? The following discussion elaborates on these five issues and illustrates why each of them creates problems for the development of healthy self-esteem. So this text is a good starting place. You might also want to log on to the National Association for Self-Esteem's website (http://www .self-esteem-nase.org). There you'll find a variety of materials for examining and bolstering self-esteem.

The basic idea behind self-esteem is that when you feel good about yourself—about who you are and what you're capable of doing—you will perform better. When you think you're a success, you're more likely to act like you're a success. Conversely, when you think you're a failure, you're more likely to act like you're a failure. When you reach for the phone to ask the most popular student in the school for a date and you visualize yourself being successful and effective, you're more likely to give a good impression. If, on the other hand, you think you're going to forget what you want to say or stutter or say something totally stupid, you're less likely to be successful. Here are five suggestions for increasing self-esteem that parallel the questions in the self-test.

Attack Self-Destructive Beliefs   Challenge **self-destructive beliefs**—ideas you have about yourself that are unproductive or that make it more difficult for you to achieve your goals (Einhorn, 2006). Here, for example, are some beliefs that are likely to prove self-destructive (Butler, 1981):

- The belief that you have to be perfect; this causes you to try to perform at unrealistically high levels at work, school, and home; anything short of perfection is unacceptable.
- The belief that you have to be strong, which tells you that weakness and any of the more vulnerable emotions—like sadness, compassion, or loneliness—are wrong.
- The belief that you have to please others and that your worthiness depends on what others think of you.
- The belief that you have to hurry up; this compels you to do things quickly, to try to do more than can be reasonably expected in any given amount of time.
- The belief that you have to take on more responsibilities than any one person can be expected to handle.

These beliefs set unrealistically high standards, and therefore almost always end in failure. As a result, you may develop a negative self-image, seeing yourself as someone who constantly fails. So, replace these self-destructive beliefs with more productive ones, such as "I succeed in many things, but I don't have to succeed in everything," and "It would be nice to be loved by everyone, but it isn't necessary to my happiness." See Table 1 for a summary and comparison of these destructive beliefs and constructive counterparts.

Seek Out Nourishing People Psychologist Carl Rogers (1970) drew a distinction between noxious and nourishing people. Noxious people criticize and find fault with just about everything. Nourishing people, on the other hand, are positive and optimistic. Most important, they reward us, they stroke us, they make us feel good about ourselves. To enhance your self-esteem, seek out these people. At the same time, avoid noxious people—those who make you feel negatively about yourself. Seek to become more nourishing yourself so that you can build up others' self-esteem.

TABLE 1 Destructive and Constructive Beliefs

Destructive Beliefs	Constructive Beliefs
I need to **be perfect.**	I'm not perfect, no one is; and I don't need to be perfect, but I'm not bad.
I need to **be strong.**	It's nice to be strong sometimes but also nice to be able to show weakness.
I need **to please** everyone.	It would be nice if I pleased everyone but that's really impossible; besides, there's no need to please everyone.
I need **to hurry**; I can't waste time.	I can stop and pause and not always be in a hurry.
I need to **do more.**	There is a limit on what one person can do; I do what I can do and don't do the rest.

Identification with people similar to yourself also seems to increase self-esteem. For example, deaf people who identified with the larger deaf community had greater self-esteem than those who didn't so identify (Jambor & Elliott, 2005). Similarly, identification with your cultural group also seems helpful in fostering positive self-esteem (McDonald, McCabe, Yeh, Lau, Garland, & Hough, 2005).

Work on Projects That Will Result in Success Some people want to fail (or so it seems). Often, they select projects that will result in failure simply because these projects are impossible to complete. Avoid this trap and select projects that will result in success. Each success will help build your self-esteem. Each success, too, will make the next success a little easier. If a project does fail, recognize that this does not mean that you're a failure. Everyone fails somewhere along the line. Failure is something that happens to you; it's not something you've created, and it's not something inside you. Further, failing once does not mean that you will fail the next time. So learn to put failure in perspective.

Remind Yourself of Your Successes Some people have a tendency to focus on and to exaggerate their failures, their missed opportunities, their social mistakes. However, others witnessing these failures give them much less importance (Savitsky, Epley, & Gilovich, 2001). If your objective is to correct what you did wrong or to identify the skills that you need to correct these failures, then focusing on failures can have some positive value. But if you just focus on failure without forming any plans for correction, then you're probably just making life more difficult for yourself and limiting your self-esteem. To counteract the tendency to recall failures, remind yourself of your successes. Recall these successes both intellectually and emotionally. Realize why they were successes, and relive the emotional experience when you sank that winning basketball, or aced that test, or helped that friend overcome personal problems. And while you're at it, recall your positive qualities.

Secure Affirmation An affirmation is simply a statement asserting that something is true. In discussions of self-concept and self-awareness, the word **affirmation** is used to refer to positive statements about yourself, statements asserting that something good or positive is true of you. It's frequently recommended that you remind yourself of your successes with

INTERPERSONAL CHOICE POINT

Understanding Rejection

You've asked several different people at school for a date, but so far all you've received have been rejections. Something's wrong; you're not that bad. What are some of your options for gaining insight into the possible reasons for these rejections?

65

VIEWPOINTS Despite its intuitive value, self-esteem has its critics (for example, Bushman & Baumeister, 1998; Baumeister, Bushman, & Campbell, 2000; Bower, 2001; Coover & Murphy, 2000; Hewitt, 1998; Epstein, 2005). Some researchers argue that high self-esteem is not necessarily desirable: It does nothing to improve academic performance, does not predict success, and may even lead to antisocial (even aggressive) behavior. Interestingly enough, a large number of criminals and delinquents are found to have high self-esteem. And conversely, many people who have low self-esteem have become quite successful in all fields (Owens, Stryker, & Goodman, 2002). How do you feel about the benefits or liabilities of self-esteem?

affirmations—that you focus on your good deeds; on your positive qualities, strengths, and virtues; and on your productive and meaningful relationships with friends, loved ones, and relatives (Aronson, Cohen, & Nail, 1998; Aronson, Wilson, & Akert, 2007).

One useful way to look at self-affirmation is in terms of "I am," "I can," and "I will" statements (www.coping.org).

- **"I am" statements** focus on your self-image—on how you see yourself—and might include, for example, "I am a worthy person," "I am responsible," "I am capable of loving," and "I am a good team player."
- **"I can" statements** focus on your abilities and might include, for example, "I can accept my past but also let it go," "I can learn to be a more responsive partner," "I can assert myself when appropriate," and "I can control my anger."
- **"I will" statements** focus on useful and appropriate goals you want to achieve and might include, for example, "I will get over my guilty feelings," "I will study more effectively," "I will act more supportively," and "I will not take on more responsibility than I can handle."

The idea behind this advice is that the way you talk to yourself will influence what you think of yourself. If you affirm yourself—if you tell yourself that you're a friendly person, that you can be a leader, that you will succeed on the next test—you will soon come to feel more positively about yourself.

Some researchers, however, argue that such affirmations—although extremely popular in self-help books—may not be very helpful. These critics contend that if you have low self-esteem, you're not going to believe your self-affirmations because you don't have a high opinion of yourself to begin with (Paul, 2001). According to this view, the alternative to self-affirmation is securing affirmation from others. You'd do this by, for example, becoming more interpersonally competent and interacting with more positive people. In this way, you'd get more positive feedback from others—which, these researchers argue, is more helpful than self-talk in raising self-esteem.

Perception in Interpersonal Communication

Perception is the process by which you become aware of objects, events, and especially people through your senses: sight, smell, taste, touch, and hearing. Perception is an active, not a passive, process. Your perceptions result both from what exists in the outside world and from your own experiences, desires, needs and wants, loves and hatreds. Among the reasons perception is so important in interpersonal communication is that it influences your communication choices. The messages you send and listen to will depend on how you see the world, on how you size up specific situations, on what you think of yourself and of the people with whom you interact.

Interpersonal perception is a continuous series of processes that blend into one another. For convenience of discussion we can separate interpersonal perception into five stages: (1) You sense, you pick up some kind of stimulation; (2) you organize the stimuli in some

Understanding *Interpersonal Theory & Research*

THE JUST WORLD HYPOTHESIS

Many people believe that the world is just: Good things happen to good people and bad things happen to bad people (Aronson, Wilson, & Akert, 2007; Hunt, 2000). Put differently, you get what you deserve! Even when you mindfully dismiss this assumption, you may use it mindlessly when perceiving and evaluating other people. Consider a particularly vivid example: In certain cultures if a woman is raped (for example, in Bangladesh, Iran, or Yemen), she is considered by many in that culture (certainly not all) to have disgraced her family and to be deserving of severe punishment—in many cases, even death. And although you may claim that this is unfair, much research shows that even in the United States many people do, in fact, blame the victim for being raped, especially if the victim is male (Adams-Price, Dalton, & Sumrall, 2004; Anderson, 2004).

The belief that the world is just creates perceptual distortions by leading us to deemphasize the influence of situational factors and to overemphasize the influence of internal factors in our attempts to explain the behaviors of other people or even our own behaviors.

Working with Theories and Research

Listen carefully to people around you and read their Facebook posts and tweets with the just world hypothesis in mind. Do the people you're listening to assume the world is just? How do they do it?

---

way; (3) you interpret and evaluate what you perceive; (4) you store it in memory; and (5) you retrieve it when needed.

Stage One: Stimulation

At this first stage, your sense organs are stimulated—you hear a new CD, see a friend, smell someone's perfume, taste an orange, receive an instant message, feel another's sweaty palm. Naturally, you don't perceive everything; rather, you engage in **selective perception**, a general term that includes selective attention and selective exposure:

- In **selective attention**, you attend to those things that you anticipate will fulfill your needs or will prove enjoyable. For example, when daydreaming in class, you don't hear what the instructor is saying until your name is called. Your selective attention mechanism then focuses your senses on your name.
- Through **selective exposure**, you expose yourself to people or messages that will confirm your existing beliefs, contribute to your objectives, or prove satisfying in some way. For example, after you buy a car, you're more apt to read and listen to advertisements for the car you just bought because these messages tell you that you made the right decision. At the same time, you'll likely avoid advertisements for the cars that you considered but eventually rejected, because these messages would tell you that you made the wrong decision.

Stage Two: Organization

At the second stage, you organize the information your senses pick up. Three interesting ways in which people organize their perceptions are by rules, by schemata, and by scripts. Let's look at each briefly.

Organization by Rules In the organization of perceptions by **rules**, one frequently used rule is that of **proximity** or physical closeness: Things that are physically close to each other are perceived as a unit. Thus, using this rule, you will tend to perceive people who are often together, or messages spoken one immediately after the other, as units, as belonging together.

Another rule is **similarity**: Things that are physically similar (they look alike) are perceived as belonging together and forming a unit. This principle of similarity may lead you to see people who dress alike as belonging together. Similarly, you may assume that people who work at the same jobs, who are of the same religion, who live in the same building, or who talk with the same accent belong together.

The rule of **contrast** is the opposite of similarity: When items (people or messages, for example) are very different from each other, you conclude that they don't belong together; they're too different from each other to be part of the same unit. If you're the only one who shows up at an informal gathering in a tuxedo, you'll be seen as not belonging to the group because you contrast too much with the other people present.

Organization by Schemata Another way you organize material is by creating **schemata**, mental templates that help you organize the millions of items of information you come into contact with every day (as well as those you already have in memory). A stereotype is a type of **schema**. Schemata, the plural of schema (though *schemas* seems to be used in many texts), may thus be viewed as general ideas about people (e.g., about Pat and Chris, Japanese people, Baptists, Texans); about yourself (your qualities, abilities, liabilities); or about social roles (the characteristics of a police officer, professor, multibillionaire CEO).

You develop schemata from your own experience—actual as well as via television, reading, the Internet, and hearsay. You might have a schema for college athletes, for example, and this might include an image of college athletes as strong, ambitious, academically weak, and egocentric.

VIEWPOINTS You've probably developed schemata for different religious, racial, and national groups; for men and women; and for people of different affectional orientations. Each of the groups that you have some familiarity with will be represented in your mind by schemata. These schemata help you organize your perceptions by enabling you to classify millions of people into a manageable number of categories or classes. What do you see as the advantages and disadvantages of schemata? If you do see disadvantages, how might you counteract their effects?

Organization by Scripts A **script** is really a type of schema, but because it's a different type, it's given a different name. A script is an organized body of information about some action, event, or procedure. It's a general idea of how some event should play out or unfold; it's the rules governing events and their sequence. For example, you probably have a script for eating in a restaurant, with the actions organized into a pattern something like this: Enter, take a seat, review the menu, order from the menu, eat your food, ask for the bill, leave a tip, pay the bill, exit the restaurant. Similarly, you probably have scripts for how you do laundry, how an interview is to be conducted, the stages you go through in introducing someone to someone else, and the way you ask for a date.

As you can see, rules, schemata, and scripts are useful shortcuts to simplify your understanding, remembering, and recalling information about people and events. They also enable you to generalize, make connections, and otherwise profit from previously acquired knowledge. If you didn't have these shortcuts, you'd have to treat every person, role, or action differently from each other person, role, or action. This would make every experience a new one, totally unrelated to anything you already know. As you'll see in the next stage, these shortcuts may mislead you; they may contribute to your remembering things that are consistent with your schemata (even if they didn't occur) and to your distorting or forgetting information that is inconsistent.

Stage Three: Interpretation–Evaluation

The **interpretation–evaluation** step in perception (a combined term because the two processes cannot be separated) is greatly influenced by your experiences, needs, wants, values, and beliefs about the way things are or should be; expectations, physical and emotional state; and so on. Your interpretation–evaluation will be influenced by your rules, schemata, and scripts as well as by your gender; for example, women have been found to view others more positively than men (Winquist, Mohr, & Kenny, 1998).

For example, on meeting a new person who is introduced to you as Ben Williams, a college football player, you're likely to apply your schema for athletes to this person and view him as strong, ambitious, academically weak, and egocentric. You will, in other words, see this person through the filter of your schema and evaluate him according to your schema for college athletes. Similarly, when viewing someone performing some series of actions (say, eating in a restaurant), you apply your script to this event and view the event through the script. You will interpret the actions of the diner as appropriate or inappropriate depending on your script for this behavior and the ways in which the diner performed the sequence of actions.

Judgments about members of other cultures are often ethnocentric—because your schemata and scripts are created on the basis of your own cultural beliefs and experiences, you can easily (but inappropriately) apply these to members of other cultures. And so it's easy to infer that when members of other cultures do things that conform to your own scripts, they're right; and when they do things that contradict your scripts, they're wrong—a classic example of ethnocentric thinking. This tendency can easily contribute to intercultural misunderstandings.

A similar problem arises when you base your scripts for different cultural groups on stereotypes that you may have derived from television or movies. For example, you may have schemata for religious Muslims that you derived from the stereotypes presented in the media. If you apply these schemata to all Muslims, you risk interpreting what you see through these schemata and distorting what does not conform.

Stage Four: Memory

Your perceptions and their interpretations–evaluations are put into memory; they're stored so that you may ultimately retrieve them at some later time. So, for example, you have in memory your schema for college athletes and the fact that Ben Williams is a football player. Ben Williams is then stored in memory with "cognitive tags" that tell you that he's strong, ambitious, academically weak, and egocentric. Despite the fact that you've not witnessed Ben's strength or ambitions and have no idea of his academic record or his psychological profile, you still may store your memory of Ben along with the qualities that make up your schema for "college athletes."

Now let's say that at different times you hear that Ben failed Spanish I, normally an A or B course at your school; that Ben got an A in chemistry (normally a tough course); and that Ben is transferring to Harvard as a theoretical physics major. Schemata act as filters or gatekeepers; they allow certain information to get stored in relatively objective form, much as you heard or read it, and may distort other information or prevent it from getting stored. As a result, these three items of information about Ben may get stored very differently in your memory.

For example, you may readily store the information that Ben failed Spanish, because it's consistent with your schema; it fits neatly into the template you have of college athletes. Information that's consistent with your schema—as in this example—strengthens your schema and make it more resistant to change (Aronson, Wilson, & Akert, 2007). Depending on the strength of your schema, you may also store in memory (even though you didn't hear it) that Ben did poorly in other courses as well. The information that Ben got an A in chemistry, because it contradicts your schema (it just doesn't seem right), may easily be distorted or lost. The information that Ben is transferring to Harvard, however, is a bit different. This information is also inconsistent with your schema, but it is so drastically inconsistent that you begin to look at this mindfully and may even begin to question your schema or perhaps view Ben as an exception to the general rule. In either case, you're going to etch Ben's transferring to Harvard very clearly in your mind.

Stage Five: Recall

The **recall** stage involves accessing the information you have stored in memory. Let's say that at some later date you want to retrieve your information about Ben, because he's the topic of discussion among you and a few friends. Memory isn't reproductive; you don't simply reproduce what you've heard or seen. Rather, you reconstruct what you've heard or seen into a whole that is meaningful to you—depending in great part on your schemata and scripts. It's this reconstruction that you store in memory. When you want to retrieve this information, you may recall it with a variety of inaccuracies:

- You're likely to recall information that is consistent with your schema; in fact, you may not even be recalling the specific information (say, about Ben) but may actually just be recalling your schema (which contains information about college athletes and, because of this, also about Ben).
- But you may fail to recall information that is inconsistent with your schema; you have no place to put that information, so you easily lose it or forget it.
- However, you may recall information that drastically contradicts your schema, because it forces you to think (and perhaps rethink) about your schema and its accuracy; it may even force you to revise your schema for college athletes in general.

Impression Formation

Impression formation (sometimes referred to as *person perception*) consists of a variety of processes that you go through in forming an impression of another person. Each of these perception processes has pitfalls and potential dangers. Before reading about these processes that you use in perceiving other people, examine your own perception strategies by taking the accompanying self-test, "How Accurate Are You at People Perception?"

Test Yourself **How Accurate Are You at People Perception?**

Respond to each of the following statements with T if the statement is usually or generally true (accurate in describing your behavior), or with F if the statement is usually or generally false (inaccurate in describing your behavior).

_____ 1. I make predictions about people's behaviors that generally prove to be true.

_____ 2. When I know some things about another person, I can pretty easily fill in what I don't know.

_____ 3. Generally my expectations are borne out by what I actually see; that is, my later perceptions usually match my initial expectations.

_____ 4. I base most of my impressions of people on the first few minutes of our meeting.

_____ 5. I generally find that people I like possess positive characteristics and people I don't like possess negative characteristics.

_____ 6. I generally take credit for the positive things that happen and deny responsibility for the negative things.

_____ 7. I generally attribute people's attitudes and behaviors to their most obvious physical or psychological characteristic.

_____ 8. When making judgments about others I emphasize looking to their personality rather than to the circumstances or context.

How Did You Do? This brief perception test was designed to raise questions to be considered in this chapter, not to provide you with a specific perception score. All statements refer to perceptual processes that many people use but that often get us into trouble, leading us to form inaccurate impressions. The questions refer to several processes to be discussed below: the self-fulfilling prophecy (statement 1), implicit personality theory (2), perceptual accentuation (3), primacy–recency (4), and consistency (5). Statements 6, 7, and 8 refer to the barriers we encounter as we attempt to determine motives for other people's and even our own behaviors: self-serving bias, overattribution, and the fundamental attribution error.

What Will You Do? As you read this chapter, think about these processes and consider how you might use them more accurately and not allow them to get in the way of accurate and reasonable people perception. At the same time, recognize that situations vary widely and that strategies for clearer perception will prove useful most of the time but not all of the time. In fact, you may want to identify situations in which you shouldn't follow the suggestions that this text will offer.

Impression Formation Processes

The way in which you perceive another person and ultimately come to some kind of evaluation or interpretation of this person is not a simple logical sequence. Instead, your perceptions seem to be influenced by a variety of processes. Here we consider some of the more significant: the self-fulfilling prophecy, implicit personality theory, perceptual accentuation, primacy–recency, consistency, and attribution of control.

Self-Fulfilling Prophecy A **self-fulfilling prophecy** is a prediction that comes true because you act on it as if it were true. Put differently, a self-fulfilling prophecy occurs when you act on your schema as if it were true and in doing so make it true. Self-fulfilling prophecies occur in such widely different situations as parent–child relationships, educational settings, and business (Merton, 1957; Rosenthal, 2002; Madon, Guyll, & Spoth, 2004; Tierney & Farmer, 2004). There are four basic steps in the self-fulfilling prophecy:

Masterfile

1. You make a prediction or formulate a belief about a person or a situation. For example, you predict that Pat is friendly in interpersonal encounters.
2. You act toward that person or situation as if that prediction or belief were true. For example, you act as if Pat were a friendly person.
3. Because you act as if the belief were true, it becomes true. For example, because of the way you act toward Pat, Pat becomes comfortable and friendly.
4. You observe your effect on the person or the resulting situation, and what you see strengthens your beliefs. For example, you observe Pat's friendliness and this reinforces your belief that Pat is in fact friendly.

The self-fulfilling prophecy also can be seen when you make predictions about yourself and fulfill them. For example, suppose you enter a group situation convinced that the other members will dislike you. Almost invariably you'll be proved right; the other members will appear to you to dislike you. What you may be doing is acting in a way that encourages the group to respond to you negatively. In this way, you fulfill your prophecies about yourself.

VIEWPOINTS Although most of the research on the self-fulfilling prophecy illustrates its distorting effect on behavior, consider how you might go about using the self-fulfilling prophecy to encourage behaviors you want to increase in strength and frequency. For example, what might you do to encourage persons who are fearful of communicating to speak up with greater confidence? What might you do to encourage people who are reluctant to self-disclose to reveal more of their inner selves?

Self-fulfilling prophecies can short-circuit critical thinking and influence others' behavior (or your own) so that it conforms to your prophecies. As a result, you may see what you predicted rather than what is really there (for example, you may perceive yourself as a failure because you have predicted it rather than because of any actual failures).

Implicit Personality Theory Each person has a subconscious or implicit theory that says which characteristics of an individual go with other characteristics. Consider, for example, the following brief statements. Note the word in parentheses that you think best completes each sentence.

- Carlo is energetic, eager, and (intelligent, unintelligent).
- Kim is bold, defiant, and (extroverted, introverted).
- Joe is bright, lively, and (thin, heavy).
- Eve is attractive, intelligent, and (likable, unlikable).
- Susan is cheerful, positive, and (outgoing, shy).
- Angel is handsome, tall, and (friendly, unfriendly).

What makes some of these choices seem right and others wrong is your **implicit personality theory**, the system of rules that tells you which characteristics go together. Your theory may, for example, have told you that a person who is energetic and eager is also intelligent, not stupid—although there is no logical reason why a stupid person could not be energetic and eager.

The widely documented **halo effect** is a function of the implicit personality theory (Dion, Berscheid, & Walster, 1972; Riggio, 1987). If you believe a person has some positive qualities, you're likely to infer that she or he also possesses other positive qualities. There is also a **reverse halo** (or "horns") **effect**: If you know a person possesses several negative qualities, you're more likely to infer that the person also has other negative qualities. For example, you're more likely to perceive attractive people as more generous, sensitive, trustworthy, and interesting than those less attractive. And the "horns effect" or "reverse halo effect" will lead you to perceive those who are unattractive as mean, dishonest, antisocial, and sneaky (Katz, 2003).

In using implicit personality theories, apply them carefully and critically so as to avoid perceiving qualities in an individual that your theory tells you should be present but aren't, or seeing qualities that are not there (Plaks, Grant, & Dweck, 2005).

Perceptual Accentuation When poor and rich children were shown pictures of coins and later asked to estimate their size, the poor children's size estimates were much greater than the rich children's. Similarly, hungry people need fewer visual cues to perceive food objects and food terms than do people who are not hungry. This process, called **perceptual accentuation**, leads you to see what you expect or want to see. You see people you like as better looking and smarter than those you don't like. You magnify or accentuate what will satisfy your needs and desires: The thirsty person sees a mirage of water, the sexually deprived person sees a mirage of sexual satisfaction.

Perceptual accentuation can lead you to perceive what you need or want to perceive rather than what is really there, and to fail to perceive what you don't want to perceive. For example, you may not perceive signs of impending relationship problems, because you're only seeing what you want to see. Another interesting distortion created by perceptual accentuation is that you may perceive certain behaviors as

Chip East/Corbis Wire/Corbis

VIEWPOINTS Racial profiling (where the police focus on members of specific races as possible crime suspects) has been widely reported and condemned as racist. In the aftermath of the September 11, 2001, attacks, profiling of Muslims and of people who looked "Arab" became viewed by many as necessary for preventing further acts of terrorism. And it still is in many quarters throughout the country. How do you feel about racial, ethnic, or religious profiling?

indicative that someone likes you simply because you want to be liked. For example, you view general politeness and friendly behavior used as a persuasive strategy (say, by a salesperson) as an indication that the person genuinely likes you.

Primacy–Recency Assume for a moment that you're enrolled in a course in which half the classes are extremely dull and half extremely exciting. At the end of the semester, you evaluate the course and the instructor. Will your evaluation be more favorable if the dull classes occurred in the first half of the semester and the exciting classes in the second? Or will it be more favorable if the order is reversed? If what comes first exerts the most influence, you have a **primacy effect**. If what comes last (or most recently) exerts the most influence, you have a **recency effect**.

In the classic study on the effects of **primacy–recency** in interpersonal perception, college students perceived a person who was described as "intelligent, industrious, impulsive, critical, stubborn, and envious" more positively than a person described as "envious, stubborn, critical, impulsive, industrious, and intelligent" (Asch, 1946). Notice that the descriptions are identical; only the order was changed. Clearly, we have a tendency to use early information to get a general idea about a person and to use later information to make this impression more specific. The initial information helps us form a schema for the person. Once that schema is formed, we're likely to resist information that contradicts it.

One interesting practical implication of primacy–recency is that the first impression you make is likely to be the most important—and is likely to be made very quickly (Sunnafrank & Ramirez, 2004; Willis & Todorov, 2006). The reason for this is that the schema that others form of you functions as a filter to admit or block additional information about you. If the initial impression or schema is positive, others are likely (1) to readily remember additional positive information because it confirms this original positive image or schema; (2) to easily forget or distort negative information because it contradicts this original positive schema; and (3) to interpret ambiguous information as positive. You win in all three ways—if the initial impression is positive.

Our tendency to give greater weight to early information and to interpret later information in light of early impressions can lead us to formulate a total picture of an individual on the basis of initial impressions that may not be typical or accurate. For example, if you judge a job applicant as generally nervous when he or she may simply be showing normal nervousness at being interviewed for a much-needed job, you will have misperceived this individual. Similarly, this tendency can lead you to discount or distort subsequent perceptions so as not to disrupt your initial impression or upset your original schema. For example, you may fail to see signs of deceit in someone you like because of your early impression that this person is a good and honest individual.

Consistency The tendency to maintain balance among perceptions or attitudes is called **consistency** (McBroom & Reed, 1992). People expect certain things to go together and other things not to go together. On a purely intuitive basis, for example, respond to the following sentences by noting your expected response.

1. I expect a person I like to (like, dislike) me.
2. I expect a person I dislike to (like, dislike) me.
3. I expect my friend to (like, dislike) my friend.
4. I expect my friend to (like, dislike) my enemy.
5. I expect my enemy to (like, dislike) my friend.
6. I expect my enemy to (like, dislike) my enemy.

According to most consistency theories, your expectations would be as follows: You would expect a person you liked to like you (1) and a person you disliked to dislike you (2). You would expect a friend to like a friend (3) and to dislike an enemy (4). You would expect your enemy

For politeness as it relates to customer–server relationships, see "Drugstore Politeness" and "Eye Contact" at tcbdevito.blogspot .com. How do you view politeness between customer and server?

INTERPERSONAL CHOICE POINT

Reversing a First Impression

You made a really bad first impression in your interpersonal communication class. You meant to be sarcastically funny but came off as merely sarcastic. What are some of the things you might say and do to lessen the impact of this first impression?

to dislike your friend (5) and to like your other enemy (6). All these expectations are intuitively satisfying.

Further, you would expect someone you liked to possess characteristics you liked or admired and would expect your enemies not to possess characteristics you liked or admired. Conversely, you would expect people you liked to lack unpleasant characteristics and those you disliked to possess unpleasant characteristics.

Uncritically assuming that an individual is consistent can lead you to ignore or distort perceptions that are inconsistent with your picture of the whole person. For example, you may misinterpret Karla's unhappiness because your image of Karla is "happy, controlled, and contented."

Attribution of Control　Research on **attribution** shows that another way in which we form impressions is through the attribution of control. For example, suppose you invite your friend Desmond to dinner for 7:00 p.m. and he arrives at 9:00. Consider how you would respond to each of these reasons:

> Reason 1: "I just couldn't tear myself away from the beach. I really wanted to get a great tan."

> Reason 2: "I was driving here when I saw some young kids mugging an old couple. I broke it up and took the couple home. They were so frightened that I had to stay with them until their children arrived. Their phone was out of order and my cell battery died, so I had no way of calling to tell you I'd be late."

> Reason 3: "I got in a car accident and was taken to the hospital."

Depending on the reason, you would probably attribute very different motives to Desmond's behavior. With reasons 1 and 2, you'd conclude that Desmond was in control of his behavior (the reasons were internal). With reason 3, you'd conclude that he was not in control of his behavior (the reason was external and not under Desmond's control). Further, you would probably respond negatively to reason 1 (Desmond was selfish and inconsiderate) and positively to reason 2 (Desmond was a Good Samaritan). Because Desmond was not in control of his behavior in reason 3, you would probably not attribute either positive or negative motivation to his behavior. Instead, you would probably feel sorry that he got into an accident.

You probably make similar judgments based on control in numerous situations. Consider, for example, how you would respond to the following situations:

- Doris fails her history midterm exam.
- Sidney's car is repossessed because he failed to keep up the payments.
- Margie has developed high blood pressure and is complaining that she feels awful.
- Thomas's wife has just filed for divorce and he is feeling depressed.

You would most likely be sympathetic to each of these people if you felt that he or she was not in control of what happened; for example, if the examination was unfair, if Sidney lost his job because of employee discrimination, if Margie's blood pressure was caused by some inherited physiological problem, and if Thomas's wife wanted to leave him for a wealthy drug dealer. On the other hand, you probably would not be sympathetic if you felt that these people were in control of what happened; for example, if Doris partied instead of studying, if Sidney gambled his payments away, if Margie ate nothing but salty junk food and refused to exercise, and if Thomas had been repeatedly unfaithful and his wife finally gave up trying to reform him.

In perceiving and especially in evaluating other people's behavior, you frequently ask if they were in control of the behavior. Generally, research shows that if you feel a person was in control of negative behaviors, you'll come to dislike him or her. If you believe the person was not in control of negative behaviors, you'll come to feel sorry for and not blame the person.

In your attribution of control—or in attributing motives on the basis of any other reasons (for example, hearsay or observations of the person's behavior) beware of several potential errors: (1) the self-serving bias, (2) overattribution, and (3) the fundamental attribution error.

For an interesting application of perception research and theory, see "Perceiving Nonverbal Cues" at tcbdevito.blogspot.com. In what other fields would knowledge of nonverbal behavior prove useful?

1. We exhibit the **self-serving bias** when we take credit for the positive and deny responsibility for the negative. For example, you're more likely to attribute your positive outcomes (say, you get an A on an exam) to internal and controllable factors—to your personality, intelligence, or hard work. And you're more likely to attribute your negative outcomes (say, you get a D) to external and uncontrollable factors—to the exam's being exceptionally difficult or to your roommate's party the night before (Bernstein, Stephan, & Davis, 1979; Duval & Silva, 2002).

2. **Overattribution** is the tendency to single out one or two obvious characteristics of a person and attribute everything that person does to this one or these two characteristics. For example, if a person is blind or was born into great wealth, there's often a tendency to attribute everything that person does to such factors. And so you might say, "Alex overeats because he's blind," or "Lillian is irresponsible because she never had to work for her money." To avoid overattribution, recognize that most behaviors and personality characteristics result from lots of factors. You almost always make a mistake when you select one factor and attribute everything to it.

3. The **fundamental attribution error** occurs when we assess someone's behavior but overvalue the contribution of internal factors (for example, a person's personality) and undervalue the influence of

Jane September/Shutterstock

VIEWPOINTS Writers to advice columnists generally attribute their problems to external sources (the economy, an inconsiderate partner), whereas the columnists' responses often focus on internal sources (what has the writer done or not done); and their advice is therefore directed at the writer (you shouldn't have done that, apologize, get out of the relationship) (Schoeneman & Rubanowitz, 1985). Do you observe the same pattern when people discuss their problems with you, whether face-to-face, in letters, or in e-mail? Do you generally respond in the same ways as the advice columnists?

external factors (for example, the context or situation the person is in). The fundamental attribution error leads us to conclude that people do what they do because that's the kind of people they are, not because of the situation they're in. When Pat is late for an appointment, for example, you're more likely to conclude that Pat is inconsiderate or irresponsible than to attribute the lateness to a bus breakdown or a traffic accident.

Increasing Accuracy in Impression Formation

Successful interpersonal communication depends largely on the accuracy of the impressions you form of others. We've already seen the potential barriers that can arise with each of the perceptual processes, such as the self-serving bias or overattribution. In addition to avoiding these barriers, here are additional ways to increase your accuracy in impression formation.

Analyze Impressions   Subject your perceptions to logical analysis, to critical thinking. Here are two suggestions:

- **Recognize your own role in perception.** Your emotional and physiological state will influence the meaning you give to your perceptions. A movie may seem hysterically funny when you're in a good mood but just plain stupid when you're in a bad mood. Understand your own biases; for example, do you tend to perceive only the positive in people you like and only the negative in people you don't like?

- **Avoid early conclusions.** On the basis of your observations of behaviors, formulate hypotheses to test against additional information and evidence; avoid drawing conclusions that you then look to confirm. Look for a variety of cues pointing in the same direction. The more cues point to the same conclusion, the more likely your conclusion will be correct. Be especially alert to contradictory cues that seem to refute your initial hypotheses. At the same time, seek validation from others. Do others see things in the same way you do? If not, ask yourself if your perceptions may be distorted in some way.

Check Perceptions   **Perception checking** is another way to reduce uncertainty and to make your perceptions more accurate. The goal of perception checking is to further explore the thoughts and feelings of the other person, not to prove that your initial perception is correct. With this simple technique, you lessen your chances of misinterpreting another's feelings. At the same time, you give the other person an opportunity to elaborate on his or her thoughts and feelings. In its most basic form, perception checking consists of two steps:

1. **Describe what you see or hear**, recognizing that descriptions are not really objective but are heavily influenced by who you are, your emotional state, and so on. At the same time, you may wish to describe what you think is happening. Try to do this as descriptively (not evaluatively) as you can. Sometimes you may wish to offer several possibilities.

   - You've called me from work a lot this week. You seem concerned that everything is all right at home.
   - You've not wanted to talk with me all week. You say that my work is fine, but you don't seem to want to give me the same responsibilities that other research assistants have.

2. **Seek confirmation**: Ask the other person if your description is accurate. Avoid mind reading; that is, don't try to read the thoughts and feelings of another person just from observing their behaviors. Regardless of how many behaviors you observe and how carefully you examine them, you can only guess what is going on in someone's mind. A person's motives are not open to outside inspection; you can only make assumptions based on overt behaviors. So be careful that your request for confirmation does not sound as though you already know the answer. Avoid phrasing your questions defensively; for example, "You really don't want to go out, do you? I knew you didn't when you turned on that lousy television." Instead, ask for confirmation in as supportive a way as possible.

   - Would you rather watch TV?
   - Are you worried about me, or the kids?
   - Are you displeased with my work? Is there anything I can do to improve my job performance?

INTERPERSONAL CHOICE POINT

Mutual Attraction Testing

You've become attracted to another student in your class but don't know if it's mutual. In what ways might you use the suggestions discussed here for increasing your own accuracy in perceiving whether or not the attraction is mutual?

Reduce Uncertainty   In every interpersonal situation there is some degree of uncertainty. A variety of strategies can help reduce uncertainty (Berger & Bradac, 1982; Gudykunst, 1993; Brashers, 2007).

- Observing another person while he or she is engaged in an active task, preferably interacting with others in an informal social situation, will often reveal a great deal about the person, as people are less apt to monitor their behaviors and more likely to reveal their true selves in informal situations.
- You can sometimes manipulate situations so as to observe the person in more specific and revealing contexts. Employment interviews, theatrical auditions, and student teaching are good examples of situations arranged to provide an accurate view of the person in action.
- When you log on to an Internet chat group and lurk, reading the exchanges between the other group members before saying anything yourself, you're learning about the people in the group and about the group itself, thus reducing uncertainty. When uncertainty is reduced, you're more likely to make contributions that will be appropriate to the group and less likely to violate the group's norms.
- Learn about a person through asking others. You might inquire of a colleague if a third person finds you interesting and might like to have dinner with you.
- Interact with the individual. For example, you can ask questions: "Do you enjoy sports?" "What did you think of that computer science course?" "What would you do if you got

fired?" You also gain knowledge of another by revealing information about yourself, which encourages the other person to also talk about himself or herself.

Increase Cultural Sensitivity **Cultural sensitivity**—recognizing and being sensitive to cultural differences—will help increase your accuracy in perception. For example, Russian or Chinese artists such as ballet dancers will often applaud their audience by clapping. Americans seeing this may easily interpret this as egotistical. Similarly, a German man will enter a restaurant before the woman in order to see if the place is respectable enough for the woman to enter. This simple custom can easily be interpreted as rude when viewed by people from cultures in which it's considered courteous for the woman to enter first (Axtell, 2007).

Within every cultural group there are wide and important differences. As all Americans are not alike, neither are all Indonesians, Greeks, or Mexicans. When you make assumptions that all people of a certain culture are alike, you're thinking in stereotypes. Recognizing differences between another culture and your own, and among members of the same culture, will help you perceive situations more accurately.

Cultural sensitivity will help counteract the difficulty most people have in understanding the nonverbal messages of people from other cultures. For example, it's easier to interpret the facial expressions of members of your own culture than those of members of other cultures (Weathers, Frank, & Spell, 2002). This "in-group advantage" will assist your perceptional accuracy for members of your own culture but will often hinder your accuracy for members of other cultures (Elfenbein & Ambady, 2002).

The suggestions for improving intercultural communication are applicable to increasing your cultural sensitivity in perception. For example, educate yourself; reduce uncertainty; recognize differences (between yourself and people from other cultures, among members of other cultures, and between your meanings and the meanings that people from other cultures may have); confront your stereotypes; and adjust your communication.

Impression Management: Goals and Strategies

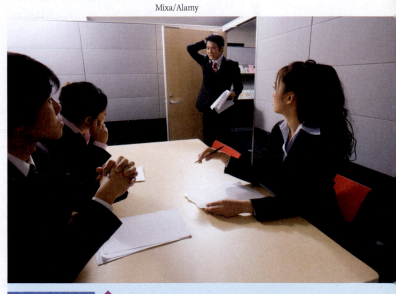

Mixa/Alamy

Impression management (some writers use the term "self-presentation" or "identity management") has to do with the processes you go through to communicate the image of yourself that you want others to have of you.

The impression you make on others is largely the result of the messages you communicate. In the same way that you form impressions of others largely on the basis of how they communicate, verbally and nonverbally, you also convey an impression of yourself through what you say (your verbal messages) and how you act and dress, as well as how you decorate your office or apartment (your nonverbal messages). Communication messages, however, are not the only means for impression formation and management. For example, you also communicate your self-image by the people with whom you associate (and judge others the same way); if you associate with A-list people, then surely you must be A-list yourself, the theory goes. Also, as illustrated in the discussion of stereotypes, you may form an impression of someone on the basis of that person's age, gender, or ethnic origin. Or you may rely on what others have said about the person and form impressions

VIEWPOINTS What one suggestion for increasing accuracy in impression formation do you wish others would follow more often when they make judgments about you?

that are consistent with these comments. And, of course, the others may do the same in forming impressions of you.

Part of the art and skill of interpersonal communication is to understand and be able to manage the impressions you give to others; mastering the art of impression management will enable you to present yourself as you want others to see you—at least to some extent.

The strategies you use to achieve this desired impression will depend on your specific goal. Here is an interpersonal typology of seven major communication goals and strategies of impression management. As you read about these goals and strategies, and about how these strategies can backfire, consider your own attempts to communicate the "right" impression to others and what you do (that is, the strategies you use) to achieve this unique kind of communication.

To Be Liked: Immediacy, Affinity-Seeking, and Politeness Strategies

If you want to be liked—say, you're new at school or on the job and you want to be well-liked, to be included in the activities of other students or work associates, and to be thought of highly by these other people—you'll likely use three sets of strategies. **Immediacy strategies** are those that connect you and the other person. The other two sets of strategies for being liked are affinity-seeking and politeness strategies.

Affinity-Seeking Strategies   As you can see from examining the list of **affinity-seeking strategies** that follows, the use of these techniques is likely to increase your chances of being liked (Bell & Daly, 1984). Such strategies are especially important in initial interactions, and their use by teachers has even been found to increase student motivation (Martin & Rubin, 1998; Myers & Zhong, 2004; Wrench, McCroskey, & Richmond, 2008).

- Be of help to Other (the other person).
- Appear to be "in control" as a leader, as one who takes charge.
- Present yourself as socially equal to Other.
- Present yourself as comfortable and relaxed when with Other.
- Allow Other to assume control over relational activities.
- Follow the cultural rules for polite, cooperative conversation with Other.
- Appear active, enthusiastic, and dynamic.
- Stimulate and encourage Other to talk about himself or herself; reinforce disclosures and contributions of Other.
- Ensure that activities with Other are enjoyable and positive.
- Include Other in your social activities and groupings.
- Show that your relationship with Other is closer than it really is.
  - Listen to Other attentively and actively.
  - Communicate interest in Other.
  - Engage in self-disclosure with Other.
  - Appear optimistic and positive rather than pessimistic and negative.
  - Appear to Other as an independent and freethinking individual.
  - Appear to Other as being as physically attractive as possible.
  - Appear to Other as an interesting person to get to know.
  - Appear as someone who is able to reward Other for associating with you.
  - Show respect for Other, and help Other to feel positively about himself or herself.
  - Arrange circumstances so that you and Other come into frequent contact.
  - Communicate warmth and empathy to Other.
  - Demonstrate that you share significant attitudes and values with Other.
  - Communicate supportiveness in Other's interpersonal interactions.
  - Appear to Other as honest and reliable.

The strongest principle of growth lies in human choice.
—*George Eliot*

Understanding *Interpersonal Skills*

OTHER-ORIENTATION

Other-orientation is a quality of interpersonal effectiveness that includes the ability to adapt your messages to the other person (Spitzberg & Hecht, 1984; Dindia & Timmerman, 2003). The more accurately you perceive another person, the more effectively you'll be able to adapt your own messages. It involves communicating attentiveness to and interest in the other person and genuine interest in what the person says.

Communicating Other-Orientation. You'll recognize the following behaviors in those with whom you enjoy talking. As you read these suggestions you'll note that these are also likely to serve the impression formation function of being liked.

- **Show consideration.** Demonstrate respect; for example, ask if it's all right to dump your troubles on someone before doing so, or ask if your phone call comes at a good time.
- **Acknowledge the other person's feelings as legitimate.** Expressions such as "You're right" or "I can understand why you're so angry" help focus the interaction on the other person and confirm that you're listening.
- **Acknowledge the other person.** Recognize the importance of the other person. Ask for suggestions, opinions, and clarification. This will ensure that you understand what the other person is saying from that person's point of view.
- **Focus your messages on the other person.** Use open-ended questions to involve the other person in the interaction (as opposed to questions that merely ask for a yes or no answer), and make statements that directly address the person. Use focused eye contact and appropriate facial expressions; smile, nod, and lean toward the other person.
- **Grant permission.** Let the other person know that it's OK to express (or to not express) her or his feelings. A simple statement such as "I know how difficult it is to talk about feelings" opens up the topic of feelings and gives the other person permission either to pursue such a discussion or to say nothing.

Working with Interpersonal Skills

On a 10-point scale, how would you rate your general other-orientation (give yourself a 10 if you are always and everywhere other-oriented)? Can you identify situations in which you are especially likely to forget other-orientation? In what ways might you become more other-oriented?

And, not surprisingly, plain old flattery goes a long way toward making you liked. Flattery has also been found to increase your chances for success in a job interview, increase the tip a customer is likely to leave, and even increase your perceived credibility (Varma, Toh, & Pichler, 2006; Seiter, 2007; Vonk, 2002).

Politeness Strategies   We can view **politeness strategies**, which are often used to make ourselves appear likeable, in terms of negative and positive types (Goffman, 1967; Brown & Levinson, 1987; Holmes 1995; Goldsmith, 2007). Both of these types of politeness are responsive to two needs that we each have:

(1) **positive face**—the desire to be viewed positively by others, to be thought of favorably, and

(2) **negative face**—the desire to be autonomous, to have the right to do as we wish.

Politeness in interpersonal communication, then, refers to behavior that allows others to maintain both positive and negative face; and impoliteness refers to behaviors that attack either positive face (for example, you criticize someone) or negative face (for example, you make demands on someone).

Ethics in Interpersonal Communication

THE ETHICS OF IMPRESSION MANAGEMENT

Impression-management strategies may also be used unethically and for less than noble purposes. For example, people may use affinity-seeking strategies to get you to like them so that they can extract favors from you. Politicians frequently portray themselves as credible (when they are not) in order to win votes. The same could be said of the stereotypical used-car salesperson or insurance agent trying to make a sale. Some people use self-handicapping strategies or self-deprecating strategies to get you to see their behavior from a perspective that benefits them rather than you. Self-monitoring strategies are often deceptive, and are designed to present a more polished image than one that might come out without this self-monitoring. And, of course, influence strategies have been used throughout history in deception as well as in truth. Even image confirming strategies can be used to deceive, as when people exaggerate their positive qualities (or make them up) and hide their negative ones.

ETHICAL CHOICE POINT

You're interviewing for a job you really want and you need to be perceived as credible and likeable. What are your ethical choices for presenting yourself as both credible and likeable?

Konstantynov/Shutterstock

VIEWPOINTS There is a negative effect that can result from the use of affinity-seeking strategies—as there is for all of the strategies discussed in this section. Using affinity-seeking strategies too often or in ways that may appear insincere may lead people to see you as attempting to ingratiate yourself for your own advantage and not really meaning "to be nice." Can you identify examples from your own interpersonal experiences?

To help another person maintain positive face, you speak respectfully to and about the person, you give the person your full attention, you say "excuse me" when appropriate. In short you treat the person as you would want to be treated. In this way you allow the person to maintain positive face through what is called positive politeness. You attack the person's positive face when you speak disrespectfully about the person, ignore the person or the person's comments, and fail to use the appropriate expressions of politeness, such as "Thank you" and "Please."

To help another person maintain negative face, you respect the person's right to be autonomous and so you request, rather than demand, that they do something; you say, "Would you mind opening a window" rather than "Open that window!" You might also give the person an "out" when making a request, allowing the person to reject your request if that is what the person wants. And so you say, "If this is a bad time, please tell me, but I'm really strapped and could use a loan of $100" rather than "Loan me a $100" or "You have to lend me $100." If you want a recommendation, you might say, "Would it be possible for you to write me a recommendation for graduate school?" rather than "You have to write me a recommendation for graduate school." In this way you enable the person to maintain negative face through what is called negative politeness.

Of course, we do this almost automatically, and asking for a favor without any consideration for the person's negative face needs would seems totally insensitive. In most situations, however, this type of attack on negative face often appears in more subtle forms. For example, your mother saying "Are you going to wear that?"—to use Deborah Tannen's (2006) example—attacks negative face by criticizing or challenging your autonomy. This comment also attacks positive face by questioning your ability to dress properly.

Like all the strategies discussed here, politeness, too, may have negative consequences. Over-politeness, for example, is likely to be seen as phony and is likely to be resented. Over-politeness will also be resented if it's seen as a persuasive strategy.

To Be Believed: Credibility Strategies

Let's say you're a politician and you want people to vote for you or to support a particular proposal you're advancing. In this case you'll probably use **credibility strategies**—a concept that goes back some 2300 years (to the ancient Greek and Roman rhetoricians) and is supported by contemporary research—and seek to establish your competence, your character, and your charisma. For example, to establish your competence, you may mention your great educational background or the courses you took that qualify you as an expert. To establish that you're of good character, you may mention how fair and honest you are or speak of your concern for enduring values or your concern for others. And to establish your charisma—your take-charge, positive personality—you may demonstrate enthusiasm, be emphatic, or focus on the positive while minimizing the negative.

Of course, if you stress your competence, character, and charisma too much, you risk being perceived as too eager—as someone who is afraid of being exposed as lacking the very qualities that you seek to present to others. For example, generally, people who are truly competent need say little directly about their own competence; their knowledgeable, insightful, and logical messages reveal their competence.

For a discussion of the functions of politeness, see "The Communication Functions of Politeness" at tcbdevito.blogspot.com. What function do you think is most important? Are there other functions that should be added here?

To Excuse Failure: Self-Handicapping Strategies

If you were about to tackle a difficult task and were concerned that you might fail, you might use what are called **self-handicapping strategies**. In the more extreme type of self-handicapping strategy, you actually set up barriers or obstacles to make the task impossible so that when you fail, you won't be blamed or thought ineffective—after all, the task was impossible. Let's say you aren't prepared for your interpersonal communication exam and you feel you're going to fail. Well, using this extreme type of self-handicapping strategy, you might go out and party the night before so that when you do poorly in the exam, you can blame it on the all-night party rather than on your intelligence or knowledge. The less extreme type involves manufacturing excuses for failure and having them ready if you do fail. "The exam was unfair" is one such popular excuse. Or you might blame a long period without a date on your being too intelligent or too shy or too poor, or blame a poorly cooked dinner on your defective stove.

Using self-handicapping strategies too often may lead people to see you as incompetent or foolish—after all, partying late into the night before an exam for which you are already unprepared doesn't make a whole lot of sense; very likely this would reflect negatively on your overall competence.

To Secure Help: Self-Deprecating Strategies

If you want to be taken care of and protected or simply want someone to come to your aid, you might use **self-deprecating strategies**. Confessions of incompetence and inability often bring assistance from others. And so you might say, "I just can't fix that drain and it drives me crazy; I just don't know anything about plumbing," with the hope that the other person will offer help.

But be careful: Using self-deprecating strategies may convince people that you are in fact as incompetent as you say you are. Or people may see you as someone who doesn't want to do something and so confesses incompetence to get others to do it for you. This is not likely to get you help in the long run.

To Hide Faults: Self-Monitoring Strategies

Much impression management is devoted not merely to presenting a positive image but to suppressing the negative via **self-monitoring strategies**. Here you carefully monitor (self-censor) what you say or do. You

INTERPERSONAL CHOICE POINT

Face-to-Face

You've been communicating with Pat over the Internet for the past seven months, and you finally have decided to meet for coffee. You really want Pat to like you. What impression-management strategies might you use?

avoid your normal slang so as to make your colleagues think more highly of you; you avoid chewing gum so you don't look juvenile or unprofessional. While you readily disclose favorable parts of your experience, you actively hide the unfavorable parts.

But, if you self-monitor too often or too obviously, you risk being seen as unwilling to reveal your true self, perhaps because you don't trust others enough to feel comfortable disclosing your weaknesses as well as your strengths. In more extreme cases you may be seen as dishonest, or as trying to fool other people.

Jeff Greenberg/Alamy

VIEWPOINTS There is some evidence that we attribute less credibility to people who have accents than we do to people who don't (Lev-Ari & Keysar, 2010). Does your experience support this? Can you think of exceptions? For example, might the chef who speaks with a French accent be seen as having more credibility than one without a French accent?

To Be Followed: Influencing Strategies

In many instances you'll want to get people to see you as a leader, as someone to be followed in thought and perhaps in behavior. Here you can use a variety of **influencing strategies**. One set of such strategies are those normally grouped under power. So, for example, to gain influence you may stress your knowledge (information power); your expertise (expert power); and/or your right to lead by virtue of your position as, say, a doctor or judge or accountant (legitimate power). Another set of influencing strategies are those of leadership, in which you might stress your prior experience, your broad knowledge, or your previous successes.

Influencing strategies, too, can easily backfire. If your influence attempts fail—for whatever reason—you will lose general influence. That is, if you try but fail to influence someone, you'll be seen to have less power than before you tried the failed influence attempt. And, of course, if you're perceived as trying to influence others for self-gain, your persuasive attempts are likely to be rejected and perhaps seen as self-serving and resented.

To Confirm Self-Image: Image-Confirming Strategies

At times you communicate to confirm your self-image. For example, if you see yourself as the life of the party, you'll tell jokes and try to amuse people. In doing so you'd be using **image-confirming strategies**. Your behaviors confirm your own self-image. By engaging in image confirming behaviors, you'll also let others know that this is who you are, this is how you want to be seen. At the same time that you reveal aspects of yourself that confirm your desired image, you will probably suppress revealing aspects of yourself that would disconfirm this image.

If you use image-confirming strategies too frequently, however, you risk being seen as "too perfect to be for real." If you try to project an all-positive image, it's likely to turn people off—people want to see their friends and associates as having some faults, some imperfections. Also recognize that image-confirming strategies invariably involve your talking about yourself, and with that comes the risk of appearing self-absorbed.

A knowledge of these impression-management strategies and the ways in which they are effective and ineffective will give you a greater number of choices for achieving such widely diverse goals as being liked, being believed, excusing failure, securing help, hiding faults, being followed, and confirming your self-image.

At the same time, recognize that these very same impression-management strategies may be used unethically and for less-than-noble purposes. For example, people may use affinity-seeking strategies to get you to like them so that they can extract favors from you. In order to get votes, politicians frequently present themselves as credible (competent, moral, and charismatic) when in fact they are not. And of course the same could be said of the stereotypical used-car salesperson or the insurance agent. Some people will use self-handicapping strategies or self-deprecating strategies to get you to see their behavior from a perspective that benefits them rather than you. Self-monitoring strategies are most often deceptive and are designed to present a more polished image than one that might come out without this self-monitoring. And, of course, influence strategies have throughout history been used in deception as well as in truth. Even image-confirming strategies can be used to deceive, as when people exaggerate their positive qualities (or make them up) and hide their negative traits.

Summary

Use your smartphone or tablet device (or log on to mycommunicationlab.com) to hear an audio summary of this chapter.

This chapter looked at the ways in which you perceive yourself and other people and how you manage the perception of yourself that you communicate to others.

The Self in Interpersonal Communication

1. Self-concept is the image you have of who you are. Sources of self-concept include others' images of you, social comparisons, cultural teachings, and your own interpretations and evaluations.
2. Self-awareness is your knowledge of yourself—the extent to which you know who you are. A useful way of looking at self-awareness is with the Johari window, which consists of four parts. The open self holds information known to self and others; the blind self holds information known only to others; the hidden self holds information known only to self; and the unknown self holds information known to neither self nor others.
3. To increase self-awareness, ask yourself about yourself, listen to others, actively seek information about yourself, see your different selves, and increase your open self.
4. Self-esteem is the value you place on yourself—your perceived self-worth.
5. To increase self-esteem, try attacking your self-destructive beliefs, seeking affirmation, seeking out nourishing people, and working on projects that will result in success.

Perception in Interpersonal Communication

6. Perception is the process by which you become aware of objects and events in the external world.

7. Perception occurs in five stages: (1) stimulation, (2) organization, (3) interpretation–evaluation, (4) memory, and (5) recall.

Impression Formation

8. Six important processes influence the way you form impressions: Self-fulfilling prophecies may influence the behaviors of others; implicit personality theory allows you to conclude that certain characteristics go with certain other characteristics; perceptual accentuation may lead you to perceive what you expect to perceive instead of what is really there; primacy–recency may influence you to give extra importance to what occurs first (a primacy effect) and may lead you to see what conforms to this judgment and to distort or otherwise misperceive what contradicts it; the tendency to seek and expect consistency may influence you to see what is consistent and not to see what is inconsistent; and attributions, through which you try to understand the behaviors of others, are made in part on the basis of your judgment of control.
9. Among the major errors of attribution are the self-serving bias, overattribution, and the fundamental attribution error.
10. In increasing your accuracy in impression formation: Analyze your impressions and recognize your role in perception; check your impressions; reduce uncertainty; and become culturally sensitive by recognizing the differences between you and others and also the differences among people from other cultures.

Impression Management: Goals and Strategies

1. Among the goals and strategies of impression management are: to be liked (immediacy, affinity-seeking, and politeness

strategies); to be believed (credibility strategies that establish your competence, character, and charisma); to excuse failure (self-handicapping strategies); to secure help (self-deprecating strategies); to hide faults (self-monitoring strategies); to be followed (influencing strategies); and to confirm your self-image (image-confirming strategies).

2. Each of these impression-management strategies can backfire and give others negative impressions. Also, each of these strategies may be used to reveal your true self or to present a false self and deceive others in the process.

Key Terms

affinity-seeking strategies	negative face	schemata
affirmation	other-orientation	script
attribution	overattribution	selective attention
consistency	perception	selective exposure
contrast, rule of	perception checking	selective perception
credibility strategies	perceptual accentuation	self-awareness
cultural sensitivity	politeness strategies	self-concept
fundamental attribution error	positive face	self-deprecating strategies
halo effect	primacy effect	self-destructive beliefs
image-confirming strategies	primacy–recency	self-esteem
immediacy strategies	proximity, rule of	self-fulfilling prophecy
implicit personality theory	recall	self-handicapping strategies
impression formation	recency effect	self-monitoring strategies
impression management	reverse halo (or "horns") effect	self-serving bias
influencing strategies	rules	similarity, rule of
interpretation–evaluation	schema	

MyCommunicationLab Explorations

MyCommunicationLab®

Communication Choice Points

Revisit the chapter-opening video, "Mike Tries to Get a Date." Recall from the video scenario that Mike is not always successful when asking girls for a date. Mike is an average guy, who is pleasant and reasonably good-looking, but he often gets rejected and isn't sure why. "Mike Tries to Get a Date" looks at how Mike's own self-expectations and impression-management skills affect the outcome of this interaction.

Log on to mycommunicationlab.com to view the video for this chapter, "Mike Tries to Get a Date," and then answer the related discussion questions.

Additional Resources

These exercises enable you to further explore the concepts of the self and perception, discussed in this chapter.

1 How Can You Attack Self-Defeating Impulses? asks you to consider your own self-destructive beliefs and how you deal with them. Other exercises focus on sensitizing you to the influences on your perceptions and on helping you make your perceptions more accurate. **2** Perceiving My Selves invites you to consider how you see yourself and how you think others see you; this exercise is also an excellent icebreaker. **3** How Might You Perceive Others' Perceptions? presents a variety of situations in which people are likely to see things very differently and sensitizes you to the variety of perceptions possible from the "same" event. **4** How Do You Make Attributions? looks at a few specific situations and asks how you might make attributions in explaining the reasons for the behaviors. **5** Barriers to Accurate Perception presents a dialogue containing a variety of perceptional errors and asks you to identify them. **6** Perspective Taking asks you to take positive and negative perspectives on the same situations to help you explore the different conclusions people may draw from the same incident.

Listening in Interpersonal Communication

Listening in Interpersonal Communication

The Importance of Listening

The Process of Listening

Listening Barriers

Culture, Gender, and Listening

Styles of Effective Listening

Pearson Education

Sue's partner Harry is visibly upset, but she doesn't know why. Sue considers the elements of the listening process and the various barriers that can interfere with effective listening as she contemplates her communication choices. See how Sue's choices play out in the video, "A Bad Day at Work" (www.mycommunicationlab.com).

Listening is one of the most important of all interpersonal communication skills. Just think of your own listening behavior during an average day. You wake up to the alarm radio, put on the television to hear the weather and the news, check your computer and listen to the latest entries on YouTube and the advertising pop-ups, go to school while talking on your cell phone, listen to fellow students and instructors, listen to music or watch television, and listen to family members at dinner. Surely listening occupies a good part of your communication day.

The Importance of Listening

The skills of listening will prove crucial to you in both your professional and relationship lives. Let's look at a few of the benefits, both professional and personal.

Professional Benefits

In today's workplace, listening is regarded as a crucial skill. Whether a temporary intern or a high-level executive, you need to listen if you're going to function effectively in today's workplace. If you're not convinced of this, take a look at the many websites that talk about the skills needed for success in today's workplace and you will find that listening consistently ranks among the most important skills (see, for example, www.career.com, www.dol.gov, www.buzzle.com, or www.ezinearticles.com).

Another important professional benefit of listening is to establish and communicate power. In much the same way that you communicate power with your words or gestures, you also communicate your power through listening.

It's also interesting to note that the effective listener is more likely to emerge as a group leader and is often a more effective salesperson, a more attentive and effective healthcare worker, and a more effective manager (Johnson & Bechler, 1998; Kramer, 1997; Castleberry & Shepherd, 1993; Lauer, 2003; Stein & Bowen, 2003; Levine, 2004). And, medical educators, claiming that doctors are not trained to listen to their patients, have introduced what they call "narrative medicine" to teach doctors not only to listen more effectively but also to recognize how their perceptions of their patients are influenced by their own emotions (D. Smith, 2003).

For a brief discussion of the importance of listening in health care, see "Listening Doctors" at tcbdevito.blogspot.com. In what other areas would you like to see people listening more effectively?

Personal Benefits

There can be little doubt that listening skills play a crucial role as we develop and maintain a variety of interpersonal relationships (Brownell, 2006). When asked what they want in a partner, women overwhelmingly identify "a partner who listens." And most men would agree that they too want a partner who listens. Among friends, listening skills consistently rank high; in fact, it would be hard to think of a person as a friend if that person was not also a good listener. Within the family, listening is perhaps at its most crucial. Children need to learn to listen to their parents and also need their parents to listen to them. And parents need to learn to listen to their children.

Another way to appreciate the importance of listening is to consider its purposes and the benefits that accrue for each of these purposes. These purposes, of course, are the same as those of communication generally: to learn, to relate, to influence, to play, and to help.

- **To learn:** One purpose of listening is to learn, something you do regularly as you listen to lectures in college. You also listen in order to learn about and understand other people and perhaps to avoid problems and make more reasonable decisions. For example, listening to how your friend dealt with an overly aggressive lover may suggest options to you or to those you know. Listening to your sales staff discuss their difficulties may help you offer more pertinent sales training.

- **To relate:** One of the communication skills most important to healthy relationships is the ability to listen to friends, romantic partners, family members, colleagues, and just about anyone with whom you come into contact. In fact, women rate listening as one of the most important qualities in a partner. We all use listening to gain social acceptance and popularity and to make people like us. As you know from your own experience, the people you want to talk most with are the people who know how to listen. When you listen attentively and supportively, you communicate a genuine concern for others; it's a way of telling others that you care about them.

- **To influence:** You also listen to influence other people's attitudes, values, beliefs, opinions, and behaviors. While at first this relationship may seem strange, think about the people who are influential in your life. Very likely these are the people who listen to you, who know you and understand you. You're more likely to follow someone's advice once you feel that you've really been listened to—that your insights and concerns have been heard and understood.

- **To play:** Listening to play, which some listening researchers refer to as appreciative listening, would include all those listening experiences where your purpose is primarily enjoyment (Worthington & Fitch-Hauser, 2012). Listening to music or the rustle of leaves often serves a play purpose. Here listening doesn't have to have a profitable outcome; it merely has to be enjoyable for the moment. Listening to the amusing stories of family members and the anecdotes of coworkers, for example, will allow you to gain a more comfortable balance between the world of work and the world of play.

INTERPERSONAL CHOICE POINT

Relationship Listening

A young nephew tells you that he can't talk with his parents. No matter how hard he tries, they don't listen. "I tried to tell them that I can't play baseball and I don't want to play baseball," he confides. "But they ignore me and tell me that all I need is practice." What are some of the things you can say or do that will show your nephew that you're listening.

Alamy

VIEWPOINT What makes a person or a message deserving of your attentive listening? For example, would you find it more difficult to listen to someone who was overjoyed because of winning the lottery for $27 million or to someone who was overcome with sadness because of the death of a loved one? How easy would it be for you to listen to someone who was depressed because an expected bonus of $60,000 turned out to be only $45,000? Put differently, what types of people and what types of message engage your listening attention?

■ **To help:** Listening to help is something we experience growing up when our parents listen (or, sometimes, don't listen) to our concerns and help us solve our problems. Sometimes just listening—with no advice and no suggestions—proves extremely helpful. Supportive and non-influential listening helps the other person clarify his or her thoughts and enables them to be seen more objectively. And of course listening is almost always a prerequisite to offering advice or help of any specific kind; after all, you really can't offer useful aid without first knowing and listening to the individual.

The Process of Listening

Listening is the process of: (1) receiving (hearing and attending to the message), (2) understanding (deciphering meaning from the message you hear), (3) remembering (retaining what you hear in memory), (4) evaluating (thinking critically about and judging the message), and (5) responding (answering or giving feedback to the speaker). This five-step process is visualized in Figure 1.

All five listening stages overlap; when you listen, you're performing all five processes at essentially the same time. For example, when listening in conversation, you're not only remaining attentive to what the other person is saying but also critically evaluating what he or she just said and perhaps giving feedback.

Listening is never perfect. There are lapses in attention, misunderstandings, lapses in memory, inadequate critical thinking, and inappropriate responding. The goal is to reduce these obstacles as best you can.

Note that the listening process is circular. The responses of Person A serve as the stimuli for Person B, whose responses in turn serve as the stimuli for Person A, and so on. As will become clear in the following discussion of the five steps, listening is not a process of transferring an idea from the mind of a speaker to the mind of a listener. Rather, it is a process in which speaker and listener work together to achieve a common understanding.

Figure 1 emphasizes that listening involves a collection of skills: attention and concentration (receiving), learning (understanding), memory (remembering), critical thinking (evaluation), and competence in giving feedback (responding). Listening can go wrong at

FIGURE 1

A Five-Stage Model of Listening

Recognize that at each stage of listening there will be lapses. For example, at the receiving stage a listener receives part of the message but, because of noise and perhaps for other reasons, fails to receive other parts. Similarly, at the stage of understanding, a listener understands part of the message but, because of each person's inability to share another's meanings exactly, fails to understand other parts. The same is true for remembering, evaluating, and responding. This model draws on a variety of previous models that listening researchers have developed (for example, Worthington & Fitch-Hauser, 2012; Barker, 1990; Brownell, 2010).

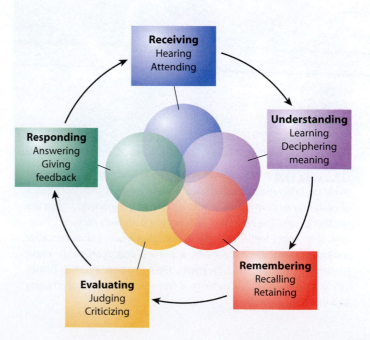

any stage—but you can improve your listening ability by strengthening the skills needed at each step of the listening process. Consequently, suggestions for listening improvement are offered with each of the five stages.

Stage One: Receiving

Listening begins with hearing, the process of receiving the messages the speaker sends. One of the great myths about listening is that it's the same as hearing. It isn't. Hearing is just the first stage of listening; it's equivalent to receiving. Hearing (and receiving) is a physiological process that occurs when you're in the vicinity of vibrations in the air and these vibrations impinge on your eardrum. Hearing is basically a passive process that occurs without any attention or effort on your part; hearing is mindless. Listening, as you'll see, is very different; listening is mindful.

At the **receiving** stage, you note not only what is said (verbally and nonverbally) but also what is omitted. You receive, for example, your boss's summary of your accomplishments as well as the omission of your shortcomings. To improve your receiving skills:

- **Focus your attention** on the speaker's verbal and nonverbal messages, on what is said and on what isn't said. Avoid focusing your attention on what you'll say next; if you begin to rehearse your responses, you're going to miss what the speaker says next.
- **Avoid distractions** in the environment; if necessary, shut off the stereo or and turn off your cell phone.
- **Maintain your role as listener** and avoid interrupting. Avoid interrupting as much as possible. It will only prevent you from hearing what the speaker is saying.

At times, you may wish to ask your listeners to receive your messages fairly and without prejudice, especially when you anticipate a negative reaction. For this purpose you're likely to use **disclaimers**, statements that aim to ensure that your messages will be understood and will not reflect negatively on you. Some of the more popular disclaimers are these (Hewitt & Stokes, 1975; McLaughlin, 1984):

- **Hedging** helps you to separate yourself from the message so that if your listeners reject your message, they need not reject you (for example, "I may be wrong here, but . . .").
- **Credentialing** helps you establish your special qualifications for saying what you're about to say ("Don't get me wrong, I'm not homophobic" or "As someone who telecommutes, I . . .").
- **Sin licenses** ask listeners for permission to deviate in some way from some normally accepted convention ("I know this may not be the place to discuss business, but . . .").
- **Cognitive disclaimers** help you make the case that you're in full possession of your faculties ("I know you'll think I'm crazy, but let me explain the logic of the case").
- **Appeals for the suspension of judgment** ask listeners to hear you out before making a judgment ("Don't hang up on me until you hear my side of the story").

Generally, disclaimers are effective when you think you might offend listeners in telling a joke ("I don't usually like these types of jokes, but . . ."). In one study, for example, 11-year-old children were read a story about someone whose actions created negative effects. Some children heard the story with a disclaimer, and others heard the same story without the disclaimer. When the children were asked to indicate how the person should be punished, those

Splash News/Newscom

VIEWPOINTS Research shows that hedging reflects negatively on both male and female speakers when it indicates a lack of certainty or conviction resulting from some inadequacy on the speaker's part. The hedging will be more positively received, however, if listeners feel it reflects the speaker's belief that tentative statements are the only kinds a person can reasonably make (Wright & Hosman, 1983; Hosman, 1989; Pearson, West, & Turner, 1995). Do you find this to be true from your experience in using and listening to hedges?

TABLE 1

INTERPERSONAL COMMUNICATION TIPS
Between People with and without Hearing Difficulties

Ludwig van Beethoven
Ludwig van Beethoven (1770-1827) Composing his "Missa Solemnis" (oil on canvas)

Thomas Edison
Stieler, Joseph Carl (1781-1858)/Private Collection/The Bridgeman Art Library

Pete Townshend
The Granger Collection

Marlee Matlin
Robert E. Klein/AP Photos

Here are some suggestions for more effective communication between people who hear well and those who have hearing problems.

If you have unimpaired hearing:

Generally	Specifically
Avoid interference.	Make sure the visual cues from your speech are clearly observable; face the person squarely and avoid smoking, chewing gum, or holding your hand over your mouth.
Speak at an adequate volume.	But avoid shouting, which can distort your speech and may insult the person. Be careful to avoid reducing volume at the ends of your sentences.
Phrase ideas in different ways.	Because some words are easier to lip-read than others, it often helps if you can rephrase your ideas in different words.
Avoid overlapping speech.	In group situations only one person should speak at a time. Similarly, direct your comments to the person with hearing loss himself or herself; don't talk to the person through a third party.
Use nonverbal cues.	Nonverbals can help communicate your meaning; gestures indicating size or location and facial expressions indicating feelings are often helpful.

If you have impaired hearing:

Do your best to eliminate background noise.	Reduce the distance between yourself and the person with a hearing impairment. Reduce background noise. Make sure the lighting is adequate.
Move closer to the speaker if this helps you hear better.	Alert the speaker that this closer distance will help you hear better.
Ask for adjustments.	If you feel the speaker can make adjustments, ask the speaker to repeat a message, to speak more slowly, or to increase volume.
Position yourself for best reception.	If you hear better in one ear than another, position yourself accordingly and, if necessary, clue the speaker in to this fact.
Ask for additional cues.	If necessary, ask the speaker to write down certain information, such as phone numbers or website addresses.

Sources: These suggestions were drawn from a variety of sources: Tips for Communicating with Deaf People (Rochester Institute of Technology, National Technical Institute for the Deaf, Division of Public Affairs), http://www.his.com/~lola/deaf.html, http://www.zak.co.il/deaf-info/old /comm_strategies.html, http://www.agbell.org/, http://www.dol.gov/odep/pubs/fact/comucate.htm, www.ndmig.com, www.mass.gov, and http://spot.pcc.edu/~rjacobs/career/communication_tips.htm.

who heard the story with the disclaimer recommended significantly lower punishments (Bennett, 1990).

Disclaimers, however, can also get you into trouble. For example, to preface remarks with "I'm no liar" may well lead listeners to think that perhaps you are lying. Also, if you use too many disclaimers, you may be perceived as someone who doesn't have any strong convictions or as one who wants to avoid responsibility for just about everything. This seems especially true of hedges.

In responding to statements containing disclaimers, it's often necessary to respond to both the disclaimer and to the statement. By doing so, you let the speaker know that you heard the disclaimer and that you aren't going to view this communication negatively. Appropriate responses might be: "I know you're no sexist, but I don't agree that ..." or "Well, perhaps we should discuss the money now even if it doesn't seem right."

In this brief discussion of receiving—and, in fact, throughout this entire chapter on listening—the unstated assumption is that both individuals can receive auditory signals without difficulty. But for the many people who have hearing impairments, listening presents a variety of problems. Table 1 provides tips for communication between people who have and people who do not have hearing difficulties.

Stage Two: Understanding

Understanding is the stage at which you learn what the speaker means—the stage at which you grasp both the thoughts and the emotions expressed. Understanding one without the other is likely to result in an unbalanced picture.

You can improve your listening understanding in a variety of ways.

Everett Collection

The term *false memory syndrome* refers to a phenomenon in which a person "remembers" past experiences that never actually occurred. Most of the studies on false memory syndrome have centered on erroneous recollections of abuse and other traumatic experiences. Often these false memories are implanted by therapists and interviewers, whose persistent questioning over a period of time can create such a realistic scenario that an individual comes to believe these things actually occurred (Porter, Brit, Yuille, & Lehman, 2000). In what other, less dramatic, ways can false memory syndrome occur?

1. **Avoid assuming you understand** what the speaker is going to say before he or she actually says it. If you do make assumptions, these will likely prevent you from accurately listening to what the speaker wants to say.
2. **See the speaker's messages from the speaker's point of view.** Avoid judging the message until you fully understand it as the speaker intended it.
3. **Ask questions** for clarification, if necessary; ask for additional details or examples if they're needed. This shows not only that you're listening—which the speaker will appreciate—but also that you want to learn more. Material that is not clearly understood is likely to be easily lost.
4. **Rephrase (paraphrase)** the speaker's ideas in your own words. This can be done silently or aloud. If done silently, it will help you rehearse and learn the material; if done aloud, it also helps you confirm your understanding of what the speaker is saying.

Right now, a large part of your listening will take place in the classroom—listening to the instructor and to other students, essentially for understanding. Take a look at Table 2, which offers a few suggestions for listening effectively in the classroom.

Stage Three: Remembering

Effective listening depends on **remembering**. For example, when Susan says she is planning to buy a new car, the effective listener remembers this and at a later meeting asks about the car. When Joe says his mother is ill, the effective listener remembers this and inquires about her health later in the week.

TABLE 2 — Listening in the Classroom

In addition to following the general guidelines for listening noted throughout this chapter, here are a few additional suggestions for making your listening for understanding in the classroom more effective.

General Suggestions	Specifically
Prepare yourself to listen.	Sit up front where you can see your instructor and any visual aids clearly and comfortably. Remember that you listen with your eyes as well as your ears.
Avoid distractions.	Avoid mental daydreaming, and put away physical distractions like your laptop, iPhone, or newspaper.
Pay special attention to the introduction.	Listen for orienting remarks and for key words and phrases (often written on the board or on PowerPoint slides), such as "another reason," "three major causes," and "first." Using these cues will help you outline the lecture.
Take notes in outline form.	Avoid writing in paragraph form. Listen for headings and then use these as major headings in your outline. When the instructor says, for example, "there are four kinds of noise," you have your heading and you will have a numbered list of four kinds of noise.
Assume relevance.	A piece of information may eventually prove irrelevant (unfortunately), but if you listen with the assumption of irrelevancy, you'll never hear anything relevant.
Listen for understanding.	Avoid taking issue with what is said until you understand fully, and then, of course, take issue if you wish. But, generally, don't rehearse in your own mind your arguments against a particular position. When you do this, you run the risk of missing additional explanation or qualification.

In some small group and public speaking situations, you can augment your memory by taking notes or by taping the messages. And in many work situations, taking notes is common and may even be expected. In most interpersonal communication situations, however, note taking is inappropriate—although you often do write down a telephone number, an appointment, or directions.

Perhaps the most important point to understand about memory is that what you remember is not what was said but what you remember was said. Memory for speech is not reproductive; you don't simply reproduce in your memory what the speaker said. Rather, memory is reconstructive; you actually reconstruct the messages you hear into a system that makes sense to you.

If you want to remember what someone says or the names of various people, this information needs to pass from your **short-term memory** (the memory you use, say, to remember a phone number just long enough to write it down) into long-term memory. Short-term memory is very limited in capacity—you can hold only a small amount of information there. **Long-term memory** is unlimited. To facilitate the passage of information from short- to long-term memory, here are four suggestions:

1. **Focus** your attention on the central ideas. Even in the most casual of conversations, there are central ideas. Fix these in your mind. Repeat these ideas to yourself as you continue to listen. Avoid focusing on minor details that often lead to detours in listening and in conversation.

2. **Organize** what you hear; summarize the message in a more easily retained form, but take care not to ignore crucial details or qualifications. If you chunk the material into categories, you'll be able to remember more information. For example, if you want to remember 15 or 20 items to buy in the supermarket, you'll remember more if you group them into chunks—produce, canned goods, and meats.

3. **Unite** the new with the old; relate new information to what you already know. Avoid treating new information as totally apart from all else you know. There's probably some relationship and if you identify it, you're more like to remember the new material.

4. **Repeat** names and key concepts to yourself or, if appropriate, aloud. By repeating the names or key concepts, you in effect rehearse these names and concepts, and as a result they'll be easier to learn and remember. If you're introduced to Alice, you'll stand a better chance of remembering her name if you say, "Hi, Alice" than if you say just "Hi." Be especially careful that you don't rehearse your own anticipated responses; if you do, you're sure to lose track of what the speaker is saying.

Stage Four: Evaluating

Evaluating consists of judging the messages in some way. At times you may try to evaluate the speaker's underlying intentions or motives. Often this evaluation process goes on without much conscious awareness. For example, Elaine tells you that she is up for a promotion and is really excited about it. You may then try to judge her intention: Perhaps she wants you to use your influence with the company president, or maybe she's preoccupied with the promotion and so she tells everyone, or possibly she's looking for a compliment.

In other situations your evaluation is more in the nature of critical analysis. For example, in listening to proposals advanced in a business meeting, you may ask: Are the proposals practical? Will they increase productivity? What's the evidence? Is there contradictory evidence?

In evaluating consider these suggestions:

1. **Resist evaluation** until you fully understand the speaker's point of view. This is not always easy, but it's almost always essential. If you put a label on what the speaker is saying (ultraconservative, bleeding-heart liberal), you'll hear the remainder of the messages through these labels.

2. **Distinguish facts from opinions** and personal interpretations by the speaker. And, most important, fix these labels in mind with the information; for example, try to remember that *Jesse thinks Pat did XYZ,* not just that *Pat did XYZ.*

3. **Identify any biases,** self-interests, or prejudices that may lead the speaker to slant unfairly what is said. It's often wise to ask if the material is being presented fairly or if this person is slanting it in some way.

4. **Recognize fallacious forms of "reasoning"** speakers may employ, such as:

   - **Name-calling:** applying a favorable or unfavorable label to color your perception—"democracy" and "soft on terrorism" are two currently popular examples.
     - **Testimonial:** using positively or negatively viewed spokespersons to encourage your acceptance or rejection of something—such as a white-coated actor to sell toothpaste or a disgraced political figure associated with an idea the speaker wants rejected.
   - **Bandwagon:** arguing that you should believe or do something because "everyone else does."

Stage Five: Responding

Responding occurs in two phases: responses you make while the speaker is talking (immediate feedback) and responses you make after the speaker has stopped talking (delayed feedback). These feedback messages send information back to the speaker and tell the speaker how you feel and what you think about his or her messages. When you nod or smile in response

Do you notice bias in your instructors? See "Teacher Bias?" at tcbdevito.blogspot.com. How might this type of research help instructors and students alike?

INTERPERSONAL CHOICE POINT

Giving Antilistening Cues

One of your friends is a storyteller; instead of talking about the world and about people, he tells endless stories—about things that happened a long time ago that he finds funny (though no one else does). You just can't deal with this any longer. What are some of your choices to help you get yourself out of these situations?

to someone you're interacting with face-to-face, you're responding with immediate feedback. When you comment on a blog post, poke a person on Facebook who has poked you, or say you like a photo or post on Facebook, you're responding with delayed feedback.

In face-to-face communication, supportive responses made while the speaker is talking are particularly effective; they acknowledge that you're listening and that you're understanding the speaker. These responses include what nonverbal researchers call *back-channeling cues*—comments such as "I see," "yes," "uh-huh," and similar signals. Back-channeling cues are especially important in face-to-face conversation.

Responses made after the speaker has stopped talking or after you read a post on a blog or on Facebook are generally more elaborate and might include expressing empathy ("I know how you must feel"), asking for clarification ("Do you mean that this new health plan is going to replace the old one?"), challenging ("I think your evidence is weak here"), agreeing ("You're absolutely right on this; I'll support your proposal"), or giving support ("good luck"). Social networks make this type of feedback especially easy with comment buttons and the thumbs up icon.

Improving listening responding involves avoiding some of the destructive patterns and practicing more constructive patterns such as the following five:

1. **Support the speaker** throughout the speaker's conversation by using and varying your listening cues, such as head nods and minimal responses such as "I see" or "mm-hmm." Using the "like" icon, poking back on Facebook, and commenting on another's photos or posts on social-networking sites will also prove supportive.
2. **Own your responses.** Take responsibility for what you say. Instead of saying, "Nobody will want to do that" say something like "I don't think I'll do that." Use the anonymity that the most social networks allow with discretion.
3. **Resist "responding to another's feelings" with "solving the person's problems"** (as men are often accused of doing) unless, of course, you're asked for advice (Tannen, 1990).
4. **Focus on the other person.** Avoid multitasking when you're listening. Show the speaker that he or she is your primary focus. Take off headphones; shut down the iPhone and the television; turn away from the computer screen. And, instead of looking around the room, look at the speaker; the speaker's eyes should be your main focus.
5. **Avoid being a thought-completing listener** who listens a little and then finishes the speaker's thought. Instead, express respect by allowing the speaker to complete his or her thoughts. Completing someone's thoughts often communicates the message that nothing important is going to be said ("I already know it").

Table 3 provides a comparison and summary of ineffective and effective listening at each of these five stages.

Listening Barriers

In addition to practicing the various skills for each stage of listening, consider some of the common general barriers to listening. Here are four such barriers and some suggestions for dealing with them as both listener and speaker—because both speaker and listener are responsible for effective listening.

Distractions: Physical and Mental

Physical barriers to listening may include, for example, hearing impairment, a noisy environment, or loud music. Multitasking (watching TV while listening to someone with the aim of being supportive, say) simply doesn't work. As

Toby Burrows/Digital Vision/Getty Images

VIEWPOINTS Research indicates that overheard cell phone conversations are rated as more intrusive than overheard conversations between two people talking face-to-face (Monk, Fellas, & Ley, 2004); one researcher argues that cell conversations are particularly annoying because you can hear only one side of the dialogue. Do you find the cell phone conversations of people near you on a bus or in a store annoying? If you do, why?

| | TABLE 3 | Ineffective and Effective Listening |

Listening Stage	Ineffective Listening	Effective Listening
At the **receiving** stage, you note not only what is said (verbally and nonverbally) but also what is omitted.	Attention wanders, distractions are attended to.	1. **Focus your attention** on the speaker's verbal and nonverbal messages. 2. **Avoid distractions** in the environment. 3. **Maintain your role as listener** and avoid interrupting.
Understanding is the stage at which you learn what the speaker means, the stage at which you grasp both the thoughts and the emotions expressed.	Assume you understand what the speaker is going to say. Interpret the speaker's message from your own point of view. Make no attempt to seek clarification.	1. **Avoid assuming you understand** what the speaker is going to say before he or she actually says it. 2. **See the speaker's messages from the speaker's point of view.** 3. **Ask questions** for clarification. 4. **Rephrase (paraphrase)** the speaker's ideas in your own words.
Effective listening depends on **remembering.**	Fail to distinguish between central and peripheral ideas.	1. **Focus** your attention on the central ideas. 2. **Organize** what you hear. 3. **Unite** the new with the old. 4. **Rehearse**; repeat names and key concepts to yourself or, if appropriate, aloud.
Evaluating consists of judging the messages in some way.	Evaluate immediately. Facts and opinions are grouped together. Biases go unnoticed. Be taken in by fallacious reasoning.	1. **Resist evaluation** until you fully understand the speaker's point of view? 2. **Distinguish facts from opinions** and personal interpretations by the speaker. 3. **Identify any biases,** self-interests, or prejudices in the speaker. 4. **Recognize some of the popular but fallacious forms of "reasoning"** speakers may employ, such as **name-calling, testimonial, and bandwagon.**
Responding occurs in two phases: responses you make while the speaker is talking and responses you make after the speaker has stopped talking.	Fail to give the speaker appropriate feedback.	1. **Support the speaker.** 2. **Own your responses.** 3. **Resist "responding to another's feelings" with "solving the person's problems."** 4. **Focus on the other person.** 5. **Avoid being a thought-completing listener.**

both listener and speaker, try to remove whatever physical barriers can be removed; for those that you can't remove, adjust your listening and speaking to lessen the effects as much as possible. As a listener, focus on the speaker; you can attend to the room and the other people later.

Mental distractions are in many ways similar to physical distractions; they get in the way of focused listening. Typical mental distractions, for example, are thinking about your upcoming Saturday night date or becoming too emotional to think (and listen) clearly. In listening, recognize that you can think about your date later. In speaking, make what you say compelling and relevant to the listener.

Biases and Prejudices

Biases and prejudices against groups, or against individuals who are members of such groups, will invariably distort listening. For example, a gender bias that assumes that only one sex has anything useful to say about certain topics will likely distort incoming messages that contradict this bias. As a listener, be willing to subject your biases and prejudices to contradictory information; after all, if they're worth having, they should stand up to differences of opinion. When you as a speaker feel that you may be facing bias, ask your listeners to suspend their attitude for the moment—*I know you don't like the Martins, and I can understand why. But, just listen to . . .*

Another type of bias is closed-mindedness, which is seen, for example, in the person who refuses to hear any feminist argument or anything about gay marriage. As a listener, assume that what the speaker is saying will be useful in some way. As a speaker, anticipate that many people will be closed-minded on a variety of issues, and remember that it often helps to simply ask for openness—*I know this is contrary to what many people think, but let's look at this logically.*

Lack of Appropriate Focus

Focusing on what a person is saying is obviously necessary for effective listening. And yet there are many influences that can lead you astray. For example, listeners often get lost because they focus on irrelevancies; say, on an especially vivid example that conjures up old memories. As a listener, try not to get detoured from the main idea; don't get hung up on unimportant details. Try to repeat the idea to yourself and see the details in relation to this main concept. As a speaker, try to avoid language or examples that may divert attention from your main idea.

At times people will listen only for information with an obvious relevance to them. But this type of listening only prevents you from expanding your horizons. After all, it's quite possible that information that you originally thought irrelevant will eventually prove helpful. Avoid interpreting everything in terms of what it means to you; see other perspectives. As a speaker, be sure to make what you say relevant to your specific listener.

Another mistake is for the listener to focus on the responses he or she is going to make while the speaker is still speaking. Anticipating how you're going to respond or what you're going to say (and perhaps even interrupting the speaker) just prevents you from hearing the message in full. Instead, make a mental note of something and then get back to listening. As a speaker, when you feel someone is preparing to argue with you, ask them to hear you out—*I know you disagree with this, but let me finish and we'll get back to that.*

Premature Judgment

Perhaps the most obvious form of premature judgment is assuming you know what the speaker is going to say—so there's no need to really listen. Let the speaker say what he or she is going to say before you decide that you already know it. As a speaker, of course, it's often wise to assume that listeners will do exactly this, so it may be helpful to make clear that what you're saying will be unexpected.

A common listener reaction is to draw conclusions or judgments on incomplete evidence. Sometimes listeners will stop listening after hearing a speaker, for example, express an attitude they disagree with or make some sexist or culturally insensitive remark. Instead, this is a situation that calls for especially concentrated listening so that you don't rush to judgment. Instead, wait for the evidence or argument; avoid making judgments before you gather all the

INTERPERSONAL CHOICE POINT

Homophobic Language

At the organization where you work, homophobic language is rampant in small groups but totally absent in formal meetings. You want to point out this hypocrisy but don't want to make enemies or have people think you're going to cause legal problems for them. What options do you have for accomplishing what you want to without incurring negative reactions?

Ethics in Interpersonal Communication

ETHICAL LISTENING

As a listener you have at a minimum these two ethical obligations:

1. You owe it to the speaker to give an honest hearing, without prejudgment, putting aside prejudices and preconceptions as best you can. At the same time, you owe the speaker your best effort at understanding emotionally as well as intellectually what he or she means.
2. You owe the speaker honest responses. Just as you should be honest with the listener when speaking, you should be honest with the speaker when listening. This means giving open and honest feedback and also reflecting honestly on the questions that the speaker raises.

ETHICAL CHOICE POINT

Your friend begins revealing deeply personal secrets—problems at home, a lack of money, no friends, and on and on. You don't want to hear all this; it depresses you. You want to avoid having to listen to these disclosures. At the same time, however, you wonder if you have an ethical obligation to listen openly and respond honestly to your friend. What would you do in this situation?

information. Listen first; judge second. As a speaker, be aware of this tendency and when you feel this is happening, ask for a suspension of judgment. A simple "*Hear me out*" is often sufficient to prevent a too-early judgment on the part of listeners.

Styles of Effective Listening

Before reading about styles of effective listening in interpersonal communication, examine your own listening habits and tendencies by taking the accompanying self-test, "How Do You Listen?"

Test Yourself   How Do You Listen?

Respond to each question using the following scale: 1 = always, 2 = frequently, 3 = sometimes, 4 = seldom, and 5 = never.

_____ 1. I listen to what the speaker is saying and feeling; I try to feel what the speaker feels.
_____ 2. I listen objectively; I focus on the logic of the ideas rather than on the emotional meaning of the message.
_____ 3. I listen without judging the speaker.
_____ 4. I listen critically, evaluating the speaker and what the speaker is saying.
_____ 5. I listen to the literal meanings that a speaker communicates; I don't look too deeply into hidden meanings.
_____ 6. I look for the hidden meanings, the meanings that are revealed by subtle verbal or nonverbal cues.
_____ 7. I listen actively, communicate acceptance of the speaker, and prompt the speaker to further explore his or her thoughts.
_____ 8. I listen without active involvement; I generally remain silent and take in what the other person is saying.

How Did You Do? These statements focus on the styles of listening discussed in this section, each of which is appropriate at some times but not at others. The only responses that are inappropriate are "always" and "never." Effective listening is listening that is tailored to the specific communication situation.

What Will You Do? Consider how you might use these statements to begin to improve your listening effectiveness. A good way to begin doing this is to review these statements and try to identify situations in which each statement would be appropriate and situations in which each statement would be inappropriate.

As the self-test emphasizes, listening is situational; your style of listening should vary with the situation, and each situation will call for a somewhat different combination of listening styles. You do (and should) listen differently depending on your purpose, your conversational partners, and the type of message; in some situations you'll need to be especially critical and in others especially supportive.

Visualize each listening situation as one in which you have to make choices among the five dimensions of listening discussed in this section. Each listening situation should call for a somewhat different configuration of listening responses. The art of effective listening is largely one of making appropriate choices along the following five dimensions: (1) empathic versus objective listening, (2) nonjudgmental versus critical listening, (3) surface versus depth listening, (4) polite versus impolite listening, and (5) active versus inactive listening. Let's take a look at each of these dimensions.

INTERPERSONAL CHOICE POINT

Listening Choices

Your friend Phil has just broken up a love affair and is telling you about it. "I can't seem to get Chris out of my mind," he says. "All I do is daydream about what we used to do and all the fun we used to have." What are some of the things you can do or say that will help Phil feel better? What are some things that are likely to make him feel worse?

Empathic and Objective Listening

If you're to understand what a person means and what a person is feeling, you need to listen with some degree of **empathy**, the feeling of another's feelings (Rogers, 1970; Rogers & Farson, 1981). To empathize with others is to feel with them, to see the world as they see it, to feel what they feel. Only when you achieve this can you fully understand another person's meaning. **Empathic listening** will also help you enhance your relationships (Barrett & Godfrey, 1988; Snyder, 1992).

Although for most communication situations empathic listening is the preferred mode of responding, there are times when you need to engage in **objective listening**—to go beyond empathy and measure meanings and feelings against some objective reality. It's important to listen as Peter tells you how the entire world hates him and to understand how Peter feels and why he feels this way. But then you need to look a bit more objectively at Peter and perhaps see the paranoia or the self-hatred. Sometimes you have to put your empathic responses aside and listen with objectivity and detachment.

In adjusting your empathic and objective listening:

- **Punctuate the message from the speaker's point of view**; see the sequence of events (which events are causes and which are effects) as the speaker does. And try to figure out how this punctuation can influence what the speaker says and does.

- **Engage in equal, two-way conversation.** To encourage openness and empathy, try to eliminate any physical or psychological barriers to equality (for example, step from behind the large desk separating you from your employees). Avoid interrupting the speaker—which sends the signal that what you have to say is more important.

- **Seek to understand both thoughts and feelings.** Don't consider your listening task finished until you've understood what the speaker is feeling as well as thinking.

- **Avoid "offensive listening,"** the tendency to listen to bits and pieces of information that will enable you to attack the speaker or find fault with something the speaker has said (Floyd, 1985).

Jose Ignacio Soto/Shutterstock

If, when, and how you listen are questions of choice.
—*Communication principle*

■ **Strive to be objective** when listening to friends and foes alike. Your attitudes may lead you to distort messages—to block out positive messages about a foe and negative messages about a friend. Guard against "expectancy hearing," when you fail to hear what the speaker is really saying and hear what you expect to hear instead.

INTERPERSONAL CHOICE POINT

Empathic Listening

Your mother has been having a difficult time at work. She was recently passed up for a promotion and received one of the lowest merit raises given in the company. "I'm not sure what I did wrong," she tells you. "I do my work, mind my own business, don't take my sick days like everyone else. How could they give that promotion to Helen, who's only been with the company for two years? Maybe I should just quit." What can you do and say that will demonstrate empathic listening?

Gary Conner/PhotoEdit

VIEWPOINTS ◆ Although empathy is almost universally considered positive, there is some evidence to show that it also can have a negative side. For example, people are most empathic with those who are similar—racially and ethnically as well as in appearance and social status. The more empathy you feel toward your own group, the less empathy—possibly even the more hostility—you feel toward other groups. The same empathy that increases your understanding of your own group decreases your understanding of other groups. So although empathy may encourage ... cohesiveness and identification, it also can create dividing ... tween your group and "them" (Angier, 1995b). Have you ... ienced or witnessed these negative effects of empathy?

Nonjudgmental and Critical Listening

Effective listening includes both nonjudgmental and critical responses. You need to listen nonjudgmentally—with an open mind toward understanding. But you also need to listen critically—with a view toward making some kind of evaluation or judgment. Clearly, engage in **nonjudgmental listening** first; listen for understanding while suspending judgment. Only after you've fully understood the relevant messages should you evaluate or judge.

Supplement open-minded listening with **critical listening**. Listening with an open mind will help you understand messages better; listening with a critical mind will help you analyze and evaluate the messages. In adjusting your nonjudgmental and critical listening:

■ **Keep an open mind and avoid prejudging.** Delay your judgments until you fully understand the intention and the content the speaker is communicating. Avoid both positive and negative evaluation until you have a reasonably complete understanding.

■ **Avoid filtering out or oversimplifying complex messages.** Similarly, avoid filtering out undesirable messages. You don't want to hear that something you believe in is untrue, that people you care for are unkind, or that ideals you hold are self-destructive. Yet it's important that you reexamine your beliefs by listening to these messages.

■ **Recognize your own biases.** These may interfere with accurate listening and cause you to distort message reception through the process of *assimilation*—the tendency to integrate and interpret what you hear (or think you hear) to fit your own biases, prejudices, and expectations. For example, are your ethnic, national, or religious biases preventing you from appreciating a speaker's point of view?

■ **Avoid sharpening.** Recognize and combat the natural human tendency toward sharpening—a process in which one or two aspects of the message become highlighted, emphasized, and perhaps embellished. Often the concepts that are sharpened are incidental remarks that somehow stand out from the rest of the message. Be sure to listen critically to the entire message when you need to make evaluations and judgments.

■ **Recognize the fallacies of language.** Take a look at Table 4; it identifies four common barriers that challenge critical listening.

Surface and Depth Listening

In Shakespeare's *Julius Caesar*, Marc Antony, in giving the funeral oration for Caesar, says: "I come to bury Caesar, not to praise him. / The evil that men do lives after them; / The good is oft interred with their bones." And later: "For Brutus is an

TABLE 4 Listening for Fallacies of Language

Here are four language fallacies that often get in the way of meaningful communication and need to be identified in critical listening. Often these fallacies are used to fool you; they are ways in which language can be used to serve less than noble purposes, to convince or persuade you without giving you any reasons. After reviewing this table, take a look at some of the commercial websites for clothing, books, music, or any such product you're interested in. Can you find examples of these fallacies?

Fallacy	Example	Notes
Weasel words are those terms whose meanings are slippery and difficult to pin down (Hayakawa & Hayakawa, 1989).	A commercial claims that Medicine M works "better than Brand X" but doesn't specify how much better or in what respect Medicine M performs better. It's quite possible that it performs better in one respect but less effectively according to nine other measures.	Other weasel words are "help," "virtually," "as much as," "like" (as in "it will make you feel like new"), and "more economical." Ask yourself, "Exactly what is being claimed?" For example, "What does 'may reduce cholesterol' mean? What exactly is being asserted?"
Euphemisms make the negative and unpleasant appear positive and appealing.	An executive calls the firing of 200 workers "downsizing" or "reallocation of resources."	Often euphemisms take the form of inflated language designed to make the mundane seem extraordinary, the common seem exotic. Don't let words get in the way of accurate firsthand perception.
Jargon is the specialized language of a professional class.	Examples of jargon include the language of the computer hacker, the psychologist, and the advertiser.	When used to intimidate or impress, as when used with people who aren't members of the profession, jargon prevents meaningful communication. Don't be intimidated by jargon; ask questions when you don't understand.
Gobbledygook is overly complex language that overwhelms the listener instead of communicating meaning.	Extra long sentences, complex grammatical constructions, and rare or unfamiliar words can constitute gobbledygook.	Some people just normally speak in complex language. But, others use complexity to confuse and mislead. Ask for simplification when appropriate.

honourable man; / So are they all, all honourable men." If we listen beyond the surface of Marc Antony's words, we can see that he does come to praise Caesar, and to convince the crowd that Brutus was dishonorable—despite the fact that at first glance his words seem to say quite the opposite.

In most messages there's an obvious meaning that you can derive from **surface listening**—a literal reading of the words and sentences. But there's often another level of meaning. Sometimes, as in *Julius Caesar*, it's the opposite of the literal meaning; at other times it seems totally unrelated. Consider some frequently heard types of messages. For example, Claire asks you how you like her new haircut. On one level the meaning is clear: Do you like the haircut? But depth listening can reveal another, perhaps more important, level: Claire is asking you to say something positive about her appearance. In the same way, the parent who complains about working hard at the office or in the home may,

INTERPERSONAL CHOICE POINT

Listening without Judging

A classmate says to you: I got a C on that paper. That's the worst grade I've ever received. I just can't believe that I got a C. This is my major. What am I going to do? What options do you have in this case for communicating without judging?

Understanding *Interpersonal Theory & Research*

LISTENING TO LYING

In normal listening you assume the speaker is telling the truth. When you do question the speaker's truthfulness, it may be because the speaker exhibits cues that often accompany lying. Research has identified numerous such cues. Typically liars smile less; respond with shorter answers, often a simple yes or no; use fewer specifics and more generalities, such as "we hung out"; shift their posture more; use more self-touching movements; use more and longer pauses; avoid direct eye contact with the listener and blink more often than normal; appear less friendly and attentive; and make more speech errors (Knapp & Hall, 2006; Knapp, 2008; O'Hair, Cody, Goss, & Krayer, 1988; Bond & Atoum, 2000; Al-Simadi, 2000; Burgoon & Bacue, 2003).

But be careful, however, that you don't fall into the trap of thinking that just because someone emits some or all of these cues, he or she is therefore lying. These cues are often used by truth tellers as well as liars. In one study, in fact, people who held stereotypical views of how liars behave (for example, "liars don't look at you" or "liars fidget") were *less* effective in detecting lying than were those who didn't hold such beliefs (Vrij & Mann, 2001).

Furthermore, lie detection is generally unreliable. Whether among nonprofessionals or professional lie detectors (for example, judges, psychiatrists, and police officers), accuracy in judging lying is quite low; accuracy is generally found to be somewhere around 45 to 60 percent (Knapp, 2008).

Most people seem to operate with a truth bias and generally assume that others are telling the truth (Levine, Kim, Park, & Hughes, 2006). But under certain circumstances (with prisoners in prison or when law enforcement personnel interrogate a suspect, for example), there is a "lie bias"; people operate on the assumption that the person is lying. This assumption, not surprisingly, does not increase accuracy in overall lie-detection ability (Knapp, 2008).

Working with Theories and Research

Recall a situation in which you assumed, on the basis of the cues described here (or others), that someone was lying. What happened? If you want to learn more about lying, log on to an online database and search for lying, deception, and similar terms. It's a fascinating subject of study.

on a deeper level, be asking for an expression of appreciation. The child who talks about the unfairness of the other children in the playground may be asking for comfort and love.

To appreciate these other meanings, listen in depth. If you listen only to the surface-level communication (the literal meaning), you'll miss the underlying message and will surely miss the opportunity to make meaningful contact with the other person's feelings and needs. If you say to your parent, "You're always complaining. I bet you really love working so hard," you fail to respond to the call for understanding and appreciation.

In regulating your surface and depth listening:

- **Focus on both verbal and nonverbal messages.** Recognize both consistent and inconsistent "packages" of messages, and use these as guides for drawing inferences about the speaker's meaning. Ask questions when in doubt. Listen also to what is omitted. Remember that speakers communicate by what they leave out as well as by what they include.
- **Listen for both content and relational messages.** The student who constantly challenges the teacher is, on one level, communicating disagreement over content. However,

Understanding *Interpersonal Skills*

OPENNESS

Openness in interpersonal communication is a person's willingness to self-disclose—to reveal information about himself or herself as appropriate. Openness also includes a willingness to listen openly and to react honestly to the messages of others. This does not mean that openness is always appropriate. In fact, too much openness is likely to lead to a decrease in your relationship satisfaction (Dindia & Timmerman, 2003).

Communicating Openness. Consider these few ideas:

- Self-disclose when appropriate. Be mindful about whatever you say about yourself. There are benefits and dangers to this form of communication. And listen carefully to the disclosures of others; these reciprocal disclosures (or the lack of them) will help guide your own disclosures.
- Listen mindfully and respond to those with whom you're interacting with spontaneity and with appropriate honesty—though also with an awareness of what you're saying and of what the possible outcomes of your messages might be.
- Communicate a clear willingness to listen. Let the other person know that you're open to listening to his or her thoughts and feelings.
- Own your own feelings and thoughts. Take responsibility for what you say. Listen to the kinds of messages you're using, and use *I*-messages instead of *you*-messages. Instead of saying, "You make me feel stupid when you don't ask my opinion," own your feelings and say, for example, "I feel stupid when you ask everyone else what they think but don't ask me." When you own your feelings and thoughts—when you use *I*-messages— you say, in effect, "This is how I feel," "This is how I see the situation." *I*-messages make explicit the fact that your feelings result from the interaction between what is going on outside your skin (what others say, for example) and what is going on inside your skin (your preconceptions, attitudes, and prejudices, for example).

Working with Interpersonal Skills

On a scale from 1 to 10, how would you describe your face-to-face communication and your social networking communication with casual friends or acquaintances in terms of closedness (1) versus openness (10)? With your best friends or a romantic partner? Are there significant differences in openness in face-to-face versus online communication?

on another level—the relationship level—the student may be voicing objections to the instructor's authority or authoritarianism. The instructor needs to listen and respond to both types of messages.

- **Make special note of self-reflexive statements**—statements that refer back to the speaker. People inevitably talk about themselves. Whatever a person says is, in part, a function of who that person is. Attending carefully to those personal, self-referential messages will give you great insight into the person and the person's messages.
- At the same time, **don't disregard the literal meaning** in trying to uncover the message's hidden meaning. Balance your listening between the surface and the underlying meaning. Respond to the different levels of meaning in the messages of others as you would like others to respond to yours—be sensitive but not obsessive, attentive but not overly eager to uncover hidden messages.

Polite and Impolite Listening

Politeness is often thought of as the exclusive function of the speaker, as solely an encoding or sending function. But, politeness (or impoliteness) may also be signaled through listening (Fukushima, 2000).

INTERPERSONAL CHOICE POINT
Giving Listening Cues

Often you're asked by a speaker if he or she is getting through or making sense. It seems as if speakers doubt that you're listening. But, usually at least, you are. What are some of the things you might do to show people you're listening to them and interested in what they're saying?

Of course, there are times when you would not want to listen politely (for example, if someone is being verbally abusive or condescending or using racist or sexist language). In these cases you might want to show your disapproval by showing that you're not even listening. But most often you'll want to listen politely and you'll want to express this politeness through your listening behavior. Here are a few suggestions for demonstrating that you are in fact listening politely. As you read these you'll notice that these are strategies designed to be supportive of the speaker's positive and negative face needs:

- **Avoid interrupting the speaker.** Avoid trying to take over the speaker's turn. Avoid changing the topic. If you must say something in response to something the speaker said and can't wait until he or she finishes, then say it as briefly as possible and pass the speaker's turn back to the speaker.
- **Give supportive listening cues.** These might include nodding your head, giving minimal verbal responses such as "I see" or "yes, it's true", or moving closer to the speaker. Listen in a way that demonstrates that what the speaker is saying is important. In some cultures, polite listening cues must be cues of agreement (Japanese culture is often used as an example); in other cultures, polite listening cues are attentiveness and support rather than cues of agreement (much of United States culture is an example).
- **Show empathy with the speaker.** Demonstrate that you understand and feel the speaker's thoughts and feelings by giving responses that show this level of understanding—smiling or cringing or otherwise echoing the feelings of the speaker. If you echo the speaker's nonverbal expressions, your behavior is likely to be seen as empathic.
- **Maintain eye contact.** In much of the United States this is perhaps the single most important rule. If you don't maintain eye contact when someone is talking to you, then you'll appear to be not listening and definitely not listening politely. This rule, however, does not hold in all cultures. In some Latin and Asian cultures, polite listening would consist of looking down and avoiding direct eye contact when, for example, listening to a superior or much older person.
- **Give positive feedback.** Throughout the listening encounter and perhaps especially after the speaker's turn (when you continue the conversation as you respond to what the speaker has said), positive feedback will be seen as polite and negative feedback as impolite. If you must give negative feedback, then do so in a way that does not attack the person's negative face. For example, first mention areas of agreement or what you liked about what the person said and stress your good intentions. And, most important, do it in private. Public criticism is especially threatening and will surely be seen as a personal attack.

A somewhat different slant on politeness and listening can be seen in "forcing" people to listen when they don't want to. Generally, the polite advice is to be sensitive to when the other person wants to leave and to stop asking the person to continue listening. And, closely related to this, is the "forced" listening that many cell phone users impose on others, a topic addressed in Table 5.

Active and Inactive Listening

One of the most important communication skills you can learn is that of active listening (Gordon, 1975). Consider the following interaction. You're disappointed that you have to redo your entire report, and you say:

INTERPERSONAL CHOICE POINT

Listening Politely

A close friend says to you, "That rotten, inconsiderate pig just up and left. He never even said goodbye. We were together for six months and after one small argument he leaves without a word. And he even took my bathrobe—that expensive one he bought for my last birthday." What are some of the things you can say to demonstrate politeness?

TABLE 5	Politeness and the Cell Phone

The ubiquity of the cell phone has led to enormous increases in telephone communication but it has also created problems, many of which are problems of politeness. Because much cell phone usage occurs in a public space, it forces people who have nothing to do with the call to listen to the conversation.

Here are just a few guidelines:

- Avoid using cell phones where inappropriate; for example, restaurants, hospitals, theatres, museums, a commuter bus or train, and the classroom. If you must make or take a call when in these various situations, try to move to a less public area.
- Put your phone on vibrate mode or let your voicemail answer and take a message when your call might interfere with others as it would in the classroom, for example.
- When you can't avoid taking a call, speak as quietly as possible and as briefly as possible.
- Don't take pictures of people who aren't posing for you and erase photos if the person you photographed requests it. Of course, if there's an accident or a robbery, you may want to photograph the events.
- Avoid extended talking when your reception is weak. Walking along a crowded street while talking on your cell is likely to result in poor reception, which is annoying to the other person and generally impolite.
- Because cell phones are always with us, it's easy to assume that when you have nothing better to do, that the person you're calling also has nothing better to do. As with any phone call, it's wise to ask if this is a good time to call—a strategy that helps maintain the autonomy (negative face) of the person you're calling.

"I can't believe I have to rewrite this entire budget report. I really worked hard on this project and now I have to do it all over again." To this, you get three different responses:

DANNY: That's not so bad; most people find they have to redo their first reports. That's the norm here.

KELLY: You should be pleased that all you have to do is a simple rewrite. Sylar and Nathan both had to completely redo their entire projects.

SUZANNE: You have to rewrite that report you've worked on for the last three weeks? You sound really angry and frustrated.

All three listeners are probably trying to make you feel better. But they go about it in very different ways and, you can be sure, with very different results. Danny tries to lessen the significance of the rewrite. This well-intended response is extremely common but does little to promote meaningful communication and understanding. Kelly tries to give the situation a positive spin. With these responses, however, both these listeners are also suggesting that you should not be feeling the way you do. They're implying that your feelings are not legitimate and should be replaced with more logical feelings.

Suzanne's response, however, is different from the others. Suzanne uses active listening. **Active listening** owes its development to Thomas Gordon (1975), who made it a cornerstone of his P-E-T (Parent Effectiveness Training) technique; it is a process of sending back to the speaker what you as a listener think the speaker meant—both in content and in feelings. Active listening, then, is not merely repeating the speaker's exact words, but rather putting together your understanding of the speaker's total message into a meaningful whole.

The Functions of Active Listening   Active listening serves several important functions. First, it helps you as a listener to check your understanding of what the speaker said and, more important, of what he or she meant. Reflecting back perceived meanings to the speaker gives the speaker an opportunity to offer clarification and correct any misunderstandings.

Second, through active listening you let the speaker know that you acknowledge and accept his or her feelings. In the sample responses given, the first two listeners challenged the speaker's feelings. Suzanne, the active listener, accepted what you were feeling. In addition, she also explicitly identified your feelings: "You sound angry and frustrated," allowing you an opportunity to correct her interpretation if necessary.

Third, active listening stimulates the speaker to explore feelings and thoughts. Suzanne's response encourages you to elaborate on your feelings and helps you deal with them by talking them through.

A word of caution: In communicating your understanding back to the person, be especially careful to avoid sending what Gordon (1975) calls "solution messages"—messages that tell the person how he or she should feel or what he or she should do. Four types of messages send solutions, and you'll want to avoid them in your active listening:

- **Ordering messages:** "Do this. . . ." "Don't touch that. . . ."
- **Warning and threatening messages:** "If you don't do this, you'll . . ." "If you do that, you'll . . ."
- **Preaching and moralizing messages:** "People should all . . ." "We all have responsibilities. . . ."
- **Advising messages:** "Why don't you . . . ?" "I think you should . . ."

The Techniques of Active Listening Three simple techniques will prove useful as you learn to practice active listening: Paraphrase the speaker's meaning, express understanding, and ask questions.

1. **Paraphrase the speaker's meaning.** Stating in your own words what you think the speaker means and feels helps ensure understanding and also shows interest in the speaker. Paraphrasing gives the speaker a chance to extend what was originally said. Thus, when Suzanne echoes your thoughts, you're given the opportunity to elaborate on why rewriting the budget report means so much to you. In paraphrasing, be objective; be especially careful not to lead the speaker in the direction you think he or she should go. Also, be careful that you don't overdo paraphrase; only a very small percentage of statements need paraphrasing. Paraphrase when you feel there's a chance for misunderstanding or when you want to express support for the other person and keep the conversation going.

2. **Express understanding of the speaker's feelings.** Echo the feelings the speaker expressed or implied ("You must have felt horrible."). This expression of empathy will help you further check your perception of the speaker's feelings. This will also allow the speaker to see his or her feelings more objectively (especially helpful when they're feelings of anger, hurt, or depression) and to elaborate on them.

3. **Ask questions.** Asking questions ensures your own understanding of the speaker's thoughts and feelings and secures additional information ("How did you feel when you read your job appraisal report?"). Ask questions to provide just enough stimulation and support for the speaker to feel he or she can elaborate on these thoughts and feelings. These questions should further confirm your interest and concern for the speaker but not pry into unrelated areas or challenge the speaker in any way.

Active listening, then, is not merely repeating the speaker's exact words, but rather putting together into some meaningful whole your understanding of the speaker's total message. And incidentally, when combined with empathic listening, it proves the most effective mode for success as a salesperson (Comer & Drollinger, 1999).

As noted earlier, listening styles need to be adjusted to the specific situation. Understanding the nature and skills of these styles should help you make more reasoned and more effective listening choices.

Not all questions are polite to ask. For a brief discussion of impolite questions, see "Impolite Questions, What Are They?" at tcbdevito .blogspot.com. Have you ever asked or been asked an impolite question?

Culture, Gender, and Listening

Listening is difficult in part because of the inevitable differences in communication systems between speaker and listener. Because each person has had a unique set of experiences, each person's meaning system is going to be different from every other person's. When speaker and listener come from different cultures or are of different genders, these differences and their effects are naturally much greater. Consider culture first.

Culture and Listening

In a global environment in which people from very different cultures work together, it's especially important to understand the ways in which cultural differences can influence listening. Three such factors may be singled out: (1) language and speech, (2) nonverbal behaviors, and (3) feedback.

Language and Speech   Even when speaker and listener speak the same language, they speak it with different meanings and different accents. No two speakers speak exactly the same language. Speakers of the same language will, at the very least, have different meanings for the same terms because they have had different experiences.

Speakers and listeners who have different native languages and who may have learned English as a second language will have even greater differences in meaning. Translations never fully capture the meaning in the other language. If your meaning for the word *house* was learned in a culture in which everyone lived in their own house with lots of land around it, then communicating with someone for whom the meaning of *house* was learned in a neighborhood of high-rise tenements is going to be difficult. Although you'll each hear the same word, the meanings you'll each develop will be drastically different. In adjusting your listening—especially in an intercultural setting—understand that the speaker's meanings may be very different from yours even though you're speaking in the same language.

In many classrooms throughout the world, there will be a wide range of accents. Students whose native language is a tonal one (in which differences in pitch signal important meaning differences), such as Chinese, may speak other languages such as English with variations in pitch that may seem puzzling to others. Those whose native language is Japanese may have trouble distinguishing *l* from *r* in English, for example, since Japanese does not include this distinction. The native language acts as a filter and influences the accent given to the second language.

Nonverbal Behaviors   Speakers from different *cultures* have different **display rules**—cultural rules that govern what nonverbal behaviors are appropriate or inappropriate in a public setting. As you listen to other people, you also "listen" to their nonverbal cues. If nonverbals are drastically different from what you expect on the basis of the verbal message, you may experience them as a kind of noise or interference or even as contradictory messages. Also, of course, different cultures may give very different meanings to the same nonverbal gesture. For example, the thumb and forefinger forming a circle means "OK" in most of the United States; but it means "money" in Japan, "zero" in some Mediterranean countries, and "I'll kill you" in Tunisia.

Feedback   Members of some cultures give very direct and very frank feedback. Speakers from these cultures—the United States is a good example—expect feedback to be an honest reflection of what their listeners are feeling. In other cultures—Japan and Korea are good examples—it's more important to be positive than to be truthful; so people may respond with positive feedback (say, in commenting on a business colleague's proposal) even though they don't agree with what is being said. Listen to feedback, as you would all messages, with a full recognition that various cultures view feedback very differently.

Gender and Listening

Men and women learn different styles of listening, just as they learn different styles for using verbal and nonverbal messages. Not surprisingly, these different styles can create major difficulties in opposite-sex interpersonal communication.

Rapport and Report Talk   According to Deborah Tannen (1990) in her best-selling *You Just Don't Understand: Women and Men in Conversation*, women seek to build rapport and establish closer relationships and use listening to achieve these ends. Men, on the other hand, will play up their expertise, emphasize it, and use it in dominating the interaction. They will talk about things; they report. Women play down their expertise and are more interested in talking about feelings and relationships and in communicating supportiveness. Tannen argues that the goal of a man in conversation is to be given respect, so he seeks to show his knowledge and expertise. A woman, on the other hand, seeks to be liked, so she expresses agreement.

Listening Cues   Men and women feed back to the speaker different types of listening cues and consequently show that they're listening in different ways. In conversation, a woman is more apt to give lots of listening cues—interjecting "Yeah" or "Uh-huh," nodding in agreement, and smiling. A man is more likely to listen quietly, without giving lots of listening cues as feedback. Women also make more eye contact when listening than do men, who are more apt to look around and often away from the speaker (Brownell, 2006). As a result of these differences, women seem to be more engaged in listening than do men.

Amount and Purposes of Listening   Tannen argues that men listen less to women than women listen to men. The reason, says Tannen, is that listening places the person in an inferior position, whereas speaking places the person in a superior position. Men may seem to assume a more argumentative posture while listening, as if getting ready to argue. They also may appear to ask questions that are more argumentative or that seek to puncture holes in your position as a way to play up their own expertise. Women are more likely to ask supportive questions and perhaps offer criticism that is more positive than men. Men and women act this way to both men and women; their customary ways of talking don't seem to change depending on whether the listener is male or female.

It's important to note that not all researchers agree that there is sufficient evidence to make the claims that Tannen and others make about gender differences (Goldsmith & Fulfs, 1999). Gender differences are changing drastically and quickly; it's best to take generalizations about gender as starting points for investigation and not as airtight conclusions (Gamble & Gamble, 2003). Further, as you no doubt have observed, gender differences—although significant—are far outnumbered by similarities between males and females. It's important to be mindful of both differences and similarities.

Summary

Use your smartphone or tablet device (or log on to mycommunicationlab.com) to hear an audio summary of this chapter.

This chapter focused on the nature of listening, the dimensions of listening that you need to consider for effective listening, the influence of culture and gender on listening, and four dimensions of effective listening.

The Importance of Listening: Professional and Relationship Benefits

1. Listening is crucial in a wide range of professions.
2. Listening is crucial to relationship success.

The Process of Listening

3. Listening is an active process of receiving, understanding, remembering, evaluating, and responding to communications.
4. Listening enables you (1) to learn, to acquire information; (2) to relate, to help form and maintain relationships; (3) to influence, to have an effect on the attitudes and behaviors of others; (4) to play, to enjoy yourself; and (5) to help, to assist others.

Listening Barriers

5. Both listener and speaker share in the responsibility for effective listening.

6. Among the obstacles to effective listening are physical and mental distractions, biases and prejudices, lack of appropriate focus, and premature judgment.

Styles of Effective Listening

7. The empathic–objective listening dimension has to do with the extent to which you focus on feeling what the speaker is feeling rather than on external reality.
8. The nonjudgmental–critical listening dimension involves the extent to which you accept and support the speaker as opposed to evaluating and analyzing.
9. The surface–depth listening dimension involves the extent to which you focus on obvious surface meanings rather than underlying hidden messages.

10. The politeness-impoliteness dimension refers to the preserving of the individuals positive and negative face.
11. The active–inactive listening dimension relates to the extent to which you reflect back what you think the speaker means in content and feeling.

Culture, Gender, and Listening

12. Members of different cultures vary on several communication dimensions that influence listening, among them speech and language, nonverbal behavioral differences, and approaches to feedback.
13. Men and women appear to listen differently; generally, women give more specific listening cues to show they're listening than do men.

Key Terms

active listening	empathic listening	long-term memory	remembering
critical listening	empathy	nonjudgmental listening	responding
disclaimers	evaluating	objective listening	short-term memory
display rules	listening	receiving	understanding

MyCommunicationLab Explorations

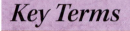

Communication Choice Points

Revisit the chapter-opening video, "A Bad Day at Work." Recall from the video scenario that Harry is upset, but Sue does not know why. "A Bad Day at Work" looks at how Sue's listening choices will affect the outcome of this interaction and potentially help Harry better cope with his issues.

Log on to mycommunicationlab.com to view the video for this chapter, "A Bad Day at Work," and then answer the related discussion questions.

Additional Resources

This group of listening experiences will help you gain new insights into listening and will help to sharpen your listening skills.

1 Listening to Other Perspectives and **2** How Might You Listen to New Ideas? present two creative thinking tools to sharpen a variety of skills, especially listening. **3** Regulating Your Listening Perspective presents different scenarios that call for different types of listening to heighten your awareness of potential listening choices. **4** Experiencing Active Listening asks you how you'd listen in a variety of situations calling for active listening. **5** Sequential Communication, which you may recognize as the game of "telephone," will help you identify some of the major errors made in listening. **6** Reducing Barriers to Listening asks how you'd listen effectively in difficult situations. **7** Typical Man, Typical Woman explores some of the differences in the way we think of men and women as listeners. **8** Paraphrasing to Ensure Understanding and **9** How Can You Express Empathy? provide practice in essential listening skills.

Verbal Messages

Verbal Messages

Principles of Verbal Messages

Guidelines for Using Verbal Messages Effectively

Pearson Education

Zach, an employee at a small office, is trying to cope with a coworker. Katie is just a little too friendly, constantly chatting. Zach does not want either of them to lose their jobs and would like to remain on good speaking terms with Katie. He tries a couple of strategies with varying levels of success. See how his choices play out in the video "We Have Work to Do" (www.mycommunicationlab.com).

As you communicate, you use two major signal systems—the verbal and the nonverbal. **Verbal messages** are those sent with words. The word *verbal* refers to words, not to orality; verbal messages consist of both oral and written words. Verbal messages do not include laughter; vocalized pauses you make when you speak, such as "er," "um," and "ah"; or responses you make to others that are oral but don't involve words, such as "ha-ha," "aha," and "ugh!" These sounds are considered nonverbal—as are, of course, facial expressions, eye movements, gestures, and so on. This chapter focuses on verbal messages; the next focuses on nonverbal messages.

Principles of Verbal Messages

To clarify the nature of verbal messages and the meanings they create in the minds of listeners, let's examine some specific principles: (1) Messages are packaged, (2) meanings are in people, (3) meanings are denotative and connotative, (4) messages vary in abstraction, (5) messages vary in politeness, (6) messages can deceive, (7) messages can criticize and praise, (8) messages vary in assertiveness, (9) messages can confirm and disconfirm, and (10) messages vary in cultural sensitivity. Throughout this discussion you'll find lots of useful suggestions for more effective interpersonal communication.

Messages Are Packaged

Both verbal and nonverbal signals occur simultaneously. Usually, verbal and nonverbal behaviors reinforce or support each other. For example, you don't usually express fear with words while the rest of your body relaxes. You don't normally express anger with your body posture while your face smiles. Your entire being works as a whole—verbally and nonverbally—to express your thoughts and feelings. Interestingly enough, this blending of verbal and nonverbal signals seems also to help you think and remember (Iverson & Goldin-Meadow, 1999). Social networking sites enable you to package your messages with simple clicks of the mouse—combining photos and videos with your verbal posts. Even

Tim Larsen/AP Photos

VIEWPOINTS When asked what they would like to change about the communication patterns of the opposite sex, men said they wanted women to be more direct, and women said they wanted men to stop interrupting and offering advice (Noble, 1994). What one change would you like to see in the communication system of the opposite sex? of your own sex?

in the text-only Twitter, you can post the URLs to photos, videos, and to sites where you elaborate on your 140-character tweet; for example, a blog post or a website.

You often fail to notice this "packaging" in others' messages because it seems so natural. But when the nonverbal messages of someone's posture or face contradict what is said verbally, you take special notice. For example, the person who says, "I'm so glad to see you," but avoids direct eye contact and looks around to see who else is present, is sending contradictory messages. You also see contradictory or mixed messages when couples say they love each other but seem to go out of their way to hurt each other nonverbally—for example, being late for important dates, flirting with others, or avoiding touching each other.

An awareness of the packaged nature of communication, then, suggests a warning against the too-easy interpretation of another's meaning, especially as revealed in nonverbal behaviors. Before you identify or guess the meaning of any bit of behavior, look at the entire package or cluster of which it's a part, the way in which the cluster is a response to its context, and the role of the specific nonverbal behavior within that cluster. That attractive person winking in your direction may be giving you the come-on—but don't rule out the possibility of ill-fitting contact lenses.

Message Meanings Are in People

Meaning depends not only on the packaging of messages (the combined verbal and nonverbal elements), but also on the interaction of these messages and the receiver's own thoughts and feelings. You don't "receive" meaning; you create meaning. You construct meaning out of the messages you receive combined with your own social and cultural perspectives (beliefs, attitudes, and values, for example) (Berger & Luckmann, 1980; Delia, 1977; Delia, O'Keefe, & O'Keefe, 1982). Words don't mean; people mean.

For example, if you wanted to know the meaning of the word *love*, you'd probably turn to a dictionary. There you'd find, according to Webster's: "the attraction, desire, or affection felt for a person who arouses delight or admiration." But where would you turn if you wanted to know what Pedro means when he says, "I'm in love"? Of course, you'd turn to Pedro to discover his meaning. It's in this sense that meanings are not in words but in people. Consequently, to uncover meaning, you need to look into people and not merely into words.

Also recognize that as you change, you also change the meanings you create. That is, although the message sent may not have changed, the meanings you created from it yesterday and the meanings you create today may be quite different. Yesterday, when a special someone said, "I love you," you created certain meanings. But today, when you learn that the same "I love you" was said to three other people, or when you fall in love with someone else, you drastically change the meanings you draw from those three words.

Because meanings are in people—and each person is unique and different from every other person—no word or message will mean the same thing to two different people. And this is why, for example, the same message may be perceived as controlling by one person and as a simple request by another. As you can appreciate, this type of misunderstanding can easily lead to interpersonal conflict if we fail to recognize that the meaning is not in the words; it's in the person. As a result, check your perceptions of another's meanings by asking questions, echoing what you perceive to be the other person's feelings or thoughts, seeking elaboration and clarification, and in general practicing the skills identified in the discussions of effective interpersonal perception and listening.

Blend Images/Shutterstock

VIEWPOINTS Consider the differences in meaning for such words as *religion* to a born-again Christian and an atheist, and *lunch* to a day-laborer and a Wall Street executive. What principles might help such diverse groups understand the different meanings?

Meanings Are Denotative and Connotative

Consider a word such as *death*. To a doctor this word may mean the moment at which the heart stops beating. This is denotative meaning—a rather objective description of an event. To a mother whose son has just died, however, the word means much more. It recalls the son's youth, his ambitions, his family, his illness, and so on. To her, the word is emotional, subjective, and highly personal. These emotional, subjective, and personal associations are the word's connotative meaning. The **denotation** of a word is its objective definition; the **connotation** is its subjective or emotional meaning. Take another example: Compare the term *migrant* (to designate Mexicans coming into the United States to better their economic condition) with the term *settlers* (to designate Europeans who came to the United States for the same reason) (Koppelman, 2005). Though both terms describe essentially the same activity (and are essentially the same denotatively), one is often negatively evaluated and the other is more often positively valued (and so differ widely in their connotations).

Now consider a simple nod of the head in answer to the question, "Do you agree?" This gesture is largely denotative and simply says yes. But what about a wink, a smile, or an overly rapid speech rate? These nonverbal expressions are more connotative; they express your feelings rather than objective information. The denotative meaning of a message is universal; most people would agree with the denotative meanings and would give similar definitions. Connotative meanings, however, are extremely personal, and few people would agree on the precise connotative meaning of a word or nonverbal behavior.

"Snarl words" and "purr words" may further clarify the distinction between denotative and connotative meaning (Hayakawa & Hayakawa, 1989; Hoffmann, 2005). Snarl words are highly negative ("She's an idiot," "He's a pig," "They're a bunch of losers"). Sexist, racist, and heterosexist language and hate speech provide lots of other examples. Purr words are highly positive ("She's a real sweetheart," "He's a dream," "They're the greatest"). Although they may sometimes seem to have denotative meaning and refer to the "real world," snarl and purr words are actually connotative in meaning. They don't describe people or events; rather, they reveal the speaker's feelings about these people or events.

In connection with this principle, also keep in mind that verbal and nonverbal messages occur in a context that, to a large extent, determines their meaning (both denotative and connotative). The same words or behaviors may have totally different meanings when they occur in different contexts. For example, the greeting, "How are you?" means "Hello" to someone you pass regularly on the street, but means "Is your health improving?" when said to a friend in the hospital. A wink to an attractive person on a bus means something completely different from a wink that signifies a put-on or a lie. The same message may be considered gracious in one culture and offensive in another culture.

Similarly, the meaning of a given signal depends on the other behavior it accompanies or is close to in time. Pounding a fist on the table during a speech in support of a politician means something quite different from that same gesture in response to news of a friend's death. Divorced from the context, both the denotative and the connotative meanings of messages can be hard to determine. Of course, even if you know the context in detail, you still may not be able to decipher the meaning of the message as the speaker intended. But understanding the context helps and also raises the chances of our accurately understanding the speaker's message.

Understanding the distinction between denotation and connotation should encourage you to clarify connotative meanings (or ask for clarification) when you anticipate potential misunderstandings; misunderstandings are almost always centered on connotative differences.

Messages Vary in Abstraction

Consider the following list of terms:

- entertainment
- film
- American film
- classic American film
- *All about Eve*

Do women communicate different messages when they change their names to their husband's, when they hyphenate their birth name with their husband's, or when they retain their birth name? Check out "Names" at tcbdevito.blogspot .com. How do you feel about this topic? Do men and women view this similarly or differently?

Understanding *Interpersonal Skills*

METACOMMUNICATION

Working with Interpersonal Skills

In what ways do you normally metacommunicate? Are these generally productive? What kinds of metacommunication messages do you wish other people would use more often?

Verbal messages may refer to the objects and things in the world (in what is called *object language*) but also to itself—you can talk about your talk, write about your writing (in what is called *metacommunication*). The prefix *meta-* can mean a variety of things, but as used in communication, philosophy, and psychology, its meaning is best translated as *about*. Thus, *metacommunication* is communication *about* communication, *metalanguage* is language *about* language, and a *metamessage* is a message *about* a message.

Actually, you use this distinction every day, perhaps without realizing it. For example, when you send someone an e-mail with a seemingly sarcastic comment and then put a smiley at the end, the smiley communicates about your communication; it says something like "this message is not to be taken literally; I'm trying to be humorous." The smiley is a metamessage; it's a message about a message. When you say, in preface to some comment, "I'm not sure about this, but . . . ," you're communicating a message about a message; you're commenting on the message and asking that it be understood with the qualification that you may be wrong. When you conclude a comment with "I'm only kidding," you're metacommunicating; you're communicating about your communication. In relationship communication you often talk in metalanguage and say things like, "We really need to talk about the way we communicate when we're out with company" or, "You're too critical" or, "I love when you tell me how much you love me."

And, of course, you can also use nonverbal messages to metacommunicate. You can wink at someone to indicate that you're only kidding or sneer after saying "Yeah, that was great," with the sneer contradicting the literal meaning of the verbal message.

Increasing Metacommunication Effectiveness. Here are a few suggestions for increasing your metacommunication effectiveness:

- Explain the feelings that go with your thoughts.
- Give clear feedforward to help the other person get a general picture of the messages that will follow.
- Paraphrase your own complex messages so as to make your meaning extra clear. Similarly, check on your understanding of another's message by paraphrasing what you think the other person means.
- Ask for clarification if you have doubts about another's meaning.
- Use metacommunication when you want to clarify the communication patterns between yourself and another person: "I'd like to talk about the way you talk about me to our friends" or, "I think we should talk about the way we talk about sex."

At the top is the general or abstract term *entertainment*. Note that entertainment includes all the items on the list plus various others—television, novels, drama, comics, and so on. *Film* is more specific and concrete. It includes all of the items below it as well as various other items, such as Indian film or Russian film. It excludes, however, all entertainment that is not film. *American film* is again more specific and excludes all films that aren't American. *Classic American film* further limits American film to a relatively small group of highly acclaimed films. And *All about Eve* specifies concretely the one item to which reference is made.

The more general term—in this case, *entertainment*—conjures up many different images. One person may focus on television, another on music, another on comic books, and still another on radio. To some, the word *film* may bring to mind the early silent films. To others, it brings to mind high-tech special effects. To still others, it recalls Disney's animated cartoons. *All about Eve* guides the listener still further—in this case to one film. But note that even though *All about Eve* identifies one film, different listeners are likely to focus on different aspects of the film: perhaps its character development, perhaps its love story, perhaps its financial success.

Effective verbal messages include words at many levels of **abstraction**. At times an abstract, general term may suit your needs best; at other times a more concrete, specific term may serve better. Generally, however, the specific term will prove the better choice. As you get more specific—less abstract—you more effectively guide the images that will come into your listeners' minds. In much the same way that you use specific terms to direct your face-to-face listeners' attention to exactly what you want them to focus on, you also use specific terms to direct an Internet search engine to narrow its focus to (ideally) just those items you want to access.

Messages Vary in Politeness

One of the best ways to look at **politeness** (consideration, respect, etc.) in interpersonal communication is in terms of both positive and negative politeness. You'll recall that both of these forms of politeness are responsive to two needs that each person has: (1) Each of us wishes to be viewed positively by others, to be thought of favorably; this is referred to as maintaining **positive face**. And (2) Each of us desires to be autonomous, to have the right to do as we wish; this is referred to as maintaining **negative face**. Politeness in interpersonal communication, then, involves behavior that allows others to maintain both positive and negative face.

Politeness and Directness
Messages that support or attack face needs (the latter are called "face-threatening acts" or FTAs) are often discussed in terms of direct and indirect language. Directness is usually less polite and may infringe on a person's need to maintain negative face—"Write me the recommendation." "Lend me $100." Indirectness allows the person to maintain autonomy (negative face) and provides an acceptable way for the person to refuse your request.

Indirect messages also allow you to express a desire or preference without insulting or offending anyone; they allow you to observe the rules of polite interaction. So instead of saying, "I'm bored with this group," you say, "It's getting late and I have to get up early tomorrow," or you look at your watch and pretend to be surprised by the time. Instead of saying, "This food tastes like cardboard," you say, "I just started my diet" or, "I just ate."

Sometimes indirect messages allow you to ask for compliments in a socially acceptable manner. In saying, "I was thinking of getting my eyes done," you hope to get the response "Your eyes? They're perfect as they are."

As noted in the Understanding Interpersonal Theory & Research box, women are more polite in their speech and, not surprisingly, use more indirect statements when making requests than do men. This difference seems to have both positive and negative implications. Indirect statements, in being more polite, are generally perceived positively; yet they may also be perceived negatively if they are seen as being weaker and less authoritative than more direct statements. Partly for cultural reasons, indirect statements also may be seen as manipulative or underhanded, whereas direct statements may be seen as straightforward and honest.

Keith Morris/Alamy

VIEWPOINTS How would you describe the level of directness you use when talking face-to-face versus the level you use in social networking? If you notice differences, to what do you attribute them?

Influences on Politeness   Politeness is considered a desirable trait across most cultures (Brown & Levinson, 1987). Cultures differ, however, in how they define politeness. For example, among English speakers politeness involves showing consideration for others and presenting yourself with confidence and polish. In Japanese it involves showing respect, especially for those in higher-status positions, and presenting yourself with modesty (Haugh, 2004). Cultures also vary in how important they consider politeness as compared with, say, openness or honesty. And, of course, cultures differ in the rules for expressing politeness or impoliteness and in the punishments for violating the accepted rules (Mao, 1994; Strecker, 1993). For example, members of Asian cultures, especially those of China and Japan, are often singled out because they emphasize politeness and mete out harsher social punishments for violations than would people in the United States or Western Europe (Fraser, 1990).

In the business world politeness is recognized as an important part of interpersonal interactions. In one study some 80 percent of employees surveyed believed that they did not get respect at work, and 20 percent felt they were victims of weekly incivility (Tsiantar, 2005). Rudeness in the workplace, it's been argued, reduces performance effectiveness, hurts creativity, and leads to increased worker turnover—all of which is costly for the organization.

Culture is, of course, not the only factor influencing politeness. Your personality and your professional training will influence your degree of politeness and how you express politeness (Edstrom, 2004). And the context of communication will influence politeness; formal situations in which there is considerable power difference call for greater politeness than informal circumstances in which the power differences are minimal (Mullany, 2004). And, as mentioned earlier, gender also influences politeness, as does your relationship stage.

For a brief discussion of some gender differences, see "Gender Differences" at tcbdevito.blogspot.com. What gender differences do you observe?

Politeness in Inclusion and Exclusion   Another perspective on politeness can be seen in messages of inclusion and exclusion. Inclusive messages include all people present and acknowledge the relevance of others and are normally considered polite. Exclusive messages shut out specific people or entire cultural groups and are normally considered impolite.

You see messages of exclusion in the use of in-group language in the presence of an out-group member. When doctors get together and discuss medicine, there's no problem. But when they get together with someone who isn't a doctor, they often fail to adjust to this new person. Instead, they may continue with discussions of procedures, symptoms, medications, and so on, excluding others present. Excluding talk also occurs when people of the same nationality get together within a larger, more heterogeneous group and use the language of their nationality. Similarly, references to experiences not shared by all (experiences such as having children, exotic vacations, and people we know) can serve to include some and exclude others. The use of these terms and experiences can exclude outsiders from full participation in the communication act (Sizemore, 2004).

Another form of excluding talk is the use of the terms of your own cultural group as universal, as applying to everyone. In using such terms, you exclude others. For example, *church* refers to the place of worship for specific religions, not all religions. Similarly, *Bible* refers to the Christian religious scriptures and is not a general term for religious scriptures. Nor does the Judeo-Christian tradition include the religious traditions of everyone. Similarly, the terms *marriage, husband*, and *wife* refer to some heterosexual relationships and exclude others; in most of the world they also exclude same-sex relationships. Instead, consider the vast array of alternative terms that are inclusive rather than exclusive. For example, the Association of American University Presses (Schwartz et al., 1995) recommends using *place of worship* instead of *church* when you wish to include the religious houses of worship of all people. Similarly, *committed relationship* is more inclusive than *marriage, couples therapy* is more inclusive than *marriage counseling*, and *life partner* is more inclusive than *husband* or *wife*. *Religious scriptures* is more inclusive than *Bible*. Of course, if you're referring to, say, a specific Baptist church or married heterosexual couples, then the terms *church* and *marriage* are perfectly appropriate.

Understanding *Interpersonal Theory & Research*

THEORIES OF GENDER DIFFERENCES

Throughout this text, gender differences are discussed in a wide variety of contexts. In regard to directness, research finds that women are more indirect in giving orders, for example, than are men; they are more likely to say something like "It would be great if these letters could go out today" than "Have these letters out by three." Men are more likely to be indirect when they express weakness, reveal a problem, or admit an error. Generally, men will speak indirectly when expressing meanings that violate the masculine stereotype. Women are generally more polite and will express empathy, sympathy, and supportiveness more than men.

One researcher distinguishes three broad sets of reasons or theories to explain gender differences in communication (Holmes, 1995):

- **Biological Differences.** Some theories argue that gender differences are due to innate biological differences. Thus, gender differences in communication, such as in politeness or in listening behavior, are the result of inherited biological factors that have evolved over millions of years.
- **Socialization.** Other theories suggest that gender differences are due to different patterns of socialization. Thus, the gender differences that you observe in communication are due to the ways in which boys and girls are raised and taught.
- **Social Power.** A third group of theories contend that gender differences are due to inequalities in social power. For example, because of women's lesser social power, they're more apt to communicate with greater deference and politeness than are men.

Working with Theories and Research

Based on your own observations of and interactions with men and women, what can you add to the discussion here?

Politeness Online   The Internet has very specific rules for politeness, called netiquette or in the case of Twitter, twittiquette. Much as the rules of etiquette provide guidance in communicating in face-to-face social situations, the rules of netiquette and twittiquette provide guidance for communicating politely online (McFedries, 2010). These rules not only make online communication more pleasant and easier but also improve your personal efficiency. Here are some key guidelines:

- **Familiarize yourself with the site before contributing.** Before asking questions about the system, read the Frequently Asked Questions (FAQs). Your question has probably been asked before and you'll put less strain on the system. Lurk before speaking; read posted notices and conversations before you contribute anything yourself. Observe the kinds of photos posted and the language used. Lurking (which, in online communication is good) will help you learn the rules of the particular group and will help you avoid saying things you'd like to take back.
- **Be brief.** Communicate only the information that is needed; communicate clearly, briefly, and in an organized way. Don't over-tweet. Communicate when you have something to say; not every one of your thoughts is worth a tweet or Facebook post. The same is true of photos; not everyone wants to see 27 photos of your cat.
- **Be gentle.** Refuse a request for friendship gently or ignore it. There's no need to go into great detail about why you don't want to be friends with this person. And if you're refused, don't ask for reasons. Social networkers consider it impolite to ask for reasons why your request is refused.

- **Don't shout.** WRITING IN CAPS IS PERCEIVED AS SHOUTING. It's okay to use caps occasionally to achieve emphasis. If you wish to give emphasis, highlight _like this_ or *like this*.
- **Be discrete.** Don't use social networking information outside the network. It's considered inappropriate and impolite to relay information that you find on Facebook, for example, to those who are not also friends with the person talked about (and who therefore would not have access to the same information about the person that you do).
- **Don't spam or flame.** Don't send unsolicited mail, repeatedly send the same mail, or post the same message (or irrelevant messages) to lots of newsgroups. Don't make personal attacks on other users. As in face-to-face conflict, personal attacks are best avoided on the Internet.
- **Avoid offensive language.** Refrain from expressions that would be considered offensive to others, such as sexist or racist terms. As you may know, software is available that will scan your e-mail, alert you if you may have broken an organizational rule, and give you a chance to revise your potentially offensive e-mail. This suggestion is especially important when you write on someone's wall in, say, Facebook or post an unflattering photo for all to see.
- **Be considerate.** Avoid asking to be friends with someone you suspect may have reason for not wanting to admit you. For example, your work associate may not want you to see her or his profile; if you ask, you put your colleague in an awkward position. In this case, you might use indirect messages; for example, you might say that you want to expand your networking to work colleagues and see how your colleague responds.
- **Don't advertise.** Don't market a product, yourself, or your services on Twitter; it's permissible on Facebook but do it discretely. It's better to direct someone to another site; say, a blog or website.
- **Don't plagiarize.** Give credit to others for the ideas you post and certainly any direct quotations.
- **Don't brag.** Social networking's norm is modesty, at least as most social networkers think about it. So, don't brag, for example, about the number of followers you have or the number of friends. Although the Twitter site includes a badge that indicates your total number of followers, it's the Twitter site that is posting the number of followers rather than you.

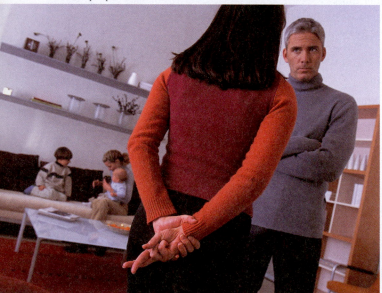

Photononstop/SuperStock

VIEWPOINTS ✛ Most often people lie to gain some benefit or reward (for example, to increase desirable relationships, to protect their self-esteem, or to obtain money) or to avoid punishment. In an analysis of 322 lies, researchers found that 75.8 percent benefited the liar, 21.7 percent benefited the person who was told the lie, and 2.5 percent benefited a third party (Camden, Motley, & Wilson, 1984). Are lies told to benefit others less unethical than lies told to benefit yourself?

Message Meanings Can Deceive

It comes as no surprise that some messages are truthful and some are deceptive. Although we operate in interpersonal communication on the assumption that people tell the truth, some people do lie. In fact, many view lying as common, whether in politics, business, or interpersonal relationships (Amble, 2005; Knapp, 2008). Lying also begets lying; when one person lies, the likelihood of the other person lying increases (Tyler, Feldman, & Reichert, 2006). Furthermore, people like people who tell the truth more than they like people who lie. So, lying needs to be given some attention in any consideration of interpersonal communication.

Lying refers to the act of (1) sending messages (2) with the intention of giving another person information you believe to be false. (1) Lying involves sending some kind of verbal and/or nonverbal message (and remember the absence of facial expression or the absence of verbal comment communicates); it also requires reception by another person. (2) The message must be sent to intentionally deceive. If you give false information to someone but you believe it to be true, then you haven't lied. You do lie when you send information that you believe to be untrue and you intend to mislead the other person.

Not surprisingly, cultural differences exist with lying—in the way lying is defined and in the way lying is treated. For example, as children get older, Chinese and Taiwanese (but not Canadians) see lying about the good deeds that they do as positive (as we'd expect for cultures that emphasize modesty), but taking credit for these same good deeds is seen negatively (Lee et al., 2002).

Some cultures consider lying to be more important than others—in one study, for example, European Americans considered lies less negatively than did Ecuadorians. Both, however, felt that lying to an out-group member was more acceptable than lying to an in-group member (Mealy, Stephan, & Urrutia, 2007).

Types of Lies   Lies vary greatly in type; each lie seems a bit different from every other lie. Here is one useful system that classifies lies into four types (McGinley, 2000).

INTERPERSONAL CHOICE POINT

Making an Excuse

Your friend is very upset over a recent breakup and wants to patch things up and so asks to borrow your car. You don't think your friend is in any position to drive and you need to refuse lending the car. What are some of the things you might say to refuse this request—a request you've always complied with on previous occasions? Would it be permissible (ethical) to make up some excuse for refusing, such as you needed the car?

Pro-social Deception: To Achieve Some Good.   These are lies that are designed to benefit the person lied to or lied about. For example, praising a person's effort to give him or her more confidence or to tell someone they look great to simply make them feel good would be examples of pro-social lies. Many of these lies are taught by the culture (Talwar, Murphy, & Kang, 2007). For example, adults might teach children about Santa Claus and the Tooth Fairy on the theory that these beliefs somehow benefit the child.

Some pro-social lies are expected and to not lie would be considered impolite. For example, it would be impolite to tell parents that their child is ugly (even if you firmly believe that the child is in fact ugly). The only polite course is to lie. Still another type of pro-social lie is when you lie to someone who would harm others. So, you'd lie to an enemy or to someone intending to hurt another person. These lies too would be expected and to not lie would likely brand you as contributing to any harm done as a result of your telling the truth. Not surprisingly children learn pro-social lying early in life and it remains the major type of lie children (and likely adults as well) tell (McGinley, 2000).

Self-Enhancement Deception: To Make Yourself Look Good.   Not all self-enhancement involves deception. For example, the impression-management strategies discussed earlier may be used to simply highlight what is already true about you and that others may not see at first glance. And so, you might mention your accomplishments to establish your credibility. If these accomplishments are true, then this impression-management effort is not deception.

At the same time, however, each of the impression-management strategies may also involve self-enhancement deception. So, for example, you might mention your good grades but omit the poorer ones; you might recount you generous acts and omit any selfish ones; or you might embellish your competence, lie about your financial situation, or present yourself as a lot more successful than you really are.

Selfish Deception: To Protect Yourself.   These lies are designed to protect yourself. Sometimes it's something as simple as not answering the phone because you are busy. In this case, no one really gets hurt. But some selfish deception strategies may involve hurting others. For example, you might imply that you did most of the work for the report—protecting yourself but also hurting the reputation of your colleague. Or you might conceal certain facts to protect yourself—previous failed relationships, an unsavory family history, or being fired. Hiding an extra-relational affair is perhaps the classic example of selfish deception.

Sometimes selfish deception is designed to protect the relationship and so, for example, you might lie about a one-time infidelity to both protect yourself (and perhaps your partner as well), but also to protect and maintain the relationship.

Anti-social Deception: To Harm Someone.   These lies are designed to hurt another person. For example, such lies might include spreading false rumors about someone you dislike or falsely accusing an opposing candidate of some wrongdoing (something you see regularly in political debates). Fighting parents may falsely accuse each other of a variety of wrongdoing to gain the affection and loyalty of the child. Falsely accusing another person of a wrong you did yourself would be perhaps the clearest example of anti-social deception.

How People Lie As you can imagine people lie in various ways (Knapp, 2008; Burgoon, Guerrero, & Floyd, 2010):

- **Exaggeration.** Here you lead people to believe that, for example, you earn more money than you do or that your grades are better than they are, or that your relationship is more satisfying than it really is.
- **Minimization.** Instead of exaggerating the facts, here you minimize them. You can minimize your lack of money (we have more than enough), the importance of poor grades, or your relationship dissatisfaction.
- **Substitution.** In this method you exchange the truth for a lie—for example, *I wasn't at the bar, I stopped in at Starbucks for coffee.*
- **Equivocation.** When you equivocate, your message is sufficiently ambiguous to lead people to think something different from your intention. *That outfit really is something, very interesting* instead of *Ugh!*
- **Omission.** And of course you can lie by not sending certain messages. So, when your romantic partner asks where you were last night, you might omit those things your partner would frown on and just include the positives.

The Behavior of Liars One of the more interesting questions about lying is how do liars act. Do they act differently from those telling the truth? And, if they do act differently, how can we tell when someone is lying to us? These questions are not easy to answer and we are far from having complete answers to such questions. But, we have learned a great deal.

For example, after an examination of 120 research studies, the following behaviors were found to most often accompany lying (DePaulo, et al, 2003; Knapp, 2008):

- **Liars hold back.** They speak more slowly (perhaps to monitor what they're saying), take longer to respond to questions (again, perhaps monitoring their messages), and generally give less information and elaboration.
- **Liars make less sense.** Liar's messages contain more discrepancies; more inconsistencies.
- **Liars give a more negative impression.** Generally, liars are seen as less willing to be cooperative, smile less than truth-tellers, and are more defensive.
- **Liars are tense.** The tension may be revealed by their higher pitched voices and excessive body movements.

It's very difficult to detect when a person is lying and when telling the truth. The hundreds of research studies conducted on this topic find that in most instances people judge lying accurately in less than 60 percent of the cases—only slightly better than chance (Knapp, 2008).

And there is some evidence to show that lie detection is even more difficult (that is, less accurate) in long-standing romantic relationships—the very relationships in which the most significant lying occurs (Guerrero, Andersen, & Afifi, 2007). One of the most important reasons for this is the **truth bias**. In most situations we assume that the person is telling the truth; as noted earlier in this chapter, we normally operate under the quality principle, which assumes that what a person says is the truth. This truth bias is especially strong in long-term relationships, where it's simply expected that each person tells the truth. There are, however, situations where there is a **lie bias**. For example, in prison where lying is so prevalent and where lie detection is a crucial survival skill, prisoners often operate with a lie bias and assume that what the speaker is saying is a lie (Knapp, 2008).

A related reason is that because of the truth bias, you may unconsciously avoid cues to lying in close relationships that you might easily notice at work, for example, simply as a kind of self-protection. After all, you wouldn't want to think that your long-term relationship partner would lie to you.

Ethics in Interpersonal Communication

LYING

Not surprisingly, lies have ethical implications. In fact, one of the earliest cultural rules children are taught is that lying is wrong. At the same time, children also learn that in some cases lying is effective—in gaining some reward or in avoiding some punishment.

Some pro-social, self-enhancement, and selfish-deception lies are considered ethical (for example, publicly agreeing with someone you really disagree with to enable the person to save face, saying that someone will get well despite medical evidence to the contrary, or simply bragging about your accomplishments). Some lies are considered not only ethical but required (for example, lying to protect someone from harm or telling the proud parents that their child is beautiful). Other lies (largely those in the anti-social category) are considered unethical (for example, lying to defraud investors or to falsely accuse someone).

However, a large group of lies are not that easy to classify as ethical or unethical, as you'll see in the Ethical Choice Points.

ETHICAL CHOICE POINTS

- Is it ethical to lie to get what you deserved but couldn't get any other way? For example, would you lie to get a well-earned promotion or raise? Would it matter if you hurt a colleague's chances of advancement in the process?

- Is it ethical to lie to your relationship partner to avoid a conflict and perhaps splitting up? In this situation, would it be ethical to lie if the issue was a minor one (you were late for an appointment because you wanted to see the end of the football game) or a major one (say, continued infidelity)?

- Is it ethical to lie to get yourself out of an unpleasant situation? For example, would you lie to get out of an unwanted date, an extra office chore, or a boring conversation?

- Is it ethical to lie about the reasons for breaking up a relationship to make it easier for you and the other person? For example, would you conceal that you've fallen in love with another person (or that you're simply bored with the relationship or that the physical attraction is gone) in your breakup speech?

- Is it ethical to exaggerate the consequences of an act in order to discourage it? For example, would you lie about the bad effects of marijuana in order to prevent your children or your students from using it?

- Is it ethical to lie about yourself in order to appear more appealing—for example, saying you were younger or richer or more honest than you really are? For example, would you lie in your profile on Facebook or MySpace or on a dating website to increase your chances of meeting someone really special?

Another reason that makes lie detection so difficult in close relationships is that the liar knows how to lie largely because he or she knows how you think and can therefore tailor lies that you'll fall for. And, of course, the liar often has considerable time to rehearse the lie, which generally makes lying more effective (that is, less easy to detect).

Nevertheless, there are some communication factors that seem to be more often associated with lying (Andersen, 2004; Leathers & Eaves, 2008). None of these, taken alone or in a group, is proof that a person is lying. Liars can be especially adept at learning to hide any signs that they might be lying. Nor is an absence of these features proof that the person is telling the truth. Generally, however, liars exhibit:

- greater pupil dilation and more eye blinks; more gaze aversion.
- higher vocal pitch; voices sound as if they were under stress.

- more errors and hesitations in their speech; they pause more and for longer periods of time.
- more hand, leg, and foot movements.
- more self-touching movements—for example, touching their face or hair—and more object touching—for example, playing with a coffee cup or pen.

In detecting lying, be especially careful that you formulate any conclusions with a clear understanding that you can be wrong, and that accusations of lying (especially when untrue but even when true) can often damage a relationship to the point where it's beyond repair. In addition, keep in mind all the cautions and potential errors in perception discussed earlier; after all, lie detection is a part of person perception.

Messages Can Criticize and Praise

Throughout your communication experiences, you're expected to criticize, evaluate, and otherwise to render judgment on some person or on something someone did or created. Especially in helping professions such as teaching, nursing, or counseling, criticism is an important and frequently used skill. The problem arises when criticism is used outside of its helping function—when it's inappropriate or excessive. An important interpersonal skill is to develop a facility for detecting when a person is asking for criticism and when that person is simply asking for a compliment. For example, when a friend asks how you like his or her new apartment, the friend may be searching for a compliment rather than wanting you to itemize all the things wrong with the place. Similarly, the person who says, "Do I look okay?" may be asking for a compliment.

Sometimes the desire to be liked (or perhaps the need to be appreciated) is so strong that we go to the other extreme and lavish praise on everything. The most ordinary jacket, the most hackneyed thought, the most average meal are given extraordinary praise, way beyond their merits. Both overly critical and overly complimentary individuals soon find that their comments are no longer met with concern or interest.

In expressing praise, keep the following in mind:

- **Use *I*-messages.** Instead of saying, "That report was good," say, "I thought that report was good" or "I liked your report."
- **Make sure your affect (facial expression of feelings) is positive.** Often, when people praise others simply because it's the socially correct response, they may betray their lack of conviction with too little or inappropriate affect.
- **Name the behavior you're praising.** Instead of saying, "That was good," say, "I liked your assertiveness" or "You really made them feel comfortable."
- **Take culture into consideration.** Many Asians, for example, feel uncomfortable when praised because they may interpret praise as a sign of veiled criticism (Dresser, 2005).

As an alternative to excessive criticism or praise, consider the principle of honest appraisal. Tell the truth—but note that there is an art to truth telling, just as there is an art to all other forms of effective communication. First, distinguish between instances in which an honest appraisal is sought and those in which the individual needs a compliment. Respond on the appropriate level. Second, if an honest appraisal is desired and if yours is negative, give some consideration to how you should phrase your criticism.

In giving criticism, focus on the event or the behavior rather than on personality; for example, say, "This paper has four typos and has to be redone" rather than "You're a lousy typist; do this over." In offering criticism, be specific. Instead of saying, "This paper is weak," say, "I think the introduction wasn't clear enough. Perhaps a more specific statement of purpose would have worked better."

INTERPERSONAL CHOICE POINT

Confronting a Lie

You ask about the previous night's whereabouts of your romantic partner of two years and are told something you know beyond any doubt to be false. You don't want to break up the relationship over this, but you do want the truth and an opportunity to resolve the problems that contributed to this situation. What are some of the things you might say to achieve your purposes? What are some types of things you'd definitely want to avoid saying?

Try to state criticism positively, if at all possible. Rather than saying, "You look terrible in black," it might be more helpful to say, "You look best in bright colors." In this way, you're also being constructive; you're explaining what can be done to make the situation better. If you do express criticism that seems to prove destructive, it may be helpful to offer a direct apology or to disclaim any harmful intentions (Baron, 1990). In your positive statement of criticism, try to demonstrate that your criticism stems from your caring and concern for the other person (Hornsey, Bath, & Gunthorpe, 2004). Instead of saying, "The introduction to your report is boring," say, "I really want your report to be great; I'd open with some humor to get the group's attention." Or say, "I want you to make a good impression. I think the dark suit would work better."

Avoid implying that because of the criticism, approval or affection will be withdrawn (Marano, 2008). When you criticize specific behavior rather than the person as a whole, this is less likely to happen.

- **Own your thoughts and feelings.** Instead of saying, "Your report was unintelligible," say, "I had difficulty following your ideas." At the same time, avoid mind reading. Instead of saying, "Don't you care about the impression you make? This report is terrible," say, "I think I would use a stronger introduction and a friendlier writing style."
- **Be clear.** Many people tend to phrase their criticism ambiguously, thinking that this will hurt less. Research suggests, however, that although ambiguous criticism may appear more polite, it also will appear less honest, less competent, and not necessarily more positive (Edwards & Bello, 2001).
- **Avoid ordering or directing** the other person to change (remember that this attacks a person's negative face); try identifying possible alternatives. Instead of saying, "Don't be so forward when you're first introduced to someone," consider saying, "I think they might respond better to a less forward approach." Also, whether with workplace colleagues or in relationships, generally avoid what one writer has called "microinequities"— subtle putdowns, sarcastic remarks, and gestures that imply a lack of concern or interest (Lubin, 2004).
- **Consider the context of the criticism.** Generally, it's best to express criticism in situations where you can interact with the person and express your attitudes in dialogue rather than monologue. By this principle, then, your first choice would be to express criticism face-to-face and your second choice would be by telephone; a distant third choice would be by letter, memo, or e-mail. Also, try to express your criticism in private. This is especially important when you are dealing with members of cultures in which public criticism can result in a serious loss of face.

As a receiver of criticism, consider the motivation behind the criticism. Some criticism, the kind discussed so far, is well intentioned and is designed to help you improve your performance or benefit you in some way. But some criticism is motivated by less noble purposes and may be designed to hurt or to humiliate you. Criticism that is not constructive needs to be examined mindfully. Criticism uttered in conflict or in times of rising emotions may be harsher and more hurtful than criticism given in calmer moments.

Messages Vary in Assertiveness

If you disagree with other people in a group, do you speak your mind? Do you allow others to take advantage of you because you're reluctant to say what you want? Do you feel uncomfortable when you have to state your opinion in a group? Questions such as these speak to your degree of **assertiveness**. Before reading further about this aspect of communication, take the following self-test, "How Assertive Are Your Messages?"

INTERPERSONAL CHOICE POINT

Criticizing

You're supervising a group of five interns who have been doing just about nothing. You don't want to discourage them or criticize them too harshly, but at the same time you have to get them to do some work. What are some of the things you can say to help turn this group around? What are some of the things you should probably avoid saying?

Test Yourself   How Assertive Are Your Messages?

Indicate how true each of the following statements is about your own communication. Respond instinctively rather than in the way you feel you should respond. Use the following scale: 5 = always or almost always true; 4 = usually true; 3 = sometimes true, sometimes false; 2 = usually false; and 1 = always or almost always false.

_____   1. I would express my opinion in a group even if my view contradicted the opinions of others.

_____   2. When asked to do something that I really don't want to do, I can say no without feeling guilty.

_____   3. I can express my opinion to my superiors on the job.

_____   4. I can start up a conversation with a stranger on a bus or at a business gathering without fear.

_____   5. I voice objection to people's behavior if I feel it infringes on my rights.

How Did You Do? All five items in this test identified characteristics of assertive communication. So high scores (say about 20 and above) would indicate a high level of assertiveness. Low scores (say about 10 and below) would indicate a low level of assertiveness.

What Will You Do? The discussion in this section clarifies the nature of assertive communication and offers guidelines for increasing your own assertiveness. Consider these suggestions as ways to increase your own assertiveness and at the same time to reduce your aggressive tendencies when appropriate.

Assertive people operate with an "I win, you win" philosophy; they assume that both parties can gain something from an interpersonal interaction, even from a confrontation. Assertive people are more positive and score lower on measures of hopelessness than do nonassertive people (Velting, 1999). Assertive people are willing to assert their own rights. Unlike their aggressive counterparts, however, they don't hurt others in the process. Assertive people speak their minds and welcome others to do likewise.

Do realize that, as with many other aspects of communication, there will be wide cultural differences when it comes to assertiveness. For example, the values of assertiveness are more likely to be extolled in individualist cultures than in collectivist cultures. Assertiveness will be valued more by those cultures that stress competition, individual success, and independence. It will be valued much less by those cultures that stress cooperation, group success, and the interdependence of all members on one another. American students, for example, are found to be significantly more assertive than Japanese or Korean students (Thompson, Klopf, & Ishii, 1991; Thompson & Klopf, 1991). Thus, for some situations, assertiveness may be an effective strategy in one culture but may create problems in another. Assertiveness with an elder in many Asian and Hispanic cultures may be seen as insulting and disrespectful.

Most people are nonassertive in certain situations. If you're one of these people and if you wish to increase your assertiveness, consider the following steps (Bower & Bower, 2005; Windy & Constantinou, 2005). (If you are always nonassertive and are unhappy about this, then you may need to work with a therapist to change your behavior.)

Analyze Assertive Communications   The first step in increasing your assertiveness skills is to understand the nature of assertive communications. Observe and analyze the messages of others. Learn to distinguish the differences among assertive, aggressive, and nonassertive messages. Focus on what makes one behavior assertive and another behavior nonassertive or aggressive. After you've gained some skills in observing the behaviors of others, turn your analysis to yourself. Analyze situations in which you're normally assertive and situations in which you're more likely to act nonassertively or aggressively. What characterizes these situations? What do the situations in which you're normally assertive have in common? How do you speak? How do you communicate nonverbally?

Rehearse Assertive Communications

One way to rehearse assertiveness is to use desensitization techniques (Dwyer, 2005; Wolpe, 1958). Select a situation in which you're normally nonassertive. Build a hierarchy that begins with a relatively nonthreatening message and ends with the desired communication. For example, let's say that you have difficulty voicing your opinion to your supervisor at work. The desired behavior then is to tell your supervisor your opinions. To desensitize yourself, construct a hierarchy of visualized situations leading up to this desired behavior. Such a hierarchy might begin with visualizing yourself talking with your boss. Visualize this scenario until you can do it without any anxiety or discomfort. Once you have mastered this visualization, visualize a step closer to your goal, such as walking into your boss's office. Again, do this until your visualization creates no discomfort. Continue with these successive visualizations until you can visualize yourself telling your boss your opinion. As with the other visualizations, do this until you can do it while totally relaxed. This is the mental rehearsal. You might add a vocal dimension to this by actually acting out (with voice and gesture) your telling your boss your opinion. Again, do this until you experience no difficulty or discomfort. Next, try doing this in front of a trusted and supportive friend or group of friends. Ideally this interaction will provide you with useful feedback. After this rehearsal, you're probably ready for the next step.

Communicate Assertively

This step is naturally the most difficult but obviously the most important. Here's a generally effective pattern to follow in communicating assertively:

1. **Describe the problem**. Don't evaluate or judge it. "We're all working on this advertising project together. You're missing half our meetings, and you still haven't produced your first report." Be sure to use *I*-messages and to avoid messages that accuse or blame the other person.
2. **State how this problem affects you.** Tell the person how you feel. "My job depends on the success of this project, and I don't think it's fair that I have to do extra work to make up for what you're not doing."
3. **Propose solutions that are workable.** Propose solutions that allow the person to save face. Describe or visualize the situation if your solution were put into effect. "If you can get your report to the group by Tuesday, we'll still be able to meet our deadline. I could give you a call on Monday to remind you."
4. **Confirm understanding**. "It's clear that we can't produce this project if you're not going to pull your own weight. Will you have the report to us by Tuesday?"

Keep in mind that assertiveness is not always the most desirable response. Assertive people are assertive when they want to be, but they can be nonassertive if the situation calls for it. For example, you might wish to be nonassertive in a situation in which assertiveness might emotionally hurt the other person. Let's say that an older relative wishes you to do something for her or him. You could assert your rights and say no, but in doing so you would probably hurt this person; it might be better simply to do as asked. Of course, there are limits that should be observed. You should be careful in such a situation that you're not hurt instead.

A note of caution should be added to this discussion. It's easy to visualize a situation in which, for example, people are talking behind you in a movie, and with your newfound enthusiasm for assertiveness, you tell them to be quiet. It's also easy to see yourself getting smashed in the teeth as a result. In applying the principles of assertive communication, be careful that you don't go beyond what you can handle effectively.

> **INTERPERSONAL CHOICE POINT**
>
> **Rejecting Directly**
>
> *Your supervisor seems never to get you the work you need early in the day; instead you receive the work late in the afternoon and invariably have to stay late to finish it. You've tried politeness and it didn't work; you need to be more forceful. In what ways can you express your feelings assertively to achieve your goal and yet not alienate or insult your colleague?*

Messages Can Confirm and Disconfirm

The language behaviors known as confirmation and disconfirmation have to do with the extent to which you acknowledge another person. Consider this situation: You've been living with someone for the last six months and you arrive home late one night. Your partner, let's say Pat, is angry and complains about your being so late. Of the following responses, which are you most likely to give?

1. Stop screaming. I'm not interested in what you're babbling about. I'll do what I want, when I want. I'm going to bed.
2. What are you so angry about? Didn't you get in three hours late last Thursday when you went to that office party? So knock it off.
3. You have a right to be angry. I should have called to tell you I was going to be late, but I got involved in a serious debate at work and I couldn't leave until it was resolved.

In response 1, you dismiss Pat's anger and even indicate dismissal of Pat as a person. In response 2, you reject the validity of Pat's reasons for being angry, although you do not dismiss either Pat's feelings of anger or of Pat as a person. In response 3, you acknowledge Pat's anger and the reasons for being angry. In addition, you provide some kind of explanation and, in doing so, show that both Pat's feelings and Pat as a person are important and that Pat has the right to know what happened. The first response is an example of disconfirmation, the second of rejection, and the third of confirmation.

Psychologist William James once observed that "no more fiendish punishment could be devised, even were such a thing physically possible, than that one should be turned loose in society and remain absolutely unnoticed by all the members thereof." In this often-quoted observation, James identifies the essence of disconfirmation (Veenendall & Feinstein, 1995; Watzlawick, Beavin, & Jackson, 1967).

Disconfirmation is a communication pattern in which you ignore a person's presence as well as that person's communications. You say, in effect, that the person and what she or he has to say aren't worth serious attention. Disconfirming responses often lead to loss of self-esteem (Sommer, Williams, Ciarocco, & Baumeister, 2001).

Note that disconfirmation is not the same as rejection. In **rejection**, you disagree with the person; you indicate your unwillingness to accept something the other person says or does. In disconfirming someone, however, you deny that person's significance; you claim that what this person says or does simply does not count.

Confirmation is the opposite communication pattern. In **confirmation**, you not only acknowledge the presence of the other person but also indicate your acceptance of this person, of this person's definition of self, and of your relationship as defined or viewed by this other person. Confirming responses often lead to gains in self-esteem and have been shown to reduce student apprehension in the classroom and indirectly to increase motivation and learning (Ellis, 2004). You can communicate both confirmation and disconfirmation in a wide variety of ways; Table 1 shows just a few.

You can gain insight into a wide variety of offensive language practices by viewing them as types of disconfirmation—as language that alienates and separates. We'll explore this important principle by looking at racism, heterosexism, ageism, and sexism. Another significant *-ism* is **ableism**—discrimination against people with disabilities. This particular practice is handled throughout the text in a series of tables offering tips for communicating between people with and without a variety of disabilities:

INTERPERSONAL CHOICE POINT

Discouraging Disconfirmation

For the last several months you've noticed how disconfirming your neighbors are toward their preteen children; it seems the children can never do anything to the parents' satisfaction. What are some of the things you might say (if you do decide to get involved) to make your neighbors more aware of their communication patterns and the possible negative effects these might have?

Jupiterimages/Comstock/Getty Images/Thinkstock

VIEWPOINTS ✥ Hate speech is speech that is hostile, offensive, degrading, or intimidating to a particular group of people. Women, African Americans, Muslims, Hispanics, and gay men and lesbians are among the major targets of hate speech in the United States. On your college campus, which would be most likely to be considered hate speech: sexist, heterosexist, racist, or ageist language? Which would be least likely? How do you respond when you hear other students using sexist language? heterosexist language? racist language? ageist language?

TABLE 1	Confirmation and Disconfirmation

This table identifies some specific confirming and disconfirming messages. As you review this table, try to imagine a specific illustration for each of the ways of communicating disconfirmation and confirmation (Galvin, Bylund, & Brommel, 2011; Pearson, 1993).

Disconfirmation	Confirmation
Ignores the presence or contributions of the other person; expresses indifference to what the other person says.	**Acknowledges** the presence and the contributions of the other person by either supporting or taking issue with what he or she says.
Makes no nonverbal contact; avoids direct eye contact; avoids touching and general nonverbal closeness.	**Makes nonverbal contact** by maintaining direct eye contact and, when appropriate, touching, hugging, kissing, and otherwise demonstrating acknowledgment of the other.
Monologues; engages in communication in which one person speaks and one person listens; there is no real interaction; there is no real concern or respect for each other.	**Dialogues**; engage in communication in which both persons are speakers and listeners; both are involved; both are concerned with and have respect for each other.
Jumps to interpretation or evaluation rather than working at understanding what the other person means.	**Demonstrates understanding** of what the other person says and means and reflects your understanding in what you say; or when in doubt ask questions.
Discourages, interrupts, or otherwise makes it difficult for the other person to express himself or herself.	**Encourages** the other person to express his or her thoughts and feelings by showing interest and asking questions.
Avoids responding or responds tangentially by acknowledging the other person's comment but shifts the focus of the message in another direction.	**Responds directly** and exclusively to what the other person says.

- Between people who are visually impaired and those who aren't
- Between people with and without disabilities
- Between people with and without hearing problems
- Between people with and without speech and language disorders

Racism   According to Andrea Rich (1974), "any language that, through a conscious or unconscious attempt by the user, places a particular racial or ethnic group in an inferior position is racist." **Racist language** expresses racist attitudes. It also, however, contributes to the development of racist attitudes in those who use or hear the language. Even when racism is subtle, unintentional, or even unconscious, its effects are systematically damaging (Dovidio, Gaertner, Kawakami, & Hodson, 2002).

Racism exists on both individual and institutional levels—distinctions made by educational researchers and used throughout this discussion (Koppelman, 2005). Individual racism involves the negative attitudes and beliefs that people hold about specific races. The assumption that certain races are intellectually inferior to others or that certain races are incapable of certain achievements are clear examples of individual racism. Prejudice against groups such as American Indians, African Americans, Hispanics, and Arabs have been with us throughout history and is still a part of many people's lives. Such racism is seen in the negative terms people use to refer to members of other races and to disparage their customs and accomplishments.

Institutionalized racism is seen in patterns—such as de facto school segregation, companies' reluctance to hire members of minority groups, and banks' unwillingness to extend mortgages and business loans to members of some races or tendency to charge higher interest rates.

Examine your own language for:

- derogatory terms for members of a particular race.
- maintaining stereotypes and interacting with members of other races based on those stereotypes.
- including reference to race when it's irrelevant, as in "the [racial name] surgeon" or "the [racial name] athlete."
- attributing an individual's economic or social problems to the individual's race rather than to, say, institutionalized racism or general economic problems that affect everyone.

Heterosexism   Heterosexism also exists on both an individual and an institutional level. Individual heterosexism consists of attitudes, behaviors, and language that disparage gay men and lesbians and includes the belief that all sexual behavior that is not heterosexual is unnatural and deserving of criticism and condemnation. These beliefs are at the heart of anti-gay violence and "gay bashing." Individual heterosexism also includes such beliefs as the notions that homosexuals are more likely to commit crimes than are heterosexuals (there's actually no difference) and to molest children than are heterosexuals (actually, child molesters are overwhelmingly heterosexual, married men) (Abel & Harlow, 2001; Koppelman, 2005). It also includes the belief that homosexuals cannot maintain stable relationships or effectively raise children, beliefs that contradict research evidence (Fitzpatrick, Jandt, Myrick, & Edgar, 1994; Johnson & O'Connor, 2002).

Tupungato/Shutterstock

The difficulty in life is the choice.
—*George Moore*

Institutional heterosexism is easy to identify. For example, the ban on gay marriage in most states and the fact that at this time only a handful of states allow gay marriage is a good example of institutional heterosexism. Other examples include the Catholic Church's ban on homosexual priests and the many laws prohibiting adoption of children by gay men or lesbians. In some cultures homosexual relations are illegal (for example, in India, Malaysia, Pakistan, and Singapore); penalties range from a "misdemeanor" charge in Liberia to life in jail in Singapore and death in Pakistan.

Heterosexist language includes derogatory terms used for lesbians and gay men. For example, surveys in the military showed that 80 percent of those surveyed heard "offensive speech, derogatory names, jokes or remarks about gays" and that 85 percent believed that such derogatory speech was "tolerated" (*New York Times*, March 25, 2000, p. A12). You also see heterosexism in more subtle forms of language usage; for example, when you qualify a professional—as in "gay athlete" or "lesbian doctor"—and, in effect, say that athletes and doctors are not normally gay or lesbian.

Still another form of heterosexism is the presumption of heterosexuality. Usually, people assume the person they're talking to or about is heterosexual. And usually they're correct, because most people are heterosexual. At the same time, however, this presumption denies the lesbian or gay identity a certain legitimacy. The practice is very similar to the presumptions of whiteness and maleness that we have made significant inroads in eliminating.

Examine your own language for possible heterosexism and consider, for example, if you do any of the following:

- use offensive nonverbal mannerisms that parody stereotypes when talking about gay men and lesbians. Do you avoid the "startled eye blink" with which some people react to gay couples (Mahaffey, Bryan, & Hutchison, 2005)?
- "compliment" gay men and lesbians by saying that they "don't look it." To gay men and lesbians, this is not a compliment. Similarly, expressing disappointment that a person is gay—often thought to be a compliment, as in comments such as "What a waste!"—is not really a compliment.
- make the assumption that every gay or lesbian knows what every other gay or lesbian is thinking. It's very similar to asking a Japanese person why Sony is investing heavily in the United States.
- stereotype—saying things like "Lesbians are so loyal" or "Gay men are so open with their feelings," which ignore the reality of wide differences within any group, and are potentially insulting to all groups.

- overattribute—the tendency to attribute just about everything a person does, says, and believes to the fact that the person is gay or lesbian. This tendency helps to activate and perpetuate stereotypes.
- forget that relationship milestones are important to all people. Ignoring anniversaries or birthdays of, say, a relative's partner is resented by everyone.

As you think about heterosexism, recognize not only that heterosexist language will create barriers to communication, but also that its absence will foster more meaningful communication: greater comfort, an increased willingness to disclose personal information, and a greater willingness to engage in future interactions (Dorland & Fisher, 2001).

Ageism   Although used mainly to refer to prejudice against older people, the word **ageism** can also refer to prejudice against other age groups. For example, if you describe all teenagers as selfish and undependable, you're discriminating against a group purely because of their age, and thus are ageist in your statements. In some cultures—some Asian and some African cultures, for example—the old are revered and respected. Younger people seek them out for advice on economic, ethical, and relationship issues.

Individual ageism is seen in the general disrespect many show toward older people and in negative stereotypes about older people. Institutional ageism is seen in mandatory retirement laws and age restrictions in certain occupations (as opposed to requirements based on demonstrated competence). In less obvious forms, ageism is seen in the media's portrayal of old people as incompetent, complaining, and, perhaps most clearly evidenced in both television and films, without romantic feelings. Rarely, for example, does a TV show or film show older people working productively, being cooperative and pleasant, and engaging in romantic and sexual relationships.

Popular language is replete with examples of **ageist language**; "little old lady," "old hag," "old-timer," "over the hill," "old coot," and "old fogy" are a few examples. As with sexism, qualifying a description of someone in terms of his or her age demonstrates ageism. For example, if you refer to "a quick-witted 75-year-old" or "an agile 65-year-old" or "a responsible teenager," you're implying that these qualities are unusual in people of these ages and thus need special mention. You're saying that "quick-wittedness" and "being 75" do not normally go together. The problem with this kind of stereotyping is that it's simply wrong. There are many 75-year-olds who are extremely quick-witted (and many 30-year-olds who aren't).

You also communicate ageism when you speak to older people in overly simple words, or explain things that don't need explaining. Nonverbally, you demonstrate ageist communication when, for example, you avoid touching an older person but touch others, or when you avoid making direct eye contact with the older person but readily do so with others, or when you speak at an overly high volume (suggesting that all older people have hearing difficulties).

One useful way to avoid ageism is to recognize and avoid the illogical stereotypes that ageist language is based on and examine your own language to see if you do any of the following:

- talk down to a person because he or she is older. Older people are not mentally slow; most people remain mentally alert well into old age.
- refresh an older person's memory each time you see the person. Older people can and do remember things.
- imply that romantic relationships are no longer important. Older people continue to be interested in relationships.
- speak at an abnormally high volume. Being older does not mean being hard of hearing or being unable to see; most older people hear and see quite well, sometimes with hearing aids or glasses.
- avoid engaging older people in conversation as you would wish to be engaged. Older people are interested in the world around them.

Even though you want to avoid ageist communication, there are times when you may wish to make adjustments when talking with someone who does have language or commu-

nication difficulties. The American Speech and Hearing Association offers several useful suggestions (www.asha.org/public/speech/development/communicating-better-with-older-people.htm):

- Reduce as much background noise as you can.
- Ease into the conversation by beginning with casual topics and then moving into more familiar topics. Stay with each topic for a while; avoid jumping too quickly from one topic to another.
- Speak in relatively short sentences and questions.
- Give the person added time to respond. Some older people react more slowly and need extra time.
- Listen actively. Practice the skills of active listening.

Sexism   Individual sexism consists of prejudicial attitudes and beliefs about men or women based on rigid beliefs about gender roles. These might include such beliefs as the idea that women should be caretakers, should be sensitive at all times, and should acquiesce to a man's decisions concerning political or financial matters. Sexist attitudes would also include the beliefs that men are insensitive, interested only in sex, and incapable of communicating feelings.

Institutional sexism, on the other hand, results from customs and practices that discriminate against people because of their gender. Clear examples in business and industry are the widespread practice of paying women less than men for the same job and the discrimination against women in the upper levels of management. Another clear example of institutionalized sexism is the courts' practice of automatically or near-automatically granting child custody to the mother rather than the father.

Of particular interest here is **sexist language**: language that puts down someone because of his or her gender (a term usually used to refer to language derogatory toward women). The National Council of Teachers of English (NCTE) has proposed guidelines for nonsexist (gender-free, gender-neutral, or sex-fair) language. These guidelines concern the use of the generic word *man,* the use of generic *he* and *his,* and sex-role stereotyping (Penfield, 1987). Consider your own communication behavior. Examine your own language for such examples of sexism as these:

- use of *man* generically. Using the term to refer to humanity in general emphasizes maleness at the expense of femaleness. Gender-neutral terms can easily be substituted. Instead of "mankind," say "humanity," "people," or "human beings." Similarly, the use of terms such as *policeman* or *fireman* that presume maleness as the norm—and femaleness as a deviation from this norm—are clear and common examples of sexist language.
- use of *he* and *his* as generic. Instead, you can alternate pronouns or restructure your sentences to eliminate any reference to gender. For example, the NCTE Guidelines (Penfield, 1987) suggest that instead of saying, "The average student is worried about his grades," you say, "The average student is worried about grades."
- use of sex-role stereotyping. When you make the hypothetical elementary school teacher female and the college professor male, or refer to doctors as male and nurses as female, you're sex-role stereotyping, as you are when you include the sex of a professional with terms such as "woman doctor" or "male nurse."

For an article on sexual equality in different countries, see "Gender Gap" at tcbdevito.blogspot.com. Do you see "gender gaps"? Where are they most prevalent?

Racist, Heterosexist, Ageist, and Sexist Listening

Just as racist, heterosexist, ageist, and sexist attitudes will influence your language, they can also influence your listening if you hear what speakers are saying through the stereotypes you hold. Prejudiced listening occurs when you listen differently to a person because of his or her gender, race, affectional orientation, or age, even though these characteristics are irrelevant to the message.

Racist, heterosexist, ageist, and sexist listening occur in lots of situations. For example, when you dismiss a valid argument—or attribute validity to an invalid argument—because the speaker is of a particular race, affectional orientation, age group, or gender, you're listening with prejudice.

Of course, there are many instances when these characteristics are relevant and pertinent to your evaluation of a message. For example, the sex of a person who is talking about pregnancy, fathering a child, birth control, or surrogate motherhood is, most would agree, probably relevant to the message. So in these cases it is not sexist listening to take the sex of the speaker into consideration. It is, however, sexist listening to assume that only one sex can be an authority on a particular topic or that one sex's opinions are without value. The same is true in relation to listening through a person's race or affectional orientation.

PhotoObjects/Thinkstock

Messages Vary in Cultural Sensitivity

Recognizing that messages vary in cultural sensitivity is a great step toward developing confirming and avoiding disconfirming messages. Perhaps the best way to develop nonracist, nonheterosexist, nonageist, and nonsexist language is to examine the preferred **cultural identifiers** to use in talking to and about members of different groups. Keep in mind, however, that preferred terms frequently change over time, so keep in touch with the most current preferences. The preferences and many of the specific examples identified here are drawn largely from the findings of the Task Force on Bias-Free Language of the Association of American University Presses (Schwartz, 1995; Faigley, 2009).

VIEWPOINTS A widely held assumption in anthropology, linguistics, and communication is that the importance of a concept to a culture can be measured by the number of words the language has for talking about the concept. So, for example, in English there are lots of words for money, transportation, and communication—all crucial to the English-speaking world. With this principle in mind, consider the findings of Julia Stanley, for example. Stanley researched English-language terms indicating sexual promiscuity and found 220 terms referring to a sexually promiscuous woman but only 22 terms for a sexually promiscuous man (Thorne, Kramarae, & Henley, 1983). What does this finding suggest about our culture's attitudes and beliefs about promiscuity in men and women?

Race and Nationality   Generally, most African Americans prefer *African American* to *black* (Hecht, Jackson, & Ribeau, 2003); although *black* is often used with *white,* as well as in a variety of other contexts (for example, Department of Black and Puerto Rican Studies, the *Journal of Black History,* and Black History Month). The American Psychological Association recommends that both terms be capitalized, but the *Chicago Manual of Style* (the manual used by most newspapers and publishing houses) recommends using lowercase. The terms *Negro* and *colored,* although used in the names of some organizations (for example, the United Negro College Fund and the National Association for the Advancement of Colored People), are no longer used outside these contexts. *People of color*—a literary-sounding term appropriate perhaps to public speaking but awkward in most conversations—is preferred to *nonwhite,* which implies that whiteness is the norm and nonwhiteness is a deviation from that norm.

White is generally used to refer to those whose roots are in European cultures and usually does not include Hispanics. Analogous to African American (which itself is based on a long tradition of terms such as Irish American and Italian American) is the phrase *European American.* Few European Americans, however, call themselves that; most prefer their national origins emphasized, as in, for example, German American or Greek American.

Generally, the term *Hispanic* refers to anyone who identifies as belonging to a Spanish-speaking culture. *Latina* (female) and *Latino* (male) refer to

INTERPERSONAL CHOICE POINT

Cultural Insensitivity

You inadvertently say something that you thought would be funny but that turns out to be culturally insensitive, causing offense to a friend. What are some of your options for making it clear that you would never intentionally talk this way?

VIEWPOINTS ✛ Many people feel that it's permissible for members of a particular subculture to refer to themselves in terms that if said by outsiders would be considered racist, sexist, or heterosexist. Some researchers suggest a possible problem with this—the idea that these terms may actually reinforce negative stereotypes that the larger society has already assigned to the group (Guerin, 2003). By using these terms members of the group may come to accept the labels with their negative connotations and thus contribute to their own stereotyping and their own deprecation. Others would argue that by using such labels groups weaken the terms' negative impact. Do you refer to yourself using terms that would be considered offensive or politically incorrect if said by "outsiders"? What effects, if any, do you think such self-talk has?

INTERPERSONAL CHOICE POINT

Discouraging Ethnocentricity

You've been dating a wonderful person for the last few months, but increasingly you are discovering that your "ideal" partner is extremely ethnocentric and sees little value in other religions, races, and nationalities. What are some things you can do to educate your possible life partner?

persons whose roots are in one of the Latin American countries, such as Haiti, the Dominican Republic, Nicaragua, or Guatemala. *Hispanic American* refers to U.S. residents whose ancestry is in a Spanish culture; the term includes people from Mexico, the Caribbean, and Central and South America. In emphasizing a Spanish heritage, however, the term is really inaccurate, because it leaves out the large numbers of people in the Caribbean and in South America whose origins are African, Native American, French, or Portuguese. *Chicana* (female) and *Chicano* (male) refer to persons with roots in Mexico, although it often connotes a nationalist attitude (Jandt, 2004) and is considered offensive by many Mexican Americans. *Mexican American* is generally preferred.

Inuk (plural *Inuit*), also spelled with two *n*'s (*Innuk* and *Innuit*), is preferred to *Eskimo* (the term the U.S. Census Bureau uses), which was applied to the indigenous peoples of Alaska and Canada by Europeans and literally means "raw meat eaters."

The word *Indian* technically refers only to someone from India, not to members of other Asian countries or to the indigenous peoples of North America. *American Indian* or *Native American* is preferred, even though many Native Americans do refer to themselves as *Indians* and *Indian people*. The word *squaw*, used to refer to a Native American woman and still used in the names of some places in the United States and in some textbooks, is clearly a term to be avoided; its usage is almost always negative and insulting (Koppelman, 2005).

In Canada indigenous people are called *first people* or *first nations*. The term *native American* (with a lowercase *n*) is most often used to refer to persons born in the United States. Although technically the term could refer to anyone born in North or South America, people outside the United States generally prefer more specific designations, such as *Argentinean, Cuban,* or *Canadian*. The term *native* describes an indigenous inhabitant; it is not used to indicate "someone having a less developed culture."

Muslim (rather than the older *Moslem*) is the preferred form to refer to a person who adheres to the religious teachings of Islam. *Quran* (rather than *Koran*) is the preferred spelling for the scriptures of Islam. *Jewish people* is often preferred to *Jews,* and *Jewess* (a Jewish female) is considered derogatory. Finally, the term *non-Christian* is to be avoided: It implies that people who have other beliefs deviate from the norm.

When history was being written from a European perspective, Europe was taken as the focal point and the rest of the world was defined in terms of its location relative to that continent. Thus, Asia became the East or the Orient, and *Asians* became *Orientals*—a term that is today considered inappropriate or "Eurocentric." Thus, people from Asia are *Asians,* just as people from Africa are *Africans* and people from Europe are *Europeans*.

Affectional Orientation

Generally, *gay* is the preferred term to refer to a man who has an affectional orientation toward other men, and *lesbian* is the preferred term for a woman who has an affectional orientation toward other women (Lever, 1995). ("Lesbian" means "homosexual woman," so the term *lesbian woman* is redundant.) *Homosexual* refers to both gay men and lesbians, and describes a same-sex sexual orientation. The definitions of *gay* and *lesbian* go beyond sexual orientation and refer to a self-identification as a gay man or lesbian. *Gay* as a noun, although widely used, may be offensive in some contexts, as in "We have two gays on the team." Because most scientific thinking holds that sexuality is not a matter of choice, the terms *sexual orientation* and *affectional orientation* are preferred to *sexual preference* or *sexual status* (which is also vague). In the case of same-sex marriages, there are two husbands or two wives. In a male-male marriage, each person is referred to as husband and in the case of female-female marriage, each person is referred to as wife. Some same-sex couples—especially those who are not married—prefer the term "partner" or "lover."

Age   *Older person* is preferred to *elder, elderly, senior,* or *senior citizen* (which technically refers to someone older than 65). Usually, however, terms designating age are unnecessary. There are times, of course, when you'll need to refer to a person's age group, but most of the time age is irrelevant—in much the same way that racial or affectional orientation terms are usually irrelevant.

Sex and Gender   Generally, the term *girl* should be used only to refer to very young females and is equivalent to *boy. Girl* is never used to refer to a grown woman, nor is *boy* used to refer to people in blue-collar positions, as it once was. *Lady* is negatively evaluated by many because it connotes the stereotype of the prim and proper woman. *Woman* or *young woman* is preferred. The term *ma'am,* originally an honorific used to show respect, is probably best avoided since today it's often used as a verbal tag to comment (indirectly) on the woman's age or marital status (Angier, 2010).

Transgendered people (people who identify themselves as members of the sex opposite to the one they were assigned at birth and who may be gay or straight, male or female) are addressed according to their self-identified sex. Thus, if the person identifies herself as a woman, then the feminine name and pronouns are used—regardless of the person's biological sex. If the person identifies himself as a man, then the masculine name and pronouns are used.

Transvestites (people who prefer at times to dress in the clothing of the sex other than the one they were assigned at birth and who may be gay or straight, male or female) are addressed on the basis of their clothing. If the person is dressed as a woman—regardless of the birth-assigned sex—she is referred to and addressed with feminine pronouns and feminine name. If the person is dressed as a man—regardless of the birth-assigned sex—he is referred to and addressed with masculine pronouns and masculine name.

INTERPERSONAL CHOICE POINT

Using Inappropriate Cultural Identifiers

Your parents use cultural identifiers that would be considered inappropriate among most social groups—not because of prejudice but mainly through ignorance and habit. You want to avoid falling into these patterns yourself. What are some of the things you might do to achieve your goal?

Guidelines for Using Verbal Messages Effectively

Our examination of the principles governing the verbal messages system has suggested a wide variety of ways to use language more effectively. Here are some additional guidelines for making your own verbal messages more effective and a more accurate reflection of the world in which we live. We'll consider six such guidelines: (1) Extensionalize: avoid intensional orientation; (2) see the individual: avoid allness, (3) distinguish between facts and inferences: avoid fact–inference confusion, (4) discriminate among: avoid indiscrimination, (5) talk about the middle: avoid polarization, and (6) update messages: avoid static evaluation.

These guidelines are derived from the work of general semanticists. For a look at this area of study concerned with the relationships among language, thought, and behavior, see "General Semantics" at tcbdevito.blogspot.com. Which of these principles/ guidelines do you see violated most often?

Extensionalize: Avoid Intensional Orientation

The term **intensional orientation** refers to a tendency to view people, objects, and events in terms of how they're talked about or labeled rather than in terms of how they actually exist. **Extensional orientation** is the opposite: It's a tendency to look first at the actual people, objects, and events and then at the labels—a tendency to be guided by what you see happening rather than by the way something or someone is talked about or labeled.

Intensional orientation occurs when you act as if the words and labels were more important than the things they represent—as if the map were more important than the territory. In its extreme form, intensional orientation is seen in the person who is afraid of dogs and who begins to sweat when shown a picture of a dog or when hearing people talk about dogs. Here the person is responding to a label as if it were the actual thing. In its more common form, intensional orientation occurs when you see people through your schemata instead of on the basis of their specific behaviors. For example, it occurs when you think of a professor as an unworldly egghead before getting to know the specific professor.

The corrective to intensional orientation is to focus first on the object, person, or event and then on the way in which the object, person, or event is talked about. Labels are certainly helpful guides, but don't allow them to obscure what they're meant to symbolize.

See the Individual: Avoid Allness

The world is infinitely complex, and because of this you can never say all there is to say about anything—at least not logically. This is particularly true when you are dealing with people. You may think you know all there is to know about certain individuals or about why they did what they did, yet clearly you don't know all. You can never know all the reasons you do something, so there is no way you can know all the reasons your parents, friends, or enemies did something.

Suppose, for example, you go on a first date with someone who, at least during the first hour or so, turns out to be less interesting than you would have liked. Because of this initial impression, you may infer that this person is dull, always and everywhere. Yet it could be that this person is simply ill at ease or shy during first meetings. The problem here is that you run the risk of judging a person on the basis of a very short acquaintanceship. Further, if you then define this person as dull, you're likely to treat the person as dull and fulfill your own prophecy.

The parable of the six blind men and the elephant is an excellent example of an **allness** orientation—the tendency to judge the whole on the basis of experience with part of the whole—and its attendant problems. You may recall from elementary school the poem by John Saxe that concerns six learned blind men of Indostan who came to examine an elephant, an animal they had only heard about. The first blind man touched the elephant's side and concluded that an elephant was like a wall. The second felt the tusk and said an elephant must be like a spear. The third held the trunk and concluded that an elephant was much like a snake. The fourth touched the knee and decided that an elephant was like a tree. The fifth felt the ear and said an elephant was like a fan. The sixth grabbed the tail and concluded that an elephant was like a rope. Each of these learned men reached his own conclusion regarding what an elephant was really like. Each argued that he was correct and that the others were wrong.

Each, of course, was correct; at the same time, however, all were wrong. The point this parable illustrates is that you can never see all of anything; you can never experience anything fully. You see part of an object, event, or person—and on that limited basis, you conclude what the whole is like. This procedure is universal, and you follow it because you cannot possibly observe everything. Yet recognize that when making judgments of the whole based on only a part, you're actually making inferences that can later be proved wrong. If you assume that you know everything there is to know about something or someone, you fall into the pattern of misevaluation called allness.

Famed British Prime Minister Benjamin Disraeli once said that "to be conscious that you are ignorant is a great step toward knowledge." This observation is an excellent example of a nonallness attitude. If you recognize that there is more to learn, more to see, more to hear, you leave yourself open to this additional information, and you're better prepared to assimilate it.

A useful extensional device that can help you avoid allness is to end each statement, sometimes verbally but always mentally, with an "etc." (et cetera)—a reminder that there is more to learn, know, and say; that every statement is inevitably incomplete. To be sure, some people overuse the "et cetera." They use it as a substitute for being specific, which defeats its purpose. It should be used to mentally remind yourself that there is more to know and more to say.

Distinguish between Facts and Inferences: Avoid Fact–Inference Confusion

Language enables us to form statements of facts and inferences without making any linguistic distinction between the two. Similarly, when we listen to such statements, we often don't make a clear distinction between statements of facts and statements of inference. Yet there are great differences between the two. Barriers to clear thinking can be created when inferences are treated as facts—a hazard called **fact–inference confusion**.

For example, you can make statements about things that you observe, and you can make statements about things that you have not observed. In form or structure these statements are similar; they cannot be distinguished from each other by any grammatical analysis. For example, you can say, "She is wearing a blue jacket" as well as "She is harboring an illogical hatred." If you diagrammed these sentences, they would yield identical structures, and yet you know that they're different types of statements. In the first sentence, you can observe the jacket and the blue color; the sentence constitutes a *factual statement.* But how do you observe "illogical hatred"? Obviously, this is not a descriptive statement but an *inferential statement,* a statement that you make not solely on the basis of what you observe but on the basis of what you observe plus your own conclusions.

There's no problem with making inferential statements; you must make them if you're to talk about much that is meaningful. The problem arises when you act as though those inferential statements are factual statements. Consider, for example, the following anecdote (Maynard, 1963):

> A woman went for a walk one day and met her friend, whom she had not seen, heard from, or heard of in ten years. After an exchange of greetings, the woman said, "Is this your little boy?" and her friend replied, "Yes. I got married about six years ago." The woman then asked the child, "What is your name?" and the little boy replied, "Same as my father's." "Oh," said the woman, "then it must be Peter."

The question, of course, is how did the woman know the boy's father's name? The answer is obvious, but only after you recognize that in reading this short passage you have, quite unconsciously, made an inference that is preventing you from arriving at the answer. You have inferred that the woman's friend is a woman. Actually, the friend is a man named Peter.

You may wish to test your ability to distinguish facts from inferences by taking the accompanying self-test, "Can You Distinguish Facts from Inferences?"

Test Yourself Can You Distinguish Facts from Inferences?

Carefully read the following account, modeled on a report developed by William Haney (1973), and the observations based on it. Indicate whether you think the observations are true, false, or doubtful on the basis of the information presented in the report. Circle T if the observation is definitely true, F if the observation is definitely false, and ? if the observation may be either true or false. Judge each observation in order. Don't reread the observations after you have indicated your judgment, and don't change any of your answers.

> A well-liked college teacher had just completed making up the final examinations and had turned off the lights in the office. Just then a tall, broad figure appeared and demanded the examination. The professor opened the drawer. Everything in the drawer was picked up and the individual ran down the corridor. The dean was notified immediately.

T F ? 1. The thief was tall and broad.
T F ? 2. The professor turned off the lights.

T F ? 3. A tall figure demanded the examination.

T F ? 4. The examination was picked up by someone.

T F ? 5. The examination was picked up by the professor.

T F ? 6. A tall figure appeared after the professor turned off the lights in the office.

T F ? 7. The man who opened the drawer was the professor.

T F ? 8. The professor ran down the corridor.

T F ? 9. The drawer was never actually opened.

T F ? 10. Three persons are referred to in this report.

How Did You Do? After you answer all 10 questions, form small groups of five or six and discuss the answers. Look at each statement from each member's point of view. For each statement, ask yourself, "How can you be absolutely certain that the statement is true or false?" You should find that only one statement can be clearly identified as true and only one as false; eight should be marked "?".

What Will You Do? This test is designed to trap you into making inferences and treating them as facts. Statement 3 is true (it's in the report); statement 9 is false (the drawer was opened); but all other statements are inferences and should have been marked "?". Review the remaining eight statements to see why you cannot be certain that any of them are either true or false.

As you continue reading this chapter, try to formulate specific guidelines that will help you distinguish facts from inferences as a speaker and as a listener.

Natalia Bratslavsky/Shutterstock

VIEWPOINTS Informal time terms (e.g., *soon, right away, early, in a while, as soon as possible*) seem to create communication problems because they're ambiguous; different people will often give the terms different meanings. How might you go about reducing or eliminating the ambiguity created by these terms?

Some of the essential differences between factual and inferential statements are summarized in Table 2. Distinguishing between these two types of statements does not imply that one type is better than the other. Both types of statements are useful; both are important. The problem arises when you treat an inferential statement as if it were fact. Phrase your inferential statements as tentative. Recognize that such statements may be wrong. Leave open the possibility of other alternatives.

Discriminate Among: Avoid Indiscrimination

Nature seems to abhor sameness at least as much as vacuums, for nowhere in the universe can you find identical entities. Everything is unique. Language, however, provides common nouns—such as *teacher, student, friend, enemy, war, politician, liberal,* and the like—that may lead you to focus on similarities. Such nouns can lead you to group together all teachers, all students, and all friends and perhaps divert attention from the uniqueness of each individual, object, and event.

The misevaluation known as **indiscrimination**—a form of stereotyping—occurs when you focus on classes of individuals, objects, or events and fail to see that each is unique and needs to be looked at individually. Indiscrimination can be seen in such statements as these:

- He's just like the rest of them: lazy, stupid, a real slob.
- I really don't want another ethnic on the board of directors. One is enough for me.
- Read a romance novel? I read one when I was 16. That was enough to convince me.

TABLE 2 Differences between Factual and Inferential Statements

These differences highlight the important distinctions between factual and inferential statements and are based on the discussions of William Haney (1973) and Harry Weinberg (1959). As you go through this table, consider how you would classify such statements as: "God exists," "Democracy is the best form of government," "This paper is white," "The Internet will grow in size and importance over the next 10 years," and "This table is based on Haney and Weinberg."

Inferential Statements	Factual Statements
May be made at any time	May be made only after observation
Go beyond what has been observed	Are limited to what has been observed
May be made by anyone	May be made only by the observer
May be about any time—past, present, or future	May be about only the past or the present
Involve varying degrees of probability	Approach certainty
Are not subject to verifiable standards	Are subject to verifiable, scientific standards

A useful antidote to indiscrimination is the extensional device called the *index*, a mental subscript that identifies each individual in a group as an individual, even though all members of the group may be covered by the same label. For example, when you think and talk of an individual politician as just a "politician," you may fail to see the uniqueness in this politician and the differences between this particular politician and other politicians. However, when you think with the index—when you think not of politician but of politician 1 or politician 2 or politician 3—you're less likely to fall into the trap of indiscrimination and more likely to focus on the differences among politicians. The same is true with members of cultural, national, or religious groups; when you think of Iraqi 1 and Iraqi 2, you'll be reminded that not all Iraqis are the same. The more you discriminate among individuals covered by the same label, the less likely you are to discriminate against any group.

Talk about the Middle: Avoid Polarization

Polarization, often referred to as the fallacy of "either/or," is the tendency to look at the world and to describe it in terms of extremes—good or bad, positive or negative, healthy or sick, brilliant or stupid, rich or poor, and so on. Polarized statements come in many forms; for example:

- After listening to the evidence, I'm still not clear who the good guys are and who the bad guys are.
- Well, are you for us or against us?
- College had better get me a good job. Otherwise, this has been a big waste of time.

Most people exist somewhere between the extremes of good and bad, healthy and sick, brilliant and stupid, rich and poor. Yet there seems to be a strong tendency to view only the extremes and to categorize people, objects, and events in terms of these polar opposites.

You can easily demonstrate this tendency by filling in the opposites for each of the following words:

							Opposite
tall	___:___:___:___:___:___:___						_____
heavy	___:___:___:___:___:___:___						_____
strong	___:___:___:___:___:___:___						_____
happy	___:___:___:___:___:___:___						_____
legal	___:___:___:___:___:___:___						_____

Filling in the opposites should have been relatively easy and quick. The words should also have been fairly short. Further, if various different people supplied the opposites, there would be a high degree of agreement among them. Now try to fill in the middle positions with words meaning, for example, "midway between tall and short," "midway between heavy and light," and so on. Do this before reading any farther.

These midway responses (compared to the opposites) were probably more difficult to think of and took you more time. The responses should also have been long words or phrases of several words. Further, different people would probably agree less on these midway responses than on the opposites.

This exercise clearly illustrates the ease with which we can think and talk in opposites and the difficulty we have in thinking and talking about the middle. But recognize that the vast majority of cases exist between extremes. Don't allow the ready availability of extreme terms to obscure the reality of what lies in between (Read, 2004).

In some cases, of course, it's legitimate to talk in terms of two values. For example, either this thing you're holding is a book or it isn't. Clearly, the classes "book" and "not-book" include all possibilities. There is no problem with this kind of statement. Similarly, you may say that a student either will pass this course or will not, as these two categories include all the possibilities.

You create problems, however, when you use this either/or form in situations in which it's inappropriate; for example, "The supervisor is either for us or against us." The two choices simply don't include all possibilities: The supervisor may be for us in some things and against us in others, or he or she may be neutral. Right now there is a tendency to group people into pro- and antiwar, for example—and into similar pro- and anti- categories on abortion, taxes, and just about every important political or social issue. Similarly, you see examples of polarization in opinions about the Middle East, with some people entirely and totally supportive of one side and others entirely and totally supportive of the other side. But clearly these extremes do not include all possibilities, and polarized thinking actually prevents us from entertaining the vast middle ground that exists on all such issues.

Update Messages: Avoid Static Evaluation

Language changes very slowly, especially when compared to the rapid pace at which people and things change. When you retain an evaluation of a person, despite the inevitable changes in the person, you're engaging in **static evaluation**.

Alfred Korzybski (1933) used an interesting illustration in this connection: In a tank there is a large fish and many small fish that are its natural food source. Given freedom in the tank, the large fish will eat the small fish. After some time, the tank is partitioned, with the large fish on one side and the small fish on the other, divided only by glass. For a time, the large fish will try to eat the small fish but will fail; each time it tries, it will knock into the glass partition. After some time it will learn that trying to eat the small fish means difficulty, and it will no longer go after them. Now, however, the partition is removed, and the small fish swim all around the big fish. But the big fish does not eat them and in fact will die of starvation while its natural food swims all around. The large fish has learned a pattern of behavior, and even though the actual territory has changed, the map remains static.

While you would probably agree that everything is in a constant state of flux, the relevant question is whether you act as if you know this. Do you act in accordance with the notion of change, instead of just accepting it intellectually? Do you treat your little sister as if she were 10 years old, or do you treat her like the 20-year-old woman she has become? Your evaluations of yourself and others need to keep pace with the rapidly changing real world. Otherwise you'll be left with attitudes and beliefs—static evaluations—about a world that no longer exists.

To guard against static evaluation, use an extensional device called the date: Mentally date your statements and especially your evaluations. Remember that Gerry Smith$_{2006}$ is not Gerry Smith$_{2013}$; academic abilities$_{2006}$ are not academic abilities$_{2013}$. T. S. Eliot, in *The Cocktail Party,* said that "what we know of other people is only our memory of the moments during which we knew them. And they have changed since then . . . at every meeting we are meeting a stranger."

These six guidelines, which are summarized in Table 3, will not solve all problems in verbal communication—but they will help you to more accurately align your language with the real world, the world of words and not words; infinite complexity; facts and inferences; sameness and difference; extremes and middle ground; and, perhaps most important, constant change.

Also, recognize that each of these six guidelines contains a warning against verbal messages that can be used to deceive you. For example, when people try to influence you to respond to people in terms of their labels (often racist, sexist, or homophobic), they are using intensional orientation unethically. Similarly, when people present themselves as knowing everything about something (gossip is often a good example), they are using your natural tendency to think in allness terms to achieve their own ends, not to present the truth. When people present inferences as if they are facts (again, gossip provides a good example) to secure your belief, or when they stereotype, they are relying on your tendency to confuse facts and inferences and to fail to discriminate. And when people talk in terms of opposites (polarize) or as if things and people don't change (static evaluation) in order to influence you to believe certain things or to do certain things, they are again assuming you won't talk about the middle or ask for updated messages.

TABLE 3 Essential Verbal Message Guidelines

Here is a brief summary of the guidelines for using verbal messages. As you review these principles, try recalling examples and the consequences of the failure to follow these principles from your own recent interactions.

Effective	Ineffective
Extensionalize; distinguish between the way people and things are talked about and what exists in reality; the word is not the thing.	**Intensionalize;** treat words and things as the same; respond to things as they are talked about rather than as they exist.
Avoid allness; no one can know or say all about anything; always assume there is more to be said, more to learn.	**Commit allness;** assume you know everything that needs to be known or that all that can be said has been said.
Distinguish between facts and inferences and respond to them differently.	**Confuse facts and inferences;** respond to inferences as if they were facts.
Discriminate among items covered by the same label.	**Indiscriminately treat** all items (people, things, and events) covered by the same label similarly.
Talk about the middle, where the vast majority of cases exist.	**Polarize;** view and talk about only the extremes; ignore the middle.
Recognize change; update messages.	**Statically evaluate;** fail to recognize the inevitable change in things and people.

Summary

 Use your smartphone or tablet device (or log on to mycommunicationlab.com) to hear an audio summary of this chapter.

This chapter introduced the verbal message system and identified some basic principles concerning how the verbal message system works and how it can be used more effectively.

Principles of Verbal Messages

1. Messages are packaged; verbal and nonverbal signals interact to produce one (ideally) unified message. Six major ways nonverbal messages can interact with verbal messages are to: (1) accent, or emphasize a verbal message; (2) complement, or add nuances of meaning; (3) contradict, or deny the verbal message; (4) control, or manage the flow of communication; (5) repeat, or restate the message; and (6) substitute, or take the place of a verbal message.

2. Message meanings are in people—in people's thoughts and feelings, not just in their words.

3. Messages are both denotative and connotative. Denotation is the dictionary-like meaning of a word or sentence. Connotation is the personal meaning of a word or sentence. Denotative meaning is relatively objective; connotative meaning is highly subjective.

4. Messages vary in abstraction; they vary from very specific and concrete to highly abstract and general.

5. Messages vary in politeness—from rude to extremely polite—and may be viewed in terms of maintaining positive and negative face. Variations in what is considered polite among cultures are often great.

6. Messages can deceive; some messages are lies.

7. Messages can criticize and praise. Criticism that is overly negative or not constructive will normally be resented, while praise that is unrealistic or unspecific may be dismissed.

8. Messages vary in assertiveness. Standing up for one's own rights without infringing on the rights of others is the goal of most assertive communication.

9. Messages can confirm and disconfirm. Disconfirmation is communication that ignores another, that denies the other person's definition of self. Confirmation expresses acknowledgment and acceptance of others and avoids racist, heterosexist, ageist, and sexist expressions that are disconfirming.

10. Messages vary in cultural sensitivity.

Guidelines for Using Verbal Messages Effectively

11. Extensionalize; the word is not the thing. Avoid intensional orientation, the tendency to view the world in the way it's talked about or labeled. Instead, respond to things first; look for the labels second.

12. See the individual; avoid allness, our tendency to describe the world in extreme terms that imply we know all or are saying all there is to say. To combat allness, remind yourself that you can never know all or say all about anything; use a mental and sometimes verbal "etc."

13. Distinguish between facts and inferences, and act differently depending on whether the message is factual or inferential.

14. Discriminate among. Avoid indiscrimination, the tendency to group unique individuals or items because they're covered by the same term or label. To combat indiscrimination, recognize uniqueness, and mentally index each individual in a group ($teacher_1$, $teacher_2$).

15. Talk with middle terms; avoid polarization, the tendency to describe the world in terms of extremes or polar opposites. To combat polarization use middle terms and qualifiers.

16. Update messages regularly; nothing is static. Avoid static evaluation, the tendency to describe the world in static terms, denying constant change. To combat static evaluation, recognize the inevitability of change; date statements and evaluations, realizing, for example, that $Gerry Smith_{2006}$ is not $Gerry Smith_{2013}$.

Key Terms

ableism	cultural identifiers,	lie bias	rejection
abstraction	denotation	lying	sexist language
ageism	disconfirmation	metacommunication	static evaluation
ageist language	extensional orientation	negative face	truth bias
allness	fact–inference confusion	polarization	verbal messages
assertiveness	heterosexist language	politeness	
confirmation	indiscrimination	positive face	
connotation	intensional orientation	racist language	

MyCommunicationLab Explorations

MyCommunicationLab®

Communication Choice Points

Revisit the chapter-opening video, "We Have Work To Do." Recall that Zach and Katie are co-workers at the same small office. Zach is becoming increasingly annoyed with Katie's over-friendliness, but does not want to alienate her. However, his work is beginning to suffer. Zach has two objectives: getting his work done and maintaining a cordial relationship with Katie. "We Have Work To Do" looks at verbal messages and at the choices available for communicating a desired message.

Log on to mycommunicationlab.com to view the video for this chapter, "We Have Work to Do," and then answer the related discussion questions.

Additional Resources

This group of experiences will help clarify the interaction and basic principles of verbal messages.

1 Integrating Verbal and Nonverbal Messages explores some of the connections between verbal and nonverbal messages. **2** Climbing the Abstraction Ladder and **3** Using the Abstraction Ladder as a Creative Thinking Tool will clarify the abstraction process and explain a useful creative thinking technique. **4** How Can You Vary Directness for Greatest Effectiveness? provides practice in varying directness. **5** How Can You Rephrase Clichés? provides an opportunity to replace trite expressions with more creative and meaningful phrases. **6** Who? is a class game/experience that asks you to identify characteristics of other people on the basis of their various verbal and nonverbal messages. This exercise can be used as an introduction to the messages section or as a conclusion. **7** Analyzing Assertiveness provides practice scenarios calling for assertiveness. **8** Identifying the Barriers to Communication provides a dialogue demonstrating the various barriers discussed in this chapter. **9** How Do You Talk? as a Woman? as a Man? and **10** Recognizing Gender Differences looks at gender differences in language and at our perceptions of the speech of others. **11** Thinking with E-Prime focuses on the difficulties that can be created when you use and think with the verb "to be." **12** How Do You Talk about the Middle? illustrates the ways in which our language makes it easy to polarize. **13** Confirming, Rejecting, and Disconfirming looks at specific examples of these types of messages. **14** "Must Lie" Situations examines scenarios in which many people would consider it ethical, even necessary, to lie.

Nonverbal Messages

Nonverbal Messages

Principles of Nonverbal Communication

Channels of Nonverbal Communication

Nonverbal Communication Competence

Pearson Education

2:13 / 5:00

Kendra is sitting alone, working on her laptop. A friend, Lori, comes into the room and Kendra lets Lori know that she'd rather be left alone; but later on, she welcomes the interruption. Watch the video "Inviting or Discouraging Conversation" (www.mycommunicationlab .com) to see how, in both cases, body language, eye contact, and other nonverbal cues communicate the message.

Because you'll learn about:

- the nature of nonverbal communication.
- the ways nonverbal messages are sent and received.
- cultural differences in nonverbal communication.

Because you'll learn to:

- send and receive nonverbal messages more effectively.
- use nonverbal messages with effectiveness and with sensitivity to cultural and gender issues.

Nonverbal communication is communication without words. You communicate non-verbally when you gesture, smile or frown, widen your eyes, move your chair closer to someone, wear jewelry, touch someone, raise your vocal volume, or even when you say nothing. The crucial aspect of nonverbal communication is that the message you send is in some way received by one or more other people. If you gesture while alone in your room and no one is there to see you, then, most theorists would argue, communication has not taken place. The same, of course, is true of verbal messages: If you recite a speech and no one hears it, then communication has not taken place.

Your ability to use nonverbal communication effectively can yield two major benefits (Burgoon & Hoobler, 2002). First, the greater your ability to send and receive nonverbal signals, the higher your attraction, popularity, and psychosocial well-being are likely to be. Second, the greater your nonverbal skills, the more successful you're likely to be in a wide variety of interpersonal communication situations, including close relationships, organizational communication, teacher-student communication, intercultural communication, courtroom communication, in politics, and in health care (Richmond, McCroskey, & Hickson, 2012; Riggio & Feldman, 2005).

Principles of Nonverbal Communication

Perhaps the best way to begin the study of nonverbal communication is to examine several principles that, as you'll see, also identify the varied functions that nonverbal messages serve (Afifi, 2007; Burgoon & Bacue, 2003; Burgoon & Hoobler, 2002).

Nonverbal Messages Interact with Verbal Messages

Verbal and nonverbal messages interact with each other in six major ways: to accent, to complement, to contradict, to control, to repeat, and to substitute for each other.

- **Accent.** Nonverbal communication is often used to accent or emphasize some part of the verbal message. You might, for example, raise your voice to underscore a particular word or phrase, bang your fist on the desk to stress your commitment, or look longingly into someone's eyes when saying, "I love you."
- **Complement.** Nonverbal communication may be used to complement, to add nuances of meaning not communicated by your verbal message. Thus, you might smile when telling a story (to suggest that you find it humorous) or frown and shake your head when recounting someone's deceit (to suggest your disapproval).
- **Contradict.** You may deliberately contradict your verbal messages with nonverbal movements; for example, by crossing your fingers or winking to indicate that you're lying.

- **Control.** Nonverbal movements may be used to control, or to indicate your desire to control, the flow of verbal messages, as when you purse your lips, lean forward, or make hand movements to indicate that you want to speak. You might also put up your hand or vocalize your pauses (for example, with "um") to indicate that you have not finished and aren't ready to relinquish the floor to the next speaker.
- **Repeat.** You can repeat or restate the verbal message nonverbally. You can, for example, follow your verbal "Is that all right?" with raised eyebrows and a questioning look, or you can motion with your head or hand to repeat your verbal "Let's go."
- **Substitute.** You may also use nonverbal communication to substitute for verbal messages. You can, for example, signal "OK" with a hand gesture. You can nod your head to indicate yes or shake your head to indicate no.

When you communicate electronically, of course, your message is communicated by means of typed letters without facial expressions or gestures that normally accompany face-to-face communication and without the changes in rate and volume that are a part of normal telephone communication. To compensate for this lack of nonverbal behavior, the emoticon was created. Sometimes called a "smiley" after the ever-present :), the emoticon is a typed symbol that communicates through a keyboard the nuances of the message normally conveyed by nonverbal expression. The absence of the nonverbal channel through which you can clarify your message—for example, smiling or winking to communicate sarcasm or humor—make such typed symbols extremely helpful. Here are some of the more popular emoticons used in computer talk (two excellent websites contain extensive examples of smileys, emoticons, acronyms, and shorthand abbreviations: www.netlingo.com/smiley.cfm and www.netlingo.com/emailsh.cfm):

:-)	= smile; I'm only kidding
:-(	= frown; I'm feeling sad; this saddens me
*	= kiss
:-	= male
>-	= female
{}	= hug
{{{***}}}	= hugs and kisses
;-)	= sly smile
this is important	= underlining, adds emphasis
this is important	= asterisks, adds emphasis
ALL CAPS	= shouting, emphasizing
<G> or <grin>	= grin

Not surprisingly, these symbols aren't used universally (Pollack, 1996). For example, because it's considered impolite for a Japanese woman to show her teeth when she smiles, the Japanese emoticon for a woman's smile is (ˆ . ˆ), where the dot signifies a closed mouth. A man's smile is written (ˆ _ ˆ). Other emoticons popular in Japan but not used in Europe or the United States are (ˆ ˆ;) for "cold sweat," (ˆ o ˆ; Ò) for "excuse me," and (ˆ o ˆ) for "happy."

Nonverbal Messages Help Manage Impressions

It is largely through the nonverbal communications of others that you form impressions of them. Based on a person's body size, skin color, and dress, as well as on the way the person smiles, maintains eye contact, and expresses himself or herself facially, you form impressions—you judge who the person is and what the person is like.

And, at the same time that you form impressions of others, you are also managing the impressions they form of you. You use different strategies to achieve different impressions, and of course many of these strategies involve nonverbal messages. For example:

- **To be liked** you might smile, pat another on the back, and shake hands warmly. See Table 1 for some additional ways in which nonverbal communication may make you seem more attractive and more likeable.

- **To be believed** you might use focused eye contact, a firm stance, and open gestures.
- **To excuse failure** you might look sad, cover your face with your hands, and shake your head.
- **To secure help** by indicating helplessness, you might use open hand gestures, a puzzled look, and inept movements.
- **To hide faults** you might avoid self-adaptors.
- **To be followed** you might dress the part of a leader or display your diploma or awards where others can see them.
- **To confirm self-image and to communicate it to others**, you might dress in certain ways or decorate your apartment with things that reflect your personality.

Nonverbal Messages Help Form Relationships

Much of your relationship life is lived nonverbally. You communicate affection, support, and love, in part at least, nonverbally (Floyd & Mikkelson, 2005). At the same time, you also communicate displeasure, anger, and animosity through nonverbal signals.

TABLE 1 **Ten Nonverbal Messages and Attractiveness**

Here are 10 nonverbal messages that can help communicate your attractiveness and 10 that will likely create the opposite effect (Andersen, 2004; Riggio & Feldman, 2005).

Attractive	Unattractive
Gesture to show liveliness and animation in ways that are appropriate to the situation and to the message.	Gesture for the sake of gesturing or gesture in ways that may prove offensive to members of other cultures.
Nod and lean forward to signal that you're listening and are interested.	Go on automatic pilot, nodding without any connection to what is said, or lean so far forward that you intrude on the other's space.
Smile and facially show your interest, attention, and positivity.	Overdo it; inappropriate smiling is likely to be perceived negatively.
Make eye contact in moderation.	Stare, ogle, glare, or otherwise make the person feel that he or she is under scrutiny.
Touch in moderation when appropriate. When in doubt, avoid touching another.	Touch excessively or too intimately.
Use vocal variation in rate, rhythm, pitch, and volume to communicate your animation and involvement in what you're saying.	Fall into a pattern in which, for example, your voice goes up and down without any relationship to what you're saying.
Use appropriate facial reactions, posture, and back-channeling cues to show that you're listening.	Listen motionlessly or in ways that suggest you're listening only halfheartedly.
Stand reasonably close to show connectedness.	Invade the other person's comfort zone.
Present a pleasant smell—and be careful to camouflage the onions, garlic, or smoke that you're so used to you can't smell.	Overdo the cologne or perfume.
Dress appropriately to the situation.	Wear clothing that's uncomfortable or that calls attention to itself.

For additional reasons why identifying lying is so difficult, see "Deception Detection" at tcbdevito .blogspot.com. Based on your own deception detection experiences, do you agree/disagree with what is said here?

You also use nonverbal signals to communicate the nature of your relationship to another person; and you and that person communicate nonverbally with each other. These signals that communicate your relationship status are known as "tie signs": They indicate the ways in which your relationship is tied together (Afifi & Johnson, 2005; Goffman, 1967; Knapp & Hall, 2009). Tie signs are also used to confirm the level of the relationship; for example, you might hold hands to see if this is responded to positively. And of course tie signs are often used to let others know that the two of you are tied together.

Tie signs vary in intimacy and may extend from the relatively informal handshake through more intimate forms—such as hand holding and arm linking—to very intimate contact—such as full mouth kissing (Andersen, 2004).

You also use nonverbal signals to communicate your relationship dominance and status (Dunbar & Burgoon, 2005; Knapp & Hall, 2009). The large corner office with the huge desk communicates high status, just as the basement cubicle communicates low status.

Nonverbal Messages Structure Conversation

When you're in conversation, you give and receive cues—signals that you're ready to speak, to listen, to comment on what the speaker just said. These cues regulate and structure the interaction. These turn-taking cues may be verbal (as when you say, "What do you think?" and thereby give the speaking turn over to the listener). Most often, however, they're nonverbal; a nod of the head in the direction of someone else, for example, signals that you're ready to give up your speaking turn and want this other person to say something. You also show that you're listening and that you want the conversation to continue (or that you're not listening and want the conversation to end) largely through nonverbal signals of posture and eye contact (or the lack thereof).

Nonverbal Messages Can Influence and Deceive

You can influence others not only through what you say but also through your nonverbal signals. A focused glance that says you're committed; gestures that further explain what you're saying; appropriate dress that says, "I'll easily fit in with this organization"—these are just a few examples of ways in which you can exert nonverbal influence.

And with the ability to influence, of course, comes the ability to deceive—to mislead another person into thinking something is true when it's false or that something is false when it's true. One common example of nonverbal deception is using your eyes and facial expressions to communicate a liking for other people when you're really interested only in gaining their support in some endeavor. Not surprisingly, you also use nonverbal signals to detect deception in others. For example, you may well suspect a person of lying if he or she avoids eye contact, fidgets, and conveys inconsistent verbal and nonverbal messages.

But be careful, research shows that it is much more difficult to tell when someone is lying than you probably think it is. So, use caution in judging deception (Knapp, 2008).

Nonverbal Messages Are Crucial for Expressing Emotions

Although people often explain and reveal emotions verbally, nonverbal signals communicate a great part of your emotional experience. For example, you reveal your level of happiness or sadness or confusion largely through facial expressions. Of course, you also reveal your feelings by posture (for example, whether tense or relaxed), gestures, eye movements, and even the dilation of your pupils. Nonverbal messages often help people communicate unpleasant messages that they might feel uncomfortable putting into words (Infante, Rancer, & Womack, 2003). For example, you might avoid eye contact and maintain large distances between yourself and someone with whom you didn't want to interact or with whom you wanted to decrease the intensity of your relationship.

At the same time, you also use nonverbal messages to hide your emotions. You might, for example, smile even though you feel sad so as not to dampen the party spirit. Or you might laugh at someone's joke even though you think it silly.

Channels of Nonverbal Communication

Nonverbal communication involves a variety of channels. Here we look at: (1) body gestures, (2) body appearance, (3) facial communication, (4) eye communication, (5) touch communication, (6) paralanguage and silence, (7) spatial messages, (8) artifactual communication, and (9) temporal communication. As you'll see nonverbal messages are heavily influenced by culture (Matsumoto, 2006; Matsumoto Yoo, 2005; Matsumoto, Yoo, Hirayama, & Petrova, 2005).

Body Gestures

An especially useful classification in **kinesics**—or the study of communication through body movement—identifies five types: emblems, illustrators, affect displays, regulators, and adaptors (Ekman & Friesen, 1969). Table 2 summarizes and provides examples of these five types of movements.

Emblems   **Emblems** are substitutes for words; they're body movements that have rather specific verbal translations, such as the nonverbal signs for "OK," "Peace," "Come here," "Go away," "Who, me?" "Be quiet," "I'm warning you," "I'm tired," and "It's cold." Emblems are as arbitrary as any words in any language. Consequently, your present culture's emblems are not necessarily the same as your culture's emblems of 300 years ago or the same as the emblems of other cultures. For example, the sign made by forming a circle with the thumb and index finger may mean "nothing" or "zero" in France, "money" in Japan, and something sexual in certain southern European cultures.

Illustrators   **Illustrators** accompany and literally illustrate verbal messages. Illustrators make your communications more vivid and help to maintain your listener's attention.

INTERPERSONAL CHOICE POINT

Inviting and Discouraging Conversation

Sometimes you want to encourage people to come into your office and chat, and at other times you want to be left alone. What are some of your options for achieving each goal nonverbally?

TABLE 2	Five Types of Body Movements

Can you identify similar gestures that mean different things in different cultures and that might create interpersonal misunderstandings?

Movement and Function	Examples
Emblems directly translate words or phrases.	"OK" sign, "Come here" wave, hitchhiker's sign
Illustrators accompany and literally "illustrate" verbal messages.	Circular hand movements when talking of a circle, hands far apart when talking of something large
Affect displays communicate emotional meaning.	Expressions of happiness, surprise, fear, anger, sadness, disgust
Regulators monitor, maintain, or control the speaking of another.	Facial expressions and hand gestures indicating "Keep going," "Slow down," or "What else happened?"
Adaptors satisfy some need.	Scratching head, chewing on pencil, adjusting glasses

They also help to clarify and intensify your verbal messages. In saying, "Let's go up," for example, you probably move your head and perhaps your finger in an upward direction. In describing a circle or a square, you more than likely make circular or square movements with your hands. Research points to another advantage of illustrators: that they increase your ability to remember. People who illustrated their verbal messages with gestures remembered some 20 percent more than those who didn't gesture (Goldin-Meadow, Nusbaum, Kelly, & Wagner, 2001).

We are aware of illustrators only part of the time; at times, they may have to be brought to our attention. Illustrators are more universal than emblems; illustrators will be recognized and understood by members of more different cultures than will emblems.

Affect Displays   **Affect displays** are the movements of the face that convey emotional meaning—the expressions that show anger and fear, happiness and surprise, eagerness and fatigue. They're the facial expressions that give you away when you try to present a false image and that lead people to say, "You look angry. What's wrong?" We can, however, consciously control affect displays, as actors do when they play a role. Affect displays may be unintentional (as when they give you away) or intentional (as when you want to show anger, love, or surprise). A particular kind of affect display is the poker player's "tell," a bit of nonverbal behavior that communicates bluffing; it's a nonverbal cue that tells others that a player is lying. In much the same way that you may want to conceal certain feelings from friends or relatives, the poker player tries to conceal any such tells.

Regulators   **Regulators** monitor, maintain, or control the speaking of another individual. When you listen to another, you're not passive; you nod your head, purse your lips, adjust your eye focus, and make various paralinguistic sounds such as "mm-mm" or "tsk." Regulators are culture-bound: Each culture develops its own rules for the regulation of conversation. Regulators also include such broad movements as shaking your head to show disbelief or leaning forward in your chair to show that you want to hear more.

Regulators communicate what you expect or want speakers to do as they're talking; for example, "Keep going," "Tell me what else happened," "I don't believe that. Are you sure?" "Speed up," and "Slow down." Speakers often receive these nonverbal signals without being consciously aware of them. Depending on their degree of sensitivity, speakers modify their speaking behavior in accordance with these regulators.

Adaptors   **Adaptors** satisfy some need and usually occur without conscious awareness; they're unintentional movements that usually go unnoticed. Nonverbal researchers identify three types of adaptors based on their focus, direction, or target: self-adaptors, alter-adaptors, and object-adaptors (Burgoon, Buller, & Woodall, 1996).

- **Self-adaptors** usually satisfy a physical need, generally serving to make you more comfortable; examples include scratching your head to relieve an itch, moistening your lips because they feel dry, or pushing your hair out of your eyes. When these adaptors occur in private, they occur in their entirety: You scratch until the itch is gone. But in public these adaptors usually occur in abbreviated form. When people are watching you, for example, you might put your fingers to your head and move them around a bit but probably not scratch with the same vigor as when in private.
- **Alter-adaptors** are the body movements you make in response to your current interactions. Examples include crossing your arms over your chest when someone unpleasant approaches or moving closer to someone you like.
- **Object-adaptors** are movements that involve your manipulation of some object. Frequently observed examples include punching holes in or drawing on a styrofoam coffee cup, clicking a ballpoint pen, or chewing on a pencil. Object-adaptors are usually signs of negative feelings; for example, you emit more adaptors when feeling hostile than when feeling friendly. Further, as anxiety and uneasiness increase, so does the frequency of object-adaptors (Burgoon, Guerrero, & Floyd, 2010).

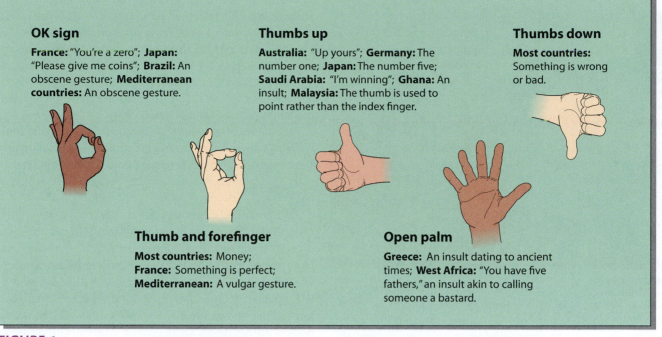

OK sign

France: "You're a zero"; **Japan:** "Please give me coins"; **Brazil:** An obscene gesture; **Mediterranean countries:** An obscene gesture.

Thumbs up

Australia: "Up yours"; **Germany:** The number one; **Japan:** The number five; **Saudi Arabia:** "I'm winning"; **Ghana:** An insult; **Malaysia:** The thumb is used to point rather than the index finger.

Thumbs down

Most countries: Something is wrong or bad.

Thumb and forefinger

Most countries: Money; **France:** Something is perfect; **Mediterranean:** A vulgar gesture.

Open palm

Greece: An insult dating to ancient times; **West Africa:** "You have five fathers," an insult akin to calling someone a bastard.

FIGURE 1
Some Cultural Meanings of Gestures

Cultural differences in the meanings of nonverbal gestures are often significant. The over-the-head clasped hands that signify victory to an American may signify friendship to a Russian. To an American, holding up two fingers to make a V signifies victory or peace. To certain South Americans, however, it is an obscene gesture that corresponds to the American's extended middle finger. This figure highlights some additional nonverbal differences. Can you identify others?

Gestures and Cultures   There is much variation in gestures and their meanings among different cultures (Axtell, 2007). Consider a few common gestures that you may often use without thinking, but that could easily get you into trouble if you used them in another culture (also, take a look at Figure 1):

- Folding your arms over your chest would be considered defiant and disrespectful in Fiji.
- Waving your hand would be insulting in Nigeria and Greece.
- Gesturing with the thumb up would be rude in Australia.
- Tapping your two index fingers together would be considered an invitation to sleep together in Egypt.
- Pointing with your index finger would be impolite in many Middle Eastern countries.
- Bowing to a lesser degree than your host would be considered a statement of your superiority in Japan.
- Inserting your thumb between your index and middle finger in a clenched fist would be viewed as a wish that evil fall on the person in some African countries.
- Resting your feet on a table or chair would be insulting and disrespectful in some Middle Eastern cultures.

Body Appearance

Of course, the body communicates even without movement. For example, others may form impressions of you from your general body build; from your height and weight; and from your skin, eye, and hair color. Assessments of your power, attractiveness, and suitability as a friend or romantic partner are often made on the basis of your body appearance (Sheppard & Strathman, 1989).

Height, for example, is significant in a wide variety of situations. Tall presidential candidates have a much better record of winning elections than do their shorter opponents. Tall people seem to be paid more and are favored by interviewers over shorter applicants (Guerrero & Hecht, 2008; Jackson & Ervin, 1992; Keyes, 1980; Knapp & Hall, 2009). Taller people also have higher self-esteem and greater career success than do shorter people (Judge & Cable, 2004).

Your body reveals your race, through skin color and tone, and also may give clues as to your more specific nationality. Your weight in proportion to your height will communicate messages to others, as will the length, color, and style of your hair.

Your general attractiveness also is a part of body communication. Attractive people have the advantage in just about every activity you can name. They get better grades in school, are more valued as friends and lovers, and are preferred as co-workers (Burgoon, Guerrero, & Floyd, 2010). Although we normally think that attractiveness is culturally determined—and to some degree it is—research seems to indicate that definitions of attractiveness are becoming universal (Brody, 1994). That is, a person rated as attractive in one culture is likely to be rated as attractive in other cultures—even in cultures whose people are widely different in appearance.

Facial Communication

Throughout your interpersonal interactions, your face communicates—especially signaling your emotions. In fact, facial movements alone seem to communicate the degree of pleasantness, agreement, and sympathy a person feels; the rest of the body doesn't provide any additional information. For other aspects, however—for example, the intensity with which an emotion is felt—both facial and bodily cues are used (Graham & Argyle, 1975; Graham, Bitti, & Argyle, 1975).

Some nonverbal communication researchers claim that facial movements may communicate at least the following eight emotions: happiness, surprise, fear, anger, sadness, disgust, contempt, and interest (Ekman, Friesen, & Ellsworth, 1972). Others propose that, in addition, facial movements may communicate bewilderment and determination (Leathers & Eaves, 2008).

Of course, some emotions are easier to communicate and to decode than others. For example, in one study, happiness was judged with an accuracy ranging from 55 percent to 100 percent, surprise from 38 percent to 86 percent, and sadness from 19 percent to 88 percent (Ekman, Friesen, & Ellsworth, 1972). Research finds that women and girls are more accurate judges of facial emotional expression than men and boys (Argyle, 1988; Hall, 1984).

As you've probably experienced, you may interpret the same facial expression differently depending on the context in which it occurs. For example, in a classic study, when a smiling face was presented looking at a glum face, the smiling face was judged to be vicious and taunting. But when the same smiling face was presented looking at a frowning face, it was judged peaceful and friendly (Cline, 1956). In general, not surprisingly, people who smile are judged to be more likable and more approachable than people who don't smile or people who pretend to smile (Gladstone & Parker, 2002; Kluger, 2005; Woodzicka & LaFrance, 2005). And women perceive men who are smiled at by other women as being more attractive than men who are not smiled at. But men—perhaps being more competitive—perceive men whom women smile at as being less attractive than men who are not smiled at (Jones, DeBruine, Little, Burriss, & Feinberg, 2007).

Facial Management   As you learned the nonverbal system of communication, you also learned certain facial management techniques that enable you to communicate your feelings to achieve the effect you want—for example, to hide certain emotions and to emphasize others. Consider your own use of such facial management techniques. As you do so, think about the types of interpersonal situations in which you would use each of these facial management techniques (Malandro, Barker, & Barker, 1989; Metts & Planalp, 2002). Would you:

- **intensify,** as when you exaggerate surprise when friends throw you a party to make your friends feel better?
- **deintensify,** as when you cover up your own joy in the presence of a friend who didn't receive such good news?
- **neutralize,** as when you cover up your sadness to keep from depressing others?
- **mask,** as when you express happiness in order to cover up your disappointment at not receiving the gift you expected?
- **simulate,** as when you express an emotion you don't feel?

These facial management techniques help you display emotions in socially acceptable ways. For example, when someone gets bad news in which you may secretly take pleasure, the display rule dictates that you frown and otherwise nonverbally signal your sorrow. If you place first in a race and your best friend barely finishes, the display rule requires that you minimize your expression of pleasure in winning and avoid any signs of gloating. If you violate these display rules, you'll be judged as insensitive. So although facial management techniques may be deceptive, they're also expected—and, in fact, required by the rules of polite interaction.

Facial Feedback   When you express emotions facially, a feedback effect is observed. This finding has given rise to what is called the **facial feedback hypothesis**, which holds that your facial expressions influence your physiological arousal (Lanzetta, Cartwright-Smith, & Kleck, 1976; Zuckerman, Klorman, Larrance, & Spiegel, 1981). For example, in one study, participants held a pen in their teeth to simulate a sad expression and then rated a series of photographs. Results showed that mimicking sad expressions actually increased the degree of sadness the subjects reported feeling when viewing the photographs (Larsen, Kasimatis, & Frey, 1992).

Generally, research finds that facial expressions can produce or heighten feelings of sadness, fear, disgust, and anger. But this effect does not occur with all emotions; smiling, for example, won't make you feel happier. And if you're feeling sad, smiling is not likely to replace your sadness with happiness. A reasonable conclusion seems to be that your facial expressions can influence some feelings, but not all (Burgoon & Bacue, 2003).

Culture and Facial Communication   The wide variations in facial communication that we observe in different cultures seem to reflect which reactions are publicly permissible rather than a fundamental difference in the way emotions are facially expressed. In one study, for example, Japanese and American students watched a film of a surgical operation (Ekman, 1985). The students were videotaped both during an interview about the film and alone while watching the film. When alone, the students showed very similar reactions; but in the interview the American students displayed facial expressions indicating displeasure, whereas the Japanese students did not show any great emotion. Similarly, it's considered "forward" or inappropriate for Japanese women to reveal broad smiles, so many Japanese women will hide their smile, sometimes with their hands (Ma, 1996). Women in the United States, on the other hand, have no such restrictions and so are more likely to smile openly. Thus, the difference may not be in the way different cultures express emotions but rather in the society's **cultural display rules**, or rules about the appropriate display of emotions in public (Aune, 2005; Matsumoto, 1991). For example, the well-documented finding that women smile more than men is likely due, at least in part, to display rules that allow women to smile more than men (Hall, 2006).

Eye Communication

Occulesis is the study of the messages communicated by the eyes, which vary depending on the duration, direction, and quality of the eye behavior. For example, in every culture there are rather strict, though unstated, rules for the proper duration for eye contact. In much of England and the United States, for example, the average length of gaze is 2.95 seconds. The average length of mutual gaze (two persons gazing at each other) is 1.18 seconds (Argyle, 1988; Argyle & Ingham, 1972). When the duration of eye contact is shorter than 1.18 seconds, you may think the person is uninterested, shy, or preoccupied. When the appropriate amount of time is exceeded, you may perceive this as showing high interest.

In much of the United States direct eye contact is considered an expression of honesty and forthrightness. But the Japanese often view eye contact as a lack of respect. The Japanese will glance at the other person's face rarely and then only for very short periods (Axtell, 2007). In many Hispanic cultures, direct eye contact signifies a certain equality and so should be avoided by, say, children when speaking to a person in authority. Try visualizing the potential misunderstandings that **eye communication** alone could create when people from Tokyo, San Francisco, and San Juan try to communicate.

The direction of the eye also communicates. Generally, in communicating with another person, you will glance alternatively at the other person's face, then away, then again at the face, and so on. When these directional rules are broken, different meanings are communicated—abnormally high or low interest, self-consciousness, nervousness over the interaction, and so on. The quality of the gaze—how wide or how narrow your eyes get during interaction—also communicates meaning, especially interest level and such emotions as surprise, fear, and disgust.

Another type of eye movement is the eye roll. Take a look at "The Eye Roll" at tcbdevito.blogspot.com. Do you use the eye roll? What messages would you be most likely to communicate with the eye roll?

Shutterstock

VIEWPOINTS Listeners gaze at speakers more than speakers gaze at listeners (Knapp & Hall, 2009. The percentage of interaction time spent gazing while listening, for example, ranges from 62 percent to 75 percent; the percentage of time spent gazing while talking, however, ranges from 38 percent to 41 percent. When these percentages are reversed—when a speaker gazes at the listener for longer than "normal" periods or when a listener gazes at the speaker for shorter than "normal" periods—the conversational interaction becomes awkard. Try this out with a friend and see what happens. Even with mutual awareness, you'll notice the discomfort caused by this seemingly minor communication change.

Eye Contact You use eye contact to serve several important functions (Knapp & Hall, 2009; Malandro, Barker, & Barker, 1989; Richmond, McCroskey, & Hickson, 2012).

- **To monitor feedback.** For example, when you talk with others, you look at them and try to understand their reactions to what you're saying. You try to read their feedback, and on this basis you adjust what you say. As you can imagine, successful readings of feedback will help considerably in your overall effectiveness.

- **To secure attention.** When you speak with two or three other people, you maintain eye contact to secure the attention and interest of your listeners. When someone fails to pay you the attention you want, you probably increase your eye contact, hoping that this will increase attention.

- **To regulate the conversation.** Eye contact helps you regulate, manage, and control the conversation. With eye movements you can inform the other person that she or he should speak. A clear example of this occurs in the college classroom, where the instructor asks a question and then locks eyes with a student. This type of eye contact tells the student to answer the question.

- **To signal the nature of the relationship.** Eye communication also can serve as a "tie sign" or signal of the nature of the relationship between two people—for example, to indicate positive or negative regard. Depending on the culture, eye contact may communicate your romantic interest in another person, or eye avoidance may indicate respect. Some researchers note that eye contact serves to enable gay men and lesbians to signal their homosexuality and perhaps their interest in some-one—an ability referred to as "gaydar" (Nicholas, 2004).

- **To signal status.** Eye contact is often used to signal status and aggression. Among many younger people, prolonged eye contact from a stranger is taken to signify aggressiveness and frequently prompts physical violence—merely because one person looked perhaps a little longer than was considered normal in that specific culture (Matsumoto, 1996).
- **To compensate for physical distance.** Eye contact is often used to compensate for increased physical distance. By making eye contact you overcome psychologically the physical distance between yourself and another person. When you catch someone's eye at a party, for example, you become psychologically closer even though you may be separated by considerable physical distance.

Eye Avoidance   The eyes, sociologist Erving Goffman observed in *Interaction Ritual* (1967), are "great intruders." When you avoid eye contact or avert your glance, you allow others to maintain their privacy. You probably do this when you see a couple arguing in the street or on a bus. You turn your eyes away, as if to say, "I don't mean to intrude; I respect your privacy." Goffman refers to this behavior as **civil inattention**.

Eye avoidance also can signal lack of interest—in a person, a conversation, or some visual stimulus. At times, like the ostrich, we hide our eyes to try to cut off unpleasant stimuli. Notice, for example, how quickly people close their eyes in the face of some extreme unpleasantness. Interestingly enough, even if the unpleasantness is auditory, we tend to shut it out by closing our eyes. At other times, we close our eyes to block out visual stimuli and thus to heighten our other senses; for example, we often listen to music with our eyes closed. Lovers often close their eyes while kissing, and many prefer to make love in a dark or dimly lit room.

Pupil Dilation   In the fifteenth and sixteenth centuries, Italian women used to put drops of belladonna (which literally means "beautiful woman") into their eyes to enlarge the pupils so that they would look more attractive. Research in the field of pupillometrics supports the intuitive logic of these women: Dilated pupils are in fact judged more attractive than constricted ones (Hess, 1975; Marshall, 1983).

In one study, for example, photographs of women were retouched (Hess, 1975). In one set of photographs the pupils were enlarged, and in the other they were made smaller. Men were then asked to judge the women's personalities from the photographs. The photos of women with small pupils drew responses such as cold, hard, and selfish; those with dilated pupils drew responses such as feminine and soft. However, the male observers could not verbalize the reasons for the different perceptions. Both pupil dilation itself and people's reactions to changes in the pupil size of others seem to function below the level of conscious awareness.

Pupil size also reveals your interest and level of emotional arousal. Your pupils enlarge when you're interested in something or when you're emotionally aroused. When homosexuals and heterosexuals were shown pictures of nude bodies, the homosexuals' pupils dilated more when viewing same-sex bodies, whereas the heterosexuals' pupils dilated more when viewing opposite-sex bodies (Hess, Seltzer, & Schlien, 1965). These pupillary responses are unconscious and are even observed in persons with profound mental retardation (Chaney, Givens, Aoki, & Gombiner, 1989). Perhaps we find dilated pupils more attractive because we judge them as indicative of a person's interest in us. That may be why models, Beanie Babies, and Teletubbies, for example, have exceptionally large pupils.

Although belladonna is no longer used, the cosmetics industry has made millions selling eye enhancers—eye shadow, eyeliner, false eyelashes, and tinted contact lenses that change eye color. These items function (ideally, at least) to draw attention to these most powerful communicators.

Culture and Eye Communication   Not surprisingly, eye messages vary with both culture and gender. Americans, for example, consider direct eye contact an expression of honesty and forthrightness, but the Japanese often view this as showing a lack of respect. A Japanese person will glance at the other person's face rarely, and then only for very short periods

Understanding *Interpersonal Skills*

IMMEDIACY

Immediacy is the creation of closeness, a sense of togetherness, of oneness, between speaker and listener. When you communicate immediacy you convey a sense of interest and attention, a liking for and an attraction to the other person. You communicate immediacy with both verbal and nonverbal messages.

Not surprisingly, people respond to communication that is immediate more favorably than to communication that is not. People like people who communicate immediacy. You can increase your interpersonal attractiveness, the degree to which others like you and respond positively toward you, by using immediacy behaviors. In addition there is considerable evidence to show that immediacy behaviors are also effective in workplace communication, especially between supervisors and subordinates (Richmond, McCroskey, & Hickson, 2012). For example, when a supervisors uses immediacy behaviors, he or she is seen by subordinates as interested and concerned; subordinates are therefore likely to communicate more freely and honestly about issues that can benefit the supervisor and the organization. Also, workers with supervisors who communicate immediacy behaviors have higher job satisfaction and motivation.

Not all cultures or all people respond in the same way to immediacy messages. For example, in the United States immediacy behaviors are generally seen as friendly and appropriate. In other cultures, however, the same immediacy behaviors may be viewed as overly familiar—as presuming that a relationship is close when only acquaintanceship exists (Axtell, 2007). Similarly, recognize that some people may take your immediacy behaviors as indicating a desire for increased intimacy in the relationship. So although you may be trying merely to signal a friendly closeness, the other person may perceive a romantic invitation. Also, recognize that because immediacy behaviors prolong and encourage in-depth communication, they may not be responded to favorably by persons who are fearful about communication and/or who want to get the interaction over with as soon as possible (Richmond, McCroskey, & Hickson, 2012).

Communicating Immediacy. Here are a few suggestions for communicating immediacy verbally and nonverbally (Mottet & Richmond, 1998; Richmond, McCroskey, & Hickson, 2012):

- Self-disclose; reveal something significant about yourself.
- Refer to the other person's good qualities of, say, dependability, intelligence, or character—"you're always so reliable."
- Express your positive view of the other person and of your relationship—"I'm so glad you're my roommate; you know everyone."
- Talk about commonalities, things you and the other person have done together or share.
- Demonstrate your responsiveness by giving feedback cues that indicate you want to listen more and that you're interested—"And what else happened?"
- Express psychological closeness and openness by, for example, maintaining physical closeness and arranging your body to exclude third parties.
- Maintain appropriate eye contact and limit looking around at others.
- Smile and express your interest in the other person.
- Focus on the other person's remarks. Make the speaker know that you heard and understood what was said, and give the speaker appropriate verbal and nonverbal feedback.

At the same time that you'll want to demonstrate these immediacy messages, try also to avoid nonimmediacy messages, such as speaking in a monotone, looking away from the person you're talking to, frowning while talking, having a tense body posture, or avoiding gestures.

Working with Interpersonal Skills

How would other people rate you on immediacy? If you have no idea, ask a few friends. How would you rate yourself? In what situations might you express greater immediacy? In what situations might you express less immediacy?

(Axtell, 2007). Interpreting another's eye contact messages according to your own cultural rules is a risky undertaking; eye movements that you may interpret as insulting may have been intended to show respect.

Women make eye contact more and maintain it longer (both in speaking and in listening) than men. This holds true whether women are interacting with other women or with men. This difference in eye behavior may result from women's greater tendency to display their emotions (Wood, 1994). When women interact with other women, they display affiliative and supportive eye contact, whereas when men interact with other men, they avert their gaze (Gamble & Gamble, 2003).

Cultural differences also exist in the ways people decode the meanings of facial expressions. For example, American and Japanese students judged the meaning of a smiling and a neutral facial expression. The Americans rated the smiling face as more attractive, more intelligent, and more sociable than the neutral face. In contrast, the Japanese rated the smiling face as more sociable but not as more attractive—and they rated the neutral face as more intelligent (Matsumoto & Kudoh, 1993).

Touch Communication

Tactile communication, or communication by touch, also referred to as **haptics**, is perhaps the most primitive form of communication. Developmentally, touch is probably the first sense to be used; even in the womb, the child is stimulated by touch. Soon after birth the child is fondled, caressed, patted, and stroked. In turn, the child explores its world through touch. In a very short time, the child learns to communicate a wide variety of meanings through touch. Not surprisingly, touch also varies with your relationship stage. In the early stages of a relationship, you touch little; in intermediate stages (involvement and intimacy), you touch a great deal; and at stable or deteriorating stages, you again touch little (Guerrero & Andersen, 1991).

VIEWPOINTS Here are a few findings from research on nonverbal gender differences (Burgoon, Guerrero, & Floyd, 2010; Gamble & Gamble, 2003; Guerrero & Hecht, 2008; KroLøkke & Sørensen, 2006; Stewart, Cooper, & Stewart, 2003): (1) Women smile more than men. (2) Women stand closer to each other than do men and are generally approached more closely than men. (3) Both men and women, when speaking, look at men more than at women. (4) Women both touch and are touched more than men. (5) Men extend their bodies more, taking up greater areas of space, than women. What problems might these differences create when men and women communicate with each other?

Monkey Business Images/Shutterstock

The Meanings of Touch Touch may communicate five major meanings (Jones, 2005; Jones & Yarbrough, 1985).

- **Positive emotions.** Touch often communicates positive emotions, mainly between intimates or others who have a relatively close relationship. Among the most important of these positive emotions are support, appreciation, inclusion, sexual interest or intent, and affection. Additional research found that touch communicated such positive feelings as composure, immediacy, trust, similarity and equality, and informality (Burgoon, 1991). Touch also has been found to facilitate self-disclosure (Rabinowitz, 1991).
- **Playfulness.** Touch often communicates a desire to play, either affectionately or aggressively. When touch is used in this manner, the playfulness deemphasizes the emotion and tells the other person that it's not to be taken seriously. Playful touches lighten an interaction.
- **Control.** Touch also may seek to control the behaviors, attitudes, or feelings of the other person. Such control may communicate various different kinds of messages. To ask for compliance, for example, we touch the other person to communicate, "Move over," "Hurry," "Stay here," or "Do it." Touching to control may also communicate status and dominance (DiBaise & Gunnoe, 2004; Henley, 1977). The higher-status and dominant person, for

example, initiates touch. In fact, it would be a breach of etiquette for the lower-status person to touch the person of higher status.

- **Ritual.** Much touching centers on performing rituals; for example, in greetings and departures. Shaking hands to say hello or goodbye is perhaps the clearest example of ritualistic touching, but we might also hug, kiss, or put an arm around another's shoulder.

- **Task-related.** Touching is often associated with the performance of a function, such as removing a speck of dust from another person's face, helping someone out of a car, or checking someone's forehead for fever. Task-related touching seems generally to be regarded positively. In studies on the subject, for example, book borrowers had a more positive attitude toward the library and the librarian when touched lightly, and customers gave larger tips when lightly touched by the waitress (Marsh, 1988). Similarly, diners who were touched on the shoulder or hand when being given their change in a restaurant tipped more than diners who were not touched (Crusco & Wetzel, 1984; Guéguen & Jacob, 2004; Stephen & Zweigenhaft, 1986).

As you can imagine, touching also can get you into trouble. For example, touching that is too positive (or too intimate) too early in a relationship may send the wrong signals. Similarly, playing too roughly or holding someone's arm to control their movements may be resented. Using ritualistic touching incorrectly or in ways that may be culturally insensitive may likewise get you into difficulty.

Touch Avoidance

Much as we have a need and desire to touch and be touched by others, we also have a tendency to avoid touch from certain people or in certain circumstances (Andersen, 2004; Andersen & Leibowitz, 1978).

Among the important findings is that **touch avoidance** is positively related to communication apprehension, or fear or anxiety about communicating: People who fear oral communication also score high on touch avoidance. Touch avoidance also is high among those who self-disclose little; touch and self-disclosure are intimate forms of communication, and people who are reluctant to get close to another person by self-disclosure also seem reluctant to get close through touch.

Older people have higher touch avoidance scores for opposite-sex persons than do younger people. Apparently, as we get older we are touched less by members of the opposite sex, and this decreased frequency of touching may lead us to avoid touching. Males score higher than females on same-sex touch avoidance. This accords well with our stereotypes: Men avoid touching other men, but women may and do touch other women. Women, it is found, have higher touch avoidance scores for opposite-sex touching than do men.

Culture and Touch

The several functions and examples of touching discussed earlier in this chapter were based on studies in North America; in other cultures these functions are not served in the same way. In some cultures, for example, some task-related touching is viewed negatively and is to be avoided. Among Koreans it is considered disrespectful for a store owner to touch a customer in, say, handing back change; it is considered too intimate a gesture. A member of another culture who is used to such touching may consider the Korean's behavior cold and aloof. Muslim children are socialized not to touch members of the opposite sex; their behavior can easily be interpreted as unfriendly by American children who are used to touching one another (Dresser, 2005).

Some cultures—including many in southern Europe and the Middle East—are contact cultures; others are noncontact cultures, such as those of northern Europe and Japan. Members of contact cultures maintain close distances, touch one another in conversation, face each other more directly, and maintain longer and more focused eye contact. Members of noncontact cultures maintain greater distance in their interactions, touch each other rarely (if at all), avoid facing each other directly, and maintain much less direct eye contact. As a result of these

VIEWPOINTS Consider, as Nancy Henley asks in her book *Body Politics* (1977), who would touch whom—say, by putting an arm on the other person's shoulder or by putting a hand on the other person's back—in the following dyads: teacher and student, doctor and patient, manager and worker, minister and parishioner, business executive and secretary. Do your answers reveal that the higher-status person initiates touch with the lower-status person? Henley argues that in addition to indicating relative status, touching demonstrates the assertion of male power, dominance, and superior status over women. When women touch men, Henley says, any suggestion of a female-dominant relationship is not acceptable (to men), so the touching is interpreted as a sexual invitation. What do you think of this position?

Bob Daemmrich/The Image Works

differences, problems may occur. For example, northern Europeans and Japanese may be perceived as cold, distant, and uninvolved by southern Europeans—who may in turn be perceived as pushy, aggressive, and inappropriately intimate.

Paralanguage

Paralanguage is the vocal but nonverbal dimension of speech. It has to do with the manner in which you say something rather than with what you say. An old exercise used to increase a student's ability to express different emotions, feelings, and attitudes was to have the student say the following sentence while accenting or stressing different words: "Is this the face that launched a thousand ships?" Significant differences in meaning are easily communicated, depending on where the stress is placed. Consider, for example, the following variations:

1. *Is* this the face that launched a thousand ships?
2. Is *this* the face that launched a thousand ships?
3. Is this the *face* that launched a thousand ships?
4. Is this the face that *launched* a thousand ships?
5. Is this the face that launched a *thousand ships*?

INTERPERSONAL CHOICE POINT

Touching

Your supervisor touches just about everyone. You don't like it and want it to stop—at least as far as you're concerned. What are some ways you can nonverbally show your aversion to this unwanted touching?

Each of these five sentences communicates something different. Each, in fact, asks a totally different question, even though the words used are identical. All that distinguishes the sentences is variation in stress, one of the aspects of paralanguage.

In addition to stress, paralanguage includes such vocal characteristics as **rate** and **volume**. Paralanguage also includes the vocalizations we make when laughing, yelling, moaning, whining, and belching; vocal segregates—sound combinations that aren't words—such as "uh-uh" and "shh"; and **pitch**, the highness or lowness of vocal tone (Argyle, 1988; Trager 1958, 1961).

Paralanguage and People Perception

When listening to people—regardless of what they're saying—we form impressions based on their paralanguage as to what kind of people they are. It does seem that certain voices are symptomatic of certain personality types or problems and, specifically, that the personality orientation gives rise to the vocal qualities. Our impressions of others from paralanguage cues span a broad range and consist of physical impressions (perhaps about body type and certainly about gender and age), personality impressions (they sound shy, they appear aggressive), and evaluative impressions (they sound like good people, they sound evil and menacing, they have vicious laughs).

One of the most interesting findings on voice and personal characteristics is that listeners can accurately judge the socioeconomic status (high, middle, or low) of speakers after hearing a 60-second voice sample. In fact, many listeners reported that they made their judgments in less than 15 seconds. It has also been found that the speakers judged to be of high status were rated as being of higher credibility than those rated of middle or low status.

It's interesting to note that listeners agree with one another about the personality of the speaker even when their judgments are in error. Listeners have similar stereotyped ideas about the way vocal characteristics and personality characteristics are related, and they use these stereotypes in their judgments.

Paralanguage and Persuasion

The rate of speech is the aspect of paralanguage that has received the most research attention—because speech rate is related to persuasiveness. Therefore, it's of interest to the advertiser, the politician, and anyone else who wants to convey information or to influence others orally—especially when time is limited or expensive. The research on rate of speech shows that in one-way communication situations, persons who talk fast are more persuasive and are evaluated more highly than those who talk at or below normal speeds (MacLachlan, 1979). This greater persuasiveness and higher regard holds true whether the person talks fast naturally or the speech is sped up electronically (as in time-compressed speech).

In one experiment, subjects were asked to listen to taped messages and then to indicate both the degree to which they agreed with the message and their opinions as to how intelligent and objective they thought the speaker was (MacLachlan, 1979). Rates of 111, 140 (the average rate), and 191 words per minute were used. Subjects agreed most with the fastest speech and least with the slowest speech. Further, they rated the fastest speaker as the most intelligent and objective and the slowest speaker as the least intelligent and objective. Even in experiments in which the speaker was known to have something to gain personally from persuasion (as would, say, a salesperson), the speaker who spoke at the fastest rate was the most persuasive. Research also finds that faster speech rates increase listeners' perceptions of speaker competence and dominance (Buller, LePoire, Aune, & Eloy, 1992).

Although generally research finds that a faster than normal speech rate lowers listener comprehension, a rapid rate may still have the advantage in communicating information (Jones, Berry, & Stevens, 2007; MacLachlan, 1979). For example, people who listened to speeches at 201 words per minute (140 is average) comprehended 95 percent of the message, and those who listened to speeches at 282 words per minute (that is, double the normal rate) comprehended 90 percent. Even though the rates increased dramatically, the comprehension rates fell only slightly. These 5 percent and 10 percent losses are more than offset by the increased speed and thus make the faster rates much more efficient in communicating information. If the speech speeds are increased more than 100 percent, however, listener comprehension falls dramatically.

Exercise caution in applying this research to your own interpersonal interactions (MacLachlan, 1979). Realize that while the speaker is speaking, the listener is generating and framing a reply. If the speaker talks too rapidly, there may not be enough time to compose this reply, and resentment may be generated. Furthermore, the increased rate may seem so unnatural that the listener may come to focus on the speed of speech rather than the thought expressed.

Culture and Paralanguage   Cultural differences also need to be taken into consideration when we evaluate the results of the studies on speech rate, because different cultures view speech rate differently. For example, investigators found that Korean male speakers who spoke rapidly were given unfavorable credibility ratings, unlike Americans who spoke rapidly (Lee & Boster, 1992). Researchers have suggested that in individualist societies a rapid-rate speaker is seen as more competent than a slow-rate speaker, whereas in collectivist cultures a speaker who uses a slower rate is judged more competent.

Silence

"Speech," wrote Thomas Mann, "is civilization itself. The word, even the most contradictory word, preserves contact; it's silence which isolates." Philosopher Karl Jaspers, on the other hand, observed that "the ultimate in thinking as in communication is silence." And philosopher Max Picard noted that "silence is nothing merely negative; it's not the mere absence of speech. It's a positive, a complete world in itself." The one thing on which these contradictory observations agree is that **silence** communicates. Your silence communicates just as intensely as anything you verbalize (Jaworski, 1993; Richmond, McCroskey, & Hickson, 2012).

The Functions of Silence   Like words and gestures, silence serves important communication functions. Here are several:

- **To provide time to think.** Silence allows the speaker *time to think*, time to formulate and organize his or her verbal communications. Before messages of intense conflict, as well as those confessing undying love, there is often silence. Again, silence seems to prepare the receiver for the importance of these future messages.
- **To hurt.** Some people use silence as a weapon *to hurt* others. We often speak of giving someone "the silent treatment." After a conflict, for example, one or both individuals may remain silent as a kind of punishment. Silence used to hurt others also may take the form of refusing to acknowledge the presence of another person, as in disconfirmation;

Ethics in Interpersonal Communication

INTERPERSONAL SILENCE

Remaining silent is at times your right. At other times, however, it may be unlawful. You have the right to remain silent so as not to incriminate yourself. You have a right to protect your privacy—to withhold information that has no bearing on the matter at hand. For example, your previous relationship history, affectional orientation, or religion is usually irrelevant to your ability to function in a job, and thus may be kept private in most job-related situations. On the other hand, these issues may be relevant when, for example, you're about to enter a more intimate phase of a relationship; then there may be an obligation to reveal information about yourself that could ethically have been kept hidden at earlier relationship stages.

You do not have the right to remain silent and to refuse to reveal information about crimes you've seen others commit. However, psychiatrists, clergy, and lawyers—fortunately or unfortunately—are often exempt from the requirement to reveal information about criminal activities when the information had been gained through privileged communication with clients.

ETHICAL CHOICE POINT

On your way to work, you witness a father verbally abusing his three-year-old child. You worry that he might psychologically harm the child, and your first impulse is to speak up and tell this man that verbal abuse can have lasting effects on the child and often leads to physical abuse. At the same time, you don't want to interfere with his right to speak to his child and you certainly don't want to make him angrier. What is your ethical obligation in this case? What would you do in this situation?

here silence is a dramatic demonstration of the total indifference one person feels toward the other.

■ **To respond to personal anxiety.** Sometimes silence is used as a *response to personal anxiety,* shyness, or threats. You may feel anxious or shy among new people and prefer to remain silent. By remaining silent you preclude the chance of rejection. Only when you break your silence and attempt to communicate with another person do you risk rejection.

■ **To prevent communication.** Silence may be used to *prevent communication* of certain messages. In conflict situations, silence is sometimes used to prevent certain topics from surfacing or to prevent one or both parties from saying things they may later regret. In such situations, silence often allows us time to cool off before expressing hatred, severe criticism, or personal attacks that we know are irreversible.

■ **To communicate emotions.** Like the eyes, face, or hands, silence can also be used to *communicate emotions* (Ehrenhaus, 1988; Lane, Koetting, & Bishop, 2002). Sometimes silence communicates a determination to be uncooperative or defiant; by refusing to engage in verbal communication, you defy the authority or the legitimacy of the other person's position. Silence is often used to communicate annoyance, usually accompanied by a pouting expression, arms crossed in front of the chest, and nostrils flared. Silence may express affection or love, especially when coupled with long and longing gazes into each other's eyes.

■ **To achieve specific effects.** Silence may also be used strategically, to *achieve specific effects.* The pause before making what you feel is an important comment or after hearing about some mishap may be strategically positioned to communicate a desired impression—to make your idea stand out among others or perhaps to give others the impression that you care a lot more than you really do. In some cases a prolonged silence after someone voices disagreement may give the appearance of control and superiority. It's a way of saying, "I can respond in my own time." Generally, research finds that people use silence strategically more with strangers than they do with close friends (Hasegawa & Gudykunst, 1998).

■ **To say nothing.** Of course, you also may use silence when you simply have *nothing to say,* when nothing occurs to you, or when you don't want to say anything. James Russell Lowell

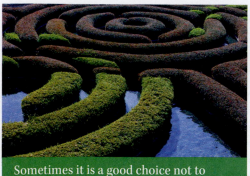

> Sometimes it is a good choice not to choose at all.
> —*Michel de Montaigne*

Laurin Rinder/Shutterstock

expressed this well: "Blessed are they who have nothing to say, and who cannot be persuaded to say it." At the same time, recall the inevitability of communication: When in an interactional situation, your silence will also communicate.

The Spiral of Silence The **spiral of silence** theory offers a somewhat different perspective on silence. Applying this theory (originally developed to explain the media's influence on opinion) to the interpersonal context, this theory argues that you're more likely to voice agreement than disagreement (Noelle-Neumann, 1973, 1980, 1991; Scheufele & Moy, 2000 Severin & Tankard, 2001). The theory claims that when a controversial issue arises, you estimate the opinions of others and figure out which views are popular and which are not. In face-to-face conversations—say with a group of five or six people—you'd have to guess about their opinions or wait until they're voiced. In social media communication, on the other hand, you're often provided statistics on opinions that eliminate the guess work. You also estimate the rewards and the punishments you'd likely get from expressing popular or unpopular positions. You then use these estimates to determine which opinions you'll express and which you won't.

Generally, you're more likely to voice your opinions when you agree with the majority than when you disagree. And there's evidence to show that this effect is stronger for minority group members (Bowen & Blackmon, 2003). You may do this to avoid being isolated from the majority, or for fear of being proved wrong or being disliked, for example. Or you may simply assume that the majority, because they're a majority, must be right.

As people with minority views remain silent, the majority position gets stronger (because those who agree with it are the only ones speaking); so, as the majority position becomes stronger and the minority position becomes weaker, the situation becomes an ever-widening spiral. The Internet (blogs and social network sites, especially) may in some ways act as a counteragent to the spiral of silence, because Internet discussions provide so many free ways for you to express minority viewpoints (anonymously if you wish) and to quickly find like-minded others (McDevitt, Kiousis, & Wahl-Jorgensen, 2003).

Radius Images/ Alamy

VIEWPOINTS Consider the operation of the spiral of silence theory on your own interpersonal interactions. For example, if you were talking with a group of new students, would you be more likely to voice opinions that agreed with the majority? Would you hesitate to voice opinions that differed greatly from what the others were expressing?

Culture and Silence Similarly, not all cultures view silence as functioning in the same way (Vainiomaki, 2004). In the United States, for example, people often interpret silence negatively. At a business meeting or even in an informal social group, others may wonder if the silent member is not listening, has nothing interesting to add, doesn't understand the issues, is insensitive, or is too self-absorbed to focus on the messages of others.

Other cultures, however, view silence more positively. In many situations in Japan, for example, silence is a response that is considered more appropriate than speech (Haga, 1988). And in this country the traditional Apache regard silence very differently than do European Americans (Basso, 1972). Among the Apache, mutual friends do not feel the need to introduce strangers who may be working in the same area or on the same project. The strangers may remain silent for several days. This period enables people to observe one another and to come to a judgment about the other individuals. Once this assessment is made, the individuals talk. When courting, especially during the initial stages, Apache couples remain silent for hours; if they do talk, they generally talk very little. Only after a couple has been dating for several months will they have lengthy conversations.

These periods of silence are generally attributed to shyness or self-consciousness. The use of silence is explicitly taught to Apache women, who are especially discouraged from engaging in long discussions with their dates. Silence during courtship is a sign of modesty to many Apache.

Spatial Messages and Territoriality

Space is an especially important factor in interpersonal communication, although we seldom think about it. Edward T. Hall (1959, 1963, 1966), who pioneered the study of spatial communication, called this area **proxemics**. We can examine this broad area by looking at proxemic distances, the theories about space, and territoriality.

Proxemic Distances Four **proxemic distances**, the distances we maintain between each other in our interactions, correspond closely to the major types of relationships. They are intimate, personal, social, and public distances (see Table 3).

Intimate Distance Within **intimate distance**, ranging from the close phase of actual touching to the far phase of 6 to 18 inches, the presence of the other person is unmistakable. You experience the sound, smell, and feel of the other's breath. The close phase is used for lovemaking and wrestling, for comforting and protecting. In the close phase, the muscles and the skin communicate, while actual words play a minor role. The far phase allows people to touch each other by extending their hands. The individuals are so close that this distance is not considered proper for strangers in public. Because of the feeling of inappropriateness and discomfort (at least for some Americans), if

INTERPERSONAL CHOICE POINT

Inappropriate Spacing

As in an episode of Seinfeld, *your friend is a "close talker" who stands much too close to others when talking and makes others feel uncomfortable. What (if anything) can you say to help your friend use space to communicate more effectively?*

TABLE 3	Relationships and Proxemic Distances

Note that these four distances can be further divided into close and far phases and that the far phase of one level (say, personal) blends into the close phase of the next level (social). Do your relationships also blend into one another? Or are, say, your personal relationships totally separate from your social relationships?

Relationship	Distance
Intimate relationship	Intimate distance 0 _____ 18 inches close phase ... far phase
Personal relationship	Personal distance 1½ _____ 4 feet close phase ... far phase
Social relationship	Social distance 4 _____ 12 feet close phase ... far phase
Public relationship	Public distance 12 _____ 25+ feet close phase ... far phase

strangers are this close (say, on a crowded bus), their eyes seldom meet but remain fixed on some remote object.

Personal Distance   You carry a protective bubble defining your **personal distance**, which allows you to stay protected and untouched by others. Personal distance ranges from 18 inches to about 4 feet. In the close phase, people can still hold or grasp each other, but only by extending their arms. You can then take into your protective bubble certain individuals—for example, loved ones. In the far phase, you can touch another person only if you both extend your arms. This far phase is the extent to which you can physically get your hands on things; hence, it defines, in one sense, the limits of your physical control over others. At times, you may detect breath odor, but generally at this distance etiquette demands that you direct your breath to some neutral area.

Social Distance   At the **social distance**, ranging from 4 to 12 feet, you lose the visual detail you had at the personal distance. The close phase is the distance at which you conduct impersonal business or interact at a social gathering. The far phase is the distance at which you stand when someone says, "Stand away so I can look at you." At this distance, business transactions have a more formal tone than they do when conducted in the close phase. In the offices of high officials, the desks are often positioned so that clients are kept at least this distance away. Unlike the intimate distance, where eye contact is awkward, the far phase of the social distance makes eye contact essential—otherwise, communication is lost. The voice is generally louder than normal at this level. This distance enables you to avoid constant interaction with those with whom you work without seeming rude.

Public Distance   **Public distance** ranges from 12 to more than 25 feet. In the close phase, a person seems protected by space. At this distance, you're able to take defensive action should you feel threatened. On a public bus or train, for example, you might keep at least this distance from a drunk. Although you lose the fine details of the face and eyes, you're still close enough to see what is happening.

At the far phase, you see others not as separate individuals but as part of the whole setting. People automatically establish a space of approximately 30 feet around important public figures, and they seem to do this whether or not there are guards preventing their coming closer. The far phase is the distance by which actors on stage are separated from their audience; consequently, their actions and voices have to be somewhat exaggerated.

The specific distance that you'll maintain between yourself and any given person depends on a wide variety of factors (Burgoon & Bacue, 2003; Burgoon, Guerrero, & Floyd, 2010). Among the most significant are: Gender (women sit and stand closer to each other than do men in same-sex dyads, and people approach women more closely than they approach men); age (people maintain closer distances with similarly aged others than they do with those much older or much younger); personality (introverts and highly anxious people maintain greater distances than do extroverts); and familiarity (you'll maintain shorter distances with people you're familiar with than with strangers, and with people you like than with those you don't like).

Territoriality   Another type of communication having to do with space is **territoriality**, the possessive reaction to an area or to particular objects. You interact basically in three types of territories (Altman, 1975):

- **Primary territories**, or **home territories**, are areas that you might call your own; these areas are your exclusive preserve and might include your room, your desk, or your office.
- **Secondary territories** are areas that don't belong to you but that you have occupied; thus, you're associated with them. Secondary territories might include the table in the cafeteria that you regularly eat at, your classroom seat, or your neighborhood turf.
- **Public territories** are areas that are open to all people; they may be owned by some person or organization, but they are used by everyone. Examples include a movie house, a restaurant, or a shopping mall.

When you operate in your own primary territory, you have an interpersonal advantage, often called the **home field advantage**. In their own home or office, people take on a kind of leadership role: They initiate conversations, fill in silences, assume relaxed and comfortable postures, and in conversations maintain their positions with greater conviction. Because the territorial owner is dominant, you stand a better chance of getting your raise, having your point accepted, or getting a contract resolved in your favor if you're in your own territory (your office, your home) rather than in someone else's (your supervisor's office, for example) (Marsh, 1988).

Like animals, humans mark both their primary and secondary territories to signal ownership. Some people—perhaps because they can't own territories—use markers to indicate pseudo-ownership or appropriation of someone else's space, or of a public territory, for their own use (Childress, 2004). Graffiti and the markings of gang boundaries come quickly to mind as examples. If you think about your own use of markers, you'll probably identify three different types of **markers**: central, boundary, and ear markers (Goffman, 1971).

- **Central markers** are items you place in a territory to reserve it for you—for example, a coffee cup on the table, books on your desk, or a sweater over a library chair.
- **Boundary markers** set boundaries that divide your territory from that of others. In the supermarket checkout line, the bar that is placed between your groceries and those of the person behind you is a boundary marker, as are fences, the armrests separating chairs in a movie theater, and the contours of the molded plastic seats on a bus.
- **Ear markers**—a term taken from the practice of branding animals on their ears—are identifying marks that indicate your possession of a territory or object. Trademarks, nameplates, and monograms are all examples of ear markers.

Markers are important in giving you a feeling of belonging. For example, students in college dormitories who marked their rooms by displaying personal items stayed in school longer than did those who didn't personalize their spaces (Marsh, 1988).

Again, like animals, humans use territory to signal their status. For example, the size and location of your territory (your home or office, say) indicates something about your status. Status is also signaled by the unwritten law granting the right of invasion, or **territorial encroachment**. Higher-status individuals have a "right" to invade the territory of lower-status persons, but the reverse is not true. The boss of a large company, for example, can barge into the office of a junior executive, but the reverse would be unthinkable. Similarly, a teacher may invade a student's personal space by looking over her or his shoulder as the student writes, but the student cannot do the same to the teacher.

At times, you may want to resist the encroachment on your territory. If so, you can react in several ways (Lyman & Scott, 1967; Richmond, McCroskey, & Hickson, 2012):

- In **withdrawal** you simply leave the scene, whether the country, home, office, or social media site.
- In **turf defense** you defend the territory against the encroachment. This may mean doing something as simple as saying, "This is my seat," or you may start a fight as nations do.
- **Insulation** involves erecting barriers between yourself and those who would encroach on your territory. Putting up a fence around your property or surrounding your desk with furniture so that others can't get close are common examples of insulation.
- **Linguistic collusion** means speaking in a language or jargon that the "invaders" don't understand and thus excluding them from your interactions.

Artifactual Communication

Artifactual communication consists of messages conveyed by objects that are made by human hands. Thus, aesthetics, color, clothing, jewelry, and hairstyle, as well as scents such as perfume, cologne, or incense, all are considered artifactual. Here are a few examples.

Space Decoration   That the decoration or surroundings of a place exert influence on perceptions should be obvious to anyone who has ever entered a hospital, with its sterile

Understanding *Interpersonal Theory & Research*

THEORIES ABOUT SPACE

Researchers studying nonverbal communication have offered numerous explanations as to why people maintain the distances they do. Prominent among these explanations are protection theory, equilibrium theory, and expectancy violation theory—rather complex names for simple and interesting concepts.

Protection theory holds that you establish a body buffer zone around yourself as protection against unwanted touching or attack (Dosey & Meisels, 1976). When you feel that you may be attacked, your body buffer zone increases; you want more space around you. For example, if you found yourself in a dangerous neighborhood at night, your body buffer zone would probably expand well beyond what it would be if you were in familiar and safe surroundings. If someone entered this buffer zone, you would probably feel threatened and seek to expand the distance by walking faster or crossing the street. In contrast, when you're feeling secure and protected, your buffer zone becomes much smaller. For example, if you're with a group of close friends and feel secure, your buffer zone shrinks, and you may welcome close proximity and mutual touching.

Equilibrium theory holds that intimacy and interpersonal distance vary together: The greater the intimacy, the closer the distance; the lower the intimacy, the greater the distance. This theory says that you maintain close distances with those with whom you have close interpersonal relationships and that you maintain greater distances with those with whom you do not have close relationships (Argyle & Dean, 1965; Bailenson, Blascovich, Beall, & Loomis, 2001).

At times, however, you're forced into close distances with someone with whom you're not intimate (or whom you may even dislike)—for example, on a crowded bus or in the dentist's chair. In these situations, you make the psychological distance greater by, for example, avoiding eye contact or turning your head in an opposite direction. In the dentist's chair, you probably close your eyes to decrease this normally intimate distance. If seated to the right of a stranger, you might cross your legs and turn your torso to the left.

Expectancy violations theory explains what happens when you increase or decrease the distance between yourself and another in an interpersonal interaction (Burgoon, Guerrero, & Floyd, 2010). The theory assumes that you have expectancies for the distance people are to maintain in their conversations. When these expectancies are violated, you try to explain to yourself why this violation occurred and it brings into focus the nature of your relationship. Perhaps the most interesting conclusion to emerge from this theory is that the meaning you give to the violation will depend on whether or not you like the person. If you like the person who violated your expectancies by, say, standing too close, you'll like the person even more as a result of this violation—probably because you'll interpret this added closeness as an indication that the person likes you. If, on the other hand, you do not like the person, you'll like the person even less as a result of the violation—perhaps because you'll interpret this added closeness as threatening.

Working with Theories and Research

Do these theories reflect the way you view space and interpersonal distance? Are there aspects of spatial distance that you'd like explained that these theories don't?

170

walls and furniture; or a museum, with its imposing columns, glass-encased exhibits, and brass plaques. Even the way a room is furnished exerts influence on us. In a classic study, researchers attempted to determine if the aesthetic conditions of a room would influence the judgments people made in it (Maslow & Mintz, 1956; Mintz, 1956). Three rooms were used: one was beautiful, one average, and one ugly. In the three different rooms, students rated art prints in terms of the fatigue/energy and displeasure/well-being depicted in them. As predicted, the students in the beautiful room rated the prints as more energetic and as displaying well-being; the prints judged in the ugly room were rated as displaying fatigue and displeasure, while those judged in the average room were perceived as somewhere between these two extremes.

The way you decorate your private spaces communicates something about who you are. The office with a mahogany desk, bookcases, and oriental rugs communicates importance and status within the organization, just as a metal desk and bare floor communicate a status much farther down in the hierarchy. At home, the cost of your furnishings may communicate your status and wealth, and their coordination may communicate your sense of style. The magazines may communicate your interests. The arrangement of chairs around a television set may reveal how important watching television is. Bookcases lining the walls reveal the importance of reading. In fact, there is probably little in your home that does not send messages to others and that others do not use for making inferences about you. Computers, wide-screen televisions, well-equipped kitchens, and oil paintings of great-grandparents, for example, all say something about the people who own them. Likewise, the absence of certain items will communicate something about you. Consider, for example, what messages you would get from a home in which there was no television, telephone, or books.

People also will form opinions about your personality on the basis of room decorations. Research, for example, finds that people will make judgments as to your openness to new experiences (distinctive decorating usually communicates this, as do different types of books and magazines and travel souvenirs) and as to your conscientiousness, emotional stability, degree of extroversion, and agreeableness. Not surprisingly, bedrooms prove more revealing than offices (Gosling, Ko, Mannarelli, & Morris, 2002).

Color Communication

When you're in debt, you speak of being "in the red"; when you make a profit, you're "in the black." When you're sad, you're "blue"; when you're healthy, you're "in the pink"; when you're covetous, you're "green with envy." To be a coward is to be "yellow," and to be inexperienced is to be "green." When you talk a great deal, you talk "a blue streak"; when you're angry, you "see red." As revealed through these timeworn clichés, language abounds in color symbolism.

Color communication takes place on many levels. For example, there is some evidence that colors affect us physiologically. Respiratory movements increase in the presence of red light and decrease in the presence of blue light. Similarly, eye blinks increase in frequency when eyes are exposed to red light and decrease when exposed to blue. This seems consistent with our intuitive feelings that blue is more soothing and red more provocative.

Color seems also to influence the expectation of taste sensation (Srivastava & More, 2011). For example, people expect pink pills to be sweeter than red pills, yellow pills to be salty, white and blue pills to be bitter, and orange pills to be sour.

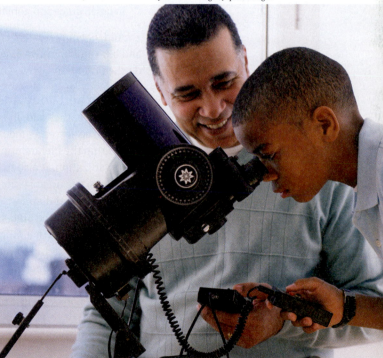

JGI/Blend Images/Jupiter Images

VIEWPOINTS The "Pygmalion gift" is a gift that is designed to change the recipient into what the donor wants that person to become. For example, the parent who gives a child books or science equipment may be asking the child to be a scholar or a scientist. What messages have you recently communicated in your gift-giving behavior? What messages do you think others have communicated to you by the gifts they gave you?

Colors vary greatly in their meanings from one culture to another. To illustrate this cultural variation, here are some of the many meanings that popular colors communicate in a variety of different cultures (Dresser, 2005; Dreyfuss, 1971; Hoft, 1995; Singh & Pereira, 2005). As you read this section, you may want to consider your own meanings for these colors and where your meanings came from.

- **Red**: In China red signifies prosperity and rebirth and is used for festive and joyous occasions. In France and the United Kingdom, red indicates masculinity, in many African countries blasphemy or death, and in Japan anger and danger. Red ink, especially among Korean Buddhists, is used only to write a person's name at the time of death or on the anniversary of the person's death; this can create problems when American teachers use red ink to mark homework.
- **Green**: In the United States green signifies capitalism, a signal to go ahead, and envy; in Ireland patriotism; among some Native Americans femininity; to the Egyptians fertility and strength; and to the Japanese youth and energy.
- **Black**: In Thailand black signifies old age, in parts of Malaysia courage, and in much of Europe death.
- **White**: In Thailand white signifies purity, in many Muslim and Hindu cultures purity and peace, and in Japan and other Asian countries death and mourning.
- **Blue**: In Iran blue signifies something negative, in Ghana joy; for the Cherokee it signifies defeat, for the Egyptian virtue and truth, and for the Greek national pride.
- **Yellow**: In China yellow signifies wealth and authority, in the United States caution and cowardice, in Egypt happiness and prosperity, and in many countries throughout the world femininity.
- **Purple**: In Latin America purple signifies death, in Europe royalty, in Egypt virtue and faith, in Japan grace and nobility, in China barbarism, and in the United States nobility and bravery.

And, of course, colors are often associated with gender, beginning with pink for baby girls and blue for baby boys. Even as adults, women are allowed great choice in clothing color. Men, on the other hand, have a more restricted palette from which to choose.

Clothing and Body Adornment

Clothing serves a variety of functions. It protects you from the weather and, in sports like football, from injury. It helps you conceal parts of your body and so serves a modesty function. In the business world it may communicate your position within the hierarchy and your willingness and desire to conform to the clothing norms of the organization. It also may communicate your professionalism, which seems to be the reason why some organizations favor dress codes (M. H. Smith, 2003). Clothing also serves as a form of **cultural display** (Morris, 2002). It communicates your cultural and subcultural affiliations. In the United States, where there are so many different ethnic groups, you regularly see examples of dress that indicate what country the wearers are from.

The very poor and the very rich don't dress in the same way, nor do white- and blue-collar workers or the young and the old (Lurie, 1983). People dress, in part at least, to identify with the groups of which they are or want to be members. At the same time, they dress to manage the impressions they give to others (Frith & Gleeson, 2004; Keating, 2006). For example, you're likely to dress conservatively if you're interviewing for a job at a conservative firm, to indicate that you share the values of the firm of which you want to be a part. On the other hand, you'd dress very differently if you were going clubbing at one of the trendy hot spots.

You probably make judgments about your college instructors on the basis of the way they dress, especially on the first day. In one study, college students perceived an instructor dressed informally as friendly, fair, enthusiastic, and flexible, and the same instructor dressed formally as prepared, knowledgeable, and organized (Malandro, Barker, & Barker, 1989). Perceptions will naturally vary with the fashions of the time and the expectations of what's appropriate and what's inappropriate. Today, with websites such as Rate My Professor, students may come into the class with a pretty firm picture of the instructor, and clothing is likely to prove less important.

INTERPERSONAL CHOICE POINT

Criticizing with Kindness

A close friend is going to an important job interview dressed totally inappropriately and asks, "How do I look?" What are some of the ways of expressing your response that will help your friend with the interview presentation but also bolster your friend's self-esteem?

Clothing also seems to influence your own behavior and the behavior of groups. For example, it has been argued that people who dress casually act more informally (Morand, 1995). Therefore, meetings with such casually dressed people are more likely to involve a freer exchange of thoughts and ideas, which in turn may stimulate creativity. This casual attire seems to work well in companies that must rely heavily on creative development, such as computer software companies. And many technology companies, like Google, Yahoo, and Apple, encourage a more informal, casual style of dress. But banks and insurance companies, which traditionally have resisted change, may prefer more formal attire that creates distance between workers as well as between employees and customers.

Your jewelry, too, communicates messages about you. Wedding and engagement rings are obvious examples of jewelry designed to communicate very specific messages. College rings and political buttons also communicate specific information. If you wear a Rolex watch or large precious stones, others are likely to infer that you're rich. Men with earrings will be judged differently from men without earrings. And the number and type of buttons you display on your Facebook page will similarly communicate something about you, your sense of humor, your passions, and your values.

Today body piercings are popular, especially among the young. Nose and nipple rings and tongue and belly-button jewelry send a variety of messages. Although people wearing such jewelry may wish to communicate meanings of their own, those interpreting these messages seem to infer that the wearer is communicating an unwillingness to conform to social norms and a willingness to take greater risks than those without such piercings (Forbes, 2001). It's worth noting that in a study of employers' perceptions, applicants with eyebrow piercings were rated and ranked significantly lower than those without such piercings (Acor, 2001). In another study, nose-pierced job candidates were given lower scores on measures of credibility, such as character and trust, as well as sociability and hirability (Seiter & Sandry, 2003). Tattoos—temporary or permanent—likewise communicate a variety of messages, often the name of a loved one or some symbol of allegiance or affiliation. Tattoos also communicate to the wearers themselves. For example, tattooed students see themselves (and perhaps others do as well) as more adventurous, creative, individualistic, and risk-prone than those without tattoos (Drews, Allison, & Probst, 2000). In addition, tattoos and piercings may communicate such undesirable traits as impulsiveness, unpredictability, and a tendency toward recklessness or violence (Rapsa & Cusack, 1990; M. H. Smith, 2003).

Although tattoos and body piercings are becoming more accepted, business experts continue to note the negative effects in terms of getting a job and suggest hiding them during job interviews (Ingegneri, 2008; Varenik, 2010).

The way you wear your hair communicates who you are. Your hair may communicate a concern for being up-to-date, a desire to shock, or perhaps a lack of concern for appearances. Men with long hair will generally be judged as less conservative than men with shorter hair.

Scent Smell is a peculiar aspect of nonverbal communication and is discussed in widely different ways by different writers. Here, because the emphasis is on using scents (for example, perfume or cologne), it's grouped with artifactual communication. But recognize that body odor also communicates, and perhaps that part of smell is best thought of as a form of body communication. You also use smells to make yourself feel better. When the smells are pleasant, you feel better about yourself; when the smells are unpleasant, you feel less good about yourself. In fact, research finds that smells can influence your body's chemistry, which, in turn, influences your emotional state. For example, the smell of chocolate results in the reduction of theta brain waves, which produces a sense of relaxation and a reduced level of attention (Martin, 1998).

Olfactory communication, or olfactics, is extremely important in a wide variety of situations. Scientists estimate that you can smell some 10,000 different odors (Angier, 1995a). There is some evidence, though not conclusive, showing that the smell of lemon contributes to a perception of health; the smells of lavender and eucalyptus seem to increase alertness, and the smell of rose oil seems to reduce blood pressure. Findings such as these have contributed to the growth of aromatherapy and to the profession of aromatherapist (Furlow, 1996). Because humans possess "denser skin concentrations of scent glands than almost any other

VIEWPOINTS A popular defense tactic in sex crimes against women, gay men, and lesbians is to blame the victim by referring to the way the victim was dressed and implying that the victim, by wearing certain clothing, provoked the attack. What do you think of this tactic? Is it likely to be effective? Is it ethical?

Photos 12/Alamy

For another function of rings, see "The Divorce Ring" at tcbdevito .blogspot.com. If you were divorced, would you wear a divorce ring?

mammal," it has been argued that it only remains for us to discover how we use scent to communicate a wide variety of messages (Furlow, 1996, p. 41). Some of the most important messages scent seems to communicate involve attraction, taste, memory, and identification.

INTERPERSONAL CHOICE POINT

Demonstrating Credibility

At work people don't attribute any credibility to you, although you're probably as competent as anyone else. You need to increase the nonverbal credibility cues you give off. What nonverbal cues will help you communicate your abilities? How might you begin to integrate these into your own communication?

Take a look at "Nonverbal Communication: Scent" at tcbdevito.blogspot.com for a brief discussion of the connection between scent and memory. Have you ever experienced this?

Mircea Bezergheanu/Shutterstock

- **To attract others.** In many animal species the female gives off a scent that draws males, often from far distances, and thus ensures the continuation of the species. Humans, too, emit sexual attractants called sex pheromones, body secretions that arouse sexual desire (Kluger, 2008). Humans, of course, supplement pheromones with perfumes, colognes, after-shave lotions, powders, and the like to further enhance attractiveness and sexuality. And if we can judge from the advertisements and the space devoted to such products, men seem to be catching up with women in the amount and diversity of such products. Women, research finds, prefer the scent of men who bear a close genetic similarity to themselves—a finding that may account in part for our attraction to people much like ourselves (Ober, Weitkamp, Cox, Dytch, Kostyu, & Elias, 1997; Wade, 2002).

- **To aid taste.** Without smell, taste would be severely impaired. For example, it would be extremely difficult to taste the difference between a raw potato and an apple without the sense of smell. Street vendors selling hot dogs, sausages, and similar foods are aided greatly by the smells that stimulate the appetites of passersby.

- **To aid memory.** Smell is a powerful memory aid; you can often recall situations from months and even years ago when you happen upon a similar smell. One reason smell can so effectively recall a previous situation is that it's often associated with significant emotional experiences (Malandro, Barker, & Barker, 1989; Rubin, Groth, & Goldsmith, 1984).

- **To create an image.** Smell is often used to create an image or an identity for a product. Advertisers and manufacturers spend millions of dollars each year creating scents for cleaning products and toothpastes, for example. These scents have nothing to do with the products' cleaning power. Instead, they function solely to help create product images or identities. There also is evidence that we can identify specific significant others by smell. For example, infants find their mothers' breasts through smell, mothers can identify their newborns solely through smell, and children are able to identify the T-shirts of their brothers and sisters solely on the basis of smell (Angier, 1995a; Porter & Moore, 1981). One researcher goes so far as to advise: "If your man's odor reminds you of Dad or your brother, you may want genetic tests before trying to conceive a child" (Furlow, 1996, p. 41).

Temporal Communication

The study of **temporal communication**, known technically as **chronemics**, concerns the use of time—how you organize it, react to it, and communicate messages through it (Bruneau, 1985, 1990, 2009/2010). Consider, for example, **psychological time**: the emphasis you place on the past, present, or future. In a past orientation, you have special reverence for the past. You relive old times and regard the old methods as the best. You see events as circular and recurring, so the wisdom of yesterday is applicable also to today and tomorrow. In a present orientation, however, you live in the present: for now, not tomorrow. In a future orientation, you look toward and live for the future. You save today, work hard in college, and deny yourself luxuries because you're preparing for the future. Before reading more about time, take the self-test, "What's Your Time?"

VIEWPOINTS As noted in the text, you're likely to dress differently depending on the situation. But exactly how would you dress:

- to interview for a job at a prestigious and conservative law firm?
- to appear friendly but serious as you teach your first class?
- to appear as the trendiest partygoer at the trendiest spot in town?

Test Yourself | What's Your Time?

For each statement indicate whether the statement is true (T) or false (F) of your general attitude and behavior.

_____ 1. I work hard today basically because of tomorrow's expected rewards.
_____ 2. I enjoy life as it comes.
_____ 3. I enjoy planning for tomorrow and the future generally.
_____ 4. I avoid looking too far ahead.
_____ 5. I'm willing to endure difficulties if there's a payoff/reward at the end.
_____ 6. I frequently put off work to enjoy the moment.
_____ 7. I prepare "to do" lists fairly regularly.
_____ 8. I am late with assignments at least 25% of the time.
_____ 9. I get very disappointed with myself when I'm late with assignments.
_____ 10. I look for immediate payoffs/rewards.

How Did You Do? These questions were designed to raise the issue of present and future time orientation, whether you focus more on the present or more on the future. Future-oriented individuals would respond with T to odd numbered statements (1, 3, 5, 7, 9) and F to even numbered questions (2, 4, 6, 8, 10). Present-oriented individuals would respond in reverse: F for odd numbered statements and T for even numbered statements.

What Will You Do? As you read more about time and nonverbal communication generally, consider how these time orientations work for or against you. For example, will your time orientation help you achieve your social and professional goals? If not, what might you do about changing these attitudes and behaviors?

The time orientation you develop depends to a great extent on your socioeconomic class and your personal experiences (Gonzalez & Zimbardo, 1985). For example, parents with unskilled and semiskilled occupations are likely to teach their children a present-orientated fatalism and a belief that enjoying yourself is more important than planning for the future. Parents who are teachers, managers, or other professionals tend to teach their children the importance of planning and preparing for the future, along with other strategies for success. In the United States, not surprisingly, future income is positively related to future orientation; the more future oriented you are, the greater your income is likely to be.

Different time perspectives also account for much intercultural misunderstanding, as different cultures often teach their members drastically different time orientations. For example, people from some Latin cultures would rather be late for an appointment than end a conversation abruptly or before it has come to a natural end. So the Latin cultures may see an individual's lateness as a result of politeness. But others may see the lateness as impolite to the person with whom the individual had the appointment (Hall & Hall, 1987).

Similarly, the future-oriented person who works for tomorrow's goals will frequently see the present-oriented person as lazy and poorly motivated for enjoying today and not planning for tomorrow. In turn, the present-oriented person may see those with strong future orientations as obsessed with amassing wealth or rising in status.

Not surprisingly, time orientation is heavily influenced by culture. Some cultures—individualistic cultures in particular—seem to emphasize a future orientation; members work

INTERPERSONAL CHOICE POINT

Smelling

Your colleague in the next cubicle wears extremely strong cologne that you find horrendous. You can't continue smelling this horrible scent any longer. What choices or options do you have to correct this situation?

hard today for a better future and without much regard for the past, for example. Collectivist cultures, on the other hand, have greater respect for the past; the past is often looked to for guidance for the present. According to some intercultural researchers, many Asian cultures (Japanese and Chinese) place great value on the past; Latinos and Native Americans place more emphasis on the present, and European Americans emphasize the future (Lustig & Koester, 2012). Different time perspectives also account for much intercultural misunderstanding, because different cultures often teach their members drastically different time orientations. The future-oriented person who works for tomorrow's goals will frequently regard the present-oriented person who focuses on enjoying today as lazy and poorly motivated. In turn, the present-oriented person may see those with strong future orientations as obsessed with accumulating wealth or rising in status. Here we look at three types of cultural time: formal and informal time, monochronism and polychronism, and the social clock.

Formal and Informal Time

Days are astronomically determined by the earth's rotation on its axis, months by the moon's movement around the earth, and years by the earth's rotation around the sun. But the rest of our time divisions are cultural (largely religious) in origin.

Formal time divisions in the United States and in most of the world include seconds, minutes, hours, days, weeks, months, and years. Some cultures, however, may use seasons or phases of the moon to demarcate their most important time periods. In the United States, if your college is on the semester system, your courses are divided into 50- or 75-minute periods that meet two or three times a week for 14-week periods. Eight semesters of 15 or 16 periods per week equal a college education. As these examples illustrate, formal time units are arbitrary. The culture establishes them for convenience.

Informal time divisions are more general, more ambiguous, and involve such informal time terms as "forever," "immediately," "soon," "right away," "as soon as possible." This type of time communication creates the most problems, because informal terms have different meanings for different people. This is especially true when these terms are used interculturally. For example, what does "late" mean when applied to a commuter train that is not on time? Apparently, it depends on your culture. In the United States (the New York area specifically), "late" means arriving six minutes or more after the scheduled time; in Britain it means five minutes or more. But in Japan it means one minute.

Not only in concepts of lateness but in other respects as well, attitudes toward time vary from one culture to another. In one study, for example, researchers measured the accuracy of clocks in six cultures—in Japan, Indonesia, Italy, England, Taiwan, and the United States. Japan had the most accurate and Indonesia had the least accurate clocks. The investigators also measured the speed at which people in these six cultures walked; results showed that the Japanese walked the fastest, the Indonesians the slowest (LeVine & Bartlett, 1984).

Monochronism and Polychronism

Another important distinction is that between **monochronic** and **polychronic time orientations** (Hall, 1959, 1976; Hall & Hall, 1987). Monochronic people or cultures—such as those of the United States, Germany, Scandinavia, and Switzerland—schedule one thing at a time. In these cultures time is compartmentalized and there is a time for everything. On the other hand, polychronic people or cultures—such as those of Latin Americans, Mediterranean peoples, and Arabs—schedule multiple things at the same time. Eating, conducting business with several different people, and taking care of family matters all may occur at the same time.

It's interesting to note that social network sites enable you to do (or at least appear to do) more things at one time by enabling you to schedule your tweets or the sending of birthday cards. So, you can be skiing down the slopes at the same time your tweets are posted or your cards are sent.

Johner Bildbyra/PhotoLibrary

VIEWPOINTS Informal time terms (e.g., *soon, right away, early, in a while, as soon as possible*) seem to create communication problems because they're ambiguous; different people will often give the terms different meanings. How might you go about reducing or eliminating the ambiguity created by these terms?

TABLE 4	Monochronic and Polychronic Time

As you read this table, based on Hall and Hall (1987), note the potential for miscommunication that these differences may create when monochronic-time and polychronic-time people interact. Have any of these differences ever created interpersonal misunderstandings for you?

The Monochronic-Time Person	The Polychronic-Time Person
Does one thing at a time.	Does several things at once.
Treats time schedules and plans very seriously; feels they may be broken only for the most serious of reasons.	Treats time schedules and plans as useful (not sacred) tools; feels they may be broken for a variety of causes.
Considers the job the most important part of life, ahead of even family.	Considers the family and interpersonal relationships more important than the job.
Considers privacy extremely important; seldom borrows or lends to others; works independently.	Is actively involved with others; works in the presence of and with lots of people at the same time.

No culture is entirely monochronic or polychronic; rather, these are general tendencies that are found across a large part of the culture. Some cultures combine both time orientations; for example, both orientations are found in Japan and in parts of American culture. Table 4 identifies some of the distinctions between these two time orientations.

Understanding these culturally different perspectives on time should make intercultural communication a bit easier, especially if these time differences are discussed in a culturally sensitive atmosphere. After all, one view of time is not any more correct than any other. However, like all cultural differences, these different time orientations have consequences. For example, the train crash in Japan might not have happened had it not been for the national obsession with time. And members of future-oriented cultures are more likely to succeed in competitive markets like the United States, but may be viewed negatively by members of cultures that stress living in and enjoying the present.

The Social Clock Your culture maintains a *social clock*—a time schedule for the right time to do various important things, such as starting dating, finishing college, buying your own home, or having a child. The social clock tells you if you're keeping pace with your peers, are ahead of them, or are falling behind (Greene, 2003; Neugarten, 1979). On the basis of this social clock, which you learned as you grew up, you evaluate your own social and professional development. If you're keeping pace with the rest of your peers (for example, you started dating at the "appropriate" age or you're finishing college at the "appropriate" age), you'll feel well-adjusted, competent, and a part of the group. If you're late, you'll probably experience feelings of dissatisfaction. Although today the social clock is becoming more flexible and more tolerant of deviations from the acceptable timetable than it was in past decades, it still exerts pressure on each of us to keep pace with our peers (Peterson, 1996).

Even the emotional tone of tweets seems to vary with the time of day. See "Tweets" at tcbdevito.blogspot .com. If you tweet, do you notice differences in emotional tone?

Nonverbal Communication Competence

Throughout the discussion of nonverbal communication, you've probably deduced a number of suggestions for improving your own nonverbal communication. Here, we bring together some suggestions for both receiving or decoding and sending or encoding nonverbal messages.

Perhaps the most general skill that applies to both receiving and sending is to become mindful of nonverbal messages—those of others as well as your own. Observe those whose nonverbal behavior you find particularly effective and those you find ineffective and try to identify exactly what makes one effective and one ineffective. Consider this chapter a brief introduction to a life-long study.

Decoding Nonverbal Messages

When you make judgments or draw conclusions about another person on the basis of her or his nonverbal messages, consider these suggestions:

- When making judgments, mindfully seek alternative judgments. Consider the vast array of choices for, say, interpreting or describing a person's behavior. Your first judgment choice may be in error, and one good way to test it is to consider alternative judgments. When your romantic partner creates a greater than normal distance between you, it may signal an annoyance with you but it can also signal that your partner needs some space to think something out.
- Be tentative. Resist the temptation to draw conclusions from nonverbal behaviors. Instead, develop hypotheses (educated guesses) about what is going on, and test the validity of your hypotheses on the basis of other evidence.
- Notice that messages come from lots of different channels and that reasonably accurate judgments can only be made when multiple channels are taken into consideration. Although textbooks must present the areas of nonverbal communication separately, the various elements all work together in actual communication situations.
- Even after you've explored the different channels, consider the possibility that you are incorrect. This is especially true when you make a judgment that another person is lying, based on, say, eye avoidance or long pauses. These nonverbal signals may mean lots of things (as well as the possibility of lying).
- Interpret your judgments and conclusions against a cultural context. Consider, for example, if you interpret another's nonverbal behavior through its meaning in your own culture. So, for example, if you interpret someone's "overly close" talking distance as intrusive or pushy because that's your culture's interpretation, you may miss the possibility that this distance is simply standard in the other person's culture, or it's a way of signaling closeness and friendliness.
- Consider the multitude of factors that can influence the way a person behaves nonverbally. For example, a person's physical condition or personality or particular situation may all influence a person's nonverbal communication. A sour stomach may be more influential in unpleasant expressions than any interpersonal factor. A low grade in an exam may make your normally pleasant roommate scowl and grumble. Without knowing these factors, it's difficult to make an accurate judgment.

Encoding Nonverbal Messages

In using nonverbal messages whether unconsciously or to express your meanings, consider these suggestions:

- Consider your choices for your nonverbal communication just as you do for your verbal messages. Identify and think mindfully about the choices you have available for communicating what you want to communicate.
- Keep your nonverbal messages consistent with your verbal messages; avoid sending verbal messages that say one thing and nonverbal messages that say something else—at least not when you want to be believed.

- Monitor your own nonverbal messages with the same care that you monitor your verbal messages. If it's not appropriate to say "this meal is terrible," then it's not appropriate to have a negative expression when you're asked if you want seconds.

- Avoid extremes and monotony. Too little nonverbal communication or too much are likely to be responded to negatively. Similarly, always giving the same nonverbal message—say, continually smiling and nodding your head when listening to a friend's long story—is likely to be seen as insincere.

- Take the situation into consideration. Effective nonverbal communication is situational; to be effective adapt your nonverbal messages to the specific situation. Nonverbal behavior appropriate to one situation may be totally inappropriate in another.

- Maintain eye contact with the speaker—whether at a meeting, in the hallway, or on an elevator; it communicates politeness and says that you are giving the person the consideration of your full attention. Eye contact that is too focused and too prolonged is likely to be seen as invasive and impolite.

- Avoid using certain adaptors in public—for example, combing your hair, picking your teeth, or putting your pinky in your ear; these will be seen as impolite. And, not surprisingly, the greater the formality of the situation, the greater the perception of impoliteness is likely to be. So, for example, combing your hair while sitting with two or three friends would probably not be considered impolite (or perhaps only mildly so), but in a classroom or at a company meeting, it would be considered inappropriate.

- Avoid strong cologne or perfume. While you may enjoy the scent, those around you may find it unpleasant and intrusive. Much like others do not want to hear your cell messages, they probably don't want to have their sense of smell invaded either.

- Be careful with touching; it may or may not be considered appropriate or polite depending on the relationship you have with the other person and on the context in which you find yourselves. The best advice to give here is to avoid touching unless it's part of the culture of the group or organization.

Summary

 Use your smartphone or tablet device (or log on to mycommunicationlab.com) to hear an audio summary of this chapter.

This chapter explored nonverbal communication and identified the varied channels of nonverbal communication, several functions of nonverbal communication that research has focused on, and the influence of culture on nonverbal messages.

Principles of Nonverbal Communication

1. Nonverbal messages interact with verbal messages in six major ways: to accent, to complement, to contradict, to control, to repeat, and to substitute for each other.

2. Nonverbal messages help manage impressions. It is largely through the nonverbal communications of others that you form impressions of them and through your nonverbals that they draw impressions of you.

3. Nonverbal messages help you form relationships. You communicate affection, support, and love, and also displeasure, anger, and animosity through nonverbal signals.

4. Nonverbal messages structure conversation. When you're in conversation, you exchange nonverbal signals indicating that you're ready to speak, to listen, to comment on what the speaker just said.

5. Nonverbal messages can influence and deceive. You can influence (and deceive) others not only through what you say but also through your nonverbal signals.

6. Nonverbal messages are crucial for emotional expression. Although people often explain and reveal emotions verbally, nonverbal signals communicate a great part of your emotional experience.

Channels of Nonverbal Communication

7. Nonverbal messages are communicated through a variety of channels and their meanings will be greatly influenced by culture.

8. Among body gestures are emblems, illustrators, affect displays, regulators, and adaptors.

9. General body appearance (e.g., height, weight, and eye and skin colors) can communicate a person's power, level of

attractiveness, and suitability as a friend or romantic partner.

10. Facial movements express emotions, such as happiness, surprise, fear, anger, sadness, disgust/contempt, interest, bewilderment, and determination. Some facial movements manage the meanings being communicated by means of intensifying, deintensifying, neutralizing, masking, and simulating.

11. Through eye contact we monitor feedback, maintain interest/attention, signal conversational turns, signal the nature of relationships, signal status, and compensate for physical distance. Through eye avoidance we may give others privacy, signal disinterest, cut off unpleasant stimuli, or heighten other senses. Pupil dilation indicates interest/arousal and increases attractiveness.

12. Among the meanings touch can communicate are positive affect, playfulness, control, ritual functions, and task-relatedness.

13. Paralanguage cues help people form impressions; identify emotional states; and make judgments of speakers' credibility, intelligence, and objectivity.

14. Silence can communicate varied meanings (for example, to hurt, to prevent communication, to achieve special effects). The spiral of silence theory offers an interesting perspective on the influence of silence.

15. The major types of distance that correspond to types of relationships are intimate distance (touching to 18 inches), personal distance (18 inches to 4 feet), social distance (4 to 12 feet), and public distance (12 or more feet).

16. Theories about space include protection theory (you maintain spatial distance to protect yourself); equilibrium theory (you regulate distance according to the intimacy level of your relationship); and expectancy violations theory (increasing or decreasing the expected distance between yourself and another can send important messages).

17. Your territories may be identified as primary (areas you own), secondary (areas that you occupy regularly), and public (areas open to everyone). Like animals, humans often mark their territories with central, boundary, and ear markers as proof of ownership. Your territory (its appearance and the way it's used) also communicates status.

18. Among the artifactual nonverbal cues are space decoration, color, clothing and body adornment, and the use of scent.

19. Three main time orientations can be distinguished: past, present, and future. These orientations influence a wide variety of behaviors, such as your willingness to plan for the future, your tendency to party, and even your potential income.

Nonverbal Communication Competence

20. You can increase your nonverbal decoding competence by mindfully seeking alternative judgments, being tentative, attending to all nonverbal channels, considering being wrong, being sensitive to the cultural context, and considering the vast array of factors that can influence what a person does or says.

21. You can increase your nonverbal encoding competence by considering your choices for communicating, being consistent in your messages, monitoring your nonverbal choices, avoiding extremes, being aware of the situation, maintaining eye contact, avoiding adaptors, avoiding strong and potentially unpleasant scents, and being cautious about touching.

Key Terms

adaptors
affect displays
artifactual
   communication
chronemics
civil inattention
color communication
cultural display
cultural display rules
emblems
equilibrium theory
expectancy violations
   theory
eye avoidance

facial feedback
   hypothesis
formal time
haptics
home field advantage
home territories
illustrators
immediacy
informal time
intimate distance
kinesics
markers
monochronic time
   orientation

nonverbal
   communication
occulesis
olfactory
   communication
paralanguage
personal distance
pitch
polychronic time
   orientation
protection theory
proxemic distances
proxemics
psychological time

public distance
rate
regulators
silence
social distance
spiral of silence
tactile communication
temporal communication
territorial encroachment
territoriality
touch avoidance
volume

MyCommunicationLab Explorations

MyCommunicationLab®

Communication Choice Points

Revisit the chapter-opening video, "Inviting or Discouraging Conversation." Recall that at first, Kendra is intently studying and doesn't really have time for her roommate. But Lori ignores her body language and keeps interrupting, frustrating both of them. Next, Kendra is trying to study, but doesn't seem focused. She's looking for any excuse to be distracted—and she makes this clear through both her words and her actions. "Inviting or Discouraging Conversation" examines how much information is communicated nonverbally through actions, tone, gestures, and even the use of silence.

Log on to mycommunicationlab.com to view the video for this chapter, "Inviting or Discouraging Conversation," and then answer the related discussion questions.

Additional Resources

This group of experiences deals with nonverbal messages and provides opportunities to work with these various channels of communication.

1 Facial Expressions and **2** Eye Contact focus on the various meanings the face and the eyes communicate. **3** Interpersonal Interactions and Space and **4** Sitting at the Company Meeting look at the meanings communicated by the way you use space. **5** The Meanings of Color helps sensitize you to the various meanings that different colors communicate. **6** Praising and Criticizing looks at how a variety of meanings can be communicated without words. **7** Artifacts and Culture: The Case of Gifts illustrates the vast cultural differences in what is considered appropriate gift giving.

Emotional Messages

From Chapter 7 of *The Interpersonal Communication Book*, Thirteenth Edition. Joseph A. DeVito. Copyright © 2013 by Pearson Education, Inc.
All rights reserved.

Emotional Messages

Principles of Emotions and Emotional Messages

Obstacles to Communicating Emotions

Skills for Expressing Emotions

Skills for Responding to the Emotions of Others

2:13 / 5:00

Pearson Education

Tobin, the manager of a small firm, has called a team leader meeting. There are going to be some unpopular changes in the work teams, and each leader will be responsible for giving the news to their respective teams. In the video "Communicating Change," you can see how Tobin's emotional state affects the choices he makes about how to deliver the message (www.mycommunicationlab.com).

Some of the more difficult interpersonal communication situations are those that involve **emotions,** which we can define simply as strong feelings. This chapter addresses this crucial topic; it offers insight into the nature of emotions and emotional expression, discusses some of the obstacles to communicating emotions, and presents suggestions for communicating emotions and for responding to the emotions of others.

Principles of Emotions and Emotional Messages

Communicating emotions, or feelings, is difficult. It's difficult because your thinking often gets confused when you're intensely emotional. It's also difficult because you probably weren't taught how to communicate emotions—and you probably have few effective models to imitate.

Communicating emotions is also important. Feelings constitute a great part of your meanings. If you leave your feelings out, or if you express them inadequately, you will fail to communicate a great part of your meaning. For example, consider what your communications would be like if you left out your feelings when talking about failing a recent test, winning the lottery, becoming a parent, getting engaged, driving a car for the first time, becoming a citizen, or being promoted to supervisor. Emotional expression is so much a part of communication that even in the cryptic e-mail message style, emoticons are becoming more popular.

So important is **emotional communication** that it is at the heart of what is now called "emotional intelligence" or "social intelligence" (Goleman, 1995a). And, it's been shown, that without emotions, decision making is impaired and often rendered impossible (Damasio, 2005).

The inability to engage in emotional communication—as sender and as receiver—is part of the learning disability known as *dyssemia,* a condition in which individuals are unable to appropriately read the nonverbal messages of others or to communicate their own meanings nonverbally (Duke & Nowicki, 2005). Persons suffering from dyssemia, for example, look uninterested, fail to return smiles, and use facial expressions that are inappropriate to the situation and the interaction. As you can

Corbis Super RF/Alamy

VIEWPOINTS *Emotional isolation* refers to the situation in which a person has no intimate with whom to share emotions. Even though the person may have a wide network of associates, there is no one person to relate to on an intimate level. In what ways might people seek to prevent or lessen emotional isolation?

Understanding *Interpersonal Theory & Research*

THREE THEORIES OF EMOTIONS

Working with Theories and Research

These theories offer considerable insight into the way in which we experience emotions, though none of them is the total explanation. From an analysis of your own emotional experience, what explanation seems the most logical? Why? How would you describe emotional arousal?

If you were to describe the events leading up to emotional arousal, you would probably describe three stages: (1) An event occurs. (2) You experience an emotion such as surprise, joy, or anger. (3) You respond physiologically; your heart beats faster, your face flushes, and so on. The process would go like this:

A An event occurs → You experience an emotion → You respond physiologically

Psychologist William James and physiologist Carl Lange offered a different explanation. Their theory places the physiological arousal before the experience of the emotion. The sequence of events according to the **James–Lange theory** is: (1) An event occurs. (2) You respond physiologically. And (3) you experience an emotion; for example, you feel joy or sadness. This process would look like this:

B An event occurs → You respond physiologically → You experience an emotion—for example, joy or sadness

According to a third explanation, the **cognitive labeling theory**, you interpret the physiological arousal and, on the basis of this, experience the emotions of joy, sadness, or whatever (Reisenzein, 1983; Schachter, 1971). The sequence goes like this: (1) An event occurs. (2) You respond physiologically. (3) You interpret this arousal—that is, you decide what emotion you're experiencing. And (4) you experience the emotion. Your interpretation of your arousal will depend on the situation you're in. For example, if you experience an increased pulse rate after someone you've been admiring smiles at you, you may interpret this as joy. If three suspicious-looking strangers approach you on a dark street, however, you may interpret that same increased heartbeat as fear. It's only after you make the interpretation that you experience the emotion; for example, the joy or the fear. This process looks like this:

C An event occurs → You respond physiologically → You interpret this arousal; you decide what emotion you are experiencing → You identify the emotion you're feeling

imagine, people who are poor senders and receivers of emotional messages will likely have problems in developing and maintaining relationships. When interacting with such people, you're likely to feel uncomfortable because of their inappropriate emotional communication (Goleman, 1995a).

Let's look first at several general principles of emotions and emotional expression; these will establish a foundation for our consideration of the skills of emotional competence.

Emotions May Be Primary or Blended

How would you feel in each of the following situations?

- You won the lottery.
- You got the job you applied for.
- Your best friend just died.
- Your parents tell you they're getting divorced.

You would obviously feel very differently in each of these situations. In fact, each feeling is unique and unrepeatable. Yet amid all these differences, there are some similarities. For example, most people would agree that the first two sets of feelings are more similar to each other than they are to the last two. Similarly, the last two are more similar to each other than they are to the first two.

To capture the similarities and differences among emotions, one researcher identifies the basic or **primary emotions** (Havlena, Holbrook, & Lehmann, 1989; Plutchik, 1980): joy, trust, fear, surprise, sadness, disgust, anger, and anticipation (Figure 1). This model of emotions is especially useful for viewing the broad scale of emotions, their relationships to each other, and their varied combinations.

Emotions that are close to each other on this wheel are also close to each other in meaning. For example, joy and anticipation are more closely related than are joy and sadness or trust and disgust. Emotions that are opposite each other on the wheel are also opposite each other in their meaning. For example, joy is the opposite of sadness; anger is the opposite of fear.

In this model there are also blends. These **blended emotions** are combinations of the primary emotions. These are noted outside the emotion wheel. For example, according to this model, love is a blend of joy and trust. Remorse is a blend of disgust and sadness. Similar but milder emotions appear in lighter shades (for example, serenity is a milder joy) and stronger emotions appear in darker shades (for example, terror is a stronger fear).

FIGURE 1
A Model of the Emotions

Do you agree with the basic assumptions of this model?

Reprinted with permission from Annette deFerrari Design.

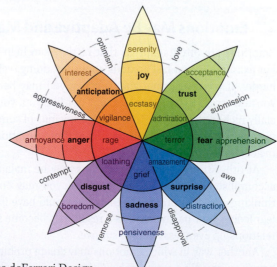

Reprinted with permission from Annette deFerrari Design

Emotions Are Influenced by Body, Mind, and Culture

Emotion involves at least three parts: bodily reactions (such as blushing when you're embarrassed); mental evaluations and interpretations (as in calculating the odds of drawing an inside straight at poker); and cultural rules and beliefs (such as the pride parents feel when their child graduates from college).

It's interesting to note that programs are available for checking the emotional tone of your e-mail, highlighting problematic terms and suggesting alternative expressions—another indication of the importance the workplace puts on emotions and their expression. See "Emotional Checker" at tcbdevito .blogspot.com. What do you think of this?

- **The Body.** Bodily reactions are the most obvious aspect of our emotional experience because we can observe them easily. Such reactions span a wide range. They include, for example, the blush of embarrassment, the sweating palms that accompany nervousness, and the gestures (such as playing with your hair or touching your face) that go with discomfort. When you judge people's emotions, you probably look to these nonverbal behaviors. You conclude that Ramon is happy to see you because of his smile and his open body posture. You conclude that Lisa is nervous from her damp hands, vocal hesitations, and awkward movements.
- **The Mind.** The mental or cognitive part of emotional experience involves the evaluations and interpretations you make on the basis of what you experience. For example, leading psychotherapist Albert Ellis (1988; Ellis & Harper, 1975), whose insights are used throughout this chapter, claims that your evaluations of what happens have a greater influence on your feelings than what actually happens. Let us say, for example, that your best friend, Sally, ignores you in the college cafeteria. The emotions you feel will depend on what you think this behavior means. You may feel pity if you figure that Sally is depressed because her father died. You may feel anger if you believe that Sally is simply rude and insensitive and snubbed you on purpose. Or you may feel sadness if you believe that Sally is no longer interested in being friends with you.
- **The Culture.** The cultural context—the culture you were raised in and/or the culture you live in—gives you a framework for both expressing feelings and interpreting the emotions of others. A colleague of mine gave a lecture in Beijing, China, to a group of Chinese college students. The students listened politely but made no comments and asked no questions after her lecture. At first my colleague concluded that the students were bored and uninterested. Later, however, she learned that Chinese students show respect by being quiet and seemingly passive. They think that asking questions would imply that she was not clear in her lecture. In other words, the culture—whether American or Chinese—influenced the interpretation of the students' feelings. Another example: In a recent study, Japanese students, when asked to judge the emotion shown in a computer icon, looked to the eyes to determine the emotion. Students from the United States, however, focused on the mouth (Masuda, Ellsworth, Mesquita, Leu, Tanida, & van de Veerdonk, 2008; Yuki, Maddux, & Masuda, 2007).

Emotions May Be Adaptive and Maladaptive

Emotions are often adaptive; that is, they can help you adjust appropriately to situations. For example, if you feel anxious about not doing well on an exam, it may lead you to study harder. If you fear losing your partner, you may behave more supportively and lovingly. If you're worried that someone might not like you, your worry may motivate you to be especially nice to the person. If you feel suspicious of someone following you down a dark street, you may take safety precautions. All of these situations are examples of emotions aiding you in accomplishing useful goals.

At other times, however, emotions may be maladaptive and may get in the way of your accomplishing your goals. For example, you may be so anxious about a test that you stop thinking and do more poorly than you would have if you walked in totally cold. Or you may fear losing your partner and as a result may become suspicious and accusatory, making your relationship even less likely to survive.

Another way in which emotions may create problems is in a tendency that some theorists have cleverly called *catastrophizing* (or *awfulizing*): taking a problem—even a minor one—and making it into a catastrophe. For example, you may feel that "If I don't do well on this test, I'll never get into law school" or "If this relationship doesn't work, I'm doomed." As you convince yourself of these impending catastrophes, your emotional responses can easily get out of hand (Bach & Wyden, 1968; Willson & Branch, 2006).

The important point is that emotions can work for you or against you. And the same is true of emotional communication. Some of it is good and is likely to lead to positive outcomes (a more secure relationship or a more positive interaction, say). But some of it is bad and may aggravate a conflict, alienate friends, or lessen your relationship satisfaction. Or emotional communication may simply be thought inappropriate and thus give others a bad impression.

Emotions Can Be Used Strategically

Although you may at first think of emotional expression as honest reflections of what a person is feeling, emotions can be and often are used strategically. In **strategic emotionality**, emotions (for example, crying, ranting, screaming, and threatening to commit self-harm) are used for one's personal ends. Such emotions can take a variety of forms and serve a variety of purposes. But, the basic idea behind strategic emotionality is to control the situation or the other person. For example, in a conflict situation, emotions are often used to win. If someone cries enough and loud enough, the other person may just give in. It works for the baby who wants to be picked up, and it often works for the adult and enables the person to win the fight. This strategy is more likely to be used by members of individualist cultures that emphasize the winning of a conflict, rather than compromise or negotiation (which would be more likely in collectivist cultures).

Not surprisingly this strategy, which is essentially one of manipulation, often creates resentment and perhaps a desire to retaliate—neither of which is good for a relationship. Another negative outcome of this strategy is that the other person can never be sure how accurate their partner's emotions reflect their true feelings, and this is likely to create communication problems whenever emotions are involved. The effect of this lack of transparency—of not knowing if one's partner is trying to manipulate or if they are expressing strong and honest feelings—is likely to be greatest in intimate relationships, where these expressions are likely to have long-term effects.

Emotions Are Communicated Verbally and Nonverbally

Although emotions are especially salient in conflict situations and in relationship development and dissolution, they are actually a part of all messages. Emotions are always present—sometimes very strongly, sometimes only mildly. Therefore, they must be recognized as a part of the communication experience. This is not to say that you should always talk about or express all the emotions you feel. Emotional feeling and emotional communication are two different things. In some instances you may want to say exactly what you feel, to reveal your emotions without any censorship. At other times, however, you may want to avoid revealing your emotions. For example, you might not want to reveal your frustration

VIEWPOINTS One implication of the cognitive labeling theory of emotions is that you and only you can make yourself feel angry or sad or anxious. This view is often phrased popularly as "Other people can hurt you physically, but only you can hurt yourself emotionally." Do you agree with this? What evidence can you advance to support or refute this position?

Design Pics Inc./Alamy

INTERPERSONAL CHOICE POINT

Mindreading

Alex and Deirdre have dated steadily for the last four years. Deirdre is extremely unexpressive but believes that Alex—because of their long and close relationship—should know how she feels without her having to spell it out. When Alex doesn't respond appropriately, Deirdre becomes angry, saying that Alex doesn't really love her; if he did, he would know what she's feeling. Alex says this is crazy: "I'm no mind reader; if Deirdre wants something, she has the obligation to say so." If you were a mediator, what are some of the things you might say to Alex and to Deirdre?

Ethics in Interpersonal Communication

MOTIVATIONAL APPEALS

Appeals to motives are commonplace. For example, if you want a friend to take a vacation with you, you're likely to appeal to such motives as the friend's desire for fun and excitement, and perhaps to the friend's hopes of meeting his or her true love. If you look at the advertisements for cruises and vacation packages, you'll see appeals to very similar motives. Fear appeals also are common: Persons who want to censor the Internet may appeal to your fear of children's accessing pornographic materials; those who want to restrict media portrayals of violence may appeal to your fear of increased violence in your community. Advertisers appeal to your vanity and your desire for increased sexual attractiveness in trying to sell you cosmetics and expensive clothing.

There can be no doubt that such motivational appeals are effective. But are they ethical?

ETHICAL CHOICE POINT

Suppose you wanted to dissuade your teenage children from engaging in sexual relationships. Would it be ethical to use emotional appeals to fear—to scare them so that they'd avoid such relationships? Would it be ethical to use the same appeals if your goal were to get them to stop smoking?

over a customer's indecision, or you might not want to share with your children your worries about finding a job.

Theorists do not agree over whether you can choose the emotions you feel. Some argue that you can; others argue that you cannot. You are, however, in control of the ways in which you express your emotions. Whether or not you choose to express your emotions will depend on your own attitudes about emotional expression. You may wish to explore these by taking the self-test.

Test Yourself How Do You Feel about Communicating Feelings?

Respond to each of the following statements with T if you feel the statement is a generally true description of your attitudes about expressing emotions, or with F if you feel the statement is a generally false description of your attitudes.

_____ 1. Expressing feelings is healthy; it reduces stress and prevents wasting energy on concealment.
_____ 2. Expressing feelings can lead to interpersonal relationship problems.
_____ 3. Expressing feelings can help others understand you.
_____ 4. Emotional expression is often an effective means of persuading others to do as you wish.
_____ 5. Expressing emotions may lead others to perceive you negatively.
_____ 6. Emotional expression can lead to greater and not less stress; expressing anger, for example, may actually increase your feelings of anger.

How Did You Do? These statements are arguments that are often made for and against expressing emotions. Statements 1, 3, and 4 are arguments made in favor of expressing emotions; 2, 5, and 6 are arguments made against expressing emotions. You can look at your responses as revealing (in part) your attitude favoring or opposing the expression of feelings. "True" responses to statements 1, 3, and 4 and "False" responses to statements 2, 5, and 6 would indicate a favorable attitude to expressing feelings. "False" responses to statements 1, 3, and 4 and "True" responses to statements 2, 5, and 6 indicate a negative attitude.

What Will You Do? There is evidence suggesting that expressing emotions can lead to all six outcomes—the positives and the negatives—so general suggestions for increasing your willingness to express your emotions are not offered. These potential consequences underscore the importance of critically assessing your options for emotional expression. Be flexible, remembering that what will work in one situation will not work in another.

If you decide to communicate your feelings, you need to make several decisions. For example, you have to choose how to do so—face-to-face or by letter, phone, e-mail, text message, or office memo. And you have to choose the specific emotions you will and will not reveal. Finally, you have to choose the language in which you'll express your emotions.

As with most meanings, emotions are encoded both verbally and nonverbally. Your words, the emphasis you give them, and the gestures and facial expressions that accompany them all help to communicate your feelings. Conversely, you decode the emotional messages of others on the basis of both verbal and nonverbal cues. And of course emotions, like all messages, are most effectively communicated when verbal and nonverbal messages reinforce and complement each other.

VIEWPOINTS People are more likely to receive expressions of positive affect positively and with approval, whereas negative affect is more likely to meet negative reactions (Metts & Planalp, 2002 Monahan, 1998; Sommers, 1984). But it's not always easy to determine how others will perceive an emotion; for example, jealousy, although a negative emotion, may be perceived positively, as a sign that you really care (Metts & Planalp, 2002, p. 359). What rule(s) do you follow in deciding whether or not to express your positive and your negative emotions?

Zefa RF/Alamy

Emotional Expression Is Governed by Display Rules

Different cultures' **display rules** govern what is and what is not permissible emotional communication. Even within U.S. culture itself, there are differences. For example, in one study Americans classified themselves into four categories: Caucasian, African American, Asian, and Hispanic/Latino. Just to make the point that different cultures teach different rules for the display of emotions, here are a few of the study's findings (Matsumoto, 1994, 2009): (1) Caucasians found the expression of contempt more appropriate than did Asians; (2) African Americans and Hispanics felt that showing disgust was less appropriate than did Caucasians; (3) Hispanics rated public displays of emotion as less appropriate than did Caucasians; and (4) Caucasians rated the expression of fear as more appropriate than did Hispanics.

Researchers agree that men and women experience emotions similarly (Cherulnik, 1979; Oatley & Duncan, 1994; Wade & Tavris, 2007). The differences that are observed are differences in the way emotions are expressed, not in the way they are felt. Men and women seem to have different **gender display rules** for what is and what isn't appropriate to express, much as different cultures have different cultural display rules.

Women talk more about feelings and emotions and use communication for emotional expression more than men (Barbato & Perse, 1992). Perhaps because of this, they also express themselves facially more than men. Even junior and senior high schoolers show this gender difference. Research findings suggest that this difference may be due to differences in the brains of men and women; women's brains have a significantly larger inferior parietal lobule, which seems to account for women's greater awareness of feelings (Barta, 1999).

Women are also more likely to express socially acceptable emotions than are men (Brody, 1985). For example, women smile significantly more than men. In fact, women smile even when smiling is not appropriate—for example, when reprimanding a subordinate. Men, on the other hand, are more likely than women to express anger and aggression (DePaulo, 1992; Fischer, 1993; Wade & Tavris, 2007). Similarly, women are more effective at communicating happiness and men are more effective at communicating anger (Coats & Feldman, 1996). Women also cry more than men (Metts & Planalp, 2002).

In an extensive survey of emotions in the workplace, women were found to cry more than men (41 percent of the women surveyed had cried on the job but only 9 percent of the men [Kreamer, 2011]). But, interestingly enough, women were more disapproving of those who cry than were men; 43 percent of the women and 32 percent of the men considered those who cry on the job to be "unstable." Further, women feel worse after crying; men feel better.

Earlier we considered the fundamental attribution error in which too much emphasis is placed on internal factors (for example, personality) and too little emphasis is placed on external factors (for example, the work load) in explaining a person's behavior. This is exactly what happens when the emotional behavior of men and women is "explained." Specifically, a woman's anger was most often attributed to her personality (she's unstable or out of control), whereas a man's anger was more often attributed to external factors (the report was inadequate or the work was late). As you can imagine, women's anger was seen as unjustified whereas men's anger was judged justifiable (Kreamer, 2011).

Emotions Have Consequences

Like all communications, emotions and emotional expression have consequences and impact on your relationships in important ways. By revealing your emotions you may create close bounds with others. At the same time, you may also scare people with too much and too intimate disclosure.

Revealing your emotions communicates important information about who you are and how you feel about those you're communicating with. If you talk about your loneliness then you're revealing important information about yourself and also expressing a confidence in the person with whom you're talking. It also tells people what's really important to you. Do realize that in revealing strongly felt emotions, you may be exposing vulnerabilities or weaknesses that conceivably could be used against you.

Emotions and emotional expression also impact on your work life and, in fact, organizations are devoting energy to dealing with worker emotion, trying to turn the negative into the positive. See Table 1.

VIEWPOINTS When workers cry on the job, the most frequent reason—for both men and women—is that stress from home spread into the workplace (Kreamer, 2011). What other reasons might account for crying (or wanting to cry) on the job? Will these reasons be different for men and women? How would you evaluate the crying of your male and female co-workers?

Sergey Peterman/Shutterstock

Emotions Are Contagious

Emotional messages are often contagious (Cappella & Schreiber, 2006). If you've ever watched an infant and mother interacting, you can readily see how quickly the infant mimics the emotional expressions of the mother. If the mother smiles, the infant smiles; if the mother frowns, the infant frowns. As children get older, they begin to pick up more subtle expressions of emotions. For example, children quickly identify and often mimic a parent's anxiety or fear. Even among college roommates, the depression of one roommate spread to the other over a period of just three weeks (Joiner, 1994). In short, in **emotional contagion** emotions pass from one person to another; women are especially prone to this process (Cappella & Schreiber, 2006; Doherty, Orimoto, Singelis, Hatfield, & Hebb, 1995). In conversation and in small groups, the strong emotions of one person can easily prove contagious to others present; this can be productive when the emotions are productive, or unproductive when the emotions are unproductive.

One view of this process goes like this (Figure 2):

1. You perceive an emotional expression of another.
2. You mimic this emotional expression, perhaps unconsciously.
3. The feedback you get from expressing the emotion creates in you a replication of the other person's feelings.

You see another variant of intentional emotional contagion in attempts at persuasion that utilize **emotional appeals**. One popular appeal, which organizations use frequently in fund-raising for needy children, is to the emotion of pity. By showing you images of hungry and destitute children, these fund-raisers hope to get you to experience so much pity that

Even loneliness seems to be contagious. See "Loneliness Is Contagious" at tcbdevito.blogspot.com. Does your experience support this view?

192

Blend Images/Alamy

Thomas Northcut/Riser/Getty Images

VIEWPOINTS Here are three theories offered to explain sex differences in emotional expression, similar to those noted in the discussion of gender differences in language. Each of these provides a useful perspective for viewing often quite pronounced sex differences (Guerrero, Jones, & Boburka, 2006).

- Biological theory claims that differences in brains and chemistry account for the differences in the ability to express and detect emotions and for the different emotions displayed.
- Evolutionary theory claims that emotional expression was basic to survival; those who were good at it lived and passed on their genes to others and those who weren't good at it often died early with the result that their genes were not passed on. And, because men and women served widely differing functions, they each came to rely on different emotions and different ways of expressing and inhibiting emotions.
- Socialization theory claims that men and women are taught differently about emotions (and this, of course, varies with the culture) and have been socialized into expressing emotions as they do. Women are taught to smile and to express positive affect (it's the "feminine" thing to do), while men are taught to inhibit expressing sadness or fear (it's not "masculine" to display "weak" emotions).

Which of these positions seems the most important based on your own observations of sex differences in communication?

TABLE 1	Negative Emotions and Work

Here are the five most frequently experienced negative emotions on the job (Fisher, 1997). Assuming these emotions are unproductive, record any recommendations you would offer a colleague who experiences each of these negative emotions. After making your recommendations, take a look at Mindtools.com (Managing Your Emotions at Work).

Negative Emotions	Recommendations
Frustration over feeling stuck in a rut	
Worry and anxiety over job security	
Anger over the actions or decisions of others	
Dislike of others you work with and for	
Disappointment over your position, accomplishments, and prospects	

FIGURE 2
Emotional Contagion

Another view of emotional contagion would hold that the process is under more conscious control. That is, you look at others who are expressing emotions to see how you should be feeling—you take nonverbal cues from those you observe—and then feel the feeling you believe you should be feeling. Which view seems more satisfying?

you'll help finance their efforts. Similarly, people who beg for money often emphasize their difficulties in an effort to evoke pity and donations.

Emotional contagion also seems the goal of certain organizational display rules. For example, a company may require (or at least expect) that the sales force cheer enthusiastically as each new product is unveiled. This cheering is extremely useful and is likely to make the sales representatives more enthusiastic about and more emotionally committed to the product than if they didn't engage in this cheering.

Another popular appeal is to guilt. If someone does something for you, he or she may try to make you feel guilty unless you do something in return. Or someone may present himself or herself as in desperate need of money and make you feel guilty for having what you have and not sharing it. Sometimes people encourage others to feel guilty to make them more easily manipulated. If you can make a person feel guilty for having a great deal of money while others have little, you are on the road to persuading the person to give some of that money away.

With these principles of emotions and emotional expression as a foundation, we can now look at some of the obstacles to effective emotional expression.

INTERPERSONAL CHOICE POINT

Emotional Frankness

Joe is extremely honest and open; he regularly says everything he feels without self-censorship. Not surprisingly, he often offends people. Joe is entering a new work environment and worries that his frankness may not be the best way to win friends and influence people. What are some things Joe can do to better understand this problem? What can he do to correct it?

Obstacles to Communicating Emotions

The expression of feelings is a part of most meaningful relationships. Yet it's often very difficult. Three major obstacles stand in the way of effective emotional communication: (1) society's rules and customs, (2) fear, and (3) inadequate interpersonal skills. Let's look more closely at each of these barriers.

Societal and Cultural Customs

If you grew up in the United States, you probably learned that many people frown on emotional expression. This attitude is especially prevalent in men and has been aptly called the "cowboy syndrome," after a pattern of behavior seen in the old Westerns (Balswick & Peck, 1971). The cowboy syndrome characterizes the closed and unexpressive male. This man is strong but silent. He never feels any of the softer emotions (such as compassion, love, or contentment). He would never ever cry, experience fear, or feel sorry for himself.

Unfortunately, many men grow up trying to live up to this unrealistic image. It's a syndrome that prevents open and honest expression. Boys are taught early in life not to cry and to not be "babies" if hurt. All of this is not to suggest that men should communicate their emotions more openly. Unfortunately, there are many who will negatively evaluate men who express emotions openly and often; such men may be judged ineffective, insecure, or unmanly. In fact, some

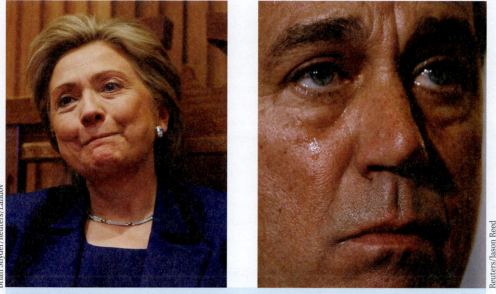

Brian Snyder/Reuters/Landov

Reuters/Jason Reed

VIEWPOINTS ⬌ Here Hillary Clinton and John Boehner both cry in public. How do you respond to a politician crying? Do you see this as a sign of compassion and caring or a sign of weakness and an inability to control oneself? Do you have different attitudes based on the sex of the person crying? Given your cultural traditions, when is it permissible for a woman to cry in public? When it is permission for a man to cry in public?

research shows that the reason men are reluctant to provide sensitive emotional support—to the degree that women do, for example—is that men don't want their behavior to be seen as feminine (Burleson, Holmstrom, & Gilstrap, 2005).

Nor are women exempt from restraints on emotional expression. At one time our society permitted and encouraged women to express emotions openly. The tide now is turning, especially for women in executive and managerial positions. Today the executive woman is being forced into the same cowboy syndrome. She is not allowed to cry or to show any of the once acceptable "soft" emotions. She is especially denied these feelings while she is on the job.

And, of course, organizations have their own cultural norms for the expression of emotions. For example, in many organizations employees are expected to pretend to be cheerful even when not and generally to display some emotions and to hide others. Unfortunately, differences between the emotions you feel and the emotions you express can create emotional dissonance, which in turn can lead to stress (Remland, 2006).

For both men and women, the best advice (as with any of the characteristics of communication effectiveness discussed in this book) is to express your emotions selectively. Carefully weigh the arguments for and against expressing your emotions. Consider the situation, the people you're with, the emotions themselves, and all of the elements that make up the communication act. And, most important, consider your choices for communicating emotions—not only what you'll say but also how you'll say it.

Fear

A variety of types of fear stand in the way of emotional expression. Emotional expression exposes a part of you that makes you vulnerable to attack. For example, if you express your love for another person, you risk being rejected. When you expose a weakness, you can more easily be hurt by uncaring or insensitive others. Of course, you may also fear hurting someone else by, say, voicing your feelings about past loves. Or you may be angry and want to say something but fear that you might hurt the person and then feel guilty yourself.

VIEWPOINTS Marie and Dave have been married for several years. Marie is extremely expressive, yelling one minute, crying the next. By comparison, Dave is nonexpressive. This difference is now causing problems. Dave feels Marie reacts impulsively without thinking her feelings through; Marie feels Dave is unwilling to share his life with her. What skills do Marie and Dave need to learn?

INTERPERSONAL CHOICE POINT

Responding Emotionally (or Not)

Your supervisor seems to constantly belittle your experience, which you thought was your strong point. Often your supervisor will say that your experiences were "in school" or "with only a few people" or some such negative phrase. You think your experience has more than prepared you for this job, and you want to make sure your supervisor knows this. What are your options for communicating this feeling? What should you say?

In addition, you may avoid revealing your emotions for fear of causing a conflict. Expressing your dislike for Pat's friends, for example, may create difficulties for the two of you, and you may not be willing to risk the argument and its aftermath. Because of fears such as these, you may deny to others and perhaps even to yourself that you have certain feelings. In fact, this kind of denial is the way many people were taught to deal with emotions.

As you can appreciate, fear can be adaptive; it may lead you to not say things you may be sorry for later. It may lead you to consider more carefully whether or not you should express yourself and how you might do it. But when it debilitates us and contradicts what logic and reason might tell us, then the fear becomes maladaptive.

Inadequate Interpersonal Skills

Perhaps the most important obstacle to effective emotional communication is lack of interpersonal skills. Many people simply don't know how to express their feelings. Some people, for example, can express anger only through violence or avoidance. Others can deal with anger only by blaming and accusing others. And many people cannot express love. They literally cannot say, "I love you."

Expressing negative feelings is doubly difficult. Many of us suppress or fail to communicate negative feelings for fear of offending the other person or making matters worse. But failing to express negative feelings will probably not help the relationship, especially if these feelings are concealed frequently and over a long time.

Both communicating your emotions and responding appropriately to the emotional expressions of others are as important as they are difficult (Burleson, 2003). And to complicate matters further, as noted in the self-test earlier in this chapter, emotional expression can be good but also can be bad. On the one hand, expressing emotions can be cathartic to you and may benefit a relationship. Expressing emotions can also help you air dissatisfactions and perhaps reduce or even eliminate them. Through emotional expression you can come to understand each other better, which may lead to a closer and more meaningful relationship.

On the other hand, expressing emotions may cause relationship difficulties. For example, expressing your dislike of a colleague's customary way of answering the phone may generate hostility; expressing jealousy when your partner spends time with friends may cause your partner to fear being controlled and losing autonomy.

Emotional Competence

Much as emotions are a part of your psychological life, emotional expression is a part of your interpersonal life; it is not something you could avoid even if you wanted to. In specific cases you may decide to hide your emotions and not express them; but in other cases you'll want to express your emotions and this calls for what we might call emotional competence, the skills for expressing and responding to the emotions of others. We can group these under

TABLE 2   Emotional Happiness

A somewhat different view of emotional competence would be emotional happiness; after all, if you're emotionally competent, it should contribute to your individual happiness, a topic addressed in this table. Here are a few "dos" (but with qualifications) for achieving emotional satisfaction, contentment, and happiness.

Do	But
Think positively.	Don't be a Pollyanna; don't gloss over problems.
Associate with positive people.	Don't avoid others because they have different ideas or backgrounds; you'll miss out on a lot.
Do what you enjoy.	Don't forget your responsibilities or ignore obligations.
Talk about your feelings.	Don't substitute talk for action or talk too much.
Imagine yourself positively.	Don't become egotistical; after all, we all have faults and these need to be addressed if we're to improve.
Think logically; keep emotions in perspective.	Don't ignore the crucial role that emotions and emotional expression often play in interpersonal communication.

three major headings: emotional understanding, emotional expression, and emotional responding (also see Table 2).

Emotional Understanding

Your first task is to develop self-awareness: recognizing what your feelings are, understanding why you feel as you do, and understanding the potential effects of your feelings (Stein & Book, 2006). Here you ask yourself a few pertinent questions:

- **"What am I feeling, and what made me feel this way?"** That is, understand your emotions. Think about your emotions as objectively as possible. Identify, in terms as specific as possible, the antecedent conditions that may be influencing your feelings. Try to answer the question, "Why am I feeling this way?" or "What happened to lead me to feel as I do?"
- **"What exactly do I want to communicate?"** Consider also whether your emotional expression will be a truthful expression of your feelings. When emotional expressions are faked—when, for example, you smile though feeling angry or say, "I forgive you" when you don't—you may actually be creating emotional and physical stress (Grandey, 2000). Remember, too, the irreversibility of communication; once you communicate something, you cannot take it back.
- **"What are my communication choices?"** Evaluate your communication options in terms of both effectiveness (what will work best and help you achieve your goal) and ethics (what is right or morally justified).

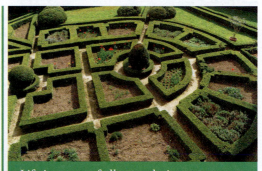

Life is a sum of all your choices.
—*Albert Camus*

Bartosz Koszowski/Shutterstock

INTERPERSONAL CHOICE POINT

The Crying Child

A young child about six or seven years old is crying because the other children won't play with her. What are some things you can say to make the child feel better but without trying to solve the child's problems by asking the other children to play with this child?

Emotional Expression

Your second step is interpersonal. Here are a few suggestions for this type of special communication. A special box on handling anger complements this discussion.

- **Be specific.** Consider, for example, the frequently heard, "I feel bad." Does it mean, "I feel guilty" (because I lied to my best friend)? "I feel lonely" (because I haven't had a date in the last two months)? "I feel depressed" (because I failed that last exam)? Specificity helps. Describe also the intensity with which you feel the emotion: "I feel so angry I'm thinking of quitting the job." "I feel so hurt I want to cry." Also describe any mixed feelings you might have. Very often feelings are a mixture of several emotions, sometimes even of conflicting emotions. Learn the vocabulary to describe your emotions and feelings in specific and concrete terms.

Here is a list of terms for describing your emotions verbally. Notice that the terms included for each basic emotion provide you with lots of choices for expressing the intensity level you're feeling. For example, if you're extremely fearful then *terror* or *dread* might be appropriate; but if your fear is mild, then perhaps *apprehension* or *concern* might be an appropriate term. Look over the list and try grouping the terms into three levels of intensity: high, middle, and low. Before doing that, however, look up the meanings of any words that are unfamiliar to you.

Take a look at a discussion of the lack of vocabulary needed to describe feelings, "alexithymia," at tcbdevito.blogspot.com. Do you see the lack of vocabulary a problem among people you know?

- **Joy:** happiness, bliss, cheer, contentment, delight, ecstasy, enchantment, enjoyment, felicity, rapture, gratification, pleasure, satisfaction, well-being
- **Trust:** confidence, belief, hope, assurance, faith, reliance
- **Fear:** anxiety, apprehension, awe, concern, consternation, dread, fright, misgiving, phobia, trepidation, worry, qualm, terror
- **Surprise:** amazement, astonishment, awe, eye-opener, incredulity, jolt, revelation, shock, unexpectedness, wonder, startle, catch off-guard, unforeseen
- **Sadness:** dejected, depressed, dismal, distressed, grief, loneliness, melancholy, misery, sorrowful, unhappiness
- **Disgust:** abhorrence, aversion, loathing, repugnance, repulsion, revulsion, sickness, nausea, offensiveness
- **Anger:** acrimony, annoyance, bitterness, displeasure, exasperation, fury, ire, irritation, outrage, rage, resentment, tantrum, umbrage, wrath, hostility
- **Anticipation:** contemplation, prospect, expectancy, hope, foresight, expectation, foreboding, forecast, forethought

- **Describe the reasons you're feeling as you are.** "I'm feeling guilty because I was unfaithful." "I feel lonely; I haven't had a date for the last two months." "I'm really depressed from failing that last exam." If your feelings were influenced by something the person you're talking to did or said, describe this also. For example, "I felt so angry when you said you wouldn't help me". "I felt hurt when you didn't invite me to the party."
- **Address mixed feelings.** If you have mixed feelings—and you really want the other person to understand you—then address these mixed or conflicting feelings. "I want so much to stay with Pat and yet I fear I'm losing my identity." Or, "I feel anger and hatred but at the same time I feel guilty for what I did."
- **In expressing feelings—inwardly or outwardly—try to anchor your emotions in the present.** Coupled with specific description and the identification of the reasons for your feelings, such statements might look like this: "I feel like a failure right now; I've erased this computer file three times today." "I felt foolish when I couldn't think of that formula." "I feel stupid when you point out my grammatical errors."

Understanding *Interpersonal Skills*

FLEXIBILITY

Flexibility is a quality of thinking and behaving, in which you vary your messages based on the unique situation in which you find yourself. One measure of flexibility asks you to consider how true you believe certain statements are, such as:

- "People should be frank and spontaneous in conversation" or
- "When angry, a person should say nothing rather than say something he or she will be sorry for later."

The "preferred" answer to all such questions is "sometimes true," underscoring the importance of flexibility in all interpersonal situations (Hart, Carlson, & Eadie, 1980).

As you can appreciate, flexibility is especially important when communicating your feelings—be they positive or negative. It's especially important in emotional communication, because it's in times of emotional arousal that you're likely to forget the varied choices you have available. And of course this is exactly the time when you need to consider your choices. The greater your flexibility, the more likely you'll be to see the varied choices you do have for communicating in any situation.

Increasing Flexibility. Here are a few ways to cultivate interpersonal flexibility:

- Realize that no two situations or people are exactly alike; consider what is different about this situation or person and take these differences into consideration as you construct your messages.
- Recognize that communication always takes place in a context discover what that unique context is and ask yourself how it might influence your messages. Communicating bad news during a joyous celebration, for example, needs to be handled quite differently from communicating good news.
- Become aware of the constant change in people and in things. Everything is in a state of flux. Even if the way you communicated last month was effective, that doesn't mean it will be effective today or tomorrow. Realize too that sudden changes (the death of a lover or a serious illness) will influence what are and what are not appropriate messages.
- Appreciate the fact that every situation offers you different options for communicating. Consider these options and try to predict the effects each option might have.

Working with Interpersonal Skills

Try applying the four suggestions for increasing flexibility in any of the following situations: (1) you're substitute teaching a ninth-grade class known for being difficult; (2) you're leading a work team designed to find ways to increase worker morale; or (3) you're responding to some negative comments on your Facebook wall.

- **Own your feelings; take personal responsibility for your feelings.** Consider the following statements: "You make me angry." "You make me feel like a loser." "You make me feel stupid." "You make me feel like I don't belong here." In each of these statements, the speaker blames the other person for the way he or she is feeling. Of course, you know, on more sober reflection, that no one can make you feel anything. Others may do things or say things to you but it is you who interpret them. That is, you develop feelings as a result of the interaction between what these people say, for example, and your own interpretations. **Owning feelings** means taking responsibility for them—acknowledging that your feelings are your feelings. The best way to own your statements is to use *I*-messages.

Handling Anger: A Special Case Illustration

As a kind of summary of the guidelines for expressing your emotions, this section looks at anger. **Anger** is one of the eight basic emotions identified in Plutchik's model (Figure 1). It's also an emotion that can create considerable problems if not managed properly. Anger varies from mild annoyance to intense rage; increases in pulse rate and blood pressure usually accompany these feelings.

Anger is not always necessarily bad. In fact, anger may help you protect yourself, energizing you to fight or flee. Often, however, anger does prove destructive—as when, for example, you allow it to obscure reality or to become an obsession.

Anger doesn't just happen; you make it happen by your interpretation of events. Yet life events can contribute mightily. There are the road repairs that force you to detour so you wind up late for an important appointment. There are the moths that attack your favorite sweater. There's the water leak that ruins your carpet. People, too, can contribute to your anger: the driver who tailgates, the clerk who overcharges you, the supervisor who ignores your contributions to the company. But it is you who interpret these events and people in ways that stimulate you to generate anger.

Writing more than a hundred years ago, Charles Darwin observed in his *The Expression of the Emotions in Man and Animals* (1872) that "The free expression by outside signs of an emotion intensifies it . . . the repression, as far as this is possible, of all outside signs softens our emotions. He who gives way to violent gestures will increase his rage." Popular psychology ignored Darwin's implied admonition in the 1960s and '70s, when the suggested prescription for dealing with anger was to "let it all hang out" and "tell it like it is." Express your anger, many people advised, or risk its being bottled up and eventually exploding. This idea is called the **ventilation hypothesis**—the notion that expressing emotions allows you to ventilate your negative feelings and that this will have a beneficial effect on your physical health, your mental well-being, and even your interpersonal relationships (Kennedy-Moore & Watson, 1999; Spett, 2004).

Later thinking has returned to Darwin, however, and suggests that venting anger may not be the best strategy (Tavris, 1989). Expressing anger doesn't get rid of it but makes it grow: Angry expression increases anger, which promotes more angry expression, which increases anger, and on and on. Some support for this idea that expressing emotions makes them stronger comes from a study that compared (a) participants who felt emotions such as happiness and anger with (b) participants who both felt and expressed these emotions. The results of the study indicated that people who felt and expressed the emotions became emotionally aroused faster than did those who only felt the emotion (Hess, Kappas, McHugo, & Lanzetta, 1992). And of course this spiral of anger can make conflicts all the more serious and all the more difficult to manage.

A better strategy seems to be to reduce the anger. With this principle in mind, here are some suggestions for managing and communicating anger.

Anger Management: SCREAM before You Scream

Perhaps the most popular recommendation for dealing with anger is to count to 10. The purpose is to give you a cooling-off period, and the advice is not bad. A somewhat more difficult but probably far more effective strategy, however, would be to use that cooling-off period not merely for counting but for mindfully analyzing and ultimately managing your anger. The **anger management** procedure offered here is similar to those available in popular books on anger management but is couched in a communication framework. It's called SCREAM, an acronym for the major issues (that is, the major components of the communication process) that you need to consider:

1. **Self.** How important is this matter to you? Is it worth the high blood pressure and the general aggravation? For example, are you interpreting the "insult" as the other person intended, or could you be misperceiving the situation or the intent? Is an "insult" to you the same as an "insult" to your mother-in-law? Are you confusing factual with inferential knowledge? Are you sure that what you think happened really happened? Or might you be filling in the gaps with what could have or might have happened or with what you expected to happen?
2. **Context.** Is this the appropriate time and place to express your anger? Do you have to express your anger right now? Do you have to express it right here? Might a better time and place be arranged?
3. **Receiver.** Is this person the one to whom you wish to express your anger? For example, do you want to express your anger to your life partner if you're really angry with your supervisor for not recommending your promotion?

4. **Effect (immediate).** What effect do you want to achieve? Do you want to express your anger to help you get the promotion? to hurt the other person? to release pent-up emotions? to stand up for your rights? Each purpose would obviously require a different communication strategy. Consider, too, what may be the likely immediate effect of your anger display. For example, will the other person also become angry? And if so, is it possible that the entire situation will snowball and get out of hand?

5. **Aftermath (long-range).** What are the likely long-term repercussions of this expression of anger? What will be the effects on your relationship? your continued employment?

6. **Messages.** Suppose that after this rather thorough analysis, you do decide to express your anger. What messages would be appropriate? How can you best communicate your feelings to achieve your desired results? This question brings us to the subject of anger communication.

Anger Communication

Anger communication is not angry communication. In fact, it might be argued that the communication of anger ought to be especially calm and dispassionate. Here, then, are a few suggestions for communicating your anger in a nonangry way.

- **Get ready to communicate calmly and logically.** First, relax. Try to breathe deeply; think pleasant thoughts; perhaps tell yourself to "take it easy," "think rationally," and "calm down." Try to get rid of any unrealistic ideas you may have that might contribute to your anger. For example, ask yourself if this person's revealing something about your past to a third party is really all that serious or was really intended to hurt you.

- **Examine your communication choices.** In most situations you'll have a range of choices. There are lots of different ways to express yourself, so don't jump to the first possibility that comes to mind. Assess your options for the form of the communication—should you communicate face-to-face? by e-mail? by telephone? Similarly, assess your options for the timing of your communication, for the specific words and gestures you might use, for the physical setting, and so on.

- **Consider the advantages of delaying the expression of anger.** For example, consider writing the e-mail but sending it to yourself, at least until the next morning. Then the options of revising it or not sending it at all will still be open to you.

- **Remember that different cultures have different display rules**—norms for what is and what is not appropriate to display. Assess the culture you're in as well as the cultures of the other people involved, especially these cultures' display rules for communicating anger.

- **Apply the relevant skills of interpersonal communication.** For example, be specific, use *I*-messages, avoid allness, avoid polarized terms, and in general communicate with all the competence you can muster.

- **Recall the irreversibility of communication.** Once you say something, you'll not be able to erase or delete it from the mind of the other person.

These suggestions are not going to solve the problems of road rage, gang warfare, or domestic violence. Yet they may help—a bit—in reducing some of the negative consequences of anger and perhaps even some of the anger itself.

Polka Dot Images/Thinkstock

VIEWPOINTS Some societies permit and even expect men (but not women) to show strong emotions such as anger. What has your culture taught you about the expression of anger and particularly about gender differences in the expression of anger?

With this acknowledgment of responsibility, the above statements would look like these: "I get angry when you come home late without calling." "I begin to think of myself as a loser when you criticize me in front of my friends." "I feel so stupid when you use medical terms that I don't understand." "When you ignore me in public, I feel like I don't belong here." These rephrased statements identify and describe your feelings about those behaviors; they don't attack the other person or demand that he or she change certain behaviors and consequently don't encourage defensiveness. With *I*-message statements, it's easier for the other person to acknowledge behaviors and to offer to change them.

For good or ill, some social network sites (and the same is true with blogs) make it very easy to *not* own your own messages by enabling you to send comments anonymously.

- **Ask for what you want.** Depending on the emotions you're feeling, you may want the listener to assume a certain role or just listen or offer advice. Let the listener know what you want. Use *I*-messages to describe what, if anything, you want the listener to do: "I'm feeling sorry for myself right now; just give me some space. I'll give you a call in a few days." Or, more directly: "I'd prefer to be alone right now." Or, "I need advice." Or, "I just need someone to listen to me."

- **Respect emotional boundaries.** Each person has a different level of tolerance for communication about emotions or communication that's emotional. Be especially alert to nonverbal cues that signal that boundaries are near to being broken. And, it's often useful to simply ask, "Would you rather change the subject?" At the same time, realize that you also have a certain tolerance for revealing your own feelings as well as for listening to and responding to the emotions of others.

Table 3 provides a comparison and summary of effective and ineffective emotional expression.

INTERPERSONAL CHOICE POINT

Responding to Betrayal

A colleague at work has revealed to other workers personal information about you that you confided in him and him alone. You're steaming as you pass a group of colleagues commenting on your current relationship problems. What are some choices you have for reacting to this? What would you do first?

TABLE 3 — Ineffective and Effective Emotional Expression

Effective Emotional Expression	Ineffective Emotional Expression
Specific; talks about emotions with specific terms and with specific examples and behavioral references.	**General;** talks about emotions and feelings in general terms and without specifics.
Describes reasons; seeks to understand the causes of emotions.	**Ignores reasons;** mindlessly accepts emotions without asking about their causes.
Present focused; concentrates on present feelings.	**Past focused;** concentrates on past feelings (perhaps as a way to avoid focusing on present feelings)
Own one's feelings and their expressions; "I feel angry, I'm hurt, I don't feel loved."	**Lacks ownership;** attributes feelings to others—"You made me angry; you hurt me; you don't love me."
Polite; talks about emotions (even anger) without anger and with respect for the other person and the relationship.	**Impolite;** lashes out in anger without regard for the feelings of the other person.

Emotional Responding

Expressing your feelings is only half of the process of emotional communication; the other half is listening and responding to the feelings of others. Here are a few guidelines for making an often difficult process a little easier. A special box on responding to the grief stricken complements this discussion.

- **Look at nonverbal cues to understand the individual's feelings.** For example, overly long pauses, frequent hesitations, eye contact avoidance, or excessive fidgeting may be a sign of discomfort that it might be wise to talk about. Similarly, look for inconsistent messages, as when someone says that, "everything is okay" while expressing facial sadness; these are often clues to mixed feelings. But be sure to use any verbal or nonverbal cues as hypotheses, never as conclusions. Check your perceptions before acting on them. Treat inferences as inferences and not as facts.

- **Look for cues as to what the person wants you to do.** Sometimes all the person wants is for someone to listen. Don't equate (as the stereotypical male supposedly does) "responding to another's feelings" with "solving the other person's problems." Instead, provide a supportive atmosphere that encourages the person to express his or her feelings.

- **Use active listening techniques.** These will encourage the person to talk should he or she wish to. Paraphrase the speaker. Express understanding of the speaker's feelings. Ask questions as appropriate.

- **Empathize.** See the situation from the point of view of the speaker. Don't evaluate the other person's feelings. For example, comments such as, "Don't cry; it wasn't worth it" or "You'll get promoted next year" can easily be interpreted to mean, "Your feelings are wrong or inappropriate."

- **Focus on the other person.** Interjecting your own similar past situations is often useful for showing your understanding, but it may create problems if it refocuses the conversation away from the other person. Show interest by encouraging the person to explore his or her feelings. Use simple encouragers like "I see" or "I understand." Or ask questions to let the speaker know that you're listening and that you're interested.

- **Remember the irreversibility of communication.** Whether expressing emotion or responding to the emotions of others, it's useful to recall the irreversibility of communication. You won't be able to take back an insensitive or disconfirming response. Responses to another's emotional expressions are likely to have considerable impact, so be especially mindful to avoid inappropriate responding.

VIEWPOINTS Research finds that sleep deprivation hinders your ability to accurately recognize the emotions expressed facially by others (Gordon, 2010). What other factors might influence your ability to accurately detect the emotions of others?

Castelao Productions/Album/Newscom

INTERPERSONAL CHOICE POINT

Giving Emotional Advice

Your best friend tells you that he suspects his girlfriend is seeing someone else. He's extremely upset; he tells you that he wants to confront her with his suspicions but is afraid of what he'll hear. What options does your friend have? What would you advise him to say?

Communicating with the Grief-Stricken: A Special Case Illustration

Communicating with people who are experiencing grief, a common but difficult type of communication interaction, requires special care (Zunin & Zunin, 1991). Consideration of this topic also will offer a useful recap of some of the principles of responding to the emotions of others.

A person may experience grief because of illness or death, the loss of a job or highly valued relationship (such as a friendship or romantic breakup), the loss of certain physical or mental abilities, the loss of material possessions (a house fire or stock losses), or the loss of some ability (for example, the loss of the ability to have children or to play the piano). Each situation seems to call for a somewhat different set of dos and don'ts.

A Problem

Before considering specific suggestions for responding to a person experiencing grief, read the following expression of sympathy, what we might call "the problem."

I just heard that Harry died—I mean—passed away. Excuse me. I'm so sorry. We all are. I know exactly how you feel. But, you know, it's for the best. I mean the man was suffering. I remember seeing him last month; he could hardly stand up, he was so weak. And he looked so sad, so lonely, so depressed. He must have been in constant pain. It's better this way; believe me. He's at peace now. And you'll get over it. You'll see. Time heals all wounds. It was the same way with me and you know how close we were. I mean we were devoted to each other. Everyone said we were the closet pair they ever saw. And I got over it. So, how about we'll go to dinner tonight? We'll take about old times. Come on. Come on. Don't be a spoilsport. I really need to get out. I've been in the house all week and you know what a drag that can be. So, do it for me; come to dinner. I won't take no for an answer; I'll pick you up at seven.

Obviously, this is not the way to talk to the grief-stricken. In fact, this paragraph was written to illustrate several popular mistakes. After you read the suggestions below, you may wish to return to this "expression of sympathy," reanalyze it, and rework it into an effective expression of sympathy.

A Solution

Here are some suggestions for communicating more effectively with the grief-stricken, offering at least some solutions to the above problem.

- **Confirm the other person and the person's emotions.** A simple, "You must be worried about finding another position" or "You must be feeling very alone right now" confirms the person's feelings. This type of expressive support lessens feelings of grief (Reed, 1993).
- **Give the person permission to grieve.** Let the person know that it's acceptable and okay with you if he or she grieves in the ways that feel most comfortable—for example, crying or talking about old times. Don't try to change the subject or interject too often. As long as the person is talking and seems to be feeling better for it, be supportive.
- **Avoid trying to focus on the bright side.** Avoid expressions such as, "You're lucky you have some vision left" or "It's better this way; Pat was suffering so much." These expressions may easily be seen as telling people that their feelings should be redirected, that they should be feeling something different.
- **Encourage the person to express feelings and talk about the loss.** Most people will welcome this opportunity. On the other hand, don't try to force people to talk about experiences or feelings they may not be willing to share.
- **Be especially sensitive to leave-taking cues.** Behaviors such as fidgeting or looking at a clock, and statements such as, "It's getting late" or "We can discuss this later," are hints that the other person is ready to end the conversation. Don't overstay your welcome.
- **Let the person know you care and are available.** Saying you're sorry is a simple but effective way to let the

person know you care. Express your empathy; let the grief-stricken person know that you can feel (to some extent) what he or she is going through. But don't assume that your feelings, however empathic you are, are the same in depth or in kind. At the same time, let the person know that you are available—"If you ever want to talk, I'm here" or "If there's anything I can do, please let me know."

Even when you follow the principles and do everything according to the book, you may find that your comments are not appreciated or are not at all effective in helping the person feel any better. Use these cues to help you readjust your messages.

Hemera Technologies/AbleStock/Thinkstock

VIEWPOINTS Can you recall a situation in which you interacted with someone who was experiencing grief, but for some reason you didn't communicate very effectively? Did you violate any of the suggestions identified here? What would you do differently if this situation occurred today?

Summary

 Use your smartphone or tablet device (or log on to mycommunicationlab.com) to hear an audio summary of this chapter.

This chapter explored the nature and principles of emotions in interpersonal communication, the obstacles to meaningful emotional communication, and some guidelines that will help you communicate your feelings and respond to the feelings of others more effectively.

Principles of Emotions and Emotional Messages

1. Emotions may be primary or blends. The primary emotions, according to Robert Plutchik, are joy, trust, fear, surprise, sadness, disgust, anger, and anticipation. Other emotions, such as love, awe, contempt, and aggressiveness, are blends of primary emotions.
2. Emotions consist of a physical part (our physiological reactions), a cognitive part (our interpretations of our feelings), and a cultural part (our cultural traditions' influence on our emotional evaluations and expressions).
3. Emotions may be adaptive or maladaptive.
4. Emotions may be used strategically.
5. Emotions are communicated verbally and nonverbally, and the way in which you express emotions is largely a matter of choice.
6. Cultural and gender display rules identify what emotions may be expressed, where, how, and by whom.
7. Emotions are often contagious.
8. There are different views as to how emotions are aroused. One proposed sequence is this: An event occurs, you respond physiologically, you interpret this arousal, and you experience emotion based on your interpretation.

Obstacles to Communicating Emotions

9. Societal and cultural customs may have taught you that emotional expression is inappropriate.

10. Fear of exposing weaknesses or causing a conflict may inhibit your emotional expression.
11. Inadequate interpersonal skills may make you feel unsure or hesitant and so you might withdraw.

Emotional Competence

12. Understand what you are feeling and what made you feel this way.
13. Formulate a communication goal; what exactly do you want to accomplish when expressing emotions?
14. Identify your communication choices and evaluate them.
15. Describe your feelings as accurately as possible, identify the reasons for your feelings, anchor your feelings and their expression in the present time, own your own feelings, and handle your anger as appropriate.
16. Look for cues to understand the person's feelings. Listen for what is said and not said; look at the nonverbals, especially those that don't match the verbals.
17. Look for cues as to what the person wants you to do. Don't assume it's to solve their problem.
18. Use active listening techniques. Paraphrase, express understanding, and ask questions as appropriate.
19. Empathize. See the situation from the other person's perspective. Ask yourself what the other person may be feeling.
20. Focus on the other person. Avoid interpreting the situation from your own experiences.
21. Remember the irreversibility of communication. Once said, messages can't be erased, mentally or emotionally.

Key Terms

anger,	emotions,	gender display rules,	strategic emotionality,
anger management,	emotional appeals,	*I*-messages,	ventilation hypothesis,
blended emotions,	emotional communication,	James-Lange theory,	
cognitive labeling theory,	emotional contagion,	owning feelings,	
display rules,	flexibility,	primary emotions,	

MyCommunicationLab Explorations

MyCommunicationLab®

Communication Choice Points

Revisit the chapter-opening video, "Communicating Change." Recall that Tobin, the manager of a small manufacturing firm, was meeting with his team leaders. He describes how upcoming changes will affect workers and how this should be communicated by team leaders. Tobin's emotional state directly affects the message he delivers and how it is received. "Communicating Change" looks at how tone and word choice affects how information is received. The video looks at three variations in delivering the same message.

Log on to mycommunicationlab.com to view the video for this chapter, "Communicating Change," and then answer the related discussion questions.

Additional Resources

Exercises to help you understand the nature of emotional communication include:

1 Communicating Emotions Nonverbally, **2** Communicating Your Emotions, **3** Expressing Negative Feelings, **4** Communicating Emotions Effectively, and **5** Emotional Advice.

Conversational Messages

From Chapter 8 of *The Interpersonal Communication Book*, Thirteenth Edition. Joseph A. DeVito. Copyright © 2013 by Pearson Education, Inc.

Conversational Messages

Principles of Conversation

Conversational Management

Conversational Disclosure: Revealing Yourself

Everyday Conversations

Pearson Education

Tim would like to initiate a conversation with his classmate Emad, but feels awkward. Tim considers some of the principles of conversation that you will read about in this chapter as he makes both effective and ineffective communication choices. See how his choices play out in the video "First Day of Class" (www.mycommunicationlab.com).

Conversation is the essence of interpersonal communication. These two concepts are so closely related that some communication researchers think of the words *conversation* and *interpersonal communication* as synonymous, as meaning essentially the same thing. Most researchers and theorists would claim that communication exists on a continuum, and that interpersonal communication occupies some significant portion of the right side of this continuum. Exactly where impersonal ends and interpersonal begins is a matter of disagreement.

Conversation can be defined as "relatively informal social interaction in which the roles of speaker and hearer are exchanged in a nonautomatic fashion under the collaborative management of all parties" (McLaughlin, 1984). Examining conversation provides an excellent opportunity to look at verbal and nonverbal messages as they're used in day-to-day communications, and thus serves as a useful culmination for this second part of the text.

Principles of Conversation

Although conversation is an everyday process and one we seldom think about, it is, like most forms of communication, governed by several principles.

The Principle of Process: Conversation Is a Developmental Process

It's convenient to divide up the process of conversation into chunks or stages and to view each stage as requiring a choice as to what you'll say and how you'll say it. Here we divide the sequence into five steps: opening, feedforward, business, feedback, and closing (see Figure 1). These stages and the way people follow them will vary depending on the personalities of the

FIGURE 1

A Five-Stage Model of Conversation

This model of the stages of conversation is best seen as a way of talking about conversation and not as a hard-and-fast depiction of stages all conversations follow. As you review the model, consider how accurately it depicts conversation as you experience it. Can you develop a more accurate and more revealing model?

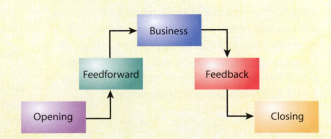

communicators, their culture, the context in which the conversation occurs, the purpose of the conversation, and the entire host of factors considered throughout this text.

When reading about the process of conversation, keep in mind that not everyone speaks with the fluency and ease that many textbooks often assume. Speech and language disorders, for example, can seriously disrupt the conversation process when some elementary guidelines aren't followed. Table 1 offers suggestions for making such conversations run more smoothly.

Opening The first step is to open the conversation, usually with some kind of greeting: A "Hi. How are you?" or "Hello, this is Joe" or a poke on Facebook. The greeting is a good example of **phatic communication**: It's a message that establishes a connection between two people and opens up the channels for more meaningful interaction. When you send a friend a photo of strawberry cheesecake, you're creating an opportunity for communication; you're saying that you're thinking of the person and want to communicate. A simple tweet or post likewise can serve as a conversation opener. Openings, of course, may be nonverbal as well as verbal. A smile, kiss, or handshake may be as clear an opening as "Hello." Greetings are so common that they often go unnoticed. But when they're omitted—as when the doctor begins the conversation by saying, "What's wrong?"—you may feel uncomfortable and thrown off guard.

In normal conversation, the greeting is reciprocated with a greeting similar in degree of formality and intensity. When it isn't—when the other person turns away or responds coldly to your friendly "Good morning"—you know that something is wrong.

Openings are also generally consistent in tone with the main part of the conversation; a cheery "How ya doing today, bud?" is not normally followed by news of a family death; and a friendly conversation is not begun with insensitive openers: "Wow, you've gained a few pounds haven't you?"

Opening References. Several approaches to opening a conversation can be derived from the elements of interpersonal communication process:

- **Self-references** say something about you. Such references may be of the "name, rank, and serial number" type—for example: "My name is Joe. I'm from Omaha." On the first day of class, students might say, "I'm worried about this class" or "I took this instructor last semester; she was excellent."
- **Other-references** say something about the other person or ask a question: "I like that sweater." "Didn't we meet at Charlie's?" Of course, there are pitfalls here. Generally, it's best not to comment on the person's race ("My uncle married a Korean"), the person's affectional orientation ("Nice to meet you; I have a gay brother"), or physical disability ("It must be awful to be so limited").
- **Relational references** say something about the two of you: for example, "May I buy you a coffee?" "Would you like to dance?" or simply "May I join you?"
- **Context references** say something about the physical, social–psychological, cultural, or temporal context. The familiar "Do you have the time?" is a reference of this type. But you can be more creative and say, for example, "This restaurant seems very friendly" or "This painting is fantastic."

As you know from experience, conversations are most satisfying when they're upbeat and positive. So it's generally best to lead off with something positive rather than something negative. Say, for example, "I like the music here" instead of "Don't you just hate this place?" Also, it's best not to be too revealing; disclosing too much too early in an interaction can make the other person feel uncomfortable.

Opening Lines. Another way of looking at the process of initiating conversations is to examine the infamous "opening line," the opener designed to begin a romantic relationship. Consider your own opening lines (or the opening lines that have been used on you). Let's say you're at a club and want to strike up a conversation—and perhaps spark a relationship. Which of the following are you most likely to use (Kleinke, 1986; Kleinke & Dean, 1990)?

For a more extended discussion of phatic communication (also and originally called phatic communion), see "ABCD: Phatic Communion" at tcbdevito.blogspot.com. In what ways do you use phatic communication/communion?

INTERPERSONAL CHOICE POINT

Prefacing to Extremes

A friend whom you talk to on the phone fairly regularly seems to take phatic communication to a new level—the preface is so long that it makes you want to get off the phone and frequently you make excuses to do just that. What are some things you might do to help your friend change this communication pattern?

TABLE 1 — INTERPERSONAL COMMUNICATION TIPS
Between People with and without Speech and Language Disorders

Demosthenes
The Granger Collection

Lewis Carroll
NYC

Winston Churchill
Al Francekevich/ Getty Images

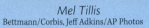

Mel Tillis
Bettmann/Corbis, Jeff Adkins/AP Photos

Speech and language disorders vary widely—from fluency problems (such as stuttering), to indistinct articulation, to difficulty in finding the right word (aphasia). Following a few simple guidelines can facilitate communication between people with and without speech and language disorders.

If you're the person without a speech or language disorder:

Generally	Specifically
Avoid finishing another's sentences.	Finishing the person's sentences may communicate the idea that you're impatient and don't want to spend the extra time necessary to interact effectively.
Avoid giving directions to the person with a speech disorder.	Saying "slow down" or "relax" will often seem insulting and will make further communication more difficult.
Maintain eye contact.	Show interest and at the same time avoid showing any signs of impatience or embarrassment.
Ask for clarification as needed.	If you don't understand what the person said, ask him or her to repeat it. Don't pretend that you understand when you don't.
Don't treat people who have language problems like children.	A person with aphasia, say, who has difficulty with names or nouns generally, is in no way childlike. Similarly, a person who stutters is not a slow thinker; in fact, stutterers differ from non-stutterers only in their oral fluency.

If you're the person with a speech or language disorder:

Generally	Specifically
Let the other person know what your special needs are.	If you stutter, you might tell others that you have difficulty with certain sounds and so they need to be patient.
Demonstrate your own comfort.	Show that you have a positive attitude toward the interpersonal situation. If you appear comfortable and positive, others will also.
Be patient.	For example, have patience with those who try to finish your sentences; they're likely just trying to be helpful.

Sources: These suggestions were drawn from a variety of sources: www.nsastutter.org/material/indep.php?matid=189, www.aphasia.org/, http://spot.pcc.edu/~rjacobs/career/communication_tips.htm, and www.dol.gov/odep/pubs/fact/comucate.htm.

Mark Liebowitz/Masterfile

- **Cute–flippant openers** are humorous, indirect, and ambiguous as to whether or not the person opening the conversation really wants an extended encounter. Examples: "Is that really your hair?" "I bet the cherries jubilee isn't as sweet as you are."
- **Innocuous openers** are highly ambiguous as to whether these are simple comments that might be made to just anyone or whether they're in fact openers designed to initiate an extended encounter. Examples: "What do you think of the band?" "Could you show me how to work this machine?"
- **Direct openers** demonstrate clearly the speaker's interest in meeting the other person. Examples: "I feel a little embarrassed about this, but I'd like to meet you." "Would you like to have coffee after dinner?"

One advantage of cute-flippant openers is that they're indirect enough to cushion any rejection. These are also, however, the lines least preferred by both men and women.

In contrast, both men and women generally like innocuous openers; they're indirect enough to allow for an easy out if the other person doesn't want to talk.

On direct openers, however, genders differ. Men like direct openers that are very clear in meaning, possibly because men are not used to having another person initiate a meeting. Women prefer openers that aren't too strong and that are relatively modest.

In e-mail conversations the situation is a bit different. Even before your message is opened, the receiver knows who the sender is, when the message was composed, and, from the title or subject line, something about the nature of your message. In addition to this general hint at the nature of the message, most e-mail users begin their e-mail with a kind of orientation or preface to what will follow; for example, "I'm writing to ask the name of your acupuncturist" or "I want to fill you in as to what happened at the party." Generally, such openers are direct and relate closely to what is to follow.

Feedforward   At the second step, you usually provide some kind of feedforward which gives the other person a general idea of the conversation's focus: "I've got to tell you about Jack," "Did you hear what happened in class yesterday?" or "We need to talk about our vacation plans." Feedforward also may identify the tone of the conversation ("I'm really depressed and need to talk with you") or the time required ("This will just take a minute") (Frentz, 1976; Reardon, 1987).

More formally we can identify at least four major functions of feedforward: to open the channels of communication, to preview the message, to disclaim, and to altercast.

- **To Open the Channels of Communication.** Phatic communication (also referred to as phatic communion) is information that tells you that the normal, expected, and accepted rules of interaction will be in effect. It tells you another person is willing to communicate. It's the "How are you?" and "Nice weather" greetings that are designed to maintain rapport and friendly relationships (Burnard, 2003; Placencia, 2004). Similarly, listeners' short comments that are unrelated to the content of the conversation but that indicate interest and attention may also be considered phatic communication (McCarthy, 2003). Not surprisingly, phatic communication is important not only in face-to-face interaction but also in e-mail (Bloch, 2002).

- **To Preview the Message.** Feedforward messages may, for example, preview the content ("I'm afraid I have bad news for you"), the importance ("Listen to this before you make a move"), the form or style ("I'll tell you all the gory details"), and the positive or negative quality of subsequent messages ("You're not going to like this, but here's what I heard"). The subject heading on your e-mail well illustrates this function of feedforward, as do the phone numbers and names that come up on your caller ID.

- **To Disclaim.** The disclaimer is a statement that aims to ensure that your message will be understood as you want it to be and that it will not reflect negatively on you. For example, you might use a disclaimer when you think that what you're going to say may be met with opposition. Thus, you say, "I'm not against immigration, but . . ." or "Don't think I'm homophobic, but . . ."

- **To Altercast.** Feedforward is often used to place the receiver in a specific role and to request responses in terms of this assumed role, a process called altercasting (McLaughlin, 1984; Weinstein & Deutschberger, 1963). For example, you might altercast by asking a friend, "As a future advertising executive, what would you think of corrective advertising?" This question casts your friend in the role of advertising executive (rather than parent, Democrat, or Baptist, for example) and asks that she or he answer from a particular perspective.

Conversational awkwardness often occurs when feedforwards are used inappropriately. For example, using overly long feedforwards may make the listener wonder whether you'll ever get to the business at hand and may make you seem disorganized and lacking in focus. Omitting feedforward before a truly shocking message (for example, the terminal illness of a friend or relative) can make you seem insensitive or uncaring.

Often the feedforward is combined with the opening, as when you see someone on campus, for example, and say, "Hey, listen to this" or when, in a work situation, someone says, "Well, folks, let's get the meeting going."

Here are a few suggestions for giving effective feedforward:

- Use feedforward to estimate the receptivity of the person to what you're going to say. For example, before asking for a date, you'd probably use feedforward to test the waters and to see if you're likely to get a "yes" response. You might ask if the other person enjoys going out to dinner or if he or she is dating anyone seriously. Before asking a friend for a loan, you'd probably feedforward your needy condition and say something like, "I'm really strapped for cash and need to get my hands on $200 to pay my car loan" and wait for the other person to say (you hope), "Can I help?"

- Use feedforward that's consistent with your subsequent message. If your main message is one of bad news, then your feedforward needs to be serious and to help to prepare the other person for this bad news. You might, for example, say something like, "I need to tell you something you're not going to want to hear. Let's sit down."

- The more important or complex the message, the more important and more extensive your feedforward needs to be. For example, in public speaking, in which the message is relatively long, the speaker is advised to give fairly extensive feedforward or what is called an orientation or preview. At the start of a business meeting, the leader may give feedforward in the form of an agenda or meeting schedule.

Business The third step is the "business," the substance or focus of the conversation. The term *business* is used to emphasize that most conversations are goal directed. That is, you converse to fulfill one or several of the general purposes of interpersonal communication: to learn, relate, influence, play, or help (see Chapter 1). The term is also sufficiently general to incorporate all kinds of interactions. Not surprisingly, however, each culture has certain conversational **taboos**—topics or language that should be avoided, especially by "outsiders." For example, discussing bullfighting or illegal aliens can easily get you into difficulty in conversations with Mexicans, and politics and religion may pose problems in conversation with those from the Middle East (Axtell, 1997, 2007). In any case, the business is conducted through an exchange of speaker and listener roles. Brief, rather than long, speaking turns characterize most satisfying conversations.

In the business stage, you talk about Jack, what happened in class, or your vacation plans. This is obviously the longest part of the conversation and the reason for the opening and the feedforward.

Feedback

The fourth step is feedback, the reverse of the second step. Here you reflect back on the conversation to signal that, as far as you're concerned, the business is completed: "So you want to send Jack a get-well card?" "Wasn't that the craziest class you ever heard of?" or "I'll call for reservations, and you'll shop for what we need."

Each feedback opportunity presents you with choices along at least the following five dimensions: positive–negative, person focused–message focused, immediate–delayed, low monitored–high monitored, and supportive–critical. To use feedback effectively, you need to make educated choices along these dimensions.

- **Positive–Negative.** Feedback may be positive (you pay a compliment or pat someone on the back) or negative (you criticize someone or scowl). Positive feedback tells the speaker that he or she is on the right track and should continue communicating in essentially the same way. Negative feedback tells the speaker that something is wrong and that some adjustment should be made.

- **Person Focused–Message Focused.** Feedback may center on the person ("You're sweet" or "You have a great smile"). Or it may center on the message ("Can you repeat that number?" or "Your argument is a good one").

- **Immediate–Delayed.** In interpersonal situations, feedback is often sent immediately after the message is received; you smile or say something in response almost simultaneously with your receiving the message. In other communication situations, however, the feedback may be delayed. Instructor evaluation questionnaires completed at the end of a course provide feedback long after the class began. When you applaud or ask questions of a public speaker at the end of a lecture, the feedback is delayed. In interview situations, the feedback may come weeks afterward. In media situations, some feedback comes immediately through Nielsen ratings, and other feedback comes much later through viewing and buying patterns.

- **Low-Monitoring–High-Monitoring Feedback.** This dimension refers to the degree to which feedback is a spontaneous and totally honest reaction (low-monitored feedback) or a carefully constructed, highly censored, response designed to serve a specific purpose (high-monitored feedback). In most interpersonal situations, you probably give feedback spontaneously; you allow your responses to show without any monitoring or self-censorship. At other times, however, you may be more guarded, as when your boss asks you how you like your job or when your grandparents ask what you think of your dinner.

  Supportive–Critical. Supportive feedback accepts the speaker and what the speaker says. It occurs, for example, when you console another, encourage him or her to talk, or otherwise confirm the person's definition of self. Critical feedback, on the other hand, is evaluative; it's judgmental. When you give critical feedback (whether positive or negative), you judge another's performance—as in, for example, coaching someone learning a new skill.

Jose Ignacio Soto/Shutterstock

It is always your next move.
—*Napoleon Hill*

Realize that these categories are not exclusive. Feedback does not have to be either critical or supportive; it can be both. For example, in talking with someone who is trying to become a more effective interviewer, you might critically evaluate a practice interview but also express support for the effort. Similarly, you might respond to a friend's question immediately and then after a day or two elaborate on your response. Because each situation is unique, it's difficult to offer specific suggestions for making your conversational feedback more effective. But, with some adjustments for the specifics of the situation, the following guides might prove helpful:

- Focus on the behavior or the message rather than the motives behind the message or behavior. Say, for example, "You forgot my birthday" rather than "You don't love me."
- If your feedback is largely negative, try to begin with something positive. There are always positives if you look hard enough. The negatives will be much easier to take, after hearing some positives.
- Ask for feedback on your feedback; for example, say, "Does this make sense?" "Do you understand what I want our relationship to be?"
- Avoid giving feedback (especially negative feedback) when you're angry and especially when your anger is likely to influence what you say (Wright, 2011).

The other half of the feedback equation is the person receiving the feedback (Robbins & Hunsaker, 2006). When you are the recipient of feedback, be sure to show your interest in feedback. This is vital information that will help you improve whatever you're doing. Encourage the feedback giver. Be open to hearing this feedback. Don't argue; don't be defensive.

Perhaps most important, check your perceptions. Do you understand the feedback? Ask questions. Not all feedback is easy to understand; after all, a wink, a backward head nod, or a smile can each signal a variety of different messages. When you don't understand the meaning of the feedback, ask for clarification (nondefensively, of course). Paraphrase the feedback you've just received to make sure you both understand it: "You'd be comfortable taking over the added responsibilities if I went back to school?"

Closing   The fifth and last step, the opposite of the first step, is the closing, the goodbye, which often reveals how satisfied the persons were with the conversation: "I hope you'll call soon" or "Don't call us, we'll call you." The closing also may be used to schedule future conversations: "Give me a call tomorrow night" or "Let's meet for lunch at twelve." When closings are indefinite or vague, conversation often becomes awkward; you're not quite sure if you should say goodbye or if you should wait for something else to be said.

In a way similar to the opening and the feedforward being combined, the closing and the feedback might be combined, as when you say: "Look, I've got to think more about this commitment, okay?"

Closing a conversation is often a difficult task. It can be an awkward and uncomfortable part of interpersonal interaction. Here are a few suggestions you might consider:

- Reflect back on the conversation and briefly summarize it so as to bring it to a close. For example: "I'm glad I ran into you and found out what happened at that union meeting. I'll probably be seeing you at the meetings next week."
- Directly state the desire to end the conversation and to get on with other things. For example: "I'd like to continue talking, but I really have to run. I'll see you around."
- Refer to future interaction. For example: "Why don't we get together next week sometime and continue this discussion?"
- Ask for closure. For example: "Have I explained what you wanted to know?"
- State that you enjoyed the interaction. For example: "I really enjoyed talking with you."

Closing a conversation in e-mail follows the same principles as closing a face-to-face conversation. But exactly when you end the e-mail exchange is often not clear, partly because the absence of nonverbal cues creates ambiguity. For example, if you ask someone a question and the other person answers, do you then e-mail again and say "thanks"? If so, should the other person e-mail you back and say, "It was my pleasure"? And, if so, should you then e-mail back and say, "I appreciate your willingness to answer my questions"? And, if so, should the other person then respond with something like "It was no problem"?

On the one hand, you don't want to prolong the interaction more than necessary; on the other, you don't want to appear impolite. So how do you signal (politely) that the e-mail exchange should stop? Here are a few suggestions (Cohen, 2002).

- Include in your e-mail the notation NRN (No Reply Necessary).
- If you're replying with information the other person requested, end your message with something like "I hope this helps."
- Title or head your message FYI (For Your Information), indicating that your message is just to keep someone in the loop.
- When you make a request for information, end your message with "thank you in advance."

With any of these closings, it should be clear to the other person that you're attempting to end the conversation. Obviously, you will have to use more direct methods with those who don't take these subtle hints or don't realize that both persons are responsible for the interpersonal interaction and for bringing it to a satisfactory close.

INTERPERSONAL CHOICE POINT

Expressing Yourself

People have told you that they never can tell what you're thinking. Although you think this may well be an asset, you also want to have the ability to allow what you're thinking and feeling to be clear to others. What are some of your options for making yourself more expressive in, say, work relationships? When first meeting another person? When meeting someone you may easily develop feelings for?

The Principle of Cooperation

During conversation you probably follow the principle of **cooperation**; you and the other person implicitly agree to cooperate in trying to understand what each is saying (Grice, 1975; Lindblom, 2001). You cooperate largely by using four **conversational maxims**—principles that speakers and listeners in the United States and in many other cultures follow in conversation. Although the names for these maxims may be new, the principles themselves will be easily recognized from your own experiences.

The Maxim of Quantity   Be as informative as necessary to communicate the intended meaning. Thus, in keeping with the **quantity maxim**, you include information that makes the meaning clear but omit what does not; you give neither too little nor too much information. You see people violate this maxim when they try to relate an incident and digress to give unnecessary information. You find yourself thinking or saying, "Get to the point; so what happened?" This maxim is also violated when necessary information is omitted. In this situation, you find yourself constantly interrupting to ask questions: "Where were they?" "When did this happen?" "Who else was there?"

This simple maxim is frequently violated in e-mail communication. Here, for example, are three ways in which e-mail often violates the maxim of quantity and some suggestions on how to avoid these violations:

- Chain e-mails (and "forwards" of jokes or pictures) often violate the maxim of quantity by sending people information they don't really need or want. Some people maintain lists of e-mail addresses and send all these people the same information. It's highly unlikely that everyone on these lists will need or want to read the long list of jokes you find so funny. *Suggestion:* Avoid chain e-mail (at least most of the time). When something comes along that you think someone you know would like to read, send it on to the specific one, two, or three people you know would like to receive it.
- When chain e-mails are used, they often contain the e-mail addresses of everyone on the chain. These extensive headers clog the system and also reveal e-mail addresses that some people may prefer to keep private or to share with others at their own discretion.

Suggestion: When you do send chain e-mails (and in some situations, they serve useful purposes), conceal the e-mail addresses of your recipients by using some general description such as "undisclosed recipients."

- Large attachments take time to download and can create problems for people who do not have the latest technology. Not everyone wants to see the two hundred photos of your last vacation. *Suggestion:* Use attachments in moderation; find out first who would like to receive photos and who would not.

The Maxim of Quality   Say what you know or assume to be true, and do not say what you know to be false. When you're in conversation, you assume that the other person's information is true—at least as far as he or she knows. When you speak with people who frequently violate the **quality maxim** by lying, exaggerating, or minimizing major problems, you come to distrust what such individuals are saying and wonder what is true and what is fabricated.

The Maxim of Relation   Talk about what is relevant to the conversation. Thus, the **relation maxim** states, if you're talking about Pat and Chris and say, for example, "Money causes all sorts of relationship problems," it's assumed by others that your comment is somehow related to Pat and Chris. This principle is frequently violated by speakers who digress widely or frequently interject irrelevant comments, causing you to wonder how these comments are related to what you're discussing.

The Maxim of Manner   Be clear, avoid ambiguities, be relatively brief, and organize your thoughts into a meaningful sequence. Thus, in accordance with the **manner maxim**, you use terms that the listener understands and clarify terms that you suspect the listener will not understand. When talking with a child, for example, you simplify your vocabulary. Similarly, you adjust your manner of speaking on the basis of the information you and the listener share. When talking to a close friend, for example, you can refer to mutual acquaintances and to experiences you've had together. When talking to a stranger, however, you'll either omit such references or explain them.

The four maxims just discussed aptly describe most conversations as they take place in much of the United States. Recognize, however, that maxims will vary from one culture to another. Here are two maxims appropriate in cultures other than that of the United States, but also appropriate to some degree throughout the United States:

- In Japanese conversations and group discussions, a maxim of preserving peaceful relationships with others may be observed (Midooka, 1990). Thus, for example, it would be considered inappropriate to argue and to directly demonstrate that another person is wrong. It would be inappropriate to contribute to another person's embarrassment or, worse, loss of face.
- The maxim of self-denigration, observed in the conversations of Chinese speakers, may require that you avoid taking credit for some accomplishment or make less of some ability or talent you have (Gu, 1990). To put yourself down in this way is a form of politeness that seeks to elevate the person to whom you're speaking.

The Principle of Politeness: Conversation Is (Usually) Polite

Not surprisingly, conversation is expected (at least in many cases) to follow the principle of politeness. Six maxims of politeness have been identified by linguist Geoffrey Leech (1983) and seem to encompass a great deal of what we commonly think of as conversational politeness. Before reading about these maxims take the following self-test to help you personalize the material that follows.

The maxim of tact (Statement 1 in the self-test) helps to maintain the other's autonomy (what we referred to earlier as negative face). Tact in your conversation would mean that you do not impose on others or challenge their right to do as they wish. For example, if you wanted to ask someone a favor, using the maxim of tact, you might say something like, "I know you're very busy but . . ." or "I don't mean to impose, but . . ." Not using the maxim of tact, you might say something like, "You have to lend me your car this weekend" or "I'm going to use your ATM card."

The maxim of generosity (Statement 2) helps to confirm the other person's importance, the importance of the person's time, insight, or talent, for example. Using the maxim of generosity, you might say, "I'll walk the dog; I see you're busy" and violating the maxim, you might say, "I'm really busy, why don't you walk the dog; you're not doing anything important."

The maxim of approbation (Statement 3) refers to praising someone or complimenting the person in some way (for example, "I was really moved by your poem") and minimizing any expression of criticism or disapproval (for example, "For a first effort, that poem wasn't half bad").

The maxim of modesty (Statement 4) minimizes any praise or compliments *you* might receive. At the same time, you might praise and compliment the other person. For example, using this maxim you might say something like, "Well, thank you, but I couldn't have done this without your input; that was the crucial element." Violating this maxim, you might say, "Yes, thank you, it was one of my best efforts, I have to admit."

The maxim of agreement (Statement 5) refers to your seeking out areas of agreement and expressing them ("That color you selected was just right; it makes the room exciting") and at the same time to avoid and not express (or at least minimize) disagreements ("It's an interesting choice, very different"). In violation of this maxim, you might say "That color—how can you stand it?"

The maxim of sympathy (Statement 6) refers to the expression of understanding, sympathy, empathy, supportiveness, and the like for the other person. Using this maxim you might say, "I understand your feelings; I'm so sorry." If you violated this maxim you might say, for example, "You're making a fuss over nothing" or "You get upset over the least little thing; what is it this time?"

The Principle of Dialogue

A **monologue** is communication in which one person speaks and the other listens; there's no real interaction among participants. The term monologic communication is an extension of this basic definition and refers to communication in which there is no genuine interaction, in which you speak without any real concern for the other person's feelings or attitudes. The monologic communicator is concerned only with his or her own goals and is interested in the other person only insofar as that person can be used to achieve those goals. In monologic interaction, you communicate what will advance your own goals, prove most persuasive, and benefit you.

Not surprisingly, effective communication is based not on monologue but on its opposite, dialogue (Brown & Keller, 1979; Buber, 1958; McNamee & Gergen, 1999; Thomlison, 1982; Yau-fair Ho, Chan, Peng, & Ng, 2001). In a **dialogue**, there is two-way interaction. Each person is both speaker and listener, sender and receiver. In dialogic communication there is deep concern for the other person and for the relationship between the two people. The objective of dialogue is mutual understanding and empathy. There is respect for the other person, not because of what this person can do or give, but simply because this person is a human being and therefore deserves to be treated honestly and sincerely.

In a dialogic interaction, you respect the other person enough to allow that person the right to make his or her own choices without coercion, without the threat of punishment, without fear or social pressure. A dialogic communicator respects other people enough to believe that they can make their own decisions and implicitly or explicitly lets them know that whatever choices they make, they will still be respected as people.

Table 2 provides a comparison and summary of some of the essential differences between monologue and dialogue.

The Principle of Turn Taking

The defining feature of conversation is that the speaker and listener exchange roles throughout the interaction. You accomplish this through a wide variety of verbal and nonverbal cues

TABLE 2 Monologue and Dialogue

Monologue	Dialogue
You frequently use negative criticism ("I didn't like that explanation") and negative personal judgments ("You're not a very good listener, are you?").	You avoid negative criticism and negative personal judgments; you practice using positive criticism ("I like those first two explanations best; they were really well-reasoned").
You frequently use dysfunctional communication, such as avoiding the topic or talking about irrelevancies.	You keep the channels of communication open ("I really don't know what I did that offended you, but tell me. I don't want to hurt you again").
You rarely demonstrate through paraphrase or summary that you understand the other person's meaning.	You frequently paraphrase or summarize what the other person has said to ensure accurate understanding.
You rarely request clarification of the other person's perspectives or ideas.	You request clarification as necessary and ask for the other person's point of view because of a genuine interest in the other person's perspective.
You frequently make positive statements about yourself or request statements of approval from others ("How did you like the way I told that guy off? Clever, no?").	You avoid requesting self-approval statements.

that signal **conversational turns**—the changing (or maintaining) of the speaker or listener role during the conversation. In hearing people, turn taking is regulated by both audio and visual signals. Among blind speakers, turn taking is governed in larger part by audio signals and often touch. Among deaf speakers, turn-taking signals are largely visual and also may involve touch (Coates & Sutton-Spence, 2001). Combining the insights of a variety of communication researchers (Burgoon, Guerrero, & Floyd, 2010; Duncan, 1972; Pearson & Spitzberg, 1990), let's look more closely at conversational turns in terms of cues that speakers use and cues that listeners use.

Speaker Cues

As a speaker, you regulate conversation through two major types of cues: turn-maintaining and turn-yielding. Turn-maintaining cues are designed to help you maintain the speaker's role. You can do this with a variety of cues; for example, by audibly inhaling to show that you have more to say, continuing a gesture or gestures to show that you have not completed the thought, avoiding eye contact with the listener so there's no indication that you're passing the speaking turn to him or her, sustaining your intonation pattern to indicate that you intend to say more, or vocalizing pauses ("er," "um") to prevent the listener from speaking and to show that you're still talking (Burgoon, Buller, & Woodall, 1996; Duncan, 1972). In most cases, speakers are expected to maintain relatively brief speaking turns and to turn over the speaking role willingly to the listener (when so signaled by the listener).

With turn-yielding cues you tell the listener that you're finished and wish to exchange the role of speaker for that of listener. These cues tell the listener (sometimes a specific listener) to take over the role of speaker. For example, at the end of a statement you might add some paralinguistic cue such as "eh?" that asks one of the listeners to assume the role of speaker. You can also indicate that you've finished speaking by dropping your intonation, by prolonged silence, by making direct eye contact with a listener, by asking some general question, or by nodding in the direction of a particular listener.

In much the same way that you expect a speaker to yield the role of speaker, you also expect the listener to willingly assume the speaking role. Those who don't may be regarded as reticent or unwilling to involve themselves and take equal responsibility for the conversation. For example, in an analysis of turn-taking violations in the conversations of marrieds, the most common violation found was that of no response. Forty-five percent of the 540 violations identified involved a lack of response to an invitation to assume the speaker role. Of these "no response" violations, 68 percent were committed by men and 32 percent by women. Other turn-taking violations include interruptions, delayed responses, and inappropriately brief responses. From this it's been argued that by means of these violations, all of which are committed more frequently by men, men often silence women in marital interactions (DeFrancisco, 1991).

Listener Cues

As a listener, you can regulate the conversation by using a variety of cues. Turn-requesting cues let the speaker know that you'd like to take a turn as speaker. Sometimes you can do this by simply saying, "I'd like to say something," but often you do it more subtly through some vocalized "er" or "um" that tells the mindful speaker that you'd now like to speak. This request to speak is also often made with facial and mouth gestures. You can, for example, indicate a desire to speak by opening your eyes and mouth widely as if to say something, by beginning to gesture with your hand, or by leaning forward.

You can also indicate your reluctance to assume the role of speaker by using turn-denying cues. For example, intoning a slurred "I don't know" or a brief grunt signals you have nothing to say. Other ways to refuse a turn are to avoid eye contact with the speaker who wishes you to take on the role of speaker or to engage in some behavior that is incompatible with speaking—for example, coughing or blowing your nose.

Back-Channeling Cues

Back-channeling cues are used to communicate various types of information back to the speaker *without* your assuming the role of speaker. Some researchers call these "acknowledgment tokens"—brief utterances such as "mm-hm," "uh-huh," and "yeah," the three most often used such tokens—that tell the speaker you're listening (Drummond &

Hopper, 1993; Schegloff, 1982). Others call them "overlaps" to distinguish them from those interruptions that are aimed at taking over the speaker's turn (Tannen, 1994b). Back-channeling cues are generally supportive and confirming and show that you're listening and are involved in the interaction (Kennedy & Camden, 1988).

You can communicate a variety of messages with these back-channeling (overlaps, acknowledgment tokens) cues; here are four of the most important messages (Burgoon, Guerrero, & Floyd, 2010; Pearson & Spitzberg, 1990).

- **To indicate agreement or disagreement.** Smiles, nods of approval, brief comments such as "Right" and "Of course," or a vocalization like "uh-huh" signal agreement. Frowning, shaking your head, or making comments such as "No" or "Never" signal disagreement.
- **To indicate degree of involvement.** An attentive posture, forward leaning, and focused eye contact tell the speaker that you're involved in the conversation. An inattentive posture, backward leaning, and avoidance of eye contact communicate a lack of involvement.

Understanding *Interpersonal Theory & Research*

ONLINE COMMUNICATION THEORIES

Here are two theories of online communication that raise issues that are unique to online communication and which other theories do not address.

Social presence theory argues that the bandwidth of communication (the number of message cues exchanged) influences the degree to which the communication is personal or impersonal (Short, Williams, & Christie, 1976; Walther & Parks, 2002; Wood & Smith, 2005). When lots of cues are exchanged (especially nonverbal cues), as in face-to-face communication, you feel great social presence—the whole person is there for you to communicate with and exchange messages. When the bandwidth is smaller (as in e-mail or chat communication), then the communication is largely impersonal. So, for example, personal communication is easier to achieve in face-to-face situations (where tone of voice, facial expressions, eye contact, and similar nonverbal cues come into play) than in computer-mediated communication, which essentially contains only written cues.

It's more difficult, the theory goes, to communicate supportiveness, warmth, and friendliness in text-based chat or e-mail exchanges because of the smaller bandwidth. Of course, as video and audio components become more widely used, this distinction will fade.

Social information processing theory (SIP) argues, contrary to social presence theory, that whether you're communicating face-to-face or online, you can communicate the same degree of personal involvement and develop similar close relationships (Walther, 1992; Walther & Parks, 2002; Walther, 2008). The idea behind this theory is that communicators are clever people: Given whatever channel they have available to send and receive messages, they will make adjustments to communicate what they want and to develop the relationships they want. It is true that when the time span studied is limited—as it is in much of the research—that it is probably easier to communicate and develop relationships in face-to-face interaction than in online situations. But when the interaction occurs over an extended time period, as it often does in ongoing chat groups and in repeated e-mail exchanges, then the communication and the relationships can be as personal as those you develop in face-to-face situations.

Working with Theories and Research

How would you compare the level of closeness that you can communicate in face-to-face and in online situations? Do you feel it's more difficult (even impossible) to communicate, say, support, warmth, and friendship in online communication than in face-to-face communication?

- **To pace the speaker.** You ask the speaker to slow down by raising your hand near your ear and leaning forward, or to speed up by repeatedly nodding your head. Or you may cue the speaker verbally by asking the speaker to slow down or to speed up.
- **To ask for clarification.** Puzzled facial expressions, perhaps coupled with a forward lean, or direct interjection of "Who?," "When?," or "Where?" signal your need for clarification.

Interruptions   In contrast to back-channeling cues, **interruptions** are attempts to take over the role of the speaker. These are not supportive and are often disconfirming. Interruptions are often interpreted as attempts to change the topic to a subject that the interrupter knows more about or to emphasize the person's authority. Interruptions are seen as attempts to assert power and to maintain control. Not surprisingly, research finds that superiors (bosses and supervisors) and those in positions of authority (police officers and interviewers) interrupt those in inferior positions more than the other way around (Ashcraft, 1998; Carroll, 1994). In fact, it would probably strike you as strange to see a worker repeatedly interrupting a supervisor or a student repeatedly interrupting a professor.

Another and even more often-studied aspect of interruption is that of gender difference. The popular belief is that men interrupt more than women. This belief, research finds, is basically accurate. Men interrupt both women and other men more than women do. For example, one analysis of 43 published studies on interruptions and gender differences showed that men interrupted significantly more than women (Anderson, 1998). In addition, the more malelike the person's gender identity—regardless of the person's biological sex—the more likely it is that the person will interrupt (Drass, 1986). Fathers, one research study shows, interrupt their children more than mothers do (Greif, 1980). These gender differences, however, are small. More important than gender in determining who interrupts is the specific type of situation; some contexts (for example, task-oriented situations) may call for more interruptions, whereas others (such as relationship discussions) may call for more back-channeling cues (Anderson, 1998).

The various turn-taking cues and how they correspond to the conversational wants of speaker and listener are summarized in Figure 2.

INTERPERSONAL CHOICE POINT

Interrupting

You're supervising a group of six people who are working to revise your college's website. But one member of the group interrupts so much that other members have simply stopped contributing. It's become a one-person group, and you can't have this. What are some of the things that you might say to correct this situation without coming across as the bossy supervisor?

FIGURE 2

Turn Taking and Conversational Wants

Each quadrant represents a different type of turn taking:

- Quadrant 1 represents the speaker who wishes to speak (or to continue speaking) and uses turn-**maintaining** cues.
- Quadrant 2 represents the speaker who wishes to listen and uses turn-**yielding** cues.
- Quadrant 3 represents the listener who wishes to speak and uses turn-**requesting** cues.
- Quadrant 4 represents the listener who wishes to listen (or to continue listening) and uses turn-**denying** cues.

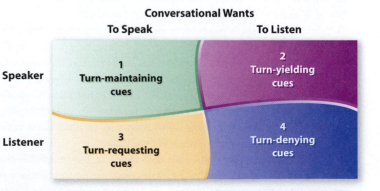

Conversational Wants

	To Speak	To Listen
Speaker	1 Turn-maintaining cues	2 Turn-yielding cues
Listener	3 Turn-requesting cues	4 Turn-denying cues

Back-channeling cues would also appear in quadrant 4, as they are cues that listeners use while they continue to listen. Interruptions would appear in quadrant 3, though they're not so much cues that request a turn as takeovers of the speaker's position.

How responsive would you say you are to the turn-taking cues of others? How responsive would you say others are to your turn-taking cues?

Conversational Disclosure: Revealing Yourself

One of the most important forms of interpersonal communication that you can engage in is talking about yourself, or self-disclosure. **Self-disclosure** means communicating information about yourself (usually information that you normally keep hidden) to another person. It may involve information about (1) your values, beliefs, and desires ("I believe in reincarnation"); (2) your behavior ("I shoplifted but was never caught"); or (3) your self-qualities or characteristics ("I'm dyslexic"). Overt and carefully planned statements about yourself as well as slips of the tongue would be classified as self-disclosing communications. Similarly, you could self-disclose nonverbally by, for example, wearing gang colors, a wedding ring, a shirt with slogans that reveal your political or social concerns, such as "Pro-Choice" or "Go Green," or photos on Facebook. Self-disclosure also may involve your reactions to the feelings of others; for example, when you tell your friend that you're sorry she was fired.

Self-disclosure occurs in all forms of communication, not just interpersonal. It frequently occurs in small group settings, in public speeches, on television talk shows such as *Maury* and *Jerry Springer*, and even on *Leno* and *Letterman.* And self-disclosure can occur not only in face-to-face settings but also through the Internet. On social network sites such as Twitter or Facebook, for example, a great deal of self-disclosure goes on, as it does when people reveal themselves in personal e-mails, newsgroups, and blog posts. In fact, research finds that reciprocal self-disclosure occurs more quickly and at higher levels online than it does in face-to-face interactions (Joinson, 2001; Levine, 2000).

You probably self-disclose for a variety of reasons. Perhaps you feel the need for catharsis—a need to get rid of feelings of guilt or to confess some wrongdoing. You may also disclose to help the listener; to show the listener, for example, how you dealt with an addiction or succeeded in getting a promotion. Of course, you may self-disclose to encourage relationship growth, or to maintain or repair a relationship, or even as a strategy for ending a relationship.

Although self-disclosure may occur as a single message—for example, you tell a stranger on a train that you're thinking about getting a divorce—it's best viewed as a developing process in which information is exchanged between people over the period of their relationship (Spencer, 1993, 1994). If we view it as a developing process, we can then appreciate how self-disclosure changes as the relationship changes; for example, as a relationship progresses from initial contact through involvement to intimacy, the self-disclosures increase. If the relationship deteriorates and perhaps dissolves, the disclosures will decrease. We can also appreciate how self-disclosure will differ depending on the type of relationship, on whether the other person is your friend, lover, parent, child, or counselor.

Self-disclosure involves at least one other individual; it cannot be an intrapersonal communication act. To qualify as self-disclosure, the information must be received and understood by another person. As you can appreciate, self-disclosure can vary from the relatively insignificant ("I'm a Sagittarius") to the highly revealing and deeply personal ("I'm currently in an abusive relationship" or "I'm almost always depressed"). It can occur face-to-face and it can occur over the Internet. It can be limited to one person or to a network of thousands on Twitter or Facebook.

The remaining discussion of this important concept will be more meaningful if you first consider your own willingness to self-disclose. How likely would you be to disclose the following items

VIEWPOINTS Some researchers have pointed to a "disinhibition effect" that occurs in online communication. We seem less inhibited in communicating in e-mail or in chat groups, for example, than we do face-to-face. Among the reasons for this seems to be the fact that in online communication there is a certain degree of anonymity and invisibility (Suler, 2004). Does your relative anonymity in online communication lead you to self-disclose differently than you do in face-to-face interactions?

Pixellover RM 6/Alamy

Take a look at "Self-disclosure" at tcbdevito.blogspot.com. What do you see as the advantages and the disadvantages of this form of disclosure?

VIEWPOINTS At times self-disclosure occurs more in temporary than in permanent relationships—for example, between strangers on a train or plane, a kind of "in-flight intimacy" (McGill, 1985). In this situation, two people set up an intimate self-disclosing relationship during a brief travel period, but they don't pursue it beyond that point. In a similar way, you might set up a relationship with one or several people on the Internet and engage in significant disclosure. Perhaps knowing that you'll never see these other people and that they will never know where you live or work or what you look like makes it easier. Do you engage in such disclosure? If so, why?

of information to, say, members of this class? Respond using a simple five-part scale (very likely, likely, not sure, unlikely, very unlikely):

1. Some of the happiest moments in your life.
2. Aspects of your personality that you don't like.
3. Your most embarrassing moment.
4. Your sexual fantasies.
5. Your greatest fears.

Thinking about your willingness to disclose these types of information—and you can easily add other things about yourself that you would and would not disclose—should get you started examining your own self-disclosing behavior.

Influences on Self-Disclosure

Many factors influence whether or not you disclose, what you disclose, and to whom you disclose. Among the most important factors are who you are, your culture, your gender, who your listeners are, and what your topic is.

- **Who you are:** Highly sociable and extroverted people self-disclose more than those who are less sociable and more introverted. People who are apprehensive about talking in general also self-disclose less than do those who are more comfortable in communicating. Competent people and those with high self-esteem engage in self-disclosure more than less competent people and those with low self-esteem (Dolgin, Meyer, & Schwartz, 1991; McCroskey & Wheeless, 1976).

- **Your culture:** Different cultures view self-disclosure differently. People in the United States, for example, disclose more than do those in Great Britain, Germany, Japan, or Puerto Rico (Gudykunst, 1983). Americans also reported greater self-disclosure when communicating with other Americans than when communicating interculturally (Allen, Long, O'Mara, & Judd, 2003). In Japan it's considered undesirable for colleagues to reveal personal information, whereas in much of the United States it's expected (Barnlund, 1989; Hall & Hall, 1987).

- **Your gender:** Research supports the popular belief that women disclose more than men (Stewart, Cooper, & Stewart, 2003). Women disclose more than men about their previous romantic relationships, their feelings about their closest same-sex friends, their greatest fears, and what they don't like about their partners (Sprecher, 1987). A notable exception occurs in initial encounters. Here men will disclose more intimately than women, perhaps "in order to control the relationship's development" (Derlega, Winstead, Wong, & Hunter, 1985).

- **Your listeners:** Because you disclose on the basis of the support you receive, you disclose to people you like (Collins & Miller, 1994; Derlega, Winstead, Greene, Serovich, & Elwood, 2004) and to people you trust and love (Wheeless & Grotz, 1977; Sprecher & Hendrick, 2004). You also come to like those to whom you disclose (Berg & Archer, 1983). Not surprisingly, you're more likely to disclose to people who are close to you in age (Parker & Parrott, 1995). Social network sites enable you to regulate who will have access to your messages. For example, Twitter enables you to keep your tweets private (open only to those who follow you) or to allow anyone, even those without a Twitter account, to read your tweets.

- **Your topic:** You're more likely to self-disclose about some topics than others; for example, you're more likely to disclose information about your job or hobbies than about your sex life or financial situation (Jourard, 1968, 1971a). You're also more likely to disclose favorable than unfavorable information. Generally, the more personal and negative the topic, the less likely you'll be to self-disclose.

Rewards and Dangers of Self-Disclosure

Research shows that self-disclosure has both significant rewards and dangers. In making choices about whether or not to disclose, consider both.

Rewards of Self-Disclosure
Self-disclosure may help increase self-knowledge, communication and relationship effectiveness, and physiological well-being.

Self-disclosure helps you gain greater self-knowledge: a new perspective on yourself, a deeper understanding of your own behavior. Through self-disclosure you may bring to consciousness a great deal that you might otherwise keep from conscious analysis. Even self-acceptance is difficult without self-disclosure. You accept yourself largely through the eyes of others. Through self-disclosure and subsequent support, you'll see the positive responses to you; you'll see, for example, that others appreciate your sense of humor or ability to tell a good story or the values you espouse. And through these positive responses, you'll likely strengthen your positive self-concept.

Because you understand the messages of another person largely to the extent that you understand the person, self-disclosure is an essential condition for communication and relationship effectiveness. Self-disclosure helps you achieve a closer relationship with the person to whom you self-disclose and increases relationship satisfaction (Meeks, Hendrick, & Hendrick, 1998; Schmidt & Cornelius, 1987; Sprecher, 1987). Within a sexual relationship, self-disclosure increases sexual rewards and general relationship satisfaction; after all, it's largely through self-disclosure that you learn what another person likes and dislikes. These two benefits increase sexual satisfaction (Byers & Demmons, 1999). Self-disclosure has also been studied as it relates to psychological abuse; research indicates that persons who engage in in-depth self-disclosure seem to experience less psychological abuse (Shirley, Powers, & Sawyer, 2007). The reason for this finding may be that people in abusive relationships tend to disclose less for fear that such disclosures will provide "reasons" for the abuse. Or it may be that freedom to disclose comes from a nonabusive, supportive, confirming relationship.

Self-disclosure seems to have a positive effect on physiological health. People who self-disclose are less vulnerable to illnesses (Pennebacker, 1991). Not surprisingly, health benefits also result from disclosing in e-mails (Sheese, Brown, & Graziano, 2004). For example, bereavement over the death of someone very close is linked to physical illness for those who bear this alone and in silence. But it's unrelated to any physical problems for those who share their grief with others.

Dangers of Self-Disclosure: Risks Ahead
There are considerable potential personal, relational, and professional risks to self-disclosure.

- **Personal risks.** If you self-disclose aspects of your life that vary greatly from the values of those to whom you disclose, you incur personal risks; you may experience rejection from even your closest

VIEWPOINTS In American culture we're more likely to disclose when the person we're with discloses. This **dyadic effect** (what one person does, the other person does likewise) probably leads us to feel more secure and reinforces our own self-disclosing behavior. Disclosures are also more intimate when they're made in response to the disclosures of others (Berg & Archer, 1983). This dyadic effect is not universal across all cultures, however. For example, although Americans are likely to follow the dyadic effect and reciprocate with explicit, verbal self-disclosure, Koreans aren't (Won-Doornick, 1985). As you can appreciate, this can easily cause intercultural differences; for example, an American might be insulted if his or her Korean counterpart didn't reciprocate with self-disclosures that were similar in depth.

Cultura Creative/Alamy

INTERPERSONAL CHOICE POINT
To Disclose or Not?

You discover that your close friend's romantic partner of the last two years is being unfaithful. You feel you have an obligation to tell your friend and decide to do so (though you still have doubts that this is the right thing to do). What are some of the choices you have for communicating this information to your friend? What choice seems the most logical for this specific situation?

227

friends and family members. Men and women who disclose that they have cheated on their relationship partner, have stolen, or are suffering from protracted depression, for example, may find their friends and family no longer wanting to be quite as close as before.

- **Relational risks.** Even in close and long-lasting relationships, self-disclosure can pose relational risks (Bochner, 1984). Total self-disclosure may prove threatening to a relationship by causing a decrease in mutual attraction, trust, or any of the bonds holding the individuals together. Self-disclosures concerning infidelity, romantic fantasies, past indiscretions or crimes, lies, or hidden weaknesses and fears could easily have such negative effects.

- **Professional risks.** Revealing political views or attitudes toward different religious or racial groups may open you to professional risks and create problems on the job, as may disclosing any health problems, such as being HIV positive (Fesko, 2001). Teachers, for example, who disclose former or current drug use or cohabitation with students may find themselves denied tenure, teaching at undesirable hours, arrested, and/or a victim of "budget cuts."

In making your choice between disclosing and not disclosing, keep in mind—in addition to the advantages and dangers already noted—the irreversible nature of communication. Regardless of how many times you may try to qualify something or take it back, once you have disclosed, you cannot undisclose. Nor can you erase the conclusions and inferences listeners have made on the basis of your disclosures.

Guidelines for Self-Disclosure

Because self-disclosure is so important and so delicate a matter, guidelines are offered here for (1) deciding whether and how to self-disclose, (2) responding to the disclosures of others, and (3) resisting pressures to self-disclose.

Guidelines for Making Self-Disclosures The following guidelines will help you ask yourself the right questions before you make a choice that must ultimately be your own.

- **Disclose out of appropriate motivation.** Self-disclosure should be motivated by a concern for the relationship, for the others involved, and for yourself. Avoid disclosing to hurt the listener; for example, people who tell their parents that they hindered their emotional development may be disclosing out of a desire to hurt and punish rather than a desire to improve the relationship.

- **Disclose in the appropriate context.** Before making any significant self-disclosure, ask whether this is the right time and place. Could a better time and place be arranged? Ask, too, whether this self-disclosure is appropriate to the relationship. Generally, the more intimate the disclosures, the closer the relationship should be. It's probably best to resist intimate disclosures (especially negative ones) with nonintimates, casual acquaintances, or in the early stages of a relationship. And, of course, ask yourself whether the forum for the disclosures is appropriate. Some disclosures may best be made in private with one person while others can be broadcasted on television or on any one of the social network sites. Not surprisingly, social networks such as Twitter and Facebook have recognized this and instituted privacy controls, enabling you to monitor who can receive your posts (that is, disclosures) and who will be blocked.

Archives du 7eme Art/Photos 12/Alamy

VIEWPOINTS Realize that the more you reveal about yourself to others, the more areas of your life you expose to possible attack. Especially in the competitive context of work (or even romance), the more that others know about you, the more they'll be able to use against you. This simple fact has prompted power-watcher Michael Korda (1975, p. 302) to advise that you "never reveal all of yourself to other people; hold something back in reserve so that people are never quite sure if they really know you." This advice is not to suggest that you be secretive; rather, Korda is advocating "remaining slightly mysterious, as if [you] were always capable of doing something surprising and unexpected." Do you agree with Korda? Why?

- **Disclose gradually.** During your disclosures, give the other person a chance to reciprocate with his or her own disclosures. If reciprocal disclosures are not made, reassess your own self-disclosures. It may be a signal that for this person at this time and in this context, your disclosures are not welcome or appropriate.
- **Disclose without imposing burdens on yourself or others.** Carefully weigh the potential problems that you may incur as a result of your disclosure. Can you afford to lose your job if you disclose your arrest record? Is it wise to burden your in-laws with promises of secrecy to your disclosures of infidelity?

Guidelines for Facilitating and Responding to Self-Disclosures   When someone discloses to you, it's usually a sign of trust and affection. In serving this most important receiver function, keep the following guidelines in mind. These guidelines will also help you facilitate the disclosures of another person.

- **Practice the skills of effective and active listening.** The skills of effective listening are especially important when you are listening to self-disclosures: Listen actively, listen for different levels of meaning, listen with empathy, and listen with an open mind. Express an understanding of the speaker's feelings to allow the speaker the opportunity to see them more objectively and through the eyes of another. Ask questions to ensure your own understanding and to signal your interest and attention.
- **Support and reinforce the discloser.** Express support for the person during and after the disclosures. Concentrate on understanding and empathizing with (rather than evaluating) the discloser. Make your supportiveness clear to the discloser through your verbal and nonverbal responses: Maintain eye contact, lean toward the speaker, ask relevant questions, and echo the speaker's thoughts and feelings.
- **Be willing to reciprocate.** When you make relevant and appropriate disclosures of your own in response to the other person's disclosures, you're demonstrating your understanding of the other's meanings and at the same time showing a willingness to communicate on this meaningful level.
- **Keep the disclosures confidential.** When a person discloses to you, it's because she or he wants you to know the feelings and thoughts that are communicated. If you reveal these disclosures to others, negative outcomes are inevitable and your relationship is almost sure to suffer. And be sure not to use the disclosures against the person. Many self-disclosures expose some kind of vulnerability or weakness. If you later turn around and use disclosures against the person who made them, you betray the confidence and trust invested in you. Regardless of how angry you may get, resist the temptation to use disclosures as weapons.

Guidelines for Resisting Pressure to Self-Disclose   You may, on occasion, find yourself in a position where a friend, colleague, or romantic partner pressures you to self-disclose. In such situations, you may wish to weigh the pros and cons of self-disclosure and then make your decision as to whether and what you'll disclose. If your decision is not to disclose and you're still being pressured, then you need to say something. Here are a few suggestions.

- **Don't be pushed.** Although there may be certain legal or ethical reasons for disclosing, generally, if you don't want to disclose, you don't have to. Don't be pushed into disclosing because others are doing it or because you're asked to.
- **Be assertive in your refusal to disclose.** Say, very directly, "I'd rather not talk about that now" or "Now is not the time for this type of discussion."

For a brief discussion of the dangers of revealing normally hidden information about others, see "Outing" at tcbdevito.blogspot.com. Have you ever been "outed"? Ever "outed" others? What were the consequences?

INTERPERSONAL CHOICE POINT

Discouraging Self-Disclosure

Your colleague at work reveals too much private information for your liking. You're really not interested in this person's sex life, financial woes, and medical problems. What can you do to prevent or discourage this too-personal self-disclosure, at least to you?

INTERPERSONAL CHOICE POINT

Refusing to Self-Disclose

You've dated this person three or four times, and each time you're pressured to self-disclose past experiences and personal information you're simply not ready to talk about—at least, not at this early stage of the relationship. What are some of the things you can say or do to resist this pressure to self-disclose? What might you say to discourage further requests that you reveal yourself?

Ethics in Interpersonal Communication

THE ETHICS OF GOSSIP

Gossip is social talk that involves making evaluations about persons who are not present during the conversation; it generally occurs when two people talk about a third party (Eder & Enke, 1991; Wert & Salovey, 2004). And at times it occurs when someone reveals a private disclosure. As you obviously know, a large part of your conversation at work and in social situations is spent gossiping (Carey, 2005; Lachnit, 2001; Waddington, 2004). In fact, one study estimates that approximately two-thirds of people's conversation time is devoted to social topics, and that most of these topics can be considered gossip (Dunbar, 2004). Gossiping seems universal among all cultures (Laing, 1993), and among some it's a commonly accepted ritual (Hall, 1993). And, not surprisingly, gossip occupies a large part of Internet communication, as demonstrated by the growing popularity of such websites as Juicy Campus (www.JuicyCampus.com), which currently link 59 college campuses (Morgan, 2008).

As you might expect, gossiping often has ethical implications, and in many instances gossip is considered unethical. Some such instances generally identified as unethical are (Bok, 1983):

- when gossip is used to unfairly hurt another person; for example, spreading gossip about an office romance or an instructor's past indiscretions.
- when you know that what you're saying is not true; for example, lying to make another person look bad.
- when no one has the right to such personal information; for example, revealing the income of neighbors to others or revealing a fellow student's poor grades to other students.
- when you've promised secrecy; for example, revealing something that you promised not to repeat to others.

ETHICAL CHOICE POINT

Your best friend's romantic partner has come on to you on several occasions. What is your ethical obligation to your friend? If you decide to tell your friend, will it be ethical to tell other mutual friends? At what point does revealing this become unethical gossip?

Another "everyday conversation" is that of introducing people. For a brief discussion, see "Introducing People" at tcbdevito.blogspot.com. What other suggestions would you offer for introducing people? What about introducing yourself?

- **Delay a decision.** If you don't want to say no directly, but still don't want to disclose, delay the decision. Say something like, "That's pretty personal; let me think about that before I make a fool of myself" or "This isn't really a good time (or place) to talk about this; I'll get back to you and we'll talk."
- **Be indirect and move to another topic.** Avoid the question and change the subject. This is a polite way of saying, "I'm not talking about it," and may be the preferred choice in certain situations. Most often people will get the hint and understand your refusal to disclose.

Everyday Conversations

Here we discuss a variety of everyday conversation situations: making small talk, excusing and apologizing, complimenting, and giving advice. In connection with this section, take a look at Table 3 on the following page, which summarizes some of the unsatisfying conversational partners that you'll want to avoid imitating.

Small Talk

Before reading about this ever-present form of conversation, take the accompanying self-test, "How Do You Small Talk?"

Understanding *Interpersonal Skills*

EXPRESSIVENESS

Expressiveness is the skill of communicating genuine involvement in the conversation; it entails, for example, taking responsibility for your thoughts and feelings, encouraging expressiveness or openness in others, and providing appropriate feedback. As you can easily appreciate, these are the qualities that make a conversation exciting and satisfying. Expressiveness includes both verbal and nonverbal messages and often involves revealing your emotions and your normally hidden self—bringing in a variety of interpersonal skills noted earlier.

Communicating Expressiveness. Here are a few suggestions for communicating expressiveness.

- **Vary your vocal rate, pitch, volume, and rhythm** to convey involvement and interest. Vary your language; avoid clichés and trite expressions, which signal a lack of originality and personal involvement.
- **Use appropriate gestures,** especially gestures that focus on the other person rather than yourself. Maintain eye contact and lean toward the person; at the same time, avoid self-touching gestures or directing your eyes to others in the room.
- **Give verbal and nonverbal feedback** to show that you're listening. Such feedback promotes relationship satisfaction.
- **Smile.** Your smile is probably your most expressive feature and it will likely be much appreciated.
- **Communicate expressiveness in ways that are culturally sensitive.** Some cultures (Italian, for example) encourage expressiveness and teach children to be expressive. Other cultures (Japanese and Thai, for example) encourage a more reserved response style (Matsumoto, 1996). Some cultures (Arab and many Asian cultures, for example) consider expressiveness by women in business settings to be inappropriate (Lustig & Koester, 2010; Axtell, 2007; Hall & Hall, 1987).

Working with Interpersonal Skills

Think about the expressiveness of the people you know who are extremely popular and those who are significantly less popular. In what ways do these groups differ in expressiveness? How would you describe your own expressiveness?

Test Yourself   How Do You Small Talk?

Examine your small talk communication by responding to the following questions.

_____ 1. On an elevator with three or four strangers, I'd be most likely to
   a. seek to avoid interacting.
   b. respond to another but not initiate interaction.
   c. be the first to talk.

_____ 2. When I'm talking with someone and I meet a friend who doesn't know the person I'm with, I'd be most apt to
   a. avoid introducing them.
   b. wait until they introduce each other.
   c. introduce them to each other.

_____ 3. At a party with people I've never met before, I'd be most likely to
   a. wait for someone to talk to me.
   b. nonverbally indicate that you're receptive to someone interacting with you.
   c. initiate interaction with others nonverbally and verbally.

_____ 4. When confronted with someone who doesn't want to end the conversation, I'd be most apt to
   a. just stick it out and listen.

    b. tune out the person and hope time goes by quickly.

    c. end it firmly myself.

_____ 5. When the other person monologues, I'd be most apt to

    a. listen politely.

    b. try to change the focus.

    c. exit as quickly as possible.

How Did You Do? The **a** responses are unassertive, the **b** responses are indirect (not totally unassertive but not assertive either), and the **c** responses are direct and assertive. Very likely, if you answered with 4 or 5 **c** responses, you're comfortable and satisfied with your small talk experiences. Lots of **a** responses would indicate some level of dissatisfaction and discomfort with the experience of small talk. If you had lots of **b** responses then you probably experience both satisfaction and dissatisfaction with small talk.

What Will You Do? If your small talk experiences are not satisfying to you, read on. The entire body of interpersonal skills will prove relevant here as will a number of suggestions unique to small talk.

TABLE 3	**Unsatisfying Conversational Partners and How Not to Become One of Them**

As you read this table, consider your own conversations. Have you met any of these people? Have you ever been one of these people?

Unsatisfying Conversational Partners	How Not to Become One of Them
The **Detour Taker** begins to talk about a topic and then goes off pursuing a totally different subject.	Follow a logical pattern in conversation, and avoid frequent and long detours.
The **Monologist** gives speeches rather than engaging in dialogue.	Engage in dialogue; give the other person a chance to speak and keep your own "lectures" short.
The **Complainer** has many complaints and rarely tires of listing each of them.	Be positive; emphasize what's good before what's bad.
The **Moralist** evaluates and judges everyone and everything.	Avoid evaluation and judgment; see the world through the eyes of the other person.
The **Inactive Responder** gives no reaction regardless of what you say.	Respond overtly with verbal and nonverbal messages; let the other person see and hear that you're listening.
The **Story Teller** tells stories, too often substituting them for two-way conversation.	Talk about yourself in moderation; be other-oriented.
The **Egotist** talks only about topics that are self-related.	Be other-oriented; focus on the other person; listen as much as you speak.
The **Thought Completer** "knows" exactly what you're going to say and so says it for you.	Don't interrupt; assume that the speaker wants to finish her or his own thoughts.
The **Self-Discloser** discloses more than you need or want to hear.	Disclose selectively, in ways appropriate to your relationship with the listener.
The **Advisor** regularly and consistently gives advice, whether you want it or not.	Don't assume that the expression of a problem is a request for a solution.

Small talk is pervasive; all of us engage in small talk. Sometimes, we use small talk as a preface to big talk. For example, before a conference with your boss or even an employment interview, you're likely to engage in some preliminary small talk. *How you doing? I'm pleased this weather has finally cleared up. That's a great looking jacket.* The purpose here is to ease into the major topic or the big talk.

Sometimes, small talk is a politeness strategy and a bit more extensive way of saying hello as you pass someone in the hallway or a neighbor you meet at the post office. And, so you might say, "Good seeing you, Jack. You're ready for the big meeting?" or, "See you in Geology at 1."

Sometimes, your relationship with another person revolves totally around small talk, perhaps with your barber or hair dresser, a colleague at work, your next door neighbor, or a student you sit next to in class. In these relationships neither person makes an effort to deepen the relationship and it remains on a small talk level.

The Topics and Contexts of Small Talk

The topics of small talk have one important characteristic and that is that the topic must be non-controversial in the sense that it must not be something that you and the other person are likely to disagree on. If a topic is likely to arouse deep emotions or different points of view, then it is probably not a small talk topic.

Most often the topics are relatively innocuous. The weather is perhaps the most popular small talk topic. "Trivial" news, for example, news about sports (although criticizing the other person's favorite team would not be considered non-controversial by many), and movie or television stars are also popular small talk topics. Current affairs—as long as there is agreement—might also be used in small talk, "Did you see the headline in the news? Horrible, isn't it?" Sometimes small talk grows out of the context; waiting on line for tickets may prompt a comment to the person next to you about your feet hurting or if they know how long it will be until the tickets go on sale.

Small talk is usually short in duration, a factor that helps make this talk non-controversial. Because of the context in which small talk occurs—waiting on line to get into a movie or for a store to open—it allows for only a brief interaction.

Another popular occasion, which contradicts this short duration characteristic, is sitting next to someone on a long plane or train ride. Here, the small talk—assuming you keep it to small talk—can last for many hours. Sometimes, this situation produces a kind of "in-flight intimacy" in which you engage in significant self-disclosure, revealing secrets you normally keep hidden, largely because you know you'll never see this person again.

Even though small talk is non-controversial and brief, it serves important purposes. One obvious purpose is to pass the time more pleasantly than you might in silence. Another purpose is that it demonstrates that the normal rules of politeness are operating. In the United States, for example, you would be expected to smile and at least say hello to people on an elevator in your apartment building and perhaps at your place of work. It also demonstrates to others that all is well with you.

Guidelines for Effective Small Talk

Although "small," this talk still requires the application of the interpersonal communication skills for "big" talk. Keep especially in mind, as already noted, that the best topics are non-controversial and that most small talk is relatively brief. Here are a few additional guidelines for more effective small talk.

For a brief list of annoying conversational phrases, see "Annoying Conversation" at tcbdevito.blogspot.com. What do you feel are the most annoying phrases?

Eric Audras/PhotoAlto/Alamy

VIEWPOINTS One of the stereotypes about gender differences in communication and widely reported in the popular writings on gender is that women talk more than men. But, a recent study of 396 college students finds that women and men talk about the same number of words per day, about 16,000; more precisely women spoke an average of 16,215 words while men spoke an average of 15,669 words, a difference that was statistically insignificant (Mehl, Vazire, Ramirez-Esparza, Slatcher, & Pennebaker, 2007). Do your own experiences support the stereotype or do they support these research findings?

- Be positive. No one likes a negative doom-sayer.
- Be sensitive to leave-taking cues. Small talk is necessarily brief, but at times one person may want it to be a preliminary to the big talk and another person may see it as the sum of the interaction.
- Stress similarities rather than differences; this is a good way to ensure that this small talk is non-controversial.
- Answer questions with enough elaboration to give the other person information that can then be used to interact with you. Let's say someone sees a book you're carrying and says, "I see you're taking interpersonal communication." If you say, simply "yes," you've not given the other person anything to talk with you about. Instead, if you say, "Yes, it's a great course; I think I'm going to major in communication" then you have given the other person information that can be addressed. The more elaborate answer also signals your willingness to engage in small talk. Of course, if you do not want to interact, then a simple one-word response will help you achieve your goal.

Excuses and Apologies

Despite your best efforts, there are times when you'll say or do the wrong thing and an excuse and/or an apology may be necessary. **Excuses** are *explanations* designed to reduce the negative effects of your behavior and help to maintain your positive image (Snyder, 1984; Snyder, Higgins, & Stucky, 1983). **Apologies**, on the other hand, are *expressions of regret or sorrow* for having done what you did or for what happened. Often the two are blended—*I didn't realize how fast I was driving* (the excuse); *I'm really sorry* (the apology). Let's separate them and look first at the excuse.

The Excuse Excuses seem especially in order when you say or are accused of saying something that runs counter to what is expected or considered "right" by the people with whom you're talking. Ideally, the excuse lessens the negative impact of the message.

The major motive for excuse making seems to be to maintain your self-esteem, to project a positive image to yourself and to others. Excuses also represent an effort to reduce stress: You may feel that if you can offer an excuse—especially a good one that is accepted by those around you—it will reduce the negative reaction and the subsequent stress that accompanies a poor performance.

Excuses also may enable you to maintain effective interpersonal relationships even after some negative behavior. For example, after criticizing a friend's behavior and observing the negative reaction to your criticism, you might offer an excuse such as, "Please forgive me; I'm really exhausted. I'm just not thinking straight." Excuses enable you to place your messages—even your possible failures—in a more favorable light.

Types of Excuses. Different researchers have classified excuses into varied categories (Cody & Dunn, 2007; Scott & Lyman, 1968). One of the best typologies classifies excuses into three main types (Snyder, 1984):

- **I didn't do it:** Here you deny that you have done what you're being accused of. You may then bring up an alibi to prove you couldn't have done it or perhaps you may accuse another person of doing what you're being blamed for ("I never said that" or "I wasn't even near the place when it happened"). These "I didn't do it" types are generally the worst excuses (unless they're true), because they fail to acknowledge responsibility and offer no assurance that this failure will not happen again.
- **It wasn't so bad:** Here you admit to doing it but claim the offense was not really so bad or perhaps that there was justification for the behavior ("I only padded the expense account by a few bucks").
- **Yes, but:** Here you claim that extenuating circumstances accounted for the behavior; for example, that you weren't in control of yourself at the time or that you didn't intend to do what you did ("I never intended to hurt him; I was actually trying to help").

Good and Bad Excuses. The most important question for most people is what makes a good excuse and what makes a bad excuse (Dunn & Cody, 2000; Slade, 1995; Snyder, 1984). How can you make good excuses and thus get out of problems, and how can you avoid bad excuses that only make matters worse?

What makes one excuse effective and another ineffective will vary from one culture to another and will depend on factors already discussed, such as the culture's individualism–collectivism, its power distance, the values it places on assertiveness, and various other cultural tendencies (Tata, 2000). But, at least in the United States, researchers seem to agree that in the best excuses in interpersonal communication you do the following (Coleman, 2002; Slade, 1995).

1. Demonstrate that you really understand the problem and that your partner's feelings are legitimate and justified. Avoid minimizing the issue or your partner's feelings ("It was only $100; you're overreacting," "I was only two hours late").
2. Acknowledge your responsibility. If you did something wrong, avoid qualifying your responsibility ("I'm sorry if I did anything wrong") or expressing a lack of sincerity ("Okay, I'm sorry; it's obviously my fault—again"). On the other hand, if you can demonstrate that you had no control over what happened and therefore cannot be held responsible, your excuse is likely to be highly persuasive (Heath, Stone, Darley, & Grannemann, 2003).
3. Acknowledge your own displeasure at what you did, your unhappiness for having done what you did.
4. Make it clear that your misdeed will never happen again.

The Apology

In its most basic form, an apology is an expression of regret for something you did; it's a statement that you're sorry. And so, the most basic of all apologies is simply: "I'm sorry." In popular usage, the apology includes some admission of wrongdoing on the part of the person making the apology. Sometimes the wrongdoing is acknowledged explicitly ("I'm sorry I lied") and sometimes only by implication ("I'm sorry you're so upset").

In many cases the apology also includes a request for forgiveness ("Please forgive my lateness") and some assurance that this won't happen again ("Please forgive my lateness; it won't happen again").

According to the Harvard Business School Working Knowledge website (http://hbswk.hbs.edu/archive/3481.html), apologies are useful for two main reasons. Apologies (1) help repair your relationships (as you can easily imagine) and, perhaps less obviously, (2) repair your reputation. So, if you do something wrong in your relationship, for example, an apology will help you repair the relationship with your partner and perhaps reduce the level of conflict. At the same time, however, realize that other people know about your behavior and an apology will help improve their image of you.

An effective apology, like an effective excuse, must be crafted for the specific situation. An effective apology to a long-time lover, to a parent, or to a new supervisor are likely to be very different because the individuals are different and your relationships are different. And so, the first rule of an effective apology is to take into consideration the uniqueness of the situation—the people, the context, the cultural rules, the relationship, the specific wrongdoing—for which you might want to apologize. Each situation will call for a somewhat different message of apology. Nevertheless we can offer some general recommendations.

Robert Koene/Photodisc/Thinkstock

VIEWPOINTS Recall the last time you made an excuse or someone made an excuse to you. What form did it take? Did it follow the suggestions identified here? What do you see as the most important ingredient of a good excuse?

- **Admit wrongdoing** (if indeed wrongdoing occurred). Accept responsibility. Own your own actions; don't try to pass them off as the work of someone else. Instead of *Smith drives so slow, it's a wonder I'm only 30 minutes late,* say *I should have taken traffic into consideration.*
  - **Be apologetic.** Say (and mean) the words *I'm sorry.* Don't justify your behavior by mentioning that everyone does it, for example, *Everyone leaves work early on Friday.* Don't justify your behavior by saying that the other person has done something equally wrong: *So I play poker; you play the lottery.*
  - **Be specific.** State, in specific rather than general terms, what you've done. Instead of *I'm sorry for what I did,* say *I'm sorry for flirting at the party.*
  - **Express understanding** of how the other person feels and acknowledge the legitimacy of these feelings, (for example, *You have every right to be angry; I should have called*). Express your regret that this has created a problem for the other person, (*I'm sorry I made you miss your appointment*). Don't minimize the problem that this may have caused. Avoid such comments as, *So the figures arrived a little late. What's the big deal?*
- **Give assurance that this will not happen again.** Say, quite simply, *It won't happen again* or better and more specifically, *I won't be late again.* And, whenever possible, offer to correct the problem, (*I'm sorry I didn't clean up the mess I made; I'll do it now*).
- **Omit the excuses.** Be careful of including excuses with your apology; for example, *I'm sorry the figures are late but I had so much other work to do.* An excuse often takes back the apology and says, in effect, I'm really not sorry because there was good reason for what I did but I'm saying "I'm sorry" to cover all my bases and to make this uncomfortable situation go away.
- **Don't take the easy way out** and apologize through e-mail (unless the wrongdoing was committed in e-mail or if e-mail is your only or main form of communication). Generally, it's more effective to use a more personal mode of communication—face-to-face or phone, for example. It's harder but it's more effective.

For suggestions on conversational turn-offs and their corresponding turn-ons, see "Conversational Coolers and Warmers" at tcbdevito .blogspot.com. What is the single most annoying conversational habit you can think of? What is the single most pleasant conversational habit?

Complimenting

A **compliment** is a message of praise, flattery, or congratulations. It's the opposite of criticism, insult, or complaint. The compliment functions like a kind of interpersonal glue; it's a way a relating to another person with positiveness and immediacy. It's also a conversation starter—"I like your watch; may I ask where you got it?" Another purpose the compliment serves is to encourage the other person to compliment you—even if not immediately (which often seems inappropriate). When you click the "like" or "recommend" buttons on social networks you're complimenting the person in much the same way as commenting favorably on a tweet or blog post.

Compliments can be unqualified or qualified. The unqualified compliment is a message that is purely positive: "Your paper was just great, an A." The qualified message is positive but with some negativity thrown in: "Your paper was great, an A; if not for a few problems, it would have been an A+." You might also give a qualified compliment by qualifying your own competence; for example, "That song you wrote sounded great, but I really don't know anything about music."

A **backhanded compliment** is really not a compliment at all; it's usually an insult masquerading as a compliment. For example, you might give a backhanded compliment as you say, "That sweater takes away from your pale complexion; it makes you look less washed out" (it compliments the color of the sweater but criticizes the person's complexion) or "Looks like you've finally lost a few pounds, am I right?" (it compliments a slimmer appearance but points out the person's being overweight).

Yet, compliments are sometimes difficult to express and even more difficult to respond to without discomfort or embarrassment. Fortunately, there are easy-to-follow guidelines. Let's consider first, some suggestions for giving compliments.

Giving a Compliment

Here are a few suggestions for giving compliments.

- **Be real and honest.** Say what you mean and omit giving compliments you don't believe in. They'll likely sound insincere and won't serve any useful purpose.
- **Compliment in moderation.** A compliment that is too extreme (say, for example, "that's the best decorated apartment I've ever seen in my life") may be viewed as dishonest. Similarly, don't compliment at every possible occasion; if you do, your compliments will seem too easy to win and not really meaningful.
- **Be totally complimentary.** Avoid qualifying your compliments. If you hear yourself giving a compliment and then adding a "but" or a "however" be careful; you're likely going to qualify your compliment. Unfortunately, in such situations many people will remember the qualification rather than the compliment and the entire compliment + qualification will appear as a criticism.
- **Be specific.** Direct your compliment at something specific rather than something general. Instead of saying something general such as, *I like your design,* you might say something more specific such, as *I like your design; the colors and fonts are perfect.*
- **Be personal in your own feelings.** For example, say *Your song really moved me; it made me recall so many good times.* At the same time, avoid any compliment that can be misinterpreted as overly sexual.

VIEWPOINTS Some interpersonal watchers recommend that you compliment people for their accomplishments rather than for who they are or for things over which they have no control. So, for example, you would compliment people for their clear reports, their poetry, their problem solving, and their tact, but not for being attractive or having green eyes. What do you think of this advice?

Digital Vision/Thinkstock

Receiving a Compliment

In receiving a compliment, people generally take either one of two options: denial or acceptance. Many people deny the compliment ("It's nice of you to say, but I know I was terrible"), minimize it ("It isn't like I wrote the great American novel; it was just an article that no one will read"), change the subject ("So, where should we go for dinner?"), or say nothing. Each of these responses creates problems. When you deny the legitimacy of the compliment you may communicate that the person isn't being sincere or doesn't know what he or she is talking about. When you minimize it, you may be interpreted as meaning that the person doesn't understand what you've done or what he or she is complimenting. When you change the subject or say nothing, you're saying that the compliment isn't having any effect; you're ignoring it because it isn't meaningful.

Accepting the compliment seems the much better alternative. An acceptance might consist simply of (1) a smile with eye contact—avoid looking at the floor; (2) a simple "thank you," and, if appropriate (3) a personal reflection where you explain (very briefly) the meaning of the compliment and why it's important to you (for example, "I appreciate your comments; I worked really hard on that design and it's great to hear it was effective").

Advice Giving

Everyone loves to give advice. Somehow it makes you seem important; after all, if you can give someone else advice, you must be pretty clever. In some cases, of course, advice giving may be part of your job description. For example, if you're a teacher, lawyer, health care provider, religious leader, or psychiatrist, you are in the advice giving business. And if you give advice that is found useful and consistently effective, you'll develop a reputation and get lots of business; if your advice is useless and consistently ineffective, you'll be out of business in short order.

Sometimes, people seek advice because they're in situations of doubt or indecision (especially important decisions) and so they seek out someone they think might have something useful to say. The greater the indecision and the more important the decision, the more likely are people to seek advice.

Sometimes people seek advice to avoid personal responsibility. So, for example, one spouse may say to the other, "I really don't know what to do with this bonus money. What do you think?" And, assuming the suggestion is followed, the advice-seeking spouse can then blame the other for "deciding" what to do with the extra money. Parents who absolve themselves of advising their child about what college to go to might also fall into this don't-blame-me class.

Sometimes, advice seeking is used as an ingratiation strategy. Saying, for example, "I know you know a great deal about finances—you're like a genius. Would you mind looking over my income tax statement?" likely makes the potential advice giver feel good about himself or herself, more positively toward the advice seeker, and, most important, more likely to comply with the request to review the income tax statement.

Advice and Meta-Advice.
Advice is best viewed as a process of giving another person a suggestion for thinking or behaving, usually to change their thinking or ways of behaving. In many ways, you can look at it as a suggestion to solve a problem. So, for example, you might advise friends to change their way of looking at broken love affairs or their financial situation or their career path. Or, you might advise someone to do something, to behave in a certain way, for example, to start dating again or to invest in certain stocks or to go back to school and take certain courses. Sometimes, the advice is to continue what the person is currently thinking or doing, for example, to stay with Pat despite the difficulties or to hold the stocks the person already has or to continue on his or her current career path.

Notice that you can give advice in at least two ways. One way is to give specific advice and another is to give **meta-advice** or advice about advice. Thus, you can give advice to a person that addresses the problem or issue directly—buy that condo, take this course, or vacation in Hawaii. But, you can also give advice about advice. At least three types of meta-advice can be identified.

- **To explore options and choices.** When confronted with a request for advice, this meta-advice would focus on helping the person explore the available options. For example, if a friend asks what he or she should do about never having a date, you might give meta-advice and help your friend explore the available options and the advantages and disadvantages (the rewards and the costs) of each.

- **To seek expert advice.** If confronted with a request for advice concerning some technical issue in which you have no competence, the best advice is often meta-advice—in this case, to seek advice from someone who is an expert in the field. When a friend asks what to do about a persistent cough, the best advice seems to be the meta-advice to "talk to your doctor."

- **To delay decision.** If confronted with a request for advice about a decision that doesn't have to be made immediately, one form of meta-advice would be to delay the decision while additional information is collected. So, for example, if you are seeking advice about taking a job at XYZ Company and you have two weeks to make a decision, then one bit of meta-advice would suggest that you delay the decision while you research the company more thoroughly.

Giving Advice.   In addition to giving meta-advice, there is also the option of giving specific advice. Here are a few suggestions:

- **Listen.** This is the first rule for advice giving. Listen to the person's thoughts and feelings. Listen to what the person wants—the person may actually want support and active listening and not advice. Or the person may simply want to ventilate in the presence of a friend.

- **Empathize.** Try to feel what the other person is feeling. Perhaps you might recall similar situations you were in or similar emotions you experienced. Think about the importance of the issue to the person and, in general, try to put yourself into the position, circumstance, and the context of the person asking your advice.

- **Be tentative.** If you give advice, give it with the qualifications it requires. The advice seeker has a right to know how sure (or unsure) you are of the advice or what evidence (or lack of evidence) you have that the advice will work.

- **Ensure understanding.** Often people seeking advice are emotionally upset and may not remember everything in the conversation. So, seek feedback after giving advice; for example, "Does that make sense?" "Is my suggestion workable?"

- **Keep the interaction confidential.** Often advice seeking is directed at very personal matters and so it's best to keep such conversations confidential, even if you're not asked to do so.

- **Avoid *should* statements.** People seeking advice still have to make their own decisions rather than being told what they should or should not do. And so, it's better to say, for example, "You *might* do X" or "You *could* do Y" rather than "You *should* do Z." Don't demand—or even imply—that the person has to follow your advice. This attacks the person's negative face, the person's need for autonomy.

> **INTERPERSONAL CHOICE POINT**
>
> **Unwanted Advice**
>
> *One of your close friends has the annoying habit of trying to give you advice that you don't want and only depresses you. What are some of your options for dealing with this problem? What are some of the things you might say to your friend? What are some of the things you'd want to avoid saying, assuming you'd like the friendship to continue?*

Responding to Advice.   Responding appropriately to advice is often a difficult process. Here are just a few suggestions for making receiving advice more effective:

- If you asked for the advice, then accept what the person says. You don't have to follow the advice, you just have to listen to it and process it.

- And even if you didn't ask for advice (and don't like it), resist the temptation to retaliate or criticize the advice giver. Instead of responding with, "Well, your hair doesn't look that great either," consider if the advice has any merit.

- Interact with the advice. Talk about it with the advice-giver. A process of asking and answering questions is likely to produce added insight into the problem.

- Express your appreciation for the advice. It's often difficult to give advice and so it's only fair that the advice-giver receive some words of appreciation.

In each of these everyday conversations, you have choices in terms of what you say and in terms of how you respond. Consider these choices mindfully, taking into consideration the variety of influencing factors discussed throughout this text, and their potential advantages and disadvantages. Once you lay out your choices in this way, you'll be more likely to select effective ones.

Summary

 Use your smartphone or tablet device (or log on to mycommunicationlab.com) to hear an audio summary of this chapter.

This chapter reviewed the process of conversation and discussed conversational stages, rules, and principles for effective conversational management, self-disclosure in conversation, and conversational repair.

The Conversation Process

1. The opening initiates and begins the conversation.
2. The feedforward previews or prefaces the major part of the conversation that is to follow.
3. The business is the major part of the conversation; it's the reason for the conversation.
4. The feedback summarizes or reflects back on the conversation.
5. The closing brings the conversation to an end.

Principles of Conversation

6. The principle of process emphasizes that conversation is a process rather than an act; it's a process with an opening, feedforward, business, feedback, and closing.
7. The principle of cooperation emphasizes that conversation proceeds with the assumption that each person is cooperating in the process.
8. The principle of politeness is designed to emphasize that there is a politeness dimension to conversation; some, probably most, are polite; others not so much.
9. The principle of dialogue emphasizes that conversation involves two involved people.
10. The principle of turn taking points to the most obvious aspect of conversation, namely that it's essentially a process of exchanging speaking and listening turns.

Conversational Disclosure: Revealing Yourself

11. Self-disclosure is revealing information about yourself to others—usually information that is normally hidden.
12. Self-disclosure is influenced by a variety of factors: who you are, your culture, your gender, your listeners, and your topic and channel.
13. Among the rewards of self-disclosure are self-knowledge, ability to cope, communication effectiveness, meaningfulness of relationships, and physiological health. Among the dangers are personal risks, relational risks, professional risks, and the fact that communication is irreversible; once something is said, you can't take it back.
14. In self-disclosing consider your motivation, the appropriateness of the disclosure to the person and context, the emergence (or absence) of reciprocal disclosure from the other person (the dyadic effect), and the possible burdens that the self-disclosure might impose on others and on yourself.
15. In responding to the disclosures of others, listen effectively, support and reinforce the discloser, keep disclosures confidential, and don't use disclosures as weapons.
16. In some situations you'll want to resist self-disclosing by being determined not to be pushed into it, being assertive and direct, or being indirect.

Everyday Conversations

17. Small talk is pervasive, non-controversial, and often serves as a polite way of introducing one's self or a topic.
18. Excuses are explanations designed to lessen any negative implications of a message. Apologies are expressions of regret or sorrow for having done what you did or for what happened.
19. A compliment is a message of praise, flattery, or congratulations and often enables you to interact with positiveness and immediacy.
20. Advice—telling another person what he or she should do—can be specific or general (meta-advice).

Key Terms

advice,	conversational turns,	manner maxim,	self-disclosure,
apologies,	cooperation,	meta-advice,	small talk,
back-channeling cues,	dialogue,	monologue,	social information
back-handed compliment,	excuses,	phatic communication,	processing theory,
compliment,	expressiveness,	quality maxim,	social presence theory,
conversation,	gossip,	quantity maxim,	taboos,
conversational maxims,	interruptions,	relation maxim,	

MyCommunicationLab Explorations

 MyCommunicationLab®

Communication Choice Points

Revisit the chapter-opening video, "First Day of Class." Recall that Tim would like to initiate a conversation with Emad but has a few false starts before making an effective choice. See how his choices played out in the video "First Day of Class" (www.mycommunicationlab.com).

Log on to mycommunicationlab.com to view the video for this chapter, "First Day of Class," and then answer the related discussion questions.

Additional Resources

This group of experiences deals with the conversation process and with a special aim to provide experience in effective and satisfying conversation.

1 How Do You Open a Conversation? and **2** How Do You Close a Conversation? provide practice in beginning and ending conversations effectively. **3** Conversational Analysis: A Chance Meeting provides a dialogue that you can analyze for the elements and principles of conversation covered in this chapter. **4** Giving and Taking Directions is a gamelike experience that will illustrate the difficulties in giving and taking directions and suggest how these difficult communication situations can be made more effective. **5** Gender and the Topics of Conversation looks at gender differences in conversation. **6** Responding Effectively in Conversation and **7** The Qualities of Effectiveness are summary-type exercises that provide the opportunity to apply the qualities of effectiveness that you've already encountered to conversation. **8** What Do You Have a Right to Know? explores a different perspective on self-disclosure; namely, the obligation to reveal parts of yourself. **9** Disclosing Your Hidden Self presents an exciting class experience on the types of behaviors people keep hidden and the potential reactions to their disclosures. **10** Weighing the Rewards and Dangers of Self-Disclosure presents a variety of scenarios of impending self-disclosure and asks you to consider the advantages and disadvantages of disclosing. **11** Time for Self-Disclosure explores the appropriateness of time in revealing certain information. **12** Formulating Excuses provides practice in developing and expressing excuses.

Interpersonal Relationship Stages, Theories, and Communication

From Chapter 9 of *The Interpersonal Communication Book*, Thirteenth Edition. Joseph A. DeVito. Copyright © 2013 by Pearson Education, Inc.

Interpersonal Relationship Stages, Theories, and Communication

Relationship Stages
Relationship Theories
Relationship Communication

2:13 / 5:00

Pearson Education

Sally is getting ready to meet someone face-to-face who she met on Match.com; so far, they've only communicated over the Internet. She likes what she has learned about this person and would like to see the relationship make it to the next stage. To make this happen, she's going to have to admit that she lied about her age and a few other things. She has to decide how to communicate these admissions in some way. See how her choices play out in the video "Coming Clean" (www.mycommunicationlab.com).

Because you'll learn about:

- the stages that relationships go through.
- the reasons you develop relationships.
- the communication patterns in relationship development, deterioration, and repair.

Because you'll learn to:

- navigate through relationships stages more comfortably and effectively.
- evaluate and assess your own relationships.
- communicate more effectively in developing, deteriorating, and repairing relationships.

Contact with other human beings is so important that when you're deprived of it for long periods, depression sets in, self-doubt surfaces, and you may find it difficult to manage even the basics of daily life. Research shows clearly that the most important contributor to happiness—outranking money, job, and sex—is a close relationship with one other person (Freedman, 1978; Laroche & deGrace, 1997; Lu & Shih, 1997). The desire for relationships is universal; interpersonal relationships are important to men and to women, to homosexuals and to heterosexuals, to young and to old (Huston & Schwartz, 1995).

A good way to begin the study of interpersonal relationships is to examine your own relationships (past, present, or those you look forward to) by asking yourself what your relationships do for you. What are the advantages and the disadvantages? Focus on your own relationships in general (friendship, romantic, family, and work); focus on one particular relationship (say, your life partner or your child or your best friend); or focus on one type of relationship (say, friendship), and respond to the following statements by indicating the extent to which your relationship(s) serve each of these functions. Visualize a 10-point scale on which 1 indicates that your relationship(s) never serves this function, 10 indicates that your relationship(s) always serves this function, and the numbers in between indicate levels between these extremes. You may wish to do this twice—once for your face-to-face relationships and once for your online relationships.

_____ 1. My relationships help to lessen my loneliness.
_____ 2. My relationships help me gain in self-knowledge and in self-esteem.
_____ 3. My relationships help enhance my physical and emotional health.
_____ 4. My relationships maximize my pleasures and minimize my pains.
_____ 5. My relationships help me to secure stimulation (intellectual, physical, and emotional).

Let's elaborate just a bit on each of these commonly accepted advantages of interpersonal communication.

1. One of the major benefits of relationships is that they help to lessen loneliness (Rokach, 1998; Rokach & Brock, 1995). They make you feel that someone cares, that someone likes you, that someone will protect you, that someone ultimately will love you.

2. Through contact with others you learn about yourself and see yourself from different perspectives and in different roles—as a child or parent, as a coworker, as a manager, as a best friend, for example. Healthy interpersonal relationships help enhance self-esteem

and self-worth. Simply having a friend or romantic partner (at least most of the time) makes you feel desirable and worthy.

3. Research consistently shows that interpersonal relationships contribute significantly to physical and emotional health (Goleman, 1995a; Pennebacker, 1991; Rosen, 1998; Rosengren, 1993) and to personal happiness (Berscheid & Reis, 1998). Without close interpersonal relationships you're more likely to become depressed—and this depression, in turn, contributes significantly to physical illness. Isolation, in fact, contributes as much to mortality as high blood pressure, high cholesterol, obesity, smoking, or lack of physical exercise (Goleman 1995a).

4. The most general function served by interpersonal relationships, and the function that encompasses all the others, is that of maximizing pleasure and minimizing pain. Your good friends, for example, will make you feel even better about your good fortune and less hurt when you're confronted with hardships.

5. As plants are heliotropic and orient themselves to light, humans are stimulotropic and orient themselves to sources of stimulation (Davis, 1973). Human contact is one of the best ways to secure this stimulation—intellectual, physical, and emotional. Even an imagined relationship seems better than none.

Now, respond to these sentences as you did to the above.

_____ 6. My relationships put uncomfortable pressure on me to expose my vulnerabilities.
_____ 7. My relationships increase my obligations.
_____ 8. My relationships prevent me from developing other relationships.
_____ 9. My relationships scare me because they may be difficult to dissolve.
_____ 10. My relationships hurt me.

These statements express what most people would consider disadvantages of interpersonal relationships.

6. Close relationships put pressure on you to reveal yourself and to expose your vulnerabilities. While this is generally worthwhile in the context of a supporting and caring relationship, it may backfire if the relationship deteriorates and these weaknesses are used against you.

7. Close relationships increase your obligations to other people, sometimes to a great extent. Your time is no longer entirely your own. And although you enter relationships to spend more time with these special people, you also incur time (and perhaps financial) obligations with which you may not be happy.

8. Close relationships can lead you to abandon other relationships. Sometimes the other relationship involves someone you like, but your partner can't stand. More often, however, it's simply a matter of time and energy; relationships take a lot of both, and you have less to give to these other and less intimate relationships.

9. The closer your relationships, the more emotionally difficult they are to dissolve—a feeling which may be uncomfortable for some people. If a relationship is deteriorating, you may feel distress or depression. In some cultures, for example, religious pressures may prevent married couples from separating. And if lots of money is involved, dissolving a relationship can often mean giving up the fortune you've spent your life accumulating.

10. And, of course, your partner may break your heart. Your partner may leave you—against all your pleading and promises. Your hurt will be in proportion to how much you care and need your partner. If you care a great deal, you're likely to experience great hurt. If you care less, the hurt will be less—it's one of life's little ironies.

Relationship Stages

It's useful to look at interpersonal relationships as created and constructed by the individuals. That is, in any interpersonal relationship—say, between Pat and Chris—there are actually several relationships: (1) the relationship that Pat sees, (2) the relationship as Chris sees it, (3) the relationship that Pat wants and is striving for, (4) the relationship that Chris wants. And of course there are the many relationships that friends and relatives see and that they reflect back in their communications; for example, the relationship that Pat's mother, who dislikes Chris, sees and reflects in her communication with Pat and Chris is very likely to influence Pat and Chris in some ways. And then there's the relationship that a dispassionate researcher/observer would see. Looked at in this way, there are many interpersonal relationships in any interpersonal relationship.

This is not to say that there is no *real* relationship; it's just to say that there are many real relationships. And because there are these differently constructed relationships, people often disagree about a wide variety of issues and evaluate the relationship very differently. Regularly, on *Jerry Springer* and *Maury,* you see couples who view their relationship very differently. The first guest thinks all is going well until the second guest comes on and explodes—often identifying long-held dissatisfactions and behaviors that shock the partner.

One of the most obvious characteristics of relationships is that they occur in stages, moving from initial contact to greater intimacy and sometimes to dissolution. You and another person don't become intimate friends immediately upon meeting. Rather, you build an intimate relationship gradually, through a series of steps or stages. The same is true of most relationships (Mongeau & Henningsen, 2008).

The six-stage model presented in Figure 1 describes the main stages in most relationships. As shown in the figure, the six stages of relationships are contact, involvement, intimacy, deterioration, repair, and dissolution with each having an early and a late phase. The arrows represent the movements that take place as relationships change. Let's first examine the six stages and then we'll look at the types of relationship movements.

Contact

At the initial phase of the **contact** stage, there is some kind of *perceptual contact*—you see, hear, read a message from, view a photo or video, or perhaps smell the person. From this you form a mental and physical picture—gender, approximate age, beliefs and values, height, and so on. After this perception, there is usually *interactional contact.* Here the contact is superficial and relatively impersonal. This is the stage at which you exchange basic information that is preliminary to any more intense involvement ("Hello, my name is Joe"), or you might send someone a request to be a friend. Here you initiate interaction ("May I join you?") and engage in invitational communication ("May I buy you a latte?"). The contact stage is the time of "first impressions." According to some researchers, it's at this stage—within the first four minutes of initial interaction—that you decide whether you want to pursue the relationship (Zunin & Zunin, 1972).

Involvement

At the **involvement** stage of a relationship, a sense of mutuality, of being connected, develops. Here you experiment and try to learn

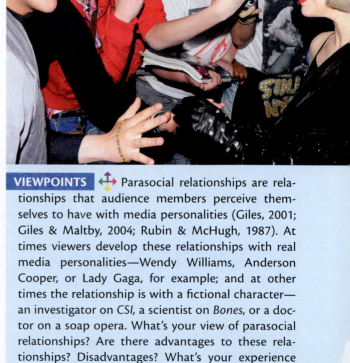

Tony Clark/Splash News/Newscom

VIEWPOINTS Parasocial relationships are relationships that audience members perceive themselves to have with media personalities (Giles, 2001; Giles & Maltby, 2004; Rubin & McHugh, 1987). At times viewers develop these relationships with real media personalities—Wendy Williams, Anderson Cooper, or Lady Gaga, for example; and at other times the relationship is with a fictional character— an investigator on *CSI*, a scientist on *Bones*, or a doctor on a soap opera. What's your view of parasocial relationships? Are there advantages to these relationships? Disadvantages? What's your experience with parasocial relationships?

FIGURE 1

A Six-Stage Model of Relationships

Because relationships differ so widely, it's best to think of any relationship model as a tool for talking about relationships rather than as a specific map that indicates how you move from one relationship position to another. As you review this figure, consider, for example, if you feel that other steps or stages would further explain what goes on in relationship development.

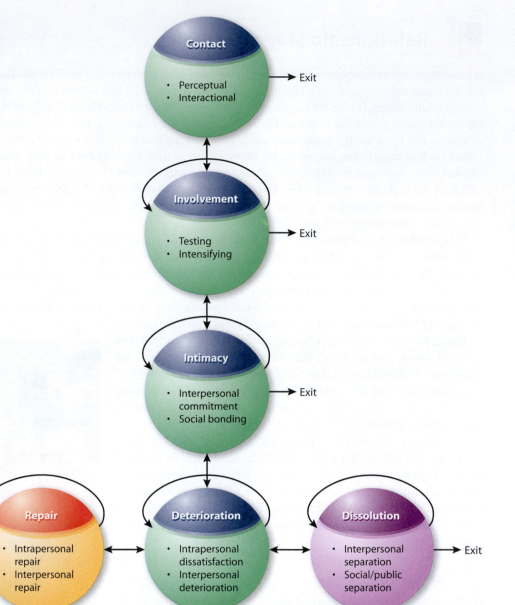

For cyberflirting, see "Cyberflirting, etc." at tcbdevito.blogspot.com. How do you see cyberflirting? What cyberflirting techniques do you find most interesting?

more about the other person. At the initial phase of involvement, a kind of *testing* goes on. You want to see whether your initial judgment proves reasonable. So you may ask questions: "Where do you work?" "What are you majoring in?" If you want to get to know the person even better, you might continue your involvement by intensifying your interaction and by beginning to reveal yourself, though in a preliminary way. In a dating relationship, you might use a variety of strategies to help you move to the next stage and perhaps to intimacy. For example, you might increase contact with your partner; give your partner tokens of affection such as gifts, cards, or flowers; increase your own personal attractiveness; do things that suggest intensifying the relationship, such as flirting or making your partner jealous; and become more sexually intimate (Tolhuizen, 1989). Table 1 provides a look at some of the popular ways we flirt.

Intimacy

At the **intimacy** stage, you commit yourself still further to the other person and establish a relationship in which this individual becomes your best or closest friend, lover, or companion.

TABLE 1	How to Flirt and Not to Flirt

Here are a few nonverbal and verbal ways people flirt and some cautions to observe. The most general caution, which applies to all the suggestions, is to recognize that different cultures view flirting very differently and to observe the prevailing cultural norms.

Flirtatious Messages	Cautions
Maintain an open posture; face the person; lean forward; tilt your head to one side (to get a clearer view of the person you're interested in).	Don't move so close that you make it uncomfortable for the other person.
Make eye contact and maintain it for a somewhat longer than normal time; raise your eyebrows to signal interest; blink and move your eyes more than usual; wink.	Be careful that your direct eye contact doesn't come off as leering or too invasive, and avoid too much blinking—people will think you have something wrong with your eyes.
Smile and otherwise displace positive emotions with your facial expressions.	Avoid overdoing this; laughing too loud at lame jokes is probably going to appear phony.
Touch the person's hand.	Be careful that the touching is appropriate and not perceived as intrusive.
Mirror the other's behaviors.	Don't overdo it. It will appear as if you're mimicking.
Introduce yourself.	Avoid overly long or overly cute introductions.
Ask a question (most commonly, "Is this seat taken?").	Avoid sarcasm or joking; these are likely to be misunderstood.
Compliment ("great jacket").	Avoid any compliment that might appear too intimate.
Be polite; respect the individuals positive and negative face needs.	But, don't be overly polite; it will appear phony.

Both the quantity and the quality of your interpersonal exchanges increase (Emmers-Sommer, 2004), and, of course, you also talk more and in greater detail about the relationship (Knobloch, Haunani, & Theiss, 2006). You also come to share each other's social networks—a practice followed by members of widely different cultures (Gao & Gudykunst, 1995). And, not surprisingly, your relationship satisfaction also increases with the move to this stage (Siavelis & Lamke, 1992).

The intimacy stage usually divides itself into two phases. In the *interpersonal commitment* phase the two people commit themselves to each other in a private way. In the *social bonding* phase the commitment is made public—perhaps to family and friends, perhaps to the public at large. Here you and your partner become a unit, an identifiable pair. The Understanding Interpersonal Theory & Research box looks at this process of commitment in more detail.

Deterioration

The **relationship deterioration** stage is characterized by a weakening of the bonds between the friends or lovers. The first phase of deterioration is usually *intrapersonal dissatisfaction*: You

INTERPERSONAL CHOICE POINT

Meeting the Parents

You're dating someone from a very different culture and have been invited to meet the parents and have a traditional ethnic dinner. What are some of the things you might do to make this potentially difficult situation go smoothly?

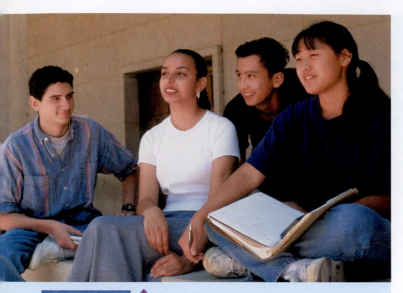

VIEWPOINTS ⬈ Some cultures consider sexual relationships to be undesirable outside of marriage; others see sex as a normal part of intimacy and chastity as undesirable. Intercultural researchers (Hatfield & Rapson, 1996, p. 36) recall a meeting at which colleagues from Sweden and the United States were discussing ways of preventing AIDS. When members from the United States suggested teaching abstinence, Swedish members asked, "How will teenagers ever learn to become loving, considerate sexual partners if they don't practice?" "The silence that greeted the question," note the researchers, "was the sound of two cultures clashing." How have your cultural beliefs and values influenced what you consider appropriate relationship and sexual behavior?

begin to experience personal dissatisfaction with everyday interactions and begin to view the future with your partner more negatively. If this dissatisfaction grows, you pass to the second phase, *interpersonal deterioration.* You withdraw and grow farther and farther apart. You share less of your free time. When you're together, there are more awkward silences, fewer disclosures, less physical contact, and a lack of psychological closeness. Conflicts become more common and their resolution more difficult. On social network sites, the deterioration stage is perhaps seen most clearly in the decline in frequency of comments, pokes, and thumbs-up liking.

Repair

Some relationship partners, sensing deterioration, may pursue the **relationship repair** stage. Others, however, may progress—without stopping, without thinking—to dissolution.

At the first repair phase, *intrapersonal repair,* you may analyze what went wrong and consider ways of solving your relational difficulties. You might, at this stage, consider changing your behaviors or perhaps changing your expectations of your partner. You might also evaluate the rewards of your relationship as it is now and the rewards to be gained if your relationship ended.

Should you decide that you want to repair your relationship, you might discuss this with your partner at the *interpersonal repair* phase—you might talk about the problems in the relationship, the changes you wanted to see, and perhaps what you'd be willing to do and what you'd want your partner to do. This is the stage of negotiating new agreements and new behaviors. You and your partner might try to repair your relationship by yourselves, or you might seek the advice of friends or family or perhaps go for professional counseling.

Dissolution

At the **relationship dissolution** stage, the bonds between the individuals are broken. In the beginning, dissolution usually takes the form of *interpersonal separation,* in which you may move into separate apartments and begin to lead lives apart from each other. If this separation proves acceptable and if the original relationship isn't repaired, you enter the phase of *social or public separation.* If the relationship is a marriage, this phase corresponds to divorce. Avoidance of each other and a return to being "single" are among the primary characteristics of dissolution. On Facebook this would be the stage where you defriend the person and/or block that person from accessing your profile.

INTERPERSONAL CHOICE POINT
Ending the Relationship

You want to break up your eight-month romantic relationship and still remain friends. What are the possible contexts in which you might do this? What types of things can you say that might help you accomplish your dual goal?

Dissolution also is the stage during which the ex-partners begin to look upon themselves as individuals rather than halves of a pair. They try to establish a new and different life, either alone or with another person. Some people, it's true, continue to live psychologically with a relationship that has already been dissolved; they frequent old meeting places, reread old love letters, daydream about all the good times, and fail to extricate themselves from a relationship that has died in every way except in their memory.

Understanding *Interpersonal Theory & Research*

RELATIONSHIP COMMITMENT

An important factor influencing the course of relationship deterioration (as well as relationship maintenance) is the degree of commitment that you and your relationship partner have toward each other and toward the relationship. Not surprisingly, commitment is especially strong when individuals are satisfied with their relationship and grows weaker as individuals become less satisfied (Hirofumi, 2003). Three types of commitment are often distinguished and can be identified from your answers to the following questions (Johnson, 1973, 1982, 1991; Knapp & Taylor, 1994; Knapp & Vangelisti, 2009; Kurdek, 1995):

- Do I have a **desire** to stay in this relationship? Do I have a desire to keep this relationship going?
- Do I have a moral **obligation** to stay in this relationship?
- Do I have to stay in this relationship? Is it a **necessity** for me to stay in this relationship?

All relationships are held together, in part, by commitment based on desire, obligation, or necessity, or on some combination of these factors. And the strength of the relationship, including its resistance to possible deterioration, is related to your degree of commitment. When a relationship shows signs of deterioration and yet there's a strong commitment to preserving it, you may well surmount the obstacles and reverse the process. For example, couples with high relationship commitment will avoid arguing about minor grievances and also will demonstrate greater supportiveness toward each other than will those with lower commitment (Roloff & Solomon, 2002). Similarly, those who have great commitment are likely to experience greater jealousy in a variety of situations (Rydell, McConnell, & Bringle, 2004). When commitment is weak and the individuals doubt that there are good reasons for staying together, the relationship deteriorates faster and more intensely.

Working with Theories and Research

Has commitment or the lack of it (on the part of either or both of you) ever influenced the progression of one of your relationships? What happened?

In cultures that emphasize continuity from one generation to the next—as in, say, China—interpersonal relationships are likely to be long-lasting and permanent. Those who maintain long-term relationships tend to be rewarded, and those who break relationships tend to be punished. But in cultures in which change is seen as positive—as in, say, the United States—interpersonal relationships are likely to be more temporary (Moghaddam, Taylor, & Wright, 1993). Here the rewards for long-term relationships and the punishments for broken relationships will be significantly less.

Movement among the Stages

Relationships are not static; we move from one stage to another largely as a result of our interpersonal interactions. Three general kinds of movement may be identified.

Airn/Shutterstock

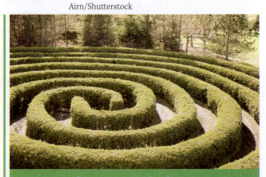

Love is a choice you make from moment to moment
—*Barbara De Angelis*

Stage Movement   The six-stage model illustrates the kinds of movement that take place in interpersonal relationships. In the model, you'll note three types of arrows:

- The **exit arrows** show that each stage offers the opportunity to exit the relationship. After saying "Hello" you can say "Goodbye" and exit. And, of course, you can end even the most intimate of relationships.
- The **vertical arrows** between the stages represent the fact that you can move to another stage: either to a stage that is more intense (say, from involvement to intimacy) or to a stage that is less intense (say, from intimacy to deterioration).
- The **self-reflexive arrows**—the arrows that return to the beginning of the same level or stage—signify that any relationship may become stabilized at any point. You may, for example, continue to maintain a relationship at the intimate level without its deteriorating or going back to the less intense stage of involvement. Or you may remain at the "Hello, how are you?" stage—the contact stage—without getting any further involved.

As you can imagine, movement from one stage to another depends largely on your communication skills—for example, your abilities to initiate a relationship, to present yourself as likable, to express affection, to self-disclose appropriately, and, when necessary, to dissolve the relationship with the least possible amount of acrimony (Dindia & Timmerman, 2003). These issues are covered in the last section of this chapter, "Relationship Communication".

Turning Points   Movement through the various stages takes place both gradually and in leaps. Often, you progress from one stage to another gradually. You don't jump from contact to involvement to intimacy; rather, you progress gradually, a few degrees at a time. In addition to this gradual movement, there are relationship turning points (Baxter & Bullis, 1986). These are significant relationship events that have important consequences for the individuals and the relationship and may turn its direction or trajectory. For example, a relationship that is progressing slowly might experience a rapid rise after the first date, the first kiss, the first sexual encounter, or the first meeting with the partner's child.

Turning points are often positive, as the examples above would indicate. But, they can also be negative. For example, the first realization that a partner has been unfaithful, lied about past history, or revealed a debilitating addiction would likely be significant turning points for many romantic relationships.

Not surprisingly, turning points vary with culture. In some cultures the first sexual experience is a major turning point; in others it's a minor progression in the normal dating process.

What constitutes a turning point will also vary with your relationship stage. For example, an expensive and intimate gift may be a turning point at the involvement or the repair stage, an ordinary event if you're at the intimate stage and such gifts are exchanged regularly, and an inappropriate gift if given too early in the relationship.

The Relationship License   Movement of a somewhat different type can be appreciated by looking at what is called the **relationship license**—the license or permission to break some relationship rule as a result of your relationship stage. As the relationship develops, so does the relationship license; as you become closer and approach the intimacy stage, you have greater permission to say and do things that you didn't have at the contact or involvement stage. The license becomes broader as the relationship develops and becomes more restrictive

For an interesting article on moving from involvement to intimacy, see "From Dating to Mating" at tcbdevito.blogspot.com. Any further suggestions?

as the relationship deteriorates. For example, long-term friends or romantic couples (say at the intimacy stage) may taste each other's food in a restaurant or may fix each other's clothing or pat each other on the rear. These are violations of rules that normally hold for non-intimates, for casual acquaintances or people in the initial stages of a relationship. In relationships that are deteriorating, the licenses become more limited or may be entirely withdrawn.

In some relationships the license is reciprocal; each person's license is the same. In other relationships it's nonreciprocal; one person has greater license than the other. For example, perhaps one person has license to come home at any time but the other is expected to stay on schedule. Or one person has license to spend the couple's money without explanation but the other has no such right. Or one perhaps has the right to be unfaithful but the other doesn't. For example, in some cultures men are expected to have intimate relationships with many women, whereas women are expected to have relationships only with a legally approved partner. In this case a nonreciprocal license is built into the culture's rules.

Part of the art of relationship communication—as you move through the various stages—is to negotiate the licenses that you want without giving up the privacy you want to retain. This negotiation is almost never made explicit; most often it is accomplished nonverbally and in small increments. The license to touch intimately, for example, is likely to be arrived at through a series of touches that increase gradually, beginning with touching that is highly impersonal.

INTERPERSONAL CHOICE POINT
Reducing Uncertainty

You've been dating this person on and off for the last six months but you'd now like to move this relationship to a more exclusive arrangement. You're just not sure how your partner would feel about this. What are some of the things you might do to reduce the uncertainty and ambiguity? Specifically, what might you say to get some indication of whether your partner would or would not like to move this relationship toward greater intimacy?

Ethics in Interpersonal Communication

YOUR OBLIGATION TO REVEAL YOURSELF

If you're in a close relationship, your influence on your partner is considerable, so you may have an obligation to reveal certain things about yourself. Conversely, you may feel that the other person—because he or she is so close to you—has an ethical obligation to reveal certain information to you. At what point in a relationship—if any—do you feel you would have an ethical obligation to reveal each of the 10 items of information listed here? Visualize a relationship as existing on a continuum, from initial contact at 1 to extreme intimacy at 10; and use the numbers from 1 to 10 to indicate at what point you would feel your romantic partner or friend would have a right to know each type of information about you. If you feel you would never have the obligation to reveal this information, use 0.

At what point do you have an ethical obligation to reveal the following information to a romantic partner (say of a year or two) and a close friend?

Romantic Partner	Friend	
_____	_____	Age
_____	_____	History of family genetic disorders
_____	_____	HIV status
_____	_____	Past sexual experiences
_____	_____	Marital history
_____	_____	Annual salary and net financial worth
_____	_____	Affectional orientation
_____	_____	Attitudes toward other races and nationalities
_____	_____	Religious beliefs
_____	_____	Past criminal activity or incarceration

ETHICAL CHOICE POINT

You're in a romantic relationship and your partner presses you to reveal your past sexual experiences. You really don't want to (you're not very proud of your past) and furthermore, you don't think it's relevant to your current relationship. Today, your partner asks you directly to reveal this part of your past. What are your ethical obligations here? Are there certain aspects that you ethically need to reveal and others aspects that you are not ethically bound to reveal?

Relationship Theories

Several theories offer insight into why and how we develop and dissolve our relationships (Baxter & Braithwaite, 2008b). Here we'll examine seven such theories: attraction, relationship rules, relationship dialectics, social penetration, social exchange, equity, and politeness.

Attraction Theory

Attraction theory holds that people form relationships on the basis of attraction. You are no doubt drawn to or attracted to some people and not to others. In a similar way, some people are attracted to you and some are not. The accompanying self-test will help you think about the factors that you consider important in interpersonal attraction.

Test Yourself   ## What Is Attractive to You?

For each of the following characteristics, indicate how important each one is to you in a potential (or actual) romantic life partner. Use the following scale:

5 = Very important

4 = Important

3 = Neither important nor unimportant

2 = Unimportant

1 = Very unimportant

_____ 1. Facial appearance

_____ 2. General body structure (weight, height, shape)

_____ 3. Grooming and general cleanliness

_____ 4. Appropriate financial resources

_____ 5. Intelligence

_____ 6. Similarity in religious beliefs

_____ 7. Sense of humor

_____ 8. Positive toward me

_____ 9. Optimistic toward life in general

_____ 10. Honest/ethical

_____ 11. Ambitious

_____ 12. Communicative

_____ 13. Similarity in cultural backgrounds, including race and nationality

_____ 14. Available

_____ 15. Sexual compatibility

How Did You Do? There are no correct or incorrect answers and people are likely to respond to such characteristics very differently. This self-test was designed simply to stimulate you to think in specific terms about the characteristics of another person that are important to you. Those given here are often mentioned in research and theory as being significant in evaluating a potential life partner.

What Will You Do? Consider the importance of these characteristics to your own relationship happiness and well-being. At the same time, consider the importance of these characteristics to your potential partner. Consider, too, other characteristics that you consider important. Another way to use this self-test is to review each of the characteristics and specify more concretely what each of them means to you. For example, how attractive must a person be for you to be attracted to him or her? What constitutes "appropriate financial resources"? How ambitious would you want your partner to be?

If you're like most people, then you're attracted to others on the basis of five major factors: similarity, proximity, reinforcement, physical attractiveness and personality, and socioeconomic and educational status. As a preface to these factors, it's important to recognize the difference between online and face-to-face relationships. Attraction to a person in an online relationship (especially one that is going to stay online) will depend on the communicated messages, photos, videos, the responsiveness to your posts, the sense of humor—all having nothing to do with the person's physical appearance. With face-to-face relationships or online relationships that will morph into face-to-face relationships, there is considerable emphasis on the physical qualities of the individual.

For a seldom-discussed view on attraction, see "Facial Attraction" at tcbdevito.blogspot.com. Does this all seem logical?

Similarity

If you could construct your mate, according to the **similarity** principle, it's likely that your mate would look, act, and think very much like you (Burleson, Samter, & Luccetti, 1992; Burleson, Kunkel, & Birch, 1994). Generally, people like those who are similar to them in nationality, race, abilities, physical characteristics, intelligence, and attitudes (Pornpitakpan, 2003).

Research also finds that you're more likely to help someone who is similar in race, attitude, general appearance, and even first name. Sometimes people are attracted to their opposites, in a pattern called **complementarity**; for example, a dominant person might be attracted to someone who is more submissive. Generally, however, people prefer those who are similar.

Proximity

If you look around at people you find attractive, you will probably find that they are the people who live or work close to you. People who become friends are the people who have the greatest opportunity to interact with each other. Proximity, or physical closeness, is most important in the early stages of interaction—for example, during the first days of school (in class or in dormitories). The importance of proximity as a factor in attraction decreases, though always remaining significant, as the opportunity to interact with more distant others increases.

Reinforcement

Not surprisingly, you're attracted to people who give rewards or reinforcements, which can range from a simple compliment to an expensive cruise. You're also attracted to people you reward (Jecker & Landy, 1969; Aronson, Wilson, & Akert, 2007). That is, you come to like people for whom you do favors; for example, you've probably increased your liking for persons after buying them an expensive present or going out of your way to do them a special favor. In these situations you justify your behavior by believing that the person was worth your efforts; otherwise, you'd have to admit to spending effort on people who don't deserve it.

Physical Attractiveness and Personality

It's easily appreciated that people like physically attractive people more

CJG - Technology/Alamy

VIEWPOINTS Among the advantages of online relationships is that they reduce the importance of physical characteristics and instead emphasize such factors as rapport, similarity, and self-disclosure, and in the process promote relationships that are based on emotional intimacy rather than physical attraction (Cooper & Sportolari, 1997). What do you see as the main advantages of online relationships?

than they like physically unattractive people. What isn't so obvious is that we also feel a greater sense of familiarity with more attractive people than with less attractive people; that is, we're more likely to think we've met a person before if that person is attractive (Monin, 2003). Also, although culture influences what people think is physical attractiveness and what isn't, some research indicates that there are certain facial features that seem to be thought attractive in all cultures—a kind of universal attractiveness (Brody, 1994). Additionally, you probably tend to like people who have a pleasant rather than an unpleasant personality (although people will differ on what is and what is not an attractive personality).

Socioeconomic and Educational Status

Popular belief holds that among heterosexual men and women, men are more interested in a woman's physical attributes than in her socioeconomic status. And indeed, research shows that women flirt on the Internet by stressing their physical attributes, whereas men stress their socioeconomic status (Whitty, 2003b). Interestingly, there is evidence that men, too, consider a woman's socioeconomic status in making romantic relationship decisions—but whereas women find higher socioeconomic status more attractive, men find just the opposite. Men report greater likelihood of a romantic relationship with a woman lower in socioeconomic status than they are. Further, men find women with a higher educational level (which is often responsible for the higher socioeconomic status) less likable and less faithful and as a result see less likelihood of a romantic relationship with such women (Greitemeyer, 2007).

Reciprocity of Liking

It will come as no surprise that research supports what you already know from your own experience: You tend to be attracted to people you think are attracted to you; you come to like those who you think like you. **Reciprocity of liking**, also known as reciprocity of attraction or reciprocal liking, is seen in a variety of situations. We initiate potential friendships and romantic relationships with people who we think like us, certainly not with those we think dislike us. Group members who are told that certain other members like them will later express greater liking for these members than for others. Public speakers are advised to compliment the audience and express liking for them largely on the theory that this liking will be reciprocated. There is even evidence to show that people like "likers"— people who like others generally—more than they like people who don't express such liking (Eastwick & Finkel, 2009).

Relationship Rules Theory

You can gain an interesting perspective on interpersonal relationships by looking at them in terms of the rules that govern them (Shimanoff, 1980). The general assumption of **rules theory** is that relationships—friendship and love in particular—are held together by adherence to certain rules. When those rules are broken, the relationship may deteriorate and even dissolve.

Relationship rules theory helps us clarify several aspects of relationships. First, these rules help identify successful versus destructive relationship behavior. In addition, these rules help pinpoint more specifically why relationships break up and how they may be repaired. Further, if we know what the rules are, we will be better able to master the social skills involved in relationship development and maintenance. And because these rules vary from one culture to another, it is important to identify those unique to each culture so that intercultural relationships may be more effectively developed and maintained.

Friendship Rules

One approach to friendship argues that friendships are maintained by rules (Argyle, 1986; Argyle & Henderson, 1984). When these rules are followed, the friendship is strong and mutually satisfying. When these rules are broken, the friendship suffers and may die. For example, the rules for keeping a friendship call for such behaviors as standing up for your friend in his or her absence, sharing information and feelings about successes, demonstrating emotional support for a friend, trusting and offering to help a friend in need, and trying to make a friend happy when you're together. On the other hand, a friendship is likely to be in trouble when one or both friends are intolerant of the other's friends, discuss confidences with third parties, fail to demonstrate positive support, nag, and/or fail to trust or confide in the other. The strategy for maintaining a friendship, then, depends on your knowing the rules and having the ability to apply the appropriate interpersonal skills (Blieszner & Adams, 1992; Trower, 1981).

Romantic Rules   Other research has identified the rules that romantic relationships establish and follow. These rules, of course, will vary considerably from one culture to another. For example, the different attitudes toward permissiveness and sexual relations with which Chinese and American college students view dating influence the romantic rules each group will establish and live by (Tang & Zuo, 2000). Leslie Baxter (1986) has identified eight major romantic rules. Baxter argues that these rules keep the relationship together—or, when broken, lead to deterioration and eventually dissolution. The general form for each rule if that if you are in a close relationship then you should:

1. recognize that each has a life beyond the relationship.
2. have and express similar attitudes and interests.
3. reinforce each other's self-esteem.
4. be real: open and genuine.
5. be faithful to each other.
6. spend substantial time together.
7. obtain rewards commensurate with your investment compared to the other party.
8. experience an inexplicable "magic" when together.

INTERPERSONAL CHOICE POINT

Virtual Infidelity

You discover that your partner of the last 15 years is being unfaithful with someone online (and in another country). You understand that generally such infidelity is seen as a consequence of a failure in communication (Young, Griffin-Shelley, Cooper, O'Mara, & Buchanan, 2000). You want to discover the extent of this online relationship and your partner's intentions in regard to this affair. What choices do you have for opening up this topic for honest conversation without making your partner defensive and hence uncommunicative?

Family Rules   Family communication research points to the importance of rules in defining and maintaining the family (Galvin, Bylund, & Brommel, 2008). Family rules concern three main interpersonal communication issues (Satir, 1983):

- **What you can talk about.** Can you talk about the family finances? grandpa's drinking? your sister's lifestyle?
- **How you can talk about something.** Can you joke about your brother's disability? Can you address directly questions of family history or family skeletons?
- **To whom you can talk.** Can you talk openly to extended family members such as cousins and aunts and uncles? Can you talk to close neighbors about family health issues?

All families teach rules for communication. Some of these are explicit, such as "Never contradict the family in front of outsiders" or "Never talk finances with outsiders." Other rules are unspoken; you deduce them as you learn the communication style of your family. For example, if financial issues are always discussed in secret and in hushed tones, then you rather logically infer that you shouldn't tell other more distant family members or neighbors about family finances.

Like the rules of friends and lovers, family rules tell you which behaviors will be rewarded (and therefore what you should do) and which will be punished (and therefore what you should not do). Rules also provide a kind of structure that defines the family as a cohesive unit and that distinguishes it from other similar families.

Not surprisingly, the rules a family develops are greatly influenced by the culture. Although there are many similarities among families throughout the world, there are also differences (Georgas et al., 2001). For example, members of collectivist cultures are more likely to restrict family information from outsiders as a way of protecting the family than are members of individualist cultures. But this tendency to protect the family can create serious problems in cases of wife abuse. Many women will not report spousal abuse because of this desire to protect the family image and not let others know that things aren't perfect at home (Dresser, 2005).

Family communication theorists argue that rules should be flexible so that special circumstances can be accommodated; for example, there are situations that necessitate changing the family dinner-time, vacation plans, or savings goals (Noller & Fitzpatrick, 1993). Rules should also be negotiable so that all members can participate in their modification and feel a part of family government.

Workplace Rules   Rules also govern your workplace relationships. These rules are usually a part of the corporate culture that an employee would learn from observing other employees (especially those who move up the hierarchy) as well as from official memos on dress, sexual harassment, and the like. Of course each organization will have different rules, so it's important to see what rules are operating in any given situation. Among the rules that you might find are:

- Work very hard.
- Be cooperative in teams; the good of the company comes first.
- Don't reveal company policies and plans to workers at competing firms.
- Don't form romantic relationships with other workers.
- Avoid even the hint of sexual harassment.
- Be polite to other workers and especially to customers.

Relationship Dialectics Theory

Relationship dialectics theory argues that someone who is engaged in a relationship experiences internal tensions between pairs of motives or desires that pull him or her in opposite directions. These tensions are much like those you experience in your daily lives. For example, you want to work this summer to earn money to get a new car but you also want to go to Hawaii and surf for two months. You want both but you can only have one. In a similar way, you experience tensions between opposites in your relationship desires. Research generally finds three such pairs of opposites (Baxter, 2004; Baxter & Braithwaite, 2007, 2008a; Baxter & Simon, 1993; Rawlins, 1989, 1992).

The tension between *closedness and openness* has to do with the conflict between the desire to be in a closed, exclusive relationship and the wish to be in a relationship that is open to different people. Not surprisingly, this tension manifests itself most during the early stages of relationship development. You like the exclusiveness of your pairing and yet you want also to relate to a larger group. Young heterosexual men, in interacting with women, use a pattern of messages that encourage closeness followed by messages that indicate a desire for distance followed by closeness messages followed by distancing messages—a clear example of the tension between the desire for closeness and the desire for autonomy (Korobov & Thorne, 2006)

The tension between *autonomy and connection*, which seems to occur more often as the relationship progresses, involves the desire to remain an autonomous, independent individual but also to connect intimately to another person and to a relationship. You want to be close and connected with another person but you also want to be independent (Sahlstein, 2004). This tension, by the way, is a popular theme in women's magazines, which teach readers to want both autonomy and connection (Prusank, Duran, & DeLillo, 1993).

The tension between *novelty and predictability* centers on the competing desires for newness, different experiences, and adventure on the one hand and for sameness, stability, and predictability on the other. You're comfortable with being able to predict what will happen, and yet you also want newness, difference, and novelty.

Doug Menuez/Thinkstock

VIEWPOINTS ⬌ In face-to-face relationships, emotional closeness compromises privacy; the closer you become, the less privacy you have. Research on online relationships, however, indicates that because you're more in control of what you reveal, you can develop close emotional relationships, but also maintain your privacy (Ben-Ze'ev, 2003). Do you find this to be true? If not, how would you express the relationship between emotional closeness and privacy online?

Each individual in a relationship may experience a somewhat different set of desires. For example, one person may want exclusivity above all, whereas that person's partner may want greater openness. There are three main ways that you can use to deal with these tensions.

First, you can simply *accept the imbalance* as part of dating or as part of a committed relationship. You may even redefine it as a benefit and tell yourself something like: "I had been spending too much time at work. It's probably better that I come home earlier and don't work weekends"—accepting the closeness and giving up the autonomy.

Second, you can simply *exit the relationship*. For example, if the loss of autonomy is so great that you can't live with it, then you may choose to simply end the relationship and achieve your desired autonomy.

A third alternative is to *rebalance your life*. For example, if you find the primary relationship excessively predictable, you may seek to satisfy the need for novelty elsewhere, perhaps with a vacation to exotic places, perhaps with a different partner. If you find the relationship too connected (even suffocating), you may seek physical and psychological space to meet your autonomy needs. You can also establish the balance you feel you need by negotiating with your partner; for example, agreeing that you will take separate vacations or that each of you will go out separately with old friends once or twice a week.

As you can appreciate, meeting your partner's needs while also meeting your own needs is one of the major relationship challenges you'll face. Knowing and empathizing with these tensions and discussing them seem useful (even necessary) tools for relationship maintenance and satisfaction.

INTERPERSONAL CHOICE POINT
Refusing a Gift Positively

A coworker with whom you're becoming friendly gives you a very intimate gift. You really don't want the relationship to progress to this level. What might you say to refuse the gift but not close off the possibility of dating?

Social Penetration Theory

Social penetration theory is a theory not of why relationships develop but of what happens when they do develop; it describes relationships in terms of the number of topics that people talk about and the degree of "personalness" of those topics (Altman & Taylor, 1973). The **breadth** of a relationship has to do with how many topics you and your partner talk about. The **depth** of a relationship involves the degree to which you penetrate the inner personality—the core—of the other individual.

We can represent an individual as a circle and divide that circle into various parts, as in Figure 2. This figure illustrates different models of social penetration. Each circle in the figure contains eight topic areas to depict breadth (identified as A through H) and five levels of intimacy to depict depth (represented by the concentric circles). Note that in circle 1, only three topic areas are penetrated. Of these, one is penetrated only to the first level and two to the second. In this type of interaction, three topic areas are discussed, and only at rather superficial levels. This is the type of relationship you might have with an acquaintance. Circle 2 represents a more intense relationship, one that has greater breadth and depth; more topics are discussed and to deeper levels of penetration. This is the type of relationship you might have with a friend. Circle 3 represents a still more intense relationship. Here there is considerable breadth (seven of the eight areas are penetrated) and depth (most of the areas are penetrated to the deepest levels). This is the type of relationship you might have with a lover or a parent.

FIGURE 2
Models of Social Penetration

How accurately do the concepts of breadth and depth express your communication in relationships of different intensities? Can you identify other aspects of messages that change as you go from talking with an acquaintance to talking with a friend or an intimate?

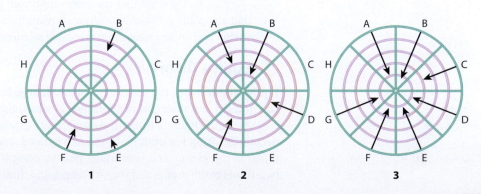

When a relationship begins to deteriorate, the breadth and depth will, in many ways, reverse themselves, in a process called **depenetration**. For example, while ending a relationship, you might cut out certain topics from your interpersonal communications. At the same time, you might discuss the remaining topics in less depth. In some instances of relational deterioration, however, both the breadth and the depth of interaction increase. For example, when a couple breaks up and each is finally free from an oppressive relationship, they may—after some time—begin to discuss problems and feelings they would never have discussed when they were together. In fact, they may become extremely close friends and come to like each other more than when they were together. In these cases the breadth and depth of their relationship may increase rather than decrease (Baxter, 1983).

Social Exchange Theory

Social exchange theory claims that you develop relationships that will enable you to maximize your profits (Chadwick-Jones, 1976; Gergen, Greenberg, & Willis, 1980; Thibaut & Kelley, 1986; Stafford, 2008)—a theory based on an economic model of profits and losses. The theory begins with the following equation: Profits = Rewards – [minus sign] Costs.

- **Rewards** are anything that you would incur costs to obtain. Research has identified six types of rewards in a love relationship: money, status, love, information, goods, and services (Baron & Byrne, 1984). For example, to get the reward of money, you might have to work rather than play. To earn the status of an A in an interpersonal communication course, you might have to write a term paper or study more than you want to.
- **Costs** are things that you normally try to avoid, that you consider unpleasant or difficult. Examples might include working overtime; washing dishes and ironing clothes; watching your partner's favorite television show, which you find boring; or doing favors for those you dislike.
- **Profit** is what results when the costs are subtracted from the rewards (Profit = Rewards – Costs).

Using this basic economic model, social exchange theory claims that you seek to develop the friendships and romantic relationships that will give you the greatest profits; that is, relationships in which the rewards are greater than the costs.

INTERPERSONAL CHOICE POINT

Complaining

Your partner complains constantly; no matter what the situation, your partner has a complaint about it. It's becoming painful to listen to this and you want to stop it. What are some of the things you might do to help lessen the complaining? Alternatively, what might you be doing to encourage the complaints, and therefore what might you stop doing?

When you enter a relationship, you have in mind a **comparison level**—a general idea of the kinds of rewards and profits that you feel you ought to get out of such a relationship. This comparison level consists of your realistic expectations concerning what you feel you deserve from this relationship. For example, a study of married couples found that most people expect high levels of trust, mutual respect, love, and commitment. Couples' expectations are significantly lower for time spent together, privacy, sexual activity, and communication (Sabatelli & Pearce, 1986). When the rewards that you get equal or surpass your comparison level, you feel satisfied with your relationship.

However, you also have a comparison level for alternatives. That is, you compare the profits that you get from your current relationship with the profits you think you could get from alternative relationships. Thus, if you see that the profits from your present relationship are below the profits that you could get from an alternative relationship, you may decide to leave your current relationship and enter a new, more profitable relationship.

Equity Theory

Equity theory uses the ideas of social exchange, but goes a step farther and claims that you develop and maintain relationships in which the ratio of your rewards relative to your costs is approximately equal to your partner's (Messick & Cook, 1983; Walster, Walster, & Berscheid, 1978). For example, if you and a friend start a business in which you put up two-thirds of the money and your friend puts up one-third, equity would demand that you get two-thirds of the profits and your friend get one-third. In an *equitable relationship*, then, each party derives rewards that are proportional to the costs they each pay. If you contribute more toward the relationship than your partner, then equity requires that you should get greater rewards. If you both work equally hard, then equity demands that you should both get approximately equal rewards. Conversely, inequity will exist in a relationship if you pay more of the costs (for example, if you do more of the unpleasant tasks) but your partner enjoys more of the rewards. Inequity also will exist if you and your partner work equally hard but your partner gets more of the rewards. In this case you'd be under-benefited and your partner would be over-benefited.

Much research supports this theory that people want equity in their interpersonal relationships (Hatfield & Rapson, 2007; Ueleke et al., 1983). The general idea behind the theory is that if you are under-benefited (you get too little in proportion to what you put in), you'll be angry and dissatisfied. If, on the other hand, you are over-benefited (you get too much in proportion to what you put in), you'll feel guilty. Some research, however, has questioned this rather neat but intuitively unsatisfying assumption and finds that the over-benefited person is often quite happy and contented; guilt from getting more than you deserve seems easily forgotten (Noller & Fitzpatrick, 1993).

Equity theory puts into clear focus the sources of relational dissatisfaction seen every day. For example, in a relationship both partners may have full-time jobs, but one partner may also be expected to do the major share of the household chores. Thus, although both may be deriving equal rewards—they have equally good cars, they live in the same three-bedroom house, and so on—one partner is paying more of the costs. According to equity theory, this partner will be dissatisfied because of this lack of equity.

Equity theory claims that you will develop, maintain, and be satisfied with relationships that are equitable. You will not develop, will terminate, or will be dissatisfied with relationships that are inequitable. The greater the inequity, the greater the dissatisfaction and the greater the likelihood that the relationship will end.

VIEWPOINTS How would you feel if you were in a relationship in which you and your partner contributed an equal share of the costs (that is, you each worked equally hard) but your partner derived significantly greater rewards?

Creatista/Shutterstock

Politeness Theory

Still another approach to relationships looks at politeness as a major force in developing, maintaining, and deteriorating relationships. **Politeness theory** would go something like this: *Two people develop a relationship when each respects, contributes to, and acknowledges the positive and negative face needs of the other and it deteriorates when they don't.* You'll recall from Chapter 3 that positive face is the need to be thought of highly—to be valued, to be esteemed. In communication terms, respect for positive face entails the exchange of compliments, praise, and general positivity. Negative face is the need to be autonomous—to be in control of one's own behavior, to not be obligated to do something. In communication terms, respect for negative face entails the exchange of permission requests (rather than demands), messages indicating that a person's time is valuable and respected, and few if any imposed obligations. It would also entail providing the other person an easy "way out" when a request is made.

Relationships develop when these needs are met. Relationships will be maintained when the rules of politeness are maintained. And relationships will deteriorate when the rules of politeness are bent, violated too often, or ignored completely. Relationship repair will be affected by a process of reinstituting the rules of politeness. Politeness, of course, is not the entire story; it's just a piece. It won't explain all the reasons for relationship development or deterioration but it explains a part of the processes. It won't explain, for example, why so many people stay in abusive and unsatisfying relationships. Its major weakness seems to be that politeness needs for specific individuals are difficult to identify—what is politeness to one person, may be perceived as rude or insensitive to another.

And, perhaps not surprisingly, politeness seems to be relaxed as the relationship becomes more intimate. As the relationship becomes more intimate and long-lasting, there is greater license to violate the normal rules of politeness. This may be a mistake, at least in certain relationships. Our needs for positive and negative face do not go away when a relationship becomes more intimate; they're still there. If the definitions of politeness are relaxed by the individuals, then there seems little problem. There is a problem when the definitions—relaxed or original—are not shared by the individuals; when one assumes the acceptability of something generally considered impolite as okay while the other does not.

When people in relationships complain that they are not respected, are not valued as they used to be when they were dating, and that their relationship is not romantic, they may well be talking about politeness. And so, on the more positive side, it offers very concrete suggestions for developing, maintaining, and repairing interpersonal relationships. Namely: Increase politeness by contributing to the positive and negative face needs of the other person.

Though each relationship is unique, relationships for many people possess similar characteristics. It is these general patterns that these theories try to explain. Taken together, the theories actually illuminate a great deal about why you develop relationships, the way relationships work, the ways you seek to maintain relationships, and the reasons why some relationships are satisfying and others are not. With an understanding of these aspects of relationships, you'll be in a better position to regulate and manage your own friendship, romantic, and family relationships—the topic of the next chapter. Table 2 compares movement toward and away from intimacy as seen by the various theories.

TABLE 2 Movement among the Stages as Predicted by Relationship Theories

You move toward intimacy when:	Relationship Stages	You move away from intimacy when:
Attraction increases	Contact	Attraction decreases
Rules are followed		Rules are broken, disregarded
Tensions are at acceptable limits	Involvement	Tensions become too high and unacceptable
Social penetration increases; the breadth and depth of conversation increases		Depenetration occurs; breadth and depth of conversation decrease
Rewards increase, costs decrease, profits increase	Intimacy	Rewards decrease, costs increase, profits decrease
Equity prevails; each derives rewards in proportion to the costs paid	Deterioration	Inequities exist and grow greater; one person is under-benefited and one person is over-benefited
Politeness increases; positive and negative face needs are met	Dissolution	Politeness decreases; positive and negative face needs are not met or are violated

Relationship Communication

Communication is the life-blood of relationships—without communication relationships could not exist. And without effective communication, effective relationships could not exist. With effective communication, however, you stand a much better chance of experiencing relationships that are productive, satisfying, supportive, open, honest, and possess all the characteristics you want in a relationships. Here we look at some of the communication patterns and guides to effectiveness in developing, deteriorating, and repairing relationships.

Communicating in Developing Relationships

Much research has focused on the communication that takes place as you make contact, become involved, and reach intimacy (Ayres, 1983; Canary & Stafford, 1994; Canary, Stafford, Hause, & Wallace, 1993; Dainton & Stafford, 1993; Dindia & Baxter, 1987; Guerrero, Eloy, & Wabnik, 1993). Here are some examples of how people communicate as they develop and seek to maintain their relationships, presented in the form of suggestions for more effective interpersonal relationships. As a preface, it should be noted that these messages may be sent over any of the available communication channels. Because many relationships develop online (Match.com commercials claim that one out of five relationships begin online), and because online contact is so easy to maintain even when partners are widely separated geographically, a great deal of relationship communication occurs through e-mail, Facebook postings, instant messaging, texting, and tweeting.

VIEWPOINTS One study found that of people who met on the Internet, those who meet in places of common interest, who communicate over a period of time before they meet in person, who manage barriers to greater closeness, and who manage conflict well are more likely to say together than couples who do not follow this general pattern (Baker, 2002). Based on your own experiences, how would you predict which couples would stay together and which would break apart?

NetPhotos/Alamy

- **Be nice.** Researchers call this *prosocial behavior.* You're polite, cheerful, and friendly; you avoid criticism; and you compromise even when it involves self-sacrifice. Prosocial behavior also includes talking about a shared future; for example, talking about a future vacation or buying a house together. It also includes acting affectionately and romantically.

- **Communicate.** You call just to say, "How are you?" or send cards or letters. Sometimes communication is merely "small talk" that is insignificant in itself but is engaged in because it preserves contact. Also included would be talking about the honesty and openness in the relationship and talking about shared feelings. Responding constructively in a conflict (even when your partner may act in ways harmful to the relationship) is another type of communicative maintenance strategy (Rusbult & Buunk, 1993).

- **Be open.** You engage in direct discussion and listen to the other—for example, you self-disclose, talk about what you want from the relationship, give advice, and express empathy.

- **Give assurances.** You assure the other person of the significance of the relationship—for example, you comfort the other, put your partner first, and express love.

- **Share joint activities.** You spend time with the other—for example, playing ball, visiting mutual friends, doing specific things as a couple (even cleaning the house), and sometimes just being together and talking with no concern for what is done. Controlling (eliminating or reducing) extrarelational activities would be another type of togetherness behavior (Rusbult & Buunk, 1993). Also included here would be ceremonial behaviors; for example, celebrating birthdays and anniversaries, discussing past pleasurable times, and eating at a favorite restaurant.

- **Be positive.** You try to make interactions pleasant and upbeat—for example, holding hands, giving in to make your partner happy, and doing favors. At the same time, you would avoid certain issues that might cause arguments.
- **Focus on improving yourself.** For example, you work on making yourself look especially good and attractive to the other person.
- **Be empathic.** This skill is covered in the accompanying Understanding Interpersonal Skills box.

Understanding *Interpersonal Skills*

EMPATHY

Empathy is feeling what another person feels from that person's point of view without losing your own identity. Empathy enables you to understand emotionally what another person is experiencing. (To sympathize, in contrast, is to feel *for* the person—to feel sorry or happy for the person, for example.) Women, research shows, are perceived as more empathic and engage in more empathic communication than do men (Nicolai & Demmel, 2007). So following these suggestions may come more easily to women.

Communicating Empathy. Empathy is best expressed in two distinct parts: thinking empathy and feeling empathy (Bellafiore, 2005). In thinking empathy you express an understanding of what the other person means. For example, when you paraphrase someone's comment, showing that you understand the meaning the person is trying to communicate, you're communicating thinking empathy. The second part is feeling empathy; here you express your feeling of what the other person is feeling. You demonstrate a similarity between what you're feeling and what the other person is feeling. Often you'll respond with both thinking and feeling empathy in the same brief response; for example, when a friend tells you of problems at home, you may respond by saying, for example, "Your problems at home do seem to be getting worse. I can imagine how you feel so angry at times."

Here are a few more specific suggestions to help you communicate both your feeling and your thinking empathy more effectively (Authier & Gustafson, 1982).

- **Be clear.** Make it clear that you're trying to understand, not to evaluate, judge, or criticize.
- **Focus.** Maintain eye contact, an attentive posture, and physical closeness to focus your concentration. Express involvement through facial expressions and gestures.
- **Reflect.** In order to check the accuracy of your perceptions and to show your commitment to understanding the speaker, reflect back to the speaker the feelings that you think are being expressed. Offer tentative statements about what you think the person is feeling; for example, "You seem really angry with your father" or "I hear some doubt in your voice."
- **Disclose.** When appropriate, use your own self-disclosures to communicate your understanding; but be careful that you don't refocus the discussion on yourself.
- **Address mixed messages.** At times you may want to identify and address any mixed messages that the person is sending as a way to foster more open and honest communication. For example, if your friend verbally expresses contentment but shows nonverbal signs of depression, it may be prudent to question the possible discrepancy.
- **Acknowledge importance.** Make it clear that you understand the depth of a person's feelings.

Working with Interpersonal Skills

In what situations would you appreciate others showing empathy? What specifically might they do to demonstrate this empathy?

Communicating in Deteriorating Relationships

Like communication in developing relationships, communication in deteriorating relationships involves special patterns and special strategies of disengagement.

Communication Patterns   These patterns are in part a response to the deterioration; you communicate the way you do because you feel that your relationship is in trouble. However, these patterns are also causative: The communication patterns you use largely determine the fate of your relationship. Here are a few communication patterns that are seen during relationship deterioration.

- **Withdrawal.** Nonverbally, withdrawal is seen in the greater space you need and in the speed with which tempers and other signs of disturbance arise when that space is invaded. Other nonverbal signs of withdrawal include a decrease in eye contact and touching; less similarity in clothing; and fewer displays of items associated with the other person, such as bracelets, photographs, and rings (Knapp & Vangelisti, 2009; Miller & Parks, 1982). Verbally, withdrawal is marked by a decreased desire to talk and especially to listen. At times, you may use small talk not as a preliminary to serious conversation but as an alternative, perhaps to avoid confronting the serious issues.

- **Decline in self-disclosure.** Self-disclosing communications decline significantly. If the relationship is dying, you may think self-disclosure not worth the effort. Or you may limit your self-disclosures because you feel that the other person may not accept them or can no longer be trusted to be supportive and empathic.

- **Deception.** Deception increases as relationships break down. Sometimes this takes the form of clear-cut lies which you or your partner may use to avoid arguments over such things as staying out all night, not calling, or being seen in the wrong place with the wrong person. At other times lies may be used because of a feeling of shame; you may not want the other person to think less of you. One of the problems with deception is that it has a way of escalating, eventually creating a climate of distrust and disbelief.

- **Positive and negative messages.** During deterioration there's an increase in negative and a decrease in positive messages. Once you praised the other's behaviors, but now you criticize them. Often the behaviors have not changed significantly; what has changed is your way of looking at them. What once was a cute habit now becomes annoying; what once was "different" now becomes inconsiderate. When a relationship is deteriorating, requests for pleasurable behaviors decrease ("Will you fix me my favorite dessert?") and requests to stop unpleasant or negative behaviors increase ("Will you stop whistling?") (Lederer, 1984). Even the social niceties that accompany requests get lost as they deteriorate from "Would you please make me a cup of coffee, honey?" to "Get me some coffee, will you?" to "Where's my coffee?"

Strategies of Disengagement   Another dimension of communicating in relationship deterioration focuses on the strategies people use in breaking up a relationship. When you wish to exit a relationship, you need some way of explaining this—to yourself as well as to your partner. You need a strategy for getting out of a relationship that you no longer find satisfying or profitable. A few such strategies are presented in the list that follows (Cody, 1982). As you read down the list, note that your choice of a strategy will depend on your goal. For example, you're more likely to remain friends if you use de-escalation than if you use justification or avoidance (Banks, Altendorf, Greene, & Cody, 1987).

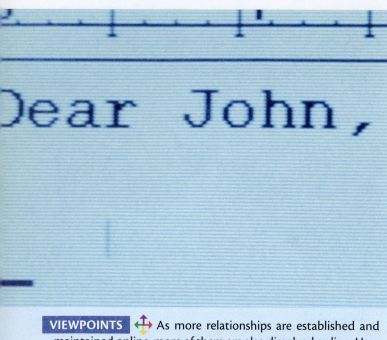

- The use of a **positive tone** to preserve the relationship and to express positive feelings for the other person. For example, "I really care for you a great deal, but I'm not ready for such an intense relationship."
- **Negative identity management** to blame the other person for the breakup and to absolve yourself of the blame for the breakup. For example, "I can't stand your jealousy, your constant suspicions, your checking up on me. I need my freedom."
- **Justification** to give reasons for the breakup. For example, "I'm going away to college for four years; there's no point in not dating others."
- **De-escalation** to reduce the intensity of the relationship. For example, you might avoid the other person, cut down on phone calls, or reduce the amount of time you spend together. Or you might de-escalate to reduce the exclusivity and hence the intensity of the relationship and say, for example, "I'm just not ready for an exclusive relationship. I think we should see other people."

Dealing with a Breakup Regardless of the specific reason for the end of the relationship, relationship breakups are difficult to deal with; invariably they cause stress and emotional problems, and they may actually create as much pain in a person's brain as physical injuries (Eisenberger, Lieberman, & Williams, 2003). Women, it seems, experience greater depression and social dysfunction than men after relationship dissolution (Chung, Farmer, Grant, Newton, Payne, Perry, Saunders, Smith, & Stone, 2002). Consequently, it's important to give attention to self-repair. Here are a few suggestions to ease the difficulty that is sure to be experienced, whether the breakup is between friends or lovers or occurs because of death, separation, or the loss of affection and connection.

- **Break the loneliness–depression cycle.** Instead of wallowing in loneliness and depression, be active, do things. Engage in social activities with friends and others in your support system. Many people feel they should bear their burdens alone. Men, in particular, have been taught that this is the only "manly" way to handle things. But seeking the support of others is one of the best antidotes to the unhappiness caused when a relationship ends. Tell your friends and family of your situation—in only general terms, if you prefer—and make it clear that you want support. Seek out people who are positive and nurturing. Avoid negative individuals who will paint the world in even darker tones. Make the distinction between seeking support and seeking advice. If you feel you need advice, seek out a professional.
- **Take time out.** Resist the temptation to jump into a new relationship while the old one is still warm or before a new one can be assessed with some objectivity. At the same time, resist swearing off all relationships. Neither extreme works well. Also, take time out for yourself. Renew your relationship with yourself. If you were in a long-term relationship, you probably saw yourself as part of a team, as part of a couple. Now get to know yourself as a unique individual—standing alone at present but fully capable of entering a meaningful relationship in the near future.
- **Bolster your self-esteem.** When relationships fail, self-esteem often declines. This seems especially true for those who did not initiate the breakup (Collins & Clark, 1989). You may feel guilty for having caused the breakup or inadequate for not holding on to the relationship. You may feel unwanted and unloved. Your task is to regain a positive self-image. Recognize, too, that having been in a relationship that failed—even if you view yourself as the main cause of the breakup—does not mean that you are a failure. Neither does it mean

that you cannot succeed in a new and different relationship. It does mean that something went wrong with this one relationship. Ideally, it was a failure from which you have learned something important about yourself and about your relationship behavior.

- **Remove or avoid uncomfortable relationship symbols.** After any breakup, there are a variety of reminders—photographs, gifts, and letters, for example. Resist the temptation to throw these out. Instead, remove them. Give them to a friend to hold or put them in a closet where you won't see them. If possible, avoid places you frequented together. These symbols will bring back uncomfortable memories. After you have achieved some emotional distance, you can go back and enjoy these as reminders of a once pleasant relationship. Support for this suggestion comes from research showing that the more vivid your memory of a broken love affair—a memory greatly aided by these relationship symbols—the greater your depression is likely to be (Harvey, Flanary, & Morgan, 1986).
- **Become mindful of your own relationship patterns.** Avoid repeating negative patterns. Many people repeat their mistakes. They enter second and third relationships with the same blinders, faulty preconceptions, or unrealistic expectations with which they entered earlier involvements. Instead, use the knowledge gained from your failed relationship to prevent repeating the same patterns. At the same time, don't become a prophet of doom. Don't see in every relationship vestiges of the old. Don't jump at the first conflict and say, "Here it goes all over again." Treat the new relationship as the unique relationship it is. Don't evaluate it through past experiences. Use past relationships and experiences as guides, not filters.

Communication in Relationship Repair

If you wish to save a relationship, you may try to do so by changing your communication patterns and, in effect, putting into practice the insights and skills learned in this course. First, we'll look at some general ways to repair a relationship, and second, we'll examine ways to deal with repair when you are the only one who wants to change the relationship.

Interpersonal Repair   We can look at the strategies for repairing a relationship in terms of the following six suggestions, whose first letters conveniently spell out the word *REPAIR*, a useful reminder that repair is not a one-step but a multistep process (see Figure 3).

FIGURE 3
The Relationship Repair Wheel

The wheel seems an apt metaphor for the repair process; the specific repair strategies—the spokes—all work together in constant process. The wheel is difficult to get moving, but once in motion it becomes easier to turn. Also, it's easier to start when two people are pushing, but it is not impossible for one to move it in the right direction. What metaphor do you find helpful in thinking about relationship repair?

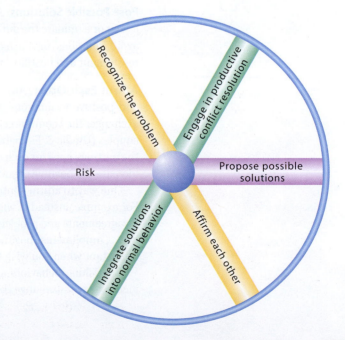

Recognize the problem

Engage in productive conflict resolution

Risk

Propose possible solutions

Integrate solutions into normal behavior

Affirm each other

Recognize the Problem Your first step is to identify the problem and to recognize it both intellectually and emotionally. Specify what is wrong with your present relationship (in concrete terms) and what changes would be needed to make it better (again, in specific terms). Create a picture of your relationship as you would want it to be, and compare that picture to the way the relationship looks now. Specify the changes that would have to take place if the ideal picture were to replace the present picture.

Also try to see the problem from your partner's point of view and to have your partner see the problem from yours. Exchange these perspectives, empathically and with open minds. Try, too, to be descriptive when discussing grievances, taking special care to avoid such troublesome terms as "always" and "never." Own your feelings and thoughts; use *I*-messages and take responsibility for your feelings instead of blaming your partner.

Engage in Productive Communication and Conflict Resolution Interpersonal communication skills such as those discussed throughout the text (for example, other-orientation, openness, confidence, immediacy, expressiveness, and empathy, considered in Understanding Interpersonal Skills boxes) are especially important during repair and are an essential part of any repair strategy. Here are several suggestions to refresh your memory.

- Look closely for relational messages that will help clarify motivations and needs. Respond to these messages as well as to the content messages.
- Exchange perspectives and see the situation as your partner does.
- Practice empathic and positive responses, even in conflict situations.
- Own your feelings and thoughts. Use *I*-messages and take responsibility for these feelings.
- Use active listening techniques to help your partner explore and express relevant thoughts and feelings.
- Remember the principle of irreversibility; think carefully before saying things you may later regret.
- Keep the channels of communication open. Be available to discuss problems, negotiate solutions, and practice new and more productive communication patterns.

Similarly, the skills of effective interpersonal conflict resolution are crucial in any attempt at relationship repair. If partners address relationship problems by deploying productive conflict resolution strategies, the difficulties may be resolved and the relationship may actually emerge stronger and healthier. If, however, unproductive and destructive strategies are used, then the relationship may well deteriorate further.

Pose Possible Solutions After the problem is identified, discuss solutions—possible ways to lessen or eliminate the difficulty. Look for solutions that will enable both of you to win. Try to avoid "solutions" in which one person wins and the other loses. With such win–lose solutions, resentment and hostility are likely to fester.

Affirm Each Other Any strategy of relationship repair should incorporate supportiveness and positive evaluations. For example, happy couples engage in greater positive behavior exchange: They communicate more agreement, approval, and positive affect than do unhappy couples (Dindia & Fitzpatrick, 1985). Clearly, these behaviors result from the positive feelings the partners have for each other. However, it can also be argued that these expressions help to increase the positive regard each person has for the other.

One way to affirm another is to talk positively. Reverse negative communication patterns. For example, instead of withdrawing, talk about the causes of and the possible cures for your disagreements and problems. Reverse the tendency to hide your inner self. Disclose your feelings. Compliments, positive stroking, and all the nonverbals that say "I care" are especially important when you wish to reverse negative communication patterns.

Cherishing behaviors are an especially insightful way to affirm another person and to increase favor exchange (Lederer, 1984). **Cherishing behaviors** are those small gestures you enjoy receiving from your partner (a smile, a wink, a squeeze, a kiss). Cherishing behaviors should be (1) specific and positive, (2) focused on the present and future rather than related to issues about which the partners have argued in the past, (3) capable of being performed daily, and (4) easily executed. People can make a list of the cherishing behaviors they each wish to receive and then exchange lists. Each person then performs the cherishing behaviors desired by the partner. At first, these behaviors may seem self-conscious and awkward. In time, however, they will become a normal part of interaction.

Integrate Solutions into Normal Behavior Often solutions that are reached after an argument are followed for only a very short time; then the couple goes back to their previous, unproductive behavior patterns. Instead, integrate the solutions into your normal behavior; make them an integral part of your everyday relationship behavior. For example, make the exchange of favors, compliments, and cherishing behaviors a part of your normal relationship behavior.

Risk Take risks in trying to improve your relationship. Risk giving favors without any certainty of reciprocity. Risk rejection by making the first move to make up or by saying you're sorry. Be willing to change, adapt, and take on new tasks and responsibilities. Risk the possibility that a significant part of the problem is you—that you're being unreasonable or controlling or stingy and that this is causing problems and needs to be changed.

Intrapersonal Repair One of the most important avenues to relationship repair originates with the principle of punctuation and the idea that communication is circular rather than linear (Duncan & Rock, 1991). Let's consider an example involving Pat and Chris: Pat is highly critical of Chris; Chris is defensive and attacks Pat for being insensitive, overly negative, and unsupportive. If you view the communication process as beginning with Pat's being critical (that is, the stimulus) and with Chris's attacks being the response, you have a pattern such as occurs in Figure 4 (A).

With this view, the only way to stop the unproductive communication pattern is for Pat to stop criticizing. But what if you are Chris and can't get Pat to stop being critical? What if Pat doesn't want to stop being critical?

You get a different view of the problem when you see communication as circular and apply the principle of punctuation. The result is a pattern such as appears in Figure 4 (B).

FIGURE 4
(A) A Stimulus–Response View of Relationship Problems
This view of the relationship process implies that one behavior is the stimulus and one behavior is the response. It implies that a pattern of behavior can be modified only if you change the stimulus, which will produce a different (more desirable) response.

(B) A Circular View of Relationship Problems
Note that in this view of relationships, as distinguished from that depicted in Figure 4 (A), relationship behaviors are seen in a circular pattern; no specific behavior is singled out as a stimulus and none as a response. The pattern can thus be broken by interference anywhere along the circle.

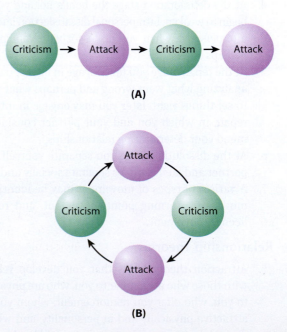

Note that no assumptions are made about causes. Instead, the only assumption is that each response triggers another response; each response depends in part on the previous response. Therefore, the pattern can be broken at any point: Chris can stop Pat's criticism, for example, by not responding with attacks. Similarly, Pat can stop Chris's attacks by not responding with criticism.

In this view, either person can break an unproductive cycle. Clearly, relationship communication can be most effectively improved when both parties change their unproductive patterns. Nevertheless, communication can be improved even if only one person changes and begins to use a more productive pattern. This is true to the extent that Pat's criticism depends on Chris's attacks and to the extent that Chris's attacks depend on Pat's criticism.

Summary

 Use your smartphone or tablet device (or log on to mycommunicationlab.com) to hear an audio summary of this chapter.

This chapter introduced interpersonal relationships and focused on two areas: the stages you go through in developing and perhaps dissolving relationships, and the various theories of how and why interpersonal relationships develop and dissolve.

Relationship Stages

1. At the contact stage of a relationship you make perceptual contact and later interact with the person.

2. At the involvement stage you test your potential partner and, if this proves satisfactory, move on to intensifying your relationship.

3. At the intimacy stage you may make an interpersonal commitment and later enter the stage of social bonding, in which you publicly reveal your relationship status.

4. At the deterioration stage the bonds holding you together begin to weaken. Intrapersonal dissatisfaction later becomes interpersonal, when you discuss it with your partner and perhaps others.

5. At the repair stage you first engage in intrapersonal repair, analyzing what went wrong and perhaps what you can do to set things right; later you may engage in interpersonal repair, in which you and your partner consider ways to mend your deteriorating relationships.

6. At the dissolution stage you separate yourself from your partner and later perhaps separate socially and publicly.

7. A variety of types of movement may be identified: stage movement, turning point movement, and relationship license movement.

Relationship Theories

8. Attraction theory holds that you develop relationships with those who are similar to you, who are physically close to you, who offer you reinforcement, whom you consider attractive physically and in personality, and who are of a desired socioeconomic and educational level.

9. Relationship rules theory holds that people maintain relationships with those who follow the rules the individuals have defined as essential to their relationship and dissolve relationships with those who don't follow the rules.

10. Relationship dialectics theory holds that relationships involve tensions between opposing needs and desires; for example, the opposing needs of connection with another person on the one hand and autonomy and independence on the other.

11. Social penetration theory focuses on the changes in breadth and depth of conversational topics that take place as partners move from one relationship stage to another.

12. Social exchange theory claims that we enter and maintain relationships in which the rewards are greater than the costs. When the costs become greater than the rewards, the relationship deteriorates.

13. Equity theory holds that you develop and maintain relationships in which your ratio of rewards compared to costs is approximately equal to your partner's.

14. Politeness theory holds that you develop and maintain relationships with those who support your positive and negative face needs.

Relationship Communication

15. Communication in developing relationships includes being nice, being open, giving assurances, sharing joint activities, being positive, and improving yourself.

16. Among the communication changes that occur during relationship deterioration are verbal and nonverbal withdrawal, a decline in self-disclosure, an increase in deception, and an increase in negative messages and decrease in positive messages.

17. General repair strategies include: Recognizing the problem, Engaging in productive communication and conflict resolution, Posing possible solutions, Affirming each other, Integrating solutions into normal behavior, and Risking.

18. Repair isn't necessarily a two-person process; one person can break unproductive and destructive cycles.

Key Terms

attraction theory,
breadth,
cherishing behaviors,
comparison level,
complementarity,
contact,
costs,
depentration,

depth,
empathy,
equity theory,
intimacy,
involvement,
politeness theory,
profit,
reciprocity of liking,

relationship
   deterioration,
relationship dialectics
   theory,
relationship
   dissolution,
relationship license,
relationship repair,

rewards,
rules theory,
similarity,
social exchange
   theory,
social penetration
   theory,
turning points,

MyCommunicationLab Explorations

MyCommunicationLab®

Communication Choice Points

Revisit the chapter-opening video, "Coming Clean." Recall that Sally and Jim have exchanged some personal information via an Internet dating site, but now they are meeting for the first time. Sally has not been completely honest and now she has to decide how she can set the record straight if she wants to pursue this relationship. "Coming Clean" presents options for how Sally might self-disclose, some of which will enhance the relationship and lead to greater intimacy, and others that will weaken its bonds.

Log on to mycommunicationlab.com to view the video for this chapter, "Coming Clean," and then answer the related discussion questions.

Additional Resources

The following exercises focus on interpersonal relationships and the communication that takes place at each stage.

1 Analyzing Stage Talk and **2** Learning to Hear Stage Talk provide opportunities to look at the various cues to the different relationship stages. **3** Giving Repair Advice looks at relationship difficulties and encourages you to offer relationship repair advice based on the discussions in this chapter. **4** Til This Do Us Part is an exercise that looks at some of the relationship issues that can break up a relationship. **5** Interpersonal Relationships in Songs and Greeting Cards explores the way cards and songs talk about relationships. **6** Applying Theories to Problems provides an opportunity to apply the theories discussed in the previous chapter to common relationship problems discussed here. **7** Male and Female looks at gender differences in relationships. **8** Changing the Distance between You illustrates how relationship changes can be made. **9** Relational Repair from Advice Columnists encourages you to critically examine the advice given by relationship columnists. **10** How Can You Get Someone to Like You? looks at affinity-seeking strategies and how they're used to change people's perceptions. **11** How Might You Repair Relationships? presents a variety of relationship problems and asks you to apply the insights gained here and from your own experience in suggesting repair strategies.

Interpersonal Conflict and Conflict Management

Interpersonal Conflict and Conflict Management

Preliminaries to Interpersonal Conflict

Principles of Interpersonal Conflict

Conflict Management Stages

Conflict Management Strategies

2:13 / 5:00

Pearson Education

Pat and Andi, a dating couple, just won the top prize in their Fantasy Football league. They have enjoyed working together to build a winning team; but now that they've won, they cannot agree on what to do with the money. See how their conflict resolution choices play out in the video "Conflict Strategies" (www.mycommunicationlab.com).

Because you'll learn about:

- interpersonal conflict, what it is and how it works.
- the stages of effective conflict management.
- the strategies used in interpersonal conflict.

Because you'll learn to:

- manage the stages of conflict resolution effectively.
- use effective conflict strategies and avoid those that are unproductive and ineffective.

This chapter addresses one of the most important topics in the study of interpersonal communication. As you'll see in this chapter, an understanding of interpersonal conflict and the skills for effective conflict management are essential to all forms of interpersonal interaction. After a few foundation concepts, this chapter focuses on the nature and principles of conflict, the stages of conflict management, and the strategies for managing conflict effectively.

Preliminaries to Interpersonal Conflict

Before considering the stages and strategies of conflict management, we need to define exactly what we mean by interpersonal conflict, some of the myths surrounding this concept, and some of the issues around which conflict often centers.

Definition of Interpersonal Conflict

You want to go to the movies with your partner. Your partner wants to stay home. Your insisting on going to the movies interferes with your partner's staying home, and your partner's determination to stay home interferes with your going to the movies. Your goals are incompatible; if your goal is achieved, your partner's goal is not. Conversely, if your partner's goal is achieved, your goal is not.

As this example illustrates, **interpersonal conflict** is disagreement between or among connected individuals who perceive their goals as incompatible: close friends, lovers, colleagues, family members (Cahn & Abigail, 2007; Folger, Poole, & Stutman, 2005; Hocker & Wilmot, 2007). More specifically, conflict occurs when people:

- are **interdependent** (they're connected in some significant way); what one person does has an impact or an effect on the other person.
- are **mutually aware that their goals are incompatible**; if one person's goal is achieved, then the other person's goal cannot be achieved. For example, if one person wants to buy a new car and the other person wants to pay down the mortgage, there is conflict. Note that this situation would not pose a conflict if the couple had unlimited resources, in which case they could both buy the car and pay down the mortgage.
- **perceive each other as interfering with the attainment of their own goals**. For example, you may want to study, but your roommate may want to party; the attainment of either goal would interfere with the attainment of the other goal.

One of the implications of this concept of interdependency is that the greater the interdependency, (1) the greater the number of issues on which conflict can center, and (2) the greater the impact of the conflict and the conflict management interaction on the individuals and on the relationship. Put in terms of the concepts of breadth and depth discussed in relation to the social penetration model of relationships: As interdependency increases, so do breadth (the number of topics) and depth (the level to which topics are penetrated). When you think about it this way, it's easy to appreciate how important understanding interpersonal conflict and mastering the strategies of effective conflict management are to your relationship life. The diagram in Figure 1 is designed to illustrate this relationship.

Myths about Interpersonal Conflict

One of the problems many people have in dealing with conflict is that they may be operating on the basis of false assumptions about what conflict is and what it means. Think about your own assumptions about interpersonal and small-group conflict, which were probably derived from the communications you witnessed in your family and in your social interactions. For example, do you think the following are true or false?

- Conflict is best avoided. Time will generally solve any problem; most difficulties blow over given time.
- If two people experience relationship conflict, it means their relationship is in trouble; conflict is a sign of a troubled relationship.
- Conflict damages an interpersonal relationship.
- Conflict is destructive because it reveals our negative selves—our pettiness, our need to be in control, our unreasonable expectations.
- In any conflict, there has to be a winner and a loser. Because goals are incompatible, someone has to win and someone has to lose.

Each of these statements is false—and, as we'll see in this chapter, these myths can easily interfere with your effectively dealing with conflict. It's not so much the conflict that creates problems as the way in which you approach and deal with the conflict. Some ways of approaching conflict can resolve difficulties and differences and can actually improve a relationship. Other ways can hurt the relationship; they can destroy self-esteem, create bitterness, and foster suspicion. And, perhaps most important, conflict does not mean that someone has to lose and someone has to win. Both can win. Your task, therefore, is not to try to create relationships that will be free of conflict, but rather to learn appropriate and productive ways of managing conflict so that neither person emerges a loser.

FIGURE 1
Conflict and Interdependency

This figure illustrates that as interdependency increases, so do the potential and the importance of conflict. How effectively does the relationship predicted in this figure depict your own interpersonal conflicts?

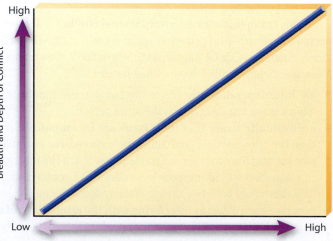

Interpersonal Conflict Issues

Interpersonal conflicts cover a wide range of issues (Canary, 2003). Such conflicts may focus on goals to be pursued (for example, parents and child disagree on what college the child should attend or what romantic partner he or she should get involved with); on the allocation of resources such as money or time (for example, partners differ on how to spend their money); on decisions to be made (for example, spouses argue about whether to save or splurge a bonus); or on behaviors that are considered appropriate or desirable by one person but inappropriate or undesirable by the other (for example, two people disagree over whether one of them was flirting or drinking or not working as hard on the relationship).

In a study on the issues argued about by gay, lesbian, and heterosexual couples, researchers found that respondents identified six major issues that were virtually identical for all couples (Kurdek, 1994). These issues are arranged here in order, with the first being the most often mentioned. As you read this list, ask yourself how many of these issues you argue about:

- **intimacy** issues, such as affection and sex
- **power** issues, such as excessive demands or possessiveness, lack of equality in the relationship, friends, and leisure time
- **personal flaws** issues, such as drinking or smoking, personal grooming, and driving style
- **personal distance** issues, such as frequent absence and heavy school or job commitments
- **social** issues, such as politics and social policies, parents, and personal values
- **distrust** issues, such as previous lovers and lying

Another study found that any (or all) of four conditions generally led up to a couple's "first big fight": uncertainty over commitment, jealousy, violation of expectations, and/or personality differences (Siegert & Stamp, 1994).

In workplace settings, the major sources of conflict among top managers revolved around the issue of executive responsibility and coordination. Other conflicts focused on differences in organizational objectives, on how resources were to be allocated, and on what constituted an appropriate management style (Morrill, 1992).

In a study of same-sex and opposite-sex friends, the four issues most often argued about were shared living space or possessions, violations of friendship rules, the sharing of activities, and disagreement about ideas (Samter & Cupach, 1998).

In large part, the same conflicts you experience in face-to-face relationships can also arise in electronic communication. Yet there are a few conflict issues that seem to be unique to electronic communication, whether via e-mail, on social networking sites such as Facebook or MySpace, in blog postings, or on the phone. For the most part, such conflict results when people violate the rules of Internet courtesy. For example, sending commercial messages to those who didn't request them often creates conflict; sending a message to an entire listserv when it's relevant to only one member may annoy other members, who expect to receive messages relevant to the entire group and not personal exchanges between two people. Sending someone unsolicited mail (spamming or spimming), repeatedly sending the same mail, or posting the same message in lots of newsgroups even when the message is irrelevant to the focus of one or more groups, also will create conflict. Putting out purposely incorrect information or outrageous viewpoints to watch other people correct you or get emotionally upset by your message (trolling) can obviously lead to conflict, though some see it as fun. Other potential causes of such conflict include ill-timed cell

Jessica Miglio/NBC/Courtesy Everett Collection

VIEWPOINTS What issues do television characters fight about? Are the issues fought over in situation comedies different from those in dramas?

Jeremy Woodhouse/PhotoLibrary

phone calls, calling someone at work just to chat, or criticizing someone unfairly or posting an unflattering photo on social network sites.

Principles of Interpersonal Conflict

The importance and influence of conflict in all interpersonal relationships can be best appreciated if we understand some fundamental principles of this particular form of interaction. Here we look at (1) the inevitability of conflict, (2) conflict's positive and negative aspects, (3) conflict's focus on content and/or on relationships, (4) differing styles of conflict and their consequences, and (5) the influence of culture on conflict.

Conflict Is Inevitable

Conflict is a part of every interpersonal relationship, whether between parents and children, brothers and sisters, friends, lovers, or coworkers. The very fact that people are different, have had different histories, and have different goals will invariably produce differences. If the individuals are interdependent, as discussed earlier (see Figure 1), these differences may well lead to conflicts—and if so, the conflicts can focus on a wide variety of issues and be extremely personal.

Conflict Can Have Negative and Positive Effects

Even though interpersonal conflict is inevitable, the way you deal with conflict is crucial, for conflict can have both negative and positive effects depending on how it is handled.

Negative Effects   Among the disadvantages of conflict is that it often leads to increased negative feelings. Many conflicts involve unfair fighting methods and focus largely on hurting the other person. If this happens, negative feelings are sure to increase. Conflict also may deplete energy better spent on other areas, especially when unproductive conflict strategies are used.

At times, conflict may lead you to close yourself off from the other individual. When you hide your feelings from your partner, you prevent meaningful communication and interaction; this, in turn, creates barriers to intimacy. Because the need for intimacy is so strong, one possible outcome is that one or both parties may seek intimacy elsewhere. This often leads to further conflict, mutual hurt, and resentment—all of which add heavily to the costs carried by the relationship. As the costs increase, the rewards may become more difficult to exchange. Here, then, is a situation in which costs increase and rewards decrease, a scenario that often results in relationship deterioration and eventual dissolution.

Positive Effects   Among the advantages of conflict is that it forces you to examine a problem and work toward a potential solution. If you use productive conflict strategies, your relationship is likely to become stronger, healthier, and more satisfying than it was before.

Conflict often prevents hostilities and resentments from festering. Say you're annoyed at your partner, who comes home from work and then talks on the phone with colleagues for two hours instead of giving that time to you. If you say nothing, your annoyance is likely to grow. Further, by saying nothing you implicitly approve of such behavior, so it's likely that the phone calls will continue. Through your conflict and its resolution, you each let your needs be known: Your partner needs to review the day's work to gain assurance that it's been properly completed, and you have a need for your partner's attention. If you both can appreciate the legitimacy of these needs, then you stand a good chance of finding workable solutions. Perhaps your partner can make the phone calls after your attention needs are met. Perhaps you can delay your need for attention until your partner gets closure about work. Perhaps you can learn to provide for your partner's closure needs and in doing so get your own attention needs met. Again, you have win–win solutions; each of you has your needs met.

Consider, too, that when you try to resolve conflict within an interpersonal relationship, you're saying that the relationship is worth the effort; otherwise, you'd walk away. Although there may be exceptions—as when you confront conflict to save face or to gratify some ego need—confronting a conflict often indicates concern, commitment, and a desire to protect and preserve the relationship.

See "Relationships and Relationship Conflict" at tcbdevito.blogspot .com for a discussion of the relationship between health and effective conflict management. What other advantages do you see for effective conflict management?

Conflict Can Focus on Content and/or Relationship Issues

Using certain concepts, you can distinguish between content and relationship conflicts.

- **Content conflict** centers on objects, events, and persons in the world that are usually external to the people involved in the conflict. These include the millions of issues that you argue and fight about every day—the merits of a particular movie, what to watch on television, the fairness of the last examination, who should get promoted, the way to spend your savings.
- **Relationship conflicts** are equally numerous and are concerned with the relationships between the individuals—with such issues as who's in charge, the equality or lack of it in the relationship, and who has the right to establish rules of behavior. Examples of relationship conflicts include those involving a younger brother who does not obey his older brother, two partners who each want an equal say in making vacation plans, or a mother and daughter who each want to have the final word concerning the daughter's lifestyle.

Relationship conflicts often are hidden and disguised as content conflicts. Thus, a conflict over where you should vacation may, on the content level, center on the advantages and disadvantages of Mexico versus Hawaii. On a relationship level, however, it may center on who has the greater right to select the place to vacation, who should win the argument, or who is the decision maker in the relationship.

INTERPERSONAL CHOICE POINT

Escalating to Relationship Conflict

Your own interpersonal conflicts often start out as content conflicts but quickly degenerate into relationship conflicts—and that's when things get ugly. What types of things might you do to keep conflicts and their resolution focused on content and not on the relationship?

Conflict Styles Have Consequences

As mentioned earlier, the way in which you engage in conflict has consequences for the resolution of the conflict and for the relationship between the conflicting parties. Conflict researchers identify five styles of engaging in conflict (Blake & Mouton, 1984). As you read through the following descriptions of these **conflict styles**, try to identify your own often-used conflict style as well as the styles of those with whom you have close relationships.

Competing—I Win, You Lose   The **competing style** represents great concern for your own needs and desires and little for those of others. As long as your needs are met, the conflict has been dealt with successfully (for you). In conflict motivated by competitiveness, you'd be likely to be verbally aggressive while blaming the other person.

This style represents an I win, you lose philosophy. With this philosophy, you attempt to manage the conflict so that you win and the other person loses. As you can tell, this style might be appropriate in a courtroom or in buying a car, two situations in which one person benefits from the other person's losses. But in interpersonal situations this philosophy can easily lead to resentment in the person who lost, which in turn can easily morph into additional conflicts. Further, the fact that you win and the other person loses probably means that the conflict really hasn't been resolved, just concluded (for now).

Avoiding—I Lose, You Lose

Using the **avoiding style** suggests that you are relatively unconcerned with your own or with the other's needs or desires. The avoider shrinks from any real communication about the problem, changes the topic when the problem is brought up, and generally withdraws from the scene both psychologically and physically.

As you can appreciate, this style does little to resolve any conflicts and may be viewed as an I lose, you lose philosophy. Interpersonal problems rarely go away of their own accord; rather, if they exist, they need to be faced and dealt with effectively. The avoidance philosophy just allows the conflict to fester and probably to grow, only to resurface in another guise.

Accommodating—I Lose, You Win

In **accommodating style**, you sacrifice your own needs for the sake of the needs of the other person. Your major purpose is to maintain harmony and peace in the relationship or group. The accommodating style may help you attain the immediate goal of maintaining peace and perhaps satisfying the other person, but it does little to meet your own needs—which are unlikely to go away.

Accommodating represents an I lose, you win philosophy. And although this style may make your partner happy (at least on this occasion), it's not likely to prove a lasting resolution to an interpersonal conflict. You'll eventually sense the unfairness and inequity inherent in this approach to conflict, and you may easily come to resent your partner and perhaps even yourself.

Collaborating—I Win, You Win

In **collaborating style**, your concern is with both your own and the other person's needs. Often considered the ideal, collaborating takes time and a willingness to communicate, and especially to listen to the perspectives and needs of the other person.

Ideally, collaborating will allow each person's needs to be being satisfied, an **I win, you win** situation. This is obviously the style that, ideally, you would use in most of your interpersonal conflict. Collaborating promotes resolutions in which both people get something.

Compromising—I Win and Lose, You Win and Lose

The **compromising style** is in the middle; there's some concern for your own needs and some concern for the other's needs. Compromising is the kind of strategy you might refer to as "meeting each other halfway," "horse trading," or "give and take." This strategy is likely to result in maintaining peace, but there also will be dissatisfaction over the inevitable losses that have to be endured.

Compromising could be called an I-win-and-lose and you-win- and-lose strategy. There are lots of times when you can't both get exactly what you want. For example, you can't both get a new car if the available funds allow for only one. Still, you might each get a better car than what you now have—so you would win something, but not everything. You wouldn't get a new car, and the same would be true of your partner.

Conflict Is Influenced by Culture

As is true with all communication processes, conflict is influenced by the culture of the participants—and especially by their beliefs and values about conflict. The accompanying Understanding Interpersonal Theory & Research box looks at the parallel issue of gender.

Topics Culture influences the topics people fight about as well as what are considered appropriate and inappropriate ways of dealing with conflict. For example, cohabiting 18-year-olds are more likely to have conflict with their parents over their living style if they live in the United States than if they live in Sweden, where cohabitation is much more accepted. Similarly, male infidelity is more likely to cause conflict among American couples than among southern European couples. Students from the United States are more likely to pursue a conflict with another United States student than with someone from another culture. Chinese students, on the other hand, are more likely to pursue a conflict with a non-Chinese than with another Chinese student (Leung, 1988).

The topics of conflicts also will depend on whether the culture is high- or low-context. In high-context cultures, conflicts are more likely to center on violations of collective

Understanding *Interpersonal Theory & Research*

CONFLICT AND GENDER

Not surprisingly, research finds significant gender differences in interpersonal conflict (Krolokke & Sorensen, 2006; Wood, 2010). For example, men are more apt to withdraw from a conflict situation than are women. It's been argued that this may be due to the fact that men become more psychologically and physiologically aroused during conflict (and retain this heightened level of arousal much longer) than do women, and so may try to distance themselves and withdraw from the conflict to prevent further arousal (Goleman, 1995b; Gottman & Carrere, 1994). Another position would argue that men withdraw because the culture has taught men to avoid conflict; still another would claim that withdrawal is an expression of power.

Women, on the other hand, want to get closer to the conflict; they want to talk about it and resolve it. Even adolescents reveal these differences. In research on boys and girls aged 11 to 17, boys withdrew more than girls (Heasley, Babbitt, & Burbach, 1995; Lindeman, Harakka, & Keltikangas-Jarvinen, 1997). Other research has found that women are more emotional and men are more logical when they argue. Women have been defined as conflict "feelers" and men as conflict "thinkers" (Sorenson, Hawkins, & Sorenson, 1995). Another difference is that women are more apt to reveal their negative feelings than are men (Canary, Cupach, & Messman, 1995; Schaap, Buunk, & Kerkstra, 1988).

It should be mentioned, however, that some research fails to support these stereotypical gender differences in conflict style—the differences that cartoons, situation comedies, and films portray so readily and so clearly. For example, several studies dealing with both college students and men and women in business found no significant differences in the ways men and women engage in conflict (Canary & Hause, 1993; Gottman & Levenson, 1999; Wilkins & Andersen, 1991).

Working with Theories and Research

New findings on gender differences continue to emerge, so update this discussion by logging on to your favorite search engine and searching for current research on "gender" and "conflict." What can you add to the discussion presented here?

---

or group norms and values. Conversely, in low-context cultures, conflicts are more likely to come up when individual norms are violated (Ting-Toomey, 1985).

Nature of Conflict   Cultures also differ in how they define what constitutes conflict. For example, in some cultures it's quite common for women to be referred to negatively and to be seen as less than equal. To most people in the United States, this would constitute a clear basis for conflict. To some Japanese women, however, this isn't uncommon and isn't perceived as abusive (*New York Times*, February 11, 1996, pp. 1, 12). Further, Americans and Japanese differ in their views of the aim or purpose of conflict. The Japanese see conflicts and their resolution in terms of compromise; Americans, on the other hand, see conflict in terms of winning (Gelfand, Nishii, Holcombe, Dyer, Ohbuchi, & Fukuno, 2001). African Americans and European Americans engage in conflict in very different ways (Hecht, Jackson, & Ribeau, 2003; Kochman, 1981). The issues that cause and aggravate conflict, the conflict strategies that are expected and accepted, and the attitudes toward conflict vary from one group to the other.

Conflict Strategies   Each culture seems to teach its members different views of conflict strategies (Tardiff, 2001). In one study, African American females were found to use more direct controlling strategies (for example, assuming control over the conflict and arguing persistently

VIEWPOINTS What does your own culture teach about conflict and its management? What strategies does it prohibit? Are some conflict strategies prohibited with certain people (say, your parents) but not with others (say, your friends)? Does your culture prescribe certain ways of dealing with conflict? Does it have different expectations for men and for women? To what degree have you internalized these teachings? What effect do these teachings have on your actual conflict behaviors?

for their point of view) than did white females. White females, on the other hand, used more solution-oriented conflict styles than did African American females. African American and white men were similar in their conflict strategies; both avoided or withdrew from relationship conflict, preferring to keep quiet about their differences or make them seem insignificant (Ting-Toomey, 1986). Another example of this cultural influence on conflict is seen in the tendency of members of collectivist cultures to avoid conflict more, and to give greater importance to saving face, than members of individualist cultures (Cai & Fink, 2002; Dsilva & Whyte, 1998; Haar & Krabe, 1999; Oetzel & Ting-Toomey, 2003).

Organizational Norms As in the wider culture, the cultural norms of organizations will influence the types of conflicts that occur and the ways in which they may be dealt with. In some work environments, for example, the expression of conflict with high-level management would not be tolerated; in others it might be welcomed. In individualist cultures there is greater tolerance for conflict within organizations, even when it may involve different levels of the hierarchy. In collectivist cultures there is less tolerance. And, not surprisingly, culture influences how conflicts will be resolved. For example, American managers (members of an individualistic culture) deal with workplace conflict by seeking to integrate the demands of the different sides; Chinese managers (members of a collectivist culture) are more likely to call on higher management to make decisions or to leave the conflict unresolved (Tinsley & Brett, 2001).

Conflict Management Stages

Before trying to manage or resolve a conflict, you need to prepare. Conflict resolution is an extremely important communication experience, and you don't want to enter it without adequate thought. Here are a few conflict management stages to prepare you to resolve conflict.

Set the Stage

First, try to fight in private. When you air your conflicts in front of others, you create a variety of other problems. You may not be willing to be totally honest when third parties are present; you may feel you have to save face and therefore must win the fight at all costs. This may lead you to use strategies to win the argument rather than to resolve the conflict. You may become so absorbed by the image that others will have of you that you forget you have a relationship problem that needs to be resolved. Also, you run the risk of embarrassing your partner in front of others, and this embarrassment may create resentment and hostility.

Be sure you're each ready to fight. Although conflicts arise at the most inopportune times, you can choose the time to resolve them. Confronting your partner when she or he comes home after a hard day of work may not be the right time for resolving a conflict. Make sure you're both relatively free of other problems and ready to deal with the conflict at hand.

Know what you're fighting about. Sometimes people in a relationship become so hurt and angry that they lash out at the other person just to vent their own frustration. The problem at the center of the conflict (for example, the uncapped toothpaste tube) is merely an excuse

Understanding *Interpersonal Skills*

EQUALITY

In interpersonal communication the term **equality** refers to an attitude or approach that treats each person as an important and vital contributor to the interaction. In any situation, of course, there will be some inequality; one person will be higher in the organizational hierarchy, more knowledgeable, or more interpersonally effective. But despite this fact, an attitude of superiority is to be avoided. Interpersonal communication is generally more effective when it takes place in an atmosphere of equality.

Communicating Equality. Here are a few suggestions for communicating equality in all interactions, and especially in those involving conflict.

- Avoid "should" and "ought" statements (for example, "You really should call your mother more often" or "You should learn to speak up"). These statements put the listener in a one-down position.
- Make requests (especially courteous ones) and avoid demands (especially discourteous ones).
- Avoid interrupting; this signals an unequal relationship and implies that what you have to say is more important than what the other person is saying.
- Acknowledge the other person's contributions before expressing your own. Saying, "I see," "I understand," or "That's right" lets the other person know you're listening and understanding.
- Recognize that different cultures treat equality very differently. In low-power-distance cultures there is greater equality than in high-power-distance cultures, in which status differences greatly influence interpersonal interactions.

Working with Interpersonal Skills

Think about your interpersonal interactions over the last few days. In what ways did you express equality? Can you identify situations in which you could have expressed greater equality? Would this have made a difference in the interaction?

to express anger. Any attempt to resolve this "problem" will be doomed to failure, because the problem addressed is not what is causing the conflict. Instead, the underlying hostility, anger, and frustration need to be addressed.

Fight about problems that can be solved. Fighting about past behaviors or about family members or situations over which you have no control solves nothing; instead, it creates additional difficulties. Any attempt at resolution will fail, because the problems are incapable of being solved. Often such conflicts are concealed attempts at expressing frustration or dissatisfaction.

Now that you're prepared for the conflict resolution interaction, refer to the model in Figure 2. It identifies the steps that will help you navigate through this process.

Define the Conflict

Your first and most essential step is to define the conflict. Here are several techniques to keep in mind.

- **Define both content and relationship issues.** Define the obvious content issues (who should do the dishes, who should take the kids to school) as well as the underlying relationship issues (who has been avoiding household responsibilities, whose time is more valuable).
- **Define the problem in specific terms.** Conflict defined in the abstract is difficult to deal with and resolve. It's one thing for a husband to say that his wife is "cold and unfeeling" and quite another to say that she does not call him at the office, kiss him when he comes home, or hold his hand when they're at a party. These behaviors can be agreed on and dealt with, but the abstract "cold and unfeeling" remains elusive.

FIGURE 2

Stages in Conflict Resolution

This 5-stage model of conflict resolution is essentially John Dewey's (1910) problem-solving sequence. The assumption made here is that a conflict to be resolved is essentially a problem to be solved and follows the same general sequence. As you read about this problem/conflict-solving sequence, try visualizing a specific conflict and how these several steps might help you resolve it.

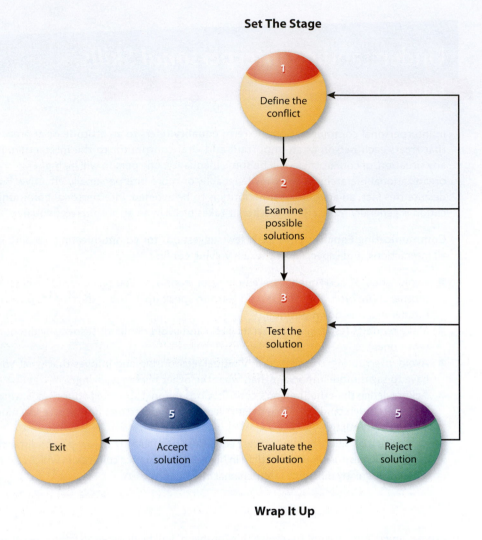

Set The Stage

1 Define the conflict

2 Examine possible solutions

3 Test the solution

4 Evaluate the solution

5 Accept solution

Exit

5 Reject solution

Wrap It Up

■ **Focus on the present.** Avoid **gunnysacking** (a term derived from the large burlap bag called a gunnysack)—the practice of storing up grievances so they may be unloaded at another time. Often, when one person gunnysacks, the other person gunnysacks; for example, the birthdays you forgot and the times you arrived late for dinner are all thrown at you. The result is two people dumping their stored-up grievances on each other with no real attention to the present problem.

■ **Empathize.** Try to understand the nature of the conflict from the other person's point of view. Why is your partner disturbed that you're not doing the dishes? Why is your neighbor complaining about taking the kids to school? Once you have empathically understood the other person's feelings, validate those feelings when appropriate. If your partner is hurt or angry and you believe such feelings are legitimate and justified, say so: "You have a right to be angry; I shouldn't have said what I did about your mother. I'm sorry. But I still don't want to go on vacation with her." In expressing validation, you're not necessarily expressing agreement; you're merely stating that your partner has feelings that you recognize as legitimate.

■ **Avoid mind reading.** Don't try to read the other person's mind. Ask questions to make sure you understand the problem as the other person is experiencing it. Ask directly and simply: "Why are you insisting that I take the dog out now, when I have to call three clients before nine o'clock?"

Examine Possible Solutions

Most conflicts can probably be resolved through a variety of solutions. Here are a few suggestions. Brainstorm by yourself or with your partner. Try not to inhibit or censor yourself or your partner as you generate these potential solutions. Once you have proposed a variety of solutions, look especially for solutions that will enable each party to win—to get something he or she wants. Avoid win–lose solutions, in which one person wins and one loses. Such outcomes will cause difficulty for the relationship by engendering frustration and resentment. Carefully weigh the costs and the rewards that each solution entails. Most solutions will involve costs to one or both parties. Seek solutions in which the costs and the rewards will be evenly shared.

Using a specific example will help us work through the various steps in the conflict resolution process. In this example, the conflict revolves around Pat's not wanting to socialize with Chris's friends. Chris is devoted to these friends, but Pat actively dislikes them. Chris thinks they're wonderful and exciting; Pat thinks they're unpleasant and boring.

For example, among the solutions that Pat and Chris might identify are these:

1. Chris should not interact with these friends anymore.
2. Pat should interact with Chris's friends.
3. Chris should see these friends without Pat.

VIEWPOINTS What changes would you like to see your relational partners (friends, family members, romantic partners) make in their own conflict management strategies? What might you do to more effectively regulate your own ways of dealing with conflict?

Bob Daemmrich/The Image Works

Clearly solutions 1 and 2 are win–lose solutions. In solution 1, Pat wins and Chris loses; in 2, Chris wins and Pat loses. Solution 3 has some possibilities. Both might win and neither must necessarily lose. This potential solution, then, needs to be looked at more closely.

Test the Solution

First, test the solution mentally. How does it feel now? How will it feel tomorrow? Are you comfortable with it? In our example, will Pat be comfortable with Chris's socializing with these friends alone? Some of Chris's friends are attractive; will this cause difficulty for Pat and Chris's relationship? Will Chris give people too much to gossip about? Will Chris feel guilty? Will Chris enjoy seeing these friends without Pat?

Second, test the solution in practice. Put the solution into operation. How does it work? If it doesn't work, then discard it and try another solution. Give each solution a fair chance, but don't hang on to a solution when it's clear that it won't resolve the conflict.

Perhaps Chris might go out without Pat once to test this solution. Afterward, the couple can evaluate the experiment. Did the friends think there was something wrong with Chris's relationship with Pat? Did Chris feel guilty? Did Chris enjoy this new experience? How did Pat feel? Did Pat feel jealous? Lonely? Abandoned?

INTERPERSONAL CHOICE POINT

Conflict Management

Your dorm mate is very popular and has an open-door policy. So, throughout the day and evening, friends drop by to chat, borrow a book, check their e-mail, and do a range of things—all of which prevent you from studying. You need to resolve this problem. What are some of the things you might say to your roommate to begin to resolve this conflict?

Evaluate the Solution

Did the solution help resolve the conflict? Is the situation better now than it was before the solution was tried? Share your feelings and evaluations of the solution.

Pat and Chris now need to share their perceptions of this possible solution. Would they be comfortable with this solution on a monthly basis? Is the solution worth the costs each will pay? Are the costs and rewards evenly distributed? Might other solutions be more effective?

Critical-thinking pioneer Edward deBono (1987) suggests that in analyzing problems, you use six "thinking hats" as a way of seeking different perspectives. With each hat you look at the problem from a different angle.

- **The fact hat** focuses attention on the facts and figures that bear on the problem. For example, how can Pat learn more about the rewards that Chris gets from the friends? How can Chris learn why Pat doesn't like these great friends?
- **The feeling hat** focuses attention on the emotional responses to the problem. How does Pat feel when Chris goes out with these friends? How does Chris feel when Pat refuses to meet them?
- **The negative argument hat** asks you to become the devil's advocate. How may this relationship deteriorate if Chris continues seeing these friends without Pat or if Pat resists interacting with Chris's friends?
- **The positive benefits hat** asks you to look at the upside. What are the opportunities that Chris's seeing friends without Pat might yield? What benefits might Pat and Chris get from this new arrangement?
- **The creative new idea hat** focuses on new ways of looking at the problem. In what other ways can Pat and Chris look at this problem? What other possible solutions might they consider?
- **The control of thinking hat** helps you analyze what you're doing; it asks you to reflect on your own thinking. Have Pat and Chris adequately defined the problem? Are they focusing too much on insignificant issues? Have they given enough attention to possible negative effects?

Accept or Reject the Solution

If you accept the solution, you're ready to put it into more permanent operation. Let's say that Pat is actually quite happy with the solution. Pat was able to use the evening to visit college friends. The next time Chris goes out with the friends Pat doesn't like, Pat intends to go out with some friends from college. Chris feels pretty good about seeing friends without Pat. Chris explains that they have both decided to see their friends separately and both are comfortable with this decision. If, however, either Pat or Chris feels unhappy with this solution, they will have to try out another solution or perhaps go back and redefine the problem and seek other ways to resolve it.

Wrap It Up

Even after the conflict is resolved, there is still work to be done. Often, after one conflict is supposedly settled, another conflict will emerge—because, for example, one person feels that he or she has been harmed and needs to retaliate and take revenge in order to restore a sense of self-worth (Kim & Smith, 1993). So it's especially important that the conflict be resolved and not be allowed to generate other, perhaps more significant conflicts.

Learn from the conflict and from the process you went through in trying to resolve it. For example, can you identify the fight strategies that merely aggravated the situation? Do you or your partner need a cooling-off period? Can you tell when minor issues are going to escalate into major arguments? Does avoidance make matters worse? What issues are particularly disturbing and likely to cause difficulties? Can they be avoided?

Keep the conflict in perspective. Be careful not to blow it out of proportion to the extent that you begin to define your relationship in terms of conflict. Avoid the tendency to see disagreement as inevitably leading to major blowups. Conflicts in most relationships actually occupy a very small percentage of the couple's time, and yet in recollection they often loom extremely large. Also, don't allow the conflict to undermine your own

INTERPERSONAL CHOICE POINT

Confronting a Problem

Your next-door neighbor never puts out the garbage in time for pickup, so the garbage—often broken into by animals—remains until the next pickup. You're fed up with the rodents the garbage attracts, the smell, and the horrible appearance. What options do you have for stopping this problem and yet not making your neighbor hate you?

or your partner's self-esteem. Don't view yourself, your partner, or your relationship as a failure just because you had an argument or even lots of arguments.

Attack your negative feelings. Negative feelings frequently arise after an interpersonal conflict. Most often they arise because one or both parties used unfair fight strategies to undermine the other person—for example, personal rejection, manipulation, or force. Resolve to avoid such unfair tactics in the future, but at the same time let go of guilt and blame toward yourself and your partner. If you think it would help, discuss these feelings with your partner or even a therapist. Apologize for anything you did wrong. Your partner should do likewise; after all, both parties are usually responsible for the conflict (Coleman, 2002).

Increase the exchange of rewards and cherishing behaviors to demonstrate your positive feelings and to show you're over the conflict and want the relationship to survive and flourish.

Conflict Management Strategies

In managing conflict you can choose from a variety of strategies, which we will explore below. First, however, realize that the strategies you choose will be influenced by a variety of factors, such as (1) the goals to be achieved, (2) your emotional state, (3) your cognitive assessment of the situation, (4) your personality and communication competence, and (5) your family history (Koerner & Fitzpatrick, 2002). Understanding these factors may help you select strategies that are more appropriate and more effective. Research finds that using productive conflict strategies can have lots of beneficial effects, whereas using inappropriate strategies may be linked to poorer psychological health (Neff & Harter, 2002; Weitzman, 2001; Weitzman & Weitzman, 2000).

- **Goals.** The short-term and long-term goals you wish to achieve will influence what strategies seem appropriate to you. If you merely want to salvage this evening's date, you may want to simply "give in" and basically ignore the difficulty. On the other hand, if you want to build a long-term relationship, you may want to fully analyze the cause of the problem and to seek strategies that will enable both parties to win.

Ethics in Interpersonal Communication

ETHICAL FIGHTING

This section focuses on conflict management strategies and attempts to point out the differences between effective and ineffective conflict management. But communication strategies also have an ethical dimension and it is important to look at the ethical implications of conflict resolution strategies. As you read this section keep the ethical dimension in mind and indicate how you would answer each of these questions:

- Does conflict avoidance have an ethical dimension? For example, is it unethical for one relationship partner to refuse to discuss disagreements?
- Can the use of physical force to influence another person ever be ethical? Can you identify a situation in which it would be appropriate for someone with greater physical strength to overpower another to compel the other to accept his or her point of view?
- Are face-detracting strategies inherently unethical, or might it be appropriate to use them in certain situations? Can you identify such situations?
- What are the ethical implications of verbal aggressiveness?

ETHICAL CHOICE POINT

At your high-powered and highly stressful job, you sometimes smoke pot. This happens several times a month, but you don't use drugs at any other times. Your relationship partner—who you know hates drugs and despises people who use any recreational drug—asks you if you take drugs. Because it's such a limited use, and because you know that admitting this will cause a huge conflict in a relationship that's already having difficulties, you wonder if you can ethically lie about this.

- **Emotional state.** Your feelings will influence your strategies. You're unlikely to select the same strategies when you're sad as when you're angry. You will choose different strategies when you're seeking to apologize than when you're looking for revenge.
- **Cognitive assessment.** Your attitudes and beliefs about what is fair and equitable will influence your readiness to acknowledge the fairness in the other person's position. Your own assessment of who (if anyone) is the cause of the problem also will influence your conflict style. You may also assess the likely effects of your various options. For example, what do you risk if you fight with your boss by using blame or personal rejection? Do you risk alienating your teenager if you use force?
- **Personality and communication competence.** If you're shy and unassertive, you may be more likely to try to avoid conflict than to fight actively. If you're extroverted and have a strong desire to state your position, then you may be more likely to fight actively and argue forcefully. And, of course, some people have greater tolerance for disagreement and consequently are more apt to let things slide and not become emotionally upset or hostile than are those with little tolerance for disagreement (Teven, Richmond, & McCroskey, 1998; Wrench, McCroskey, & Richmond, 2008).
- **Family history.** The topics you choose to fight about, and perhaps your tendencies to obsess or to forget about interpersonal conflicts, are likely influenced by your family history and the way conflicts were handled as you grew up.

There are a wide variety of conflict resolution skills. For example, active listening is a skill that has wide application in conflict situations. Similarly, using I-messages rather than accusatory you-messages will contribute to effective interpersonal conflict resolution (Noller & Fitzpatrick, 1993). Of course, the characteristics of interpersonal competence covered in the Understanding Interpersonal Skills boxes throughout the text are clear and effective conflict resolution techniques.

The following discussion identifies additional strategies, detailing both the unproductive and destructive strategies that you'll want to avoid and the productive and constructive strategies that you'll want to use. It's important to see at the outset that the strategic choices you make (and do realize that you do have choices, something people frequently try to deny) will greatly affect both the specific interpersonal conflict and your relationship as a whole. For example, refusal messages, insults, accusations, and commands are likely to lead to conflict as well as to add to existing conflicts, delaying and perhaps preventing effective conflict management (Canary, Cody, & Manusov, 2003).

Before reading about the various conflict management strategies, examine your own interpersonal conflict behavior by taking following self-test.

Jose Ignacio Soto/Shutterstock

There is little choice in a barrel of rotten apples.
—*William Shakespeare*

Test Yourself | **Conflict Management Styles**

The following statements refer to ways in which people engage in interpersonal conflict. Respond to each statement with T if this is a generally accurate description of your interpersonal conflict behavior and F if the statement is a generally inaccurate description of your behavior.

_____ 1. I strive to seek solutions that will benefit both of us.

_____ 2. I look for solutions that will give me what I want.

_____ 3. I confront conflict situations as they arrive.

_____ 4. I avoid conflict situations as best I can.

_____ 5. My messages are basically descriptive of the events leading up to the conflict.

_____ 6. My messages are often judgmental.

_____ 7. I take into consideration the face needs of the other person.

_____ 8. I advance the strongest arguments I can find even if these attack the other person.

_____ 9. I center my arguments on issues rather than on personalities.

_____ 10. I use messages that may attack a person's self-image if this will help me win the argument.

How Did You Do? This conflict management styles test was designed to sensitize you to some of the conflict strategies to be discussed in this section of the chapter. It is not intended to give you a specific score. However, in general, you would be following the general principles of effective interpersonal conflict management if you answered True to the odd-numbered statements (1, 3, 5, 7, and 9) and False to the even-numbered statements (2, 4, 6, 8, and 10).

What Will You Do? As you think about your responses and read the text discussion, ask yourself what you can do to improve your own conflict management skills.

Win–Lose and Win–Win Strategies

As indicated in the discussion of conflict styles, when you look at interpersonal conflict in terms of winning and losing, you get four basic types: (1) A wins, B loses; (2) A loses, B wins; (3) A loses, B loses; and (4) A wins, B wins.

Obviously, win–win solutions are the most desirable. Perhaps the most important reason is that win–win solutions lead to mutual satisfaction and prevent the resentment that **win–lose strategies** often engender. Looking for and developing **win–win strategies** makes the next conflict less unpleasant; it becomes easier to see the conflict as "solving a problem" rather than as a "fight." Still another benefit of win–win solutions is that they promote mutual face-saving; both parties can feel good about themselves. Finally, people are more likely to abide by the decisions reached in a win–win outcome than they are in win–lose or lose–lose resolutions.

In sum, you can look for solutions in which you or your side wins and the other person or side loses (win–lose solutions). Or you can look for solutions in which you and the other person both win (win–win solutions). Win–win solutions are always better. Too often, however, we fail even to consider the possibility of win–win solutions and what they might be.

Take an interpersonal example: Let's say that I want to spend our money on a new car (my old one is unreliable), but you want to spend it on a vacation (you're exhausted and feel the need for a rest). Through our conflict and its resolution, ideally, we learn what each really wants and may then be able to figure out a way for each of us to get what we want. I might accept a good used car, and you might accept a less expensive vacation. Or we might buy a used car and take an inexpensive road trip. Each of these win–win solutions will satisfy both of us; each of us wins, each of us gets what we wanted.

Take a look at "Conflict Management" at tcbdevito.blogspot.com for some additional suggestions. What management strategies do you find especially effective?

Avoidance and Active Fighting Strategies

Avoidance of conflict may involve actual physical flight; for example, leaving the scene of the conflict (walking out of the apartment or going to another part of the office), falling asleep, or blasting the stereo to drown out all conversation. It may also take the form of emotional or intellectual avoidance, whereby you leave the conflict psychologically by not dealing with the issues raised. Not surprisingly, as avoidance increases, relationship satisfaction decreases (Meeks, Hendrick, & Hendrick, 1998). Sometimes avoidance is a response to demands—a conflict pattern known as *demand–withdrawal*. Here one person makes demands and the other person, unwilling to accede to the demands, withdraws from the interaction (Canary, Cupach, & Messman, 1995; Guerrero, Andersen, & Afifi, 2007; Sagrestano, Heavey, & Christensen, 2006). This pattern is obviously unproductive, but either individual can easily break it—either by not making demands or by not withdrawing and instead participating actively in conflict management.

Although avoidance is an unproductive approach, this does not mean that taking time out to cool off is not a useful first strategy. Sometimes it is. When conflict is waged through e-mail or some social network site, for example, this is an easy-to-use and often effective strategy. By delaying your response until you've had time to think things out more logically and calmly, you'll be better able to respond constructively and to address possible resolutions to the conflict and get the relationship back to a less hostile stage.

Nonnegotiation is a special type of avoidance. Here you refuse to direct any attention to managing the conflict or to listen to the other person's argument. At times, nonnegotiation takes the form of hammering away at your own point of view until the other person gives in.

Another unproductive conflict strategy is the use of silencers. **Silencers** are conflict techniques that literally silence the other individual. Among the wide variety of silencers that exist, one frequently used technique is crying. When a person is unable to deal with a conflict or when winning seems unlikely, he or she may cry and thus silence the other person. Another silencer consists of feigning extreme emotionalism—yelling and screaming and pretending to be losing control. Still another is developing some physical reaction—headaches and shortness of breath are probably the most popular. One of the major problems with silencers is that you can never be certain whether they're strategies to win the argument or real physical reactions to which you should pay attention. Either way, however, the conflict remains unexamined and unresolved.

Instead of avoiding the issues or resorting to nonnegotiation or silencers, consider taking an active role in your interpersonal conflicts. If you wish to resolve conflicts, you need to confront them actively. Involve yourself on both sides of the communication exchange. Be an active participant as a speaker and as a listener; voice your own feelings and listen carefully to your partner's feelings.

An important part of active fighting involves taking responsibility for your thoughts and feelings. For example, when you disagree with your partner or find fault with her or his behavior, take responsibility for these feelings. Say, for example, "I disagree with . . ." or "I don't like it when you. . . ." Avoid statements that deny your responsibility, such as "Everybody thinks you're wrong about . . ." or "Chris thinks you shouldn't. . . ."

Force and Talk Strategies

When confronted with conflict, many people prefer not to deal with the issues but rather to force their position on the other person. The force may be emotional or physical. In either case, however, the issues are avoided, and the person who "wins" is the one who exerts the most force. This is the technique of warring nations, children, and even some normally sensible adults. It seems also to be the technique of those who are dissatisfied with the power they perceive themselves to have in a relationship (Ronfeldt, Kimerling, & Arias, 1998).

In one study more than 50 percent of single and married couples reported that they had experienced physical violence in their relationship. If we add symbolic violence (for example, threatening to hit the other person or throwing something), the percentages are above 60 percent for singles and

G90/G90/ZUMA Press/Newscom

VIEWPOINTS One of the most puzzling findings on violence is that many victims interpret it as a sign of love. For some reason, they see being beaten or verbally abused as a sign that their partner is fully in love with them. Also, many victims blame themselves for the violence instead of blaming their partners (Gelles & Cornell, 1985). Why do you think this is so? What part does force or violence play in conflicts in your own interpersonal relationships?

above 70 percent for marrieds (Marshall & Rose, 1987). In other research 47 percent of a sample of 410 college students reported some experience with violence in a dating relationship (Deal & Wampler, 1986). In most cases the violence was reciprocal—each person in the relationship used violence.

The only real alternative to force is talk. For example, the qualities of openness, positiveness, and empathy are suitable starting points. In addition, be sure to listen actively and openly. This may be especially difficult in conflict situations; tempers may run high, and you may find yourself being attacked or at least disagreed with. Here are some suggestions for talking and listening more effectively in the conflict situation.

- **Act the role of the listener.** Also, think as a listener. Turn off the television, stereo, or computer; face the other person. Devote your total attention to what the other person is saying. Make sure you understand what the person is saying and feeling. One way to make sure is obviously to ask questions. Another way is to paraphrase what the other person is saying and ask for confirmation: "You feel that if we pooled our money and didn't have separate savings accounts, the relationship would be more equitable. Is that the way you feel?"
- **Express your support or empathy** for what the other person is saying and feeling: "I can understand how you feel. I know I control the finances and that can create a feeling of inequality." If appropriate, indicate your agreement: "You're right to be disturbed."
- **State your thoughts and feelings** on the issue as objectively as you can; if you disagree with what the other person said, then say so: "My problem is that when we did have equal access to the finances, you ran up so many bills that we still haven't recovered. To be honest with you, I'm worried the same thing will happen again."

VIEWPOINTS Cultures vary widely in their responses to physical and verbal abuse. In some Asian and Hispanic cultures, for example, the fear of losing face or embarrassing the family is so great that people prefer not to report or reveal abuses. When looking over statistics, it may at first appear that little violence occurs in the families of certain cultures. Yet we know from research that wife beating is quite common in India, Taiwan, and Iran, for example (Counts, Brown, & Campbell, 1992; Hatfield & Rapson, 1996). In much of the United States and in many other cultures as well, such abuse would not be tolerated no matter who was embarrassed or insulted.

AbleStock.com/Thinkstock

Face-Attacking and Face-Enhancing Strategies: Politeness in Conflict

Face-attacking strategies are those that attack a person's positive face (for example, comments that criticize the person's contribution to a relationship or any of the person's abilities) or a person's negative face (for example, making demands on a person's time or resources or comments that attack the person's autonomy). **Face-enhancing strategies** are those that support and confirm a person's positive (praise, a pat on the back, a sincere smile) or negative face (giving the person space and asking rather than demanding), for example.

One popular but destructive face-attacking strategy is **beltlining** (Bach & Wyden, 1968). Much like fighters in a ring, each of us has a "beltline," (here, an emotional one). When you hit below this emotional beltline, you can inflict serious injury. When you hit above the belt, however, the person is able to absorb the blow. With most interpersonal relationships, especially those of long standing, you know where the beltline is. You know, for example, that to hit Kristen or Matt with the inability to have children is to hit below the belt. You know that to hit Jack or Jill with the failure to get a permanent job is to hit below the belt. This type of face-attacking strategy causes all persons involved added problems.

Another such face-attacking strategy is blame. Instead of focusing on a solution to a problem, some members try to affix blame on the other person. Whether true or not, blaming is unproductive; it diverts attention away from the problem and from its potential solution and it creates resentment that is likely to be responded to with additional resentment. The conflict then spirals into personal attacks, leaving the individuals and the relationship worse off than before the conflict was ever addressed.

Strategies that enhance a person's self-image and that acknowledge a person's autonomy will not only be polite, they're likely to be more effective than strategies that attack a person self image and deny a person's autonomy. Even when you get what you want, it's wise to help the other person retain positive face because it makes it less likely that future conflicts will arise (Donahue & Kolt, 1992).

Instead of face-attacking, try face-enhancing strategies:

- Use messages that enhance a person's self-image
- Use messages that acknowledge a person's autonomy
- Compliment the other person even in the midst of a conflict
- Make few demands, respect another's time, give the other person space especially in times of conflict
- Keep blows to areas above the belt
- Avoid blaming the other person
- Express respect for the other's point of view even when it differs greatly from your own

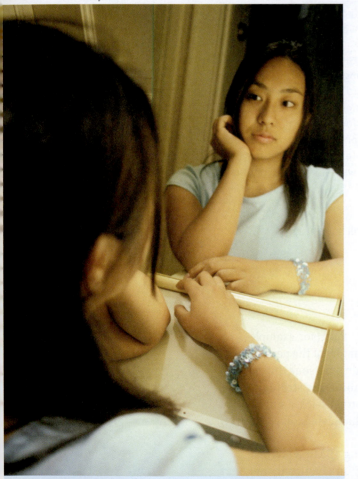

Rhoda Sidney/PhotoEdit

VIEWPOINTS Take a good look at your own conflict behaviors. What changes would you make? What conflict skills and strategies would you seek to integrate into your own interpersonal and small group conflict resolution behavior?

Verbal Aggressiveness and Argumentativeness Strategies

An especially interesting perspective on conflict has emerged from work on verbal aggressiveness and argumentativeness (Infante, 1988; Infante & Rancer, 1982; Infante & Wigley, 1986; Rancer, 1998). Understanding these concepts will help you understand some of the reasons things go wrong and some of the ways in which you can use conflict to actually improve your relationships.

Verbal Aggressiveness **Verbal aggressiveness** is an unproductive conflict strategy, in which one person tries to win an argument by inflicting psychological pain by attacking the other person's self-concept. It's a type of disconfirmation (and the opposite of confirmation) in that it seeks to discredit the individual's view of self.

Character attack, perhaps because it's extremely effective in inflicting psychological pain, is the most popular tactic of verbal aggressiveness. Other tactics include attacking the person's abilities, background, and physical appearance; cursing; teasing; ridiculing; threatening; swearing; and using various nonverbal emblems (Infante, Sabourin, Rudd, & Shannon, 1990).

Some researchers have argued that "unless aroused by verbal aggression, a hostile disposition remains latent in the form of unexpressed anger" (Infante, Chandler, & Rudd, 1989). There is some evidence to show that people in violent relationships are more often verbally aggressive than people in nonviolent relationships (Sutter & Martin, 1998).

Because verbal aggressiveness does not help to resolve conflicts, results in loss of credibility for the person using it, and actually increases the credibility of the target of the aggressiveness, you may wonder why people act aggressively (Infante, Hartley, Martin, Higgins, et al., 1992; Infante, Riddle, Horvath, & Tumlin, 1992; Schrodt, 2003).

Communicating with an affirming style (for example, with smiles, a pleasant facial expression, touching, physical closeness, eye contact, nodding, warm and sincere voice, vocal variety) leads others to perceive less verbal aggression in an interaction than communicating with a nonaffirming style. The assumptions people seem to make is that if your actions are affirming, then your messages are also, and if your actions are nonaffirming, then your messages are also (Infante, Rancer, & Jordan, 1996).

Argumentativeness   Contrary to popular usage, the term **argumentativeness** refers to a quality to be cultivated rather than avoided. Argumentativeness is your willingness to argue for a point of view, your tendency to speak your mind on significant issues. It's the preferred alternative to verbal aggressiveness (Infante & Rancer, 1996; Hample, 2004). Table 1 offers a comparison and summary of verbal aggressiveness and argumentativeness.

Strategies for Cultivating Argumentativeness   The following are some suggestions for cultivating argumentativeness. Ideally, most of these guidelines are already part of your interpersonal behavior (Infante, 1988; Rancer & Avtgis, 2006). If any are not a part of your conflict behavior, consider how you can integrate them.

- Treat disagreements as objectively as possible. Avoid assuming that because someone takes issue with your position or your interpretation, they're attacking you as a person.
- Avoid attacking the other person (rather than the person's arguments), even if this would give you a tactical advantage. Center your arguments on issues rather than personalities.
- Reaffirm the other person's sense of competence. Compliment the other person as appropriate.
- Avoid interrupting. Allow the other person to state her or his position fully before you respond.
- Stress equality, and stress the similarities that you have with the other person. Stress your areas of agreement before attacking the disagreements.
- Express interest in the other person's position, attitude, and point of view.
- Avoid presenting your arguments too emotionally. Avoid using a loud voice or interjecting vulgar expressions, which will prove offensive and eventually ineffective.
- Allow the other person to save face. Never humiliate the other person. Argue politely and respectfully.

INTERPERSONAL CHOICE POINT

Talking Aggressively

Your relationship partner is becoming more and more verbally aggressive and you're having trouble with this new communication pattern. You want your partner to realize that this way of communicating is not productive and may ultimately destroy the relationship. What options do you have for trying to lessen or even eliminate this verbal aggressiveness?

Take a look at "Interpersonal Communication and . . ." at tcbdevito.blogspot.com for a discussion of interpersonal conflict training. Would interpersonal conflict training be useful to people in the profession you're in or hope to enter?

Gerald Holubowicz/Abacusa/Newscom

VIEWPOINTS   Men generally score higher both in argumentativeness and in verbal aggressiveness than women. Men are also more apt to be perceived (by both men and women) as more argumentative and verbally aggressive than women (Nicotera & Rancer, 1994). Why do you think this is so?

TABLE 1 Differences between Verbal Aggressiveness and Argumentativeness

As you can appreciate, there are numerous differences between argumentativeness and verbal aggressiveness. Here are just a few (Infante & Rancer, 1996; Rancer & Atvgis, 2006).

Verbal Aggressiveness	Argumentativeness
Is destructive; the outcomes are negative in a variety of communication situations (interpersonal, group, organizational, family, and intercultural)	Is constructive; the outcomes are positive in a variety of communication situations (interpersonal, group, organizational, family, and intercultural)
Leads to relationship dissatisfaction, not surprising for a strategy that aims to attack another's self-concept	Leads to relationship satisfaction
May lead to relationship violence	May prevent relationship violence especially in domestic relationships
Damages organizational life and demoralizes workers on varied levels	Enhances organizational life; for example, subordinates prefer supervisors who encourage argumentativeness
Prevents meaningful parent–child communication and makes corporal punishment more likely	Enhances parent–child communication and enables parents to gain greater compliance
Decreases the user's credibility, in part because it's seen as a tactic to discredit the opponent rather than address the argument	Increases the user's credibility; argumentatives are seen as trustworthy, committed, and dynamic
Decreases the user's power of persuasion	Increases the user's power of persuasion in varied communication contexts; argumentatives are more likely to be seen as leaders

Summary

Use your smartphone or tablet device (or log on to mycommunicationlab.com) to hear an audio summary of this chapter.

This chapter examined principles of interpersonal conflict, conflict management stages, and some of the popular productive and unproductive conflict strategies.

Preliminaries to Interpersonal Conflict

1. Interpersonal conflict is a disagreement between connected individuals who each want something that is incompatible with what the other wants.
2. Interpersonal conflict is neither good nor bad; but, depending on how the disagreements are resolved, the conflict can strengthen or weaken a relationship.
3. Interpersonal conflicts arise from a variety of issues, including intimacy issues such as sex and affection, power issues such as possessiveness or lack of equity, and personal flaws issues such as drinking or smoking.

Principles of Interpersonal Conflict

4. Interpersonal conflict is inevitable; it's a fact of all relationships.
5. Conflict may have both negative and positive effects.
6. Conflict may focus on content (matters external to the relationship) or on relationship issues (matters integral to the nature of the relationship).
7. Conflict may be pursued with different styles, each of which has different consequences.
8. Conflict and the strategies used to resolve it are heavily influenced by culture.

Conflict Management Stages

9. Before the conflict: Try to fight in private, fight when you're ready, know what you're fighting about, and fight about problems that can be solved.
10. Define the conflict: Define the content and relationship issues in specific terms, avoiding gunnysacking and

mind reading; and try to empathize with the other person.

11. Examine the possible solutions: Try to identify as many solutions as possible, look for win–win solutions, and carefully weigh the costs and rewards of each solution.

12. Test the solution mentally and in practice to see if it works.

13. Evaluate the tested solution from a variety of perspectives.

14. Accept the solution and integrate it into your behavior. Or reject the solution and begin again; for example, define the problem differently or look in other directions for possible solutions.

15. After the conflict: Learn something from the conflict, keep the conflict in perspective, attack your negative feelings, and increase the exchange of rewards.

Conflict Management Strategies

16. Seek out win–win solutions.

17. Become an active participant in the conflict; don't avoid the issues or the arguments of the other person.

18. Use talk to discuss the issues rather than trying to force the other person to accept your position.

19. Try to enhance the face, the self-esteem, of the person you're arguing with; avoid strategies that may cause the other person to lose face.

20. Argue the issues, focusing as objectively as possible on the points of disagreement; avoid being verbally aggressive or attacking the other person.

Key Terms

accommodating style	collaborating style	face-attacking strategies	nonnegotiation
argumentativeness	competing style	face-enhancing	silencers
avoidance	compromising style	strategies	verbal aggressiveness
avoiding style	conflict styles	gunnysacking	win–lose strategies
beltlining	equality	interpersonal conflict	win–win strategies

MyCommunicationLab Explorations

MyCommunicationLab®

Communication Choice Points

Revisit the chapter-opening video, "Conflict Strategies." Recall that Pat and Andi are a dating couple who have enjoyed entering a Fantasy Football league together. But now that they've won, they need to resolve their conflict about how to spend their winnings. In the video "Conflict Strategies," you can witness the consequences for the relationship of the various conflict styles they choose.

Log on to mycommunicationlab.com to view the video for this chapter, "Conflict Strategies," and then answer the related discussion questions.

Additional Resources

These experiences focus on interpersonal conflict, especially on understanding the nature of conflict and how you can more effectively resolve and manage conflict.

1 Analyzing a Conflict Episode provides an opportunity to think critically about the messages used in a conflict interaction. **2** Dealing with Conflict Starters looks at some of the messages that often begin conflicts. **3** Generating Win–Win Solutions provides opportunities to experiment with strategies that can make conflict and its resolution more effective.

Glossary of Interpersonal Communication Concepts and Skills

Glossary of Interpersonal Communication Concepts and Skills

The definitions for interpersonal communication concepts are printed in roman type. *The skill components for selected terms are printed in italic type.*

Abstract terms. Words that refer to concepts and ideas that have no physical dimensions (friendship, value, fear). *See also* **concrete terms.** *Use both abstract and concrete language when describing or explaining.*

Ableism. Discrimination against people with disabilities.

Accommodation. The process of adjusting your communication patterns to those with whom you're interacting. *Accommodate to the speaking style of your listeners in moderation; too much mirroring of the other's style may appear manipulative.*

Accommodating style. A conflict management style where you sacrifice your own needs for the sake of the needs of the other person.

Acculturation. The process by which one culture is modified or changed through contact with or exposure to another culture.

Active listening. The process by which a listener expresses his or her understanding of the speaker's total message, including the verbal and nonverbal, the thoughts and feelings. *Be an active listener: Paraphrase the speaker's meaning, express understanding of the speaker's feelings, and ask questions when necessary.*

Adaptors. Nonverbal behaviors that, when engaged in, either in private or in public, serve some kind of need and occur in their entirety—for example, scratching one's head until the itch is relieved. *Generally, avoid adaptors; they may make you appear uncomfortable or ill at ease.*

Adjustment (principle of). The principle of verbal interaction that claims that effective communication depends on the extent to which communicators share the same system of signals.

Advice. Messages that tell another person what he or she should do.

Affect displays. Movements of the facial area that convey emotional meaning, such as anger, fear, and surprise.

Affinity-seeking strategies. Behaviors designed to increase interpersonal attractiveness.

Affirmation. The communication of support and approval.

Agape. A love that is compassionate and selfless.

Ageism. Discrimination based on age, usually against older people.

Ageist language. Language that discriminates based on the age of the person.

Aggression. *See* **verbal aggression.**

Allness. The illogical assumption that all can be known or said about a given person, issue, object, or event. *Avoid allness statements; they invariably misstate the reality and will often offend the other person.*

Alter-adaptors. Body movements you make in response to your current interactions—for example, crossing your arms over your chest when someone unpleasant approaches or moving closer to someone you like.

Altercasting. Placing a person in a specific role for a specific purpose and asking that he or she assume the perspective of this specific role; for example, "As a professor of communication, what do you think of . . ."

Ambiguity. The condition in which a message or relationship may be interpreted as having more than one meaning.

Ambiguity tolerance. A characteristic of culture referring to the degree to which members of a culture feel comfortable with ambiguity and uncertainty.

Anger. A generally unproductive emotion of strong feelings of displeasure, annoyance, or hostility.

Anger management. The methods and techniques by which anger is controlled and managed. *Calm down as best you can; then consider your communication options and the relevant communication skills for expressing your feelings.*

Apology. An expression of regret or sorrow for having done what you did or for what happened.

Apprehension. *See* **communication apprehension.**

Argumentativeness. A willingness to argue for a point of view, to speak one's mind. Distinguished from **verbal aggressiveness.** *Avoid aggressiveness (attacking the other person's* *self-concept); instead, focus logically on the issues, emphasize finding solutions, and work to ensure that what is said will result in positive self-feelings for both individuals.*

Artifactual communication. Messages that are conveyed by objects made by human hands. Art, color, clothing, jewelry, hairstyle, and smell would be examples of artifactual messages. *Use artifacts to communicate desired messages and avoid those that may communicate negative or unwanted meanings.*

Assertiveness. A willingness to stand up for your rights but with respect for the rights of others. *Increase assertiveness by analyzing the assertive messages of others, rehearsing assertive messages, and communicating assertively. In communicating assertively: Describe the problem, say how the problem affects you, propose solutions, confirm your understanding, and reflect on your own assertiveness.*

Assimilation. A process of message distortion in which messages are reworked to conform to your own attitudes, prejudices, needs, and values. *See also* **cultural assimilation.**

Association. A transitory type of friendship, often described as a friendly relationship.

Asynchronous communication. Communication in which the individuals send and receive messages at different times (as in e-mail communication). Opposed to **synchronous communication.**

Attention. The process of responding to a stimulus or stimuli; usually some consciousness of responding is implied.

Attitude. A predisposition to respond for or against an object, person, or position.

Attraction. The process by which one individual is emotionally drawn to another and finds that person satisfying to be with.

Attraction theory. A theory holding that you develop relationships on the basis of three major factors: attractiveness (physical appearance and personality), proximity, and similarity.

Attractiveness. A person's visual appeal and/or pleasantness in personality.

Attribution. The processes by which we assign causation or motivation to a person's behavior.

Attribution theory. A theory concerned with the process of assigning causation or motivation to a person's behavior.

Avoidance. An unproductive conflict strategy in which you take mental or physical flight from the actual conflict.

Avoiding style. A conflict management style that suggests that you are relatively unconcerned with your own or with the other's needs or desires.

Back-channeling cues. Responses a listener makes to a speaker (while the speaker is speaking) but which do not ask for the speaking role; for example, interjections such as "I understand" or "You said what?" *Generally, give backchanneling cues to show that you're listening actively.*

Backhanded compliment. An insult masquerading as a compliment.

Barriers to intercultural communication. Physical or psychological factors that prevent or hinder effective communication.

Behavioral synchrony. The similarity in the behavior (usually nonverbal; for example, postural stance or facial expressions) of two persons; generally taken as an indicator of liking.

Belief. Confidence in the existence or truth of something; conviction.

Beltlining. An unproductive conflict strategy in which one person hits the other at a vulnerable level—at the level at which the other person cannot withstand the blow.

Blame. An unproductive conflict strategy in which we attribute the cause of the conflict to the other person or devote our energies to discovering who is the cause, avoiding talking about the issues at hand. *Avoid it; generally, it diverts attention from solving the problem and only serves to alienate the other person.*

Blended emotions. Emotions that are combinations of the primary emotions; for example, disappointment is a blend of surprise and sadness.

Boundary marker. A marker that sets boundaries around or divides one person's territory from another's—for example, a fence.

Breadth. The number of topics about which individuals in a relationship communicate.

Bullying. A pattern of abusive behavior (verbal or nonverbal) repeatedly committed by one person (or group) against another.

Bypassing. A pattern of miscommunication that occurs when the speaker and the listener miss each other with their meanings.

Captology. The study of the ways in which electronic means of communication influence people's attitudes and behaviors.

Censorship. Restrictions imposed on a person's right to produce, distribute, or receive various communications.

Central marker. A marker or item that is placed in a territory to reserve it for a specific person—for example, the sweater thrown over a library chair to signal that the chair is taken.

Certainty. An attitude of closed-mindedness that creates defensiveness among communicators. Opposed to **provisionalism.**

Channel. The vehicle or medium through which signals are sent; for example, the vocal–auditory channel. *Assess your channel options (for example, face-to-face, e-mail, leaving a voicemail message) before communicating important messages.*

Cherishing behaviors. Small behaviors you enjoy receiving from others, especially from your relational partner—for example, a kiss before you leave for work.

Choice points. Moments when you have to make a choice as to whom you communicate with, what you say, what you don't say, how you phrase what you want to say, and so on.

Chronemics. The study of the communicative nature of time, of how a person's or a culture's treatment of time reveals something about the person or culture. Often divided into psychological and cultural time.

Civil inattention. Polite ignoring of others (after a brief sign of awareness) so as not to invade their privacy.

Cliché. An expression whose overuse calls attention to itself.

Closed-mindedness. An unwillingness to receive certain communication messages.

Code. A set of symbols used to translate a message from one form to another.

Coercive power. Power derived from an individual's ability to punish or to remove rewards from another person.

Cognitive labeling theory. A theory of emotions that holds that emotional feelings begin with the occurrence of an event; you respond physiologically to the event, then you interpret the arousal (you in effect decide what it is you're feeling), and then you experience (give a name to) the emotion.

Collaborating. style A conflict management style in which your concern is with both your own and the other person's needs.

Collectivist culture. A culture in which the group's goals are given greater importance than the individual's and in which, for example, benevolence, tradition, and conformity are given special emphasis. Opposed to **individualist culture.**

Color communication. The use of color to communicate different meanings; each culture seems to define the meanings colors communicate somewhat differently.

Communication. (1) The process or act of communicating; (2) the actual message or messages sent and received; (3) the study of the processes involved in the sending and receiving of messages.

Communication accommodation theory. A theory of communication holding that conversationalists adjust to (or accommodate to) the speaking styles of each other.

Communication apprehension. Fear or anxiety of communicating. *To reduce anxiety, acquire necessary communication skills and experiences, focus on prior successes, reduce unpredictability, and put apprehension in perspective.*

Communicology. The study of communication, particularly the subsection concerned with human communication.

Comparison level. A general idea of the kinds of rewards and profits that you feel you ought to get out of a relationship.

Competence. "Language competence" is a speaker's ability to use the language; it is a knowledge of the elements and rules of the language. "Communication competence" generally refers both to the knowledge of communication and also to the ability to engage in communication effectively.

Competing style. A conflict management style that represents great concern for your own needs and desires and little for those of others.

Complementarity. A principle of attraction holding that you are attracted by qualities that you do not possess or wish to possess, and to people who are opposite or different from yourself. Opposed to **similarity.**

Complementary relationship. A relationship in which the behavior of one person serves as the stimulus for the complementary behavior of the other; in complementary relationships, behavioral differences are maximized.

Compliance-gaining strategies. Behaviors designed to gain the agreement of others, to persuade others to do as you wish.

Compliance-resisting strategies. Behaviors directed at resisting the persuasive attempts of others.

Compliment. A message of praise, flattery, or congratulations.

Compromising style. A conflict management style that is in the middle; there's some concern for your own needs and some concern for the other's needs.

Computer-mediated communication. Communication between individuals that takes place through computer; usually refers to, for example, e-mail, chat groups, instant messaging, multiplayer video games.

Concrete terms. Words that refer to objects, people, and happenings that you perceive with your senses of sight, smell, touch, hearing, or taste. *See also* **abstract terms.**

Confidence. A quality of interpersonal effectiveness (and a factor in interpersonal power); a comfortable, at-ease feeling in interpersonal communication situations.

Confirmation. A communication pattern that acknowledges another person's presence and indicates an acceptance of this person, this person's self-definition, and the relationship as defined or viewed by this other person. Opposed to **rejection** and **disconfirmation.** *When you wish to be confirming, acknowledge (verbally and/or nonverbally) others in your group and their contributions.*

Conflict. A disagreement or difference of opinion; a form of competition in which one person tries to bring a rival to surrender; a situation in which one person's behaviors are directed at preventing something or at interfering with or harming another individual. *See also* **interpersonal conflict.** *Engage in interpersonal conflict actively; be appropriately revealing, see the situation from your partner's perspective, and listen to your partner. Approach conflict with an understanding of the cultural and gender differences in attitudes toward what constitutes conflict and toward how it should be pursued.*

Conflict styles. The approach to conflict resolution; for example, competing, avoiding, accommodating, collaborating, and compromising. *Chose your conflict style carefully; each style has consequences. In relationship conflict, look for win–win (collaborating) solutions rather than solutions in which one person wins and the other loses (competing, avoiding, or accommodating).*

Conformity-orientation. The degree to which family members express similar or dissimilar attitudes, values, and beliefs.

Congruence. A condition in which both verbal and nonverbal behaviors reinforce each other.

Connotation. The feeling or emotional aspect of a word's meaning; generally viewed as consisting of evaluation (for example, good–bad), potency (strong–weak), and activity (fast–slow) dimensions. Opposed to **denotation.** *Clarify your connotative meanings if you have any concern that your listeners might misunderstand you; as a listener, ask questions if you have doubts about the speaker's connotations.*

Consensual families. Families who encourage open communication and agreement; high in conversation and high in conformity.

Consistency. A tendency to maintain balance in your perception of messages or people; because of this process, you tend to see what you expect to see and to be uncomfortable when your perceptions run contrary to expectations.

Contact. The first stage in relationship development, consisting of perceptual contact (you see or hear the person) and interactional contact (you talk with the person).

Content and relationship dimensions. Two aspects to which messages may refer: the world external to both speaker and listener (content) and the connections existing between the individuals who are interacting (relationship). *Listen to both the content and the relationship aspects of messages, distinguish between them, and respond to both. Analyze conflict messages in terms of content and relationship dimensions, and respond to each accordingly.*

Context of communication. The physical, psychological, social, and temporal environment in which communication takes place. *Adjust your messages to the physical, cultural, social–psychological, and temporal context.*

Contrast, principle of. A principle of perception that holds that items that are very distinct from each other are seen as separate and not belonging to the same group.

Control. An approach to interpersonal relationships in which one person tries to control what the other person does.

Conversation. Two-person communication, usually following five stages: opening, feedforward, business, feedback, and closing.

Conversation-orientation. The degree to which family members can speak their mind.

Conversational management. The management of the way in which messages are exchanged in conversation; consists of procedures for opening, maintaining, repairing, and closing conversations.

Conversational maxims. Principles that participants in conversation follow to ensure that the goal of the conversation is achieved. *Follow (generally) the basic maxims of conversation, such as the maxims of quantity, quality, relations, manner, and politeness.*

Conversational turns. The process of passing the speaker and listener roles back and forth during conversation. *Maintain relatively short conversational turns; after taking your turn, pass the speaker's turn to another person nonverbally or verbally. Respond to both the verbal and the nonverbal conversational turn-taking cues given you by others, and make your own cues clear to others.*

Conversational rules. The socially accepted ways of engaging in conversation. *Observe the general rules for conversation (for example, keeping speaking turns relatively short and avoiding interrupting), but break them when there seems logical reason to do so.*

Cooperation. An interpersonal process by which individuals work together for a common end; the pooling of efforts to produce a mutually desired outcome.

Cooperation (principle of). In conversation, an implicit agreement between speaker and listener to cooperate in trying to understand each other.

Costs. Anything that you normally try to avoid—things you consider unpleasant or difficult. *See also* **rewards.**

Credibility. The degree to which people see a person as believable; competence, character, and charisma (dynamism) are major factors in credibility.

Credibility strategies. Techniques by which you seek to establish your competence, character, and charisma. *Use these to establish your credibility but do so in moderation; too many will make you appear to be bragging.*

Critical listening. Listening with an open mind.

Critical thinking. The process of logically evaluating reasons and evidence and reaching a judgment on the basis of this analysis.

Cultural assimilation. The process by which people leave behind their culture of origin and take on the values and beliefs of another culture; as when, for example, immigrants give up their native culture to become members of their new adopted culture.

Cultural display. Sign that communicates a person's cultural identification, such as clothing or religious jewelry.

Cultural display rules. Rules that identify what are and what are not appropriate forms of expression for members of the culture.

Cultural identifiers. The terms used to talk about cultural identifications; for example, race or religion. *Use cultural identifiers that are sensitive to the desires of others; when appropriate, make clear the cultural identifiers you prefer.*

Cultural rules. Rules that are specific to a given culture.

Cultural sensitivity. An attitude and way of behaving in which you're aware of and acknowledge cultural differences. *Cultivate cultural sensitivity by learning about other cultures and interacting with people who are culturally different.*

Culture. The lifestyle of a group of people; their values, beliefs, artifacts, ways of behaving, and ways of communicating. Culture includes everything that members of a social group have produced and developed—their language, ways of thinking, art, laws, and religion—and that is transmitted from one generation to another through communication rather than genes. *Look at cultural differences not as deviations or deficiencies but as the differences they are. Recognizing different ways of doing things, however, does not necessarily mean accepting them. Communicate with an understanding that culture influences communication in all its forms. Increase your cultural sensitivity by learning about different cultures, recognizing and facing your fears, recognizing relevant differences, and becoming conscious of the cultural rules of other cultures.*

Culture shock. The reactions people experience at being in a culture very different from their own and from what they are used to.

Cultural time. The meanings given to the ways time is treated in a particular culture.

Date. An extensional device used to emphasize the notion of constant change and symbolized by a subscript: For example,

John Smith$_{2000}$ is not John Smith$_{2007}$. *Date your statements to avoid thinking of the world as static and unchanging. Reflect the inevitability of change in your messages.*

Decoder. Something that takes a message in one form (for example, sound waves) and translates it into another form (for example, nerve impulses) from which meaning can be formulated. In human communication the decoder is the auditory mechanism; in electronic communication the decoder is, for example, the telephone earpiece. Decoding is the process of extracting a message from a code—for example, translating speech sounds into nerve impulses. *See also* **encoder.**

Defensiveness. An attitude of an individual or an atmosphere in a group characterized by threats, fear, and domination; messages evidencing evaluation, control, strategy, neutrality, superiority, and certainty are thought to lead to defensiveness. Opposed to **supportiveness.**

Delayed reaction. A reaction that a person consciously delays while analyzing the situation and evaluating possible choices for communication.

Denial. One of the obstacles to the expression of emotion; the process by which you deny your emotions to yourself or to others.

Denotation. The objective or descriptive aspect of a word's meaning; the meaning you'd find in a dictionary. Opposed to **connotation.**

Depenetration. A reversal of penetration; a condition in which the breadth and depth of a relationship decrease.

Depth. The degree to which the inner personality—the inner core of an individual—is penetrated in interpersonal interaction.

Deterioration. In the stage model of relationships, the stage during which the connecting bonds between the partners weaken and the partners begin drifting apart.

Dialogue. A form of communication in which each person is both speaker and listener; communication characterized by involvement, concern, and respect for the other person. Opposed to **monologue.**

Direct speech. Speech in which the speaker's intentions are stated clearly and directly.

Disclaimer. Statement that asks the listener to receive what you say without its reflecting negatively on you. *Use disclaimers if you feel you might be misunderstood. But avoid them when they're not necessary; too many disclaimers can make you appear unprepared or unwilling to state an opinion.*

Disconfirmation. The process by which someone ignores or denies the right of another individual even to define himself or herself. Opposed to **rejection** and **confirmation.** *Generally, avoid disconfirmation along with sexist, heterosexist, racist, and ageist language, which is insulting and invariably creates communication barriers.*

Display rule. Rule or custom (of a culture or an organization) that governs what is and what is not permissible communication.

Disqualifiers. Statements that claim some lack of responsibility and signal a lack of competence and a degree of uncertainty.

Dissolution. In the stage model of relationships, the termination or end of the relationship. *In dealing with relationship dissolution, break the loneliness–depression cycle, take time out, bolster self-esteem, seek support from nourishing others, and avoid repeating negative patterns.*

Downward communication. Communication sent from the higher levels of a hierarchy to the lower levels—for example, messages sent by managers to workers or from deans to faculty members.

Dyadic coalition. A two-person group formed from some larger group to achieve a particular goal.

Dyadic communication. Two-person communication.

Dyadic consciousness. An awareness on the part of the participants that an interpersonal relationship or pairing exists between them; distinguished from situations in which two individuals are together but do not see themselves as a unit or twosome.

Dyadic effect. The tendency for the behaviors of one person to stimulate similar behaviors in the other interactant; often refers to the tendency of one person's self-disclosures to prompt the other also to self-disclose.

Dyadic primacy. The significance or centrality of the two-person group, even when there are many more people interacting.

Dyssemia. A condition in which an individual is unable to appropriately read the nonverbal messages of others or to communicate his or her own meanings nonverbally.

Earmarker. A marker that identifies an item as belonging to a specific person—for example, a nameplate on a desk or initials on an attaché case. *Observe the markers of others; they often reveal a person's thinking about his or her territory.*

Effect. The outcome or consequence of an action or behavior; communication is assumed always to have some effect.

Emblems. Nonverbal behaviors that directly translate words or phrases—for example, the signs for OK and peace.

Emotion. The feelings we have—for example, our feelings of guilt, anger, or love.

Emotional appeals. Persuasive tactics directed at arousing emotional responses.

Emoticon. Visual representation of emotion produced by a short sequence of keyboard characters.

Emotional abuse. Behavior that is humiliating, isolating, or overly critical. *Avoid it.*

Emotional communication. The expression of feelings—for example, feelings of guilt, happiness, or sorrow. *Identify and describe emotions (both positive and negative) clearly and specifically. Learn the vocabulary of emotional expression. Communicate emotions effectively: (1) confront the obstacles to emotional expression; (2) describe your feelings, identifying the reasons behind them; (3) anchor feelings to the present; and (4) own your feelings and messages.*

Emotional contagion. The process by which the strong emotions of one person are taken on by another person; the assumption that, like the flu, emotions may be contagious.

Emotional display. Expressing emotions and interpreting the emotions of others in light of the cultural rules dictating what is and what isn't "appropriate."

Emotionality in interpersonal communication. Recognizing the inevitable emotionality in your thoughts and feelings, and including emotion as appropriate in your verbal and nonverbal messages.

Empathic listening. Listening to understand what a person means and what a person is feeling.

Empathy. A quality of interpersonal effectiveness that involves sharing others' feelings; an ability to feel or perceive things from others' points of view. *Communicate empathy when appropriate: Resist evaluating the person, focus on the person, express active involvement through facial expressions and gestures, reflect back the feelings you think are being expressed, self-disclose, and address mixed messages.*

Encoder. Something that takes a message in one form (for example, nerve impulses) and translates it into another form (for example, sound waves). In human communication the encoder is the speaking mechanism; in electronic communication the encoder is, for example, the telephone mouthpiece. Encoding is the process of putting a message into a code—for example, translating nerve impulses into speech sounds. *See also* **decoder.**

Enculturation. The process by which culture is transmitted from one generation to another.

E-prime. A form of the language that omits the verb "to be" except when used as an auxiliary or in statements of existence. *Be careful of the verb "to be"; use it with an understanding of how it might incorporate illogical assumptions.*

Equality. An attitude that recognizes that each individual in a communication interaction is equal, that no one is superior to any other; encourages supportiveness. Opposed to **superiority.**

Equilibrium theory. A theory of proxemics holding that intimacy and physical closeness are positively related; as a relationship becomes more intimate, the individuals will maintain shorter distances between themselves.

Equity theory. A theory claiming that people experience relational satisfaction when there is an equal distribution of rewards and costs between the two persons in the relationship.

Equivocation. A deceptive message that is purposely ambiguous and designed to lead people to think something different from your intention. *You sure made a statement* instead of *You made a complete fool of yourself!*

Eros. A type of love that emphasizes beauty and sexuality.

Et cetera (etc.). An extensional device used to emphasize the notion of infinite complexity; because you can never know all about anything, any statement about the world or an event must end with an explicit or implicit "etc." *Use an implicit, or sometimes an explicit, etc. to remind yourself and others that there is more to say.*

Ethics. The branch of philosophy that deals with the rightness or wrongness of actions; the study of moral values; in communication, the morality of message behavior.

Ethnic identity. The commitment to the beliefs and philosophy of one's culture; the degree to which a person identifies with his or her cultural group.

Ethnocentrism. The tendency to see others and their behaviors through your own cultural filters, often as distortions of your own behaviors; the tendency to evaluate the values and beliefs of your own culture more positively than those of another culture. *Recognize your own ethnocentric thinking and be aware of how it influences your verbal and nonverbal messages.*

Euphemism. A polite word or phrase used to substitute for some taboo or less polite term or phrase.

Evaluation. A process whereby we place a value on some person, object, or event.

Exaggeration. A common deceptive message where you, for example, lead people to believe that, for example, you earn more money than you do or that your grades are better than they are, or that your relationship is more satisfying than it really is.

Excuse. An explanation designed to lessen the negative consequences of something done or said. *Repair conversational problems by offering excuses that demonstrate understanding, acknowledge your responsibility, acknowledge your regret, request forgiveness, and make clear that this will never happen again.*

Expectancy violations theory. A theory of proxemics holding that people have a certain expectancy for space relationships. When that is violated (say, a person stands too close to you or a romantic partner maintains abnormally large distances from you), the relationship comes into clearer focus and you wonder why this "normal distance" is being violated.

Expert power. Power that a person has because others believe the individual to have expertise or special knowledge.

Expressiveness. A quality of interpersonal effectiveness that consists of genuine involvement in speaking and listening, conveyed verbally and nonverbally. *Communicate expressiveness and active involvement by using active listening, addressing mixed messages, using I-messages, and using appropriate variations in paralanguage and gestures.*

Extensional devices. Linguistic devices proposed by Alfred Korzybski to make language a more accurate means for talking about the world. The extensional devices include et cetera, date, and index. *Use them; they help make language more descriptive of the world as we know it.*

Extensional orientation. A point of view in which primary consideration is given to the world of experience and only secondary consideration is given to labels. Opposed to **intensional orientation.**

Face-attacking conflict strategies. Strategies that attack a person's positive face (for example, comments that criticize the person's contribution to a relationship or the person's ability) or a person's negative face (for example, making demands on a person's time or resources that attack the person's autonomy). *Avoid using these strategies; they're likely to cause additional conflict and resentment.*

Face-enhancing strategies. Strategies that support and confirm a person's positive face (praise, a pat on the back, a sincere smile) or negative face (giving the person space and asking rather than demanding), for example. *Use strategies that allow others, even your opponents in conflict, to save face.*

Facial feedback hypothesis. The hypothesis or theory that your facial expressions can produce physiological and emotional effects via a feedback mechanism.

Facial management techniques. Techniques used to mask certain emotions and to emphasize others; for example, intensifying your expression of happiness to make a friend feel good about a promotion. *Use these in moderation; too much excitement, for example, can appear phony.*

Fact–inference confusion. A misevaluation in which a person makes an inference, regards it as a fact, and acts upon it as if it were a fact. *Distinguish facts (verifiably true past events) from inferences (guesses or hypotheses), and act on inferences with tentativeness.*

Factual statement. A statement made by the observer after observation and limited to what is observed. Opposed to **inferential statement.**

Family. A group of people with defined roles, recognition of mutual responsibilities, a shared history and future, shared living space (usually), and rules for communicating.

Fear appeal. The appeal to fear to persuade an individual or group of individuals to believe or to act in a certain way.

Feedback. Information that is given back to the source. Feedback may come from the source's own messages (as when you hear what you're saying) or from the receiver(s)—in forms such as applause, yawning, puzzled looks, questions, letters to the editor of a newspaper, or increased or decreased subscriptions to a magazine. *See also* **negative feedback, positive feedback.** *Listen to both verbal and nonverbal feedback—from yourself and from others—and use these cues to help you adjust your messages.*

Feedforward. Information that is sent before a regular message, telling the listener something about what is to follow; messages that are prefatory to more central messages. *Use feedforward when you feel your listener needs background or when you want to ease into a particular topic, such as bad news.*

Feminine culture. A culture that encourages both men and women to be modest, oriented to maintaining the quality of life, and tender. Feminine cultures emphasize the quality of life and so socialize their people to be modest and to emphasize close interpersonal relationships. Opposed to **masculine culture.**

Flexibility. The ability to adjust communication strategies and skills on the basis of the unique situation. *Because no two communication situations are identical, because everything is in a state of flux, and because everyone is different, cultivate flexibility and adjust your communication to the unique situation.*

Flirting. A type of communication in which you signal romantic interest.

Force. An unproductive conflict strategy in which you try to win an argument by emotionally or physically overpowering the other person—either by threat or by actual behavior. *Avoid it; it attacks a person's negative face and almost invariably will create resentment.*

Formal time. Temporal divisions that are measured objectively, such as seconds, minutes, hours, days, weeks, months, and years.

Friendship. An interpersonal relationship between two persons that is mutually productive, established and maintained through perceived mutual free choice, and characterized by mutual positive regard. *Establish friendships to help serve such needs as utility, ego support, stimulation, and security. At the same time, seek to serve your friends' similar needs.*

Fundamental attribution error. The tendency to overvalue and overweight the contribution of internal factors (i.e., a person's personality) to behavior, and to undervalue and underweight the contribution of external factors (i.e., the situation the person is in or the surrounding events). *Avoid the fundamental attribution error, whereby you attribute someone's behavior solely to internal factors while minimizing or ignoring situational forces.*

Gender. The cultural roles of "masculine" and "feminine" that are learned from one's culture. *See also* **sex.**

Gender display rules. The cultural rules that identify what are appropriate and what are not appropriate forms of expression for men and for women.

General semantics. The study of the relationships among language, thought, and behavior.

Gobbledygook. Overly complex language that fails to communicate meanings clearly and specifically. *When you suspect gobbledygook is being used to confuse rather than clarify, ask for simplification.*

Gossip. Oral or written communication about someone not present, some third party, usually about matters that are private to this third party. *Generally, avoid it; it's likely to make others see you more negatively.*

Grapevine messages. Organizational messages that don't follow any of the formal lines of communication established in an organization; rather, they cross organizational lines. *Listen carefully to these messages; they often contain crucial information.*

Gunnysacking. An unproductive conflict strategy of storing up grievances—as if in a gunnysack—and holding them in readiness to dump on the other person in the conflict. *Avoid it; it leads you away from considering a workable solution to a problem.*

Halo effect. The tendency to generalize a person's virtue or expertise from one area to other areas. *Beware of this tendency; it can lead you to misperceive a situation or person.*

Haptics. The study of touch or tactile communication.

Hesitations. Verbal expressions such as "er" or "ah" that signal a lack of preparation and certainty.

Heterosexism. Negative attitudes and beliefs about gay men and lesbians; the belief that all sexual behavior that is not heterosexual is unnatural and deserving of criticism and condemnation.

Heterosexist language. Language that denigrates lesbians and gay men. *Avoid it; it will make you appear a bigot or, at best, ill-informed.*

High-ambiguity tolerant cultures. Cultures that are accepting of ambiguity and do not feel threatened by unknown situations; uncertainty is a normal part of life, and people accept it as it comes.

High-context culture. A culture in which much of the information in communication messages is left implied; it's "understood." Much information is considered to be in the context or in the person rather than explicitly coded in the verbal messages. Collectivist cultures are generally high context. Opposed to **low-context culture.** *Adjust your messages and your listening in light of the differences between high- and low-context cultures.*

High-power distance culture. Cultures in which power is concentrated in the hands of a few, and there's a great difference between the power held by these people and the power of the ordinary citizen. *See* **low-power distance culture.**

Home field advantage. The increased power that comes from being in your own territory.

Home territory. Territory in which an individual has a sense of intimacy and over which he or she exercises control—for example, a teacher's office.

Hostile environment harassment. A type of sexual harassment in which verbal and nonverbal messages about sex make a worker uncomfortable.

Identity management. *See* **impression management.**

Illustrators. Nonverbal behaviors that accompany and literally illustrate verbal messages—for example, upward movements of the head and hand that accompany the verbal "It's up there."

Image-confirming strategies. Techniques you use to communicate or to confirm your self-image, the image you want others to see.

I-messages. Messages in which the speaker accepts responsibility for personal thoughts and behaviors and states his or her point of view explicitly. Opposed to ***you*-messages.** *Use I-messages when communicating your feelings; take responsibility for your own feelings rather than attributing them to others.*

Immediacy. A quality of interpersonal effectiveness that conveys a sense of contact and togetherness, a feeling of interest in and liking for the other person. *Maintain immediacy through close physical distances and eye contact and by smiling, using the other person's name, and focusing on the other's remarks.*

Immediacy strategies. Steategies that connect you and another person.

Impression formation. The process by which you perceive another person and ultimately come to some kind of evaluation or interpretation of this person.

Impression management. The process you go through to communicate the impression you want the other person to have of you. Some writers use the term "self-presentation" or "identity management."

Inclusion (principle of). The principle of verbal interaction holding that all members should be a part of (included in) the interaction.

Independent couples. Couples for whom the relationship is important, but never more important than each person's individual identity.

Index. An extensional device symbolized by a subscript and used to emphasize the assumption that no two things are the same; for example, even though two people may both be politicians, politician1$_{[Smith]}$ is not politician2$_{[Jones]}$. *Use the index to remind yourself that even though people are covered by the same label, they are each individuals.*

Indirect speech. Speech that hides the speaker's true intentions; speech in which requests and observations are made indirectly. *Use indirect messages when a more direct style might prove insulting or offensive, but be aware that indirect messages also may create misunderstanding.*

Indiscrimination. A misevaluation that results when you categorize people, events, or objects into a particular class and respond to them only as members of the class; a failure to recognize that each individual is unique. *Treat each situation and each person as unique (when possible) even when they're covered by the same label. Index key concepts.*

Individualist culture. A culture in which the individual's rather than the group's goals and preferences are given greater importance. Opposed to **collectivist culture.** *Adjust your messages and your listening with an awareness of differences between individualist and collectivist cultures.*

Indulgence. A cultural orientation that emphasizes the gratification of desires and a focus on having fun and enjoying life. Opposed to **restraint.**

Inevitability. A principle of communication holding that communication cannot be avoided; all behavior in an interactional setting is communication.

Inferential statement. A statement that can be made by anyone, is not limited to what is observed, and can be made at any time. Opposed to **factual statement.**

Influencing strategies. Strategies designed to influence the attitudes or behaviors of others.

Informal time. Temporal divisions that are approximate and that are referred to with such general terms as, for example, forever, immediately, soon, right away, as soon as possible. *Clarify your informal time terms; ask others for clarification when they use such terms, as appropriate.*

Information or persuasion power. Power that a person has because others see that individual as having significant information and the ability to communicate logically and persuasively.

Information overload. A condition in which the amount or complexity of information is too great to be dealt with effectively by an individual, group, or organization.

In-group talk. Talk about a subject or in a vocabulary that some people present understand and others do not; has the effect of excluding those who don't understand.

Insulation. A reaction to territorial encroachment in which you erect some sort of barrier between yourself and the invaders, such as a stone wall around your property, an unlisted phone number, or caller ID.

Intensifiers. Adjectives or adverbs that emphasize extremes, too many of which signal a lack of power.

Intensional orientation. A point of view in which primary consideration is given to the way things are labeled and only secondary consideration (if any) to the world of experience. Opposed to **extensional orientation.** *Avoid intensional orientation; look to people and things first and to labels second.*

Interaction management. A quality of interpersonal effectiveness in which the interaction is controlled and managed to the satisfaction of both parties; effectively managing conversational turns, fluency, and message consistency. *Speak in relatively short conversational turns, avoid long and/or frequent pauses, and use verbal and nonverbal messages that are consistent.*

Intercultural communication. Communication that takes place between persons of different cultures or between persons who have different cultural beliefs, values, or ways of behaving. *In communicating in intercultural situations, prepare yourself, reduce your ethnocentrism, confront your stereotypes, become mindful, avoid overattribution, reduce uncertainty, and recognize (1) differences between yourself and people who are culturally different, (2) differences within other cultural groups, and (3) cultural differences in meanings.*

Interpersonal communication. Communication between two persons or among a small group of persons and distinguished from public or mass communication; communication of a personal nature and distinguished from impersonal communication; communication between or among connected persons or those involved in a close relationship.

Interpersonal competence. The knowledge of and the ability to communicate effectively in interpersonal interactions.

Interpersonal conflict. Disagreement between two connected persons.

Interpersonal effectiveness. The ability to accomplish interpersonal goals; interpersonal communication that is satisfying to both individuals.

Interpersonal perception. The perception of people; the processes through which you interpret and evaluate people and their behavior.

Interpretation–evaluation. A step in perception that is influenced by experiences, needs, wants, values, and beliefs about the way things are or should be.

Interruptions. Verbal and nonverbal attempts to take over the role of the speaker.

Intimacy. The closest interpersonal relationship; usually characterizes close primary relationships.

Intimacy claims. Obligations incurred by virtue of being in a close and intimate relationship.

Intimate distance. The closest distance in proxemics, ranging from touching to 18 inches.

Intrapersonal communication. Communication with self.

Involvement. The second stage in relationship development, in which you further advance the relationship, first testing each other and then intensifying your interaction.

Irreversibility. A principle of communication holding that communication cannot be reversed; once something has been communicated, it cannot be uncommunicated.

James-Lange theory. A theory of emotions which holds that you experience emotions in the following way: (1) An event occurs. (2) You respond physiologically. (3) You experience an emotion; for example, you feel joy or sadness.

Jargon. The technical language of any specialized group, often a professional class, which is unintelligible to individuals not belonging to the group; shop talk. This glossary is an example of the jargon of part of the communication field.

Jealousy. A reaction (consisting of feelings, thoughts, and behaviors) to a physical or emotional threat to one or more of your significant relationships. *Be careful in displaying jealousy; it can be scary.*

Johari window. A diagram of the four selves (open, blind, hidden, and unknown).

Justification. A strategy to resist compliance by giving reasons as to why you should not comply.

Kinesics. The study of the communicative dimensions of facial and bodily movements.

Laissez-faire families. Families who avoid interaction and communication, encourage privacy, and maintain a "do what you want" attitude; low in confirmation and low in conversation.

Language. The rules of syntax, semantics, and phonology by which sentences are created and understood; a language refers to the sentences that can be created in any language, such as English, Bantu, or Italian.

Language relativity. See **linguistic relativity.**

Lateral communication. Messages between equals—manager to manager, worker to worker.

Leave-taking cues. Verbal and nonverbal signals that indicate a desire to terminate a conversation. *Be especially alert to these types of cues, lest you be thought a conversational bore.*

Legitimate power. Power a person possesses because others believe he or she has a right—by virtue of his or her position—to influence or control their behavior.

Leveling. A process of message distortion in which the number of details in a message is reduced as the message gets repeated from one person to another.

Lie bias. The assumption that the person is most likely lying. Opposed to **truth bias.**

Linguistic collusion. A response to territorial encroachment in which you speak in a language or jargon that the "invaders" don't understand and thus exclude them from the interaction. *See also* **withdrawal**, **turf defense**, and **insulation.**

Linguistic relativity. The theory that the language you speak influences your perceptions of the world and your behaviors and that therefore people speaking widely differing languages will perceive and behave differently.

Listening. An active process of receiving aural stimuli consisting of five stages: receiving, understanding, remembering, evaluating, and responding. *Be especially flexible when listening in a multicultural setting, realizing that people from other cultures give different listening cues and may operate with different rules for listening.*

Long-term memory. Memory that is (theoretically) unlimited in storage capacity and that holds information for long periods of time. Opposed to **short-term memory.**

Long-term orientation. A cultural orientation that promotes the importance of future rewards and so, for example, members of these cultures are more apt to save for the future and to prepare for the future academically. Opposed to **short-term orientation.**

Love. A relationship with another person in which you feel closeness, caring, warmth, and excitement.

Low-ambiguity tolerant cultures. Cultures that are uncomfortable with ambiguity, do much to avoid uncertainty, and have a great deal of anxiety about not knowing what will happen next.

Low-context culture. A culture in which most of the information in communication is explicitly stated in the verbal message rather than being left implied or assumed to be "understood." Low-context cultures are usually individualist cultures. Opposed to **high-context culture.**

Low-power distance culture. Culture in which power is relatively evenly distributed throughout the citizenry. *See* **high-power distance culture.**

Ludus. A type of love that stresses entertainment and excitement.

Lying. The act of sending messages with the intention of giving another person information you believe to be false.

Machiavellianism. The belief that people can be manipulated easily; also, manipulative techniques or tactics one person uses to control another.

Mania. A type of love characterized by elation and depression, extreme highs and extreme lows.

Manipulation. An unproductive conflict strategy; a manipulative individual avoids engaging in open conflict but instead attempts to divert the conflict by being especially charming and getting the other person into a noncombative frame of mind.

Manner maxim. A principle of conversation that holds that speakers cooperate with listeners by being clear and by organizing their thoughts into meaningful and coherent patterns.

Markers. Devices that signify that a certain territory belongs to a particular person. *See also* **boundary marker, central marker,** and **earmarker.**

Masculine culture. A culture that views men as assertive, oriented to material success, and strong; such a culture views women, on the other hand, as modest, focused on the quality of life, and tender. Masculine cultures emphasize success and so socialize their people to be assertive, ambitious, and competitive. Opposed to **feminine culture.**

Matching hypothesis. An assumption that you date and mate people who are comparable to yourself—who match you—in physical attractiveness.

Meaningfulness. A principle of perception that assumes that the behavior of people is sensible, stems from some logical antecedent, and therefore is meaningful rather than meaningless.

Mentoring relationship. A relationship in which an experienced individual helps train someone who is less experienced; for example, an accomplished teacher might mentor a younger teacher who is newly arrived or who has never taught before.

Mere exposure hypothesis. The theory that repeated or prolonged exposure to a stimulus may result in a change in attitude toward the stimulus object, generally in the direction of increased positiveness.

Message. Any signal or combination of signals that serves as a stimulus for a receiver. *See also* **stimulus.**

Meta-advice. Advice about advice; for example, suggesting that one seek more expert advice.

Metacommunication. Communication about communication. *Metacommunicate when you want to clarify the way you're talking or what you're talking about by, for example, giving clear feedforward and paraphrasing your complex messages.*

Metalanguage. Language that refers to language.

Metamessage. A message that makes reference to another message, such as "Did I make myself clear?" or "That's a lie."

Micromomentary expressions. Extremely brief movements that are not consciously controlled or recognized and that are thought to be indicative of your true emotional state.

Mindfulness. A state of awareness in which you are conscious of the logic and rationality of your behaviors and of the logical connections existing among elements.

Mindlessness. A lack of conscious awareness of the logic or reasons behind your thoughts or behaviors. *Increase your mindfulness by creating and re-creating categories and being open to new information and points of view; also, beware of relying too heavily on first impressions.*

Minimization. A deceptive message in which the facts or their importance are minimized.

Mixed message. A message that communicates two different and often contradictory meanings—for example, a message that asks for two different (often incompatible) responses, such as "leave me alone" and "show me more attention." Often, one meaning (usually the socially acceptable meaning) is communicated verbally and the other (usually the less socially acceptable meaning) nonverbally.

Model. A representation of an object or process.

Monochronic time orientation. A view of time in which things are done sequentially; one thing is scheduled at a time. Opposed to **polychronic time orientation.**

Monologue. A form of communication in which one person speaks and the other listens; there's no real interaction among participants. Opposed to **dialogue.**

Negative face. The desire to be autonomous, to have the right to do as you wish.

Negative face strategies. Messages that recognize a person's right to autonomy. *Avoid messages that impose on others or otherwise encroach upon their independence and autonomy.*

Negative feedback. Feedback that serves a corrective function by informing the source that his or her message is not being received in the way intended. Looks of boredom, shouts of disagreement, letters critical of newspaper policy, and teachers' instructions on how better to approach a problem are examples of negative feedback and will (ideally) serve to redirect behavior. *See also* **positive feedback.**

Negative identity management. A strategy for resisting power and influence in which you portray the person as unreasonable. Opposed to **positive identity management.**

Negative power. Power that has the opposite effect to that which is intended.

Negotiation. A strategy for resisting compliance in which you attempt to accommodate or compromise in some way.

Nonnegotiation. An unproductive conflict strategy in which an individual refuses to discuss the conflict or to listen to the other person; a strategy to resist compliance without any attempt to compromise; you simply state your refusal to do as asked without any qualification.

Netiquette. Rules of politeness for online communication.

Network convergence. The blending or sharing of one individual's circle of friends with another person's circle of friends.

Networking. Connecting with people who can help you accomplish a goal or help you find information related to your goal; for example, to your search for a job. Establish a network of relationships to provide insights into issues relevant to your personal and professional life, and be willing to lend your expertise to others.

Neutrality. A response pattern lacking in personal involvement; encourages defensiveness. Opposed to **empathy.**

Noise. Anything that interferes with your receiving a message as the source intended the message to be received. Noise is present in communication to the extent that the message received is not the message sent. *In managing noise, reduce physical, physiological, psychological, and semantic noise as best you can; use repetition and restatement, and, when in doubt, ask if you're clear.*

Nonallness. A point of view holding that you can never know all about anything and that what you know, say, or hear is only a part of what there is to know, say, or hear.

Nonjudgmental listening. Listening with an open mind and a view toward understanding.

Nonnegotiation. An unproductive conflict strategy in which an individual refuses to discuss the conflict or to listen to the other person.

Nonverbal communication. Communication without words; communication by means of space, gestures, facial expressions, touching, vocal variation, or silence, for example.

Nonverbal dominance. Nonverbal behavior through which one person achieves psychological dominance over another.

Object-adaptors. Movements that involve manipulation of some object; for example, punching holes in a Styrofoam coffee cup, clicking a ballpoint pen, or chewing on a pencil.

Object language. Language used to communicate about objects, events, and relations in the world (rather than about words as in metalanguage).

Objective listening. Listening with detachment to measure meanings and feelings against some objective reality.

Occulesics. The study of the messages communicated by the eyes.

Olfactory communication. Communication by smell. *Become mindful of your own scent messages; they can serve as attractants and as repellants.*

Omission. As a form of deception, omission occurs when you omit crucial details to hide the truth and to mislead the other person.

Openness. A quality of interpersonal effectiveness involving a person's willingness (1) to interact openly with others, self-disclosing as appropriate; (2) to react honestly to incoming stimuli; and (3) to own his or her own feelings and thoughts. *Increase openness when appropriate by self-disclosing, responding spontaneously and honestly to those with whom you're interacting, and owning your own feelings and thoughts.*

Opinion. A tentative conclusion concerning some object, person, or event.

Other talk. Talk about the listener or some third party. Opposed to **self-talk.**

Other-orientation. A quality of interpersonal effectiveness involving attentiveness, interest, and concern for the other person. *Acknowledge the importance of the other person: use focused eye contact and appropriate facial expressions; smile, nod, and lean toward the other person.*

Outing. The process whereby a person's affectional orientation is made public by another person without the gay man or lesbian's consent.

Overattribution. The tendency to attribute to one or two characteristics most or even all of what a person does. *Avoid overattribution; rarely is any one factor an accurate explanation of complex human behavior.*

Owning feelings. The process of taking responsibility for your own feelings instead of attributing them to others. *Do it.*

Paralanguage. The vocal but nonverbal aspects of speech. Paralanguage consists of voice qualities (for example, pitch range, resonance, tempo); vocal characterizers (laughing or crying, yelling or whispering); vocal qualifiers (intensity, pitch height); and vocal segregates ("uh-uh" meaning "no," or "sh" meaning "silence"). *Vary paralinguistic features to communicate nuances of meaning and to add interest and color to your messages.*

Passive listening. Listening that may be attentive and supportive but that occurs without the listener's talking or directing the speaker in any nonverbal way; also (used negatively), inattentive and uninvolved listening.

Pauses. Interruptions in the normally fluent stream of speech. Pauses are of two types: filled pauses (interruptions filled with such vocalizations as "er" or "um") and unfilled pauses (silences of unusually long duration).

Peaceful relations principle. A principle of communication advising that you say only what preserves peaceful relationships with others.

Perception. The process by which you become aware of objects and events through your senses. *Increase accuracy in interpersonal perception by identifying the influence of your physical and emotional states, making sure that you're not drawing conclusions from too little information, and checking your perceptions.*

Perception checking. The process of verifying your understanding of some message, situation, or feeling. *Increase accuracy in perception by checking your perceptions: (1) describe what you see or hear and the meaning you assign to it and (2) ask the other person if your perceptions are accurate.*

Perceptual accentuation. A process that leads you to see what you expect or want to see—for example, seeing people you like as better looking and smarter than people you don't like.

Personal distance. The second closest distance in proxemics, ranging from 18 inches to 4 feet.

Personality theory. A theory of personality, complete with rules about what characteristics go with what other characteristics, that you maintain and through which you perceive others.

Personal rejection. An unproductive conflict strategy in which you withhold love and affection and seek to win the argument by getting the other person to break down under this withdrawal. *Avoid it; it invariably creates more problems.*

Persuasion. The process of influencing attitudes and behavior.

Phatic communication. Communication that is primarily social; communication designed to open the channels of communication rather than to communicate something about the external world. "Hello" and "How are you?" in everyday interaction are examples.

Physical abuse. Behavior that involves threats of violence as well as pushing, hitting, slapping, kicking, choking, throwing things, and breaking things. *Avoid it; it will not only create relationship problems, it may have very unpleasant legal consequences.*

Physical noise. Interference that is external to both speaker and listener and that interferes with the physical transmission of a signal or message.

Physiological noise. Interference within the sender or receiver of a message, such as visual impairments, hearing loss, articulation problems, and memory loss.

Pitch. In relation to voice qualities, the highness or lowness of the vocal tone.

Pluralistic families. Families whose members are encouraged to express different attitudes and points of view and to engage in open communication while being supportive of each other.

Polarization. A form of fallacious reasoning in which only two extremes are considered; also referred to as black-and-white or either/or thinking or as a two-valued orientation. *Avoid thinking and talking in extremes by using middle terms and qualifiers. But remember that too many qualifiers may make you appear unsure of yourself.*

Politeness. Civility, consideration, refinement, respect, and regard for others as expressed verbally and nonverbally; interaction that follows the socially accepted rules for interpersonal interaction.

Politeness principle. A principle advising that you treat others respectfully. *Communicate positiveness by expressing your own satisfaction with the interaction and by complimenting others.*

Politeness strategies. Strategies that are often used to make ourselves appear likeable, in terms of negative and positive types.

Polychronic time orientation. A view of time in which several things may be scheduled or engaged in at the same time. Opposed to **monochronic time orientation.**

Positive face. The desire to be viewed positively by others, to be thought of favorably.

Positive face strategies. Messages that compliment and praise another. *Use these as appropriate.*

Positive feedback. Feedback that supports or reinforces the continuation of behavior along the same lines in which it is already proceeding—for example, applause during a speech, which encourages the speaker to continue speaking the same way. *See also* **negative feedback.**

Positive identity management. A strategy for resisting power and influence in which you make the other person feel good about himself or herself. Opposed to **negative identity management.**

Positiveness. A characteristic of interpersonal effectiveness involving positive attitudes and the use of positive messages expressing these attitudes (as in complimenting others) along with acceptance and approval.

Power. The ability to influence or control the behavior of another person; A has power over B when A can influence or control B's behavior; an inevitable part of interpersonal relationships. *In communicating power: Avoid powerless message forms, such as hesitations, excessive intensifiers, disqualifiers, tag questions, one-word answers, self-critical statements, overly polite statements, and vulgar and slang expressions.*

Power distance. The degree to which differences in power exist among a people. *Adjust your messages and listening on the basis of the power-distance orientation of the culture in which you find yourself.*

Power play. A consistent pattern of behavior in which one person tries to control the behavior of another. *Respond to power plays with cooperative strategies: Express your feelings, describe the behavior to which you object, and state a cooperative response.*

Pragma. A type of love that is practical and traditional.

Pragmatic implication. An assumption that is logical (and therefore appears true) but is actually not necessarily true.

Pragmatics. In interpersonal communication, an approach that focuses on communication behaviors and effects and on communication effectiveness.

Primacy effect. Giving more importance to that which occurs first instead of that which occurs last or more recently (recency).

Primary affect displays. The communication of the six primary emotions: happiness, surprise, fear, anger, sadness, and disgust or contempt.

Primary emotions. Basic emotions; usually identified are joy, acceptance, fear, surprise, sadness, disgust, anger, and anticipation.

Primary relationship. The relationship between two people that they consider their most (or one of their most) important; for example, the relationship between husband and wife or domestic partners.

Primary territory. Areas that you consider your exclusive preserve—for example, your room or office.

Process. Ongoing activity; communication is referred to as a process to emphasize that it's always changing, always in motion.

Profit. The result of the rewards or benefits one derives from a relationship minus the costs.

Projection. A psychological process whereby you attribute characteristics or feelings of your own to others; often, the process whereby you attribute your faults to others.

Protection theory. A theory of proxemics holding that people establish a body-buffer zone to protect themselves from unwanted closeness, touching, or attack.

Protective families. Families who stress agreement and strive to avoid conflict but with little communication.

Provisionalism. An attitude of open-mindedness that leads to the development of a supportive relationship and atmosphere. Opposed to **certainty.**

Proxemic distance. The distance we maintain between each other in our interactions.

Proxemics. The study of the communicative function of space; the study of how people unconsciously structure their space—the distance between people in their interactions, the organization of space in homes and offices, and even the design of cities. *Maintain distances that are comfortable and that are appropriate to the situation and to your relationship with the other person.*

Proximity. As a principle of perception, the tendency to perceive people or events that are physically close as belonging together or representing some unit; physical closeness—one of the qualities influencing interpersonal attraction.

Psychological noise. Mental interference in the speaker or listener, such as preconceived ideas, wandering thoughts, biases and prejudices, closed-mindedness, and extreme emotionalism.

Psychological time. An emphasis on or orientation toward past, present, or future time; varies from person to person.

Public distance. The farthest distance in proxemics, ranging from 12 feet to 25 feet or more.

Public territory. Areas that are open to all people—for example, restaurants or parks.

Punctuation of communication. The breaking up of continuous communication sequences into short sequences with identifiable beginnings and endings or stimuli and responses.

Pupil dilation. The extent to which the pupil of the eye widens; generally, large pupils indicate positive reactions.

Pupillometrics. The study of communication messages reflected by changes in the size of the pupils of the eyes.

Pygmalion effect. The condition in which you make a prediction of success, act as if it is true, and thereby make it come true (as when, for example, acting toward students as if they'll be successful influences them to become successful); a type of self-fulfilling prophecy.

Quality maxim. A principle of conversation that holds that speakers cooperate with listeners by saying what they think is true and by not saying what they think is false.

Quantity maxim. A principle of conversation that holds that speakers cooperate with listeners by being only as informative as necessary to communicate their intended meanings.

Quid pro quo harassment. A type of sexual harassment in which employment opportunities (as in hiring and promotion) are made dependent on the granting of sexual favors.

Racism. Negative attitudes and beliefs that individuals or a society as a whole hold about specific ethnic groups.

Racist language. Language that denigrates, demeans, or is derogatory toward members of a particular ethnic group.

Rate. In relation to voice qualities, the speed at which you speak, generally measured in words per minute.

Recall. The perception stage that involves accessing the information stored in memory.

Receiver. Any person or thing that takes in messages. Receivers may be individuals listening to or reading a message, a group of persons hearing a speech, a scattered television audience, or machines that store information.

Receiving. A stage in listening involving the hearing of and attending to the message.

Recency effect. Giving more importance to that which occurs last or more recently instead of that which occurs first (primacy).

Receptivity. As a type of friendship, it is characterized by one person being the primary giver and the other the primary receiver.

Reciprocity. As a type of friendship, it is characterized by loyalty, self-sacrifice, and generosity.

Reciprocity of liking. The tendency to like those who like us, to find attractive people who find us attractive.

Reconciliation strategies. Behaviors designed to repair a broken relationship.

Referent power. Power that a person possesses because others desire to identify with or be like that individual.

Regulators. Nonverbal behaviors that regulate, monitor, or control the communications of another person.

Rejection. A response to an individual that acknowledges the person but expresses disagreement. Opposed to **confirmation** and **disconfirmation.**

Relational dialectics theory. A theory that describes relationships as defined by a series of competing opposite desires or motivations, such as the desires for autonomy and belonging, for novelty and predictability, and for closedness and openness.

Relation maxim. A principle of conversation that holds that speakers cooperate with listeners by talking about what is relevant and by not talking about what isn't.

Relationship communication. Communication between or among intimates or those in close relationships; the term is used by some theorists as synonymous with interpersonal communication.

Relationship deterioration. The stage of a relationship during which the connecting bonds between the partners weaken and the partners begin drifting apart.

Relationship development. The initial or beginning stage of a relationship; the stage at which two people begin to form an interpersonal relationship.

Relationship dialectics theory. An explanation of the conflicting motives that people in close relationships often experience.

Relationship dimension. The dimension of messages that comments on the relationship between the speakers rather than on matters external to them.

Relationship dissolution. The termination or end of an interpersonal relationship.

Relationship license. Permission to violate some relationship expectation, custom, or rule.

Relationship maintenance. A condition of relationship stability in which the relationship does not progress or deteriorate significantly; a continuation as opposed to a dissolution (or an intensification) of a relationship.

Relationship messages. Messages that comment on the relationship between the speakers rather than on matters external to them.

Relationship repair. That stage of relationships in which one or both parties seek to resolve problems.

Relationship rules theory. A theory that holds that people maintain relationships with those who follow the rules the individuals have defined as essential to their relationship and dissolve relationships with those who don't follow the rules.

Relationship violence. Generally considered to consist of verbal or emotional abuse, physical abuse, or sexual abuse.

Repair. In the stage model of relationships, a stage in which one or both parties seek to improve the relationship. *In repairing relationships, recognize the problem, engage in productive conflict resolution, pose possible solutions, affirm each other, integrate solutions into normal behavior, and take risks as appropriate.*

Remembering. A stage in listening referring to the retention of what you hear.

Research. A systematic process of discovering an answer (or answers) to a question (in scientific terms, an hypothesis).

Resemblance. As a principle of perception, the tendency to perceive people or events that are similar in appearance as belonging together.

Responding. Listening stage that occurs in two phases: responses you make while the speaker is talking (immediate feedback) and responses you make after the speaker has stopped talking (delayed feedback).

Response. Any bit of overt or covert behavior.

Restraint. A cultural orientation that fosters the curbing of immediate gratification and regulates it by social norms. Opposed to **indulgence.**

Reverse halo effect. The tendency to judge a person you know to have several negative qualities to also have other negative qualities (that you have not observed); also known as the "horns" effect. *See also* **halo effect.**

Reward power. Power derived from an individual's ability to give another person what that person wants or to remove what that person wants removed.

Rewards. Anything that you want, that you enjoy, and that you'd be willing to incur costs to obtain.

Role. The part an individual plays in a group; an individual's function or expected behavior.

Rhythm. The recurring patterns of emphasis in a stream of speech.

Rules theory. *See* **relationship rules theory.**

Schemata. Ways of organizing perceptions; mental templates or structures that help you organize the millions of items of information you come into contact with every day as well as those you already have in memory; general ideas about groups of people or individuals, about yourself, or about types of social roles. The word schemata is the plural of schema.

Script. A type of schema; an organized body of information about some action, event, or procedure. A script provides a general idea of how some event should play out or unfold, the rules governing the events and their sequence.

Secondary territory. An area that does not belong to you but that you've occupied and that is therefore associated with you—for example, the seat you normally take in class.

Selective attention. The tendency to attend to those things that you want to see or that you expect to see.

Selective exposure. The tendency to expose your senses to certain things and not others, to actively seek out information that supports your beliefs and to actively avoid information that contradicts these beliefs.

Selective perception. The tendency to perceive certain things and not others; includes selective attention and selective exposure.

Self-acceptance. Being satisfied with yourself, your virtues and vices, your abilities and limitations.

Self-adaptors. Movements that usually satisfy a physical need, especially to make you more comfortable; for example, scratching your head to relieve an itch, moistening your lips because they feel dry, or pushing your hair out of your eyes.

Self-attribution. A process through which you seek to account for and understand the reasons and motivations for your own behaviors.

Self-awareness. The degree to which you know yourself. *Increase self-awareness by listening to others, increasing your open self, and seeking out information to reduce blind spots.*

Self-concept. Your self-image, the view you have of who you are. *To increase your understanding of self, try to see yourself, as objectively as you can, through the eyes of others; compare yourself to similar (and admired) others; examine the influences of culture; and observe and evaluate your own message behaviors.*

Self-critical statements. Statements that reflect negatively on the self.

Self-denigration principle. A principle of communication advising you to put the other person above yourself; to praise the other person rather than taking credit yourself.

Self-deprecating strategies. Techniques you use to signal your inability to do some task or your incompetence to encourage another to help you out. *Avoid these or use in moderation; such strategies can easily backfire and simply make you seem incompetent.*

Self-destructive beliefs. Beliefs that create problems; often beliefs that are unrealistic and set goals that are impossible to achieve.

Self-disclosure. The process of revealing something about yourself to another; usually refers to information that you'd normally keep hidden. *When thinking of disclosing, consider the legitimacy of your motives, the appropriateness of the disclosure, the listener's responses (is the dyadic effect operating?), and the potential burdens such disclosures might impose.*

Self-esteem. The value (usually, the positive value) you place on yourself; your self-evaluation. *Increase your self-esteem by attacking self-destructive beliefs, seeking out nourishing people, working on projects that will result in success, and securing affirmation.*

Self-fulfilling prophecy. The situation in which you make a prediction or prophecy and fulfill it yourself. For example, expecting a person to be hostile, you act in a hostile manner toward this person, and in doing so elicit hostile behavior in the person, thus confirming your prophecy that the person will be hostile. *Take a second look at your perceptions when they correspond very closely to your initial expectations; the self-fulfilling prophecy may be at work.*

Self-handicapping strategies. Techniques you use to excuse possible failure; for example, setting up barriers or obstacles to make the task impossible and so when you fail, you won't be blamed or thought ineffective.

Self-monitoring. Manipulating the image you present to others in interpersonal interactions so as to create the most favorable impression of yourself.

Self-monitoring strategies. Techniques you use to carefully monitor (self-censor) what you say or do.

Self-presentation. *See* **impression management.**

Self-serving bias. A bias that operates in the self-attribution process, leading you to take credit for the positive consequences of your behaviors and to deny responsibility for the negative consequences. *Become mindful of giving too much weight to internal factors (when explaining your positives) and too little weight to external factors (when explaining your negatives).*

Semantic noise. Interference created when a speaker and listener have different meaning systems; such noise can include language or dialectical differences, the use of jargon or overly complex terms, or ambiguous or overly abstract terms whose meanings can be easily misinterpreted.

Semantics. The area of language study concerned with meaning.

Separate couples. Couples who live together but view their relationship more as a matter of convenience than a result of their mutual love or closeness.

Sex. The biological distinction between males and females; the genetic distinction between men and women. *See also* **gender.**

Sexism. Negative attitudes and beliefs about a particular gender; prejudicial attitudes and beliefs about men or women based on rigid beliefs about gender roles.

Sexist language. Language derogatory to members of one gender, generally women.

Sexual abuse. Behavior that is unwanted and directed at a person's sexuality; for example, touching, accusations of sexual infidelity without reason, forced sex, and references to a person by abusive sexual terms.

Sexual harassment. Unsolicited and unwanted verbal or nonverbal sexual messages. *The first generally recommended option for dealing with sexual harassment is to talk to the harasser. If this doesn't stop the behavior, then consider collecting evidence, using appropriate channels within the organization, and filing a complaint.*

Sharpening. A process of message distortion in which the details of messages, when repeated, are crystallized and heightened.

Short-term memory. Memory that is very limited in capacity; contains information that is quickly lost if it is not passed on to **long-term memory.**

Short-term orientation. A cultural dimension in which people look more to the past and the present; these cultural members spend their resources for the present and want quick results from their efforts. Opposed to **long-term orientation.**

Shyness. A condition of discomfort and uneasiness in interpersonal situations.

Signal and noise, relativity of. The principle of verbal interaction that holds that what is signal (meaningful) and what is noise (interference) is relative to the communication analyst, the participants, and the context.

Signal reaction. A conditioned response to a signal; a response to some signal that is immediate rather than delayed. Opposed to **delayed reaction.**

Signal-to-noise ratio. A measure of the relationship between meaningful information (signal) and interference (noise).

Silence. The absence of vocal communication; often misunderstood to refer to the absence of communication. *Examine silence for meanings just as you would eye movements or body gestures.*

Silencers. Unproductive conflict strategies (such as crying) that literally silence your opponent.

Similarity. A principle of attraction holding that you're attracted to qualities similar to your own and to people who are similar to you. Opposed to **complementarity.**

Skills. Proficiencies; interpersonal skills are those abilities and competencies for creating and responding to interpersonal messages effectively.

Slang. Language used by special groups, often not considered standard in general society.

Small talk. Noncontroversial talk that is usually short in duration and often serves as a polite way of introducing one's self or a topic.

Social comparison. The processes by which you compare yourself (for example, your abilities, opinions, and values) with others and then assess and evaluate yourself on the basis of the comparison; one of the sources of self-concept.

Social distance. The next-to-farthest distance in proxemics, ranging from 4 feet to 12 feet; the distance at which business is usually conducted.

Social exchange theory. A theory hypothesizing that you cultivate profitable relationships (those in which your rewards are greater than your costs) and that you avoid or terminate unprofitable relationships (those in which your costs exceed your rewards).

Social information processing theory. A theory that claims, contrary to social presence theory, that whether you're communicating face to face or online, you can communicate the same degree of personal involvement and develop similar close relationships.

Social network. An organizational structure that allows people to communicate, popularly used to refer to the online sites such as Facebook and MySpace, which enable people to communicate with others who share a common interest.

Social penetration theory. A theory concerned with relationship development from the superficial to the intimate levels (depth) and from few to many areas of interpersonal interaction (breadth). *See also* **depenetration.**

Social presence theory. A theory that argues that the bandwidth (the number of message cues exchanged) of communication influences the degree to which the communication is personal or impersonal. When lots of cues are exchanged (especially nonverbal cues) as in face-to-face communication, there is great social presence; when fewer cues are exchanged, as in e-mail, there is less social presence.

Source. Any person or thing that creates messages—for example, an individual speaking, writing, or gesturing, or a computer solving a problem.

Source–receiver. A communication term that emphasizes that both functions are performed by each individual in an interpersonal message.

Speech. Messages conveyed via a vocal–auditory channel.

Spiral of silence. A theory that argues that you're more likely to voice agreement than disagreement.

Spontaneity. The communication pattern in which you say what you're thinking without attempting to develop strategies for control; encourages supportiveness. Opposed to **strategy.**

Stability. Principle of perception that states that your perceptions of things and of people are relatively consistent with your previous conceptions.

Static evaluation. An orientation that fails to recognize that the world is constantly changing; an attitude that sees people and events as fixed rather than as ever changing.

Status. The level a person occupies in a hierarchy relative to the levels occupied by others. In the United States, occupation, financial position, age, and educational level are significant determinants of social status.

Stereotype. In communication, a fixed impression of a group of people through which we then perceive specific individuals. Stereotypes are most often negative but may also be positive. *To avoid stereotypes, focus on the individual rather than on the individual's membership in one group or another.*

Stimulus. Any external or internal change that impinges on or arouses an organism.

Stimulus–response models of communication. Models of communication that assume that the process of communication is linear, beginning with a stimulus that then leads to a response.

Storge. A type of love that is peaceful and slow.

Strategic emotionality. Using emotions (for example, crying, ranting, screaming, and threatening to commit self-harm) for one's personal ends.

Strategy. The use of some plan for control of other members of a communication interaction, often through manipulation; often encourages defensiveness. Opposed to **spontaneity.**

Stress. The relative emphasis that is put on a word in a sentence and that can often change the meaning of the sentence.

Subjectivity. The principle of perception that refers to the fact that your perceptions are not objective but are influenced by your wants and needs, expectations and predictions.

Substitution. A deceptive message where you exchange the truth for a lie—for example, *I wasn't at Pat's, I was at my sister's.*

Superiority. A point of view or attitude that assumes that others are not equal to yourself; encourages defensiveness. Opposed to **equality.**

Supportiveness. An attitude of an individual or an atmosphere in a group that is characterized by openness, absence of fear, and a genuine feeling of equality. Opposed to **defensiveness.**

Symmetrical relationship. A relation between two or more persons in which one person's behavior serves as a stimulus for the same type of behavior in the other person(s)—for example, a relationship in which anger in one person encourages anger in the other, or in which a critical comment by one person leads the other to respond in kind.

Synchronous communication. Communication that takes place in real time; sending and receiving take place at the same time (as in face-to-face communication). Opposed to **asynchronous communication.**

Taboo. Forbidden; culturally censored; frowned upon by "polite society." Taboos may include entire topics as well as specific words—for example, death, sex, certain forms of illness, and various words denoting sexual activities and excretory functions.

Tactile communication. Communication by touch; communication received by the skin.

Tag questions. Questions that ask for agreement.

Temporal communication. The messages that your time orientation and treatment of time communicate.

Territorial encroachment. The trespassing on, use of, or appropriation of one person's territory by another.

Territoriality. A possessive or ownership reaction to an area of space or to particular objects.

Theory. A general statement or principle applicable to related phenomena.

Touch avoidance. The tendency to avoid touching and being touched by others.

Touch communication. *See* **tactile communication.**

Traditional couples. Couples who share a basic belief system and philosophy of life; they see themselves as a blending of two persons into a single couple rather than as two separate individuals.

Transactional perspective. A view of communication as an ongoing process in which all elements are interdependent and influence one another.

Truth bias. The assumption most people operate under that the messages they hear are truthful. Opposed to **lie bias.**

Turf defense. A response to territorial encroachment in which you defend the territory against the invasion, sometimes with something as simple as saying "this is my seat," or you might start a fight as nations do. *See also* **withdrawal, insulation,** and **linguistic collusion.**

Turning points. Significant relationship events that have important consequences for the individuals and the relationship and may turn its direction or trajectory.

Uncertainty reduction theory. Theory that, as interpersonal relationships develop, uncertainty is reduced; relationship development is seen as a process of reducing uncertainty about each other. *To reduce uncertainty, use passive, active, and interactive strategies.*

Understanding. A stage in listening involving deciphering meaning from the message you hear.

Universal of interpersonal communication. A feature of communication common to all interpersonal communication acts.

Unproductive conflict strategies. Ways of engaging in conflict that generally prove counterproductive—for example, avoidance, force, blame, silencers, gunnysacking, manipulation, personal rejection, and fighting below the belt.

Upward communication. Communication sent from the lower levels of a hierarchy to the upper levels—for example, from line worker to manager or from faculty member to dean.

Unrepeatability. A characteristic of communication referring to the fact that all communication acts are unique and can never be repeated exactly.

Value. Relative worth of an object; a quality that makes something desirable or undesirable; ideal or custom about which we have emotional responses, whether positive or negative.

Ventilation hypothesis. The assumption that expressing emotions (that is, giving vent to the emotions) lessens their intensity.

Verbal aggressiveness. A method of arguing in which one person attacks the other person's self-concept.

Verbal or emotional abuse. Behavior that is humiliating, isolating, or overly critical.

Verbal messages. Messages that are sent using words.

Visual dominance. The use of your eyes to maintain a superior or dominant position; for example, when making an especially important point, you might look intently at the other person.

Voice qualities. Aspects of paralanguage—specifically, pitch range, lip control, glottis control, pitch control, articulation control, rhythm control, resonance, and tempo.

Volume. In relation to voice qualities, the relative loudness of the voice.

Vulgar expressions. Language that is considered obscene by the general culture.

Weasel words. Words whose meanings are slippery and difficult to pin down to specifics. *Ask yourself, "Exactly what the word means?" Is someone (say an advertiser) attempting to put something over on you?*

Win-lose strategies. Conflict management strategies that seek a resolution in which one person wins and the other loses.

Win-win strategies. Conflict management strategies that seek a resolution in which both parties win.

Withdrawal. A response to territorial encroachment by which you leave the scene, the country, home, office, or classroom. *See also* **turf defense, insulation,** and **linguistic collusion.**

You-messages. Messages in which you deny responsibility for your own thoughts and behaviors; messages that attribute your perception to another person; messages of blame. Opposed to **I-messages.** *Avoid using you-messages that blame or accuse; invariably these will be resented and may easily cut off further communication.*

References

Abel, G. G., & Harlow, N. (2001). *The stop child molestation book*. Xlibris.. Retrieved from www.stopchildmolestation.org/pdfs/study.pdf.

Acor, A. A. (2001). Employers' perceptions of persons with body art and an experimental test regarding eyebrow piercing. Ph.D. dissertation, Marquette University. *Dissertation Abstracts International: Second B: The Sciences and Engineering* 61, 3885.

Adams-Price, C. E., Dalton, W. T., & Sumrall, R. (2004). Victim blaming in young, middle-aged, and older adults: Variations on the severity effect. *Journal of Adult Development* 11 (October), 289–295.

Afifi, W. A. (2007). Nonverbal communication. In *Explaining communication: Contemporary theories and exemplars* (pp. 39–60), B. B. Whaley & W. Samter (eds.). Mahwah, NJ: Erlbaum.

Afifi, W. A., & Johnson, M. L. (2005). The nature and function of tie-signs. In *The sourcebook of nonverbal measures: Going beyond words* (pp. 189–198), V. Manusov (ed.). Mahwah, NJ: Erlbaum.

Alessandra, T. (1986). How to listen effectively. *Speaking of success* (Video Tape Series). San Diego, CA: Levitz Sommer Productions.

Allen, J. L., Long, K. M., O'Mara, J., & Judd, B. B. (2003). Verbal and nonverbal orientations toward communication and the development of intracultural and intercultural relationships. *Journal of Intercultural Communication Research* 32 (September–December), 129–160.

Al-Simadi, F. A. (2000). Detection of deception behavior: A cross-cultural test. *Social Behavior & Personality* 28, 455–461.

Alsop, R. (2004). How to get hired: We asked recruiters what M.B.A. graduates are doing wrong. Ignore their advice at your peril. *Wall Street Journal* (September 22), R8.

Altman, I. (1975). *The environment and social behavior.* Monterey, CA: Brooks/Cole.

Altman, I., & Taylor, D. (1973). *Social penetration: The development of interpersonal relationships.* New York, NY: Holt, Rinehart & Winston.

Amato, P. R. (1994). The impact of divorce on men and women in India and the United States. *Journal of Comparative Family Studies* 25, 207–221.

Andersen, P. A. (1991). Explaining intercultural differences in nonverbal communication. In *Intercultural communication: A reader,* 6th ed., L. A. Samovar & R. E. Porter (eds.). Belmont, CA: Wadsworth, pp. 286–296.

Andersen, P. A. (2004). *The complete idiot's guide to body language.* New York, NY: Penguin Group.

Andersen, P. A., & Leibowitz, K. (1978). The development and nature of the construct touch avoidance. *Environmental Psychology and Nonverbal Behavior* 3, 89–106.

Anderson, I. (2004). Explaining negative rape victim perception: Homophobia and the male rape victim. *Current Research in Social Psychology* 10 (November), np.

Anderson, K. J. (1998). Meta-analysis of gender effects on conversational interruption: Who, what, when, where, and how. *Sex Roles* 39 (August), 225–252.

Angier, N. (1995a). Powerhouse of senses: Smell, at last, gets its due. *New York Times* (February 14), C1, C6.

Angier, N. (1995b). Scientists mull role of empathy in man and beast. *New York Times* (May 9), C1, C6.

Angier, N. (2010). Just don't call me. . . . *New York Times* (August 29), Weekend, p. 3.

Aquinis, H., & Henle, C. A. (2001). Effects of nonverbal behavior on perceptions of a female employee's power bases. *Journal of Social Psychology* 141 (August), 537–549.

Argyle, M. (1986). Rules for social relationships in four cultures. *Australian Journal of Psychology* 38, 309–318.

Argyle, M. (1988). *Bodily communication,* 2nd ed. New York, NY: Methuen.

Argyle, M., & Dean, J. (1965). Eye contact, distance and affiliation. *Sociometry* 28, 289–304.

Argyle, M., & Henderson, M. (1984). The rules of friendship. *Journal of Social and Personal Relationships* 1, 211–237.

Argyle, M., & Ingham, R. (1972). Gaze, mutual gaze, and distance. *Semiotica* 1, 32–49.

Armour, S. (2003). Cupid finds work as office romance no longer taboo. *USA Today* (February 11), Money Section, 1.

Arnold, L. B. (2008). *Family communication: Theory and research.* Boston, MA: Allyn & Bacon.

Aronson, E., Wilson, T. D., & Akert, R. M. (2007). *Social psychology,* 6th ed. Boston, MA: Allyn & Bacon.

Aronson, J., Cohen, J., & Nail, P. (1998). Self-affirmation theory: An update and appraisal. In *Cognitive dissonance theory: Revival with revisions and controversies,* E. Harmon-Jones & J. S. Mills (eds.). Washington, DC: American Psychological Association.

Asch, S. (1946). Forming impressions of personality. *Journal of Abnormal and Social Psychology* 41, 258–290.

Ashcraft, M. H. (1998). *Fundamentals of cognition.* New York, NY: Longman.

Aspinwall, L. G., & Taylor, S. E. (1993). Effects of social comparison direction, threat, and self-esteem on affect, evaluation, and expected success. *Journal of Personality and Social Psychology* 64, 708–722.

Authier, J., & Gustafson, K. (1982). Microtraining: Focusing on specific skills. In *Interpersonal helping skills: A guide to training methods, programs, and resources,* E. K. Marshall, P. D. Kurtz, and Associates (eds.). San Francisco: Jossey-Bass, pp. 93–130.

Axtell, R. E. (2007). *Essential do's and taboos: The complete guide to international business and leisure travel.* Hoboken, NJ: Wiley.

Ayres, J. (1983). Strategies to maintain relationships: Their identification and perceived usage. *Communication Quarterly* 31, 62–67.

Babcock, J. C, Waltz, J., Jacobson, N. S., & Gottman, J. M. (1993). Power and violence: The relation between communication patterns, power discrepancies, and domestic violence. *Journal of Marriage and the Family* 60 (February), 70–78.

Bach, G. R., & Wyden, P. (1968). *The intimate enemy.* New York, NY: Avon.

Bacon, B. (2004). *Meet me don't delete me: Internet dating: I've made all the mistakes so you don't have to.* Burbank, CA: Slapstick Publications.

Bailenson, J. N., Blascovich, J., Beall, A. C., & Loomis, J. M. (2001). Equilibrium theory revisited: Mutual gaze and personal space in virtual environments. *Presence: Teleoperators and Virtual Environments* 10 (December), 583–595.

Baker, A. (2002). What makes an online relationship successful? Clues from couples who met in cyberspace. *CyberPsychology and Behavior* 5 (August), 363–375.

Balswick, J. O., & Peck, C. (1971). The inexpressive male: A tragedy of American society? *The Family Coordinator* 20, 363–368.

Banks, S. P., Altendorf, D. M., Greene, J. O., & Cody, M. J. (1987). An examination of relationship disengagement: Perceptions, breakup strategies, and outcomes. *Western Journal of Speech Communication* 51, 19–41.

Barbato, C. A., & Perse, E. M. (1992). Interpersonal communication motives and the life position of elders. *Communication Research* 19, 516–531.

Barker, L. L. (1990). *Communication,* 5th ed. Upper Saddle River, NJ: Prentice-Hall.

Barna, L. M. (1997). Stumbling blocks in intercultural communication. In *Intercultural communication: A reader,* 7th ed., L. A. Samovar & R. E. Porter (eds.). Belmont, CA: Wadsworth, pp. 337–346.

Barnlund, D. C. (1989). *Communicative styles of Japanese and Americans: Images and realities.* Belmont, CA: Wadsworth.

Baron, R. (1990). Countering the effects of destructive criticism: The relative efficacy of four interventions. *Journal of Applied Psychology* 75 (3), 235–245.

Baron, R. A., & Byrne, D. (1984). *Social psychology: Understanding human interaction* (4th ed.). Boston, MA: Allyn & Bacon.

Barrett, L., & Godfrey, T. (1988). Listening. *Person Centered Review* 3 (November), 410–425.

Barta, P. (1999, December 16). Sex differences in the inferior parietal lobe. *Cerebral Cortex.* Retrieved from www.wired.com/news/technology/0,1282,33033,00.html

Bartholomew, K. (1990). Avoidance of intimacy: An attachment perspective. *Journal of Social and Personal Relationships* 7, 147–178.

Basso, K. H. (1972). To give up on words: Silence in Apache culture. In *Language and social context,* Pier Paolo Giglioli (ed.). New York, NY: Penguin.

Bateson, G. (1972). *Steps to an ecology of mind.* New York, NY: Ballantine.

Baumeister, R. F., Bushman, B. J., & Campbell, W. K. (2000). Self-esteem, narcissism, and aggression: Does violence result from low self-esteem or from threatened egotism? *Current Directions in Psychological Science* 9 (February), 26–29.

Bavelas, J. B. (1990). Can one not communicate? Behaving and communicating: A reply to Motley. *Western Journal of Speech Communication* 54, 593–602.

Baxter, L. A. (1983). Relationship disengagement: An examination of the reversal hypothesis. *Western Journal of Speech Communication* 47, 85–98.

Baxter, L. A. (1986). Gender differences in the heterosexual relationship rules embedded in break-up accounts. *Journal of Social and Personal Relationships* 3, 289–306.

Baxter, L. A. (2004). Relationships as dialogues. *Personal Relationships* 11 (March), 1–22.

Baxter, L. A., & Braithwaite, D. O. (2007). Social dialectics: The contradiction of relating. In *Explaining communication: Contemporary theories and exemplars* (pp. 275–292), B. B. Whaley & W. Samter (eds.). Mahwah, NJ: Erlbaum.

Baxter, L. A., & Braithwaite, D. O. (2008a). Relational dialectics theory. In *Engaging theories in interpersonal communication: Multiple perspectives* (pp. 349–362), L. A. Baxter & D. O. Braithwaite (eds.). Los Angeles, CA: Sage.

Baxter, L. A., & Braithwaite, D. O., eds. (2008b). *Engaging theories in interpersonal communication: Multiple perspectives.* Los Angeles, CA: Sage.

Baxter, L. A., & Bullis, C. (1986). Turning points in developing romantic relationships. *Human Communication Research* 12, 469–493.

Baxter, L. A., & Simon, E. P. (1993). Relationship maintenance strategies and dialectical contradictions in personal relationships. *Journal of Social and Personal Relationships* 10, 225–242.

Baxter, L. A., & Wilmot, W. W. (1984). Secret tests: Social strategies for acquiring information about the state of the relationship. *Human Communication Research* 11, 171–201.

Beach, W. A. (1990). On (not) observing behavior interactionally. *Western Journal of Speech Communication* 54, 603–612.

Beatty, M. J., Rudd, J. E., & Valencic, K. M. (1999). A re-evaluation of the verbal aggressiveness scale: One factor or two? *Communication Research Reports* 16, 10–17.

Bell, R. A., & Buerkel-Rothfuss, N. L. (1990). S(he) loves me, s(he) loves me not: Predictors of relational information-seeking in courtship and beyond. *Communication Quarterly* 38, 64–82.

Bell, R. A., & Daly, J. A. (1984). The affinity-seeking function of communication. *Communication Monographs* 51, 91–115.

Bellafiore, D. (2005). *Interpersonal conflict and effective communication.* Retrieved from http://www.drbalternatives.com/articles/cc2.html

Bennett, M. (1990). Children's understanding of the mitigating function of disclaimers. *Journal of Social Psychology* 130, 29–37.

Ben-Ze'ev, A. (2003). Primacy, emotional closeness, and openness in cyberspace. *Computers in Human Behavior* 19 (July), 451–467.

Berg, J. H., & Archer, R. L. (1983). The disclosure-liking relationship. *Human Communication Research* 10, 269–281.

Berger, C. R., & Bradac, J. J. (1982). *Language and social knowledge: Uncertainty in interpersonal relations.* London: Edward Arnold.

Berger, C. R., & Calabrese, R. J. (1975). Some explorations in initial interaction and beyond: Toward a theory of interpersonal communication. *Human Communication Research* 1, 99–112.

Berger, P. L., & Luckmann, T. (1980). *The social construction of reality.* New York, NY: Irvington.

Bernstein, W. M., Stephan, W. G., & Davis, M. H. (1979). Explaining attributions for achievement: A path analytic approach. *Journal of Personality and Social Psychology* 37, 1810–1821.

Berry, J. N. III (2004). Can I quote you on that? *Library Journal* 129, 10.

Berry, J. W., Poortinga, Y. H., Segall, M. H., & Dasen, P. R. (1992). *Cross-cultural psychology: Research and applications.* Cambridge: Cambridge University Press.

Berscheid, E., & Reis, H. T. (1998). Attraction and close relationships. In *The handbook of social psychology,* 4th ed., Vol. 2, D. Gilbert, S. Fiske, & G. Lindzey (eds.). New York, NY: W. H. Freeman, pp. 193–281.

Bierhoff, H. W., & Klein, R. (1991). Dimensionen der Liebe: Entwicklung einer Deutschsprachigen Skala zur Erfassung von Liebesstilen. *Zeitschrift for Differentielle und Diagnostische Psychologie* 12, 53–71.

Bishop, J. E. (1993). New research suggests that romance begins by falling nose over heels in love. *Wall Street Journal* (April 7), B1.

Black, H. K. (1999). A sense of the sacred: Altering or enhancing the self-portrait in older age? *Narrative Inquiry* 9, 327–345.

Blake, R. R., & Mouton, J. S. (1984). *The managerial grid III* (3rd ed.). Houston, TX: Gulf Publishing.

Blieszner, R., & Adams, R. G. (1992). *Adult friendship.* Thousand Oaks, CA: Sage.

Blumstein, P., & Schwartz, P. (1983). *American couples: Money, work, sex.* New York, NY: Morrow.

Bochner, A. (1984). The functions of human communication in interpersonal bonding. In *Handbook of rhetorical and communication theory,* C. C. Arnold & J. W. Bowers (eds.). Boston, MA Allyn & Bacon, pp. 544–621.

Bochner, S. (1994). Cross-cultural differences in the self-concept: A test of Hofstede's individualism/collectivism distinction. *Journal of Cross-Cultural Psychology* 25, 273–283.

Bochner, S., & Hesketh, B. (1994). Power distance, individualism/collectivism, and job-related attitudes in a culturally diverse work group. *Journal of Cross-Cultural Psychology* 25, 233–257.

Bodon, J., Powell, L., & Hickson III, M. (1999). Critiques of gatekeeping in scholarly journals: An analysis of perceptions and data. *Journal of the Association for Communication Administration* 28 (May), 60–70.

Bok, S. (1983). *Secrets.* New York, NY: Vintage.

Bond, Jr., C. F., & Atoum, A. O. (2000). International deception. *Personality & Social Psychology Bulletin* 26 (March), 385–395.

Boneva, B., Kraut, R., & Frohlich, D. (2001). Using e-mail for personal relationships: The difference gender makes. *American Behavioral Scientist* 45, 530–549.

Borden, G. A. (1991). *Cultural orientation: An approach to understanding intercultural communication.* Upper Saddle River, NJ: Prentice-Hall.

Bowen, F., & Blackmon, K. (2003). Spirals of silence: The dynamic of diversity on organizational voice. *Journal of Management Studies* 40 (September), 1393–1417.

Bower, B. (2001). Self-illusions come back to bite students. *Science News* 159, 148.

Bower, S. A., & Bower, G. H. (2005). *Asserting yourself: A practical guide for positive change.* Cambridge, MA: DaCapo Press.

Brashers, D. E. (2007). A theory of communication and uncertainty management. In *Explaining communication: Contemporary theories and exemplars* (pp. 201–218), B. B. Whaley & W. Samter (eds.). Mahwah, NJ: Erlbaum.

Bravo, E., & Cassedy, E. (1992). *The 9 to 5 guide to combating sexual harassment.* New York, NY: Wiley.

Bridges, C. R. (1996). The characteristics of career achievement perceived by African American college administrators. *Journal of Black Studies* 26, 748–767.

Britnell, A. (2004). Culture shock-proofing. *Profit* 23 (November), 79–80.

Briton, N. J., & Hall, J. A. (1995). Beliefs about female and male nonverbal communication. *Sex Roles* 32, 79–90.

Brody, J. F. (1994). Notions of beauty transcend culture, new study suggests. *New York Times* (March 21), A14.

Brody, L. R. (1985). Gender differences in emotional development: A review of theories and research. *Journal of Personality* 53 (June), 102–149.

Brown, C. T., & Keller, P. W. (1979). *Monologue to dialogue: An exploration of interpersonal communication*, 2nd ed. Upper Saddle River, NJ: Prentice-Hall.

Brown, P., & Levinson, S. C. (1987). *Politeness: Some universals of language usage.* Cambridge: Cambridge University Press.

Brownell, J. (2010). *Listening: Attitudes, principles, and skills*, 4th ed. Boston, MA: Allyn & Bacon.

Buber, M. (1958). *I and thou*, 2nd ed. New York, NY: Scribner's.

Bugental, J., & Zelen, S. (1950). Investigations into the "self-concept." I. The W-A-Y technique. *Journal of Personality* 18, 483–498.

Bull, R., & Rumsey, N. (1988). *The social psychology of facial appearance.* New York, NY: Springer-Verlag.

Buller, D. B., LePoire, B. A., Aune, R. K., & Eloy, S. (1992). Social perceptions as mediators of the effect of speech rate similarity on compliance. *Human Communication Research* 19, 286–311.

Buller, D. J. (2005). *Adapting minds: Evolutionary psychology and the persistent quest for human nature.* Cambridge, MA: MIT Press.

Bumby, K. M., & Hansen, D. J. (1997). Intimacy deficits, fear of intimacy, and loneliness among sexual offenders. *Criminal Justice and Behavior* 24, 315–331.

Bunz, U., & Campbell, S. W. (2004). Politeness accommodation in electronic mail. *Communication Research Reports* 21 (winter), 11–25.

Burgoon, J. K. (1991). Relational message interpretations of touch, conversational distance, and posture. *Journal of Nonverbal Behavior* 15, 233–259.

Burgoon, J. K., & Bacue, A. E. (2003). Nonverbal communication skills. In *Handbook of communication and social interaction skills,* (pp. 179–220), J. O. Greene & B. R. Burleson (eds.). Mahwah, NJ: Lawrence Erlbaum.

Burgoon, J. K., Berger, C. R., & Waldron, V. R. (2000). Mindfulness and interpersonal communication. *Journal of Social Issues* 56, 105–127.

Burgoon, J. K., Guerrero, L. K., & Floyd, K. (2010). *Nonverbal Communication.* Boston, MA: Allyn & Bacon.

Burgoon, J. K., & Hoobler, G. D. (2002). Nonverbal signals. In *Handbook of Interpersonal Communication,* 3rd ed. (pp. 240–299), M. L. Knapp & J. A. Daly (eds.). Thousand Oaks, CA: Sage.

Burgstahler, S. (2007). Managing an e-mentoring community to support students with disabilities: A case study. *Distance Education Report* 11 (July), 7–15.

Burleson, B. R. (2003). Emotional support skills. In *Handbook of communication and social interaction skills* (pp. 551–594), J. O. Greene & B. R. Burleson (eds.), Mahwah, NJ: Erlbaum.

Burleson, B. R., Holmstrom, A. J., & Gilstrap, C. M. (2005). 'Guys can't say *that* to guys': Four experiments assessing the normative motivation account for deficiencies in the emotional support provided by men. *Communication Monographs* 72 (December), 468–501.

Burleson, B. R., Kunkel, A. W., & Birch, J. D. (1994). Thoughts about talk in romantic relationships: Similarity makes for attraction (and happiness, too). *Communication Quarterly* 42 (summer), 259–273.

Burleson, B. R., Samter, W., & Luccetti, A. E. (1992). Similarity in communication values as a predictor of friendship choices: Studies of friends and best friends. *Southern Communication Journal* 57, 260–276.

Bushman, B. J., & Baumeister, R. F. (1998). Threatened egotism, narcissism, self-esteem, and direct and displaced aggression: Does self-love or self-hate lead to violence? *Journal of Personality and Social Psychology* 75, 219–229.

Buss, D. M. (2000). *The dangerous passion: Why jealousy is as necessary as love and sex.* New York, NY: Free Press.

Buss, D. M., Shackelford, T. K., Kirkpatrick, L. A., Choe, J. C., Lim, H. K., Hasegawa, M., Hasegawa, T., & Bennett, K. (1999). Jealousy and the nature of beliefs about infidelity: Tests of competing hypotheses about sex differences in the United States, Korea, and Japan. *Personal Relationships* 6, 125–150.

Butler, P. E. (1981). *Talking to yourself: Learning the language of self-support.* New York, NY: Harper & Row.

Buunk, B. P., & Dijkstra, P. (2004). Gender differences in rival characteristics that evoke jealousy in response to emotional versus sexual infidelity. *Personal Relationships* 11 (December), 395–408.

Byers, E. S., & Demmons, S. (1999). Sexual satisfaction and sexual self-disclosure within dating relationships. *Journal of Sex Research* 36, 180–189.

Cahn, D. D., & Abigail, R. A. (2007). *Managing conflict through communication,* 3rd ed. Boston, MA: Allyn & Bacon.

Cai, D. A., & Fink, E. L. (2002). Conflict style differences between individualists and collectivists. *Communication Monographs* 69 (March), 67–87.

Callan, V. J. (1993). Subordinate–manager communication in different sex dyads: Consequences for job satisfaction. *Journal of Occupational & Organizational Psychology,* 66 (March), 1–15.

Camden, C., Motley, M. T., & Wilson, A. (1984). White lies in interpersonal communication: A taxonomy and preliminary investigation of social motivations. *Western Journal of Speech Communication* 48, 309–325.

Campbell, T. A., & Campbell, D. E. (2007). Outcomes of mentoring at-risk college students: Gender and ethnic matching effects. *Mentoring and Tutoring* 15 (May), 135–148.

Campbell, W. K., Foster, C. A., & Finkel, E. J. (2002). Does self-love lead to love for others? A story of narcissistic game playing. *Journal of Personality and Social Psychology* 83 (August), 340–354.

Canary, D. J. (2003). Managing interpersonal conflict: A model of events related to strategic choices. In *Handbook of communication and social interaction skills,* (pp. 515–550), J. O. Greene & B. R. Burleson (eds.). Mahwah, NJ: Lawrence Erlbaum.

Canary, D. J., Cody, M. J., & Manusov, V. L. (2003). *Interpersonal communication: A goals-based approach,* 3rd ed. Boston, MA: St. Bedford/St. Martins.

Canary, D. J., Cupach, W. R., & Messman, S. J. (1995). *Relationship conflict: Conflict in parent-child, friendship, and romantic relationships.* Thousand Oaks, CA: Sage.

Canary, D. J., & Hause, K. S. (1993). Is there any reason to research sex differences in communication? *Communication Quarterly* 41, 129–144.

Canary, D. J., & Stafford, L. (1994). Maintaining relationships through strategic and routine interaction. In *Communication and relational maintenance,* D. J. Canary & L. Stafford (eds.). New York, NY: Academic Press.

Canary, D. J., Stafford, L., Hause, K. S., & Wallace, L. A. (1993). An inductive analysis of relational maintenance strategies: Comparisons among lovers, relatives, friends, and others. *Communication Research Reports* 10, 5–14.

Cappella, J. N., & Schreiber, D. M. (2006). The interaction management function of nonverbal cues. In *The Sage handbook of nonverbal communication* (pp. 361–379), V. Manusov & M. L. Patterson (eds.). Thousand Oaks, CA: Sage.

Caproni, P. J. (2012). *Management skills for everyday life: The practical coach.* Upper Saddle River, NJ: Prentice-Hall.

Carey, B. (2005). Have you heard? Gossip turns out to serve a purpose. *New York Times* (August 16), F1, F6.

Carli, L. L. (1999). Gender, interpersonal power, and social influence. *Journal of Social Issues* 55 (spring), 81–99.

Carlock, C. J., ed. (1999). *Enhancing self-esteem,* 3rd ed. Philadelphia, PA: Accelerated Development, Inc.

Carroll, D. W. (1994). *Psychology of language,* 2nd ed. Pacific Grove, CA: Brooks/Cole.

Carson, J. W., Carson, K. M., Gil, K. M., & Baucom, D. H. (2004). Mindfulness-based relationship enhancement. *Behavior Therapy* 35 (summer), 471–494.

Cashdan, E. (2001). Ethnocentrism and xenophobia: A cross-cultural study. *Current Anthropology* 42, 760–765.

Castleberry, S. B., & Shepherd, C. D. (1993). Effective interpersonal listening and personal selling. *Journal of Personal Selling and Sales Management* 13, 35–49.

Cawthon, S. W. (2001). Teaching strategies in inclusive classrooms with deaf students. *Journal of Deaf Studies and Deaf Education* 6, 212–225.

Chadwick-Jones, J. K. (1976). *Social exchange theory: Its structure and influence in social psychology.* New York, NY: Academic Press.

Chan, D., K., & Cheng, G. H. (2004). A comparison of offline and online friendship qualities at different stages of relationship development. *Journal of Social and Personal Relationships* 21 (June), 305–320.

Chaney, R. H., Givens, C. A., Aoki, M. F., & Gombiner, M. L. (1989). Pupillary responses in recognizing awareness in persons with profound mental retardation. *Perceptual and Motor Skills* 69, 523–528.

Chang, H., & Holt, G. R. (1996). The changing Chinese interpersonal world: Popular themes in interpersonal communication books in modern Taiwan. *Communication Quarterly* 44, 85–106.

Chanowitz, B., & Langer, E. (1981). Premature cognitive commitment. *Journal of Personality and Social Psychology* 41, 1051–1063.

Chapdelaine, R. F., & Alexitch, L. R. (2004). Social skills difficulty: Model of culture shock for international graduate students. *Journal of College Student Development* 45 (March–April), 167–184.

Chen, G. (1992). Differences in self-disclosure patterns among Americans versus Chinese: A comparative study. Paper presented at the annual meeting of the Eastern Communication Association, Portland, ME.

Cheney, G., & Tompkins, P. K. (1987). Coming to terms with organizational identification and commitment. *Central States Speech Journal* 38, 1–15.

Cherulnik, P. D. (1979). Sex differences in the expression of emotion in a structured social encounter. *Sex Roles* 5 (August), 413–424.

Childress, H. (2004). Teenagers, territory and the appropriation of space. *Childhood: A Global Journal of Child Research* 11 (May), 195–205.

Cho, H. (2000). Asian in America: Cultural shyness can impede Asian Americans' success. *Northwest Asian Weekly* 19 (December 8), 6.

Christians, C. G., & Traber, M., eds. (1997). *Communication ethics and universal values.* Urbana, IL: University of Illinois Press.

Chung, L. C., & Ting-Toomey, S. (1999). Ethnic identity and relational expectations among Asian Americans. *Communication Research Reports* 16 (spring), 157–166.

Chung, M. C., Farmer, S., Grant, K., Newton, R., Payne, S., Perry, M., Saunders, J., Smith, C., & Stone, N. (2002). Gender differences in love styles and post traumatic reactions following relationship dissolution. *European Journal of Psychiatry* 16 (October–December), 210–220.

Clement, D. A., & Frandsen, K. D. (1976). On conceptual and empirical treatments of feedback in human communication. *Communication Monographs* 43, 11–28.

Cline, M. G. (1956). The influence of social context on the perception of faces. *Journal of Personality* 2, 142–185.

Cloud, J. (2008, January). Are gay relationships different? *Time,* 78–80.

Coates, J., & Sutton-Spence, R. (2001). Turn-taking patterns in deaf conversation. *Journal of Sociolinguistics* 5 (November), 507–529.

Coats, E. J., & Feldman, R. S. (1996, October). Gender differences in nonverbal correlates of social status. *Personality and Social Psychology Bulletin* 22, 1014–1022.

Cody, M. J. (1982). A typology of disengagement strategies and an examination of the role intimacy, reactions to inequity, and relational problems play in strategy selection. *Communication Monographs* 49, 148–170.

Cody, M. J., & Dunn, D. (2007). Accounts. In *Explaining communication: Contemporary theories and exemplars* (pp. 237–256), B. B. Whaley and W. Samter (eds.). Mahwah, NJ: Erlbaum.

Cohen, J. (2002, May 9). An e-mail affliction: The long goodbye. *New York Times*, G6.

Cohen, J. (2003). Parasocial breakups: Measuring individual differences in responses to the dissolution of parasocial relationships. *Mass Communication and Society* 6, 191–202.

Cohen, J. (2004). Parasocial break-up from favorite television characters: The role of attachment styles and relationship intensity. *Journal of Social and Personal Relationships* 21 (April), 187–202.

Coleman, P. (2002). *How to say it for couples: Communicating with tenderness, openness, and honesty.* Upper Saddle River, NJ: Prentice-Hall.

Colley, A., Todd, Z., Bland, M., Holmes, M., Khanom, N., & Pike, H. (2004). Style and content in e-mails and letters to male and female friends. *Journal of Language and Social Psychology* 23 (September), 369–378.

Collins, J. E., & Clark, L. F. (1989). Responsibility and rumination: The trouble with understanding the dissolution of a relationship. *Social Cognition* 7, 152–173.

Collins, N. L., & Miller, L. C. (1994). Self-disclosure and liking: A meta-analytic review. *Psychological Bulletin* 116 (November), 457–475.

Comer, L. B., & Drollinger, T. (1999). Active empathic listening and selling success: A conceptual framework. *Journal of Personal Selling and Sales Management,* 19, 15–29.

Conlin, M. (2002). Watch what you put in that office e-mail. *Business Week* (September 9), 114–115.

Constantine, M. G., Anderson, G. M., Berkel, L. A., Caldwell, L. D., & Utsey, S. O. (2005). Examining the cultural adjustment experiences of African international college students: A qualitative analysis. *Journal of Counseling Psychology* 52 (January), 57–66.

Cooley, C. H. (1922). *Human nature and the social order.* Rev. ed. New York, NY: Scribner's.

Cooper, A., & Sportolari, L. (1997). Romance in cyberspace: Understanding online attraction. *Journal of Sex Education and Therapy* 22, 7–14.

Coover, G. E., & Murphy, S. T. (2000). The communicated self: Exploring the interaction between self and social context. *Human Communication Research* 26, 125–147.

Copeland, L., & Griggs, L. (1985). *Going international: How to make friends and deal effectively in the global marketplace.* New York, NY: Random House.

Cornwell, B., & Lundgren, D. C. (2001). Love on the Internet: Involvement and misrepresentation in romantic relationships in cyberspace vs. realspace. *Computers in Human Behavior* 17, 197–211.

Counts, D. A., Brown, J. K., & Campbell, J. C. (1992). *Sanctions and sanctuary: Cultural perspectives on the beating of wives.* Boulder, CO: Westview Press.

Cramer, D. (2004). Emotional support, conflict, depression, and relationship satisfaction in a romantic partner. *Journal of Psychology: Interdisciplinary and Applied* 138 (November), 532–542.

Crampton, S. M., Hodge, J. W., & Mishra, J. M. (1998). The informal communication network: Factors influencing grapevine activity. *Public Personnel Management* 27 (winter), 569–584.

Crohn, J. (1995). *Mixed matches: How to create successful interracial, interethnic, and interfaith relationships.* New York, NY: Fawcett.

Cross, E. E., & Madson, L. (1997). Models of the self: Self-construals and gender. *Psychological Bulletin* 122, 5–37.

Crusco, A. H., & Wetzel, C. G. (1984). The Midas touch: The effects of interpersonal touch on restaurant tipping. *Personality and Social Psychology Bulletin* 10, 512–517.

Dahle, C. (2004). Choosing a mentor? Cast a wide net. *New York Times* (July 25), BU 9.

Dainton, M., & Stafford, L. (1993). Routine maintenance behaviors: A comparison of relationship type, partner similarity, and sex differences. *Journal of Social and Personal Relationships* 10, 255–272.

Damasio, A. (2005). *Descartes' error: Emotion, reason, and the human brain.* New York, NY: Penguin.

Darwin, C. (1872). *The expression of the emotions in man and animals.* Chicago: University of Chicago Press (reprinted 1965).

Davis, K. (1980). Management communication and the grapevine. In *Intercom: Readings in organizational communication* (pp. 55–66), S. Ferguson & S. D. Ferguson (eds.). Rochelle Park, NJ: Hayden Books.

Davis, M. S. (1973). *Intimate relations.* New York, NY: Free Press.

Davitz, J. R. (ed.). (1964). *The communication of emotional meaning.* New York, NY: McGraw-Hill.

Deal, J. E., & Wampler, K. S. (1986). Dating violence: The primacy of previous experience. *Journal of Social and Personal Relationships* 3, 457–471.

Deaux, K., & LaFrance, M. (1998). Gender. In *The handbook of social psychology,* 4th ed., Vol. 1, D. Gilbert, S. Fiske, & G. Lindzey (eds.). New York, NY: Freeman, pp. 788–828.

deBono, E. (1987). *The six thinking hats.* New York, NY: Penguin.

DeFrancisco, V. (1991). The sound of silence: How men silence women in marital relations. *Discourse and Society* 2, 413–423.

Delia, J. G. (1977). Constructivism and the study of human communication. *Quarterly Journal of Speech* 63, 66–83.

Delia, J. G., O'Keefe, B. J., & O'Keefe, D. J. (1982). The constructivist approach to communication. In *Human communication theory: Comparative essays,* Frank E. X. Dance (ed.). New York, NY: Harper & Row, pp. 147–191.

Dell, K. (2005). Just for dudes. *Time* (February, 14), B22.

DePaulo, B. M. (1992). Nonverbal behavior and self-presentation. *Psychological Bulletin* 111, 203–212.

Dereshiwsky, M. I., Moan, E. R., & Gahungu, A. (2002). Faculty perceptions regarding issues of civility in online instructional communication. *USDLA Journal* 16, No. 6 (June).

Derlega, V. J., Winstead, B. A., Greene, K., Serovich, J., & Elwood, W. N. (2004). Reasons for HIV disclosure/nondisclosure in close relationships: Testing a model of HIV-disclosure decision making. *Journal of Social and Clinical Psychology* 23 (December), 747–767.

Derlega, V. J., Winstead, B. A., Wong, P. T. P., & Hunter, S. (1985). Gender effects in an initial encounter: A case where men exceed women in disclosure. *Journal of Social and Personal Relationships* 2, 25–44.

DeVito, J. A. (1989). *The nonverbal communication workbook.* Prospect Heights, IL: Waveland Press.

DeVito, J. A. (2003a). MEDUSA messages. *Etc: A Review of General Semantics* 60 (fall), 241–245.

DeVito, J. A. (2003b). SCREAM before you scream. *Etc: A Review of General Semantics* 60 (spring), 42–45.

Dewey, J. (1910). *How we think.* Boston, MA: Heath.

DiBaise, R., & Gunnoe, J. (2004). Gender and culture differences in touching behavior. *Journal of Social Psychology* 144 (February), 49–62.

Dillard, J. P., ed. (1990). *Seeking compliance: The production of interpersonal influence messages.* Scottsdale, AZ: Gorsuch Scarisbrick

Dillard, J. P., Anderson, J. W., & Knobloch, L. K. (2002). Interpersonal influence. In *Handbook of interpersonal communication,* 3rd ed. (pp. 425–474), M. L. Knapp & J. A. Daly (eds.). Thousand Oaks, CA: Sage.

Dillard, J. P., & Marshall, L. J. (2003). Persuasion as a social skill. In *Handbook of communication and social interaction skills* (pp. 479–514), J. O. Greene & B. R. Burleson (eds.). Mahwah, NJ: Lawrence Erlbaum.

Dindia, K., & Baxter, L. A. (1987). Strategies for maintaining and repairing marital relationships. *Journal of Social and Personal Relationships* 4, 143–158.

Dindia, K., & Fitzpatrick, M. A. (1985). Marital communication: Three approaches compared. In *Understanding personal relationships: An interdisciplinary approach,* S. Duck & D. Perlman (eds.). Thousand Oaks, CA: Sage, pp. 137–158.

Dindia, K., & Timmerman, L. (2003). Accomplishing romantic relationships. In *Handbook of communication and social interaction skills* (pp. 685–721), J. O. Greene & B. R. Burleson (eds.). Mahwah, NJ: Erlbaum.

Dion, K., Berscheid, E., & Walster, E. (1972). What is beautiful is good. *Journal of Personality and Social Psychology* 24, 285–290.

Dion, K. K., & Dion, K. L. (1993a). Individualistic and collectivist perspectives on gender and the cultural context of love and intimacy. *Journal of Social Issues* 49, 53–69.

Dion, K. K., & Dion, K. L. (1996). Cultural perspectives on romantic love. *Personal Relationships* 3, 5–17.

Dion, K. L., & Dion, K. K. (1993b). Gender and ethnocultural comparisons in styles of love. *Psychology of Women Quarterly* 17, 464–473.

Doherty, R. W., Orimoto, L., Singelis, T. M., Hatfield, E., & Hebb, J. (1995). Emotional contagion: Gender and occupational differences. *Psychology of Women Quarterly* 19, 355–371.

Dolgin, K. G., Meyer, L., & Schwartz, J. (1991). Effects of gender, target's gender, topic, and self-esteem on disclosure to best and middling friends. *Sex Roles* 25, 311–329.

Donahue, W. A. (with Kolt, R.). (1992). *Managing interpersonal conflict.* Thousand Oaks, CA: Sage.

Dorland, J. M., & Fisher, A. R. (2001). Gay, lesbian, and bisexual individuals' perception: An analogue study. *Counseling Psychologist* 29 (July), 532–547.

Dosey, M., & Meisels, M. (1976). Personal space and self-protection. *Journal of Personality and Social Psychology* 38, 959–965.

Douglas, W. (1994). The acquaintanceship process: An examination of uncertainty, information seeking, and social attraction during initial conversation. *Communication Research* 21, 154–176.

Dovidio, J. F., Gaertner, S. E., Kawakami, K., & Hodson, G. (2002). Why can't we just get along? Interpersonal biases and interracial distrust. *Cultural Diversity and Ethnic Minority Psychology* 8, 88–102.

Drass, K. A. (1986). The effect of gender identity on conversation. *Social Psychology Quarterly* 49, 294–301.

Dresser, N. (2005). *Multicultural manners: Essential rules of etiquette for the 21st Century, rev. ed.* New York, NY: Wiley.

Drews, D. R., Allison, C. K., & Probst, J. R. (2000). Behavioral and self-concept differences in tattooed and nontattooed college students. *Psychological Reports* 86, 475–481.

Dreyfuss, H. (1971). *Symbol sourcebook.* New York, NY: McGraw-Hill.

Drummond, K., & Hopper, R. (1993). Acknowledgment tokens in series. *Communication Reports* 6, 47–53.

Dsilva, M., & Whyte, L. O. (1998). Cultural differences in conflict styles: Vietnamese refugees and established residents. *The Howard Journal of Communication* 9, 57–68.

Duck, S. (1986). *Human relationships.* Thousand Oaks, CA: Sage.

Duke, M., & Nowicki, S., Jr. (2005). The Emory dyssemia index. In *The sourcebook of nonverbal measures: Going beyond words* (pp. 35–46), V. Manusov (ed.). Mahwah, NJ: Erlbaum.

Dunbar, N. E., & Burgoon, J. K. (2005). Measuring nonverbal dominance. In *The sourcebook of nonverbal measures: Going beyond words* (pp. 361–374), V. Manusov (ed.). Mahwah, NJ: Erlbaum.

Dunbar, R. I. M. (2004). Gossip in evolutionary perspective. *Review of General Psychology* 8 (June), 100–110.

Duncan, B. L., & Rock, J. W. (1991). *Overcoming relationship impasses: Ways to initiate change when your partner won't help.* New York, NY: Plenum Press/Insight Books.

Duncan, S. D., Jr. (1972). Some signals and rules for taking speaking turns in conversation. *Journal of Personality and Social Psychology* 23, 283–292.

Dunn, D., & Cody, M. J. (2000). Account credibility and public image: Excuses, justifications, denials, and sexual harassment. *Communication Monographs* 67 (December), 372–391.

Durst, U. (2003). Evidence for linguistic relativity. *Pragmatics and Cognition* 11, 379–386.

Duval, T. S., & Silva, P. J. (2002). Self-awareness, probability of improvement, and the self-serving bias. *Journal of Personality and Social Psychology* 82, 49–61.

Dwyer, K. K. (2005). *Conquer your speech anxiety: Learning how to overcome your nervousness about public speaking,* 2nd ed. Belmont, CA: Wadsworth.

Eastwick, P. W. & Finkel, E. J. (2009). Reciprocity of Liking. In Harry T. Reis & Susan Sprecher (Eds.), *Encyclopedia of human relationships* (pp. 1333–1336). Thousand Oaks, CA: Sage.

Eder, D., & Enke, J. L. (1991). The structure of gossip: Opportunities and constraints on collective expression among adolescents. *American Sociological Review* 56, 494–508.

Edstrom, A. (2004). Expression of disagreement by Venezuelans in conversation: Reconsidering the influence of culture. *Journal of Pragmatics* 36 (August), 1499–1508.

Edwards, R., & Bello, R. (2001). Interpretations of messages: The influence of equivocation, face-concerns, and ego-involvement. *Human Communication Research* 27, 597–631.

Ehrenhaus, P. (1988). Silence and symbolic expression. *Communication Monographs* 55, 41–57.

Einhorn, L. (2006). Using e-prime and English minus absolutisms to provide self-empathy. *Etc.: A Review of General Semantics* 63 (April), 180–186.

Eisenberger, N. I., Liberman, M. D., & Williams, K. D. (2003). Does rejection hurt? An fMRI study of social exclusion. *Science* 302 (October), 290–292.

Ekman, P. (1985). *Telling lies: Clues to deceit in the marketplace, politics, and marriage.* New York, NY: Norton.

Ekman, P., & Friesen, W. V. (1969). The repertoire of nonverbal behavior: Categories, origins, usage, and coding. *Semiotica* 1, 49–98.

Ekman, P., Friesen, W. V., & Ellsworth, P. (1972). *Emotion in the human face: Guidelines for research and an integration of findings.* New York, NY: Pergamon Press.

Elfenbein, H. A., & Ambady, N. (2002). Is there an in-group advantage in emotion recognition? *Psychological Bulletin* 128, 243–249.

Ellis, A. (1988). *How to stubbornly refuse to make yourself miserable about anything, yes anything.* Secaucus, NJ: Lyle Stuart.

Ellis, A., & Harper, R. A. (1975). *A new guide to rational living.* Hollywood, CA: Wilshire Books.

Ellis, K. (2004). The impact of perceived teacher confirmation on receiver apprehension, motivation, and learning. *Communication Education* 53 (January), 1–20.

Elmes, M. B., & Gemmill, G. (1990). The psychodynamics of mindlessness and dissent in small groups. *Small Group Research* 21, 28–44.

Emmers-Sommer, T. M. (2004). The effect of communication quality and quantity indicators on intimacy and relational satisfaction. *Journal of Social and Personal Relationships* 21 (June), 99–411.

Epstein, R. (2005). The loose screw awards: Psychology's top 10 misguided ideas. *Psychology Today* (February), 55–62.

Epstein, R. M., & Hundert, E. M. (2002). Defining and assessing professional competence. *JAMA: Journal of the American Medical Association* 287, 226–235.

Exline, R. V., Ellyson, S. L., & Long, B. (1975). Visual behavior as an aspect of power role relationships. In *Nonverbal communication of aggression,* P. Pliner, L. Krames, & T. Alloway (eds.). New York, NY: Plenum Press.

Fagan, J., & Barnett, M. (2003). The relationship between maternal gatekeeping, paternal competence, mothers' attitudes about the father role, and father involvement. *Journal of Family Issues* 24 (November), 1020–1043.

Faigley, L. (2009). *The Penguin handbook,* 3rd ed. New York, NY: Longman.

Feeley, T. H., & deTurck, M. A. (1995). Global cue usage in behavioral lie detection. *Communication Quarterly* 43, 420–430.

Fehr, B. (2004). Intimacy expectations in same-sex friendships: A prototype interaction-pattern model. *Journal of Personality and Social Psychology* 86 (February), 265–284.

Fehr, B., & Broughton, R. (2001). Gender and personality differences in concepts of love: An interpersonal theory analysis. *Personal Relationships* 8, 115–136.

Fengler, A. P. (1974). Romantic love in courtship: Divergent paths of male and female students. *Journal of Comparative Family Studies* 5, 134–139.

Fernald, C. D. (1995). When in London . . . : Differences in disability language preferences among English-speaking countries. *Mental Retardation* 33, 99–103.

Ferraro, G. (2005). *Cultural dimension of international business,* 5th ed. Upper Saddle River, NJ: Prentice-Hall.

Fesko, S. L. (2001). Disclosure of HIV status in the workplace: Considerations and strategies. *Health and Social Work* 26 (November), 235–244.

Fife, E. M. (2007). Male friendship and competition: A dialectical analysis. *Ohio Communication Journal* 45, 41–64.

Finn, J. (2004). A survey of online harassment at a university campus. *English* 19 (April), 468–483.

Fischer, A. H. (1993). Sex differences in emotionality: Fact or stereotype? *Feminism & Psychology* 3, 303–318.

Fisher, C. (1998). Mood and emotions while working—missing pieces of job satisfaction. *School of Business Discussion Papers.* Available at: http://works.bepress.com/cynthia_fisher/3

Fisher, D. (1995). *People power: 12 power principles to enrich your business, career, and personal networks.* Austin, TX: Bard & Stephen.

Fitzpatrick, M. A. (1983). Predicting couples' communication from couples' self-reports. In *Communication yearbook 7,* R. N. Bostrom (ed.). Thousand Oaks, CA: Sage, pp. 49–82.

Fitzpatrick, M. A. (1988). *Between husbands and wives: Communication in marriage.* Thousand Oaks, CA: Sage.

Fitzpatrick, M. A. (1991). Sex differences in marital conflict: Social psychophysiological versus cognitive explanations. *Text* 11, 341–364.

Fitzpatrick, M. A., & Caughlin, J. P. (2002). Interpersonal communication in family relationships. In *Handbook of interpersonal communication,* 3rd ed., (pp. 726–777), M. L. Knapp & J. A. Daly. (eds.). Thousand Oaks, CA: Sage.

Fitzpatrick, M. A., Jandt, F. E., Myrick, F. L., & Edgar, T. (1994). Gay and lesbian couple relationships. In *Queer words, queer images: Communication and the construction of homosexuality* (pp. 265–285), Ringer, R. J. (ed.). New York, NY: New York University Press.

Floyd, J. J. (1985). *Listening: A practical approach.* Glenview, IL: Scott, Foresman.

Floyd, K., & Mikkelson, A. C. (2005). In *The sourcebook of nonverbal measures: Going beyond words* (pp. 47–56), V. Manusov (ed.). Mahwah, NJ: Erlbaum.

Folger, J. P., Poole, M. S., & Stutman, R. K. (2009). *Working through conflict: A communication perspective,* 6th ed. Boston, MA: Allyn & Bacon.

Forbes, G. B. (2001). College students with tattoos and piercings: Motives, family experiences, personality factors, and perception by others. *Psychological Reports* 89, 774–786.

Ford, S. (2003). "Dear Mr. Shawn": A lesson in e-mail pragmatics (netiquette). *TESOL Journal* 12 (spring), 39–40.

Foster, D. (2004). Standing on ceremony. *National Geographic Traveler* 21 (May–June), 97–99

Fox, A. B., Bukatki, D., Hallahan, M., & Crawford, M. (2007). The medium makes a difference: Gender similarities and differences in instant messaging. *Journal of Language and Social Psychology* 26, 389–397.

Franklin, C. W., & Mizell, C. A. (1995). Some factors influencing success among African-American men: A preliminary study. *Journal of Men's Studies* 3, 191–204.

Franklin, R. (2002). Office romances: Conduct unbecoming? *Business Week Online* (February 14), np.

Fraser, B. (1990). Perspectives on politeness. *Journal of Pragmatics* 14, 219–236.

Freedman, J. (1978). *Happy people: What happiness is, who has it, and why.* New York, NY: Ballantine.

French, J. R. P., Jr., & Raven, B. (1968). The bases of social power. In *Group dynamics: Research and theory,* 3rd ed., D. Cartwright & A. Zander (eds.). New York, NY: Harper & Row, pp. 259–269.

Frentz, T. (1976). A general approach to episodic structure. Paper presented at the Western Speech Association Convention, San Francisco. Cited in Reardon (1987).

Friedman, J., Boumil, M. M., & Taylor, B. E. (1992). *Sexual harassment.* Deerfield Beach, FL: Health Communications, Inc.

Frith, H. & Gleeson, K. (2004). Clothing and embodiment: Men managing body image and appearance. *Psychology of Men and Masculinity,* 5(1), 40–48.

Frone, M. R. (2000). Interpersonal conflict at work and psychological outcomes: Testing a model among young workers. *Journal of Occupational Health Psychology* 5, 246–255.

Fu, H., Watkins, D., & Hui, E. K. P. (2004). Personality correlates of the disposition towards interpersonal forgiveness: Chinese perspective. *International Journal of Psychology* 39 (August), 305–316.

Fuller, D. (2004). Electronic manners and netiquette. *Athletic Therapy Today* 9 (March), 40–41.

Furlow, F. B. (1996). The smell of love. *Psychology Today* 29, 38–45.

Galvin, K. M., Bylund, C. L., & Brommel, B. J. (2008). *Family communication: Cohesion and change,* 7th ed. Boston, MA: Allyn & Bacon.

Gamble, T. K., & Gamble, M. W. (2003). *The gender communication connection.* Boston, MA: Houghton Mifflin.

Gamson, J. (1998). Publicity traps: Television talk shows and lesbian, gay, bisexual, and transgender visibility. *Sexualities* 1 (February), 11–41.

Gao, G., & Gudykunst, W. B. (1995). Attributional confidence, perceived similarity, and network involvement in Chinese and American romantic relationships. *Communication Quarterly* 43, 431–445.

Gattis, K. S., Berns, S., Simpson, L. E., & Christensen, A. (2004). Birds of a feature or strange birds? Ties among personality dimensions, similarity, and marital quality. *Journal of Family Psychology* 18 (December), 564–574.

Gelfand, M. J., Nishii, L. H., Holcombe, K. M., Dyer, N., Ohbuchi, K., & Fukuno, M. (2001). Cultural influences on cognitive representations of conflict: Interpretations of conflict episodes in the United States and Japan. *Journal of Applied Psychology* 86, 1059–1074.

Gelles, R., & Cornell, C. (1985). *Intimate violence in families.* Thousand Oaks, CA: Sage.

Georgas, J., Mylonas, K., Bafiti, T., & Poortinga, Y. H. (2001). Functional relationships in the nuclear and extended family: A 16-culture study. *International Journal of Psychology* 36, 289–300.

Gergen, K. J., Greenberg, M. S., and Willis, R. H. (1980). *Social exchange: Advances in theory and research.* New York, NY: Plenum Press.

Gibb, J. (1961). Defensive communication. *Journal of Communication* 11, 141–148.

Gibbs, N. (2005). Parents behaving badly. *Time* (February 21), 40–49.

Giles, D. C. (2001). Parasocial interaction: A review of the literature and a model for future research. *Media Psychology* 4, 279–305.

Giles, D. C., & Maltby, J. (2004). The role of media figures in adolescent development: Relations between autonomy, attachment, and interest in celebrities. *Personality and Individual Differences* 36 (March), 813–822.

Giles, H. (2008). Communication accommodation theory. In *Engaging theories in interpersonal communication: Multiple perspectives* (pp. 161–174), L. A. Baxter & D. O. Braithwaite (eds.). Los Angeles, CA: Sage.

Giles, H., & Ogay, T. (2007). In *Explaining communication: Contemporary theories and exemplars* (pp. 293–310), B. B. Whaley, & W. Samter (eds.). Mahwah, NJ: Erlbaum.

Gladstone, G. L., & Parker, G. B. (2002). When you're smiling, does the whole world smile with you? *Australasian Psychiatry* 10 (June), 144–146.

Goffman, E. (1967). *Interaction ritual: Essays on face-to-face behavior.* New York, NY: Pantheon.

Goffman, E. (1971). *Relations in public: Microstudies of the public order.* New York, NY: Harper Colophon.

Goldin-Meadow, S., Nusbaum, H., Kelly, S. D., & Wagner, S. (2001). Gesture—Psychological aspects. *Psychological Science* 12, 516–522.

Goldsmith, D. J. (2007). Brown and Levinson's politeness theory. In *Explaining communication: Contemporary theories and exemplars* (pp. 219–236), B. B. Whaley & W. Samter (eds.). Mahwah, NJ: Erlbaum.

Goldsmith, D. J. (2008). Politeness theory. In *Engaging theories in interpersonal communication: Multiple perspectives* (pp. 255–268), L. A. Baxter & D. O. Braithwaite (eds.). Los Angeles, CA: Sage.

Goldsmith, D. J., & Fulfs, P. A. (1999). "You just don't have the evidence": An analysis of claims and evidence. In *Communication yearbook, 22* (pp. 1–49), M. E. Roloff (ed.). Thousand Oaks, CA: Sage.

Goleman, D. (1992). Studies find no disadvantage in growing up in a gay home. *New York Times* (December 2), C14.

Goleman, D. (1995a). *Emotional intelligence.* New York, NY: Bantam.

Goleman, D. (1995b). For man and beast, language of love shares many traits. *New York Times* (February 14), C1, C9.

[KS3]Gonzaga, G. C., Keltner, D., Londahl, E. A., & Smith, M. D. (2001). Love and the commitment problem in romantic relationships and friendships. *Journal of Personality and Social Psychology* 81 (August), 247–262.

Gonzalez, A., & Zimbardo, P. G. (1985). Time in perspective. *Psychology Today* 19, 20–26. Goodwin, R., & Findlay, C. (1997). "We were just fated together" . . . Chinese love and the concept of *yuan* in England and Hong Kong. *Personal Relationships* 4, 85–92.

Goodwin, R., & Gaines, S. O., Jr. (2004). Relationships beliefs and relationship quality across cultures: Country as a moderator of dysfunctional beliefs and relationship quality in three former Communist societies. *Personal Relationships* 11 (September), 267–279.

Gordon, A. (2010). Facing up to Fatigue. *Psychology Today* (July/August), 29.

Gordon, T. (1975). *P.E.T.: Parent effectiveness training.* New York, NY: New American Library.

Gosling, S. D., Ko, S. J., Mannarelli, T., & Morris, M. E. (2002). A room with a cue: Personality judgments based on offices and bedrooms. *Journal of Personality and Social Psychology* 82 (March), 379–398.

Gottman, J. M., & Carrere, S. (1994). Why can't men and women get along? Developmental roots and marital inequities. In D. J. Canary and L. Stafford (eds.). *Communication and relational maintenance,* San Diego, CA: Academic Press, pp. 203–229.

Gottman, J. M., & Levenson, R. W. (1999). Dysfunctional marital conflict: Women are being unfairly blamed. *Journal of Divorce and Remarriage* 31, 1–17.

Gould, S. J. (1995). No more "wretched refuse." *New York Times* (June 7), A27.

Grace, S. L., & Cramer, K. L. (2003). The elusive nature of self-measurement: The self-construal scale versus the twenty statements test. *Journal of Social Psychology* 143 (October), 649–668.

Graham, E. E., Barbato, C. A., & Perse, E. M. (1993). The interpersonal communication motives model. *Communication Quarterly* 41, 172–186.

Graham, J. A., & Argyle, M. (1975). The effects of different patterns of gaze, combined with different facial expressions, on impression formation. *Journal of Movement Studies* 1, 178–182.

Graham, J. A., Bitti, P. R., & Argyle, M. (1975). A cross-cultural study of the communication of emotion by facial and gestural cues. *Journal of Human Movement Studies* 1, 68–77.

Graham, J. L. & Hernandez Requejo, W. (2008). *Global negotiation: The new rules.* New York, NY: Macmillan.

Grandey, A. A. (2000). Emotion regulation in the workplace: A new way to conceptualize emotional labor. *Journal of Occupational Health and Psychology* 5 (January), 95–110.

Greene, J. O. (2003). Models of adult communication skill acquisition: Practice and the course of performance improvement. In *Handbook of communication and social interaction skills,* J. O. Greene & B. R. Burleson (eds.). Mahwah, NJ: Erlbaum, pp. 51–92.

Greene, J. O., & Burleson, B. R. (eds.). (2003). *Handbook of communication and social interaction skills.* Mahwah, NJ: Erlbaum.

Greif, E. B. (1980). Sex differences in parent-child conversations. *Women's Studies International Quarterly* 3, 253–258.

Greitemeyer, T. (2007). What do men and women want in a partner? Are educated partners always more desirable? *Journal of Experimental Social Psychology* 43 (March), 180–194.

Grice, H. P. (1975). Logic and conversation. In *Syntax and semantics,* Vol. 3, *Speech acts,* P. Cole & J. L. Morgan (eds.). New York, NY: Seminar Press, pp. 41–58.

Gross, T., Turner, E., & Cederholm, L. (1987). Building teams for global operation, *Management Review* (June), 32–36.

Gu, Y. (1990). Polite phenomena in modern Chinese. *Journal of Pragmatics* 14, 237–257.

Gudykunst, W. B., ed. (1983). *Intercultural communication theory: Current perspectives.* Thousand Oaks, CA: Sage.

Gudykunst, W. B. (1989). Culture and the development of interpersonal relationships. In *Communication yearbook 12,* J. A. Anderson (ed.). Thousand Oaks, CA: Sage, pp. 315–354.

Gudykunst, W. B. (1991). *Bridging differences: Effective intergroup communication.* Newbury Park, CA: Sage.

Gudykunst, W. B. (1993). Toward a theory of effective interpersonal and intergroup communication: An anxiety/uncertainty management (AUM) perspective. In *Intercultural communication competence,* R. L. Wiseman (ed.). Thousand Oaks, CA: Sage.

Gudykunst, W. B. (1994). *Bridging differences: Effective intergroup communication,* 2nd ed. Thousand Oaks, CA: Sage.

Gudykunst, W. B., & Kim, Y. W. (1992). *Communicating with strangers: An approach to intercultural communication,* 2nd ed. New York, NY: Random House.

Gudykunst, W. B., & Ting-Toomey, S. (with Chua, E.) (1988). *Culture and interpersonal communication.* Thousand Oaks, CA: Sage.

Guéguen, N. (2003). Help on the Web: The effect of the same first name between the sender and the receptor in a request made by e-mail. *Psychological Record* 53 (summer), 459–466.

Guéguen, N., & Jacob, C. (2004). The effect of touch on tipping: An evaluation in a French bar. *International Journal of Hospitality Management* 24 (June), 295–299.

Guerin, B. (2003). Combating prejudice and racism: New interventions from a functional analysis of racist language. *Journal of Community and Applied Social Psychology* 13 (January), 29–45.

Guerrero, L. K. (1997). Nonverbal involvement across interactions with same-sex friends, opposite-sex friends, and romantic partners: Consistency or change? *Journal of Social and Personal Relationships* 14, 31–58.

Guerrero, L. K., & Andersen, P. A. (1991). The waxing and waning of relational intimacy: Touch as a function of relational stage, gender and touch avoidance. *Journal of Social and Personal Relationships* 8, 147–165.

Guerrero, L. K., Andersen, P. A., & Afifi, W. A. (2007). *Close encounters: Communication in relationships,* 2nd ed. Thousand Oaks, CA: Sage.

Guerrero, L. K., Andersen, P. A., Jorgensen, P. F., Spitzberg, B. H., & Eloy, S. V. (1995). Coping with the green-eyed monster: Conceptualizing and measuring communicative response to romantic jealousy. *Western Journal of Communication* 59, 270–304.

Guerrero, L. K., & Hecht, M. L., eds. (2008). *The nonverbal communication reader: Classic and contemporary readings,* 3rd ed.. Prospect Heights, IL: Waveland Press.

Guerrero, L. K., Eloy, S. V., & Wabnik, A. I. (1993). Linking maintenance strategies to relationship development and disengagement: A reconceptualization. *Journal of Social and Personal Relationships* 10, 273–282.

Guerrero, L. K., Jones, S. M., & Boburka, R. R. (2006). Sex differences in emotional communication. In *Sex differences and similarities in communication* (2nd ed., pp. 241–262), K. Dindia & D. J. Canary (eds.). Mahwah, NJ: Erlbaum.

Haar, B. F., & Krabe, B. (1999). Strategies for resolving interpersonal conflicts in adolescence: A German-Indonesian comparison. *Journal of Cross-Cultural Psychology* 30, 667–683.

Haga, Y. (1988). Traits de langage et caractere japonais. *Cahiers de Sociologie Economique et Culturelle* 9, 105–109.

Haidar-Yassine, H. (2002). Internet friendships: Can virtual be real? *Dissertation Abstracts International: Section B: The Sciences & Engineering* 63 (5-B), 2651.

Hall, E. T. (1959). *The silent language.* Garden City, NY: Doubleday.

Hall, E. T. (1963). System for the notation of proxemic behavior. *American Anthropologist* 65, 1003–1026.

Hall, E. T. (1966). *The hidden dimension.* Garden City, NY: Doubleday.

Hall, E. T. (1976). *Beyond culture.* Garden City, NY: Anchor Press.

Hall, E. T., & Hall, M. R. (1987). *Hidden differences: Doing business with the Japanese.* New York, NY: Anchor Books.

Hall, J. A. (1984). *Nonverbal sex differences.* Baltimore: Johns Hopkins University Press.

Hall, J. A. (2006). Women's and men's nonverbal communication: Similarities, differences, stereotypes, and origins. In *The Sage handbook of nonverbal communication* (pp. 201–218), V. Manusov & M. L. Patterson (eds.). Thousand Oaks, CA: Sage.

Hall, J. K. (1993). Tengo una bomba: The paralinguistic and linguistic conventions of the oral practice Chismeando. *Research on Language and Social Interaction* 26, 55–83.

Hamlin, J. K., Wynn, K., & Bloom, P. (2007). Babies prefer helpful to unhelpful social types. *Nature* 450 (November), 557–559.

Hample, D. (2004). Arguing skills. In *Handbook of communication and social interaction skills* (pp. 439–477), J. O. Greene & B. R. Burleson (eds.). Mahwah, NJ: Erlbaum.

Han, S., & Shavitt, S. (1994). Persuasion and culture: Advertising appeals in individualistic and collectivistic societies. *Journal of Experimental Social Psychology* 30, 326–350.

Haney, W. (1973). *Communication and organizational behavior: Text and cases,* 3rd ed. Homewood, IL: Irwin.

Harris, C. R. (2003). A review of sex differences in sexual jealousy, including self-report data, psychophysiological responses, interpersonal violence, and morbid jealousy. *Personality and Social Psychology Review* 7, 102–128.

Harris, M. (1993). *Culture, people, nature: An introduction to general anthropology,* 6th ed. Boston, MA: Allyn & Bacon.

Hart, F. (1990). The construction of masculinity in men's friendships: Misogyny, heterosexism and homophobia. *Resources for Feminist Research* 19, 60–67.

Hart Research Associates (2010). Raising the bar: Employers' views on college learning in the wake of the economic downturn: A survey among employers conducted on behalf of the Association of American Colleges and Universities. Washington, D.C.

Hart, R. P., Carlson, R. E., & Eadie, W. F. (1980). Attitudes toward communication and the assessment of rhetorical sensitivity. *Communication Monographs* 47, 1–22.

Harvey, J. H., Flanary, R., & Morgan, M. (1986). Vivid memories of vivid loves gone by. *Journal of Social and Personal Relationships* 3, 359–373.

Hasart, J. K., & Hutchinson, K. L. (1993). The effects of eyeglasses on perceptions of interpersonal attraction. *Journal of Social Behavior and Personality* 8, 521–528.

Hasegawa, T., & Gudykunst, W. B. (1998). Silence in Japan and the United States. *Journal of Cross-Cultural Psychology* 29, 668–684.

Hatfield, E., & Rapson, R. L. (1996). *Love and sex: Cross-cultural perspectives.* Boston, MA: Allyn & Bacon.

Hatfield, E., & Rapson, R. L. (2007). Equity theory. In *Encyclopedia of Social Psychology*, R. Baumeister & K. D. Vohs (eds.). Los Angeles: Sage.

Haugh, M. (2004). Revisiting the conceptualization of politeness in English and Japanese. *Multilingua* 23, 85–109.

Havlena, W. J., Holbrook, M. B., & Lehmann, D. R. (1989). Assessing the validity of emotional typologies. *Psychology and Marketing* 6 (Summer), 97–112.

Hayakawa, S. I., & Hayakawa, A. R. (1989). *Language in thought and action,* 5th ed. New York, NY: Harcourt Brace Jovanovich.

Hays, R. B. (1989). The day-to-day functioning of close versus casual friendships. *Journal of Social and Personal Relationships* 6, 21–37.

Heasley, J. B. S., Babbitt, C. E., & Burbach, H. J. (1995). The role of social context in students' anticipatory reaction to a "fighting word." *Sociological Focus* 27, 281–283.

Heath, W. P., Stone, J., Darley, J. M., & Grannemann, B. D. (2003). Yes, I did it, but don't blame me: Perceptions of excuse defenses. *Journal of Psychiatry and Law* 31 (summer), 187–226.

Hecht, M. L., Jackson, R. L., & Ribeau, S. (2003). *African American communication: Exploring identity and culture,* 2nd ed. Mahwah, NJ: Erlbaum.

Hellweg, S. A. (1992). Organizational grapevines. In *Readings in organizational communication* (pp. 159–172), K. L. Hutchinson (ed.). Dubuque, IA: William. C. Brown.

Hendrick, C., & Hendrick, S. (1990). A relationship-specific version of the love attitudes scale. In *Handbook of replication research in the behavioral and social sciences* (special issue), J. W. Heulip (ed.), *Journal of Social Behavior and Personality* 5, 239–254.

Hendrick, C., Hendrick, S., Foote, F. H., & Slapion-Foote, M. J. (1984). Do men and women love differently? *Journal of Social and Personal Relationships* 1, 177–195.

Henley, N. M. (1977). *Body politics: Power, sex, and nonverbal communication.* Upper Saddle River, NJ: Prentice-Hall.

Hensley, W. E. (1996). A theory of the valenced other: The intersection of the looking-glass-self and social penetration. *Social Behavior and Personality* 24, 293–308.

Hess, E. H. (1975). *The tell-tale eye.* New York, NY: Van Nostrand Reinhold.

Hess, E. H., Seltzer, A. L., & Schlien, J. M. (1965). Pupil response of hetero- and homosexual males to pictures of men and women: A pilot study. *Journal of Abnormal Psychology* 70, 165–168.

Hess, U., Kappas, A., McHugo, G. J., Lanzetta, J. T., et al. (1992). The facilitative effect of facial expression on the self-generation of emotion. *International Journal of Psychophysiology* 12, 251–265.

Hewitt, J. P. (1998). *The myth of self-esteem: Finding happiness and solving problems in America.* New York, NY: St. Martin's Press.

Hewitt, J. P., & Stokes, R. (1975). Disclaimers. *American Sociological Review* 40, 1–11.

Hilton, L. (2000). They heard it through the grapevine. *South Florida Business Journal* 21 (August), 53.

Hinduja, S., & Patchin, J. W. (2010). Cyberbullying: Identification, prevention, and response. Retrieved from http://www.cyberbullying.us

Hirofumi, A. (2003). Closeness and interpersonal outcomes in same-sex friendships: An improvement of the investment model and explanation of closeness. *Japanese Journal of Experimental Social Psychology* 42 (March), 131–145.

Hocker, J. L., & Wilmot, W. W. (2007). *Interpersonal conflict*, 7th ed. New York, NY: McGraw Hill.

Hoffmann, G. (2005). Rhetoric of Bush speeches: Purr words and snarl words. *Etc: A Review of General Semantics* 62 (April), 198–201.

Hofstede, G. (1983). National culture revisited. *Behavior Science Research* 18, 285–305.

Hofstede, G. (1997). *Cultures and organizations: Software of the mind.* New York, NY: McGraw-Hill.

Hofstede, G. (2000). Masculine and feminine cultures. *Encyclopedia of psychology,* Vol. 5 (pp. 115–118), A. E. Kazdin (ed.). Washington, DC: American Psychological Association and Oxford University Press.

Hofstede, G., ed. (1998). *Masculinity and femininity: The taboo dimension of national cultures.* Thousand Oaks, CA: Sage.

Hoft, N. L. (1995). *International technical communication: How to export information about high technology.* New York, NY: Wiley.

Holden, J. M. (1991). The most frequent personality priority pairings in marriage and marriage counseling. *Individual Psychology Journal of Adlerian Theory, Research, and Practice* 47, 392–398.

Holmes, J. (1995). *Women, men and politeness.* New York, NY: Longman.

Hopper, R., Knapp, M. L., & Scott, L. (1981). Couples' personal idioms: Exploring intimate talk. *Journal of Communication* 31, 23–33.

Hornsey, J. J., Bath, M. T., & Gunthorpe, S. (2004). "You can criticize because you care": Identity attachment, constructiveness, and the intergroup sensitivity effect. *European Journal of Social Psychology* 34 (September–October), 499–518.

Hosman, L. A. (1989). The evaluative consequences of hedges, hesitations, and intensifiers: Powerful and powerless speech styles. *Human Communication Research* 15, 383–406.

How Americans Communicate (1999). Retrieved from http://www.natcom.org/Research/Roper/how_Americans_communicate.htm

Howard, P. E. N., Rainie, L., & Jones, S. (2001). Days and nights on the Internet: The impact of a diffusing technology. *American Behavioral Scientist* 45, 383–404.

Hu, Y., Wood, J. F., Smith, V., & Westbrook, N. (2004). Friendships through IM: Examining the relationship between instant messaging and intimacy. *Journal of Computer-Mediated Communication* 10 (November), np.

Hunt, M. O. (2000). Status, religion, and the "belief in a just world": Comparing African Americans, Latinos, and whites. *Social Science Quarterly* 81 (March), 325–343.

Huston, M., & Schwartz, P. (1995). The relationships of lesbians and gay men. In *Under-studied relationships: Off the beaten track*, J. T. Wood, & S. Duck (eds.). Thousand Oaks, CA: Sage, pp. 89–121.

Imwalle, D. B., & Schillo, K. K. (2004). Masculinity and femininity: The taboo dimension of national cultures. *Archives of Sexual Behavior* 33 (April), 174–176.

Infante, D. A. (1988). *Arguing constructively.* Prospect Heights, IL: Waveland Press.

Infante, D. A., Chandler, T. A., & Rudd, J. E. (1989). Test of an argumentative skill deficiency model of interspousal violence. *Communication Monographs* 56, 163–177.

Infante, D. A., Hartley, K. C., Martin, M. M., Higgins, M. A., Bruning, S. D., & Hur, G. (1992). Initiating and reciprocating verbal aggression: Effects on credibility and credited valid arguments. *Communication Studies* 43, 182–190.

Infante, D. A., & Rancer, A. S. (1982). A conceptualization and measure of argumentativeness. *Journal of Personality Assessment* 46, 72–80.

Infante, D. A., & Rancer, A. S. (1996). Argumentativeness and verbal aggressiveness: A review of recent theory and research. In *Communication yearbook 19* (pp. 319–351), B. R. Burleson (ed.). Thousand Oaks, CA: Sage.

Infante, D. A., Rancer, A. S., & Jordan, F. F. (1996). Affirming and nonaffirming style, dyad sex, and the perception of argumentation and verbal aggression in an interpersonal dispute. *Human Communication Research* 22, 315–334.

Infante, D. A., Rancer, A. S., & Womack, D. F. (2003). *Building communication theory,* 4th ed. Prospect Heights, IL: Waveland Press.

Infante, D. A., Riddle, B. L., Horvath, C. L., & Tumlin, S. A. (1992). Verbal aggressiveness: Messages and reasons. *Communication Quarterly* 40, 116–126.

Infante, D. A., Sabourin, T. C., Rudd, J. E., & Shannon, E. A. (1990). Verbal aggression in violent and nonviolent marital disputes. *Communication Quarterly* 38, 361–371.

Infante, D. A., & Wigley, C. J. (1986). Verbal aggressiveness: An interpersonal model and measure. *Communication Monographs* 53, 61–69.

Ingegneri, R. (2008). How should you handle tattoos and body piercing during a job interview. http://ezinearticles.com/?expert=Rachel_Ingegneri.

Iverson, J. M., & Goldin-Meadow, S., eds. (1999). *The nature and functions of gesture in children's communication.* San Francisco: Jossey-Bass.

Ivy, D. K., & Backlund, P. (2000). *Exploring gender-speak: Personal effectiveness in gender communication,* 2nd ed. New York, NY: McGraw-Hill.

Jackson, L. A., & Ervin, K. S. (1992). Height stereotypes of women and men: The liabilities of shortness for both sexes. *Journal of Social Psychology* 132, 433–445.

Jacobson, D. (1999). Impression formation in cyberspace: Online expectations and offline experiences in text-based virtual communities. *Journal of Computer Mediated Communication* 5, np.

Jaksa, J. A., & Pritchard, M. S. (1994). *Communication ethics: Methods of analysis,* 2nd ed. Belmont, CA: Wadsworth.

Jambor, E., & Elliott, M. (2005). Self-esteem and coping strategies among deaf students. *Journal of Deaf Studies and Deaf Education* 10 (winter), 63–81.

Jandt, F. E. (2004). *An introduction to intercultural communication: Identities in a global community,* 4th ed. Thousand Oaks, CA: Sage.

Jandt, F. E. (2007). *An introduction to intercultural communication: Identities in a global community,* 5th ed. Thousand Oaks, CA: Sage.

Janus, S. S., & Janus, C. L. (1993). *The Janus report on sexual behavior.* New York, NY: Wiley.

Jaworski, A. (1993). *The power of silence: Social and pragmatic perspectives.* Thousand Oaks, CA: Sage.

Jecker, J., & Landy, D. (1969). Liking a person as a function of doing him a favor. *Human Relations* 22, 371–378.

Johannesen, R. L. (2001). *Ethics in human communication,* 5th ed. Prospect Heights, IL: Waveland Press.

Johnson, A. J., Wittenberg, E., Villagran, M. M., Mazur, M., & Villagran, P. (2003). Relational progression as a dialectic: Examining turning points in communication among friends. *Communication Monographs* 70 (September), 230–249.

Johnson, C. E. (1987). An introduction to powerful and powerless talk in the classroom. *Communication Education* 36, 167–172.

Johnson, M. P. (1973). Commitment: A conceptual structure and empirical application. *Sociological Quarterly* 14, 395–406.

Johnson, M. P. (1982). Social and cognitive features of the dissolution of commitment to relationships. In *Personal Relationships 4: Dissolving Personal Relationships,* (pp. 51–73), S. Duck (ed.). New York, NY: Academic Press.

Johnson, M. P. (1991). Commitment to personal relationships. In *Advances in personal relationships, Vol. 3* (pp. 117–143), W. H. Jones, & D. Perlman (eds.). London: Jessica Kingsley.

Johnson, S. D., & Bechler, C. (1998). Examining the relationship between listening effectiveness and leadership emergence: Perceptions, behaviors, and recall. *Small Group Research* 29, 452–471.

Johnson, S. M., & O'Connor, E. (2002). *The gay baby boom: The psychology of gay parenthood.* New York, NY: New York University Press.

Joiner, T. E. (1994). Contagious depression: Existence, specificity to depressed symptoms, and the role of reassurance seeking. *Journal of Personality and Social Psychology* 67, 287–296.

Joinson, A. N. (2001). Self-disclosure in computer-mediated communication: The role of self-awareness and visual anonymity. *European Journal of Social Psychology* 31, 177–192.

Jones, B. C., DeBruine, L. M., Little, A. C., Burriss, R. P., & Feinberg, D. R. (2007). Social transmission of face preferences among humans. *Proceedings of the Royal Society* 274 (March 22), 899–903.

Jones, C., Berry, L., & Stevens, C. (2007). Synthesized speech intelligibility and persuasion: Speech rate and non-native listeners. *Computer Speech and Language* 21 (October), 641–651.

Jones, D. (2004). Cupid lurks in cubicles, so what's a worker to do? *USA Today* (April 2), Money Section, 5.

Jones, S. (2005). The touch log record: A behavioral communication measure. In *Applications of nonverbal communication* (pp. 67–82), R. E. Riggio & R. S. Feldman (eds.). Mahwah, NJ: Erlbaum.

Jones, S., & Yarbrough, A. E. (1985). A naturalistic study of the meanings of touch. *Communication Monographs* 52, 19–56.

Jörn, R. (2004). How to overcome ethnocentrism: Approaches to a culture of recognition by history in the twenty-first century. *History and Theory* 43 (December), 118–129.

Jourard, S. M. (1968). *Disclosing man to himself.* New York, NY: Van Nostrand Reinhold.

Jourard, S. M. (1971). *Self-disclosure.* New York, NY: Wiley.

Judge, T. A., & Cable, D. M. (2004). The effect of physical height on workplace success and income. *Journal of Applied Psychology* 89, 428–441.

Kallos, J. (2005). *Because netiquette matters! Your comprehensive reference guide to e-mail etiquette and proper technology use.* Philadelphia: Xlibris Corporation.

Kanemasa, Y., Taniguchi, J., Daibo, I., & Ishimori, M. (2004). Love styles and romantic love experiences in Japan. *Social Behavior and Personality: An International Journal* 32, 265–281.

Kanner, B. (1989). Color schemes. *New York Magazine* (April 3), 22–23.

Kapoor, S., Wolfe, A., & Blue, J. (1995). Universal values structure and individualism–collectivism: A U.S. test. *Communication Research Reports* 12, 112–123.

Katz, S. (2003). *Down to earth sociology: Introductory readings,* 12th ed. (pp. 313–320), J. W. Henslin (ed.). New York, NY: Free Press.

Kearney, P., Plax, T. G., Richmond, V. P., & McCroskey, J. C. (1984). Power in the classroom IV: Alternatives to discipline. In *Communication Yearbook 8,* R. N. Bostrom (ed.). Thousand Oaks, CA: Sage, pp. 724–746.

Kearney, P., Plax, T. G., Richmond, V. P., & McCroskey, J. C. (1985). Power in the classroom III: Teacher communication techniques and messages. *Communication Education* 34, 19–28.

Keating, C. F. (2006). Why and how the silence self speaks volumes: Functional approaches to nonverbal impression management. In *The Sage handbook of nonverbal communication* (pp. 321–340), V. Manusov & M. L. Patterson (eds.). Thousand Oaks, CA: Sage.

Kellerman, K., & Cole, T. (1994). Classifying compliance gaining messages: Taxonomic disorder and strategic confusion. *Communication Theory* 1, 3–60.

Kennedy, C. W., & Camden, C. T. (1988). A new look at interruptions. *Western Journal of Speech Communication* 47, 45–58.

Kennedy-Moore, E., & Watson, J. C. (1999). *Expressing emotion: Myths, realities, and therapeutic strategies.* New York, NY: Guilford Press.

Kenrick, D. T., Neuberg, S. L., and Cialdini, R. B. (2007). *Social psychology: Goals in interaction,* 4th ed. Boston, MA: Allyn & Bacon.

Keyes, R. (1980). *The height of your life.* New York, NY: Warner Books.

Kim, M., & Sharkey, W. F. (1995). Independent and interdependent construals of self: Explaining cultural patterns of interpersonal communication in multi-cultural organizational settings. *Communication Quarterly* 43, 20–38.

Kim, S. H., & Smith, R. H. (1993). Revenge and conflict escalation. *Negotiation Journal* 9, 37–43.

Kim, Y. Y. (1988). Communication and acculturation. In *Intercultural communication: A reader* (4th ed., pp. 344–354), L. A. Samovar & R. E. Porter (eds.). Belmont, CA: Wadsworth.

Kindred, J., & Roper, S. L. (2004). Making connections via instant messaging (IM): Student use of IM to maintain personal relationships. *Qualitative Research Reports in Communication* 5, 48–54.

Kirn, W. (2005). It's a glad, sad, mad world. *Time* (January 17), A65–A67.

Kleinke, C. L. (1986). *Meeting and understanding people.* New York, NY: W. H. Freeman.

Kleinke, D. L., & Dean, G. O. (1990). Evaluation of men and women receiving positive and negative responses with various acquaintance strategies. *Journal of Social Behavior and Personality* 5, 369–377.

Kluger, J. (2005). The funny thing about laughter. *Time* (January 17), A25–A29.

Kluger, J. (2008), January 28). Why we love. *Time*, pp. 54–61.

Knapp, M. L. (1978). *Social intercourse: From greeting to goodbye.* Boston, MA: Allyn & Bacon.

Knapp, M. L. (2008). *Lying and deception in human interaction.* Boston, MA: Pearson.

Knapp, M. L., Ellis, D., & Williams, B. A. (1980). Perceptions of communication behavior associated with relationship terms. *Communication Monographs* 47, 262–278.

Knapp, M. L., & Hall, J. (2002). *Nonverbal behavior in human interaction,* 3rd ed. New York, NY: Holt, Rinehart & Winston.

Knapp, M. L., & Taylor, E. H. (1994). Commitment and its communication in romantic relationships. In *Perspectives on close relationships,* A. L. Weber & J. H. Harvey (eds.). Boston, MA: Allyn & Bacon, pp. 153–175.

Knapp, M. L., & Vangelisti, A. (2009). *Interpersonal communication and human relationships,* 6th ed. Boston, MA: Allyn & Bacon.

Knobloch, L. K., & Carpenter-Theune, K. E. (2004). Topic avoidance in developing romantic relationships. *Communication Research* (April), 173–205.

Knobloch, L. K., Haunani, D., & Theiss, J. A. (2006). The role of intimacy in the production and perception of relationship talk within courtship. *Communication Research* 33 (August), 211–241.

Knobloch, L. K., & Solomon, D. H. (1999). Measuring the sources and content of relational uncertainty. *Communication Studies* 50 (winter), 261–278.

Knobloch, L. K., & Solomon, D. H. (2005). Measuring conversational equality at the relational level. In *The sourcebook of nonverbal measures: Going beyond words* (pp. 295–304), V. Manusov (ed.). Mahwah, NJ: Erlbaum.

Knox, D., Daniels, V., Sturdivant, L., & Zusman, M. E. (2001). College student use of the Internet for mate selection. *College Student Journal* 35, 158–160.

Kochman, T. (1981). *Black and white: Styles in conflict.* Chicago: University of Chicago Press.

Koerner, A. F., & Fitzpattrick, M. A. (1997). Family type and conflict: The impact of conversation orientation and conformity orientation on conflict in the family. *Communication Studies,* 48, 59-76.

Koerner, A. F., & Fitzpatrick, M. A. (2002). You never leave your family in a fight: The impact of family of origin on conflict behavior in romantic relationships. *Communication Studies* 53 (fall), 234–252.

Koerner, A. F., & Fitzpatrick, M. A. (2004). Communication in intact families. In A. L. Vangelisti (Eds), *Handbook of family communication* (pp. 177–195). Mahwah, NJ: Erlbaum.

Kollock, P., & Smith, M. (1996). Managing the virtual commons: Cooperation and conflict in computer communities. In *Computer-mediated communication: Linguistic, social, and cross-cultural perspectives* (pp. 109–128), S. Herring (ed.). Amsterdam: John Benjamins.

Koppelman, K. L., with Goodhart, R. L. (2005). *Understanding human differences: Multicultural education for a diverse America.* Boston, MA: Allyn & Bacon.

Korda, M. (1975). *Power! How to get it, how to use it.* New York, NY: Ballantine.

Korobov, N., & Thorne, A. (2006). Intimacy and distancing: Young men's conversations about romantic relationships. *Journal of Adolescent Research* 21, 27–55.

Korzybski, A. (1933). *Science and sanity.* Lakeville, CT: The International Non-Aristotelian Library.

Kposowa, A. J. (2000). Marital status and suicide in the National Longitudinal Mortality Study. *Journal of Epidemiology and Community Health,* 54 (April), 254–261.

Kramer, R. (1997). Leading by listening: An empirical test of Carl Rogers's theory of human relationship using interpersonal assessments of leaders by followers. *Dissertation Abstracts, International Section A. Humanities and Social Sciences* 58, 514.

Kraut, R., Patterson, M., Lundmarle, V., Kiesler, S., Mukopadhyay, & Scherlis, W. (1999). Internet paradox. *American Psychologist* 53, 1017–1031.

Kreamer, A. (2011). *It's always personal.* New York, NY: Random House.

Krebs, G. L. (1989). *Organizational communication,* 2nd ed. Boston, MA: Allyn & Bacon.

Krivonos, P. D., & Knapp, M. L. (1975). Initiating communication: What do you say when you say hello? *Central States Speech Journal* 26, 115–125.

Krоløkke, C., & Sørensen, A. S. (2006). *Gender communication theories and analyses: From silence to performance.* Thousand Oaks, CA: Sage.

Kurdek, L. A. (1994). Areas of conflict for gay, lesbian, and heterosexual couples: What couples argue about influences relationship satisfaction. *Journal of Marriage and the Family* 56, 923–934.

Kurdek, L. A. (1995). Developmental changes in relationship quality in gay and lesbian cohabiting couples. *Developmental Psychology* 31, 86–93.

Kurdek, L. A. (2000). Attractions and constraints as determinants of relationship commitment: Longitudinal evidence from gay, lesbian, and heterosexual couples. *Personal Relationships* 7, 245–262.

Lachnit, C. (2001). Giving up gossip. *Workforce* 80 (July), 8.

Laing, M. (1993). Gossip: Does it play a role in the socialization of nurses? *Journal of Nursing Scholarship* 25, 37–43.

Lane, R. C., Koetting, M. G., & Bishop, J. (2002). Silence as communication in psychodynamic psychotherapy. *Clinical Psychology Review* 22 (September), 1091–1104.

Langer, E. J. (1989). *Mindfulness.* Reading, MA: Addison-Wesley.

Lantz, A. (2001). Meetings in a distributed group of experts: Comparing face-to-face, chat and collaborative virtual environments. *Behaviour and Information Technology* 20, 111–117.

Lanzetta, J. T., Cartwright-Smith, J., & Kleck, R. E. (1976). Effects of nonverbal dissimulations on emotional experience and autonomic arousal. *Journal of Personality and Social Psychology* 33, 354–370.

Laroche, C., & deGrace, G. R. (1997). Factors of satisfaction associated with happiness in adults. *Canadian Journal of Counseling* 31, 275–286.

Larsen, R. J., Kasimatis, M., & Frey, K. (1992). Facilitating the furrowed brow: An unobtrusive test of the facial feedback hypothesis applied to unpleasant affect. *Cognition and Emotion* 6, 321–338.

Lau, I., Chiu, C., & Hong, Y. (2001). I know what you know: Assumptions about others' knowledge and their effects on message construction. *Social Cognition* 19, 587–600.

Lauer, C. S. (2003). Listen to this. *Modern Healthcare* 33 (February 10), 34.

Lea, M., & Spears, R. (1995). Love at first byte? Building personal relationships over computer networks. In *Understudied relationships: Off the beaten track*, J. T. Wood & S. Duck (eds.). Thousand Oaks, CA: Sage, pp. 197–233.

Leathers, D., & Eaves, M. H. (2008). *Successful nonverbal communication: Principles and applications*, 4th ed. Boston, MA: Allyn & Bacon.

Leavitt, H. J. (2005). *Top down: Why hierarchies are here to stay and how to manage them more effectively.* Cambridge, MA: Harvard Business School Publishing.

Lederer, W. J. (1984). *Creating a good relationship.* New York, NY: Norton.

Lee, H. O., & Boster, F. J. (1992). Collectivism-individualism in perceptions of speech rate: A cross-cultural comparison. *Journal of Cross-Cultural Psychology* 23, 377–388.

Lee, J. (2005). Romance beckons (in case you missed it). *New York Times* (February 23), B4.

Lee, J. A. (1976). *The colors of love.* New York, NY: Bantam.

Lee, J. A. (1988). Forbidden colors of love: Patterns of love and gay liberation. In *Gay relationships* (pp. 11–32), J. P. DeCecco (ed.). San Francisco: Haworth Press.

Lee, R. M. (2005). Resilience against discrimination: Ethnic identity and other-group orientation as protective factors for Korean Americans. *Journal of Counseling Psychology* 52 (January), 36–44.

Lemonick, M. D. (2005a). A smile doesn't always mean happy. *Time* (January 17), A29.

Lemonick, M. D. (2005b). Stealth attack on evaluation. *Time* (January 31), 53–54.

Lenhart, A., & Madden, M. (2007). Social Networking Websites and teens: An overview. *Pew Internet & American Life Project.* Retrieved from www.pewinternet.org

Lenhart, A., Madden, M., Macgill, A. R., & Smith, A. (2007). Teens and social media: The use of social media gains a greater foothold in teen life as they embrace the conversational nature of inteaction online media. *Pew Internet & American Life Project.* Retrieved from http://www.pewinternet.org

Leon, J. J., Philbrick, J. L., Parra, F., Escobedo, E., et al. (1994). Love styles among university students in Mexico. *Psychological Reports* 74, 307–310.

Leonhardt, D. (2011). A better way to measure Twitter influence. *New York Times* (March, 27), Magazine, 18.

Leung, K. (1987). Some determinants of reactions to procedural models for conflict resolution: A cross-national study. *Journal of Personality and Social Psychology* 53, 898–908.

Leung, S. A. (2001). Editor's introduction. *Asian Journal of Counseling* 8, 107–109.

Lev-Ari, S. & Keysar, B. (2010). Why don't we believe non-native speakers? The influence of accent on credibility. *Journal of Experimental Social Psychology,* 46, 1093-1096.

Levine, D. (2000). Virtual attraction: What rocks your boat. *CyberPsychology and Behavior* 3, 565–573.

Levine, M. (2004). Tell the doctor all your problems, but keep it to less than a minute. *New York Times* (June 1), F6.

LeVine, R., Bartlett, K. (1984). Pace of life, punctuality, and coronary heart disease in six countries. *Journal of Cross-Cultural Psychology* 15, 233–255.

LeVine, R., Sato, S., Hashimoto, T., & Verma, J. (1994). Love and marriage in eleven cultures. Unpublished manuscript. California State University, Fresno, cited in Hatfield & Rapson (1996).

Levine, T. R., Beatty, M. J., Limon, S., Hamilton, M. A., Buck, R., & Chory-Assad, R. M. (2004). The dimensionality of the verbal aggressiveness scale. *Communication Monographs* 71 (September), 245–268.

Levine, T. R., Kim, R. K., Park, H. S., & Hughes, M. (2006). Deception detection accuracy is a predictable linear function of message veracity base-rate: A formal test of Park and Levine's probability model. *Communication Monographs* 73, 243–260.

Lewin, K. (1947). *Human relations.* New York, NY: Harper & Row.

Lewis, D. (1989). *The secret language of success.* New York, NY: Carroll & Graf.

Lewis, P. H. (1995). The new Internet gatekeepers. *New York Times* (November 13), D1, D6.

Li, H. Z. (1999). Communicating information in conversations: A cross-cultural comparison. *International Journal of Intercultural Relations* 23 (May), 387–409.

Lindblom, K. (2001). Cooperating with Grice: A cross-disciplinary metaperspective on uses of Grice's cooperative principle. *Journal of Pragmatics* 33, 1601–1623.

Lindeman, M., Harakka, T., & Keltikangas-Jarvinen, L. (1997). Age and gender differences in adolescents' reactions to conflict situations: Aggression, prosociality, and withdrawal. *Journal of Youth and Adolescence* 26, 339–351.

Lu, L., & Shih, J. B. (1997). Sources of happiness: A qualitative approach. *Journal of Social Psychology* 137, 181–188.

Lubin, J. S. (2004). How to stop the snubs that demoralize you and your colleagues. *Wall Street Journal* (December 7), B1.

Luft, J. (1984). *Group processes: An introduction to group dynamics,* 3rd ed. Palo Alto, CA: Mayfield.

Lukens, J. (1978). Ethnocentric speech. *Ethnic Groups* 2, 35–53.

Lurie, A. (1983). *The language of clothes.* New York, NY: Vintage.

Luscombe, B. (2008, January 28). Why we flirt. *Time*, pp. 62–65.

Lustig, M. W., & Koester, J. (2010). *Intercultural competence: Interpersonal communication across cultures,* 7th ed. Boston, MA: Allyn & Bacon.

Lyman, S. M., & Scott, M. B. (1967). Territoriality: A neglected sociological dimension. *Social Problems* 15, 236–249.

Lyons, A., & Kashima, Y. (2003). How are stereotypes maintained through communication? The influence of stereotype sharedness. *Journal of Personality and Social Psychology* 85 (December), 989–1005.

Ma, K. (1996). *The modern Madame Butterfly: Fantasy and reality in Japanese cross-cultural relationships.* Rutland, VT: Charles E. Tuttle.

Mackey, R. A., Diemer, M. A., & O'Brien, B. A. (2000). Psychological intimacy in the lasting relationships of heterosexual and same-gender couples. *Sex Roles* 43, 201–227.

MacLachlan, J. (1979). What people really think of fast talkers. *Psychology Today* 13, 113–117.

MacMillan, D., & Lehman, P. (2007, November 15). Social networking with the elite. *Business Week* Retrieved from www.businessweek.com

Madon, S., Guyll, M., & Spoth, R. L. (2004). The self-fulfilling prophecy as an intrafamily dynamic. *Journal of Family Psychology* 18, 459–469.

Mahaffey, A. L., Bryan, A., & Hutchison, K. E. (2005). Using startle eye blink to measure the affective component of antigay bias. *Basic and Applied Social Psychology* 27 (March), 37–45.

Main, F., & Oliver, R. (1988). Complementary, symmetrical, and parallel personality priorities as indicators of marital adjustment. *Individual Psychology Journal of Adlerian Theory, Research, and Practice* 44, 324–332.

Malandro, L. A., Barker, L. L., & Barker, D. A. (1989). *Nonverbal communication,* 2nd ed. New York, NY: Random House.

Manusov, V. (ed.) (2005). *The sourcebook of nonverbal measures: Going beyond words.* Mahwah, NJ: Erlbaum.

Mao, L. R. (1994). Beyond politeness theory: "Face" revisited and renewed. *Journal of Pragmatics* 21, 451–486.

Marano, H. E. (2004). Unconventional wisdom. *Psychology Today* 37 (May/June), 10–11.

Marano, H. E. (2008). The making of a perfectionist. *Psychology Today* 41 (March/April), 80–86.

Marsh, P. (1988). *Eye to eye: How people interact.* Topside, MA: Salem House.

Marshall, E. (1983). *Eye language: Understanding the eloquent eye.* New York, NY: New Trend.

Marshall, L. L., & Rose, P. (1987). Gender, stress, and violence in the adult relationships of a sample of college students. *Journal of Social and Personal Relationships* 4, 229–316.

Marston, P. J., Hecht, M. L., & Robers, T. (1987). True love ways: The subjective experience and communication of romantic love. *Journal of Personal and Social Relationships* 4, 387–407.

Martin, G. N. (1998). Human electroencephalographic (EEG) response to olfactory stimulation: Two experiments using the aroma of food. *International Journal of Psychophysiology* 30, 287–302.

Martin, J. L. (2005). Is power sexy? *American Journal of Sociology* 111 (September), 408–446.

Martin, J. S., & Chaney, L. H. (2008). *Global business etiquette: A guide to international communication and customs.* Westport, CT: Praeger.

Martin, M. M., & Anderson, C. M. (1995). Roommate similarity: Are roommates who are similar in their communication traits more satisfied? *Communication Research Reports* 12, 46–52.

Martin, M. M., & Anderson, C. M. (1998). The cognitive flexibility scale: Three validity studies. *Communication Reports* 11 (winter), 1–9.

Martin, M. M., & Rubin, R. B. (1994). A new measure of cognitive flexibility. *Psychological Reports* 76, 623–626.

Martin, M. M., & Rubin, R. B. (1998). Affinity-seeking in initial interactions. *Southern Communication Journal* 63, 131–143.

Marwell, G., & Schmitt, D. R. (1967). Dimensions of compliance-gaining behavior: An empirical analysis. *Sociometry* 39, 350–364.

Marwell, G., & Schmitt, D. R. (1990). An introduction. In *Seeking compliance: The production of interpersonal influence messages,* J. P. Dillard (ed.). Scottsdale, AZ.: Gorsuch Scarisbrick, pp. 3–5.

Maslow, A., & Mintz, N. L. (1956). Effects of esthetic surroundings: I. Initial effects of three esthetic conditions upon perceiving energy and well-being in faces. *Journal of Psychology* 41, 247–254.

Masuda, T., Ellsworth, P. C., Mesquita, B., Leu, J., Tanida, S., & van de Veerdonk, E. (2008). Placing the face in context: Cultural differences in the perception of facial emotion. *Journal of Personality and Social Psychology* 94, 365–381.

Matsumoto, D. (1991). Cultural influences on facial expressions of emotion. *Southern Communication Journal* 56, 128–137.

Matsumoto, D. (1994). *People: Psychology from a cultural perspective.* Pacific Grove, CA: Brooks/Cole.

Matsumoto, D. (1996). *Culture and psychology.* Pacific Grove, CA: Brooks/Cole.

Matsumoto, D. (2006). Culture and nonverbal behavior. In *The Sage handbook of nonverbal communication* (pp. 219–236), V. Manusov & M. L. Patterson (eds.). Thousand Oaks, CA: Sage.

Matsumoto, D. (2009). Culture and emotional expression. In R. S. Wyer, C. Chiu, & Y. Hong (Eds.). *Understanding Culture: Theory, Research, and Application* (pp. 263–279). London: Psychology Press.

Matsumoto, D., & Kudoh, T. (1993). American-Japanese cultural differences in attributions of personality based on smiles. *Journal of Nonverbal Behavior* 17, 231–243.

Matsumoto, D., & Yoo, S. H. (2005). Culture and applied nonverbal communication. In *Applications of nonverbal communication* (pp. 259–277), R. E. Riggio & R. S. Feldman (eds.). Mahwah, NJ: Erlbaum.

Matsumoto, D., Yoo, S. H., Hirayama, S., & Petrova, G. (2005). Development and validation of a measure of display rule knowledge: The display rule assessment inventory. *Emotion* 5, 23–40.

Maynard, H. E. (1963). How to become a better premise detective. *Public Relations Journal* 19, 20–22.

McBroom, W. H., & Reed, F. W. (1992). Toward a reconceptualization of attitude-behavior consistency. Special Issue. Theoretical advances in social psychology. *Social Psychology Quarterly* 55, 205–216.

McCroskey, J. C. (1998). *Why we communicate the ways we do: A communibiological perspective.* Boston, MA: Allyn & Bacon.

McCroskey, J. C. (2007). *An introduction to rhetorical communication,* 9th ed. Boston, MA: Allyn & Bacon.

McCroskey, J. C., & Wheeless, L. (1976). *Introduction to human communication.* Boston, MA: Allyn & Bacon.

McDevitt, M., Kiousis, S., & Wahl-Jorgensen, K. (2003). Spiral of moderation: Opinion expression in computer-mediated discussion. *International Journal of Public Opinion Research* 15 (winter), 454–470.

McDonald, E. J., McCabe, K., Yeh, M., Lau, A., Garland, A., & Hough, R. L. (2005). Cultural affiliation and self-esteem as predictors of internalizing symptoms among Mexican American adolescents. *Journal of Clinical Child and Adolescent Psychology* 34 (February), 163–171.

McGill, M. E. (1985). *The McGill report on male intimacy.* New York, NY: Harper & Row.

McLaughlin, M. L. (1984). *Conversation: How talk is organized.* Thousand Oaks, CA: Sage.

McLaughlin, M. L., Cody, M. L., & Robey, C. S. (1980). Situational influences on the selection of strategies to resist compliance-gaining attempts. *Human Communication Research* 1, 14–36.

McNamee, S., & Gergen, K. J., eds. (1999). *Relational responsibility: Resources for sustainable dialogue.* Thousand Oaks, CA: Sage.

Medora, N. P., Larson, J. H., Hortascu, N., & Dave, P. (2002). Perceived attitudes towards romanticism: A cross-cultural study of American, Asian-Indian, and Turkish young adults. *Journal of Comparative Family Studies,* 33 (spring), 155–178.

Meeks, B. S., Hendrick, S. S., & Hendrick, C. (1998). Communication, love and relationship satisfaction. *Journal of Social and Personal Relationships* 15, 755–773.

Mehl, M. R., Vazire, S., Ramirez-Esparza, N., Slatcher, R. B., & Pennebaker, J. W. (2007, July). Are women really more talkative than men? *Science* 6, 82.

Merton, R. K. (1957). *Social theory and social structure.* New York, NY: Free Press.

Messick, R. M., & Cook, K. S., eds. (1983). *Equity theory: Psychological and sociological perspectives.* New York, NY: Praeger.

Messmer, M. (1999). Skills for a new millennium: Accounting and financial professionals. *Strategic Finance Magazine* (August), 10ff.

Metts, S., & Cupach, W. R. (2008). Face theory. In *Engaging theories in interpersonal communication: Multiple perspectives* (pp. 203–214), L. A. Baxter & D. O. Braithwaite (eds.). Los Angeles, CA: Sage.

Metts, S., & Planalp, S. (2002). Emotional communication. In *Handbook of Interpersonal Communication*, 3rd ed., (pp. 339–373), M. L. Knapp & J. A. Daly (eds.). Thousand Oaks, CA: Sage.

Midooka, K. (1990). Characteristics of Japanese style communication. *Media, Culture and Society* 12, 477–489.

Miller, G. R. (1978). The current state of theory and research in interpersonal communication. *Human Communication Research* 4, 164–178.

Miller, G. R. (1990). Interpersonal communication. In *Human communication: Theory and research* (pp. 91–122), G. L. Dahnke & G. W. Clatterbuck (eds.). Belmont, CA: Wadsworth.

Miller, G. R., & Parks, M. R. (1982). Communication in dissolving relationships. In *Personal relationships 4. Dissolving personal relationships,* S. Duck (ed.). New York, NY: Academic Press, pp. 127–154.

Mintz, N. L. (1956). Effects of esthetic surroundings: II. Prolonged and repeated experience in a beautiful and ugly room. *Journal of Psychology* 41, 459–466.

Moghaddam, F. M., Taylor, D. M., & Wright, S. C. (1993). *Social psychology in cross-cultural perspective.* New York, NY: W. H. Freeman.

Molloy, J. (1981). *Molloy's live for success.* New York, NY: Bantam.

Monahan, J. L. (1998). I don't know it but I like you. *Human Communication Research* 24, 480–500.

Mongeau, P. A., & Henningsen, M. L. M. (2008). Stage theories of relationship development. In *Engaging theories in interpersonal communication: Multiple perspectives* (pp. 363–375), L. A. Baxter & D. O. Braithwaite (eds.). Los Angeles, CA: Sage.

Monin, B. (2003). The warm glow heuristic: When liking leads to familiarity. *Journal of Personality and Social Psychology* 85 (December), 1035–1048.

Monk, A., Fellas, E., & Ley, E. (2004). Hearing only one side of normal and mobile phone conversations. *Behaviour & Information Technology* 23 (September–October), 301–306.

Moon, D. G. (1996). Concepts of "culture": Implications for intercultural communication research. *Communication Quarterly* 44, 70–84.

Morahan-Martin, J., & Schumacher, P. (2003). Loneliness and social uses of the Internet. *Computers in Human Behavior* 19 (November), 659–671.

Moran, R. T., Harris, P. R., & Moran, S. V. (2010). *Managing cultural differences: Global leadership strategies for cross-cultural business success,* 8th ed. Butterworth-Heinemann.

Morand, David (1995). Cited in When Style Is Vile, *Psychology Today* (March), 16.

Morgan, R. (2008, March 16). A crash course in online gossip. *New York Times*, Styles, p. 7.

Morreale, S. P., Osborn, M. M., & Pearson, J. C. (2000). Why communication is important: A rationale for the centrality of the study of communication. *Journal of the Association for Communication Administration* 29 (January), 1–25.

Morreale, S. P., & Pearson, J. C. (2008). Why communication education is important: The centrality of the discipline in the 21st century. *Communication Education* 57 (April), 224–240.

Morrill, C. (1992). Vengeance among executives. *Virginia Review of Sociology* 1, 51–76.

Morris, D. (1977). *Manwatching: A field guide to human behavior.* New York, NY: Abrams.

Morris, D. (2002). *Peoplewatching.* New York, NY: Vintage.

Morrison, E. W., Chen, Y., & Salgado, S. R. (2004). Cultural differences in newcomer feedback seeking: A comparison of the United States and Hong Kong. *Applied Psychology: An International Review* 53 (January), 1–22.

Morrison, R. (2004). Informal relationships in the workplace: Associations with job satisfaction, organizational commitment and turnover intentions. *New Zealand Journal of Psychology* 33, 114–128.

Morrow, G. D., Clark, E. M., & Brock, K. F. (1995). Individual and partner love styles: Implications for the quality of romantic involvements. *Journal of Social and Personal Relationships* 12, 363–387.

Mosteller, T. (2008). *Relativism: A guide for the perplexed.* London: Continuum.

Motley, M. T. (1990a). On whether one can(not) not communicate: An examination via traditional communication postulates. *Western Journal of Speech Communication* 54, 1–20.

Motley, M. T. (1990b). Communication as interaction: A reply to Beach and Bavelas. *Western Journal of Speech Communication* 54, 613–623.

Mottet, T., & Richmond, V. P. (1998). Verbal approach and avoidance items. *Communication Quarterly* 46, 25–40.

Mullen, C. A. (2005). *Mentorship primer.* New York, NY: Peter Lang.

Murstein, B. I., Merighi, J. R., & Vyse, S. A. (1991). Love styles in the United States and France: A cross-cultural comparison. *Journal of Social and Clinical Psychology* 10, 37–46.

Myers, S. A., & Zhong, M. (2004). Perceived Chinese instructor use of affinity-seeking strategies and Chinese college student motivation. *Journal of Intercultural Communication Research* 33 (September–December), 119–130.

Neff, K. D., & Harter, S. (2002). The authenticity of conflict resolutions among adult couples: Does women's other-oriented behavior reflect their true selves? *Sex Roles* 47 (November), 403–417.

Nelson, P. E., Pearson, J. C., & Kurylo, A. (2008). Developing an intellectual communication. In *Getting the most from your graduate education in communication: A student's handbook,* Morreale, S., & Arneson, P. (eds.). Washington, DC: National Communication Association.

Neugarten, B. (1979). Time, age, and the life cycle. *American Journal of Psychiatry* 136, 887–894.

Neuliep, J. W., & Grohskopf, E. L. (2000). Uncertainty reduction and communication satisfaction during initial interaction: An initial test and replication of a new axiom. *Communication Reports* 13 (summer), 67–77.

Neuliep, J. W., & McCroskey, J. C. (1997). The development of a U.S. and generalized ethnocentrism scale. *Communication Research Reports* 14, 385–398.

Ng, S. H., He, A., & Loong, C. (2004). Tri-generational family conversations: Communication accommodation and brokering. *British Journal of Social Psychology* 43 (September), 449–464.

Nicholas, C. L. (2004). Gaydar: Eye-gaze as identity recognition among gay men and lesbians. *Sexuality and Culture: An Interdisciplinary Quarterly* 8 (winter), 60–86.

Nicolai, J., & Demmel, R. (2007). The impact of gender stereotypes on the evaluation of general practitioners' communication skills: An experimental study using transcripts of physician–patient encounters. *Patient Education and Counseling* 69 (December), 200–205.

Nicotera, A. M., & Rancer, A. S. (1994). The influence of sex on self-perceptions and social stereotyping of aggressive communication predispositions. *Western Journal of Communication* 58, 283–307.

Niemeier, S., & Dirven, R. (eds.). (2000). *Evidence for linguistic relativity.* Philadelphia: John Benjamins.

Noble, B. P. (1994, August 14). The gender wars: Talking peace. *New York Times,* p. 21.

Noelle-Neumann, E. (1973). Return to the concept of powerful mass media. In *Studies in broadcasting: An international annual of broadcasting science,* H. Eguchi & K. Sata (eds.). Tokyo: Nippon Hoso Kyokai, pp. 67–112.

Noelle-Neumann, E. (1980). Mass media and social change in developed societies. In *Mass communication review yearbook,* Vol. 1, G. C. Wilhoit & H. de Bock (eds.). Thousand Oaks, CA: Sage, pp. 657–678.

Noelle-Neumann, E. (1991). The theory of public opinion: The concept of the spiral of silence. *Communication yearbook/14,* J. A. Anderson (ed.). Thousand Oaks, CA: Sage, pp. 256–287.

Noller, P., & Fitzpatrick, M. A. (1993). *Communication in family relationships.* Upper Saddle River, NJ: Prentice-Hall.

Norton, M. I., Frost, J. H., & Ariely, D. (2007). Less is more: The lure of ambiguity, or why familiarity breeds contempt. *Journal of Personality and Social Psychology* 92 (January), 97–105.

O'Hair, D., Cody, M. J., Goss, B., & Krayer, K. J. (1988). The effect of gender, deceit orientation and communicator style on macro-assessments of honesty. *Communication Quarterly* 36, 77–93.

O'Hair, D., Cody, M. J., & McLaughlin, M. L. (1981). Prepared lies, spontaneous lies, Machiavellianism, and nonverbal communication. *Human Communication Research* 7, 325–339.

O'Hair, M. J., Cody, M. J., & O'Hair, D. (1991). The impact of situational dimensions on compliance-resisting strategies: A comparison of methods. *Communication Quarterly* 39, 226–240.

Oatley, K., & Duncan, E. (1994). The experience of emotions in everyday life. *Cognition and Emotion* 8, 369–381.

Ober, C., Weitkamp, L. R., Cox, N., Dytch, H., Kostyu, D., & Elias, S. (1997). *American Journal of Human Genetics* 61, 494–496.

Oberg, K. (1960). Cultural shock: Adjustment to new cultural environments. *Practical Anthropology* 7, 177–182.

Oetzel, J. G., & Ting-Toomey, S. (2003). Face concerns in interpersonal conflict: A cross-cultural empirical test of the face negotiation theory. *Communication Research* 30 (December), 599–624.

Okrent, D. (2005). Numbed by the numbers, when they just don't add up. *New York Times* (January 23), Section 4, 2.

Olson, E. (2002). Switzerland tells its men: Wash that pot! Mop that floor! *New York Times*, A14.

Olson, E. (2006, April 6). Better not miss the buss. *New York Times*, pp. G1–G2.

Onishi, N. (2005). In Japan crash, time obsession may be culprit. *New York Times* (April 27), A1, A9.

Oswald, D. L., Clark, E. M., & Kelly, C. M. (2004). Friendship maintenance: An analysis of individual and dyad behaviors. *Journal of Social and Clinical Psychology* 23 (June), 413–441.

Owens, T. J., Stryker, S., & Goodman, N. (eds.). (2002). *Extending self-esteem research: Sociological and psychological currents.* Cambridge, MA: Cambridge University Press.

Palmer, M. T. (1989). Controlling conversations: Turns, topics, and interpersonal control. *Communication Monographs* 56, 1–18.

Parker, J. G. (2004). Planning and communication crucial to preventing workplace violence. *Safety and Health* 170 (September), 58–61.

Parker, R. G., & Parrott, R. (1995). Patterns of self-disclosure across social support networks: Elderly, middle-aged, and young adults. *International Journal of Aging and Human Development* 41, 281–297.

Parks, M. R. (1995). Webs of influence in interpersonal relationships. In *Communication and social influence processes*, C. R. Berger & M. E. Burgoon (eds.). East Lansing: Michigan State University Press, pp. 155–178.

Parks, M. R., & Floyd, K. (1996). Making friends in cyberspace. *Journal of Communication* 46, 80–97.

Pasley, K., Kerpelman, J., & Guilbert, D. E. (2001). Gendered conflict, identity disruption, and marital instability: Expanding Gottman's model. *Journal of Personal and Social Relationships* 18, 5–27.

Patterson, C. (2000). Family relationships of lesbians and gay men. *Journal of Marriage and the Family* 62, 1052–1067.

Paul, A. M. (2001). Self-help: Shattering the myths. *Psychology Today* 34, 60ff.

Pearson, J. C. (1993). *Communication in the family,* 2nd ed. Boston, MA: Allyn & Bacon.

Pearson, J. C., & Spitzberg, B. H. (1990). *Interpersonal communication: Concepts, components, and contexts,* 2nd ed. Dubuque, IA: William C. Brown.

Pearson, J. C., Turner, L. H., & Todd-Mancillas, W. (1991). *Gender and communication,* 2nd ed. Dubuque, IA: William C. Brown.

Pearson, J. C., West, R., & Turner, L. H. (1995). *Gender and communication,* 3rd ed. Dubuque, IA: William C. Brown.

Penfield, J., ed. (1987). *Women and language in transition.* Albany: State University of New York Press.

Pennebacker, J. W. (1991). *Opening up: The healing power of confiding in others.* New York, NY: Morrow.

Peplau, L. A. (1988). Research on homosexual couples: An overview. In *Gay relationships,* J. DeCecco (ed.). New York, NY: Harrington Park Press, pp. 33–40.

Peterson, C. C. (1996). The ticking of the social clock: Adults' beliefs about the timing of transition events. *International Journal of Aging and Human Development* 42, 189–203.

Petrocelli, W., & Repa, B. K. (1992). *Sexual harassment on the job.* Berkeley, CA: Nolo Press.

Pinker, S. (1994). *The language instinct: How the mind creates language.* New York, NY: Morrow.

Plaks, J. E., Grant, H., & Dweck, C. S. (2005). Violations of implicit theories and the sense of prediction and control: Implications for motivated person perception. *Journal of Personality and Social Psychology* 88 (February), 245–262.

Plutchik, R. (1980). *Emotion: A psycho-evolutionary synthesis.* New York, NY: Harper & Row.

Pollack, A. (1996). Happy in the East (^—^) or smiling (:—) in the West. *New York Times* (August 12), D5.

Pornpitakpan, C. (2003). The effect of personality traits and perceived cultural similarity on attraction. *Journal of International Consumer Marketing* 15, 5–30.

Porter, R. H., & Moore, J. D. (1981). Human kin recognition by olfactory cues. *Physiology and Behavior* 27, 493–495.

Porter, S., Brit, A. R., Yuille, J. C., & Lehman, D. R. (2000). Negotiating false memories: Interviewer and rememberer characteristics relate to memory distortion. *Psychological Science* 11 (November), 507–510.

Powell, M. (2005). *Behave yourself!: The essential guide to international etiquette.* Guilford, CT: Globe Pequot.

Prosky, P. S. (1992). Complementary and symmetrical couples. *Family Therapy* 19, 215–221.

Prusank, D. T., Duran, R. L., & DeLillo, D. A. (1993). Interpersonal relationships in women's magazines: Dating and relating in the 1970s and 1980s. *Journal of Social and Personal Relationships* 10, 307–320.

Rabinowitz, F. E. (1991). The male-to-male embrace: Breaking the touch taboo in a men's therapy group. *Journal of Counseling and Development* 69, 574–576.

Radford, M. H., Mann, L., Ohta, Y., & Nakane, Y. (1993). Differences between Australian and Japanese students in decisional self-esteem, decisional stress, and coping styles. *Journal of Cross-Cultural Psychology* 24, 284–297.

Rancer, A. S. (1998). Argumentativeness. In *Communication and Personality: Trait Perspectives,* J. C. McCroskey, J. A. Daly, M. M. Martin, & M. J. Beatty (eds.). Cresskill, NJ: Hampton Press, pp. 149–170.

Rancer, A. S., & Avtgis, T. A. (2006). *Argumentative and aggressive communication: Theory, research, and application.* Thousand Oaks, CA: Sage.

Raney, R. F. (2000). Study finds Internet of social benefit to users. *New York Times* (May 11), G7.

Rappaport, H., Enrich, K., & Wilson, A. (1985). Relation between ego identity and temporal perspective. *Journal of Personality and Social Psychology* 48, 1609–1620.

Rapsa, R., & Cusack, J. (1990). Psychiatric implications of tattoos. *American Family Physician* 41, 1481–1486.

Raven, B., Centers, C., & Rodrigues, A. (1975). The bases of conjugal power. In *Power in families,* R. E. Cromwell & D. H. Olson (eds.). New York, NY: Halsted Press, pp. 217–234.

Raven, B. H., Schwarzwald, J., & Koslowsky, M. (1998). Conceptualizing and measuring a power/interaction model of interpersonal influence. *Journal of Applied Social Psychology* 28, 307–332.

Rawlins, W. K. (1983). Negotiating close friendship: The dialectic of conjunctive freedoms. *Human Communication Research* 9, 255–266.

Rawlins, W. K. (1989). A dialectical analysis of the tensions, functions, and strategic challenges of communication in young adult friendships. In *Communication yearbook 12,* (pp. 157–189), J. A. Andersen (ed.), Thousand Oaks, CA: Sage.

Rawlins, W. K. (1992). *Friendship matters: Communication, dialectics, and the life course.* Hawthorne, NY: Aldine DeGruyter.

Rawlins, W. K. (2008). *The compass of friendship: Narratives, identities, and dialogues.* Thousand Oaks, CA: Sage.

Read, A. W. (2004). Language revision by deletion of absolutisms. *ETC: A Review of General Semantics* 61 (December), 456–462.

Reardon, K. K. (1987). *Where minds meet: Interpersonal communication.* Belmont, CA: Wadsworth.

Rector, M., & Neiva, E. (1996). Communication and personal relationships in Brazil. In *Communication in personal relationships across cultures,* W. B. Gudykunst, S. Ting-Toomey, & T. Nishida (eds.). Thousand Oaks, CA: Sage, pp. 156–173.

Reed, M. D. (1993, Fall). Sudden death and bereavement outcomes: The impact of resources on grief, symptomatology and detachment. *Suicide and Life-Threatening Behavior* 23, 204–220.

Regan, P. C., Durvasula, R., Howell, L., Ureno, O., & Rea, M. (2004). Gender, ethnicity, and the developmental timing of first sexual and romantic experiences. *Social Behavior and Personality: An International Journal* 32 (November), 667–676.

Regan, P. C., Kocan, E. R., & Whitlock, T. (1998). Ain't love grand! A prototype analysis of the concept of romantic love. *Journal of Social and Personal Relationships* 15, 411–420.

Rehman, A. A. (2007) *Dubai & Co.: Global Strategies for doing business in the Gulf states.* New York, NY: McGraw-Hill.

Reiner, D., & Blanton, K. (1997). *Person to person on the Internet.* Boston, MA: AP Professional.

Reisenzein, R. (1983). The Schachter theory of emotion: Two decades later. *Psychological Bulletin* 94, 239–264.

Reisman, J. (1979). *Anatomy of friendship.* Lexington, MA: Lewis.

Reisman, J. M. (1981). Adult friendships. In *Personal relationships. 2: Developing personal relationships,* S. Duck & R. Gilmour (eds.). New York, NY: Academic Press, pp. 205–230.

Remland, M. S. (2006). Uses and consequences of nonverbal communication in the context of organizational life. In *The Sage handbook of nonverbal communication* (pp. 501–519), V. Manusov & M. L. Patterson (eds.). Thousand Oaks, CA: Sage.

Rhee, K. Y., & Kim, W-B (2004). The adoption and use of the Internet in South Korea. *Journal of Computer Mediated Communication* 9 (4, July).

Rhee, S., Chang, J., & Rhee, J. (2003). Acculturation, communication patterns, and self-esteem among Asian and Caucasian American adolescents. *Adolescence* 38 (winter), 749–768.

Rice, M. (2007). Domestic violence. *National Center for PTSD Fact Sheet.* Retrieved from www.ncptsd.va.gov/ncmain/ncdocs/fact_shts/fs_domestic_violence.html

Rich, A. L. (1974). *Interracial communication.* New York, NY: Harper & Row.

Richards, I. A. (1951). Communication between men: The meaning of language. In *Cybernetics, Transactions of the Eighth Conference,* Heinz von Foerster (ed.).

Richmond, V. P., Davis, L. M., Saylor, K., & McCroskey, J. C. (1984). Power strategies in organizations: Communication techniques and messages. *Human Communication Research* 11, 85–108.

Richmond, V. P., & McCroskey, J. C. (1984). Power in the classroom II: Power and learning. *Communication Education* 33, 125–136.

Richmond, V. P., McCroskey, J. C., & Hickson, M. L. (2012). *Nonverbal behavior in interpersonal relations*, 7th ed. Boston, MA: Allyn & Bacon.

Richmond, V. P., Smith, R., Heisel, A., & McCroskey, J. C. (2001). Nonverbal immediacy in the physician/patient relationship. *Communication Research Reports* 18, 211–216.

Riggio, R. E. (1987). *The charisma quotient.* New York, NY: Dodd, Mead.

Riggio, R. E., & Feldman, R. S. (eds.). (2005). *Applications of nonverbal communication.* Mahwah, NJ: Erlbaum.

Rivlin, G. (2005). Hate Messages on Google Site Draw Concern. *New York Times* (February 7), C1, C7.

Roeher Institute (1995). *Harm's way: The many faces of violence and abuse against persons with disabilities.* North York (Ontario): Roeher Institute.

Rogers, C. (1970). *Carl Rogers on encounter groups.* New York, NY: Harrow Books.

Rogers, C., & Farson, R. (1981). Active listening. In *Communication: Concepts and Processes,* 3rd ed., J. DeVito (ed.). Upper Saddle River, NJ: Prentice-Hall, pp. 137–147.

Rohlfing, M. E. (1995). "Doesn't anybody stay in one place anymore?" An exploration of the under-studied phenomenon of long-distance relationships. In *Under-studied relationships: Off the beaten track,* J. T. Wood & S. Duck (eds.). Thousand Oaks, CA: Sage, pp. 173–196.

Rokach, A. (1998). The relation of cultural background to the causes of loneliness. *Journal of Social and Clinical Psychology* 17, 75–88.

Rokach, A., & Brock, H. (1995). The effects of gender, marital status, and the chronicity and immediacy of loneliness. *Journal of Social Behavior and Personality* 19, 833–848.

Roloff, M. E., & Solomon, D. H. (2002). Conditions under which relational commitment leads to expressing or withholding relational complaints. *International Journal of Conflict Management* 13, 276–291.

Ronfeldt, H. M., Kimerling, R., & Arias, I. (1998). Satisfaction with relationship power and the perpetration of dating violence. *Journal of Marriage and the Family* 60 (February), 70–78.

Rosen, E. (1998). Think like a shrink. *Psychology Today* (October), 54–59.

Rosenbaum, M. E. (1986). The repulsion hypothesis. On the nondevelopment of relationships. *Journal of Personality and Social Psychology* 51, 1156–1166.

Rosengren, A., Orth-Gomér, K., Wedel, H., & Wilhelmsen, L. (1993). Stressful life events, social support, and mortality in men born in 1933. *British Medical Journal* (October 19). Cited in Goleman (1995a).

Rosenthal, R. (2002). The Pygmalion effect and its mediating mechanism. In *Improving academic achievement: Impact of psychological factors on education* (pp. 25–36), J. Aronson (ed.). San Diego, CA: Academic Press.

Rowland-Morin, P. A., & Carroll, J. G. (1990). Verbal communication skills and patient satisfaction: A study of doctor-patient interviews. *Evaluation and the Health Professions* 13, 168–185.

Ruben, B. D. (1985). Human communication and cross-cultural effectiveness. In *Intercultural Communication: A Reader,* 4th ed., L. A. Samovar & R. E. Porter (eds.). Belmont, CA: Wadsworth, pp. 338–346.

Rubenstein, C. (1993). Fighting sexual harassment in schools. *New York Times* (June 10), C8.

Rubin, D. C., Groth, E., & Goldsmith, D. J. (1984). Olfactory cues of autobiographical memory. *American Journal of Psychology* 97, 493–507.

Rubin, R. B., & Graham, E. E. (1988). Communication correlates of college success: An exploratory investigation. *Communication Education* 37, 14–27.

Rubin, R. B., & Martin, M. M. (1994). Development of a measure of interpersonal communication competence. *Communication Research Reports* 11, 33–44.

Rubin, R. B., & McHugh, M. (1987). Development of parasocial interaction relationships. *Journal of Broadcasting and Electronic Media* 31, 279–292.

Rubin, Z. (1973). *Liking and loving: An invitation to social psychology.* New York, NY: Holt, Rinehart & Winston.

Rusbult, C. E., & Buunk, B. P. (1993). Commitment processes in close relationships: An interdependence analysis. *Journal of Social and Personal Relationships* 10, 175–204.

Rushe, R. H. (1996). Tactics of power and influence in violent marriages. *Dissertation abstracts international: Section B: The Sciences and Engineering* (University of Washington), 57, 1453.

Rydell, R. J., McConnell, A. R., & Bringle, R. G. (2004). Jealousy and commitment: Perceived threat and the effect of relationship alternatives. *Personal Relationships* 11 (December), 451–468.

Sabatelli, R. M., & Pearce, J. (1986). Exploring marital expectations. *Journal of Social and Personal Relationships* 3, 307–321.

Sagrestano, L. M., Heavey, C. L., & Christensen, A. (2006). Individual differences versus social structural approaches to explaining demand–withdrawal and social influence behaviors. In *Sex differences and similarities in communication,* 2nd ed. (pp. 379–395), K. Dindia & D. J. Canary (eds.). Mahwah, NJ: Erlbaum.

Sagula, D., & Rice, K. G. (2004). The effectiveness of mindfulness training on the grieving process and emotional well-being of chronic pain patients. *Journal of Clinical Psychology in Medical Settings* 11 (December), 333–342.

Sahlstein, E. M. (2004). Relating at a distance: Negotiating being together and being apart in long-distance relationships. *Journal of Social and Personal Relationships* 21 (October), 689–710.

Samter, W. (2004). Friendship interaction skills across the life span. In *Handbook of communication and social interaction skills* (pp. 637–684), J. O. Greene & B. R. Burleson (eds.). Mahwah, NJ: Lawrence Erlbaum.

Samter, W., & Cupach, W. R. (1998). Friendly fire: Topics variations in conflict among same- and cross-sex friends. *Communication Studies* 49, 121–138.

Sanders, J. A., Wiseman, R. L., & Matz, S. I. (1991). Uncertainty reduction in acquaintance relationships in Ghana and the United States. In *Cross-cultural interpersonal communication,* S. Ting-Toomey & F. Korzenny (eds.). Thousand Oaks, CA: Sage, pp. 79–98.

Sapadin, L. A. (1988). Friendship and gender: Perspectives of professional men and women. *Journal of Social and Personal Relationships* 5, 387–403.

Sarwer, D. B., Kalichman, S. C., Johnson, J. R., Early, J., et al. (1993). Sexual aggression and love styles: An exploratory study. *Archives of Sexual Behavior* 22, 265–275.

Satir, V. (1983). *Conjoint Family Therapy,* 3rd ed. Palo Alto, CA: Science and Behavior Books.

Savitsky, K., Epley, N., & Gilovich, T. (2001). Do others judge us as harshly as we think? Overestimating the impact of our failures, shortcomings, and mishaps. *Journal of Personality and Social Psychology* 81 (July), 44–56.

Scandura, T. (1992). Mentorship and career mobility: An empirical investigation. *Journal of Organizational Behavior* 13, 169–174.

Schaap, C., Buunk, B., & Kerkstra, A. (1988). Marital conflict resolution. In *Perspectives on marital interaction,* P. Noller & M. A. Fitzpatrick (eds.). Philadelphia: Multilingual Matters, pp. 203–244.

Schachter, S. (1971). *Emotion, obesity and crime.* New York, NY: Academic Press.

Schegloff, E. (1982). Discourses as an interactional achievement: Some uses of "uh huh" and other things that come between sentences. In *Georgetown University roundtable on language and linguistics,* Deborah Tannen (ed.). Washington, DC: Georgetown University Press, pp. 71–93.

Scheufele, D. A., & Moy, P. (2000). Twenty-five years of the spiral of silence: A conceptual review and empirical outlook. *International Journal of Public Opinion Research* 12 (spring), 3–28.

Schmidt, T. O., & Cornelius, R. R. (1987). Self-disclosure in everyday life. *Journal of Social and Personal Relationships* 4, 365–373.

Schoeneman, T. J., & Rubanowitz, E. E. (1985). Attributions in the advice columns: Actors and observers, causes and reasons. *Personality and Social Psychology Bulletin* 11, 315–325.

Schott, G., & Selwyn, N. (2000). Examining the "male, antisocial" stereotype of high computer users. *Journal of Educational Computing Research* 23, 291–303.

Schrodt, P. (2003). Students' appraisals of instructors as a function of students' perceptions of instructors' aggressive communication. *Communication Education* 52 (April), 106–121.

Schutz, A. (1999). It was your fault! Self-serving biases in autobiographical accounts of conflicts in married couples. *Journal of Social and Personal Relationships* 16, 193–208.

Schwartz, E. (2005). Watch what you say. *InfoWorld* 27 (February 28), 8.

Schwartz, M., and the Task Force on Bias-Free Language of the Association of American University Presses (1995). *Guidelines for bias-free writing.* Bloomington: Indiana University Press.

Scott, M. L., & Lyman, S. M. (1968). Accounts. *American Sociological Review* 33, 46–62.

Seiter, J. S. (2007). Ingratiation and gratuity: The effect of complimenting customers on tipping behavior in restaurants. *Journal of Applied Social Psychology* 37 (March), 478–485.

Seiter, J. S., & Sandry, A. (2003). Pierced for success?: The effects of ear and nose piercing on perceptions of job candidates' credibility, attractiveness, and hirability. *Communication Research Reports* 20 (Fall), 287–298.

Serewicz, M. C. M., & Petronio, S. (2007). Communication privacy management theory. In *Explaining communication: Contemporary theories and exemplars* (pp. 257–274), B. B. Whaley & W. Samter (eds.). Mahwah, NJ: Erlbaum.

Severin, W. J. & Tankard, J. W., Jr. (2001). *Communication theories: Origins, methods, and uses in the mass media.* Boston, MA: Allyn & Bacon.

Shaw, L. H., & Grant, L. M. (2002). Users divided? Exploring the gender gap in Internet use. *CyberPsychology & Behavior* 5 (December), 517–527.

Sheese, B. E., Brown, E. L., & Graziano, W. G. (2004). Emotional expression in cyberspace: Searching for moderators of the Pennebaker disclosure effect via e-mail. *Health Psychology* 23 (September), 457–464.

Shelton, J. N., & Richeson, J. A. (2005). Intergroup contact and pluralistic ignorance. *Journal of Personality and Social Psychology* 88 (January), 91–107.

Sheppard, J. A., & Strathman, A. J. (1989). Attractiveness and height: The role of stature in dating preferences, frequency of dating, and perceptions of attractiveness. *Personality and Social Psychology* 15, 617–627.

Shibazaki, K., & Brennan, K. A. (1998). When birds of different features flock together: A preliminary comparison of intra-ethnic and inter-ethnic dating relationships. *Journal of Social and Personal Relationships* 15, 248–256.

Shimanoff, S. (1980). *Communication rules: Theory and research.* Thousand Oaks, CA: Sage.

Shirley, J. A., Powers, W. G., & Sawyer, C. R. (2007). Psychologically abusive relationships and self-disclosure orientations. *Human Communication* 10, 289–302.

Short, J., Williams, E., & Christie, B. (1976). *The social psychology of telecommunication.* London: Wiley.

Siavelis, R. L., & Lamke, L. K. (1992). Instrumentalness and expressiveness: Predictors of heterosexual relationship satisfaction. *Sex Roles* 26, 149–159.

Siegert, J. R., & Stamp, G. H. (1994). "Our first big fight" as a milestone in the development of close relationships. *Communication Monographs* 61, 345–360.

Silverman, T. (2001). Expanding community: The Internet and relational theory. *Community, Work and Family* 4, 231–237.

Singelis, T. M. (1994). The measurement of independent and interdependent self-construals. *Personality and Social Psychology Bulletin* 20, 580–591.

Singh, N., & Pereira, A. (2005). *The culturally customized web site.* Oxford, UK: Elsevier Butterworth-Heinemann.

Sizemore, D. S. (2004). Ethnic inclusion and exclusion. *Journal of Contemporary Ethnography* 33 (October), 534–570.

Skinner, M. (2002). In search of feedback. *Executive Excellence* (June), 18.

Slade, M. (1995). We forgot to write a headline. But it's not our fault. *New York Times* (February 19), 5.

Smith, A., & Williams, K. D. (2004). R U There? Ostracism by cell phone text messages. *Group Dynamics* 8 (December), 291–301.

Smith, B. (1996). Care and feeding of the office grapevine. *Management Review* 85 (February), 6.

Smith, C. S. (2002). Beware of green hats in China and other cross-cultural faux pas. *New York Times* (April 30), C11.

Smith, D. (2003, December 2). Doctors cultivate a skill: Listening. *New York Times*, p. 6.

Smith, M. H. (2003). Body adornment: Know the limits. *Nursing Management* 34 (February), 22–23.

Smith, R. (2004). The teaching of communication skills may be misguided. *British Medical Journal* 328 (April 10), 1–2.

Smith, S. M., & Shaffer, D. R. (1991). Celerity and cajolery: Rapid speech may promote or inhibit persuasion through its impact on message elaboration. *Personality and Social Psychology Bulletin* 17 (December), 663–669.

Smith, S. M., & Shaffer, D. R. (1995). Speed of speech and persuasion: Evidence for multiple effects. *Personality and Social Psychology Bulletin* 21 (October), 1051–1060.

Snyder, C. R. (1984). Excuses, excuses. *Psychology Today* 18, 50–55.

Snyder, C. R., Higgins, R. L., and Stucky, R. J. (1983). *Excuses: Masquerades in search of grace.* New York, NY: Wiley.

Snyder, M. (1992). A gender-informed model of couple and family therapy: Relationship enhancement therapy. *Contemporary Family Therapy: An International Journal* 14 (February), 15–31.

Solomon, C. & Schell, M. S. (2009). *Managing across cultures: the seven keys to doing business with a global mindset.* New York, NY: McGraw-Hill.

Solomon, D. H., & Samp, J. A. (1998). Power and problem appraisal: Perceptual foundations of the chilling effect in dating relationships. *Journal of Social and Personal Relationships* 15, 191–209.

Sommer, K. L., Williams, K. D., Ciarocco, N. J., & Baumeister, R. F. (2001). When silence speaks louder than words: Explorations into the intrapsychic and interpersonal consequences of social ostracism. *Basic and Applied Social Psychology* 23, 225–243.

Sommers, S. (1984). Reported emotions and conventions of emotionality among college students. *Journal of Personality and Social Psychology* 46, 207–215.

Sorenson, P. S., Hawkins, K., & Sorenson, R. L. (1995). Gender, psychological type and conflict style preference. *Management Communication Quarterly* 9, 115–126.

Spencer, T. (1993). A new approach to assessing self-disclosure in conversation. Paper presented at the Annual Convention of the Western Speech Communication Association, Albuquerque, New Mexico.

Spencer, T. (1994). Transforming relationships through everyday talk. In *The Dynamics of Relationships: Vol. 4. Understanding Relationships,* S. Duck (ed.). Thousand Oaks, CA: Sage.

Spett, M. (2004). Expressing negative emotions: Healthy catharsis or sign of pathology? Retrieved from http://www.nj-act.org/article2.html

Spitzberg, B. H. (1991). Intercultural communication competence. In *Intercultural communication: A reader,* L. A. Samovar & R. E. Porter (eds.). Belmont, CA: Wadsworth, pp. 353–365.

Spitzberg, B. H., & Cupach, W. R. (1989). *Handbook of interpersonal competence research.* New York, NY: Springer-Verlag.

Spitzberg, B. H., & Hecht, M. L. (1984). A component model of relational competence. *Human Communication Research* 10, 575–599.

Sprecher, S. (1987). The effects of self-disclosure given and received on affection for an intimate partner and stability of the relationship. *Journal of Social and Personal Relationships* 4, 115–127.

Sprecher, S. (2001). Equity and social exchange in dating couples: Associations with satisfaction, commitment, and stability. *Journal of Marriage and the Family* 63 (August), 599–613.

Sprecher, S., & Hendrick, S. S. (2004). Self-disclosure in intimate relationships: Associations with individual and relationship characteristics over time. *Journal of Social and Clinical Psychology* 23 (December), 857–877.

Sprecher, S., & Metts, S. (1989). Development of the "Romantic Beliefs Scale" and examination of the effects of gender and gender-role orientation. *Journal of Social and Personal Relationships* 6, 387–411.

Sprecher, S., & Toro-Morn, M. (2002). A study of men and women from different sides of earth to determine if men are from Mars and women are from Venus in their beliefs about love and romantic relationships. *Sex Roles* 46 (March), 131–147.

Srivastava, K., & More, A. T. (2010). Some aesthetic considerations for over the-counter (OTC) pharmaceutical products. *International Journal of Biotechnology* 11 (3/4): 267. doi:10.1504/IJBT.2010.036600

Stafford, L. (2004). *Maintaining long-distance and cross-residential relationships.* Mahwah, NJ: Erlbaum.

Stafford, L. (2008). Social exchange theories. In *Engaging theories in interpersonal communication: Multiple perspectives* (pp. 377–390), L. A. Baxter & D. O. Braithwaite (eds.). Los Angeles, CA: Sage.

Stafford, L., Kline, S. L., & Dimmick, J. (1999). Home e-mail: Relational maintenance and gratification opportunities. *Journal of Broadcasting and Electronic Media* 43, 659–669.

Stafford, L., & Merolla, A. J. (2007). Idealization, reunions, and stability in long-distance dating relationships. *Journal of Social and Personal Relations* 24, 37–54.

Stein, M. M., & Bowen, M. (2003). Building a customer satisfaction system: Effective listening when the customer speaks. *Journal of Organizational Excellence* 22 (summer), 23–34.

Steiner, C. (1981). *The other side of power.* New York, NY: Grove.

Stephan, W. G., & Stephan, C. W. (1985). Intergroup anxiety. *Journal of Social Issues* 41, 157–175.

Stephen, R., & Zweigenhaft, R. L. (1986). The effect of tipping of a waitress touching male and female customers. *Journal of Social Psychology* 126 (February), 141–142.

Stephens, G. K., & Greer, C. R. (1995). Doing business in Mexico: Understanding cultural differences. *Organizational Dynamics* 24, 39–55.

Sternberg, R. J. (1986). A triangular theory of love. *Psychological Review* 93, 119–135.

Sternberg, R. J. (1988). *The triangle of love: Intimacy, passion, commitment.* New York, NY: Basic Books.

Sternberg, R. J., & Weis, K. (2008). *The new psychology of love.* New Haven, CT: Yale University Press.

Sternglanz, R. W., & DePaulo, B. (2004). Reading nonverbal cues to emotions: The advantages and liabilities of relationship closeness. *Journal of Nonverbal Behavior* 28 (winter), 245–266.

Stewart, L. P., Cooper, P. J., & Stewart, A. D. (with Friedley, S. A.). (2003). *Communication and gender,* 4th ed. Boston, MA: Allyn & Bacon.

Stewart, S. (2006). A pilot study of email in an e-mentoring relationship. *Journal of Telemedicine and Telecare* 12 (October), 83–85.

Strassberg, D. S., & Holty, S. (2003). An experimental study of women's Internet personal ads. *Archives of Sexual Behavior* 32 (June), 253–260.

Strecker, I. (1993). Cultural variations in the concept of "face." *Multilingua* 12, 119–141.

Suler, J. (2004). The online disinhibition effect. *CyberPsychology and Behavior* 7 (June), 321–326.

Sunnafrank, M., & Ramirez, A. (2004). At first sight: Persistent relational effects of get-acquainted conversations. *Journal of Social and Personal Relationships* 21 (June), 361–379.

Sutcliffe, K., Lewton, E., & Rosenthal, M. M. (2004). Communication failures: An insidious contributor to medical mishaps. *Academic Medicine* 79 (February), 186–194.

Sutter, D. L., & Martin, M. M. (1998). Verbal aggression during disengagement of dating relationships. *Communication Research Reports* 15, 318–326.

Tang, S., & Zuo, J. (2000). Dating attitudes and behaviors of American and Chinese college students. *The Social Science Journal* 37 (January), 67–78.

Tannen, D. (1990). *You just don't understand: Women and men in conversation.* New York, NY: Morrow.

Tannen, D. (1994a). *Gender and discourse.* New York, NY: Oxford University Press.

Tannen, D. (1994b). *Talking from 9 to 5.* New York, NY: Morrow.

Taraban, C. B., & Hendrick, C. (1995). Personality perceptions associated with six styles of love. *Journal of Social and Personal Relationships* 12, 453–461.

Tardiff, T. (2001). Learning to say "no" in Chinese. *Early Education and Development* 12, 303–323.

Tata, J. (2000). Toward a theoretical framework of inter-cultural account-giving and account evaluation. *International Journal of Organizational Analysis* 8, 155–178.

Tavris, C. (1989). *Anger: The misunderstood emotion* (2nd ed.). New York, NY: Simon & Schuster.

Teven, J. J., Richmond, V. P., & McCroskey, J. C. (1998). Measuring tolerance for disagreement. *Communication Research Reports* 15, 209–221.

Thelen, M. H., Sherman, M. D., & Borst, T. S. (1998). Fear of intimacy and attachment among rape survivors. *Behavior Modification* 22, 108–116.

Thibaut, J. W., & Kelley, H. H. (1959). *The social psychology of groups.* New York, NY: Wiley. Reissued (1986). New Brunswick, NJ: Transaction Books.

Thomlison, D. (1982). *Toward interpersonal dialogue.* New York, NY: Longman.

Thompson, C. A., & Klopf, D. W. (1991). An analysis of social style among disparate cultures. *Communication Research Reports* 8, 65–72.

Thompson, C. A., Klopf, D. W., & Ishii, S. (1991). A comparison of social style between Japanese and Americans. *Communication Research Reports* 8, 165–172.

Thorne, B., Kramarae, C., & Henley, N. (eds.). (1983). *Language, gender and society.* Rowley, MA: Newbury House.

Tierney, P., & Farmer, S. M. (2004). The Pygmalion process and employee creativity. *Journal of Management* 30 (June), 413–432.

Ting-Toomey, S. (1981). Ethnic identity and close friendship in Chinese-American college students. *International Journal of Intercultural Relations* 5, 383–406.

Ting-Toomey, S. (1985). Toward a theory of conflict and culture. *International and Intercultural Communication Annual* 9, 71–86.

Ting-Toomey, S. (1986). Conflict communication styles in black and white subjective cultures. In *Interethnic communication: Current research,* Y. Y. Kim (ed.). Thousand Oaks, CA: Sage, pp. 75–88.

Tinsley, C. H., & Brett, J. M. (2001). Managing workplace conflict in the United States and Hong Kong. *Organizational Behavior and Human Decision Processes* 85, 360–381.

Tolhuizen, J. H. (1986). Perceiving communication indicators of evolutionary changes in friendship. *Southern Speech Communication Journal* 52, 69–91.

Tolhuizen, J. H. (1989). Communication strategies for intensifying dating relationships: Identification, use, and structure. *Journal of Social and Personal Relationships* 6, 413–434.

Trager, G. L. (1958). Paralanguage: A first approximation. *Studies in Linguistics* 13, 1–12.

Trager, G. L. (1961). The typology of paralanguage. *Anthropological Linguistics* 3, 17–21.

Trower, P. (1981). Social skill disorder. In *Personal Relationships* 3, S. Duck & R. Gilmour (eds.). New York, NY: Academic Press, pp. 97–110.

Tsiantar, D. (2005). The cost of incivility. *Time* (February 14), B5.

Tynes, B. M. (2007). Internet safety gone wild? Sacrificing the educational and psychosocial benefits of online social environments. *Journal of Adolescent Research* 22, 575–584.

Ueleke, W., et al. (1983). Inequity resolving behavior as a response to inequity in a hypothetical marital relationship. *A Quarterly Journal of Human Behavior* 20, 4–8.

Unger, F. L. (2001). Speech directed at able-bodied adults, disabled adults, and disabled adults with speech impairments. *Dissertation Abstracts International: Second B: The Sciences and Engineering*, 62, 1146.

Vainiomaki, T. (2004). Silence as a cultural sign. *Semiotica* 150, 347–361.

Valkenburg, P. M., & Peter, J. (2007). Online communication and adolescent well-being: Testing the stimulation versus the displacement hypothesis. *Journal of Computer-Mediated Communication* 12, article 2. http://jcmc.indiana.edu/vol12/issue4/Valkenburg.html. Accessed May 28, 2008.

VanHyning, M. (1993). *Crossed signals: How to say no to sexual harassment.* Los Angeles, CA: Infotrends Press.

Varenik, T. (2010). How tattoos and body piercing affect your career. Retrieved from http://www.resumark.com/blog/tatiana/how-tattoos-and-body-piercing-affect-your-career.

Varma, A., Toh, S. M, & Pichler, S. (2006). Ingratiation in job applications: Impact on selection decisions. *Journal of Managerial Psychology* 21, 200–210.

Veenendall, T. L., & Feinstein, M. C. (1995). *Let's talk about relationships: Cases in study.* Prospect Heights, IL: Waveland Press.

Velting, D. M. (1999). Personality and negative expectations: Trait structure of the Beck Hopelessness Scale. *Personality and Individual Differences* 26, 913–921.

Victor, D. (1992). *International business communication.* New York, NY: HarperCollins.

von Tetzchner, S., & Jensen, K. (1999). Interacting with people who have severe communication problems: Ethical considerations. *International Journal of Disability, Development and Education* 46 (December), 453–462.

Vonk, R. (2002). Self-serving interpretations of flattery: Why ingratiation works. *Journal of Personality and Social Psychology* 82 (April), 515–526.

Voo, J. (2007). How to handle an office romance. Retrieved from http://www.cnn.com/2007/living/worklife/08/29/office.romance/index.html.

Vrij, A., & Mann, S. (2001). Telling and detecting lies in a high-stake situation: The case of a convicted murderer. *Applied Cognitive Psychology*, 15 (March–April), 187–203.

Waddington, K. (2004). Psst—spread the word—gossiping is good for you. *Practice Nurse* 27, 7–10.

Wade, C., & Tavris, C. (2007). *Psychology,* 9th ed. Upper Saddle River, NJ: Prentice-Hall.

Wade, N. (2002). Scent of a man is linked to a woman's selection. *New York Times* (January 22), F2.

Walster, E., Walster, G. W., & Berscheid, E. (1978). *Equity: Theory and research.* Boston, MA: Allyn & Bacon.

Walster, E., Walster, G. W., & Traupmann, J. (1978). Equity and premarital sex. *Journal of Personality and Social Psychology* 36, 82–92.

Walther, J. B. (2008). Social information processing theory. In *Engaging theories in interpersonal communication: Multiple perspectives* (pp. 391–404), L. A. Baxter & D. O. Braithwaite (eds.). Los Angeles, CA: Sage.

Walther, J. B., & Parks, M. R. (2002). Cues filtered out, cues filtered in: Computer-mediated communication and relationships. In *Handbook of interpersonal communication,* (pp. 529–563), M. L. Knapp and J. A. Daly (eds.). Thousand Oaks, CA: Sage.

Walther, J. D. (1992). Interpersonal effects in computer-mediated interaction: A relational perspective. *Communication Research* 19, 52–90.

Wan, C. (2004). The psychology of culture shock. *Asian Journal of Social Psychology* 7 (August), 233–234.

Ward, C., Bochner, S., & Furnham, A. (eds.). (2001). *The psychology of culture shock.* Hove, UK: Routledge.

Ward, S. F. (2003). Lawyers in love. *ABA Journal* 89 (September), 37.

Watzlawick, P. (1977). *How real is real? Confusion, disinformation, communication: An anecdotal introduction to communications theory.* New York, NY: Vintage.

Watzlawick, P. (1978). *The language of change: Elements of therapeutic communication.* New York, NY: Basic Books.

Watzlawick, P., Beavin, J. H., & Jackson, D. D. (1967). *Pragmatics of human communication: A study of interactional patterns, pathologies, and paradoxes.* New York, NY: Norton.

Weathers, M. D., Frank, E. M., & Spell, L. A. (2002). Differences in the communication of affect: Members of the same race versus members of a different race. *Journal of Black Psychology* 28, 66–77.

Weigel, D. J., & Ballard-Reisch, D. S. (1999). Using paired data to test models of relational maintenance and marital quality. *Journal of Social and Personal Relationships* 16, 175–191.

Weinberg, H. L. (1959). *Levels of knowing and existence.* New York, NY: Harper & Row.

Weitzman, P. F. (2001). Young adult women resolving interpersonal conflicts. *Journal of Adult Development* 8, 61–67.

Weitzman, P. F., & Weitzman, E. A. (2000). Interpersonal negotiation strategies in a sample of older women. *Journal of Clinical Geropsychology* 6, 41–51.

Wert, S. R., & Salovey, P. (2004). A social comparison account of gossip. *Review of General Psychology* 8 (June), 122–137.

Wertz, D. C., Sorenson, J. R., & Heeren, T. C. (1988). Can't get no (dis)satisfaction: Professional satisfaction with professional-client encounters. *Work and Occupations* 15, 36–54.

Westwood, R. I., Tang, F. F., & Kirkbride, P. S. (1992). Chinese conflict behavior: Cultural antecedents and behavioral consequences. *Organizational Development Journal* 10, 13–19.

Wheeless, L. R., & Grotz, J. (1977). The measurement of trust and its relationship to self-disclosure. *Human Communication Research* 3, 250–257.

Whitty, M. T. (2003a). Cyber-flirting: Playing at love on the Internet. *Theory and Psychology* 13 (June), 339–357.

Whitty, M. T. (2003b). Logging onto love: An examination of men's and women's flirting behaviour both offline and on the Internet. *Australian Journal of Psychology* 55, 68–72.

Whitty, M., & Gavin, J. (2001). Age/sex/location: Uncovering the social cues in the development of online relationships. *CyberPsychology and Behavior* 4, 623–630.

Wiederman, M. W., & Hurd, C. (1999). Extradyadic involvement during dating. *Journal of Social and Personal Relationships* 16, 265–274.

Wilkins, B. M., & Andersen, P. A. (1991). Gender differences and similarities in management communication: A meta-analysis. *Management Communication Quarterly* 5, 6–35.

Willis, J., & Todorov, A. (2006). First impressions: Making up your mind after a 100-Ms exposure to a face. *Psychological Science* 17 (July), 592–598.

Willson, R., & Branch, R. (2006). *Cognitive behavioural therapy for dummies.* West Sussex, England: Wiley.

Wilson, S. R., & Sabee, C. M. (2003). Explicating communicative competence as a theoretical term. In *Handbook of communication and social interaction skills* (pp. 3–50), J. O. Greene & B. R. Burleson (eds.). Mahwah, NJ: Erlbaum.

Windy, D., & Constantinou, D. (2005). *Assertiveness step by step.* London: Sheldon Press.

Winquist, L. A., Mohr, C. D., & Kenny, D. A. (1998). The female positivity effect in the perception of others. *Journal of Research in Personality* 32, 370–388.

Witcher, S. K. (1999, August 9–15). Chief executives in Asia find listening difficult. *Asian Wall Street Journal Weekly* 21, p. 11.

Wolak, J., Mitchell, K. J., & Finkelhor, D. (2003). Escaping or connecting? Characteristics of youth who form close online relationships. *Journal of Adolescence* 26 (February), 105–119.

Wolpe, J. (1958). *Psychotherapy by reciprocal inhibition.* Stanford, CA: Stanford University Press.

Won-Doornink, M. J. (1985). Self-disclosure and reciprocity in conversation: A cross-national study. *Social Psychology Quarterly* 48, 97–107.

Wood, A. F., & Smith, M. J. (2005). *Online communication: Linking technology, identity, and culture.* Mahwah, NJ: Lawrence Erlbaum.

Wood, J. T. (1994). *Gendered lives: Communication, gender, and culture.* Belmont, CA: Wadsworth.

Wood, J. T. (2010). Gendered Lives: Communication, Gender and Culture. Belmont, CA: Wadsworth.

Woodzicka, A. A., & LaFrance, M. (2005). Working on a smile: Responding to sexual provocation in the workplace. In *Applications of nonverbal communication* (pp. 141–160), R. E. Riggio & R. S. Feldman (eds.). Mahwah, NJ: Erlbaum.

Worthington, D. L., & Fitch-Hauser, M. E. (2012). *Listening: Processes, functions, and competency.* Boston, MA: Allyn & Bacon.

Wrench, J. S., McCroskey, J. C., & Richmond, V. P. (2008). *Human communication in everyday life: Explanations and applications.* Boston, MA: Allyn & Bacon.

Wright, J., & Chung, M. C. (2001). Mastery or mystery? Therapeutic writing: A review of the literature. *British Journal of Guidance and Counseling* 29 (August), 277–291.

Wright, J. W., & Hosman, L. A. (1983). Language style and sex bias in the courtroom: The effects of male and female use of hedges and intensifiers on impression formation. *Southern Speech Communication Journal* 48, 137–152.

Wright, K. (2011). A chick critique. *Psychology Today* 44, 54-62.

Wright, P. H. (1978). Toward a theory of friendship based on a conception of self. *Human Communication Research* 4, 196–207.

Wright, P. H. (1984). Self-referent motivation and the intrinsic quality of friendship. *Journal of Social and Personal Relationships* 1, 115–130.

Wright, P. H. (1988). Interpreting research on gender differences in friendship: A case for moderation and a plea for caution. *Journal of Social and Personal Relationships* 5, 367–373.

Yau-fair Ho, D., Chan, S. F., Peng, S., & Ng, A. K. (2001). The dialogical self: Converging East–West constructions. *Culture and Psychology* 7, 393–408.

Yela, C. (2000). Predictors of and factors related to loving and sexual satisfaction for men and women. *European Review of Applied Psychology* 50, 235–243.

Young, K. S., Griffin-Shelley, E., Cooper, A., O'Mara, J., & Buchanan, J. (2000). Online infidelity: A new dimension in couple relationships with implications for evaluation and treatment. *Sexual Addiction and Compulsivity* 7, 59–74.

Yuki, M., Maddux, W. W., Masuda, T. (2007). Are the windows to the soul the same in the East and West? Cultural differences in using the eyes and mouth as cues to recognize emotions in Japan and the United States. *Journal of Experimental Social Psychology* 43, 303–311.

Zhang, S., & Merolla, A. (2006). Communicating dislike of close friends' romantic partners. *Communication Research Reports* 23 (3), 179–186.

Zimmer, T. A. (1986). Premarital anxieties. *Journal of Social and Personal Relationships* 3, 149–159.

Zornoza, A., Ripoll, P., & Peiró, J. M. (2002). Conflict management in groups that work in two different communication contexts: Face-to-face and computer-mediated communication. *Small Group Research* 33 (October), 481–508.

Zuckerman, M., Klorman, R., Larrance, D. T., & Spiegel, N. H. (1981). Facial, autonomic, and subjective components of emotion: The facial feedback hypothesis versus the externalizer-internalizer distinction. *Journal of Personality and Social Psychology* 41, 929–944.

Zunin, L. M., & Zunin, H. S. (1991). *The art of condolence: What to write, what to say, what to do at a time of loss.* New York, NY: Harper Perennial.

Zunin, L. M., & Zunin, N. B. (1972). *Contact: The first four minutes.* Los Angeles, CA: Nash.

Index

1

1984, 61-62, 78-79, 92, 122, 156, 162, 174, 176, 191, 211, 215, 228, 234-235, 256, 260, 265, 268, 279, 315-318, 320, 325-326, 328, 330, 332, 335-336, 338, 341

A

Ableism, 130, 145, 298
Abstract terms, 14, 298, 300, 312
Abstraction, 115, 117, 119, 144-145
Accent, 9, 68, 82, 109, 144, 149, 179, 330
Accenting, 163
Accommodation, 51, 298, 300, 318, 324, 333
    conflict and, 300
Acculturation, 32-33, 53-54, 298, 328, 335
Accuracy, 9, 18, 21, 70, 75-77, 83, 104, 156, 176, 264, 309, 330
Accuracy in impression formation, 75, 77, 83
Acknowledgment tokens, 222-223, 321
Acronyms, 150
Action, 24, 68, 76, 168, 197, 302, 311, 326
Active fighting, 289-290
Active listening, 106-108, 111, 134, 203, 206, 229, 239, 268, 288, 298, 303, 336
Adaptors, 151, 153-154, 179-180, 298, 308, 311
Advice, 20, 44, 66, 75, 90-91, 97, 106, 115, 133, 179, 195, 200, 202-203, 207, 228, 230, 232, 237-240, 250, 263, 266, 271, 298, 307, 315, 337
Affect displays, 153-154, 179-180, 298, 310
Affection, 116, 124, 127, 151, 161, 165, 179, 229, 248, 252, 266, 277, 294, 309, 338
Affectional orientation, 44, 135-137, 165, 212, 253, 308
    terms for, 135
Affinity-seeking strategies, 78, 80, 82, 84, 298, 333
Affirmation, 65-66, 83-84, 298, 312, 315
Agape, 298
Age, 3, 9, 34, 42, 60, 62, 77, 133, 135, 137, 163, 168, 172, 177, 226, 244, 247, 253, 298, 313, 317, 330, 333, 341
Ageism, 130, 133, 145, 298
Agenda, 34, 215
Aggression, 22, 159, 191, 292-293, 298, 316, 318, 322, 327, 330, 336, 339
Aggressive, 21, 41, 48, 66, 90, 128, 163, 279, 293, 295, 333, 335, 337
Aggressiveness, 21-22, 37, 41, 51, 159, 187, 206, 287, 292-295, 298, 314, 317, 327, 330
    verbal, 51, 287, 292-295, 298, 314, 317, 327, 330
Allness, 137-138, 143-145, 201, 298
Allness orientation, 138
Alter-adaptors, 154, 298
Altman, I., 315
Amazon.com, 46
Ambiguity, 20-21, 26-27, 36-37, 41-42, 54, 140, 176, 217, 253, 298, 305, 307, 333
Analysis, 53, 75, 96, 122, 128, 139, 186, 201, 222, 224, 227, 241, 301, 315, 317, 319-320, 322, 324-325, 327, 331, 334-336, 339, 341
    of perceptions, 317
Anderson, K., 315
Anecdotes, 90
Anonymity, 9, 97, 225, 328
Apologies, 234-235, 240
Apology, 127, 234-236, 298
Appearance, 40, 102-103, 153, 155-156, 165, 179-180, 236, 254-255, 286, 292, 299, 311, 318, 323
appreciative listening, 90
Apprehension, 130, 162, 187, 198, 298, 300, 322
    about public speaking, 322
    in small groups, 322
Appropriateness, 10, 240-241, 312
    of self-disclosure, 241
Argentina, 45

Argument, 12, 23, 39, 99, 106, 135, 196, 216, 269, 279, 282, 286-287, 289-290, 292, 294, 304, 309
    sign, 290
Argumentativeness, 292-295, 298, 327, 335
Arguments, 23, 95, 190, 195, 264-265, 286-287, 289, 293, 295, 327
Arousal, 42, 157, 159, 180, 186, 199, 281, 300, 329
Arrangement, 42, 171, 253, 286
Articulation, 14, 213, 309, 314
Artifacts, 31, 53, 181, 299, 301
Artifactual communication, 153, 169, 173, 180, 299
Assertive, 40-41, 54, 59, 127-129, 144, 229, 232, 240, 299, 307
Assertive behavior, 40
Assertiveness, 34-35, 40, 115, 126-129, 144-145, 235, 299, 341
Assimilation, 102, 299, 301
Assumptions, 4-5, 39-40, 76-77, 94, 187, 270, 276, 293, 303, 330
Assurance, 198, 234-236, 278
Asynchronous communication, 27, 299, 314
Attack, 64, 79-80, 84, 101, 106, 119, 170, 173, 195, 200, 202, 228, 269, 287, 289, 291-292, 294-295, 303, 310, 330
    character, 84, 119, 173, 292
    personal, 64, 106, 202, 287, 292, 294, 330
Attention, 35, 63, 67, 80, 84, 90-92, 95, 98-99, 119, 122, 127, 130, 140, 151, 153-154, 158-160, 163, 173, 179-180, 214, 229, 266, 279, 284, 286, 290-292, 299, 307, 311
    gaining, 35
    listening and, 95, 98, 151
    selective, 67, 84, 311
    styles of, 279
Attitude, 33-34, 40, 44, 50, 99, 136, 138, 162, 175, 190, 194, 213, 255, 283, 293, 299, 301-303, 306-307, 310, 313, 332
    cultural, 33-34, 40, 44, 50, 194, 299, 301, 303, 306-307, 332
    implicit, 301, 303
Attitudes, 8, 11, 19, 31-32, 34-35, 42-43, 45-46, 60, 62, 70, 73, 78, 90, 102, 105, 116, 127, 131-132, 134-135, 143, 161, 163, 175-176, 190, 195, 221, 228, 253, 255, 257, 281, 288, 299-300, 304-305, 309-310, 312, 317-318, 322, 326, 332, 339
Attraction, 18, 76, 116, 125, 149, 160, 174, 228, 254-256, 262, 270-271, 299-300, 310, 313, 317-318, 320-321, 326, 330, 334
Attraction theory, 254, 270-271, 299
Attractiveness, 151, 155-156, 160, 174, 180, 190, 248, 255-256, 298-299, 307, 337
    physical, 156, 160, 180, 255-256, 298-299, 307
Attribution, 71, 74-75, 83-84, 192, 299, 304, 312
Attribution error, 71, 74-75, 83-84, 192, 304
Attribution of control, 71, 74
Attribution theory, 299
Audience, 7, 77, 168, 247, 256, 310
    beliefs and values, 247
    culture, 77, 256
    information about, 77
    knowledge of, 77
    secondary, 168
    size of, 310
    universal, 256
Authoritarianism, 105
Authority, 5, 105, 135, 158, 165, 172, 224
Avoidance, 42, 50-51, 158-159, 162, 178, 180, 196, 203, 223, 250, 265, 280, 286-287, 289-290, 295, 299, 314, 315-316, 325, 329, 333
    and conflict, 280, 286-287, 289-290, 295, 329
    touch, 162, 180, 314, 315, 325
    uncertainty, 42, 314, 325, 329, 333
Ayres, J., 316

B

Backchanneling cues, 299
Backhanded compliment, 236, 299
Barriers to listening, 89, 97, 111
Baxter, Leslie, 257
Behavior, 6, 10, 16-17, 21-24, 26, 32, 35, 37, 40, 48, 50-51, 60-61, 66, 69-75, 79-80, 82-83, 89, 106, 116-117, 119, 121, 124, 126-129, 132, 134, 137, 142, 150, 154, 158-159, 161-162, 171, 173, 175, 178-179, 188, 192, 194-195, 217, 220, 222, 225-227, 234-236, 250, 255-256, 261, 263, 267-270, 278-279, 288, 290, 292-293, 295, 299-300, 302-309, 311-314, 315-322, 324-337, 339-341
    cherishing, 268-269, 299
Belief, 18, 35, 37, 64, 67, 71, 92, 132, 143, 175, 198, 224, 226, 256, 299, 304, 307, 314, 327
Beliefs, 5, 11, 16-17, 19, 31-32, 35, 38, 44-46, 49, 53-55, 60-61, 64-65, 67, 69, 71, 83-84, 90, 102, 104, 116, 123, 131-132, 134-136, 143, 188, 225, 247, 250, 253-254, 280, 288, 300-301, 303-304, 306, 310-312, 317-318, 324, 334, 338
    changes in, 19, 310
    self-destructive, 64, 83-84, 102, 312
Bell, R. A., 317
Beltlining, 291, 295, 299
Berger, C. R., 317-318
Berry, J. W., 317
Bias, 34-35, 71, 74-75, 83-84, 96, 99, 104, 124, 135, 145, 306, 312, 314, 322, 331, 337, 341
Blame, 67, 74, 81, 129, 173, 238, 266, 287-288, 290, 292, 299, 314, 326
Blind self, 61-63, 83
Blogs, 7, 19, 166, 202
body, 12, 35, 62, 68, 115, 124, 148, 150, 153-156, 160, 162-163, 170, 172-174, 179-181, 188, 232, 254, 298, 310-311, 313, 315, 323, 326-327, 338, 340
Body adornment, 172, 180, 338
Body appearance, 153, 155-156, 179
Body communication, 156, 173
Body language, 148, 181, 315
Body movement, 153
Body movements, 124, 153-154, 298
Body type, 163
Books, 46, 66, 103, 118, 169, 171, 200, 319-322, 325, 328, 335-336, 339-340
Boundary markers, 169
Bridge, 13, 26
Brownell, J., 318
Buber, M., 318
Burgoon, J. K., 318, 321
Business, 16, 34, 39, 46, 60, 71, 92, 96, 102, 109, 120, 122, 128, 131, 134, 152, 161-162, 166, 168, 172-173, 176, 211, 215-216, 231, 235, 238, 240, 260, 281, 301, 313, 316, 320, 322-323, 325-326, 330-332, 335, 338-340
    relationships in, 260, 301, 320, 323, 335
Bypassing, 299

C

Calabrese, R. J., 317
Capitalism, 35, 172
Catharsis, 225, 338
Cell phones, 12, 107
Central markers, 169
Certainty, 92, 141, 269, 299, 302, 304, 310
Changes, 17, 19, 32-33, 53, 62, 142, 159, 184, 199, 207, 225, 250, 268, 270-271, 280, 285, 292, 310, 329, 339
Channel, 9, 13, 26-27, 223, 240, 299, 313
    organizational, 313
Channels, 8, 10, 13, 16, 26, 148, 153, 178-181, 212, 214, 221, 263, 268, 309, 312
Channels of communication, 181, 214, 221, 268, 309
    nonverbal, 181, 221, 309
Character, 81, 84, 116, 119, 160, 173, 247, 292, 301

Charisma, 81, 84, 301, 335
Chat groups, 223, 225, 300
Cherishing behaviors, 268-269, 271, 287, 299
Chronemics, 174, 180, 299
Churchill, Winston, 213
Cialdini, R. B., 328
Civil inattention, 159, 180, 299
Claim, 17, 67, 130, 156, 211, 234, 263, 265, 281, 302
Claims, 103, 110, 166, 188, 193, 260-261, 270, 298, 306, 324
Climate, 265
Clinton, Hillary, 195
Close relationships, 19, 50, 124-125, 149, 170, 223, 246, 279, 311, 313, 317, 321, 329, 336-337
Closure, 217, 279
Co-culture, 33
Coercive power, 300
Cognitive disclaimers, 92
Cohesion, 323
Cohesiveness, 102
Colleagues, 10, 35, 59, 82, 90, 122, 127, 202, 226, 250, 275, 278, 330
Collectivism, 38, 235, 317, 328, 330
Collectivist culture, 38-39, 54, 63, 282, 300, 305
Collectivist cultures, 38-39, 128, 164, 176, 189, 257, 282, 305
   conflict and, 282
Color communication, 171, 180, 300
Commitment, 11, 21, 25, 32, 53, 149, 217, 248-249, 251, 260, 264, 270, 277, 279, 303, 319, 324, 327-329, 333, 336, 338-339
Commitments, 277
Communication, 1-27, 29-55, 57-85, 87-111, 113, 115-116, 118-122, 125-131, 133-135, 140, 143-145, 147-150, 153, 156-171, 173-181, 183, 185, 189-191, 193-204, 206-207, 209-214, 216, 218, 220-223, 225, 227-228, 230-231, 233-236, 240-241, 243-271, 273, 275, 277-278, 280, 282-283, 287-288, 290, 293-295, 297-314, 315-341
   and diversity, 174
   and emotion, 330, 334
   and feedback, 14
   and noise, 14, 312
   anxiety, 12-13, 41-42, 129, 162, 165, 193, 198, 236, 300, 307, 322, 325, 338
   apprehension, 130, 162, 198, 298, 300, 322
   assertive, 40-41, 54, 59, 127-129, 144, 240, 299, 307
   barriers to, 85, 89, 97, 101, 111, 115, 133, 263, 278, 299
   channels of, 148, 153, 179, 181, 214, 221, 268, 309
   competence, 4, 10, 12, 27, 33-34, 51, 81, 84, 91, 133, 148, 164, 177, 180, 196-197, 201, 206, 236, 287-288, 293, 300-302, 306, 322, 325, 331, 336, 338, 341
   components of, 200, 341
   confidence in, 299
   context, 9-10, 14, 16-17, 26-27, 36-40, 54, 70, 75, 120, 127, 156, 166, 178-180, 199-200, 212, 228, 233, 235, 240, 246, 280, 301, 305, 307, 312, 316, 319-321, 326, 331, 335
   defensive, 62, 168, 257, 269, 323
   defined, 22, 25, 31, 37, 130, 211, 270, 283, 300, 304, 311
   definition, 5, 21, 130, 144, 216, 221, 275, 300
   definition of, 5, 21, 130, 144, 216, 275
   definitions of, 156, 262
   dyadic, 5, 227, 240, 302, 312
   effective, 3, 5, 13-14, 26, 30, 34, 36, 44-46, 49, 53-55, 59-60, 64, 82, 88-89, 92-95, 97-102, 104, 108, 110-111, 115-116, 119, 125-126, 128-129, 143, 160, 173, 178-179, 185, 190-191, 194, 196, 199-200, 202, 204, 210, 220-221, 233-236, 240-241, 263, 268, 275, 283, 287-288, 290, 295, 298-299, 317, 319, 325, 338
   ethical, 16-17, 27, 35, 60, 80, 100, 125, 133, 145, 165, 173, 190, 230, 253-254, 287, 340
   ethics and, 319
   evaluative, 50, 163, 216, 327
   explanation of, 308, 311, 326
   forms of, 6, 9, 20, 34, 36, 42, 53, 96, 98, 119, 126, 162, 211, 225, 275, 301, 304, 314
   formula, 198
   foundations of, 1-2, 4-27, 338

functions of, 81, 107, 164, 179, 214, 317, 327
good, 3-5, 16-17, 20, 26, 34, 36, 42, 44, 48-49, 52, 60-61, 64-67, 73-76, 79, 81, 84, 89-90, 97, 101-102, 106-107, 109, 121, 126-127, 143, 157, 160, 163, 166, 173, 178, 189, 193, 196, 199, 202, 212, 216, 221, 227, 230, 233-236, 245-246, 250-251, 258, 261, 264, 294, 300, 304, 309, 321, 330, 340
human, 3, 9, 17, 31, 33, 78, 102, 134, 169, 221, 245-246, 299-300, 302-303, 308, 316-322, 324, 327, 329-341
hurtful, 6, 127
impersonal, 6-7, 26, 168, 211, 223, 247, 253, 306, 313
in families, 323, 335
in society, 130
in workplace, 160, 277
influence of culture, 110, 179, 278, 322
intentional, 12, 24
interaction and, 111, 145, 218, 248, 306, 309, 317
intercultural, 16, 30-31, 33-35, 39-40, 44-46, 49-51, 53-55, 69, 77, 109, 149, 175-177, 227, 250, 256, 294, 299, 306, 315-317, 325, 327-328, 330-333, 336, 338-339
interpersonal, 1-27, 29-55, 57-85, 87-111, 113, 115-116, 118-122, 125-130, 135, 147, 149, 153, 156-157, 160, 163-167, 169-170, 174-175, 177-178, 181, 183, 185, 189-190, 194, 196-203, 206, 209, 211-213, 216, 218, 220, 223, 225, 227, 230-231, 233-236, 243-271, 273, 275, 277-278, 280, 282-283, 287-288, 290, 293-295, 297-298, 300-306, 308-314, 315-329, 331-332, 334-336, 338-340
intrapersonal, 10, 225, 248-250, 269-270, 306
language and, 47, 109, 145, 181, 316-317, 320, 323, 325, 337
listening and, 14, 95, 97-98, 102, 106, 111, 203, 223, 283, 319-320
mass, 10, 15, 93, 306, 320, 333, 337
mediated, 9, 18, 25, 223, 278, 300, 327-329, 332, 335, 340-341
models of, 27, 259, 313, 320, 324, 340
myths about, 92
nonverbal, 5, 7, 9-10, 14-15, 18, 23, 26, 48, 51, 63, 74, 77, 92-93, 97-98, 100, 104, 106, 109, 111, 115-116, 118, 122, 131, 145, 147-150, 153, 156-171, 173-181, 191, 194, 202-203, 211-212, 221, 223, 231, 249, 264-265, 270, 298-306, 308-310, 312-313, 315, 317-323, 325-326, 328-331, 333, 335, 339, 341
overly critical, 126, 302, 314
people with disabilities, 130, 298
perception and, 59, 116
persuasive, 20, 73, 80, 82, 163-164, 221, 235, 300, 302
power of, 12, 40, 294, 305, 327, 334
principles of, 2-3, 5, 17, 26, 31, 45, 115, 129, 144-145, 148-149, 179, 185, 194, 204, 206, 210-211, 240-241, 275, 278, 294
public, 10, 13, 25, 35-36, 39, 45, 53, 93, 95, 106-107, 109, 127, 134-135, 157, 167-169, 179-180, 191, 195, 202, 216, 225, 248-250, 256, 298, 306, 308, 310, 320, 322, 324, 332-333, 337
public communication, 45
repertoire of, 322
self-concept and, 65
small group, 10, 95, 118, 225, 306, 322, 328, 341
supportive, 4, 6, 13, 76, 91, 97, 101, 106, 110, 129, 161, 203-204, 216, 223, 227, 263, 265, 308-310
transaction, 339
types of, 12-14, 17, 27, 79, 90, 92, 103, 105, 108, 110-111, 126, 130, 134, 140, 145, 153, 157, 167-169, 171, 176, 180, 222, 234, 241, 247, 250-252, 254, 260, 270, 282, 306, 311
unintentional, 12, 16, 131
verbal, 5, 7, 9, 26, 51, 54, 63, 77, 92, 98, 100, 104, 106, 109, 113, 115-116, 118-122, 125-131, 133-135, 140, 143-145, 149-150, 153, 160, 164-165, 178-179, 191, 203, 211-212, 221, 227, 231, 249, 270, 287, 293-295, 298-301, 303-307, 311-312, 314, 315, 317, 327, 330, 333, 336, 339

Communication accommodation theory, 51, 300, 324
Communication apprehension, 162, 298, 300
   defined, 300
Communication effectiveness, 53, 195, 240, 310
Communication ethics, 319, 327
Communication irreversibility, 27
Communication principles, 2
Communication privacy management theory, 337
Communication process, 12, 200, 212, 269
   context in, 212
   elements of, 212
   feedback and, 12
   people in, 200
communication skills, 3-4, 18, 89-90, 106, 233, 252, 268, 298, 300, 318, 333, 336, 338
Communication studies, 327, 329, 336
communicator, 3, 5, 44, 221, 333
   elements of, 3
Communities, 327, 329
   communication and, 329
Comparisons, 59-61, 83, 319, 321
Competence, 4, 10, 12, 27, 33-34, 51, 81, 84, 91, 123, 133, 148, 164, 177, 180, 187, 196-197, 201, 206, 236, 238, 287-288, 293, 300-302, 306, 322, 325, 331, 336, 338, 341
   conflict and, 287-288, 293, 300
Competition, 34, 37, 128, 300, 322
Complementarity, 255, 271, 300, 313
Complementary relationship, 22, 27, 300
Compliance, 161, 294, 300, 306, 308, 318, 321, 328, 331, 334
Compliance gaining, 328
Complimenting, 220, 230, 236-237, 309, 337
Compliments, 119, 220, 236-237, 261, 268-269
Compromise, 37, 41, 189, 263, 281, 308
Compromising, 280, 295, 300
Computer software, 173
Computer-mediated communication, 9, 18, 223, 278, 300, 327-329, 340-341
   instant messaging and, 327
   self-disclosure and, 341
Computers, 12, 49, 171, 317, 320, 332
concrete language, 298
Concrete terms, 198, 268, 298, 300
Confirmation, 76, 129-131, 144-145, 291-292, 300, 302, 306, 311, 322
Conflict, 5, 11, 17, 24-25, 37-38, 41, 55, 116, 122, 125, 127, 164-165, 178, 189, 196, 206, 235, 258, 263, 267-268, 270, 273-295, 298-301, 303-304, 306-311, 313-314, 317-321, 323-324, 326, 328-330, 333-334, 336-341
   accommodation and, 333
   active, 206, 268, 288-290, 295, 298, 303, 307, 314, 320, 336
   aggression and, 336
   and culture, 321, 326, 333, 339, 341
   argumentativeness and, 293-294
   avoidance of, 289
   causes of, 268, 277, 336
   competition in, 300
   compromise and, 41
   content, 268, 278-279, 294, 301, 320, 329
   control and, 165
   culture and, 37-38, 41, 55, 164, 341
   defined, 25, 37, 270, 281, 283, 286, 300, 304, 311
   demand-withdrawal and, 336
   elements of, 340
   ethics and, 319
   evaluation and, 336, 341
   explanation of, 308, 311, 326
   gender and, 318, 321, 334, 338-339, 341
   group, 25, 38, 125, 127, 196, 258, 276-277, 280-281, 292, 294, 299-301, 303-304, 306, 310-311, 313, 317, 323, 328-330, 334, 337, 341
   gunnysacking and, 294
   in families, 323
   interpersonal conflict, 116, 268, 273-295, 300, 306, 317-318, 321, 323, 326, 334
   issues of, 321
   management of, 301
   myths about, 276
   online, 258, 263, 278, 308, 313, 319-321, 323, 330, 339-341
   principles of, 5, 17, 206, 274-275, 278, 289, 294
   process of, 298-299, 301, 306-309, 311, 313-314
   relationship, 5, 11, 17, 25, 55, 125, 165, 189, 196, 235, 258, 263, 267-268, 270, 276-280, 282-283, 285-295, 298-301, 303-304,

344

306-307, 309-311, 313-314, 317,
319-321, 324, 326, 328-330, 336-340
status and, 329
styles of, 278-279, 300, 339
types of, 17, 270, 279, 282, 306, 311
verbal aggressiveness and, 292-294
violence in, 290-291, 323
Conflict management, 273-295, 298-300, 314, 336,
341
skills for, 275, 298
styles of, 278-279, 300
Conflict styles, 279, 282, 289, 295, 300, 321
Connotation, 117, 144-145, 300, 302
Connotative meaning, 117, 144
Connotative meanings, 117, 300
Consensual families, 300
Constraints, 322, 329
Construct, 10, 39, 116, 199, 255, 315
Content conflict, 279
Content messages, 22, 268
Context, 9-10, 14, 16-17, 26-27, 36-40, 54, 70, 75,
117, 120, 127, 156, 166, 178-180, 188,
199-200, 212, 228-229, 233, 235, 239-240,
246, 280-281, 301, 305, 307, 312, 316,
319-321, 326, 331, 335
characteristics of, 75
culture and, 36-40, 54, 117, 331
explanation of, 326
high- and low-context cultures, 38-39
of communication, 9, 14, 16, 26-27, 36, 120, 127,
166, 228, 301, 305, 307, 312, 321, 326,
335
of messages, 16, 117, 301, 312
of small talk, 233
rhetorical, 326
words and, 326
Contradicting, 118
Contrast, 61, 68, 84, 161, 170, 214, 224, 264, 301
Control, 8, 21-22, 37, 43, 46, 66, 71, 74, 78, 83, 135,
144, 149-150, 153-154, 158, 161-162, 165,
168, 179-180, 189-190, 192, 194-195, 224,
226, 234-235, 237, 258, 261, 276, 281, 283,
286, 290-291, 301-302, 305-307, 309-310,
313-314, 334
attribution of, 71, 74
conflict and, 276, 281, 283, 286, 290-291
Conversation, 3, 6, 31, 34, 62, 78, 91, 95, 97, 101,
106-108, 110, 125, 128, 133-134, 148,
152-154, 158-159, 162, 175, 178-179, 181,
192, 199, 203-204, 210-212, 214-223,
230-233, 236, 239-241, 257, 262, 265, 289,
300-301, 306-307, 310-311, 319, 321-322,
324, 329, 332, 338-339, 341
advice and, 91
culture and, 31, 34, 110, 159, 162, 332, 341
in conflict, 178, 289, 321, 329
nonverbal communication and, 179
principles of, 3, 31, 148, 179, 204, 210-211,
240-241, 289
small talk as, 233
Conversational maxims, 218, 240, 301
Conversational rules, 301
Conversational turns, 180, 222, 240, 301, 306
Cooper, P. J., 339
Cooperation, 34, 128, 218, 240, 301, 329
Cooperative principle, 330
Coordination, 171, 277
Credibility, 34, 79-80, 82, 84, 123, 163-164, 173-174,
180, 293-294, 301, 322, 327, 330, 337
culture and, 34, 164
Critical listening, 101-103, 111, 301
Critical thinking, 5, 72, 75, 91, 115, 301
Criticism, 39, 106, 110, 126-127, 132, 144, 165,
220-221, 234, 236-237, 263, 269-270, 304,
316
behavior and, 234
constructive, 127
culture and, 39, 110
evaluating, 110
listening to, 106, 110
Critiques, 317
Cues, 9, 15, 49-51, 72, 74-75, 93, 95-97, 100,
104-106, 109-111, 124, 148, 151-152, 156,
160, 163, 174, 180, 191, 194, 202-206, 217,
221-224, 234, 240, 271, 299, 301, 304,
306-307, 313, 319, 324, 334, 336, 339-341
backchanneling, 299
listening, 93, 95-97, 100, 104-106, 109-111,
151-152, 163, 202-203, 206, 222-224,

240, 299, 301, 307, 319, 336, 341
speaker, 9, 15, 93, 95-97, 100, 104-106, 109-111,
124, 152, 160, 163, 203, 221-224, 299,
301, 306
turn-denying, 222, 224
turn-maintaining, 222, 224
turn-requesting, 222, 224
turn-taking, 15, 152, 192, 224, 301, 319
turn-yielding, 222, 224
Cultural context, 16, 178, 180, 188, 321
Cultural diversity, 33, 35, 321
Cultural identifiers, 135, 137, 145, 301
Culture, 4, 16-17, 29-55, 59-60, 63, 67, 77, 88-89,
106, 109-111, 117, 120, 123, 126, 128,
135-136, 153-159, 162, 164, 172, 175-179,
181, 188, 191, 193, 201, 212, 216, 219,
226-227, 235, 240, 249, 252-253, 256-258,
278, 280-282, 294, 298-305, 307, 309, 312,
314, 316-317, 319, 321-323, 325-326, 328,
331-333, 339-341
and emotional expression, 331
and nonverbal communication, 175, 326, 333
and self-disclosure, 162
assertiveness and, 128
attitudes about, 42, 322
characteristics of, 49, 128, 317, 332, 341
collectivist, 36-39, 54, 63, 128, 164, 176, 257, 282,
300, 305, 321
competence and, 51, 164, 302
conflict and, 17, 55, 278, 280-282, 294, 300, 303,
317, 339
conversation and, 216, 240, 300
cooperation and, 34
credibility and, 322
criticism and, 126, 304
defined, 31, 37, 136, 281, 300, 304
dimensions of, 36, 110, 331
ethnocentric, 49-50, 136, 303
ethnocentrism and, 50, 319
explanation of, 326
eye contact and, 249, 305
feminine, 37, 40-41, 54, 159, 193, 304, 307, 326
gender and, 109, 321-322, 325, 339, 341
gestures and, 155, 191
goals and, 77, 305
groups and, 34, 49, 120
high-context, 38-39, 54, 280, 305, 307
high-power-distance, 40, 53-54
individualist, 36-39, 54, 63, 128, 164, 257, 282,
300, 305, 307
language and, 47, 109, 117, 181, 316-317, 323,
325
listening, 67, 88-89, 106, 109-111, 135, 158, 179,
240, 298-299, 301, 303, 305, 307, 309,
312, 314, 316, 319, 323, 328, 341
listening and, 106, 111, 319
low-context, 37-40, 54, 280-281, 305, 307
low-power-distance, 40, 53-54
masculine, 37, 40-41, 54, 193, 304, 307, 326
nonverbal, 48, 51, 63, 77, 106, 109, 111, 117,
153-159, 162, 164, 172, 175-179, 181,
188, 191, 212, 249, 298-305, 309, 312,
317, 319, 321-323, 325-326, 328, 331,
333, 339, 341
nonverbal communication and, 179
nonverbal messages and, 181
organizational, 45, 282, 294, 304, 317, 319,
325-326, 328, 333, 339-340
paralanguage and, 153, 303
perception and, 59
physical appearance and, 299
politeness and, 106, 120, 179
relationships and, 39, 41, 110, 120
self-disclosure, 63, 162, 226-227, 240, 312, 319,
328, 340-341
self-disclosure and, 227, 341
sensitivity to, 33, 53
silence and, 322
small group, 322, 328, 341
speech and, 111, 164, 212, 328
time and, 50, 172, 175, 177, 280
touch and, 162
words and, 50, 164, 181, 201, 326
Culture shock, 46-47, 301, 317, 319, 340
Cyberbullying, 326

D

Daly, J. A., 317
Dangers of self-disclosure, 227, 241

Darwin, Charles, 200
Data, 18, 317, 325, 340
Databases, 41
Dating, 21, 40, 125, 136, 155, 166, 177, 215, 238,
248-249, 252-253, 257, 259, 262, 266, 271,
274, 291, 316, 318, 320, 334, 336-339, 341
Debates, 124
Deception, 80, 83, 104, 123-125, 152, 265, 270, 308,
315, 317, 329-330
effects of, 125, 315, 329
reasons for, 124-125
Decoding, 8, 10, 12, 26-27, 45, 177-178, 180, 302
Defensive communication, 323
Definition, 5, 21, 117, 130, 144, 216, 221, 275, 300
Definitions, 48, 117, 136, 156, 262
research, 156
use of, 48
DeFrancisco, V., 320
Demand-withdrawal, 289, 336
democracy, 96, 141
Denial, 196, 237, 302
Denotation, 117, 144-145, 300, 302
Denotative meaning, 116-117, 144
Depenetration, 260, 262, 302, 313
Depth listening, 101-104, 111
Description, 76, 117, 133, 190, 198, 219-220, 238, 288
desensitization techniques, 129
Dewey, John, 284
Dialectics, 254, 258, 270-271, 311, 316, 335
Dialogue, 22-23, 63, 85, 97, 127, 145, 221, 232,
240-241, 302, 307, 318, 332, 339
Directness, 119, 121, 145
verbal, 119, 121, 145
verbal messages and, 145
Disclaimers, 92, 94, 111, 215, 302, 317, 326
Disconfirmation, 129-131, 144-145, 164, 292, 300,
302, 311
Disconfirming response, 203
Disconfirming responses, 130
Discourse, 320, 339
Discrimination, 32, 74, 130, 134, 298, 330
Disinhibition, 225, 339
Disinhibition effect, 225, 339
Dismissal, 130
Display rules, 109, 111, 157, 180, 191, 194, 201, 206,
301, 304
Dissatisfaction, 124, 177, 232, 248-250, 261, 280,
283, 294
Distancing, 329
Distractions, 92, 95, 97-98, 111
Diversity, 33, 35, 48, 174, 317, 321
and communication, 317
communication and, 33, 48, 317, 321
cultural, 33, 35, 48, 317, 321
perceptions and, 317
respect for, 48
Dominance, 152, 161-162, 164, 308, 314, 321
Downward communication, 302
Dress, 68, 77, 80, 137, 150-152, 172-174, 258
Dyad, 327, 334
Dyadic communication, 302
Dyadic effect, 227, 240, 302, 312
Dyads, 55, 162, 168, 318
Dynamism, 301

E

Ear markers, 169, 180
Effective listening, 88, 94, 97-102, 108, 110-111, 229,
338
elements of, 88
guidelines for, 229
Electronic databases, 41
Ellis, Albert, 188
E-mail, 9, 13, 16, 34, 51, 75, 118, 122, 127, 185, 188,
191, 201, 214-215, 217-219, 223, 225, 236,
263, 277, 285, 290, 299-300, 317, 320, 323,
325, 328, 337-338
Email, 313, 339
Emblems, 153-154, 179-180, 292, 302
Emoticons, 150, 185
Emotion, 7, 48, 156-157, 161, 185-188, 191-192, 198,
200, 203, 206, 298, 300, 302-303, 306,
319-320, 322, 324, 326, 328, 330-332,
334-335, 337, 339, 341
and communication, 306, 331, 334
expression of, 157, 191-192, 200, 298, 302,
319-320, 322
theories of, 186, 332
universal, 156, 319, 328

Emotional appeals, 190, 192, 206, 302
Emotional contagion, 192, 194, 206, 302, 321
Emotional expression, 156, 179, 185, 187, 189-198, 202, 206, 302, 331, 337
Emotional intelligence, 185, 324
Emotional intimacy, 255
Emotional states, 180, 309
Emotions, 7, 43, 64, 89, 94, 98, 127, 152-153, 156-158, 161, 163, 165, 179-180, 184-198, 200-204, 206-207, 231, 233, 239, 249, 299-300, 302-304, 306, 310, 313-314, 320, 322, 334, 338-339, 341
  appeals to, 190
  conflict and, 300, 303, 339
  emoticons, 185
  listening to, 94, 163, 179, 202, 303, 310
  nonverbal messages and, 231
Empathic listening, 101-102, 108, 111, 303, 320
Empathizing, 229, 259
Empathy, 24, 44, 78, 97, 101-102, 106, 108, 111, 121, 205, 220-221, 229, 263-265, 268, 271, 291, 303, 308, 315, 322
  conflict and, 291, 303
  explanation of, 308
  feeling, 24, 101, 108, 111, 264-265, 291, 303
  listening and, 97, 102, 106, 111
  listening with, 102, 308
  responding with, 97
  thinking, 44, 101, 106, 111, 264, 303
Emphasis, 4, 21, 23, 35-36, 39, 43, 122, 150, 173-174, 176, 191-192, 255, 300, 310-311, 313
Employment interview, 233
  interview, 233
Employment interviews, 76
Encoding, 8, 10, 12, 26-27, 45, 105, 177-178, 180, 303
Encoding-decoding, 8, 12, 26
Encouragers, 203
Enculturation, 32, 53-54, 303
Enthusiasm, 81, 129
Environment, 14, 16-17, 20, 26, 92, 97-98, 109, 194, 301, 305, 315
Envy, 171-172
Episode, 167, 295
Episodes, 323
Equality, 21-22, 40, 50, 101, 134, 158, 161, 277, 279, 283, 293, 295, 303, 313, 329
Equity theory, 260-261, 270-271, 303, 326, 332
Eros, 303
Ethics, 8, 16-17, 26-27, 35, 80, 100, 125, 165, 190, 197, 230, 253, 287, 303, 319, 327
  approaches to, 27
  communication and, 17, 319
  intercultural communication, 35, 327
  interpersonal, 8, 16-17, 26-27, 35, 80, 100, 125, 165, 190, 197, 230, 253, 287, 303, 319, 327
  listening and, 319
  of gossip, 230
  of impression management, 80
  of listening, 100
  of silence, 327
  organizational, 319
  relationship, 17, 26-27, 35, 125, 165, 190, 253, 287, 303, 319, 327
  subjective view of, 17
Ethnic identity, 32, 53-54, 303, 319, 330, 339
Ethnicity, 335
Ethnocentrism, 32, 49-50, 54, 303, 306, 319, 328, 333
Euphemism, 303
Euphemisms, 103
Evaluating, 67, 74, 91, 96, 98, 100, 110-111, 229, 254, 301-303, 307
evaluation, 69, 71, 73, 83-84, 91, 96, 98, 102, 131, 135, 137, 142-145, 216, 232, 300, 302-303, 305-306, 312-313, 316-317, 325, 328, 330, 333, 336, 339, 341
  conflict and, 300, 303, 317, 339
  in groups, 341
  in perception, 69, 83, 306
  listening and, 98, 102
  static, 137, 142-145, 302, 313
Evidence, 17, 25, 35, 42-43, 75, 82, 96-97, 99, 102, 110, 124-125, 132, 141, 160, 166, 171, 173-174, 178, 189-190, 239, 256, 293, 301, 312, 322, 324, 329, 333, 338
Exaggeration, 124, 303
Examples, 13-14, 20, 33, 35, 38-39, 46, 48, 76, 80, 94, 96, 99, 103, 109, 117, 123, 133-135,

142-143, 145, 150, 152-154, 162, 168-169, 172-173, 176, 188, 202, 214, 220, 252, 260, 279, 299, 308-309
  brief, 13, 48, 94, 143, 299
  evaluating, 96
  explanation of, 308
  hypothetical, 134
  illustration, 142
  restatement, 308
  using, 80, 96, 109, 134-135, 143, 145, 152, 162, 173, 220, 260, 279, 309
Excuses, 47, 81, 212, 215, 234-236, 240-241, 303, 322, 338
Expectancy hearing, 102
Expectancy violation theory, 170
Experiments, 164, 318, 331
Expert power, 82, 303
Expression, 43, 104, 108, 122, 126, 150, 156-159, 161, 165, 179, 185, 187-198, 200-202, 204, 206, 220, 232, 235, 281-282, 293, 298-299, 301-302, 304, 319-320, 322, 326, 331-332, 337
  ethnic, 319, 337
  facial, 122, 126, 150, 156-157, 161, 191, 293, 298-299, 304, 326, 331
Expressiveness, 231, 240, 268, 303, 337
Extended family, 5, 30, 42, 55, 257, 323
Extensional devices, 303
Extensional orientation, 137, 145, 303, 306
Eye behavior, 158, 161
Eye communication, 153, 158-159
Eye contact, 7, 9, 35, 48, 51, 73, 79, 104, 106, 110, 116, 131, 133, 148, 150-152, 158-162, 168, 170, 179-181, 203, 213, 222-223, 229, 231, 237, 249, 264-265, 293, 305, 308, 315
  and listening, 106, 116
  culture and, 35, 48, 51, 110, 159, 162, 249
  meaning of, 7, 116, 161, 237

F
Face, 3, 6-9, 11-13, 15-16, 18, 24-26, 39, 44, 46, 75, 79-81, 84, 93, 97, 105-107, 111, 115-116, 119, 121-122, 125-127, 129, 144-145, 150-151, 154, 156, 158-159, 161-163, 165-166, 168, 181, 186, 188, 191, 201, 214, 217, 219-220, 223, 225, 236, 239, 244-245, 249, 255, 258-259, 261-262, 266, 270, 277-279, 282, 287, 289, 291-293, 295, 299, 303-304, 308-309, 313-314, 322, 324, 328-329, 331-332, 334, 339, 341
Face-attacking strategy, 291-292
Facebook, 5-6, 8, 11-14, 16, 18-21, 25, 43, 46, 60-61, 67, 97, 121-122, 125, 173, 199, 212, 225, 228, 250, 263, 277, 313
Face-saving, 39, 289
Face-threatening acts, 119
Face-to-face communication, 9, 13, 18, 25, 97, 105-106, 223, 313-314
Facial communication, 153, 156-157
  culture and, 157
Facial expression, 122, 126, 156, 161, 293, 326
Facial expressions, 7, 15, 77, 79, 93, 115, 150, 152-154, 157, 161, 181, 191, 223-224, 249, 264, 299, 303-304, 308, 324, 331
Facial feedback hypothesis, 157, 180, 304, 330, 341
Facial management techniques, 157, 304
Fact, 12, 16, 19-20, 23, 25, 32-33, 38, 40, 47, 49-50, 53, 62, 67, 69-71, 81, 83, 90, 93-94, 103-106, 122-123, 125, 132-133, 137, 139-140, 142, 145, 156-157, 159, 162-163, 171, 173, 187, 191-192, 194, 196, 199-201, 204, 213-214, 224-225, 228, 230, 240, 246, 252, 260, 265, 278-279, 281, 283, 286, 294, 304, 313-314, 322, 335
Fact-inference confusion, 137, 139, 145, 304
facts, 23, 96, 98, 123-124, 137, 139-140, 143-144, 203, 286, 304, 307
  evaluating, 96, 98, 307
  using, 96, 137, 143-144
Fallacies, 102-103
  listening to, 102
  of language, 102
Fallacy, 103, 141
False memory, 94
Familiarity, 68, 168, 256, 332-333
Family, 3, 5, 7, 12, 16, 30, 32, 34, 38, 42-43, 55, 67, 89-90, 117, 123, 176-177, 212, 228, 245, 249-250, 253, 257-258, 262, 266, 275-276, 283, 285, 287-288, 291, 294, 300-301, 304,

315-316, 322-323, 329, 331-338
  and emotional expression, 331
  and interpersonal communication, 7, 30, 32, 34, 38, 42-43, 55
  conflict and, 55, 275-276, 283, 285, 287-288, 291, 294, 300
  definition of, 5, 275
  relationships in, 12, 245, 301, 315, 323, 333-336
  rules of, 16, 257, 262, 300-301, 315
  types of, 12, 90, 123, 176, 250
Family of origin, 329
Fear appeals, 190
fears, 44, 46, 196, 226, 228, 301
Feedback, 8, 10, 12-14, 19, 26-27, 51, 63, 66, 91, 96-98, 100, 106, 109-111, 129, 157-158, 160, 180, 192, 211, 216-217, 231, 239-240, 301, 304, 308-309, 311, 319, 330, 333, 337, 341
  culture and, 51, 109-110, 157, 341
  explanation of, 308, 311
  facial feedback hypothesis, 157, 180, 304, 330, 341
  interpersonal, 8, 10, 12-14, 19, 26-27, 51, 63, 66, 91, 96-98, 100, 106, 109-111, 129, 157, 160, 211, 216-217, 231, 239, 301, 304, 308-309, 311, 319
  listening and, 14, 97-98, 106, 111, 239, 319
Feedforward, 8, 10, 12-13, 26-27, 118, 211, 214-217, 240, 301, 304, 307
Feeling empathy, 264
Feminine culture, 41, 54, 304, 307
Feminine cultures, 40-41, 54, 304, 326
Fields, 66, 74
films, 118-119, 133, 281
Filtering, 102
First impressions, 11, 247, 307, 341
Flexibility, 199, 206, 304, 331
Flirting, 23-24, 116, 236, 248-249, 277, 304, 340-341
Followers, 19, 60, 122, 329
Fonts, 237
Force, 70, 135, 194, 200, 204, 261, 287-288, 290-291, 295, 304, 314, 337
  and listening, 291
  in conflict, 288, 291, 304
Forcing, 106
Formality, 16, 179, 212
Forum, 228
Friendship, 5-6, 12, 19, 40, 43, 47, 121, 155, 204, 223, 239, 245, 256-257, 262, 277, 298-299, 304, 310, 315, 317-319, 322, 334-336, 339, 341
  and interpersonal communication, 40, 43, 47, 318
  in workplace, 277
  rules of, 6, 121, 257, 262, 277, 315
Friendships, 3, 13, 43, 256, 260, 304, 322, 324-327, 335
Fundamental attribution error, 71, 74-75, 83-84, 192, 304
Future orientations, 175-176

G
Gatekeepers, 69, 330
  media, 69, 330
Gatekeeping, 317, 322
Gaze, 125, 158, 161, 315-316, 324, 333
Gender, 31-32, 40, 43-44, 55, 69, 77, 88-89, 99, 109-111, 120-121, 134-135, 137, 145, 149, 159, 161, 163, 168, 172, 191, 193, 201, 206, 224, 226, 233, 240-241, 247, 271, 280-281, 300, 304, 312, 315-323, 325, 327, 329-331, 333-339, 341
  and conflict, 280-281, 329, 338
  and culture, 321, 325, 333, 339, 341
  and dating, 40
  and language, 31, 111, 334
  and nonverbal communication, 333
  and touch, 325
  conflict and, 55, 280-281, 300, 317, 339
  culture and, 31-32, 40, 43-44, 55, 77, 89, 109-110, 159, 325, 331, 341
  language and, 109, 145, 316-317, 320, 323, 325, 337
  listening and, 111, 319-320
  politeness and, 120
  relationships and, 110, 120, 271, 337
  self-concept, 40, 312, 317, 321
  self-disclosure, 161, 226, 233, 240-241, 312, 318-320, 334, 337-338, 341
  self-disclosure and, 241, 320, 341
  sexism and, 134
  stereotypes about, 233